New Perspectives on

THE INTERNET

3ʳᵈ Edition

WITHDRAWN

Comprehensive

Internet Tutorials
GARY P. SCHNEIDER
University of San Diego

JESSICA EVANS

HTML Tutorials
PATRICK CAREY
Carey Associates

**COURSE
TECHNOLOGY**
THOMSON LEARNING

Australia • Canada • Mexico • Singapore • Spain • United Kingdom • United States

COURSE TECHNOLOGY
TM
THOMSON LEARNING

New Perspectives on The Internet—Comprehensive, 3rd Edition
is published by Course Technology.

Managing Editor:
Rachel Crapser

Senior Editor:
Donna Gridley

Senior Product Manager:
Kathy Finnegan

Product Manager:
Melissa Hathaway

Technology Project Manager:
Amanda Young

Associate Product Manager:
Jessica Engstrom

Marketing Manager:
Sean Teare

Developmental Editors:
Jane Pedicini
Lisa Ruffolo

Production Editor:
Daphne Barbas

Composition:
GEX Publishing Services

Text Designer:
Meral Dabcovich

Cover Designer:
Efrat Reis

Preface

Course Technology is the world leader in information technology education. The New Perspectives Series is an integral part of Course Technology's success. Visit our Web site to see a whole new perspective on teaching and learning solutions.

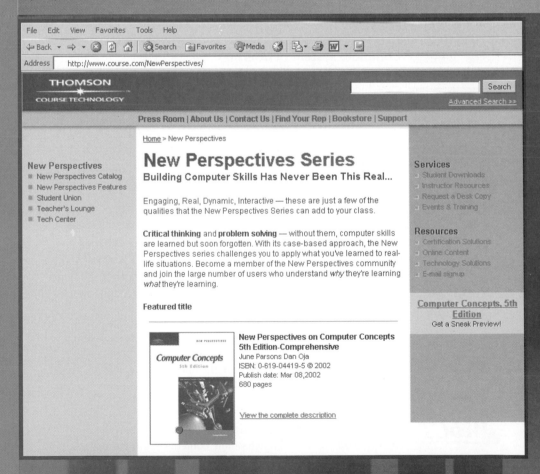

New Perspectives—Building Computer Skills Has Never Been This Real

Why New Perspectives will work for you.

Critical thinking and **problem solving**—without them, computer skills are learned but soon forgotten. With its **case-based** approach, the New Perspectives Series challenges students to apply what they've learned to real-life situations. Become a member of the New Perspectives community and watch your students not only **master** computer skills, but also **retain** and carry this **knowledge** into the world.

New Perspectives catalog
Our online catalog is never out of date! Go to the Catalog link on our Web site to check out our available titles, request a desk copy, download a book preview, or locate online files.

Complete system of offerings
Whether you're looking for a Brief book, an Advanced book, or something in between, we've got you covered. Go to the Catalog link on our Web site to find the level of coverage that's right for you.

Instructor materials
We have all the tools you need—data files, solution files, figure files, a sample syllabus, and ExamView, our powerful testing software package.

How well do your students know Microsoft Office?
Experience the power, ease, and flexibility of SAM XP and TOM. These innovative software tools provide the first truly integrated technology-based training and assessment solution for your applications course. Click the Tech Center link to learn more.

Get certified
If you want to get certified, we have the titles for you. Find out more by clicking the Teacher's Lounge link.

Interested in online learning?
Enhance your course with rich online content for use through MyCourse 2.0, WebCT, and Blackboard. Go to the Teacher's Lounge to find the platform that's right for you.

Your link to the future is at www.course.com/NewPerspectives

What you need to know about this book.

- Student Online Companion takes students to the Web for additional work.

- ExamView testing software gives you the option of generating a printed test, LAN-based test, or test over the Internet.

- New Perspectives Labs provide students with self-paced practice on computer-related topics.

- There are many NEW cases in this edition!

- Introduces latest Internet technologies such as satellite connectivity and Internet Protocol version 6.

- Coverage includes both major Web browsers in use today.

- New Session 3.4 covers Web-based e-mail clients and provides steps students can follow to create their own accounts.

- New Session 6.3 includes coverage of using online storage services to store and transfer files.

- New Session 7.2 is on wireless networks; using a PDA, notebook computer, wireless telephone, or other device to send and receive e-mail messages; and creating personal and organizational wireless networks.

- New coverage of creating your own chat room in Tutorial 8.

- Expanded coverage of electronic commerce topics in Tutorial 10.

CASE	TROUBLE?	SESSION 1.1	QUICK CHECK	RW
Tutorial Case Each tutorial begins with a problem presented in a case that is meaningful to students. The case sets the scene to help students understand what they will do in the tutorial.	**TROUBLE? Paragraphs** These paragraphs anticipate the mistakes or problems that students may have and help them continue with the tutorial.	**Sessions** Each tutorial is divided into sessions designed to be completed in about 45 minutes each. Students should take as much time as they need and take a break between sessions.	**Quick Check Questions** Each session concludes with conceptual Quick Check questions that test students' understanding of what they learned in the session.	**Reference Windows** Reference Windows are succinct summaries of the most important tasks covered in a tutorial. They preview actions students will perform in the steps to follow.

BRIEF CONTENTS

TABLE OF CONTENTS

The Internet

Tutorial 4   WEB 4.03

Searching the Web

Using Search Engines and Directories Effectively

The Internet

Tutorial 7 — WEB 7.03

Advanced E-Mail

Using Mailing Lists and Exploring Wireless E-Mail Options

Tutorial 8 — WEB 8.01

Advanced Communication Tools

Using Chat, Virtual Worlds, and Newsgroups

Creating Web Pages with HTML

Tutorial 1   HTML 1.03

Creating a Web Page

Web Fundamentals and HTML

Tutorial 2   HTML 2.01

Adding Hypertext Links to a Web Page

Developing an Online Resume with Hypertext Links

Acknowledgments

Creating a textbook is a collaborative effort—authors and publisher work as a team to provide the highest quality book possible. The authors want to acknowledge the major contributions of the Course Technology editorial team members. We thank Mac Mendelsohn for his initial interest in and continual support of this book. It was Mac's vision for a book focused on the Internet, rather than on a specific software application, that motivated us to take on this project. We offer a special thank you to Martha Wagner, former Course Technology sales representative, for introducing us to Mac. We are grateful to Melissa Hathaway, Product Manager; Amanda Young, Associate Product Manager; Daphne Barbas, Production Editor; and John Bosco's team of Quality Assurance testers for being terrific, positive, and supportive members of a great publishing team. We also thank Jane Pedicini and Lisa Ruffolo, our Developmental Editors. Their sharp eyes caught many mistakes and they contributed excellent ideas for making the manuscript more readable. We offer our heartfelt thanks to the Course Technology organization as a whole. The people at Course Technology have been, by far, the best publishing team with which we have ever worked.

We want to thank the following reviewers for their insightful comments and suggestions at various stages of the book's development: Risa Blair, Champlain College; Donna Occhifinto, County College of Morris; Cathy Fothergill, Kilgore College; Don Lopez, The Clovis Center; Suzanne Nordhaus, Lee College; Sorel Reisman, California State University, Fullerton; T. Michael Smith, Austin Community College; and Bill Wagner, Villanova University. Margaret Beeler and Pamela Drotman provided helpful comments on early drafts of the outline for the first edition of this book.

Finally, we want to express our deep appreciation for the continuous support and encouragement of our spouses, Cathy Cosby and Richard Evans. They demonstrated remarkable patience as we worked to complete this book on a very tight schedule. We also thank our children for tolerating our absences while we were busy writing.

Gary P. Schneider

Jessica Evans

Dedication

To the memory of my brother, Bruce. — G.P.S.

To my little buddy, Hannah, who is "wise and talented." And to the memories of Ed and Lottie Evans, may you touch as many lives in heaven as you touched on earth. — J.E.

New Perspectives on

THE
INTERNET

3rd Edition

Read This Before You Begin

To the Student

Data Disks

To complete the Level I tutorials, Review Assignments, and Case Problems in this book, you need one Data Disk. Your instructor will either provide you with a Data Disk or ask you to make your own.

If you are making your own Data Disk, you will need **one** blank, formatted, high-density disk. You will need to copy a set of files and/or folders from a file server, a standalone computer, or the Web onto your disk. Your instructor will tell you which computer, drive letter, and folders contain the files you need. You could also download the files by going to **www.course.com** and following the instructions on the screen.

The information below shows you which folders go on your disk, so that you will have enough disk space to complete all the tutorials, Review Assignments, and Case Problems:

Data Disk 1

Write this on the disk label:
Data Disk 1: Tutorials 2 and 3
Put these folders on the disk:
Tutorial.02
Tutorial.03

When you begin each tutorial, be sure you are using the correct Data Disk. Refer to the "File Finder" chart at the back of this text for more detailed information on which files are used in the tutorials. See the inside front or inside back cover of this book for more information on Data Disk files, or ask your instructor or technical support person for assistance.

Course Labs

The tutorials in this book feature two interactive Course Labs to help you understand Internet and e-mail concepts. There are Lab Assignments at the end of Tutorials 2 and 3 that relate to these Labs.

To start a Lab, click the **Start** button on the Windows taskbar, point to **Programs**, point to **Course Labs**, point to **New Perspectives Course Labs**, and click the name of the Lab you want to use.

Using Your Own Computer

If you are going to work through this book using your own computer, you need:

■ **Computer System** Netscape Navigator 4.0 or higher or Microsoft Internet Explorer 4.0 or higher and Windows 95 or higher must be installed on your computer. This book assumes a complete installation of the Web browser software and its components, and that you have an existing e-mail account and an Internet connection. Because your Web browser may be different from the ones used in the figures or the book, your screens may differ slightly at times.

■ **Data Disk** You will not be able to complete the tutorials or exercises in this book using your own computer until you have a Data Disk.

■ **Course Labs** See your instructor or technical support person to obtain the Course Lab software for use on your own computer.

Visit Our World Wide Web Site

Additional materials designed especially for you are available on the World Wide Web.
Go to www.course.com/NewPerspectives.

To the Instructor

The Data Disk files and Course Labs are available on the Instructor's Resource Kit for this title. Follow the instructions in the Help file on the CD-ROM to install the programs to your network or standalone computer. For information on creating the Data Disk, see the "To the Student" section above. To complete the tutorials in this book, students must have a Web browser, an e-mail account, and an Internet connection.

You are granted a license to copy the Data Disk files and Course Labs to any computer or computer network used by students who have purchased this book.

In this tutorial you will:

- Obtain an overview of the tools and information that are available on the Internet

- Learn what computer networks are and how they work

- Find out how the Internet and World Wide Web began and grew

- Compare and evaluate different methods for connecting to the Internet

INTRODUCTION
TO THE INTERNET AND THE WORLD WIDE WEB

History, Potential, and Getting Connected

CASE

Tropical Exotics Produce Company

Lorraine Tomassini, the owner of the Tropical Exotics Produce Company (TEPCo), is concerned about the firm's future. She started TEPCo 10 years ago to import organically grown exotic fruits and vegetables from South America, Africa, and Asia to the U.S. market. The TEPCo product line includes items such as Asian pear, cherimoya, feijoa, African horned melon, sapote, and tamarillo. The business has grown rapidly and thrived financially, but Lorraine is worried that TEPCo is failing to use technology effectively. She already knows that this weakness has caused TEPCo to lose customers and suppliers to competitors.

You started work as an intern at TEPCo six months ago to learn more about international business while you attend college. Justin Jansen has been with the firm for about five years and is Lorraine's key assistant. During this week's meeting with you and Justin, Lorraine expressed concern that TEPCo has become internally focused and might be missing major market trends that affect its worldwide suppliers. She worries that reading newspapers for market information and staying in touch with suppliers by telephone are time-consuming, ineffective strategies. She recalled this past year, when bad weather in Costa Rica destroyed most of their suppliers' sapote crop, TEPCo received the reports too late to change its customer price schedule, in effect, wiping out almost all of the company's second quarter profit.

Justin explained that people can follow weather reports from all over the world using the Internet. He then suggested that TEPCo might be able to attract new customers by creating a Web site on the Internet, but he also explained that first TEPCo's five computers would need to be connected to each other. Lorraine also knew that colleges and universities had been involved in the Internet for years. She asked you to research ways that TEPCo might use the Internet, and you agreed to begin the research immediately.

SESSION 1.1

In this session, you will learn about the Internet and World Wide Web. You will learn how they have grown from their beginnings in the military and research communities. You will learn about the vast array of resources they provide and how the Internet has become one of the most powerful communication tools the world has ever known.

Internet and World Wide Web: Amazing Developments

The **Internet**—a large collection of computers all over the world that are connected to one another in various ways—is one of the most amazing technological developments of the twentieth century. Using the Internet you can communicate with other people throughout the world through **electronic mail** (or **e-mail**); read online versions of newspapers, magazines, academic journals, and books; join discussion groups on almost any conceivable topic; participate in games and simulations; and obtain free computer software. In recent years, the Internet has allowed commercial enterprises to connect. Today, all kinds of businesses provide information about their products and services on the Internet. Many of these businesses use the Internet to market and sell their products and services. The part of the Internet known as the **World Wide Web** (or the **Web**), is a subset of the computers on the Internet that are connected to each other in a specific way that makes those computers and their contents easily accessible to all computers in that subset. The Web has helped to make Internet resources available to people who are not computer experts. Figure 1-1 shows some of the tools and resources available on the Internet today.

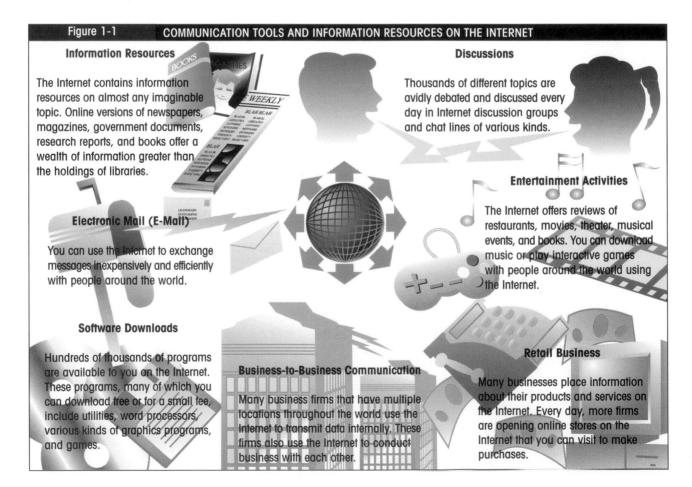

Figure 1-1   COMMUNICATION TOOLS AND INFORMATION RESOURCES ON THE INTERNET

Information Resources

The Internet contains information resources on almost any imaginable topic. Online versions of newspapers, magazines, government documents, research reports, and books offer a wealth of information greater than the holdings of libraries.

Discussions

Thousands of different topics are avidly debated and discussed every day in Internet discussion groups and chat lines of various kinds.

Electronic Mail (E-Mail)

You can use the Internet to exchange messages inexpensively and efficiently with people around the world.

Entertainment Activities

The Internet offers reviews of restaurants, movies, theater, musical events, and books. You can download music or play interactive games with people around the world using the Internet.

Software Downloads

Hundreds of thousands of programs are available to you on the Internet. These programs, many of which you can download free or for a small fee, include utilities, word processors, various kinds of graphics programs, and games.

Business-to-Business Communication

Many business firms that have multiple locations throughout the world use the Internet to transmit data internally. These firms also use the Internet to conduct business with each other.

Retail Business

Many businesses place information about their products and services on the Internet. Every day, more firms are opening online stores on the Internet that you can visit to make purchases.

As you begin Lorraine's research project, you remember her comment that TEPCo does not have its computers connected to each other. You decide to learn more about what computer networks are and how to connect computers to each other to form those networks.

Computer Networks

After talking with Adolfo Segura, the director of your school's computer lab, you realize that you will have some good news for Lorraine. Adolfo explained to you that he linked the lab computers to each other by inserting a network interface card into each computer and connecting cables from each card to the lab's main computer, called a server. Adolfo told you that a **network interface card** (often called a **NIC** or simply network card) is a card or other device used to connect a computer to a network of other computers. A **server** is a general term for any computer that accepts requests from other computers that are connected to it and shares some or all of its resources, such as printers, files, or programs, with those computers.

Client/Server Local Area Networks

The server runs software that coordinates the information flow among the other computers, which are called **clients**. The software that runs on the server computer is called a **network operating system**. Connecting computers this way, in which one server computer shares its resources with multiple client computers, is called a **client/server network**. Client/server networks commonly are used to connect computers that are located close together (for example, in the same room or building). Because the direct connection from one computer to another through network cards only works over relatively short distances (no more than a few thousand feet), this kind of network is called a **local area network** (**LAN**). Figure 1-2 shows a typical client/server LAN.

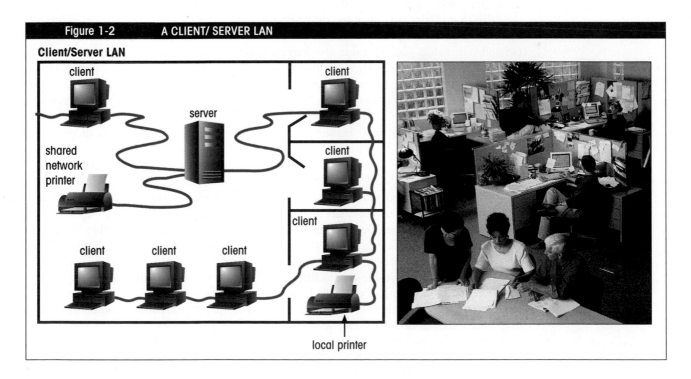

Figure 1-2   A CLIENT/ SERVER LAN

Client/Server LAN

local printer

The good news for Lorraine is that both the network cards and the cable that connects them are fairly inexpensive. Lorraine's first step in creating a LAN will be to select one of TEPCo's more powerful computers to be the server. A server can be a powerful personal computer (PC) or a minicomputer or a mainframe computer. **Minicomputers** and **mainframe computers** are larger, more expensive computers that businesses and other organizations use to process large volumes of work at high speeds. For many years, even the largest PCs were not powerful enough to be servers, but this has changed in recent years. Today, most PCs can handle server duties if they are equipped with enough memory and large enough disk drives.

Next, TEPCo will need to buy the network operating system software and have a network technician install it on the server. This software is more expensive than the operating system software for a standalone computer; however, having computers connected in a client/server network will offer TEPCo some cost savings. For example, by connecting each computer to the server, each computer can share the network printer and one tape drive for backups because a client/server network lets any computer on the network use a printer connected to the server and tape drives that are installed in the server.

Connecting Computers to a Network

As you talk with Adolfo, you learn more about computer networks. You find that not all LANs use the same kind of cables to connect their computers. The oldest cable type is called **twisted-pair**, which is the type of cable that telephone companies have used for years to wire residences and businesses. Twisted-pair cable has two or more insulated copper wires that are twisted around each other and enclosed in another layer of plastic insulation. The wires are twisted to reduce interference from other nearby current-carrying wires. The type of twisted-pair cable that telephone companies have used for years to transmit voice signals is called **Category 1** cable. Category 1 cable transmits information more slowly than the other cable types, but it is also much less expensive. **Coaxial cable** is an insulated copper wire that is encased in a metal shield that is enclosed with plastic insulation. The signal-carrying wire is completely shielded, so it resists electrical interference much better than twisted-pair cable. Coaxial cable also carries signals about 20 times faster than Category 1 twisted-pair; however, it is considerably more expensive. Because coaxial cable is thicker and less flexible than twisted-pair, it is harder for installation workers to handle and thus is more expensive to install. You might have seen coaxial cable because most cable television connections still use it.

In the past 20 years, cable manufacturers have developed better versions of twisted-pair cable. The current standards for twisted-pair cable used in computer networks are Category 5 and Category 5e cable. **Category 5** twisted-pair cable carries signals between 10 and 100 times faster than coaxial cable and is just as easy to install as Category 1 cable. Category 5e (the "e" stands for "enhanced") cable looks almost exactly like plain Category 5 cable, but it is constructed of higher quality materials so it can carry more signals even faster—up to 10 times faster—than regular Category 5 cable. Many businesses have Category 5 cable installed, but they are gradually replacing it with Category 5e. You may hear either of these cable types called Cat-5 cable by network technicians.

The most expensive cable type is **fiber-optic cable**, which does not use an electrical signal at all. Fiber-optic cable (also called simply fiber) transmits information by pulsing beams of light through very thin strands of glass. Fiber-optic cable transmits signals much faster than either coaxial cable or Category 5 twisted-pair cable. Because it does not use electricity, fiber-optic cable is completely immune to electrical interference. Fiber-optic cable is lighter and more durable than coaxial cable, but it is harder to work with and more expensive than either coaxial cable or Category 5 twisted-pair cable. The price of fiber-optic cable and the equipment that sends and receives the light-bearing signals at each end has dropped dramatically in the past few years. Thus, companies are using fiber-optic cable in more and more networks as the cost becomes more affordable. Figure 1-3 shows these three types of cable.

| Figure 1-3 | TWISTED-PAIR, COAXIAL, AND FIBER-OPTIC CABLES |

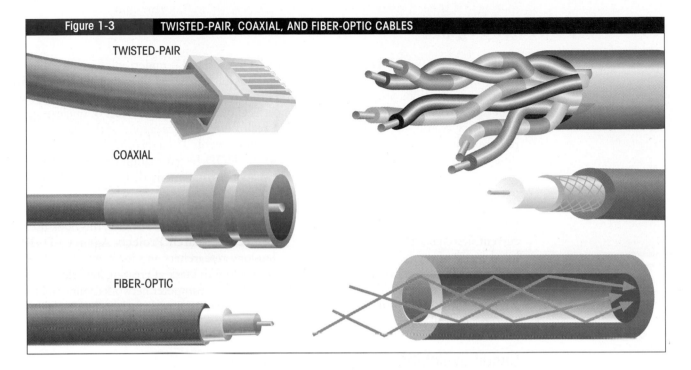

TWISTED-PAIR

COAXIAL

FIBER-OPTIC

Perhaps the most intriguing way to connect computers in a LAN is to avoid cable all together. **Wireless networks** are becoming more common as the cost of the wireless transmitters and receivers that plug into or replace network cards continues to drop. Wireless LANs are especially welcome in organizations that occupy old buildings. Many cities have structures that were built before electricity and telephones were widely available. These buildings have no provision for running wires through walls or between floors, so a wireless network can be the best option for connecting resources. Wireless connections are especially popular with companies whose employees use laptop computers and take them from meeting to meeting. A wireless network can really help workers be more effective and productive in flexible team environments. The cost of wireless networks is dropping, and many people are even installing them in their homes.

Wide Area Networks

You know that your school has several computer labs in different buildings, so you ask Adolfo whether the individual labs are connected to each other as a larger LAN. Adolfo explains that each computer lab is its own client/server LAN, but that these individual networks are connected to each other as part of the school's **wide area network (WAN)**. Adolfo remembers that you came to him with questions about the Internet and tells you that **internet** (lowercase "i") is short for **interconnected network**. The computer lab LANs are networks, and the school's WAN is a network of networks, or an internet. You look a little puzzled, so Adolfo continues to explain that *any* network of networks is called an internet. However, the school's WAN is connected to an internet called the Internet (capital "I"). The **Internet** is a specific worldwide collection of interconnected networks whose owners have voluntarily agreed to share resources and network connections with one another. You decide that your project is starting to become interesting and head toward the campus library to find out more about this huge interconnected network called the Internet.

How the Internet Began

In the early 1960s, the U.S. Department of Defense (DOD) undertook a major research project. Because this was a military project and was authorized as a part of national security, the true motivations are not known with certainty, but most people close to the project believe it arose from the government's concerns about the possible effects of nuclear attack on military computing facilities. The DOD realized that the weapons of the future would require powerful computers for coordination and control. The powerful computers of that time were all large mainframe computers, so the DOD began examining ways to connect these computers to each other and also to weapons installations that were distributed all over the world.

The agency charged with this task was the **Advanced Research Projects Agency** (**ARPA**). (During its lifetime, this agency has used two acronyms, ARPA and DARPA; this book uses its current acronym, **DARPA**, for **Defense Advanced Research Projects Agency**.) DARPA hired many of the best communications technology researchers and for many years funded research at leading universities and institutes to explore the task of creating a worldwide network. DARPA researchers soon became concerned about computer networks' vulnerability to attack and worked hard to devise ways to eliminate the need for network communications to rely on a central control function.

Circuit Switching vs. Packet Switching

The first networks among computers were created in the 1950s. The models for those early networks were the telephone companies because most early WANs used leased telephone company lines to connect computers to each other. In telephone company systems of that time, a telephone call established a single connection between sender and receiver. Once the connection was established, all data then traveled along that single path. The telephone company's central switching system selected specific telephone lines, or circuits, that would be connected to create the single path. This centrally controlled, single-connection method is called **circuit switching**. Most local telephone traffic today is still handled using circuit switching technologies.

Although the circuit switching is efficient and economical, it relies on a central point of control and a series of connections that form a single path. This makes circuit-switched communications vulnerable to the destruction of the central control point or any link in the series of connections that make up the single path that carries the signal. DARPA researchers turned to a different method of sending information, packet switching. In a **packet switching** network, files and messages are broken down into packets that are labeled electronically with codes for their origin and destination. The packets travel from computer to computer along the network until they reach their destination. The destination computer collects the packets and reassembles the original data from the pieces in each packet. Each computer that an individual packet encounters on its trip through the network determines the best way to move the packet forward to its destination. Computers that perform this function on networks are often called **routers**, or routing computers, and the programs they use to determine the best path for packets are called **routing algorithms**. Thus, packet-switched networks are inherently more reliable than circuit-switched networks because they rely on multiple routers instead of a central point of control and because each router can send individual packets along different paths if parts of the network are not operating.

By 1967, DARPA researchers had published their plan for a packet switching network, and in 1969, they connected the first computer switches at the University of California at Los Angeles, SRI International, the University of California at Santa Barbara, and the University of Utah. This experimental WAN, called the **ARPANET**, grew over the next three years to include over 20 computers and used the **Network Control Protocol (NCP)**. A **protocol** is a collection of rules for formatting, ordering, and error-checking data sent across a network.

Open Architecture Philosophy

As more researchers connected their computers and computer networks to the ARPANET, interest in the network grew in the academic community. The next several years saw many technological developments that increased the speed and efficiency with which the network operated. One reason for the project's success was its adherence to an **open architecture** philosophy; that is, each network could continue using its own protocols and data-transmission methods internally. Conversion to NCP occurred only when the data moved out of the local network and onto the ARPANET. The original purpose of the ARPANET was to connect computers in the field that were controlling a wide range of diverse weapons systems, so the ARPANET could not force its protocol or structure onto those individual component networks. This open approach was quite different from the closed architecture designs that companies such as IBM and Digital Equipment Corporation were using to build networks for their customers during this period. The open architecture philosophy included four key points:

- Independent networks should not require any internal changes to be connected to the Internet.
- Packets that do not arrive at their destinations must be retransmitted from their source network.
- The router computers do not retain information about the packets they handle.
- No global control will exist over the network.

One of the new developments of this time period that was rapidly adopted throughout the ARPANET was a set of new protocols developed by Vincent Cerf and Robert Kahn. These new protocols were the **Transmission Control Protocol** and the **Internet Protocol**, which usually are referred to by their combined acronym, **TCP/IP**. TCP includes rules that computers on a network use to establish and break connections; IP includes rules for routing of individual data packets. These two protocols were technically superior to the NCP that ARPANET had used since its inception and gradually replaced that protocol. TCP/IP continues to be used today in LANs and on the Internet. The term *Internet* was first used in a 1974 article about the TCP protocol written by Cerf and Kahn. The importance of the TCP/IP protocol in the history of the Internet is so great that many people consider Vincent Cerf to be the Father of the Internet.

ARPANET's successes were not lost on other network researchers. Many university and research institution computers used the UNIX operating system. When TCP/IP was included in a version of UNIX, these institutions found it easier to create networks and interconnect them. A number of TCP/IP-based networks—independent of the ARPANET—were created in the late 1970s and early 1980s. The National Science Foundation (NSF) funded the **Computer Science Network (CSNET)** for educational and research institutions that did not have access to the ARPANET. The City University of New York started a network of IBM mainframes at universities, called the **Because It's Time** (originally, "**There**") **Network (BITNET)**.

Birth of E-Mail: A New Use for Networks

Although the goals of ARPANET were still to control weapons systems and transfer research files, other uses for this vast network began to appear in the early 1970s. In 1972, an ARPANET researcher named Ray Tomlinson wrote a program that could send and receive messages over the network. E-mail had been born and became widely used in 1976; the Queen of England sent an e-mail message over the ARPANET. By 1981, the ARPANET had expanded to include over 200 networks and was continuing to develop faster and more effective network technologies; for example, ARPANET began sending packets via satellite in 1976.

More New Uses for Networks Emerge

The number of network users in the military and education research communities continued to grow. Many of these new participants used the networking technology to transfer files and access computers remotely. The TCP/IP suite included two tools for performing these tasks. **File Transfer Protocol** (**FTP**) enabled users to transfer files between computers, and **Telnet** let users log in to their computer accounts from remote sites. Both FTP and Telnet still are widely used on the Internet today for file transfers and remote logins, even though more advanced techniques facilitate multimedia transmissions such as real-time audio and video clips. The first e-mail mailing lists also appeared on these networks. A **mailing list** is an e-mail address that takes any message it receives and forwards it to any user who has subscribed to the list.

Although file transfer and remote login were attractive features of these new TCP/IP networks, their improved e-mail and other communications facilities attracted many users in the education and research communities. For example, BITNET would run mailing list software (called **LISTSERV**) on its IBM mainframe computers that provided automatic control and maintenance for mailing lists. In 1979, a group of students and programmers at Duke University and the University of North Carolina started Usenet, an acronym for **User's News Network**. Usenet allows anyone that connects with the network to read and post articles on a variety of subjects.

Usenet survives on the Internet today, with more than a thousand different topic areas, called **newsgroups**. Going even farther from the initial purpose of TCP/IP networks, researchers at the University of Essex wrote a program that allowed users to assume character roles and play an adventure game. This adventure game let multiple users play at the same time and interact with each other. These text-based games are much more primitive than the video games that many people play today on their computers or gaming devices, however a surprising number of people continue to play them on the Internet. These games are called **MUDs**, which originally stood for **multiuser dungeon**, although many users now consider the term an acronym for **multiuser domain** or **multiuser dimension**.

Although the people using these networks were developing many creative applications, the number of persons who had access to the networks was relatively small and limited to members of the research and academic communities. The decade from 1979 to 1989 would be the time in which these new and interesting network applications were improved and tested with an increasing number of users. The TCP/IP set of protocols would become more widely used as academic and research institutions realized the benefits of having a common communications network. The explosion of PC use during that time also would help more people become comfortable with computing.

Interconnecting the Networks

The early 1980s saw continued growth in the ARPANET and other networks. The **Joint Academic Network** (**Janet**) was established in the United Kingdom to link universities there. Traffic increased on all of these networks, and in 1984, the Department of Defense

(DOD) split the ARPANET into two specialized networks: ARPANET would continue its advanced research activities, and **MILNET** (for **Military Network**) would be reserved for military uses that required greater security. That year also saw a new addition to CSNET, named the **National Science Foundation Network (NSFnet)**. By 1987, congestion on the ARPANET caused by a rapidly increasing number of users on the limited-capacity leased telephone lines was becoming severe. To reduce the government's traffic load on the ARPANET, the NSFnet merged with BITNET and CSNET to form one network. The resulting NSFnet awarded a contract to Merit Network, Inc., IBM, Sprint, and the State of Michigan to upgrade and operate the main NSFnet backbone. A **network backbone** includes the long-distance lines and supporting technology that transports large amounts of data between major network nodes. The NSFnet backbone connected 13 regional WANs and six supercomputer centers. By the late 1980s, many other TCP/IP networks had merged or established interconnections. Figure 1-4 summarizes how the individual networks described in this section combined to become the Internet as it is known today.

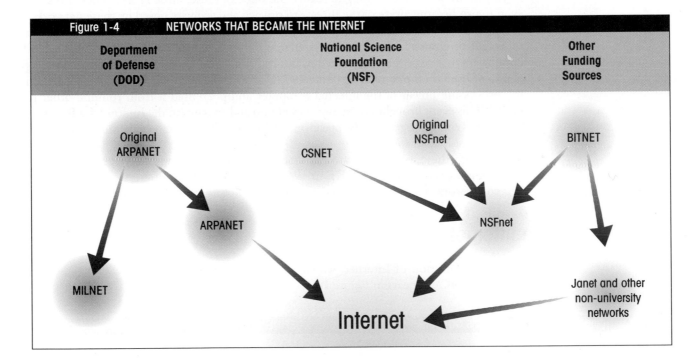

Figure 1-4   NETWORKS THAT BECAME THE INTERNET

Commercial Interest Increases

As PCs became more powerful, affordable, and available during the 1980s, firms increasingly used them to construct LANs. Although these LANs included e-mail software that employees could use to send messages to each other, businesses wanted their employees to be able to communicate with people outside their corporate LANs. The National Science Foundation (NSF) prohibited commercial network traffic on the networks it funded, so businesses turned to commercial e-mail services. Larger firms built their own TCP/IP-based WANs that used leased telephone lines to connect field offices to corporate headquarters. Today, people use the term **intranet** to describe LANs or WANs that use the TCP/IP protocol but do not connect to sites outside the firm. Although most companies allow only their employees to use the company intranet, some companies give specific outsiders, such as customers, vendors, or business partners, access to their intranets. These outside parties agree to respect the confidentiality of the information on the network. An intranet that allows selected outside parties to connect is often called an **extranet**.

In 1989, the NSF permitted two commercial e-mail services, MCI Mail and CompuServe, to establish limited connections to the Internet that allowed their commercial subscribers to exchange e-mail messages with the members of the academic and research communities who were connected to the Internet. These connections allowed commercial enterprises to send e-mail directly to Internet addresses and allowed members of the research and education communities on the Internet to send e-mail directly to MCI Mail and CompuServe addresses. The NSF justified this limited commercial use of the Internet as a service that would primarily benefit the Internet's noncommercial users.

People from all walks of life—not just scientists or academic researchers—started thinking of these networks as a global resource that we now know as the Internet. Information systems professionals began to form volunteer groups such as the **Internet Engineering Task Force (IETF)**, which first met in 1986. The IETF is a self-organized group that makes technical contributions to the engineering of the Internet and its technologies. IETF is the main body that develops new Internet standards.

Just as the world was coming to realize the value of these interconnected networks, however, it also became aware of the threats to privacy and security posed by these networks. In 1988, Robert Morris launched a program called the **Internet Worm** that used weaknesses in e-mail programs and operating systems to distribute itself to over 6,000 of the 60,000 computers that were then connected to the Internet. The Worm program created multiple copies of itself on the computers it infected. The large number of program copies consumed the processing power of the infected computer and prevented it from running other programs. This event brought international attention and concern to the Internet. Unfortunately, worms and other programs still appear on the Internet from time to time today, and they still can do considerable damage.

Although the network of networks that is now known as the Internet had grown from four computers on the ARPANET in 1969 to over 300,000 computers on many interconnected networks by 1990, the greatest growth in the Internet was yet to come.

Growth of the Internet

A formal definition of Internet, which was adopted in 1995 by the Federal Networking Council (FNC), appears in Figure 1-5.

| Figure 1-5 | THE FNC'S OCTOBER 1995 RESOLUTION TO DEFINE THE TERM INTERNET |

RESOLUTION: The Federal Networking Council (FNC) agrees that the following language reflects our definition of the term Internet. Internet refers to the global information system that

(i) is logically linked together by a globally unique address space based on the Internet Protocol (IP) or its subsequent extensions/follow-ons;

(ii) is able to support communications using the Transmission Control Protocol/Internet Protocol (TCP/IP) suite or its subsequent extensions/follow-ons, and/or other IP-compatible protocols; and

(iii) provides, uses or makes accessible, either publicly or privately, high level services layered on the communications and related infrastructure described herein.

Source: *http://www.fnc.gov/Internet_res.html*

Many people find it interesting that a formal definition of the term did not appear until 1995. The Internet was a phenomenon that surprised an unsuspecting world. The researchers who had been so involved in the creation and growth of the Internet accepted it as part of their working environment. People outside the research community were largely unaware of the potential offered by a large interconnected set of computer networks.

From Research Project to Information Infrastructure

By 1990, the Internet had become a well-functioning grid of useful technology. Much of the funding for these networks had come from the U.S. government, through the DOD and NSF. The NSFnet alone consumed over $200 million from 1986 to 1995 on research and development. Realizing that the Internet was no longer a research project, the DOD finally closed the research portion of its network, the ARPANET. The NSF also wanted to turn over the Internet to others so it could return its attention and funds to other research projects.

In 1991, the NSF further eased its restrictions on Internet commercial activity and began implementing plans to eventually privatize much of the Internet. The first parts of the NSFnet on which it encouraged commercial activity were the local and regional nodes, which allowed time for private firms to develop long-haul network capacity similar to that of the NSFnet national network backbone. Businesses and individuals connected to the Internet in ever-increasing numbers. Although nobody really knows how big the Internet is, one commonly used measure is the number of Internet hosts. An **Internet host** is a computer that connects a LAN or a WAN to the Internet. Each Internet host might have any number of computers connected to it. Figure 1-6 shows the rapid growth in the number of Internet host computers from 1991 through 2001. As you can see, the growth has been dramatic.

| Figure 1-6 | GROWTH IN THE NUMBER OF INTERNET HOSTS |

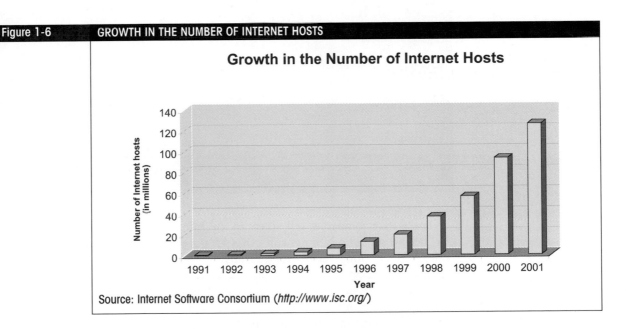

Source: Internet Software Consortium (*http://www.isc.org/*)

The numbers in Figure 1-6 probably understate the true growth of the Internet in recent years for two reasons. First, the number of hosts connected to the Internet includes only directly connected computers. In other words, if a LAN with 100 PCs is connected to the Internet through only one host computer, those 100 computers appear as one host in the count. Because the number and size of LANs has increased steadily in recent years, the host count probably is understated. Second, the number of computers is only one measure of growth. Internet traffic now carries more files that contain graphics, sound, and video, so Internet files have become larger. A given number of users sending video clips will use much more of the Internet's capacity than the same number of users will use by sending e-mail messages or text files. Many people are surprised to learn that no one knows how many users are on the Internet. The Internet has no central management or coordination, and the routing computers do not maintain records of the packets they handle. Although some companies and research organizations regularly estimate the Internet population, no one really knows how many individual e-mail messages or files travel on the Internet, and no one really knows how many people use the Internet today.

New Structure for the Internet

As NSFnet converted the main traffic-carrying backbone portion of its network to private firms, it organized the network around four network access points (NAPs). However, a different company now operates each of these NAPs, as shown in Figure 1-7.

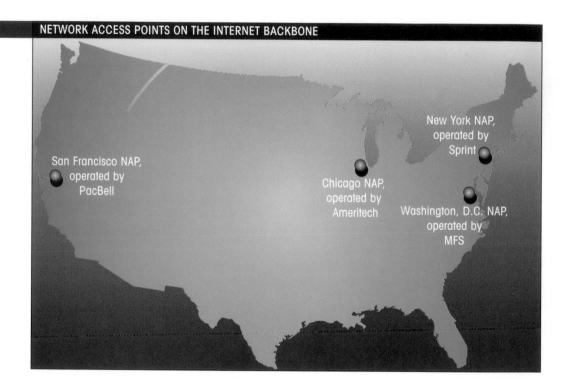

Figure 1-7   NETWORK ACCESS POINTS ON THE INTERNET BACKBONE

These four companies sell access to the Internet through their NAPs to organizations and businesses. The NSFnet still exists for government and research use, but it uses these same NAPs for long-range data transmission.

With more than 120 million connected Internet host computers and more than 500 million worldwide Internet users, the Internet faces some challenges. The firms that sell network access have enough incentive to keep investing in the network architecture because they can recoup their investments by attracting new Internet users. However, the existing TCP/IP numbering system that identifies users will run out of addresses in a few years if the Internet continues its current rate of growth. The version of the protocol that most router computers use today is IP version 4 (IPv4), which provides a maximum of about 4 billion addresses. In 1997, the IETF approved a new version of the protocol, IP version 6 (IPv6) that permits many more addresses (the actual number is 134 followed by 152 zeroes). The new addressing scheme will allow existing users to continue accessing the Internet while the new system is implemented. Although some organizations have rebuilt their networks to use IPv6, full adoption by all Internet users will take many years.

In just over 30 years, the Internet has become one of the most amazing technological and social accomplishments of the century. Millions of people use a complex, interconnected network of computers that run thousands of different software packages. The computers are located in almost every country of the world. Billions of dollars change hands every year over the Internet in exchange for all kinds of products and services. All of this activity occurs with no central coordination point or control. Even more interesting is that the Internet most likely began as a way for the military to maintain control while under attack.

The opening of the Internet to business enterprise helped increase its growth dramatically in recent years. However, another development worked hand-in-hand with the commercialization of the Internet to spur its growth. That development was the technological advance known as the World Wide Web.

World Wide Web

The World Wide Web (the Web) is more a way of thinking about information storage and retrieval than it is a technology. Because of this, its history goes back many years. Two important innovations played key roles in making the Internet easier to use and more accessible to people who were not research scientists: hypertext and graphical user interfaces (GUIs).

Origins of Hypertext

In 1945, Vannevar Bush, who was Director of the U.S. Office of Scientific Research and Development, wrote an *Atlantic Monthly* article about ways that scientists could apply the skills they learned during World War II to peacetime applications. The article included a number of visionary ideas about future uses of technology to organize and facilitate efficient access to information. He speculated that engineers eventually would build a machine that he called the **Memex**, a memory extension device that would store all of a person's books, records, letters, and research results on microfilm. Bush's Memex would include mechanical aids to help users consult their collected knowledge fast and in a wide variety of ways. In the 1960s, Ted Nelson described a similar system in which text on one page links to text on other pages. Nelson called his page-linking system **hypertext**. Douglas Englebart, who also invented the computer mouse, created the first experimental hypertext system on one of the large computers of the 1960s. Twenty years later, Nelson published *Literary Machines*, in which he outlined project Xanadu, a global system for online hypertext publishing and commerce.

Hypertext and Graphical User Interfaces Come to the Internet

In 1989, Tim Berners-Lee and Robert Calliau were working at CERN-The European Laboratory for Particle Physics and were trying to improve the laboratory's research document-handling procedures. CERN had been connected to the Internet for two years, but its scientists wanted to find better ways to circulate their scientific papers and data among the high-energy physics research community throughout the world. Independently, they each proposed a hypertext development project.

Over the next two years, Berners-Lee developed the code for a hypertext server program and made it available on the Internet. A **hypertext server** is a computer that stores files written in the hypertext markup language and lets other computers connect to it and read those files. **Hypertext Markup Language** (**HTML**) is a language that includes a set of codes (or tags) attached to text. These codes describe the relationships among text elements. For example, HTML includes tags that indicate which text is part of a header element, which text is part of a paragraph element, and which text is part of a numbered list element. One important type of tag is the hypertext link **tag**. A **hypertext link**, or **hyperlink**, points to another location in the same or another HTML document. You can use several different types of software to read HTML documents, but most people use a Web browser such as Netscape Navigator or Microsoft Internet Explorer. A **Web browser** is software that lets users read (or browse) HTML documents and move from one HTML document to another through the text formatted with hypertext link tags in each file. If the HTML documents are on computers connected to the Internet, you can use a Web browser to move from an HTML document on one computer to an HTML document on any other computer on the Internet. HTML is a subset of **Standard Generalized Markup Language** (**SGML**), which organizations have used for many years to manage large document-filing systems.

An HTML document differs from a word-processing document because it does not specify *how* a particular text element will appear. For example, you might use word-processing software to create a document heading by setting the heading text font to Arial, its font size to 14 points, and its position to centered. The document would display and print these exact settings whenever you opened the document in that word processor. In contrast, an HTML document would simply include a heading tag with the text. Many different programs can read an HTML document. Each program recognizes the heading tag and displays the text in whatever manner each program normally displays headers. Different programs might display the text differently.

A Web browser presents an HTML document in an easy-to-read format in its graphical user interface. A **graphical user interface** (**GUI,** pronounced "gooey") is a way of presenting program output using pictures, icons, and other graphical elements instead of just displaying text. Almost all PCs today use a GUI such as Microsoft Windows or the Macintosh user interface. Researchers have found that computer users—especially new users—learn new programs more quickly when they have a GUI interface instead of a text interface. Because each Web page has its own set of controls (hyperlinks, buttons to click, and blank text boxes in which to type text), every person who visits a Web site for the first time becomes a "new user" of that site. Thus, the GUI interface presented in Web browsers has been an important element in the rapid growth of the Web.

Berners-Lee and Calliau called their system of hyperlinked HTML documents the World Wide Web. The Web caught on rapidly in the scientific research community, but few people outside that community had software that could read the HTML documents. In 1993, a group of students led by Marc Andreessen at the University of Illinois wrote **Mosaic**, the first GUI program that could read HTML and use HTML documents' hyperlinks to navigate from page to page on computers anywhere on the Internet. Mosaic was the first Web browser that became widely available for PCs.

The Web and Commercialization of the Internet

Programmers quickly realized that a functional system of pages connected by hypertext links would provide many new Internet users with an easy way to locate information on the Internet. Businesses quickly recognized the profit-making potential offered by a worldwide network of easy-to-use computers. In 1994, Andreessen and other members of the University of Illinois Mosaic team joined with James Clark of Silicon Graphics to found Netscape Communications. Their first product, the Netscape Navigator Web browser program based on Mosaic, was an instant success. Netscape became one of the fastest growing software companies ever.

Microsoft created its Internet Explorer Web browser and entered the market soon after Netscape's success became apparent. Microsoft offered its browser at no cost to computer owners that used its Windows operating system. Within a few years, many users had switched to Internet Explorer, and Netscape was unable to earn enough money to continue in business. Microsoft was accused of wielding its monopoly power to drive Netscape out of business; these accusations led to the trial of Microsoft on charges that it violated the U.S. anti-trust laws. Parts of Netscape were sold to America Online, but the Netscape Navigator browser became open-source software. Open-source software is created and maintained by volunteer programmers, often hundreds of them, who work together using the Internet to build and refine a program. The program is made available to users at no charge. A few other Web browsers exist, but most people today use either Internet Explorer or Netscape Navigator.

The number of **Web sites**, which are computers connected to the Internet that store HTML documents, has grown even more rapidly than the Internet itself to include more than 30 million sites. Each Web site might have hundreds, or even thousands, of individual Web pages, so the amount of information on the Web is astounding. Figure 1-8 shows the phenomenal growth in the Web during its short lifetime.

Figure 1-8	GROWTH OF THE WORLD WIDE WEB

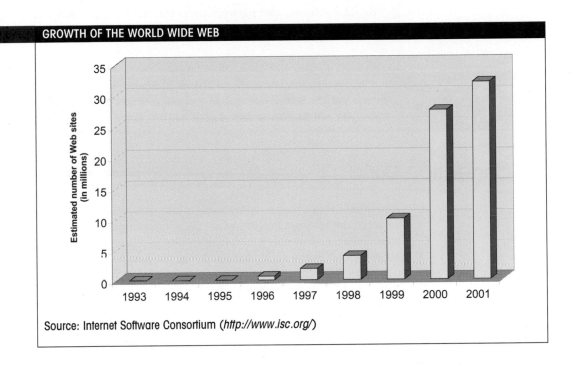

Source: Internet Software Consortium (*http://www.isc.org/*)

As more people obtain access to the Web, commercial uses of the Web and a variety of non-business uses will continue to increase. Although the Web has grown rapidly, many experts believe that it will grow at an increasing rate for the foreseeable future.

You have obtained a good background for your report on how TEPCo might use the Internet and the Web by learning about their histories. You are convinced that the Internet can help Lorraine and her staff manage the company better, identify new customers, and stay in contact with suppliers. You decide that the next logical step in your research is to identify ways that TEPCo can connect to the Internet. In the next session, you will learn how to evaluate Internet connection options.

Session 1.1 QUICK CHECK

1. Name three resources that computers connected to a client/server LAN can share.

2. The fastest and most expensive way to connect computers in a network is _____ cable.

3. Telephone companies use centrally controlled circuit switching to connect telephone callers and transmit data. The Internet uses the _____ switching method.

4. The technical term for the collection of rules that computers follow when formatting, ordering, and error-checking data sent across a network is _____.

5. The networks that became the Internet were originally designed to transmit files; however, early in its history, people found other uses for the Internet. Name one of those uses.

6. A network that uses the TCP/IP protocol, but only connects computers within one company is called a(n) _____.

7. Two key factors that contributed to the Internet's rapid growth in the 1990s are _____ and _____.

8. The software that network users can run on their computers to access HTML documents stored on other computers is called a(n) _____.

SESSION 1.2

In this session, you will learn about how to connect your computer to the Internet. You will learn about the connection options that are available and their advantages and disadvantages. You will be able to then choose the one that is right for you.

Connection Options

Remember that the Internet is a set of interconnected networks. Thus, you cannot become a part of the Internet unless you are part of a communications network, whether it is a LAN, an intranet, or through a telephone connection. Each network that joins the Internet must accept some responsibility for operating the network by routing message packets that other networks pass along. As you consider your project for TEPCo, you become concerned that Justin and Lorraine are not going to want to become involved in something this complex. After all, they are exotic-produce experts—not computer wizards!

Business of Providing Internet Access

As you continue your research, you learn more about the NAPs (network access points) that maintain the core operations and long-haul backbone of the Internet. You find that they do not offer direct connections to individuals or small businesses. Instead, they offer connections to large organizations and businesses that, in turn, provide Internet access to other businesses and individuals. These firms are called **Internet access providers (IAPs)** or **Internet service providers (ISPs)**. Most of these firms call themselves ISPs because they offer more than just access to the Internet. ISPs usually provide their customers with the software they need to connect to the ISP, browse the Web, send and receive e-mail messages, and perform other Internet-related functions such as file transfer and remote login to other computers. ISPs often provide network consulting services to their customers and help them design Web pages. Some ISPs have developed a full range of services that include network management, training, and marketing advice. Some larger ISPs not only sell Internet access to end users, but also market Internet access to other ISPs, which then sell access and service to their own business and individual customers. This hierarchy of Internet access appears in Figure 1-9.

Figure 1-9	THE HIERARCHY OF INTERNET SERVICE OPTIONS

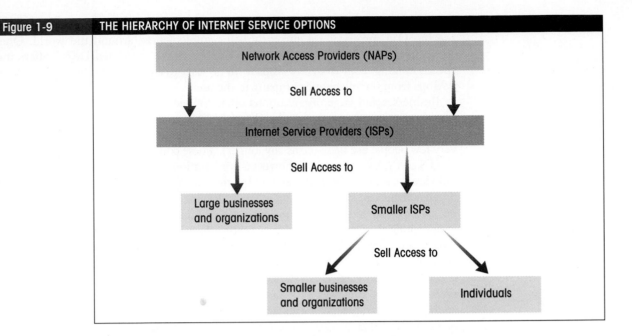

Connection Bandwidth

Of the differences that exist among service providers at different levels of the access hierarchy, one of the most important is the connection bandwidth that an ISP can offer. **Bandwidth** is the amount of data that can travel through a communications circuit in one second. The bandwidth that an ISP can offer you depends on the type of connection it has to the Internet and the kind of connection you have to the ISP.

The bandwidth for a network connection between two points is always limited to the narrowest bandwidth that exists in any part of the network. For example, if you connect to an ISP through a regular telephone line, your bandwidth is limited to the bandwidth of that telephone line, regardless of the bandwidth connection that the ISP has to the Internet. Bandwidth is measured in multiples of **bits per second (bps)**. Discussions of Internet bandwidth often use the terms **kilobits per second (Kbps)**, which is 1,024 bps; **megabits per second (Mbps)**, which is 1,048,576 bps; and **gigabits per second (Gbps)**, which is 1,073,741,824 bps. Most LANs run either an Ethernet network, which has a bandwidth of 10 Mbps, or Fast Ethernet, which operates at 100 Mbps. Some companies are starting to install the latest technology, Gigabit Ethernet, which operates at 1 Gbps. When you extend your network beyond a local area, the speed of the connection depends on what type of connection you use.

One way to connect computers or networks over longer distances is to use regular telephone service (sometimes referred to as **POTS**, or **plain old telephone service**). Regular telephone service to most U.S. residential and business customers provides a maximum bandwidth of between 28.8 Kbps and 56 Kbps. These numbers vary because the United States has a number of different telephone companies that do not all use the same technology. Some telephone companies offer a higher grade of service that uses one of a series of protocols called **Digital Subscriber Line** or **Digital Subscriber Loop (DSL)**. The first technology that was developed using a DSL protocol is called **Integrated Services Digital Network (ISDN)**. ISDN service has been available in various parts of the United States since 1984. Although considerably more expensive than regular telephone service, ISDN offers bandwidths of up to 256 Kbps. ISDN is much more widely available in Australia, France, Germany, Japan, and Singapore than in the United States because the regulatory structure of the telecommunications industries in those countries encouraged rapid deployment of this new technology. All technologies based on the DSL protocol require the implementing telephone company to install modems at its switching stations, which can be very expensive. New technologies that use the DSL protocol are currently being implemented around the world. One of those, **Asymmetric Digital Subscriber Line** (**ADSL**, also abbreviated **DSL**), offers transmission speeds ranging from 16 to 640 Kbps from the user to the telephone company and from 1.5 to 9 Mbps from the telephone company to the user.

Businesses and large organizations often connect to an ISP using higher-bandwidth telephone company connections called **T1** (1.544 Mbps) and **T3** (44.736 Mbps) connections (the names T1 and T3 were originally acronyms for Telephone 1 and Telephone 3, respectively, but very few people use these terms any longer). These connections are much more expensive than POTS or ISDN connections; however, organizations that must link hundreds or thousands of individual users to the Internet require the greater bandwidth of T1 and T3 connections. Smaller firms can share space on a T1 or T3 line. The NAPs currently operate the Internet backbone using a variety of connections. In addition to T1 and T3 lines, the NAPs use newer connections that have bandwidths of more than 1 Gbps—in some cases reaching 10 Gbps. These new connection options are numbered OC3, OC12, and so forth because when these technologies were developed they were the only connections that used optical fiber. The OC is short for optical carrier. NAPs also use high-bandwidth satellite and radio communications links to transfer data over long distances. The NAPs are working with a group of universities and the National Science Foundation (NSF) to develop a network called Internet 2 that will have backbone bandwidths that soon will exceed 10 Gbps.

A connection option that is available in parts of the United States and in some other countries is to connect to the Internet through a cable television company. The cable company transmits data in the same cables it uses to provide television service. Cable can deliver up to 10 Mbps to an individual user and can accept up to 768 Kbps from an individual user. These speeds far exceed those of existing POTS and ISDN connections and are comparable to speeds provided by the ADSL technologies currently being implemented by telephone companies and other companies that rent facilities from the telephone companies.

An option that is particularly appealing to users in remote areas is connecting via satellite. Using a satellite-dish receiver, you can download at a bandwidth of approximately 400 Kbps. Until recently, you could not send information to the Internet using a satellite dish antenna, so you needed to also have an ISP account to send files or e-mail. Very recently, two satellite companies began offering two-way satellite connections to the Internet. Figure 1-10 summarizes the bandwidths, costs, and typical uses for the various types of connections currently in use on the Internet.

Figure 1-10	BANDWIDTHS FOR VARIOUS TYPES OF INTERNET CONNECTIONS				
Service	Upstream Speed (Kbps)	Downstream Speed (Kbps)	Capacity (Number of Simultaneous Users)	One-time Startup Costs	Continuing Monthly Costs
Residential-Small Business Services					
Modem (POTS)	28–56	28–56	1	$0–$20	$12–$20
ISDN	128–256	128–256	1–3	$60–$300	$50–$90
ADSL	100–640	4,500–9,000	1–4	$50–$100	$40–$90
Cable modem	300–1,000	1,000–10,000	1–4	$0–$100	$40–$70
Satellite	125–150	400–500	1–3	$600–$1,200	$60–$70
Business Services					
Leased digital line (DS0)	64	64	1–10	$50–$200	$40–$150
Fractional T1 leased line	128–1,544	128–1,544	5–180	$50–$800	$100–$1,000
T1 leased line	1,544	1,544	100–200	$100–$2,000	$900–$1,600
T3 leased line	44,700	44,700	1,000–10,000	$1,000–$9,000	$5,000–$12,000
Large Business, ISP, NAP, and Internet 2 Services					
OC3 leased line	156,000	156,000	1,000–50,000	$3,000–$12,000	$9,000–$22,000
OC12 leased line	622,000	622,000	Backbone	Negotiated	$25,000–$100,000
OC48 leased line	2,500,000	2,500,000	Backbone	Negotiated	Negotiated
OC192 leased line	10,000,000	10,000,000	Backbone	Negotiated	Negotiated

As you evaluate the information you have gathered about ways Lorraine might connect TEPCo to the Internet, you realize that there are four ways that individuals or small businesses can link to the Internet. The first way, which is only for individuals, is a connection through your school or employer. The second option is to connect through an ISP. The third option is to connect through a cable television company. The fourth option is to use a satellite service provider. Next, you will learn about some of the advantages and disadvantages of each connection method that you have identified for your analysis and report to Lorraine.

Connecting Through Your School or Employer

One of the easiest ways to connect to the Internet is through your school or employer, if it already has an Internet connection. The connection is either free or very reasonably priced. If you do use your school or employer to connect to the Internet, you must comply with its rules. In some cases, this can outweigh the cost advantage.

Connecting Through Your School

Most universities and community colleges are connected to the Internet, and many offer Internet access to their students, faculty members, and other employees. In most schools, you can use computers in computing labs or in the library to access the Internet. Many schools provide a way to connect your own computer through the school's network to the Internet. The form of connection will depend on what your school offers. An increasing number of schools have dormitory rooms wired with LAN connections so students can connect using their own computers. Some schools even provide the computers as part of their tuition or housing charge.

Dialing In

Some schools and businesses still provide telephone numbers that students or employees can use to connect their computers to the Internet through a modem. **Modem** is short for **modulator-demodulator**. When you connect your computer, which communicates using digital signals, to another computer through a telephone line, which uses analog signals, you must perform a signal conversion. Converting a digital signal to an analog signal is **modulation**; converting that analog signal back into digital form is called **demodulation**. A modem performs both functions; that is, it acts as a modulator-demodulator. When you connect to the Internet through your school or employer, your computer's modem converts your computer's digital signals into analog signals that can travel on the telephone system's wires (POTS). A modem at your school or employer converts the analog signal back into a digital signal and sends it through a LAN and a router to the Internet for you.

Connecting Through Your Employer

Your employer might offer you a connection to the Internet through the computer you use in your job. This computer might be connected through a LAN to the Internet, or you might have to use a modem to connect it. Before you attempt to connect to the Internet this way, make sure that your employer permits personal use of company computing facilities. Remember, your employer owns the computers you use as an employee. In most of the world, this gives your employer the right to examine any e-mail or files that you transmit or store using those computers. A number of schools retain similar rights under the law or through policies they publish in their student handbooks.

Acceptable Use Policies

Most schools and employers have an **acceptable use policy (AUP)** that specifies the conditions under which you can use their Internet connections. Some organizations require you to sign a copy of the AUP before they permit you to use their computing facilities; others simply include it as part of your student or employee contract. AUPs often include provisions that require you to respect copyright laws, trade secrets, the privacy of other users, and standards of common decency. Many AUPs expressly prohibit you from engaging in commercial activities, criminal activities, or specific threat-making or equipment-endangering practices.

Many provisions in AUPs are open to honest misunderstanding or disagreement in interpretation. It is extremely important for you to read and understand any AUP with which you must comply when you use computing facilities at your school or employer. AUPs often include punitive provisions that include revocation of user accounts and all rights to use the network. Some AUPs state that a user can be expelled or fired for serious violations.

Advantages and Disadvantages

Although accessing the Internet through your school or employer might be the least expensive option, you might decide that the restrictions on your freedom of expression and actions are too great. For example, if you wanted to start a small business on the Web, you would not want to use your school account if its AUP has a commercial-activity exclusion. An important concern when using your employer's computing facilities to access the Internet is that the employer generally retains the right to examine any files or e-mail messages that you transmit through those facilities. You should carefully consider whether the limitations placed on your use of the Internet are greater than the benefits of the low cost of this access option. For example, you may not want to use your employer's Internet connection when you are sending your resume to another company in hopes of landing a different job.

Connecting Through an Internet Service Provider

Depending on where you live, you might find that an ISP is the best way for you to connect to the Internet. In major metropolitan areas, many ISPs compete for customers and, therefore connection fees often are reasonable. Smaller towns and rural areas have fewer ISPs and, thus might be less competitive. When you are shopping for an ISP, you will want to find information such as:

- The monthly base fee and number of hours it provides
- The hourly rate for time used over the monthly base amount
- Whether the telephone access number is local or long distance
- Which specific Internet services are included
- What software is included
- What user-support services are available

Advantages and Disadvantages

ISPs are the best option for many Internet users, in part, because they usually provide reliable connectivity at a reasonable price. The terms of their AUPs often are less restrictive than those imposed by schools on their students or employers on their employees. You should examine carefully the terms of the service agreement, and you always should obtain references from customers who use an ISP before signing any long-term contract.

Some ISPs limit the number of customers they serve, whereas others guarantee that you will not receive a busy signal when you dial in. These are significant factors in the quality of service you will experience. Remember, each ISP has a limited amount of bandwidth in its connection to the Internet. If your ISP allows more new customers to subscribe to its service than leave each month, each remaining user will have proportionally less bandwidth available. Be especially wary of ISPs that offer a large discount if you sign a long-term agreement. The quality of service might deteriorate significantly over time if the ISP adds many new customers without expanding its bandwidth.

You also should find out whether the ISP has an AUP and, if so, you should examine its terms carefully. Some ISPs have restrictive policies. For example, an ISP might have an entirely different fee structure for customers who use their Internet access for commercial purposes. Carefully outline how you plan to use your Internet connection, and decide what services you want before signing any long-term contract with an ISP.

Connecting Through Your Cable Television Company

One of the fastest growing means of Internet access is the cable modem. A **cable modem** performs a function similar to that of a regular modem; that is, it converts digital computer signals to analog signals. However, instead of converting the digital signals into telephone-line analog signals, a cable modem converts them into radio-frequency analog signals that are similar to television transmission signals. The converted signals travel to and from the cable company on the same lines that carry your cable television service. The cable company maintains a connection to the Internet and otherwise operates much like the ISPs discussed previously, which deliver an Internet connection through telephone lines.

To install a cable modem, the cable company first installs a **line-splitter,** a device that divides the combined cable signals into their television and data components, and then connects the television (or televisions) and the cable modem to the line-splitter. Most cable companies that offer this service rent the required line-splitter and cable modem to each customer.

Advantages and Disadvantages

The main advantage of a cable television connection to the Internet is its high bandwidth. A cable connection can provide very fast downloads to your computer from the Internet, as much as 170 times faster than a telephone line connection. Although upload speeds are not as fast, they are still about 14 times faster than a telephone line connection. The cost usually is higher than—and often more than double—what competing ISPs charge. However, if you consider that the cable connection might save you the cost of a second telephone line, the net benefit can be significant. The greatest disadvantage for most people right now is that the cable connection is simply not available in their area yet. Because cable companies must invest in expensive upgrades to offer this service, it might not become available in some parts of the U.S. for many years. Another problem arises from the shared nature of the cable connection. As more people in your neighborhood subscribe to cable modem service, they share the bandwidth of your connection. This can slow down your access speeds significantly. The cable company should monitor the traffic and, when needed, add more equipment to handle the increased load. Not all cable companies have been diligent in doing this. You should remember that, other than the nature of the connection, a cable company is the same as any other ISP. Therefore, all of the issues outlined in the previous section about contracting with ISPs apply equally to dealing with your cable company.

Connecting Through a DSL Provider

DSL connections (today, ADSL and other types of DSL connection are referred to as simply DSL) are increasingly available in the United States and a few other countries. These services are sold by telephone companies and in some locations by other companies. These other companies are called third-party DSL providers, and they are companies that lease lines from the local telephone company and resell Internet connection service through those lines to individuals and small businesses.

Advantages and Disadvantages

DSL providers often claim that their service is better than that offered by cable companies. Because the part of the DSL service that runs from the customer to the telephone company is not shared, the traffic loading problems that can occur with cable modem access cannot occur with DSL service. Of course, once the packets enter the DSL provider's network, the bandwidth is then shared and heavy traffic loads can slow down access for everyone using the service. DSL's speeds are similar to cable modems and the subscription rates are similar. The biggest drawback for most DSL users is that they are buying the service from either their local telephone company or a third-party provider that must work with the telephone company. Many people have experienced long delays in getting DSL service installed or in having repairs completed. Telephone companies have not done a very good job in training their employees to sell, install, and maintain DSL services. The third-party providers must depend on the telephone companies to install the service because it uses the telephone company's lines. A number of large DSL providers have gone out of business recently because they were unable to deliver the services they promised and make a profit. In many cases, their subscribers were left without an Internet connection for months before another company entered the market.

Connecting Via Satellite

Many rural areas in the United States do not have cable television service and may never have it because their low population density makes it too expensive—a cable company cannot afford to run miles of cable to reach one or two isolated customers. People in these areas often buy satellite receivers to obtain television signals. Recently, Internet connections via satellite became available. Some services provide a satellite connection for downlinks only, so you also must have another connection through an ISP that uses telephone lines to handle the uplink half of the connection. Recently, two companies have started offering satellite connections that are two-way. The satellite dish is a transmitting antenna as well as being a receiving antenna.

Advantages and Disadvantages

These services offer speeds and charge monthly fees that are similar to those of cable and DSL providers. The installation fee is usually considerably higher for a satellite connection because the dish must be installed and aimed at the satellite, tasks that often require the skills of a professional installer. Most satellite customers choose the option because they do not have cable or DSL service available and satellite is their only high-speed connection option.

You now have collected a great deal of information about the origins and history of the Internet and the Web. As you conducted your research project for TEPCo, you learned about some of the information and tools that exist on the Internet. You also gathered information about ways to connect to the Internet. Now you are ready to prepare your report for Lorraine and recommend a plan of action for connecting TEPCo to the Internet.

Session 1.2 QUICK CHECK

1. To connect to the Internet, your computer must be part of a(n) _____.

2. The acronym typically used when referring to a company that provides Internet access to individuals and small businesses is _____.

3. How much greater bandwidth does ISDN offer over plain old telephone service (POTS)?

4. A T3 leased line would be a good Internet connection option for a(n) _____.

5. The device that converts digital computer signals into analog signals that can travel over a standard telephone line is called a(n) _____.

6. A document that specifies the conditions under which you can use your school's or your employer's Internet connection is called a(n) _____.

7. Persons living in remote areas can have a fast connection to the Internet if they subscribe to a _____ service.

PROJECTS

1. *Diagramming School Networks* Your school probably has a number of computer networks. At most schools, you can find information about computing facilities from the department of academic computing or the school library. Identify what LANs and WANs you have on your campus, and determine whether any or all of them are interconnected. Draw a diagram that shows the networks, their connections to each other, and their connection to the Internet.

2. *DARPA Alternatives* The DARPA researchers that laid the foundation for the Internet were conducting research on ways to coordinate weapons control. They chose to develop a computer network that could operate without a central control mechanism. The DARPA researchers might have chosen to develop a centrally controlled system instead. Discuss whether you think that approach would have given birth to something similar to the Internet. Describe how you think the result would differ from the Internet and Web that exist today.

3. *School Cabling Choices* Select two or three buildings on your campus that have computers in offices, dormitory rooms, or computing labs. Find out from the appropriate office administrator, dormitory official, or lab supervisor what kind of computer cable the school uses to connect the computers. Evaluate the school's cabling choices. Would you make the same decisions? Why or why not?

4. *Using the Web and E-Mail* Describe three ways in which you might use the Web or e-mail to identify part-time job and internship opportunities that relate to your major.

5. *Acceptable Use Policy Evaluation* Obtain a copy of your school's or employer's acceptable use policy (AUP). Outline the main restrictions it places on student (or employee) activities. Compare those restrictions with the limits it places on faculty (or employer) activities. Analyze and evaluate any differences in treatment. If there are no differences, discuss whether the policy should be rewritten to include differences. If your school or employer has no policy, outline the key elements that you believe should be included in such a policy for your school or employer.

6. *Commercialization of the Internet*   Many people who have been involved with the Internet for many years believe that the National Science Foundation (NSF) made a serious mistake when it opened the Internet to commercial traffic. Discuss the advantages and disadvantages of this policy decision. Do you think that the Internet would be as successful as it is today if no commercial activity had been allowed?

7. *The Web and the Memex Machine*   Vannevar Bush died before the Web came into existence. Speculate on what he would have thought about the Web. Would he have seen it as the embodiment of his Memex machine? Why or why not?

8. *Evaluating   ISPs* Contact three ISPs in your area and obtain information about their Internet access and related services. You can find ISPs in your local telephone directory (try headings such as "Internet Services," "Computer Networks," or "Computer On-Line Services"), or look for advertisements in your local or student newspaper. Summarize the services and the charges for each service by ISP. Which ISP would you recommend for an individual? Why? Which ISP would you recommend for a small business? Why?

QUICK | CHECK ANSWERS

Session 1.1

1. printers, scanners, digital cameras, data files, programs (or similar equipment or files)
2. fiber-optic
3. packet
4. protocol
5. e-mail, mailing lists, Usenet newsgroups, adventure gaming
6. intranet
7. commercialization, the development of the WWW
8. Web browser

Session 1.2

1. network
2. ISP
3. two to ten times
4. large company or other organization, an ISP, or a network backbone services provider
5. modem
6. acceptable use policy or AUP
7. satellite

BROWSER BASICS

Introduction to Microsoft Internet Explorer and Netscape Navigator

OBJECTIVES

In this tutorial you will:

- Learn about Web browser software and Web pages

- Learn about Web addresses and URLs

- Save and organize Web addresses

- Navigate the Web

- Use the Web to find information

- Configure and use the Microsoft Internet Explorer Web browser

- Configure and use the Netscape Navigator Web browser

LAB

The Internet: World Wide Web

CASE

Sunset Wind Quintet

The Sunset Wind Quintet is a group of five musicians who have played together for eight years. At first, the group began by playing free concerts for local charitable organizations, and as the group's reputation grew, the musicians were soon in demand at art gallery openings and other functions.

Each member of the quintet is an accomplished musician. The instruments in a wind quintet include flute, oboe, clarinet, bassoon, and French horn, which are all orchestral instruments. Each quintet member has experience as a player in a symphony orchestra as well. Three quintet members—the flutist, bassoonist, and the French horn player—currently hold positions with the local orchestra. The other two quintet members—the clarinetist and the oboist—teach classes in their respective instruments at the local university.

This past summer, a booking agent asked the quintet to do a short regional tour. Although the tour was successful, the quintet members realized that none of them had any business-management skills. Marianna Rabinovich, the clarinetist, handles most of the business details for the group. The quintet members realized that business matters related to the tour were overwhelming Marianna and that they wanted to do more touring, so they hired you as their business manager.

One of your tasks will be to help market the Sunset Wind Quintet. To do this, you must learn more about how other wind quintets operate and sell their services. At one of your early meetings with the group, you found that each member of the quintet had different priorities. In addition to marketing the quintet's performances, some members felt it would be a good idea to record and sell CDs, whereas others were concerned about finding instrument-repair facilities on the road when tours extended beyond the local area.

As you discussed these issues with the quintet members, you started thinking of ways to address their concerns. Your first idea was to find trade magazines and newspapers that might describe what other small classical musical ensembles were doing. As you considered the time and cost of this alternative, you realized that the Internet and World Wide Web might offer a better way to get started.

SESSION 2.1

In this session, you will learn how Web pages and Web sites make up the World Wide Web. You will learn what you should consider when selecting and using a specific software tool to find information on the Web. Finally, you will learn some basic browser concepts, which will help your browsing experience.

Web Browsers

The Internet: World Wide Web

As you start to consider how you might use the Web to gather information for the Sunset Wind Quintet, you remember that one of your college friends, Maggie Beeler, earned her degree in library science. You meet with Maggie at the local public library, where she is working at the reference desk. She is glad to assist you.

Maggie begins by explaining that the Web is a collection of files that reside on computers, called Web servers, that are located all over the world and are connected to each other through the Internet. Most files on computers, including computers that are connected to the Internet, are private; that is, only the computer's users can access those files. The owners of the computer files that make up the Web have made those files publicly available. Anyone who has a computer connected to the Internet can obtain access to those files.

Client/Server Structure of the World Wide Web

When you use your Internet connection to become part of the Web, your computer becomes a **Web client** in a worldwide client/server network. A **Web browser** is the software that you run on your computer to make it work as a Web client. The Internet connects many different types of computers running different operating system software. Web browser software lets your computer communicate with all of these different types of computers easily and effectively.

Computers that are connected to the Internet and that contain files that their owners have made available publicly through their Internet connections are called **Web servers**. Figure 2-1 shows how this client/server structure uses the Internet to provide multiple interconnections among the various kinds of client and server computers.

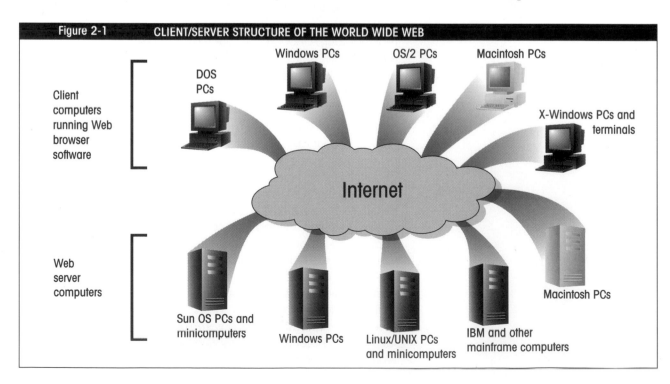

Figure 2-1   CLIENT/SERVER STRUCTURE OF THE WORLD WIDE WEB

Hypertext, Links, and Hypermedia

The public files on Web servers are ordinary text files, much like the files created and used by word-processing software. To enable Web browser software to read these files, however, the text must be formatted according to a generally accepted standard. The standard used on the Web is **Hypertext Markup Language** (**HTML**). HTML uses codes, or **tags**, that tell the Web browser software how to display the text contained in the text file. For example, a Web browser reading the following line of text

```
<B>A Review of the Book <I>Wind Instruments of the
18th Century</I></B>
```

recognizes the <B> and </B> tags as instructions to display the entire line of text in bold and the <I> and </I> tags as instructions to display the text enclosed by those tags in italics. Different Web clients that connect to this Web server might display the tagged text differently. For example, one Web browser might display text enclosed by bold tags in a blue color instead of displaying the text in bold. A text file that contains HTML tags is called an HTML document.

HTML provides a variety of text formatting tags that can be used to indicate headings, paragraphs, bulleted lists, numbered lists, and other text enhancements in an HTML document. The real power of HTML, however, lies in its anchor tag. The **HTML anchor tag** enables Web designers to link HTML documents to each other. Anchor tags in HTML documents create **hypertext links** to other HTML documents. Hypertext links can also connect one part of an HTML document to other sections of that document. Hypertext links also are called **hyperlinks** or **links**. Figure 2-2 shows how these hyperlinks can join multiple HTML documents to create a web of HTML documents across computers on the Internet. The HTML documents shown in the figure can be on the same computer or on different computers. The computers can be in the same room or an ocean away.

| Figure 2-2 | HYPERLINKS CREATE A WEB OF HTML TEXT ACROSS MULTIPLE FILES |

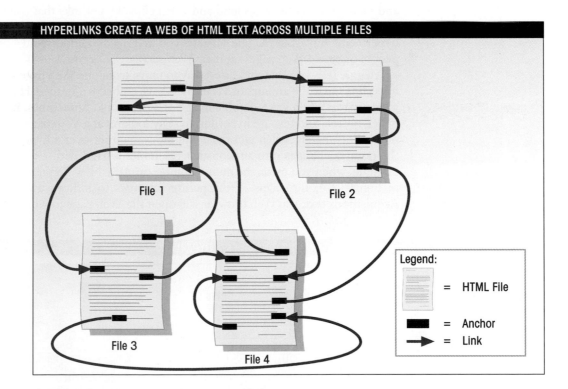

Most Web browsers display hyperlinks in a color that is different from other text in an HTML document and underline the hyperlinks so they are easy to distinguish. When a

Web browser displays an HTML document, it is often referred to as a Web page. Maggie shows you the Web page for the Lawrence Public Library (see Figure 2-3). The hyperlinks on this Web page are easy to identify because the Web browser software that displayed this page shows the hyperlinks as blue, underlined text.

Figure 2-3	LAWRENCE PUBLIC LIBRARY WEB PAGE

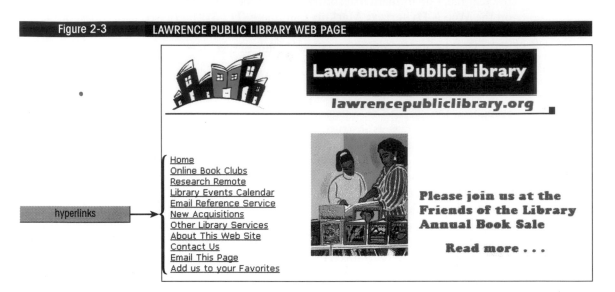

Each of the hyperlinks on the Web page shown in Figure 2-3 enables the user to connect to another Web page. In turn, each of those Web pages contains hyperlinks to other pages, including one hyperlink that leads back to the first Web page. Hyperlinks often connect to other Web pages, and these links can lead to computer files that contain pictures, graphics, and media objects such as sound and video clips. Hyperlinks that connect to these types of files often are called **hypermedia links**. You are especially interested in learning more about hypermedia links, but Maggie suggests you first need to understand a little more about how people organize Web pages on their Web servers.

Maggie tells you that the easiest way to move from one Web page to another is to use the hyperlinks that the authors of Web pages have embedded in their HTML documents. Web page authors often use a graphic image as a hyperlink. Sometimes, it is difficult to identify which objects and text are hyperlinks just by looking at a Web page displayed on your computer. Fortunately, when you move the mouse pointer over a hyperlink in a Web browser, the pointer changes into an icon that resembles a hand with a pointing index finger. For example, when you move the mouse pointer over the New Acquisitions hyperlink, as shown in Figure 2-4, the shape of the pointer changes to indicate that if you click the New Acquisitions text, the Web browser will open the Web page to which that hyperlink points.

Figure 2-4	MOUSE POINTER HOVERING OVER A HYPERLINK

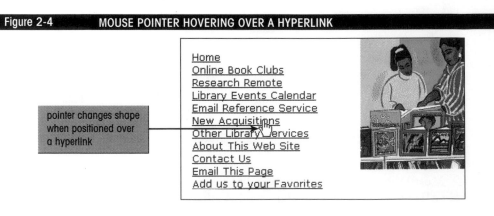

You might encounter an error message when you click on a hyperlink. Two common messages that you might see are "server busy" and "DNS entry not found". Either of these messages means that your browser was unable to communicate successfully with the Web server that stores the page you requested. The cause for this inability might be temporary—in which case, you might be able to use the hyperlink later—or the cause might be permanent. The browser has no way of determining the cause of the connection failure, so the browser provides the same types of error messages in either case. Another error message that you might receive appears as a Web page and includes the text "Error 404: File not Found." This error message usually means that the Web page's location has changed permanently or that the Web page no longer exists.

Web Pages and Web Sites

Maggie explains that people who create Web pages usually have a collection of pages on one computer that they use as their Web server. A collection of linked Web pages that has a common theme or focus is called a **Web site**. The main page that all of the pages on a particular Web site are organized around and link back to is called the site's **home page**.

Home Pages

Maggie warns you that the term *home page* is used at least three different ways on the Web and that it is sometimes difficult to tell which meaning people intend when they use the term. The first definition of home page indicates the main page for a particular site. This home page is the first page that opens when you visit a particular Web site. The second definition of home page is the first page that opens when you start your Web browser. This type of home page might be an HTML document on your own computer. Some people create such home pages and include hyperlinks to Web sites that they frequently visit. If you are using a computer on your school's or employer's network, its Web browser might be configured to open the main page for the school or firm. The third definition of home page is the Web page that a particular Web browser loads the first time you use it. This page usually is stored at the Web site of the firm or other organization that created the Web browser software. Home pages that meet the second or third definitions are sometimes called **start pages**.

Web Sites

Most Web sites store all of the site's pages in one location, either on one computer or on one LAN. Some large Web sites, however, are distributed over a number of locations. In fact, it is sometimes difficult to determine where one Web site ends and another begins. One common definition of a Web site is any group of Web pages that relates to one specific topic or organization, regardless of where the HTML documents are located.

Addresses on the Web

Maggie reminds you that there is no centralized control over the Internet. Therefore, no central starting point exists for the Web, which is a part of the Internet. However, each computer on the Internet does have a unique identification number, called an **IP (Internet Protocol) address**.

IP Addressing

The IP addressing system currently in use on the Internet is **IP version 4 (IPv4)**. IPv4 uses a 32-bit number to label each address on the Internet. The 32-bit IP address is usually written in four 8-bit parts. In most computer applications, an 8-bit number is called a **byte**; however, in networking applications, an 8-bit number is often called an **octet**. In the binary (base 2) numbering system, an octet can have values from 00000000 to 11111111; the decimal equivalents of these binary numbers are 0 and 255, respectively. Each part of a 32-bit IP address is separated from the previous part by a period, such as 106.29.242.17. You might hear a person pronounce this address as "one hundred six dot twenty-nine dot two four two dot seventeen." This notation is often called **dotted decimal** notation. The combination of these four parts provides 4.2 billion possible addresses ($256 \times 256 \times 256 \times 256$). Because each of the four parts of a dotted decimal number can range from 0 to 255, IP addresses range from 0.0.0.0 (which would be written in binary as 16 zeros) to 255.255.255.255 (which would be written in binary as 16 ones). Although many people find dotted decimal notation to be somewhat confusing at first, most do agree that writing, reading, and remembering a computer address as 216.115.108.245 is easier than 11010000111011000110100101011000 or its full decimal equivalent, which is 674,962,008.

In the mid-1990s, the accelerating growth of the Internet created concern that the world could run out of IP addresses within a few years. In the early days of the Internet, the 4 billion addresses provided by the IPv4 rules certainly seemed to be more addresses than an experimental research network would ever need. However, about 2 billion of those addresses today are either in use or unavailable for use because of the way blocks of addresses were assigned to organizations. The addition of new kinds of devices to the Internet's many networks, such as wireless personal digital assistants and cell phones that can access the Web, promises to keep the demand for IP addresses high.

Network engineers have devised a number of stop-gap techniques, such as **subnetting**, which is the use of reserved private IP addresses within LANs and WANs to provide additional address space. **Private IP addresses** are series of IP numbers that have been set aside for subnet use and are not permitted on packets that travel on the Internet. In subnetting, a computer called a **network address translation (NAT)** device converts those private IP addresses into normal IP addresses when the packets move from the LAN or WAN onto the Internet.

The **Internet Engineering Task Force (IETF)** worked on several new protocols that could solve the limited addressing capacity of IPv4 and, in 1997, approved **IP version 6 (IPv6)** as the protocol that would replace IPv4. The new IP is being implemented gradually because the two protocols are not directly compatible. However, network engineers have devised ways to run both protocols together on interconnected networks. The major advantage of IPv6 is that it uses a 128-bit hexadecimal (base 16) number for addresses instead of the 32-bit binary (base 2) number used in IPv4. A **hexadecimal numbering system** uses 16 digits (0, 1, 2, 3, 4, 5, 6, 7, 8, 9, a, b, c, d, e, and f). For example, the dotted-decimal IP address 216.115.108.245 would be written as 283b1a58 in hexadecimal. The number of available addresses in IPv6 is 134 followed by 152 zeros—many billions of times larger than the address space of IPv4. The new IP also changes the format of the packet itself. Improvements in networking technologies over the past 20 years have made many of the fields in the IPv4 packet unnecessary. IPv6 eliminates those fields and adds news fields for security and other optional information.

Domain Name Addressing

Although each computer connected to the Internet has a unique IP address, most people do not use the IP address to locate Web sites and individual pages. Instead, the browsers use domain name addressing. A **domain name** is a unique name associated with a specific IP address by a program that runs on an Internet host computer. This program, which coordinates the IP addresses and domain names for all computers attached to it, is called

DNS (domain name system) software, and the host computer that runs this software is called a **domain name server**. Domain names can include any number of parts separated by periods; however, most domain names currently in use have only three or four parts. Domain names follow a hierarchical model that you can follow from top to bottom if you read the domain names from right to left. For example, the domain name gsb.uchicago.edu is the computer connected to the Internet at the Graduate School of Business (gsb), which is an academic unit of the University of Chicago (uchicago), which is an educational institution (edu). No other computer on the Internet has the same domain name.

The last part of a domain name is called its **top-level domain (TLD)**. For example, DNS software on the Internet host computer that is responsible for the "edu" domain keeps track of the IP address for all of the educational institutions in its domain, including "uchicago." Similar DNS software on the "uchicago" Internet host computer would keep track of the academic units' computers in its domain, including the "gsb" computer.

Since 1998, the **Internet Corporation for Assigned Names and Numbers (ICANN)** has had responsibility for managing domain names. In the United States, the six most common TLDs have been .com, .edu, .gov., mil, .net, and .org. Internet host computers outside the United States often use two-letter country domain names instead of, or in addition to, the six general TLDs. For example, the domain name uq.edu.au is the domain name for the University of Queensland (uq), which is an educational institution (edu) in Australia (au). State and local government organizations in the United States frequently use an additional domain name "us." The "us" domain is also used by U.S. primary and secondary schools because the "edu" domain is reserved for postsecondary educational institutions.

In 2000, ICANN added seven new TLDs to the general domain category. Although these new domain names were chosen after much deliberation and consideration of more than 100 possible new names, a number of people were highly critical of the selections. Figure 2-5 presents a list of the general TLDs, including the seven new additions, and some of the more popular country TLDs.

Figure 2-5	COMMON TOP-LEVEL DOMAINS (TLDS)				

Original General TLDs		Country TLDs		General TLDs Approved in 2000	
TLD	**Use**	**TLD**	**Country**	**TLD**	**Use**
.com	U.S. Commercial	.au	Australia	.aero	Air-transport industry
.edu	U.S. Four-year educational institution	.ca	Canada	.biz	Businesses
		.de	Germany	.coop	Cooperatives
.gov	U.S. Federal government	.fi	Finland	.info	General use
.mil	U.S. Military	.fr	France	.museum	Museums
.net	U.S. General use	.jp	Japan	.name	Individual persons
.org	U.S. Not-for-profit organization	.se	Sweden	.pro	Professionals (accountants, lawyers, physicians)
		.uk	United Kingdom		

Uniform Resource Locators

The IP address and the domain name each identify a particular computer on the Internet, but they do not indicate where a Web page's HTML document resides on that computer. To identify a Web page's exact location, Web browsers rely on Uniform Resource Locators. A **Uniform Resource Locator (URL)** is a four-part addressing scheme that tells the Web browser:

- The transfer protocol to use when transporting the file
- The domain name of the computer on which the file resides
- The pathname of the folder or directory on the computer on which the file resides
- The name of the file

The **transfer protocol** is the set of rules that the computers use to move files from one computer to another on an internet. The most common transfer protocol used on the Internet is the hypertext transfer protocol (HTTP). You can indicate the use of this protocol by typing http:// as the first part of the URL. People do use other protocols to transfer files on the Internet, but most of these protocols were used more frequently before the Web became part of the Internet. Two protocols that you still might see on the Internet are the file transfer protocol (FTP), which is indicated in a URL as ftp://, and the Telnet protocol, which is indicated in a URL as telnet://. FTP is just another way to transfer files, and Telnet is a set of rules for establishing a remote terminal connection to another computer.

The domain name is the Internet address of the computer described in the preceding section. The pathname describes the hierarchical directory or folder structure on the computer that stores the file. Most people are familiar with the structure used on Windows and DOS PCs, which uses the back slash character (\) to separate the structure levels. URLs follow the conventions established in the UNIX operating system that use the forward slash character (/) to separate the structure levels. The forward slash character works properly in a URL, even when it is pointing to a file on a Windows or DOS computer.

The filename is the name that the computer uses to identify the Web page's HTML document. On most computers, the filename extension of an HTML document is either .html or .htm. Although many PC operating systems are not case-sensitive, computers that use the UNIX operating system *are* case-sensitive. Therefore, if you are entering a URL that includes mixed-case and you do not know the type of computer on which the file resides, it is safer to retain the mixed-case format of the URL.

Not all URLs include a filename. If a URL does not include a filename, most Web browsers will load the file named index.html. The **index.html** filename is the default name for a Web site's home page on most computer systems. Figure 2-6 shows an example of a URL annotated to show its four parts.

Figure 2-6	STRUCTURE OF A UNIFORM RESOURCE LOCATOR (URL)

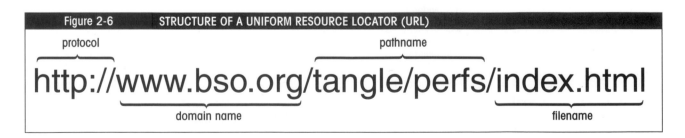

The URL shown in Figure 2-6 uses the HTTP protocol and points to a computer that is connected to the Web (www) at the Boston Symphony Orchestra (bso), which is a not-for-profit organization (org). The Boston Symphony's Web page contains many different kinds of information about the orchestra. The path shown in Figure 2-6 includes two levels. The first level indicates that the information is about the orchestra's summer home at Tanglewood (tangle), and the second level indicates that the page will contain information about the orchestra's performances (perfs) at Tanglewood. The filename (index.html) indicates that this page is the home page in the Tanglewood performances folder or directory.

You tell Maggie how much you appreciate all of the help she has given you by explaining how you can use Internet addresses to find information on the Web. Now you understand that the real secret to finding good information on the Web is to know the right URLs. Maggie tells you that you can find URLs in many places; for example, newspapers and magazines often publish URLs of Web sites that might interest their readers. Friends who know about the subject area in which you are interested also are good sources. The best source, however, is the Web itself.

You are eager to begin learning how to use a Web browser, so Maggie explains some elements common to all Web browsers. Most Web browsers have similar functions, which make it easy to use any Web browser after you have learned how to use one.

Main Elements of Web Browsers

Now that you know a little more about Web sites, you start to wonder how you can make your computer communicate with the Internet. Maggie tells you that there are a number of different Web browsers. Web browser software turns your computer into a Web client that can communicate through an Internet service provider (ISP) or a network connection with Web servers all over the world. Two popular browsers are **Microsoft Internet Explorer**, or simply **Internet Explorer**, and **Netscape Navigator**, or simply **Navigator**. Each browser has been released in different versions, however, the steps in this book are designed so they should work for most browsers.

Maggie reminds you that most Windows programs use a standard graphical user interface (GUI) design that includes a number of common screen elements. Figures 2-7 and 2-8 show the main elements of the Internet Explorer and Navigator program windows. These two Web browsers share many common Windows elements: a title bar at the top of the window, a scroll bar on the right side of the window, and a status bar at the bottom of the window.

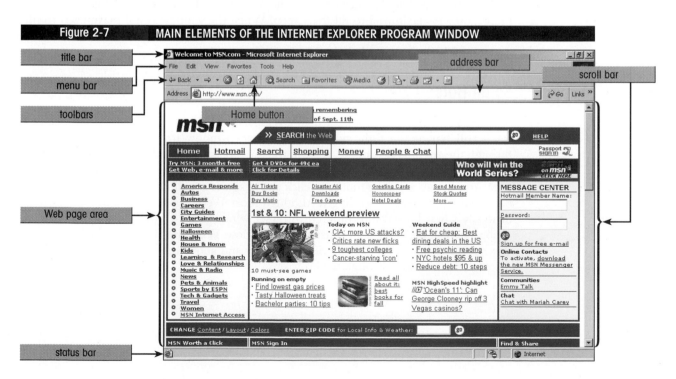

Figure 2-7 MAIN ELEMENTS OF THE INTERNET EXPLORER PROGRAM WINDOW

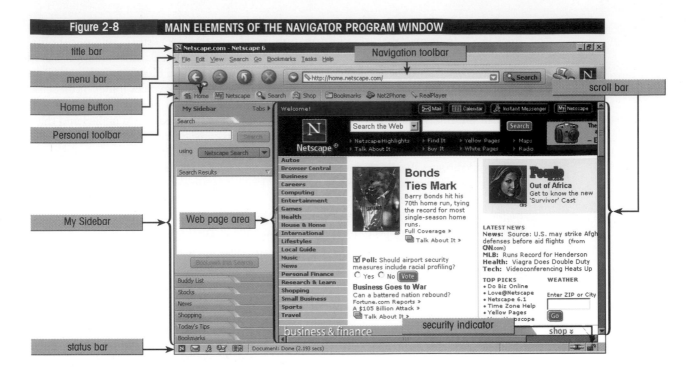

Figure 2-8   MAIN ELEMENTS OF THE NAVIGATOR PROGRAM WINDOW

In each program window, the menu bar appears below the title bar, and below the menu bar is a toolbar. Many of the toolbar button functions in Internet Explorer and Navigator are very similar. Next, Maggie describes each of these elements.

Title Bar

A Web browser's **title bar** shows the name of the open Web page and the Web browser's program name. As in all Windows programs, you can double-click the title bar to resize the window quickly. The title bar contains the **Minimize**, **Restore**, and **Close** buttons when the window is maximized to fill the screen. When the window is not maximized to fill the screen, the Restore button changes into a Maximize button. To expand such a browser window so it fills the screen, click the **Maximize** button.

Scroll Bars

A Web page can be much longer than a regular-sized document, so you often need to use the **scroll bar** at the right side of the program window to move the page up or down through the document window. You can use the mouse to click the **Up scroll button** or the **Down scroll button** to move the Web page up or down through the window's **Web page area**. You can also use the mouse to click and drag the **scroll box** up and down in the scroll bar to move the page accordingly. Although most Web pages are designed to resize automatically when loaded into different browser windows with different display areas, some Web pages can be wider than your browser window. When this happens, the browser places another scroll bar at the bottom of the window and above the status bar, so you can move the page horizontally through the browser.

Status Bar

The **status bar** at the bottom of the browser window includes information about the browser's operations. Each browser uses the status bar to deliver different information, but generally, the status bar indicates the name of the Web page that is loading, the load status (partial or complete), and important messages, such as "Document: Done." Some Web sites send messages as part of their Web pages that are displayed in the status bar as well. You will learn more about the specific functions of the status bar in Internet Explorer and Navigator in Sessions 2.2 and 2.3, respectively.

Menu Bar

The browser's **menu bar** provides a convenient way for you to execute typical File, Edit, View, and Help commands. In addition to these common Windows command sets, the menu bar also provides specialized commands for the browser that enable you to navigate the Web.

Home Button

Clicking the **Home** button in Internet Explorer or in Navigator displays the home (or start) page for the browser. Most Web browsers let you specify a page that loads automatically every time you start the program. You might not be able to do this if you are in your school's computer lab because schools often set the start page for all browsers on campus and then lock that setting. Some companies do the same thing on their employees' computers. If you are using your own computer, you can choose your own start page. Some people like to use a Web page that someone else has created and made available for others to use. One example of a start page that many people use as their start page is the refdesk.com Web page, shown in Figure 2-9.

Figure 2-9   REFDESK.COM WEB PAGE

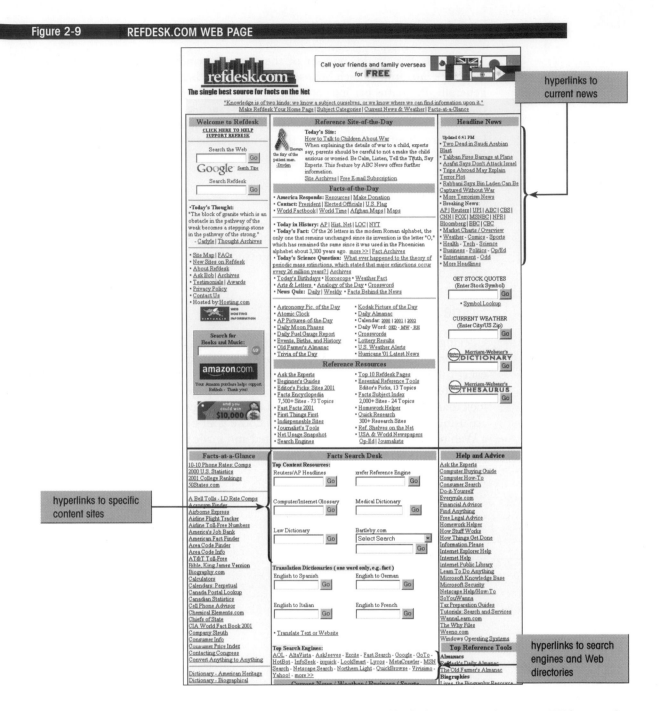

Pages such as the one shown in Figure 2-9 offer links to pages that many Web users frequently visit. The people and organizations that create these pages often sell advertising space on their pages to pay the cost of maintaining their sites.

Quick Access to Web Page Directories and Guides

You are starting to understand how to use the Internet to gather information. Maggie explains that a **Web directory** is a Web page that contains a list of Web page categories, such as education or recreation. The hyperlinks on a Web directory page lead to other pages that contain lists of subcategories that lead to other category lists and Web pages that relate to the category topics. **Web search engines** are Web pages that conduct searches of the Web to find the words or expressions that you enter. The result of such a search is a Web page that contains hyperlinks to Web pages that contain matching text or expressions. These pages can give new users an easy way to find information on the Web. Internet Explorer and Netscape each include a **Search** (the Internet) button. Clicking this button in either browser opens search engines and Web directories chosen by the companies that wrote the browser software. However, many people prefer to select their own tools for searching the Internet.

Web addresses can be long and hard to remember—even if you are using domain names instead of IP addresses. In Internet Explorer, you save the URL as a **favorite** in the Favorites folder. In Netscape, you use a **bookmark** to save the URL of a specific page so you can return to it. You realize that using the browser to remember important pages will be a terrific asset as you start collecting information for the quintet, so you ask Maggie to explain more about how to return to a Web page.

Using the History List

As you click the hyperlinks to go to new Web pages, the browser stores the locations of each page you visit during a single session in a **history list**. You click the **Back** button and the **Forward** button in both Internet Explorer and Navigator to move through the history list.

When you start your browser, both buttons are inactive (dimmed) because no history list for your new session exists yet. After you follow one or more hyperlinks, the Back button lets you retrace your path through the hyperlinks you have followed. Once you use the Back button, the Forward button becomes active and lets you move forward through the session's history list.

In most Web browsers, you can right-click either the Back or Forward button to display a portion of the history list. You can reload any page on the list by clicking its name in the list. The Back and Forward buttons duplicate the functions of commands on the browser's menu commands. You will learn more about the history list in Sessions 2.2 and 2.3.

Reloading a Web Page

Clicking the **Refresh** button in Internet Explorer or the **Reload** button in Navigator loads the same Web page that appears in the browser window again. The browser stores a copy of every Web page it displays on your computer's hard drive in a **cache** folder, which increases the speed at which the browser can display pages as you navigate through the history list. The cache folder lets the browser load the pages from the client instead of from the remote Web server.

When you click the Refresh or the Reload button, the browser contacts the Web server to see if the Web page has changed since it was stored in the cache folder. If it has changed, the browser gets the new page from the Web server; otherwise, the browser loads the cache folder copy. If you want to force the browser to load the page from the Web server, hold down the Shift key as you click the Refresh or Reload button.

Stopping a Web Page Transfer

Sometimes a Web page takes a long time to load. When this occurs, you can click the **Stop** button in Internet Explorer or Navigator to halt the Web page transfer from the server; you can then click the hyperlink again. A second attempt may connect and transfer the page more quickly. You also might want to use the Stop button to abort a transfer when you accidentally click a hyperlink that you do not want to follow.

Returning to a Web Page

You can use Internet Explorer's Favorites feature or a Navigator bookmark to store and organize a list of Web pages that you have visited so you can return to them easily without having to remember the URL or search for the page again. Internet Explorer favorites and Navigator bookmarks work very much like a paper bookmark that you might use in a printed book: They mark the page at which you stopped reading.

You can save as many Internet Explorer favorites or Navigator bookmarks as you want to mark all of your favorite Web pages, so you can return to pages that you frequently use or pages that are important to your research or tasks. You could bookmark every Web page you visit!

Keeping track of many favorites and bookmarks requires an organizing system. You store favorites or bookmarks in a system folder. Internet Explorer stores *each* favorite as a separate file on your computer, and Netscape stores bookmarks in one file on your computer. Storing each favorite separately, instead of storing all bookmarks together, offers somewhat more flexibility but uses more disk space. You can organize your favorites or bookmarks in many different ways to meet your needs. For example, you might store all of the favorites or bookmarks for Web pages that include information about wind quintets in a folder named "Wind Quintet Information."

Printing and Saving Web Pages

As you use your browser to view Web pages, you will find some pages that you want to print or store for future use. Web browsers include both the print and save capabilities. Web browsers allow you to save entire Web pages or just parts of the Web page, such as selections of text or graphics.

Printing a Web Page

The easiest way to print a Web page in Internet Explorer or Navigator is to click the browser's **Print** button. In either case, the current page (or part of a page, called a **frame**) that appears in the Web page area of the browser is sent to the printer. If the page contains light colors or many graphics, you might consider changing the printing options so the page prints without the background or with all black text. You will learn how to change the print settings for Internet Explorer and Navigator in Sessions 2.2 and 2.3, respectively.

Although printing an entire Web page is often useful, there are times when you will want to save all or part of the page to disk.

Saving a Web Page

When you save the HTML code of a Web page to disk, you save only the text portion. If the Web page contains graphics, such as photos, drawings, or icons, they will not be saved with the HTML document. To save a graphic separately, right-click the graphic in the browser window, click Save Picture As (in Internet Explorer) or Save Image (in Navigator) on the shortcut menu, and then save the graphic to the same location to which you saved the Web's HTML document. The graphics file is referenced in the HTML document as a hyperlink. Depending on how the Web page designer created the reference, you might have to edit the HTML code in the Web page to identify the new location of the graphic. Copying the graphics files to the same disk (or the same folder on a hard disk) as the HTML document will *usually* work. You will learn more about saving a Web page and its graphics in Sessions 2.2 and 2.3.

Reproducing Web Pages and Copyright Law

Maggie explains that there can be significant restrictions on the way that you can use information or images that you copy from another entity's Web site. Because of the way a Web browser works, it copies all of the HTML code and most of the graphics and media files to your computer before it can display them in the browser. Just because copies of these files are stored temporarily on your computer does not mean that you have the right to use them in any way other than having your computer display them in the browser window. The United States and other countries have copyright laws that govern the use of photocopies, audio or video recordings, and other reproductions of authors' original work. A **copyright** is the legal right of the author or other owner of an original work to control the reproduction, distribution, and sale of that work. A copyright comes into existence as soon as the work is placed into a tangible form, such as a printed copy, an electronic file, or a Web page. The copyright exists even if the work does not contain a copyright notice. If you do not know whether material that you find on the Web is copyrighted, the safest course of action is to assume that it is.

You can use limited amounts of copyrighted information in term papers and other reports that you prepare in an academic setting, but you must cite the source. Commercial use of copyrighted material is much more restricted. You should obtain permission from the copyright holder before using anything you copy from a Web page. It can be difficult to determine the owner of a source's copyright if no notice appears on the Web page; however, most Web pages provide a hyperlink to the e-mail address of the person responsible for maintaining the page. That person, often called a **webmaster**, usually can provide information about the copyright status of materials on the page.

Now that you understand the basic function of a browser and how to find information on the Web, you are ready to start using your browser to find information for the quintet. If you are using Internet Explorer, your instructor will assign Session 2.2; if you are using Navigator, your instructor will assign Session 2.3. The authors recommend, however, that you read both sessions because you might encounter a different browser on a public or employer's computer in the future.

Session 2.1 QUICK CHECK

1. True or False: Web browser software runs on a Web server computer.

2. True or False: You can format text using HTML tags.

3. The Web page that opens when you start your browser is called a(n) _____ or a(n) _____.

4. The general term for graphic images, sound clips, or video clips that appear in a Web page is _____.

5. A local political candidate is creating a Web site to help in her campaign for office. Describe three things she might want to include in her Web site.

6. What is the difference between IP addressing and domain name addressing?

7. Identify and interpret the meaning of each part of the following URL: http://www.savethetrees.org/main.html.

8. What is the difference between a Web directory and a Web search engine?

SESSION 2.2

In this session, you will learn how to configure the Microsoft Internet Explorer Web browser and use it to display Web pages. You will learn how to use Internet Explorer to follow hyperlinks from one Web page to another and how to record the URLs of sites to which you would like to return. Finally, you will print and save Web pages.

Starting Microsoft Internet Explorer

Microsoft Internet Explorer is Microsoft's Web browser that installs with Windows 95, Windows 98, Windows 2000, or Windows XP. This introduction assumes that you have Internet Explorer installed on your computer. You should have your computer turned on so the Windows desktop is displayed.

To start Internet Explorer:

1. Click the **Start** button on the taskbar, point to **Programs**, point to **Internet Explorer**, and then click **Internet Explorer**. After a moment, Internet Explorer opens.

   TROUBLE? If you cannot find Internet Explorer on the Programs menu, check to see if an Internet Explorer shortcut icon appears on the desktop, and then double-click it. If you do not see the shortcut icon, ask your instructor or technical support person for help. The program might be installed in a different folder on your computer.

2. If the program does not fill the screen entirely, click the **Maximize** button on the Internet Explorer program's title bar. Your screen should look like Figure 2-10.

Figure 2-10	INTERNET EXPLORER MAIN PROGRAM WINDOW

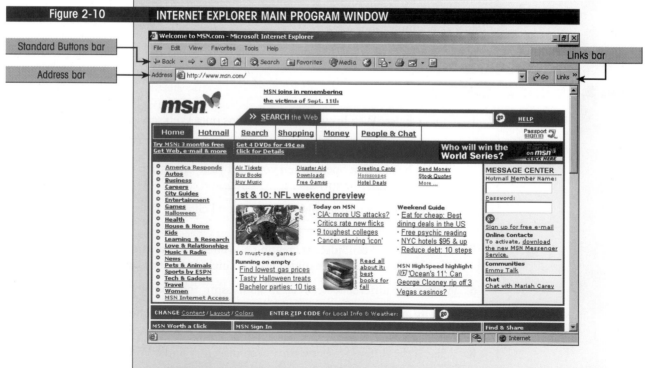

TROUBLE? Figure 2-10 shows the Microsoft home page, which is the page that Internet Explorer opens the first time it starts. Your computer might be configured to open to a different Web page or no page at all.

TROUBLE? If you do not see the bars shown in Figure 2-10, click View on the menu bar, point to Toolbars, and then click the name of the bar that is not displayed on the screen. A toolbar that is displayed has a check mark to the left of its name.

Internet Explorer includes a **Standard Buttons toolbar** with 13 buttons. Many of these buttons execute frequently used commands for browsing the Web. Figure 2-11 shows these buttons and describes the functions of the most commonly used buttons.

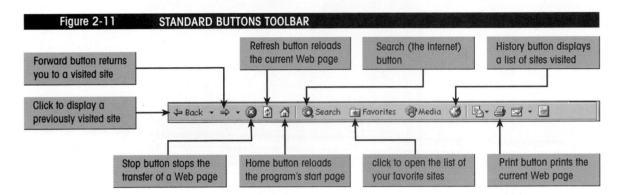

Figure 2-11   STANDARD BUTTONS TOOLBAR

Now that you understand how to start Internet Explorer, you want to learn more about components of the Internet Explorer program window.

Status Bar

The **status bar** at the bottom of the window includes several panels that give you information about Internet Explorer's operations. The first panel—the **transfer progress report**—presents status messages that show, for example, the URL of a page while it is loading. When a page is completely loaded, this panel displays the text "Done" until you move the mouse over a hyperlink. This panel displays the URL of any hyperlink on the page when you move the mouse pointer over it. A second panel that opens when a Web page is loading displays a blue **graphical transfer progress indicator** that moves from left to right in the right side of the panel to indicate how much of a Web page has loaded while Internet Explorer is loading it from a Web server. This indicator is especially useful for monitoring progress when you are loading large Web pages.

Another status bar panel displays a locked padlock icon when the browser loads a Web page that has a security certificate. You can double-click on the padlock icon to open a dialog box that contains information about the security certificate for a Web page.

The last (rightmost) status bar panel displays the **security zone** to which the page you are viewing has been assigned. As part of its security features, Internet Explorer lets you classify Web pages by the security risk you believe they present. You can open the Internet Security Properties dialog box shown in Figure 2-12 by double-clicking the last (rightmost) status bar panel. This window lets you set four levels of security-enforcing procedures: High, Medium, Medium-Low, and Low. In general, the higher level of security you set for your browser, the slower it will operate. Higher security settings also disable some of the browser features. You can click the Custom Level button to configure the way each security level operates on your computer.

Figure 2-12   INTERNET SECURITY PROPERTIES DIALOG BOX

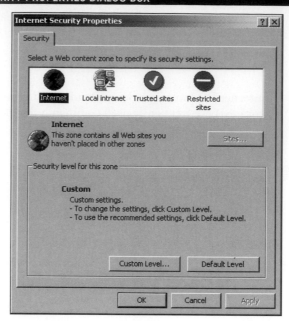

Menu Bar

In addition to the standard Windows commands, the menu bar also provides access to Favorites. The Favorites menu command lets you store and organize URLs of sites that you have visited and want or need to return to on regular basis.

Hiding and Showing the Internet Explorer Toolbars

Internet Explorer lets you hide its menu bar and toolbars to show more of the Web page area. To hide the menu bar, you can select the Full Screen option on the View menu. When the window is in **Full Screen**, the menu bar is no longer visible, and a smaller version of the Standard Buttons toolbar appears at the top of the screen. To hide the small Standard Buttons toolbar, right-click the toolbar and click Auto-Hide to give you some room for displaying the Web page. To restore the screen so both the menu bar and Standard Buttons toolbar are visible, press the F11 key.

REFERENCE WINDOW   **RW**

<u>Hiding and Restoring the Toolbars in Internet Explorer</u>

- To hide a toolbar, click View on the menu bar, point to Toolbars, and deselect the toolbar you want to hide; or right-click a toolbar, and deselect the toolbar listed in the shortcut menu that you want to hide.
- To hide a toolbar in Full Screen, right-click the small Standard Buttons toolbar that appears at the top of the screen, and then click Auto-Hide on the shortcut menu.
- To restore a toolbar, click View on the menu bar, point to Toolbars, and click to select the toolbar you want to restore; or right-click a toolbar, and click the toolbar listed in the shortcut menu that you want to restore.
- To temporarily restore the small Standard Buttons toolbar in Full Screen, move the mouse to the top of the screen until the toolbar displays.
- To restore the small Standard Buttons toolbar in Full Screen, move the mouse to the top of the screen until the toolbar displays, and then click the Restore button at the far right of the toolbar.

You will switch to Full Screen and try hiding and then restoring the small Standard Buttons toolbar.

To use the Full Screen and Auto Hide commands:

1. Click **View** on the menu bar, then click **Full Screen**.

2. Right-click the small Standard Buttons toolbar that appears at the top of the screen to open the shortcut menu, and then click **Auto-Hide** on the shortcut menu if it is not already checked.

3. Move the mouse pointer away from the top of the screen for a moment. Now, you can see more of the Web page area. When the toolbar disappears, return the mouse pointer to the top of the screen to display it again.

4. With the toolbar displayed, right-click the toolbar and then click **Auto-Hide** on the shortcut menu. This removes the check mark from the Auto-Hide entry on the menu and turns the toolbar on again.

5. Click the **Restore** button to return to the normal Internet Explorer window.

You can use the Customize command on the View Toolbars menu to change the appearance of the toolbars. For example, you can choose to show the Standard Buttons toolbar buttons with large icons or small icons.

You may have noticed that there is another option on the shortcut menu that opens when you right-click a toolbar—Lock the Toolbars. If there is a check mark next to the Lock the Toolbars option, then you cannot move the toolbars. To unlock the toolbars, click Lock the Toolbars again to clear the check mark.

Entering a URL in the Address Bar

Maggie explains that you can use the **Address bar** to enter URLs directly into Internet Explorer. As you learned in Session 2.1, you must enter the URL to identify a Web page's exact location. Although a complete URL includes the name of a file, entering just the IP address and the domain name should be enough information to find the home page of the site.

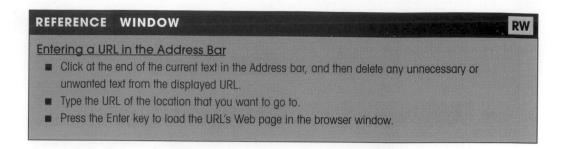

REFERENCE WINDOW   **RW**

Entering a URL in the Address Bar

■ Click at the end of the current text in the Address bar, and then delete any unnecessary or unwanted text from the displayed URL.

■ Type the URL of the location that you want to go to.

■ Press the Enter key to load the URL's Web page in the browser window.

Marianna has asked you to start your research by examining the Web page for the Miami Wind Quintet. She has given you the URL so that you can find its Web page.

To load the Miami Wind Quintet's Web page:

1. Click at the end of the text in the Address bar, and then delete any unnecessary or unwanted text by pressing the **Backspace** key.

   TROUBLE? Make sure that you delete all of the text in the Address bar so the text you type in Step 2 will be correct.

2. Type **www.course.com/newperspectives/internet3** in the Address bar. This URL will take you to the Student Online Companion page on the Course Technology Web site, and then you can click the hyperlinks provided in the steps in this tutorial to go to individual Web pages.

3. Press the **Enter** key. The Student Online Companion Web page loads, as shown in Figure 2-13. When the entire page has loaded, the graphical transfer progress indicator in the status bar will stop moving and the transfer progress report panel will display the text "Done."

Figure 2-13   STUDENT ONLINE COMPANION PAGE AT COURSE.COM

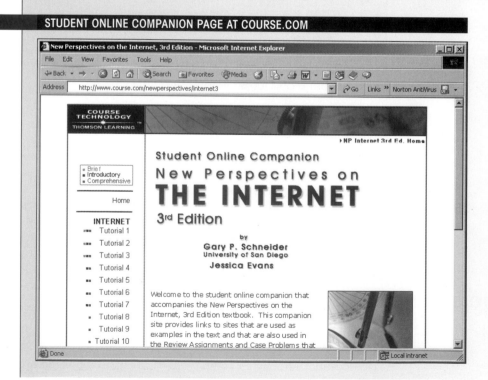

4. Click the hyperlink for your book, click the **Tutorial 2** link, and then click the **Session 2.3** link.

5. Click the link to the **Miami Wind Quintet** in the right frame. The Web page opens, as shown in Figure 2-14.

Figure 2-14	MIAMI WIND QUINTET WEB PAGE

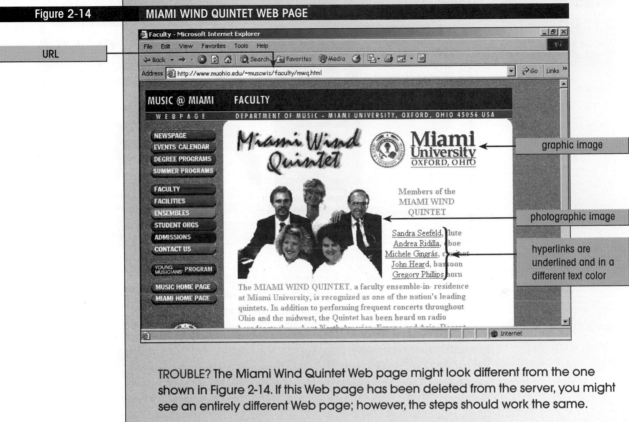

TROUBLE? The Miami Wind Quintet Web page might look different from the one shown in Figure 2-14. If this Web page has been deleted from the server, you might see an entirely different Web page; however, the steps should work the same.

6. Read the Web page, and then click the **Back** button on the toolbar to return to the Student Online Companion page.

You like the format of the Miami Wind Quintet's home page, so you want to make sure that you can go back to that page later if you need to review its contents. Maggie explains that you can write down the URL so you can refer to it later, but an easier way is to store the URL in the Favorites list for future use.

Using the Favorites List

Internet Explorer's **Favorites** feature lets you store and organize a list of Web pages that you have visited so you can return to them easily. The Favorites button on the Standard Buttons toolbar opens the Favorites bar shown in Figure 2-15. You can use the Favorites bar to open URLs you have stored as Favorites.

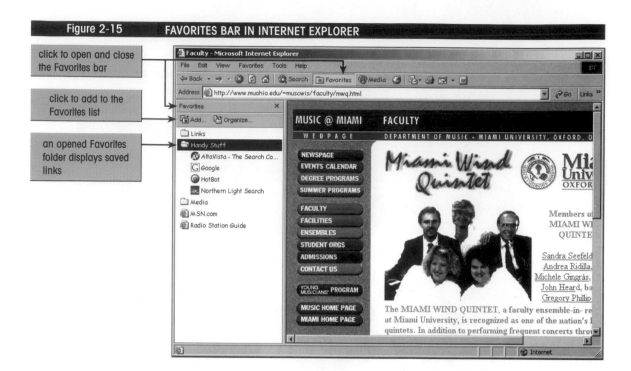

| Figure 2-15 | FAVORITES BAR IN INTERNET EXPLORER |

click to open and close the Favorites bar

click to add to the Favorites list

an opened Favorites folder displays saved links

Figure 2-15 shows the hierarchical structure of the Favorites feature. There are four search engine Web pages stored in a folder named "Handy Stuff." You can organize your favorites in the way that best suits your needs and working style.

REFERENCE WINDOW   RW

Creating a New Favorites Folder

- Open the Web page in Internet Explorer.
- Click the Favorites button on the Standard Buttons toolbar to open the Favorites bar.
- Click the Add button in the Favorites bar (or click Favorites on the menu bar, and then click Add to Favorites).
- If necessary, click the Create in button.
- Click the Favorites folder, and then click the New Folder button.
- Type the name of the new folder in the Folder name text box, and then click the OK button.
- Click the OK button.

You will save the URL for the Miami Wind Quintet Web page as a favorite in a Wind Quintet Information folder.

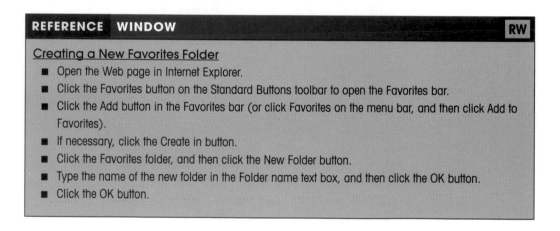

To create a new Favorites folder:

1. Click the **Forward** button on the Standard Buttons toolbar to return to the Miami Wind Quintet Web page.

2. Click the **Favorites** button on the Standard Buttons toolbar to open the Favorites bar.

3. Click the **Add** button at the top of the Favorites bar. The Add Favorite dialog box opens.

4. Delete the text in the Name field, and then type **Miami Wind Quintet**.

   If the symbols on the Create in button appear as >>, you will need to expand the dialog box so you can select the Favorites folder in which you will create a new folder.

5. If necessary, click the **Create in** button. Note that the dialog box expands to display a list of Favorites folders and that the symbols now appear as <<.

6. Click the **Favorites** folder in the Create in box, and then click the **New Folder** button. The new folder will be stored as a subfolder in the Favorites folder.

7. Type **Wind Quintet Information** in the Folder name text box, and then click the **OK** button. See Figure 2-16. Notice that the page name appears automatically in the Name text box in the Add Favorite dialog box. You can edit the suggested page name.

Figure 2-16	CREATING A NEW FAVORITES FOLDER

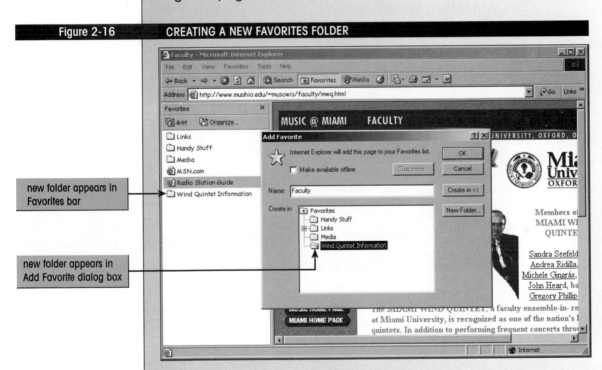

new folder appears in Favorites bar

new folder appears in Add Favorite dialog box

8. Click the **OK** button to close the Add Favorite dialog box. Now, the favorite is saved in Internet Explorer. You can test the favorite by opening it from the Favorites bar.

9. Click the **Back** button on the Standard Buttons toolbar to return to the previous page, click the **Wind Quintet Information** folder in the Favorites bar to open the folder, and then click **Miami Wind Quintet**. The Miami Wind Quintet page opens in the browser.

TROUBLE? If the Miami Wind Quintet page does not open, click Favorites on the menu bar, click the Wind Quintet Information folder, right-click the Miami Wind Quintet favorite, and then click Properties. Click the Internet Shortcut tab, and make sure that a URL appears in the Target URL text box; if there is no URL, then click the OK button to close the dialog box. Click Favorites on the menu bar, click the Wind Quintet Information folder, right-click the Miami Wind Quintet folder, and then click Delete. Repeat the steps to re-create the favorite, and then try again. If you still have trouble, ask your instructor or technical support person for help.

As you use the Web to find information about wind quintets and other sites of interest for the group, you might find yourself creating many favorites so you can return to sites of interest. When you start accumulating favorites, it is important to keep them organized. Internet Explorer helps you keep your favorites organized.

Organizing Favorites

Internet Explorer offers an easy way to organize your folders in a hierarchical structure—even after you have stored them. To rearrange URLs or even folders within folders, you use the Organize Favorites command on the Favorites menu.

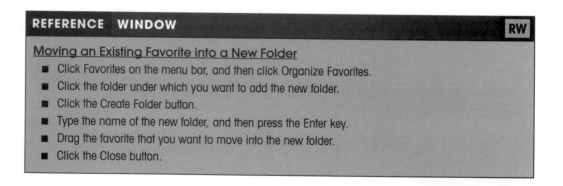

REFERENCE WINDOW   RW

Moving an Existing Favorite into a New Folder
- Click Favorites on the menu bar, and then click Organize Favorites.
- Click the folder under which you want to add the new folder.
- Click the Create Folder button.
- Type the name of the new folder, and then press the Enter key.
- Drag the favorite that you want to move into the new folder.
- Click the Close button.

You explain to Maggie that you have created a new folder for Wind Quintet Information in the Internet Explorer Favorites bar and stored the Miami Wind Quintet's URL in that folder. Maggie suggests that you might not want to keep all of the wind quintet-related information you gather in one folder. She notes that you are just beginning your work for Marianna and the quintet and that you might be collecting all types of information for them. Maggie suggests that you might want to put information about the Miami Wind Quintet in a separate folder named Midwestern Ensembles under the Wind Quintet Information folder. As you collect information about other performers, you might add folders for categories such as East Coast and West Coast ensembles, too.

To move an existing favorite into a new folder:

1. Click **Favorites** on the menu bar, and then click **Organize Favorites**.

2. Click the **Wind Quintet Information** folder in the Organize Favorites dialog box.

3. Click the **Create Folder** button. The default "New Folder" text is automatically selected.

4. Type **Midwestern Ensembles** to replace the text, and then press the **Enter** key to rename the folder.

5. Click and drag the **Miami Wind Quintet** favorite to the new Midwestern Ensembles folder, and then release the mouse button. Now, the Midwestern Ensembles folder contains the favorite, as shown in Figure 2-17.

| Figure 2-17 | REORGANIZING FAVORITES IN FOLDERS |

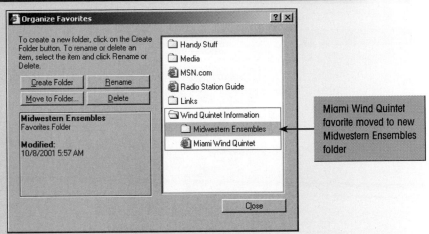

6. Click the **Close** button. The Favorites bar is updated automatically to reflect your changes.

7. Click the **Favorites** button on the Standard Buttons toolbar to close the Favorites bar.

Hyperlink Navigation Using the Mouse

Now you know how to use the Internet to find information that will help you with the Sunset Wind Quintet. Maggie tells you that the easiest way to move from one Web page to another is to use the mouse to click hyperlinks that the authors of Web pages embed in their HTML documents. You can also right-click the mouse on the background of a Web page to open a shortcut menu that includes navigation options.

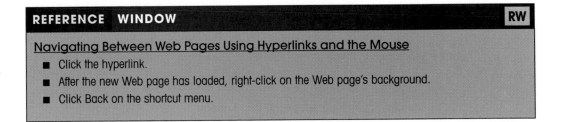

REFERENCE WINDOW | RW

Navigating Between Web Pages Using Hyperlinks and the Mouse
- Click the hyperlink.
- After the new Web page has loaded, right-click on the Web page's background.
- Click Back on the shortcut menu.

To follow a hyperlink to a Web page and return using the mouse:

1. Click the **Back** button on the Standard Buttons toolbar to return to the Student Online Companion page, click the **Lewis Music** link, and then point to the **Instrument Accessories** hyperlink shown in Figure 2-18. Note that your pointer changes to the shape of a hand with a pointing index finger.

| Figure 2-18 | LEWIS MUSIC HOME PAGE |

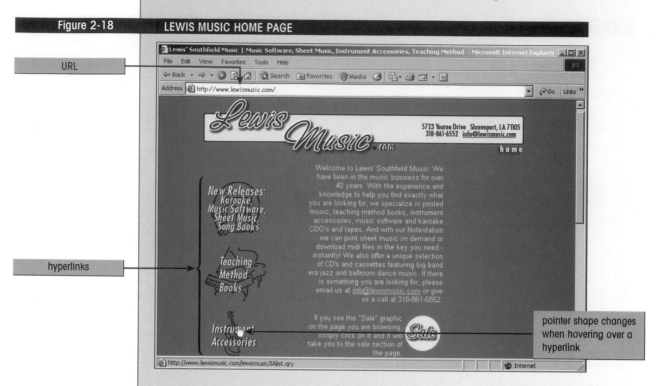

URL

hyperlinks

pointer shape changes when hovering over a hyperlink

2. Click the **Instrument Accessories** hyperlink. Watch the first panel in the status bar—when it displays the text "Done," you know that Internet Explorer has loaded the full page.

3. Right-click anywhere in the Web page area that is not a hyperlink to display the shortcut menu, as shown in Figure 2-19.

Figure 2-19 | USING THE SHORTCUT MENU TO GO BACK TO THE PREVIOUS PAGE

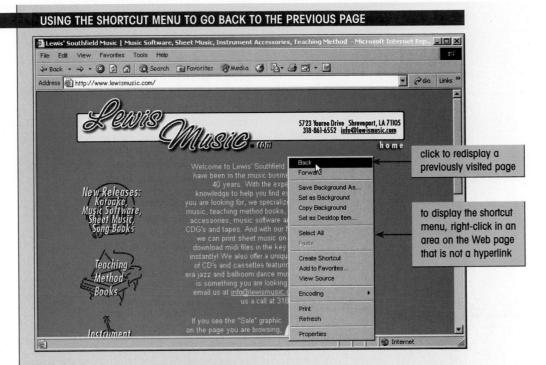

TROUBLE? If you right-click a hyperlink, your shortcut menu will display a list that differs from the one shown in Figure 2-19; therefore the Back item might not appear in the same position on the menu or not appear at all. If you do not see the shortcut menu shown in Figure 2-19, click anywhere outside of the shortcut menu to close it, and then repeat Step 3.

TROUBLE? Web pages change frequently, so the Instrument Accessories page you see might look different from the one shown in Figure 2-19, but right-clicking anywhere on the Web page area that is not a hyperlink will still work.

4. Click **Back** on the shortcut menu to return to the Lewis Music home page.

5. Repeat Step 4 to return to the Student Online Companion page.

Using the History List

The Back and Forward buttons on the Standard Buttons toolbar enable you to move to and from previously visited pages. As you move back and forth between pages, Internet Explorer records these visited sites in the history list. To see where you have been during a session, you also can open the history list by clicking the **History** button on the Standard Buttons toolbar.

To view the history list for this session:

1. Click the **History** button on the Standard Buttons toolbar. The history list opens in a hierarchical structure in a separate window on the left side of the screen. The history list stores each URL you visited during the past week or during a specified time period. It also maintains the hierarchy of each Web site; that is, pages you visit at a particular Web site are stored in a separate folder for that site. To return to a particular page, click that page's entry in the list. You can see the full URL of any item in the History bar by moving the mouse pointer over the history list item.

2. Click the **Close** button on the History bar title bar to close it.

You can right-click any entry in the history list and then copy the URL or delete it from the list. Internet Explorer stores each history entry as a shortcut in a History folder, which is in the Windows folder.

Refreshing a Web Page

The Refresh button on the Standard Buttons toolbar loads a new copy of the current Web page that currently appears in the browser window. Internet Explorer stores a copy of every Web page it displays on your computer's hard drive in a **Temporary Internet Files** folder in the Windows folder. Storing this information increases the speed at which Internet Explorer can display pages as you move back and forth through the history list because the browser can load the pages from a local disk drive instead of reloading the page from the remote Web server. When you click the Refresh button, Internet Explorer contacts the Web server to see if the Web page has changed since it was stored in the cache folder. If it has changed, Internet Explorer gets the new page from the Web server; otherwise, it loads the cache folder copy.

Returning to the Home Page

The Home button on the Standard Buttons toolbar displays the home (or start) page for your copy of Internet Explorer. You can change the setting for the Home toolbar button to display the page you want to use as the default home page.

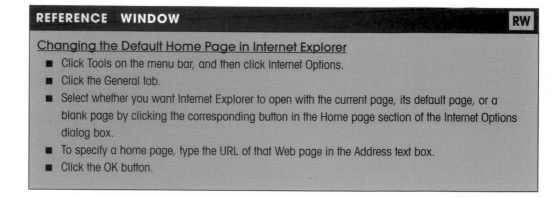

REFERENCE WINDOW · RW

Changing the Default Home Page in Internet Explorer
- Click Tools on the menu bar, and then click Internet Options.
- Click the General tab.
- Select whether you want Internet Explorer to open with the current page, its default page, or a blank page by clicking the corresponding button in the Home page section of the Internet Options dialog box.
- To specify a home page, type the URL of that Web page in the Address text box.
- Click the OK button.

To view the settings for the default home page:

1. Click **Tools** on the menu bar, and then click **Internet Options**. The Internet Options dialog box opens, as shown in Figure 2-20. To use the currently loaded Web page as your home page, click the Use Current button. To use the default home page that was installed with your copy of Internet Explorer, click the Use Default button. If you don't want a page to open when you start your browser, click the Use Blank button. If you want to specify a home page other than the current, default, or blank page, type the URL for that page in the Address box.

Figure 2-20	CHANGING THE DEFAULT HOME PAGE

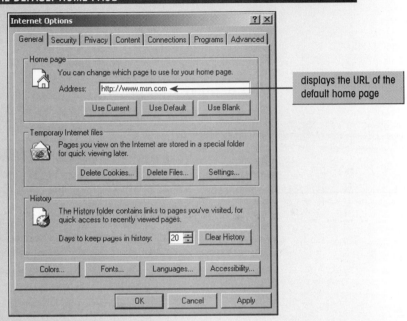

displays the URL of the default home page

TROUBLE? Do not change any settings unless you are instructed to do so by your instructor. Many organizations set the home page defaults on all of their computers and then lock those settings.

2. Click the **Cancel** button to close the dialog box without making any changes.

Printing a Web Page

The Print button on the Standard Buttons toolbar lets you print the current Web frame or page. You can use the Print command to make a printed copy of most Web pages (some Web pages disable the Print command).

REFERENCE WINDOW   **RW**

Printing the Current Web Page
- Click the Print button on the Standard Buttons toolbar to print the current Web page with the default print settings.

or

- Click File on the menu bar, and then click Print.
- Select the printer you want to use, and indicate the pages you want to print and the number of copies you want to make of each page.
- To print a range of pages, click the Pages option button, and then type the first page of the range in the from box and the last page of the range in the to box.
- Click the OK button.

To print a Web page:

1. Click in the main (right) frame of the Student Online Companion page to select it.

2. Click **File** on the menu bar, and then click **Print** to open the Print dialog box.

3. Make sure that the printer in the Name list box display the printer you want to use; if not, click the Name list arrow to change the selection.

4. Click the **Pages** option button in the Print range section of the Print dialog box, type **1** in the from text box, press the **Tab** key, and then type **1** in the to text box to specify that you only want to print the first page.

5. Make sure that the Number of copies text box displays **1**.

6. Click the **OK** button to print the Web page and close the Print dialog box.

Changing the Settings for the Page Setup

You have seen how to print a Web page using the basic options available in the Print dialog box. Usually, the default settings in the Print dialog box are fine for printing a Web page, but you can use the Page Setup dialog box to change the way a Web page prints. Figure 2-21 shows the Page Setup dialog box, and Figure 2-22 describes its settings.

Figure 2-21   **PAGE SETUP DIALOG BOX**

Figure 2-22   **PAGE SETUP DIALOG BOX OPTIONS**

OPTION	DESCRIPTION	USE
Paper Size	Changes the size of the printed page.	Use the Letter size default unless you are printing to different paper stock, such as Legal.
Paper Source	Changes the printer's paper source.	Use the default Auto Select unless you want to specify a different tray or manual feed for printing on heavy paper.
Header	Prints the Web page's title, URL, date/time printed, and page numbers at the top of each page.	To obtain details on how to specify exact header printing options, click the Header text box to select it, and then press the F1 key.
Footer	Prints the Web page's title, URL, date/time printed, and page numbers at the bottom of each page.	To obtain details on how to specify exact footer printing options, click the Footer text box to select it, and then press the F1 key.
Orientation	Selects the orientation of the printed output.	Portrait works best for most Web pages, but you can use landscape orientation to print the wide tables of numbers included on some Web pages.
Margins	Changes the margin of the printed page.	Normally, you should leave the default settings, but you can change the right, left, top, or bottom margins as needed.

When printing long Web pages, another print option that is extremely useful for saving paper is to reduce the font size of the Web pages before you print them. To do this, click View on the menu bar, point to Text Size, and then click Smaller or Smallest on the menu.

Checking Web Page Security

You can check some of the security elements of a Web page by clicking File on the menu bar, clicking Properties, and then clicking the Certificates button. Internet Explorer will display security information for the page, if it is available, to advise you of the overall security of the page that appears in the browser window. An example of this type of security information appears in Figure 2-23.

Figure 2-23   WEB PAGE SECURITY INFORMATION

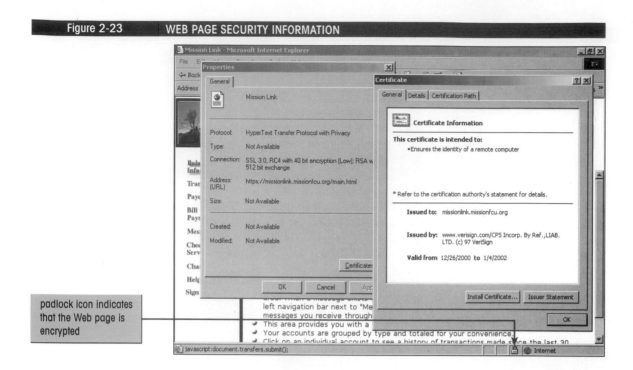

padlock icon indicates that the Web page is encrypted

Encryption is a way of scrambling and encoding data transmissions that reduces the risk that a person who intercepts the Web page as it travels across the Internet will be able to decode and read the page's contents. Web sites use encrypted transmission to send and receive information, such as credit card numbers, to ensure privacy. When Internet Explorer loads an encrypted Web page, a padlock symbol appears in the fourth pane (second from the right) of the status bar at the bottom of the Internet Explorer window.

Getting **Help in Internet Explorer**

Internet Explorer includes a comprehensive online Help system. You can open the Help Contents window to learn more about the Help options that are available.

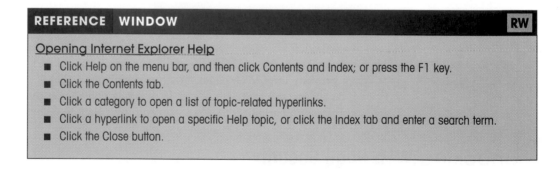

REFERENCE WINDOW   **RW**

Opening Internet Explorer Help

- Click Help on the menu bar, and then click Contents and Index; or press the F1 key.
- Click the Contents tab.
- Click a category to open a list of topic-related hyperlinks.
- Click a hyperlink to open a specific Help topic, or click the Index tab and enter a search term.
- Click the Close button.

To open the Internet Explorer Help:

1. Click **Help** on the menu bar, and then click **Contents and Index** to open the Internet Explorer Help window.

2. If necessary, click the **Maximize** button on the Internet Explorer Help window so it fills the desktop.

3. Click the **Contents** tab, click **Finding the Web Pages You Want**, and then click **Listing your favorite pages for quick viewing** to open that help topic in the Help window. Notice that the page that opens in a Help window contains links to related categories that you can explore, as shown in Figure 2-24.

Figure 2-24	INTERNET EXPLORER HELP WINDOW

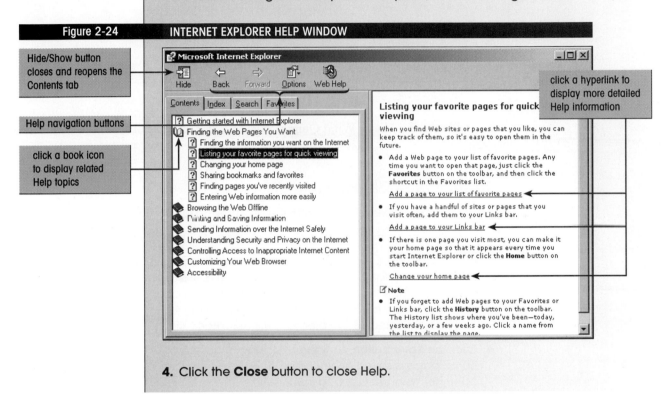

4. Click the **Close** button to close Help.

You feel confident that you have the tools you need to successfully find information on the Web. Marianna probably will be interested in seeing the Miami Wind Quintet Web page, but you are not sure if she will have Internet access while she is touring. Maggie says that you can save the Web page on disk, so Marianna can open the page locally in her Web browser using the files you save on that disk.

Using **Internet Explorer to Save a Web Page**

There will be times when you will want to refer to the information that you have found on a Web page without having to search the site. In Internet Explorer you can store entire Web pages, selected portions of Web page text, or particular graphics from a Web page to a disk.

Saving a Web Page

You like the Miami Wind Quintet's Web site and want to save a copy of the page to a disk so you can show the Web page to Marianna. That way, she can review it without having an Internet connection. To save a Web page, you must have the page open in Internet Explorer.

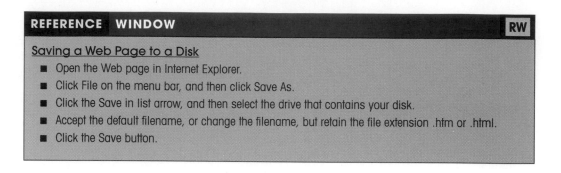

REFERENCE WINDOW   **RW**

Saving a Web Page to a Disk
- Open the Web page in Internet Explorer.
- Click File on the menu bar, and then click Save As.
- Click the Save in list arrow, and then select the drive that contains your disk.
- Accept the default filename, or change the filename, but retain the file extension .htm or .html.
- Click the Save button.

You will save the Miami Wind Quintet page to a disk so you can send it to Marianna for her review.

To save the Web page to a disk:

1. Use your Favorites list to return to the Miami Wind Quintet page.

2. Click **File** on the menu bar, and then click **Save As**. The Save As dialog box opens.

3. If necessary, click the **Save in** list arrow, select the drive that contains your disk, select the **Tutorial.02** folder, and then type **MiamiWindQuintet.htm** in the File name box. Note that you can select the Web Page option in the Save as type list and type the name of the file without typing the file extension; with the Web Page option selected the program will automatically add the file extension.

4. Click the **Save** button. Now the HTML document for the Miami Wind Quintet's home page is saved on your disk. When you send it to Marianna, she can open her Web browser and then use the Open command on the File menu to open the Web page.

If the Web page contains graphics, such as photos, drawings, or icons, they might not be saved with the HTML document. To save a graphic, right-click it in the browser window, click Save Picture As on the shortcut menu, and then save the graphic to the same location as the Web's HTML document. The graphics file will appear on the HTML document as a hyperlink; therefore, you might have to change the HTML code in the Web page to identify the location of the graphic. Copying the graphics files to the same disk as the HTML document will *usually* work. In Internet Explorer, you can make sure that a graphic is stored with the text file by selecting Web Page as the Save as type field. With this setting, Internet Explorer will create a separate folder for all of the graphic page elements and will rewrite the HTML of the Web page to ensure that its links to the graphics files are rewritten if necessary. If the page has many graphics elements, however, it is possible that the files containing those elements will not all fit on a standard 3 ½-inch disk.

Saving Web Page Text to a File

You can save portions of Web page text to a file, so that you can use the file in other programs. You will use WordPad to save text that you will copy from a Web page; however, any word processor or text editor will work.

REFERENCE   WINDOW   **RW**

Copying Text from a Web Page to a WordPad Document
- Open the Web page in Internet Explorer.
- Use the mouse pointer to select the text you want to copy.
- Click Edit on the menu bar, and then click Copy.
- Open WordPad (or another word processor or text editor if WordPad is not available).
- Click Edit on the WordPad menu bar, and then click Paste (or click the Paste button).
- Click the Save button, select the folder where you want to store the file, and then enter a new filename, if necessary.
- Click the Save button.

Marianna just called to let you know that the quintet will play a concert in Grand Rapids on a Friday night, and she asks you to identify other opportunities for scheduling local concerts during the following weekend. Often, museums are willing to book small ensembles for weekend afternoon programs, and Marianna has given you the URL for the Grand Rapids Art Museum. You will visit the site and then get the museum's address and telephone number so you can contact it about scheduling a concert.

To copy text from a Web page and save it as a WordPad document:

1. Use the **Back** button to return to the Student Online Companion page, and then click the **Grand Rapids Art Museum** link to open that Web page in the browser window.

2. Click the **address** hyperlink in the left frame on the Web page to open the museum information page in the main (right) frame.

3. Drag the mouse pointer over the address and telephone number to select it, as shown in Figure 2-25.

Figure 2-25   SELECTING TEXT ON A WEB PAGE

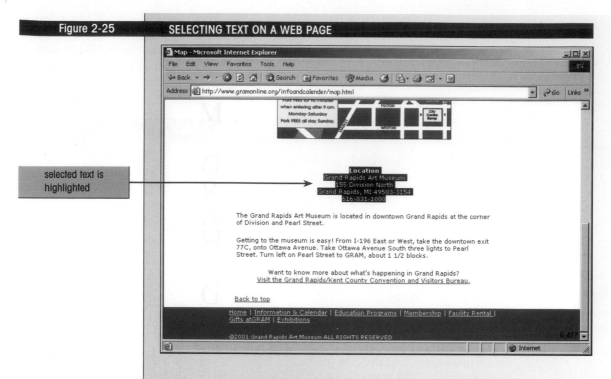

selected text is
highlighted

4. Click **Edit** on the menu bar, and then click **Copy** to copy the selected text to the Clipboard.

Now, you will start WordPad and then paste the copied text into a new document.

5. Click the **Start** button on the taskbar, point to **Programs**, point to **Accessories**, and then click **WordPad** to start the program and open a new document.

6. Click the **Paste** button on the WordPad toolbar to paste the text into the WordPad document, as shown in Figure 2-26.

TROUBLE? If the WordPad toolbar does not appear, click View on the menu bar, click Toolbar to turn it on, and then repeat Step 2. Your WordPad program window might be a different size from the one shown in Figure 2-26, which does not affect the steps.

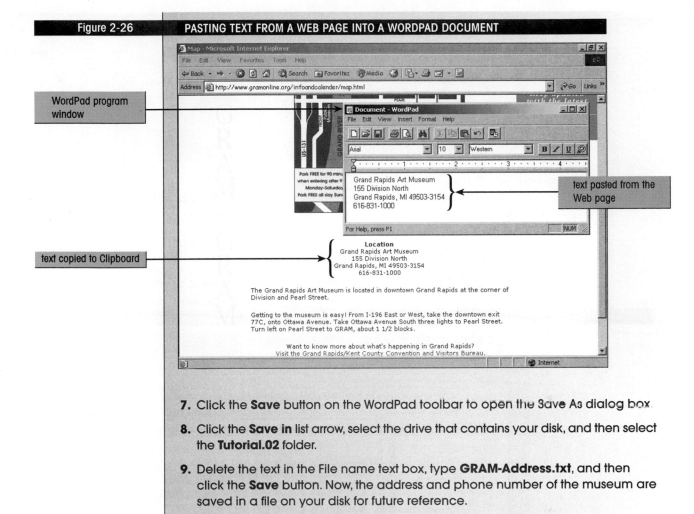

Figure 2-26 | PASTING TEXT FROM A WEB PAGE INTO A WORDPAD DOCUMENT

7. Click the **Save** button on the WordPad toolbar to open the Save As dialog box.

8. Click the **Save in** list arrow, select the drive that contains your disk, and then select the **Tutorial.02** folder.

9. Delete the text in the File name text box, type **GRAM-Address.txt**, and then click the **Save** button. Now, the address and phone number of the museum are saved in a file on your disk for future reference.

TROUBLE? If a dialog box opens, asking if you want to replace the existing GRAM-Address.txt file on your disk, click the Yes button.

10. Click the **Close** button on the WordPad title bar to close it.

You will use this information to contact the museum at a later time. As you examine the Web page, you notice a street map of the area surrounding the museum, which Marianna might like to have.

Saving a Web Page Graphic to a Disk

The Web page with directions and transportation information will be helpful to Marianna, so you decide to save the map graphic to your disk. You can then send the file to Marianna so she has a resource for getting to the museum.

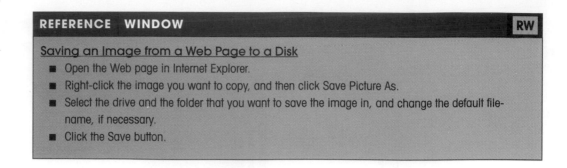

REFERENCE WINDOW   RW

Saving an Image from a Web Page to a Disk
- Open the Web page in Internet Explorer.
- Right-click the image you want to copy, and then click Save Picture As.
- Select the drive and the folder that you want to save the image in, and change the default file-name, if necessary.
- Click the Save button.

Now you will save the image of the street map to your disk, which you will later send to Marianna.

To save the street map image to a disk:

1. Right-click the map image to open its shortcut menu, as shown in Figure 2-27.

Figure 2-27	SAVING THE MAP IMAGE TO A DISK

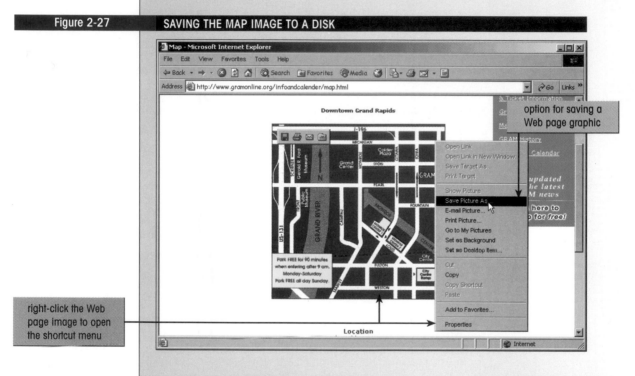

2. Click **Save Picture As** on the shortcut menu to open the Save As dialog box. Internet Explorer also opens a shortcut bar whenever you move the mouse pointer over a downloadable graphic on a Web page. This shortcut bar includes three buttons that you can click to save the image to a disk, print the image, or e-mail the image. A fourth button opens the My Pictures folder on your computer.

3. Click the **Save in** list arrow, select the drive that contains your disk, and then select the **Tutorial.02** folder.

4. Delete the text in the File name text box, type **GRAM-Map.jpg**, and then click the **Save** button to save the file.

5. Close your Web browser, and if necessary, log off your Internet connection.

Now, you can send a disk to Marianna so she will have the Miami Wind Quintet Web page and a map to show how to get to the museum. She will be able to use her Web browser to open the files and print them.

Session 2.2 QUICK CHECK

1. Describe two ways to increase the Web page area in Internet Explorer.

2. You can use the _____ button in Internet Explorer to visit previously visited sites during your Web session.

3. Clicking the _____ button on the Standard Buttons toolbar opens a search frame that contains a number of different searching options.

4. List the names of two additional Favorites folders you might want to add to the Wind Quintet Information folder as you continue to gather information for the Sunset Wind Quintet.

5. To ensure that Internet Explorer loads a Web page from the server rather than from its cache, you can hold down the _____ key as you click the Refresh button.

6. True or False: You can identify encrypted Web pages when viewing them in Internet Explorer.

7. Describe two ways to obtain help on a specific topic in Internet Explorer.

If your instructor assigns Session 2.3, continue reading. Otherwise complete the Review Assignments at the end of this tutorial.

SESSION 2.3

In this session, you will learn how to configure the Netscape Navigator Web browser and use it to display Web pages and follow hyperlinks to other Web pages. You will learn how to copy text and images from Web pages and how to mark pages so you can return to them easily.

Starting Netscape Navigator

To effectively search the Web for the Sunset Wind Quintet, you need to become familiar with Netscape Navigator. The other programs in Netscape provide e-mail, instant messaging, Web page creation tools, and other functions. This introduction assumes that you have Navigator installed on your computer. You should have your computer turned on so the Windows desktop is displayed.

To start Navigator:

1. Click the **Start** button on the taskbar, point to **Programs**, point to **Netscape Navigator** or **Netscape**, and then click **Netscape 6**. After a moment, Netscape opens.

TROUBLE? If you cannot find Netscape on the Programs menu, check to see if a Netscape Navigator shortcut icon appears on the desktop, and then double-click it. If you do not see the shortcut icon, ask your instructor or technical support person for help. The program might be installed in a different folder on the computer you are using.

2. If the program does not fill the screen entirely, click the **Maximize** button on the Navigator program's title bar. Your screen should look like Figure 2-28.

| Figure 2-28 | NETSCAPE NETCENTER HOME PAGE |

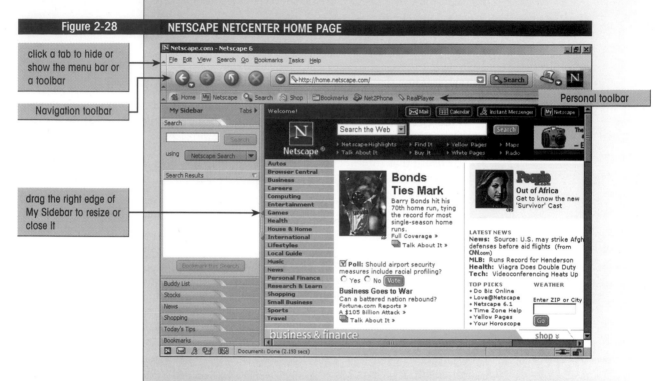

click a tab to hide or show the menu bar or a toolbar

Navigation toolbar

Personal toolbar

drag the right edge of My Sidebar to resize or close it

TROUBLE? Figure 2-28 shows the Netscape Netcenter home page, which is the page that Netscape Navigator opens the first time it starts. Your computer might be configured to open to a different Web page, or no page at all.

TROUBLE? If the Personal toolbar is not displayed on your screen, click View on the menu bar, point to Show/Hide, and then click Personal Toolbar to display the toolbar as shown in Figure 2-28.

3. Click **View** on the menu bar, and then click **My Sidebar** (or drag the right edge of the My Sidebar frame to the left side of the browser window to close My Sidebar). This will give you more room to view Web pages when using the Navigator browser. You can reopen My Sidebar at any time using the View menu or by clicking and dragging the left edge of the browser window to the right.

Now that you understand how to start Navigator, you want to learn more about the components of the Navigator program window.

Using the Navigation and Personal Toolbars

The **Navigation toolbar** includes six buttons that execute frequently used commands for browsing the Web. Figure 2-29 shows the Navigation toolbar buttons and describes their functions. (Depending on which version of Navigator you are using, you might see different toolbar buttons. Use online Help to get more information about buttons not pictured in Figure 2-29.)

Figure 2-29	NAVIGATOR NAVIGATION TOOLBAR

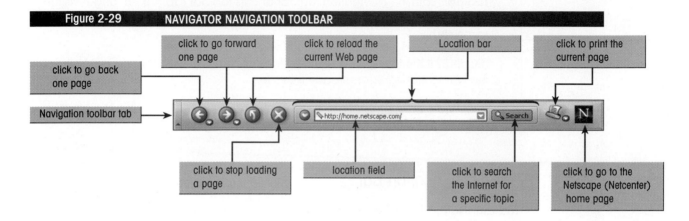

In addition to the toolbar buttons, the Navigation toolbar contains a Location bar. The Location bar is in the center of the Navigation toolbar and includes a location field and a Search (the Internet) button. You can type a URL in the location bar and then click the Search button to load a Web page. The Navigation toolbar also has a toolbar tab that you can click to hide the toolbar so there is more room to display a Web page in the Web page area. You can hide the Navigation toolbar so that the toolbar tab folds up and remains visible, or you can hide the toolbar completely by using the options on the View menu, as you will see next.

REFERENCE WINDOW   **RW**

Hiding or Showing a Toolbar In Navigator

- To hide the toolbar, click the toolbar tab for the toolbar that you want to hide; or click View on the menu bar, point to Show/Hide, and then click the name of the toolbar that you want to hide.
- To show a hidden toolbar, click the toolbar tab for the toolbar you want to show; or click View on the menu bar, click Show/Hide, and then click the name of the toolbar that you want to show.

To hide the Navigation toolbar and then show it again:

1. Click the **Navigation toolbar** tab. The toolbar disappears, but its tab redisplays under the Personal toolbar, which moves up under the menu bar.

2. Move the pointer to the Navigation toolbar tab below the Personal toolbar.

3. Click the **Navigation toolbar** tab. The Navigation toolbar appears above the Personal toolbar.

You can use the toolbar tabs to hide or show the toolbars quickly. However, if you want to hide the toolbars and their tabs, you must use the View menu. The View menu commands are toggles. A **toggle** is like a pushbutton switch on a television set; you press the button once to turn on the television and press it a second time to turn it off.

To hide the Navigation toolbar using the View menu:

1. Click **View** on the menu bar, point to **Show/Hide**, and then click **Navigation Toolbar**. Both the Navigation toolbar and its toolbar tab are no longer visible on the screen. To redisplay the Navigation toolbar and its tab, you repeat the same steps.

   TROUBLE? If the Navigation Toolbar does not have a check mark next to it, then the Navigation toolbar already is hidden.

2. Click **View** on the menu bar, point to **Show/Hide**, and then click **Navigation Toolbar**. The toolbar and its tab are displayed again.

Using the Location Bar

You can use the **Location bar** to enter URLs directly into Navigator. As you learned in Session 2.1, you must enter the URL to identify a Web page's exact location. Although a complete URL includes the name of a file, entering just the IP address or the domain name will usually be sufficient to take you to the home page of the site.

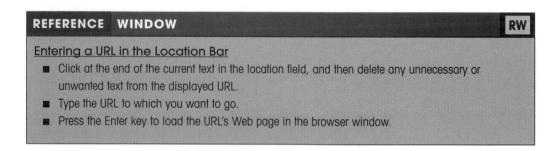

REFERENCE WINDOW   RW

Entering a URL in the Location Bar
- Click at the end of the current text in the location field, and then delete any unnecessary or unwanted text from the displayed URL.
- Type the URL to which you want to go.
- Press the Enter key to load the URL's Web page in the browser window.

Marianna has asked you to start your research by examining the Web page for the Miami Wind Quintet. She has given you the URL so that you can find its Web page.

To load the Miami Wind Quintet's Web page:

1. Click at the end of the text in the location field, and then delete any unnecessary or unwanted text by pressing the **Backspace** key.

   TROUBLE? Make sure that you delete all of the text in the location field so the text you type in Step 2 will be correct.

2. Type **www.course.com/newperspectives/internet3** in the location field. This URL will take you to the Student Online Companion page on the Course Technology Web site, and then you can click the hyperlinks provided in the steps in this tutorial to go to individual Web pages.

3. Press the **Enter** key. The Student Online Companion Web page loads, as shown in Figure 2-30.

Figure 2-30   STUDENT ONLINE COMPANION PAGE AT COURSE.COM

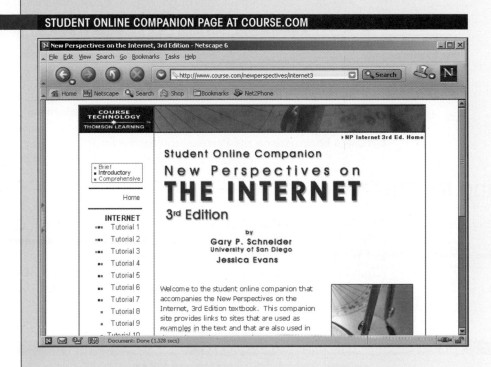

4. Click the hyperlink for your book, click the **Tutorial 2** link, and then click the **Session 2.2** link.

5. Click the **Miami Wind Quintet** link. The Web page opens, as shown in Figure 2-31.

Figure 2-31   MIAMI WIND QUINTET WEB PAGE

> **TROUBLE?** The Miami Wind Quintet Web page might look different from the one shown in Figure 2-31. If this Web page has been deleted from the server, you might see an entirely different Web page; however, the steps should work the same.
>
> **6.** Read the Web page, and then click the **Back** button on the toolbar to return to the Student Online Companion page.

You like the format of the Miami Wind Quintet's home page, so you want to make sure that you can go back to that page later if you need to review its contents. Maggie explains that you can write down the URL so you can refer to it later, but an easier way is to store the URL as a bookmark on the Personal toolbar for future use.

Using the Personal Toolbar

The **Personal toolbar** works very much like the Navigation toolbar, but with one significant difference. You can customize the Personal toolbar to meet your needs by adding and removing toolbar buttons. Because each person who installs Navigator can place a different set of buttons on the Personal toolbar, yours may look somewhat different from the one shown in Figure 2-32, depending on who installed the program on the computer you are using.

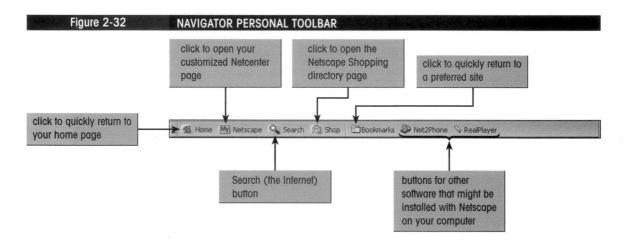

Figure 2-32   NAVIGATOR PERSONAL TOOLBAR

click to open your customized Netcenter page

click to open the Netscape Shopping directory page

click to quickly return to a preferred site

click to quickly return to your home page

Search (the Internet) button

buttons for other software that might be installed with Netscape on your computer

The Home button loads the program's defined start page. The **My Netscape** button opens a version of the Netscape's Netcenter page that you can customize. The **Search** button opens a Web page that has hyperlinks to Web search engines and directories. The **Shop** button opens the Netscape Shopping directory page, which contains links to featured products. The **Bookmarks** button opens a list of Web sites whose URLs you have saved. You will learn how to save bookmarks later in this session. Your Personal toolbar may have other buttons that lead to specific Web pages or that open other programs. For example, the Personal toolbar shown in Figure 2-32 is the default toolbar that results from a Navigator installation, which also includes the Net2Phone program (which allows the user to place telephone calls through the browser) and the RealPlayer program (which enables Navigator to play sound and video clips that have been stored on Web servers in the Real format).

Hiding and Showing the Personal Toolbar

You can click the Personal toolbar tab or use the View menu to hide and show the toolbar, just as you did to hide and show the Navigation toolbar and its tab. Clicking the Personal toolbar tab hides the toolbar, but keeps the tab visible so you can redisplay the toolbar quickly.

Creating a Bookmark for a Web Site

You use a **bookmark** to store and organize a list of Web pages that you have visited so you can return to them easily. Figure 2-33 shows an open Bookmarks window, which contains bookmarks sorted into categories according to the user's needs.

Figure 2-33	BOOKMARKS SORTED INTO CATEGORIES

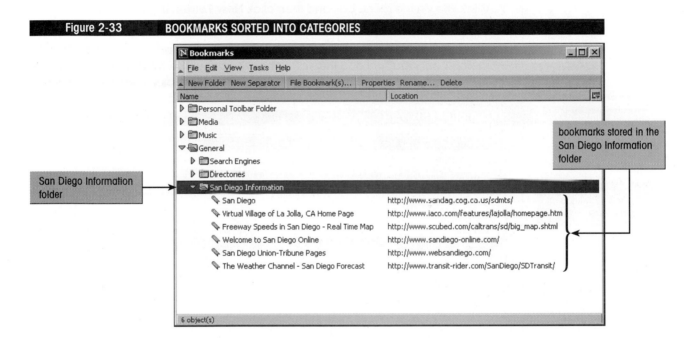

The hierarchical structure of the bookmark file is easy to see in Figure 2-33. For example, the six Web pages shown in the San Diego Information folder provide information about San Diego.

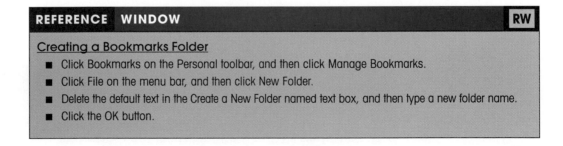

REFERENCE WINDOW **RW**

Creating a Bookmarks Folder
- Click Bookmarks on the Personal toolbar, and then click Manage Bookmarks.
- Click File on the menu bar, and then click New Folder.
- Delete the default text in the Create a New Folder named text box, and then type a new folder name.
- Click the OK button.

You will create a bookmark for the Miami Wind Quintet Web page, but first, you need to create a folder in which to store your bookmarks. You will then save your bookmark in that folder. You might not work on the same computer again, so you will save a copy of the bookmark file to a floppy disk for future use.

To create a new Bookmarks folder:

1. Click the **Bookmarks** button on the Personal toolbar, and then click **Manage Bookmarks**. The Bookmarks window opens. Note that the title bar of the Bookmarks window indicates that this window is "for" a specific user. The title bar of the Bookmarks window on your computer might display your name or the name provided by the system administrator or technical support person.

2. Click **File** on the menu bar, and then click **New Folder**. The Create New Folder dialog box opens.

3. Delete the default text in the Create a New Folder named text box, type **Wind Quintet Information**, and then click the **OK** button. The Wind Quintet Information folder appears in the Bookmarks window, as shown in Figure 2-34.

Figure 2-34	WIND QUINTET INFORMATION FOLDER

the folders in the Bookmarks window on your screen might differ

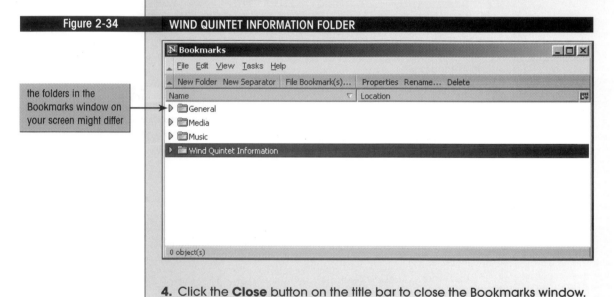

4. Click the **Close** button on the title bar to close the Bookmarks window.

Now that you have created a folder, you can save your bookmark for the Miami Wind Quintet Web page in the new folder.

REFERENCE WINDOW   **RW**

Saving a Bookmark in a Bookmarks Folder
- Open the page that you want to bookmark in Navigator.
- Click Bookmarks on the menu bar, and then click File Bookmark.
- Type a descriptive name in the box.
- Select the folder in which you want to save the bookmark.
- Click the OK button.

Before you save the bookmark, first you must return to the Web page that you want to bookmark.

To save a bookmark for the Miami Wind Quintet Web page in the Bookmarks folder:

1. Click the **Forward** button on the Navigation toolbar to return to the Miami Wind Quintet Web page.

2. Click **Bookmarks** on the menu bar, and then click **File Bookmark**. The Add Bookmark dialog box opens.

3. Type **Miami Wind Quintet** in the Name text box.

   TROUBLE? If necessary, delete any unnecessary text that appears in the Name text box before you begin typing the name for the bookmark.

4. Click the **Wind Quintet Information** folder in the Create in box, and then click the **OK** button. Now, the bookmark is saved in the correct folder. You can test your bookmark by using the bookmark to visit the site.

5. Click the **Back** button on the Navigation toolbar to go to the previous Web page.

6. Click **Bookmarks** on the menu bar, point to **Wind Quintet Information**, and then click **Miami Wind Quintet**. The Miami Wind Quintet page opens in the browser.

   TROUBLE? If the Miami Wind Quintet page does not open, click Edit Bookmarks on the menu bar, make sure that you have the correct URL for the page, and then repeat Steps 6. If you still have trouble, ask your instructor or technical support person for help.

Because you might need to visit a Web page when you are working at another computer, you can save your bookmark file on a disk.

REFERENCE WINDOW `RW`

Saving a Bookmark File to a Disk
- Click Bookmarks on the menu bar, and then click Manage Bookmarks.
- Click File on the menu bar, and then click Export Bookmarks.
- Click the Save in list arrow, and then select the drive that contains your disk.
- Type a name for the bookmark file.
- Click the Save button.

Because you might need to visit the Miami Wind Quintet page when you are working at another computer, you will save your bookmark file on a disk.

To store the Miami Wind Quintet bookmark file to a disk:

1. Click **Bookmarks** on the menu bar, and then click **Manage Bookmarks**. When you save a bookmark, you save all of the bookmarks, not just the one that you need.

2. Click **File** on the menu bar in the Bookmarks window, and then click Export Bookmarks. The Export bookmark file dialog box opens.

   TROUBLE? If prompted to, insert a disk in the appropriate drive on your computer.

3. If necessary, click the **Save in** list arrow, select the drive that contains your disk, and then select the **Tutorial.02** folder.

   TROUBLE? If you were prompted to insert a disk in Step 2, then the correct drive and disk should automatically appear in the Save in list box.

   The filename that you give the bookmark file should indicate the Web page you have marked. The file extension must be .htm or .html so the browser into which you load this file will recognize it as an HTML file. Most browsers will recognize either file extension; however, some do not. Also note that the filename cannot contain spaces.

4. Type **WindQuintetBookmarks.html** in the File name text box. Note that you can select the Web Page option in the Save as type list and type the name of the file without typing the file extension; with the Web Page option selected, the program will automatically add the file extension.

5. Click the **Save** button, and then close the Bookmarks window.

When you use another computer, you can open the bookmark file from your disk by starting Navigator, clicking Bookmarks on the menu bar, clicking Manage Bookmarks, clicking File on the menu bar, and then clicking Import Bookmarks. Change to the drive that contains your disk, and then open the HTML file. Your bookmark file will open in the Bookmarks window.

Hyperlink **Navigation Using the Mouse**

Now you know how to use Navigator to find information that will help you with the Sunset Wind Quintet. Maggie tells you that the easiest way to move from one Web page to another is to use the mouse to click hyperlinks that the authors of Web pages embed in their HTML documents. You can also right-click the mouse on the background of a Web page to open a shortcut menu that includes navigation options.

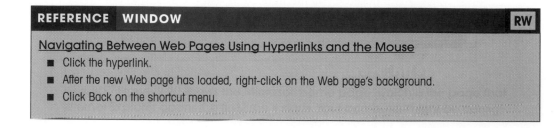

REFERENCE WINDOW   RW

Navigating Between Web Pages Using Hyperlinks and the Mouse
- Click the hyperlink.
- After the new Web page has loaded, right-click on the Web page's background.
- Click Back on the shortcut menu.

To follow a hyperlink to a Web page and return using the mouse:

1. Click the **Back** button on the Navigation toolbar to return to the Student Online Companion page, click the **Lewis Music** link to open that page, and then point to the **Instrument Accessories** hyperlink shown in Figure 2-35 so your pointer changes to an icon of a hand with a pointing index finger.

Figure 2-35	LEWIS MUSIC WEB PAGE

URL

hyperlinks

pointer shape changes when hovering over a hyperlink

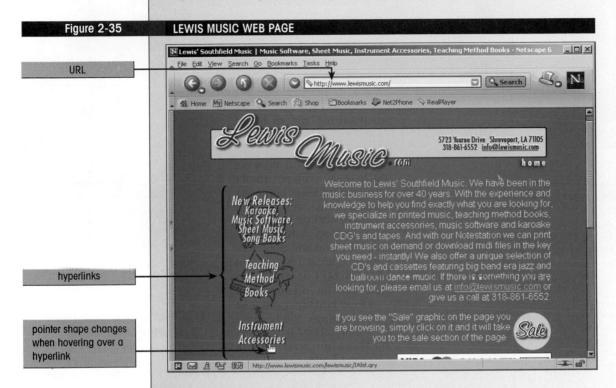

2. Click the **Instrument Accessories** link to load the page. Watch the second panel in the status bar. When the shadow disappears, you know that Navigator has loaded the full page.

3. Right-click anywhere in the Web page area to open the shortcut menu, as shown in Figure 2-36.

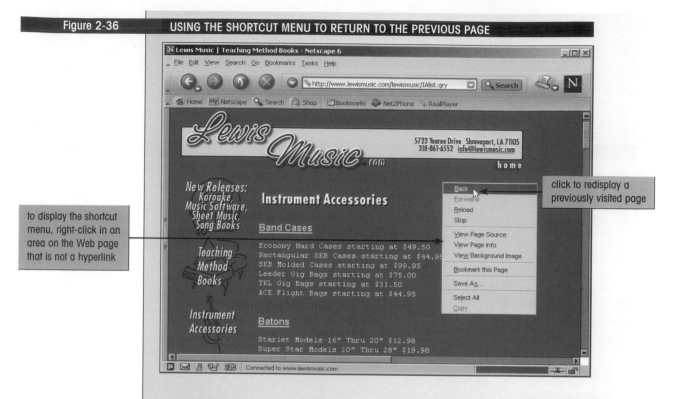

Figure 2-36   USING THE SHORTCUT MENU TO RETURN TO THE PREVIOUS PAGE

to display the shortcut menu, right-click in an area on the Web page that is not a hyperlink

click to redisplay a previously visited page

TROUBLE? If you right-click a hyperlink, your shortcut menu displays a list that differs from the one shown in Figure 2-36; therefore, the Back option might not appear in the same position on the menu. If you don't see the shortcut menu shown in Figure 2-36, click anywhere outside of the shortcut menu to close it, and then repeat Step 3.

TROUBLE? Web pages change frequently. The Instrument Accessories page you see might look different from the one shown in Figure 2-36, however, right-clicking anywhere on the Web page area will still work.

4. Click **Back** on the shortcut menu to go back to the Lewis Music home page.

5. Repeat Step 4 to return to the Student Online Companion page.

Using the History List

The Back and Forward buttons on the Navigation toolbar enable you to move to and from recently visited pages. These buttons duplicate the functions of the commands on the Go menu. The options on the Go menu enable you to move back and forward through a portion of the history list and allow you to choose a specific Web page from that list. To see where you have been during a session, you also can open the history list for your current session.

To view the history list for this session:

1. Click **Tasks** on the menu bar, click **Tools**, and then click **History** to open the history list in its own window.

2. Click the small arrow next to the **Today** folder to open the list of Web sites visited today, as shown in Figure 2-37.

Figure 2-37   **VIEWING THE HISTORY LIST**

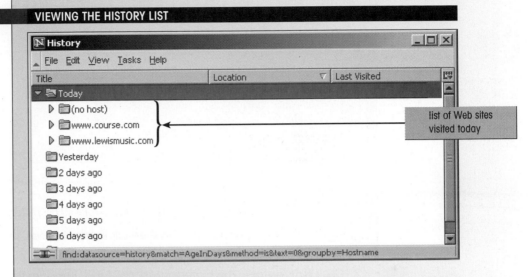

TROUBLE? The History window that appears on your computer might be a different size and contain different entries from the one that appears in Figure 2-37. You can resize the History window as you would any window by dragging its edges, and you can resize the columns in the window by dragging on the edges of the column headers.

To return to a previously visited Web page, double-click the page in the list.

3. Click the **Close** button on the History window title bar to close it.

You can change the way that pages are listed in the History window by using the commands on the View menu; for example, you can list the pages by title or in the order in which you visited them.

Reloading a Web Page

The Reload button on the Navigator toolbar loads again the Web page that currently appears in the browser window. You can force Navigator to load the page from the Web server instead of your computer's temporary storage cache by pressing the Shift key when you click the Reload button.

Returning to the Home Page

The Home button on the Personal toolbar displays the home (or start) page for your copy of Navigator. You can go to the Netscape Netcenter page, which is the software's default installation home page, by clicking the **Netscape** button on the Navigator toolbar. You cannot change the page that loads when you click the Netscape button, but you can change the default URL that opens when you click the Home button by using the Preferences dialog box.

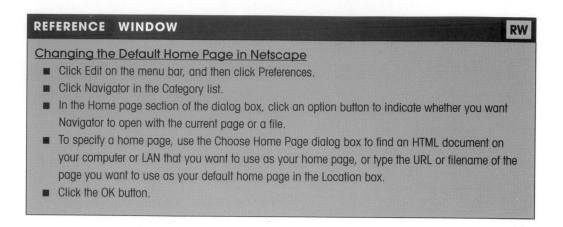

REFERENCE WINDOW   RW

<u>Changing the Default Home Page in Netscape</u>
- Click Edit on the menu bar, and then click Preferences.
- Click Navigator in the Category list.
- In the Home page section of the dialog box, click an option button to indicate whether you want Navigator to open with the current page or a file.
- To specify a home page, use the Choose Home Page dialog box to find an HTML document on your computer or LAN that you want to use as your home page, or type the URL or filename of the page you want to use as your default home page in the Location box.
- Click the OK button.

To view the settings for the default home page:

1. Click **Edit** on the menu bar, and then click **Preferences**. The Preferences dialog box opens.

2. Click **Navigator** in the Category list, as shown in Figure 2-38.

| Figure 2-38 | PREFERENCES DIALOG BOX |

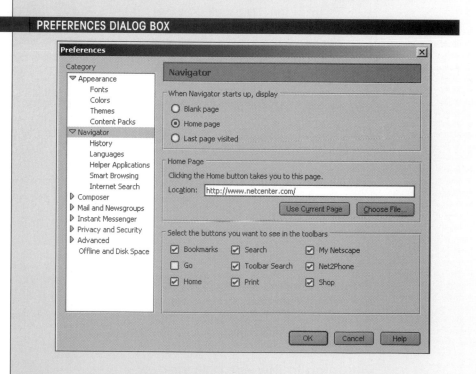

3. To open with the current page or a home page you specify, click the corresponding option button in the Home Page section of the Preferences dialog box.

TROUBLE? Do not change any settings unless you are instructed to do so by your instructor. Many organizations set the home page defaults on all of their computers and lock those settings.

To specify a home page, you would select the text in the Location box and then enter the URL of the Web page you want to use. If you load the Web page that you want as your new home page before beginning these steps, you can click the Use Current Page button to place the page's URL in the Location box. You also can specify an HTML document on your computer or LAN by clicking the Choose File button and selecting the disk drive and folder location of that HTML document.

4. Click the **Cancel** button to close the dialog box without making any changes.

Printing a Web Page

The Print button on the Navigation toolbar lets you print the current Web frame or page. You can use this button to make a printed copy of most Web pages (some Web pages disable the Print command). Navigator uses a default layout for printing Web pages that cannot be changed. The default print layout includes information about the Web page you are printing. The name of the Web page, which is the text that the Web page designer has included within the page's TITLE tags, appears at the top left of the printed page (not all Web designers give their pages such titles). The URL of the Web page appears at the top right of the printed page. A page number appears at the lower left of the page and the date and time the page was printed appear at the lower right of the page.

REFERENCE WINDOW　　　　　　　　　　　　　　　　　　　　　　　　　　　**RW**

Printing the Current Web Page
- Click the Print button on the Navigation toolbar (or click File on the menu bar, and then click Print).
- Select the printer you want to use and indicate the pages you want to print and the number of copies you want to make of each page.
- Click the OK button.

To print a Web page:

1. Click in the main (right) frame of the Student Online Companion page to select it.

2. Click the **Print** button on the Navigation toolbar to open the Print dialog box, as shown in Figure 2-39.

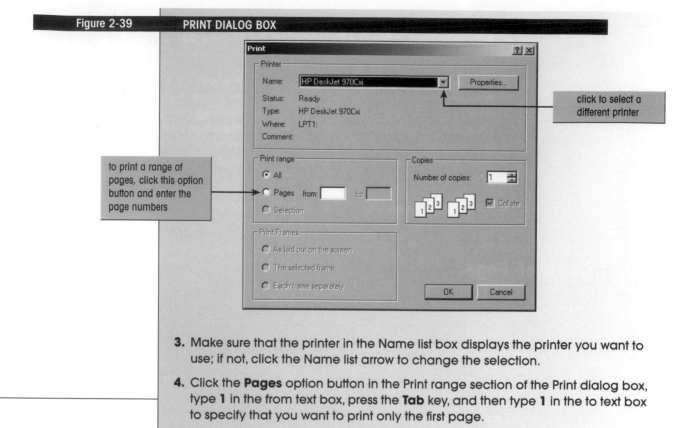

Figure 2-39 **PRINT DIALOG BOX**

click to select a different printer

to print a range of pages, click this option button and enter the page numbers

3. Make sure that the printer in the Name list box displays the printer you want to use; if not, click the Name list arrow to change the selection.

4. Click the **Pages** option button in the Print range section of the Print dialog box, type **1** in the from text box, press the **Tab** key, and then type **1** in the to text box to specify that you want to print only the first page.

5. Make sure that the Number of copies text box displays **1**.

6. Click the **OK** button to print the Web page and close the Print dialog box.

Checking Web Page Security

The **Security indicator button** is a small picture of a padlock that appears at the right edge of the status bar at the bottom of the Navigator browser window. This button lets you check some of the security elements of a Web page. The button will display as either an open padlock icon or a closed padlock icon to indicate whether the Web page was encrypted during transmission from the Web server. The closed padlock icon indicates that the page was encrypted.

Encryption is a way of scrambling and encoding data transmissions that reduces the risk that a person who intercepts the Web page as it travels across the Internet will be able to decode and read the page's contents. Web sites use encrypted transmission to send and receive information, such as credit card numbers, to ensure privacy. You can obtain more information about the details of the encryption used on a Web page by examining the Page Info dialog box that opens when you click the Security indicator button. Figure 2-40 shows the Page Info dialog box for an encrypted Web page after the user clicked the Security indicator button.

Figure 2-40	PAGE INFO DIALOG BOX FOR AN ENCRYPTED WEB PAGE

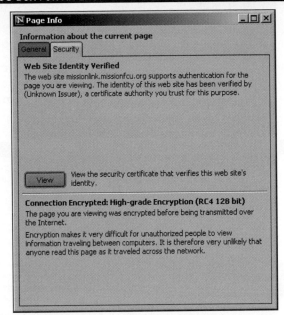

Managing Cookies

Another issue that concerns many Web users is the use of cookies. A **cookie** is a small file that a Web server writes to the disk drive of the client computer (the computer on which the Web browser is running). The cookie can contain information about the user such as login names and passwords. By storing this information on the user's computer, the Web server can perform functions such as automatic login. Often, the user is unaware that these files are being written to their computer's disk drive. Navigator stores all of these cookies in one file and gives the user a tool to manage that file called the **Cookie Manager**.

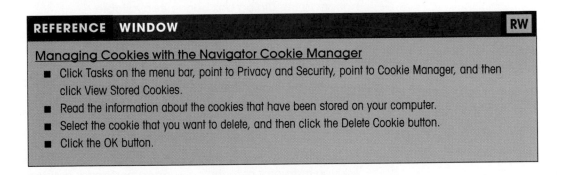

REFERENCE WINDOW   **RW**

Managing Cookies with the Navigator Cookie Manager
- Click Tasks on the menu bar, point to Privacy and Security, point to Cookie Manager, and then click View Stored Cookies.
- Read the information about the cookies that have been stored on your computer.
- Select the cookie that you want to delete, and then click the Delete Cookie button.
- Click the OK button.

You will delete a cookie stored on your computer using the Cookie Manager.

To manage cookies with the Cookie Manager:

1. Click **Tasks** on the menu bar, point to **Privacy and Security**, point to **Cookie Manager**, and then click **View Stored Cookies**.

2. Examine the cookies in the list that appears in the Cookie Manager dialog box. If your computer has many cookies stored on it, you can use the scroll bar to move up and down in the list. An example of a Cookie Manager dialog box with five cookies appears in Figure 2-41.

Figure 2-41 **COOKIE MANAGER DIALOG BOX**

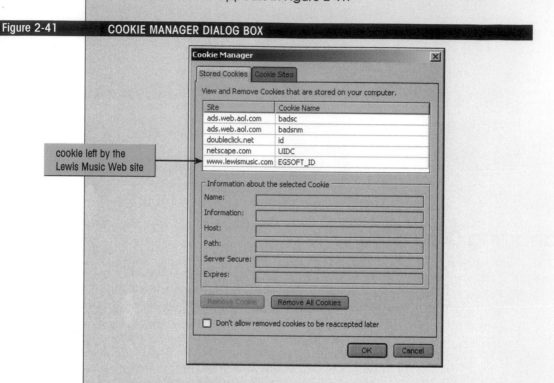

cookie left by the
Lewis Music Web site

3. Click any cookie in the list to select it. Note the Remove Cookie button near the bottom of the dialog box becomes available.

4. Find a cookie that you want to delete, click to select it, and then click the **Remove Cookie** button. You may notice that many of the cookies on your computer are placed there by companies that sell banner advertising on Web pages (such as doubleclick.net). These companies use cookies to record which ads have appeared on pages you have viewed so that they can present different ads the next time you open a Web page. In Figure 2-41, you can see that the Lewis Music Web site left a cookie on this computer.

   TROUBLE? You may be instructed to delete specific cookies or no cookies at all. Ask you instructor or technical support person for assistance if you are unsure which cookies can be deleted.

5. When you are finished exploring and deleting cookies, click the **OK** button to close the Cookie Manager dialog box.

If you want to delete all the cookies that have been stored on your computer, click the Remove All Cookies button. You can also indicate whether or not you want cookies that you have removed to be stored again.

Getting Help in Navigator

Navigator includes a limited Help system. You can open the Help Contents window to learn more about the Help options that are available.

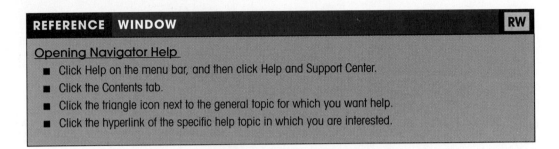

REFERENCE WINDOW   **RW**

Opening Navigator Help
- Click Help on the menu bar, and then click Help and Support Center.
- Click the Contents tab.
- Click the triangle icon next to the general topic for which you want help.
- Click the hyperlink of the specific help topic in which you are interested.

You will use Navigator Help to read about browsing the Web.

To use Navigator Help:

1. Click **Help** on the menu bar, and then click **Help and Support Center**.

2. If necessary, click the **Contents** tab to display the Contents window.

3. Click the triangle icon next to the **Browsing the Web** category to open a list of specific help topics in that category. Examine the page, which should be similar to the one shown in Figure 2-42, and use the scroll box or scroll down button to move down the page.

Figure 2-42   NETSCAPE HELP WINDOW

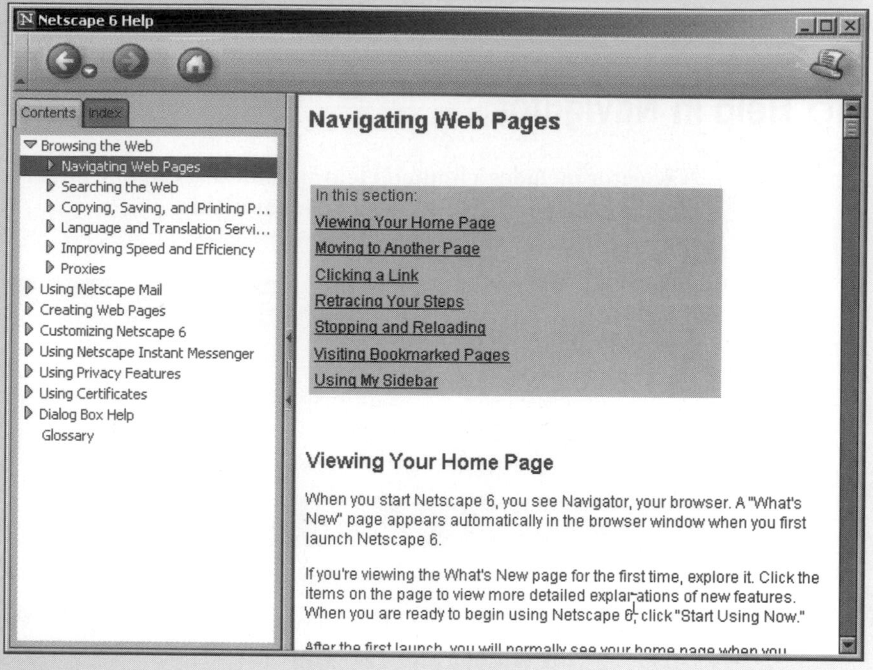

You can click any of the hyperlinks to obtain help on the specific topics listed. You can also click the Index tab to obtain an alphabetized list of hyperlinks to specific terms used in the Help pages.

4. Click the **Close** button to close Help.

You feel confident that you have the tools you need to successfully find information on the Web. Marianna probably will be interested in seeing the Miami Wind Quintet Web page, but you are not sure if she will have Internet access while she is touring. Maggie says that you can save the Web page to a disk, so Marianna can open the page locally in her Web browser using the files you saved on that disk.

Using Navigator to Save a Web Page

There will be times when you will want to refer to the information that you have found on a Web page without having to search the site. In Netscape, you can store entire Web pages, selected portions of Web page text, or particular graphics from a Web page to a disk.

Saving a Web Page

You like the Miami Wind Quintet's Web site and want to save a copy of the page to a disk so you can show the Web page to Marianna. That way, she can review it without having an Internet connection. To save a Web page, you must have the page open in Navigator.

REFERENCE   WINDOW   RW

Saving a Web Page to a Disk
- Open the Web page in Navigator.
- Click File on the menu bar, and then click Save As.
- Click the Save in list arrow, and then select the drive that contains your disk.
- Accept the default filename, or change the filename, but retain the file extension .htm or .html.
- Click the Save button.

You will save the Miami Wind Quintet page to a disk so you can send it to Marianna for her review.

To save the Web page to a disk:

1. Use your bookmark to return to the Miami Wind Quintet page.

2. Click **File** on the menu bar, and then click **Save As**. The Save As dialog box opens.

3. Click the **Save in** list arrow, click the drive that contains your disk, select the **Tutorial.02** folder, and then type the name **MiamiWindQuintet.htm** in the File name box.

4. Click the **Save** button. Now the HTML document for the Miami Wind Quintet's home page is saved on your disk. When you send it to Marianna, she can open her Web browser and then use the Open command on the File menu to open the Web page.

If the Web page contains graphics, such as photos, drawings, or icons, they will not be saved with the HTML document. To save a graphic, right-click it in the browser window, click Save Image on the shortcut menu, and then save the graphic to the same location as the Web's HTML document. The graphics file will appear on the HTML document as a hyperlink; therefore, you might have to change the HTML code in the Web page to identify the location of the graphic. Copying the graphics files to the same disk as the HTML document will *usually* work.

Saving Web Page Text to a File

You can save portions of Web page text to a file, so that you can use the file in other programs. You will use WordPad to save text that you will copy from a Web page; however, any word processor or text editor will work.

REFERENCE   WINDOW   RW

Copying Text from a Web Page to a WordPad Document
- Open the Web page in Navigator.
- Use the mouse pointer to select the text you want to copy.
- Click Edit on the menu bar, and then click Copy.
- Start WordPad (or another word processor or text editor if WordPad is not available).
- Click Edit on the WordPad menu bar, and then click Paste (or click the Paste button).
- Click the Save button, select the folder where you want to store the file, and then enter a new filename, if necessary.
- Click the Save button.

Marianna just called to let you know that the quintet will play a concert in Grand Rapids on a Friday night, and she asks you to identify other opportunities for scheduling local concerts during the following weekend. Often museums are willing to book small ensembles for weekend afternoon programs, and Marianna has given you the URL for the Grand Rapids Art Museum. You will visit the site and then get the museum's address and telephone number so you can contact it about scheduling a concert.

To copy text from a Web page and save the text as a WordPad document:

1. Use the **Back** button to return to the Student Online Companion page, and then click the **Grand Rapids Art Museum** link to open that Web page in the browser window.

2. Click the **Information & Calendar** hyperlink to open the museum information page, and then click the **Map** hyperlink.

3. Scroll down to display the text below the map image, and then drag the mouse pointer over the address and telephone number to select it, as shown in Figure 2-43.

Figure 2-43	SELECTING TEXT ON A WEB PAGE

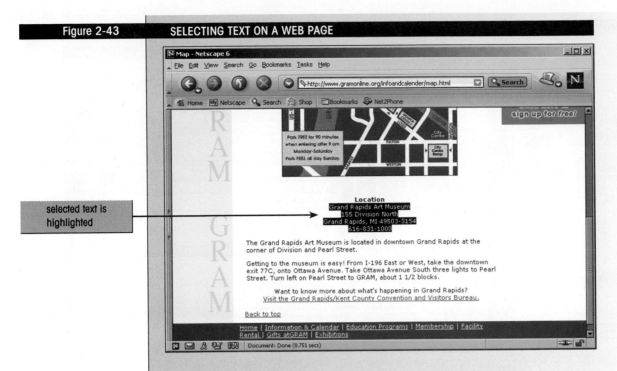

selected text is highlighted

4. Click **Edit** on the menu bar, and then click **Copy** to copy the selected text to the Clipboard.

Now, you will start WordPad and then paste the copied text into a new document.

5. Click the **Start** button on the taskbar, point to **Programs**, point to **Accessories**, and then click **WordPad** to start the program and open a new document.

6. Click the **Paste** button on the WordPad toolbar to paste the text into the WordPad document, as shown in Figure 2-44

TROUBLE? If the WordPad toolbar does not appear, click View on the menu bar, click Toolbar, and then repeat Step 2. Your WordPad program window might be a different size from the one shown in Figure 2-44, which does not affect the steps.

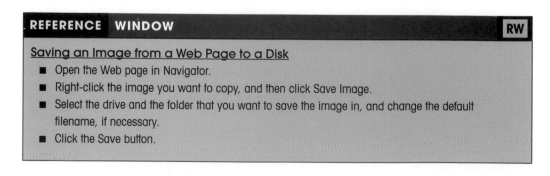

Figure 2-44   PASTING TEXT FROM A WEB PAGE INTO A WORDPAD DOCUMENT

7. Click the **Save** button on the WordPad toolbar to open the Save As dialog box.

8. Click the **Save in** list arrow, select the drive that contains your disk, and then select the Tutorial.02 folder.

9. Delete the text in the File name text box, type **GRAM-Address.txt**, and then click the **Save** button to save the file. Now, the address and phone number of the museum is saved in a file on your disk for future reference.

10. Click the **Close** button on the WordPad title bar to close it.

You will use this information to contact the museum at a later time. As you examine the Web page, you notice a street map of the area surrounding the museum, which Marianna might like to have.

Saving a Web Page Graphic to a Disk

The Web page with directions and transportation information will be helpful to Marianna, so you decide to save the map graphic to your disk. You can then send the file to Marianna so she has a resource for getting to the museum.

REFERENCE WINDOW   **RW**

<u>Saving an Image from a Web Page to a Disk</u>
- Open the Web page in Navigator.
- Right-click the image you want to copy, and then click Save Image.
- Select the drive and the folder that you want to save the image in, and change the default filename, if necessary.
- Click the Save button.

Now you will save the image of the street map to your disk, which you will later send to Marianna.

To save the street map image to a disk:

1. Right-click the map image to open its shortcut menu, as shown in Figure 2-45.

| Figure 2-45 | SAVING THE MAP IMAGE TO A DISK |

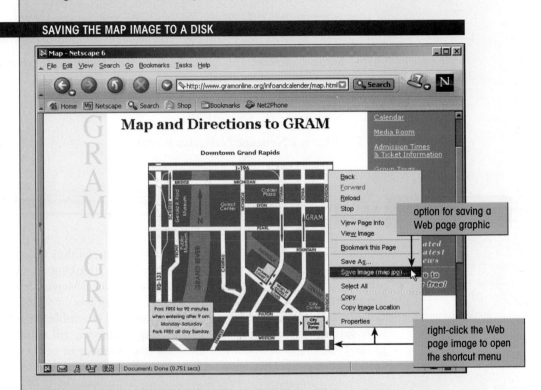

2. Click **Save Image** on the shortcut menu to open the Save As dialog box.

3. Click the **Save in** list arrow, select the drive that contains your disk, and then select the Tutorial.02 folder.

4. Delete the text in the File name text box, type **GRAM-Map.jpg**, and then click the **Save** button to save the file.

5. Close your Web browser, and if necessary, log off your Internet connection.

Now, you can send a disk to Marianna so she will have the Miami Wind Quintet Web page and a map to show how to get to the museum. She will be able to use her Web browser to open the files and print them.

Session 2.3 QUICK CHECK

1. Describe three ways to load a Web page in the Navigator browser.

2. You can use the _____ in Navigator to visit previously visited sites during your Web session.

3. When would you use the Reload command?

4. What happens when you click the Home button on the Navigation toolbar?

5. Some Web servers _____ Web pages before returning them to the client to prevent unauthorized access.

6. True or False: You can identify an encrypted Web page when viewing it in Navigator.

7. What is a Netscape Navigator bookmark?

REVIEW ASSIGNMENTS

Marianna is pleased with the information you gathered thus far about other wind quintet Web pages and potential recital sites. In fact, she is thinking about hiring someone to create a Web page for the Sunset Wind Quintet. Because Marianna wants to be prepared for her meetings with potential Web designers, she has asked you to compile some information about the Web pages that other small musical ensembles have created. Although you have searched for information about wind quintets, you will search for additional background information, which will include a large number of string quartets (two violinists, a violist, and a cellist) that play similar venues by completing the following steps.

1. Start your Web browser, open the Student Online Companion page at www.course.com/newperspectives/internet3, click the hyperlink for your book, click the Tutorial 2 link, and then click the Review Assignments link.

2. Click the hyperlinks listed under the category heading Small Musical Ensembles to explore the Web pages for these types of organizations.

3. Choose three interesting home pages, and print the first page of each. Create a bookmark or favorite for each of these sites, and then answer the following questions for these three sites:

   a. Which sites include a photograph of the ensemble?
   b. Which photographs are in color and black and white?
   c. Which sites show the ensemble members dressed in formal concert dress?

4. Choose your favorite ensemble photograph and save it to a floppy disk.

5. Do any of the three sites you have chosen provide information about the ensemble's CDs? If so, which ones? Is this information on the home page, or did you click a hyperlink to find it?

6. Do any of the sites offer CDs or other products for sale? If so, which ones? Is this information on the home page, or did you click a hyperlink to find it?

7. Write a one-page report that summarizes your findings for Marianna. Include a recommendation regarding what the Sunset Wind Quintet should consider including in its Web site.

8. Close your Web browser and, if necessary, log off your Internet connection.

CASE PROBLEMS

Case 1. Businesses on the Web Business Web sites range from very simple informational sites to comprehensive sites that offer information about the firm's products or services, history, current employment openings, and financial information. An increasing number of business sites offer products or services for sale using their Web sites. You just started a position on the public relations staff of Value City Central, a large retail chain of television and appliance stores. Your first assignment is to research and report on the types of information that other large firms offer on their Web sites, which you will do by completing the following steps.

1. Start your Web browser, open the Student Online Companion page at www.course.com/ newperspectives/internet3, click the hyperlink for your book, click the Tutorial 2 link, and then click the Case Problems link.

2. Use the Case Problem 1 hyperlinks to open the business sites on that page.

3. Choose three of those business sites that you believe would be most relevant to your assignment.

4. Print the home page for each Web site that you have chosen.

5. Select one site that you feel does the best job in each of the following five categories:

   a. overall presentation of the corporate image
   b. description of products or services offered
   c. presentation of the firm's history
   d. description of employment opportunities
   e. presentation of financial statements or other financial information about the company.

6. Prepare a report that includes one paragraph describing why you believe each of the sites you identified in the preceding step did the best job.

7. Close your Web browser, and log off the Internet, if necessary.

Case 2. Browser Wars Your employer, Bristol Mills, is a medium-sized manufacturer of specialty steel products. The firm has increased its use of computers in all of its office operations and in many of its manufacturing operations. Many of Bristol's computers currently run either Microsoft Internet Explorer or Netscape Navigator; however, the chief financial officer (CFO) has decided the firm can support only one of these products. The CFO has also heard some good things about another browser named Opera and is wondering if that might be the right product for the company. As the CFO's special assistant, you have been asked to recommend which of these three Web browsers the company should choose to support. You will research the browsers for your report by completing the following steps.

1. Start your Web browser, open the Student Online Companion page at www.course.com/ newperspectives/internet3, click the hyperlink for your book, click the Tutorial 2 link, and then click the Case Problems link.

2. Use the Case Problem 2 hyperlinks to learn more about these three Web browser software packages.

3. Write a one-page memo to the CFO (your instructor) that outlines the strengths and weaknesses of each product. Recommend one program and support your decision using the information you collected.

4. Prepare a list of features that you would like to see in a new Web browser software package that would overcome important limitations in Opera, Internet Explorer, or Navigator. Do you think it would be feasible for a firm to develop and use such a product? Why or why not?

5. Close your Web browser, and log off the Internet, if necessary.

Case 3. Citizens Fidelity Bank   You are a new staff auditor at the Citizens Fidelity Bank. You have had more recent computer training than other audit staff members at Citizens, so Sally DeYoung, the audit manager, asks you to review the bank's policy on Web browser cookie settings. Some of the bank's board members expressed concerns to Sally about the security of the bank's computers. They understand that the bank has PCs on its networks that are connected to the Internet. One of the board members learned about browser cookies and was afraid that a naive bank employee might open a Web site that would write a dangerous cookie file on the bank's computer network. Not all Web servers write cookies, but those that do can read the cookie file the next time the Web browser on that computer connects to the Web server. The Web server can then retrieve information about the Web browser's last connection to the server. None of the bank's board members knows very much about computers, but all of them became concerned that a virus-laden cookie could significantly damage the bank's computer system. Sally asks you to help inform the board of directors about cookies and to establish a policy on using them. You will accomplish these tasks by completing the following steps.

1. Start your Web browser, open the Student Online Companion page at www.course.com/newperspectives/internet3, click the hyperlink for your book, click the Tutorial 2 link, and then click the Case Problems hyperlink.

2. Use the Case Problem 3 hyperlinks to Cookie Information Resources to learn more about cookie files.

3. Prepare a brief outline of the content on each Web page you visit.

4. List the risks that Citizens Fidelity Bank might face by allowing cookie files to be written to their computers.

5. List the benefits that individual users obtain by allowing Web servers to write cookies to the computers that they are using at the bank to access the Web.

6. Close your Web browser, and log off the Internet, if necessary.

Case 4. Columbus Suburban Area Council   The Columbus Suburban Area Council is a charitable organization devoted to maintaining and improving the general welfare of people living in Columbus suburbs. As the director of the council, you are interested in encouraging donations and other support from area citizens and would like to stay informed of grant opportunities that might benefit the council. You are especially interested in developing an informative and attractive presence on the Web and will pursue that goal by completing the following steps.

1. Start your Web browser, open the Student Online Companion page at www.course.com/newperspectives/internet3, click the hyperlink for your book, click the Tutorial 2 link, and then click the Case Problems link.

2. Follow the Case Problem 4 hyperlinks to charitable organizations to find out more about what other organizations are doing with their Web sites.

3. Select three of the Web sites you visited and, for each, prepare a list of the site's contents. Note whether each site included financial information and whether the site disclosed how much the organization spent on administrative or nonprogram-related activities.

4. Identify which site you believe would be a good model for the Council's new Web site. Explain why you think your chosen site would be the best example to follow.

5. Close your Web browser, and log off the Internet, if necessary.

Case 5. *Emma's Start Page* Your neighbor, Emma Inkster, was an elementary school teacher for many years. She is now retired and has just purchased her first personal computer. Emma is excited about getting on the Web and exploring its resources. She has asked for your help. After you introduce her to what you have learned in this tutorial about Web browsers, she is eager to spend more time gathering information on the Web. Although she is retired, Emma has continued to be very active. She is an avid bridge player, enjoys golf, and is one of the neighborhood's best gardeners. Although she is somewhat limited by her schoolteacher's pension, Emma loves to travel to foreign countries and especially likes to learn the languages of her destinations. She would like to have a start page for her computer that would include hyperlinks that would help her easily visit and return regularly to Web pages related to her interests. Her nephew knows HTML and can create the page, but Emma would like you to help her design the layout of her start page. You know that Web directory sites are designed to help people find interesting Web sites, so you begin your search with them by completing the following steps.

1. Start your Web browser, open the Student Online Companion page at www.course.com/newperspectives/internet3, click the hyperlink for your book, click the Tutorial 2 link, and then click the Case Problems link.

2. Use the Case Problem 5 hyperlinks to Web directories to learn what kind of organization they use for their hyperlinks.

3. You note that many of the Web directories use a similar organization structure for their hyperlinks and categories; however, you are not sure if that organization structure would be ideal for Emma. You decide to create categories that suit Emma's specific interests. List five general categories around which you would organize Emma's start page. For each of those five general categories, list three subcategories that would help Emma find and return to Web sites she would find interesting.

4. Write a report of 100 words in which you explain why the start page you designed for Emma would be more useful to her than a publicly available Web directory.

5. Close your Web browser, and log off the Internet, if necessary.

LAB ASSIGNMENTS

The Internet: World Wide Web

One of the most popular services on the Internet is the World Wide Web. This Lab is a Web simulator that teaches you how to use Web browser software to find information. You can use this Lab whether or not your school provides you with Internet access.

1. Click the Steps button to learn how to use Web browser software. As you proceed through the Steps, answer all of the Quick Check questions that appear. After you complete the Steps, you will see a Quick Check Summary Report. Follow the instructions on the screen to print this report.

2. Click the Explore button on the Welcome screen. Use the Web browser to locate a weather map of the Caribbean Virgin Islands. What is its URL?

3. A SCUBA diver named Wadson Lachouffe has been searching for the fabled treasure of Greybeard the pirate. A link from the Adventure Travel Web site, www.atour.com, leads to Wadson's Web page called "Hidden Treasure." In Explore, locate the Hidden Treasure page and answer the following questions:

   a. What was the name of Greybeard's ship?
   b. What was Greybeard's favorite food?
   c. What does Wadson think happened to Greybeard's ship?

4. In the steps, you found a graphic of Jupiter from the photo archives of the Jet Propulsion Laboratory. In the Explore section of the Lab, you can also find a graphic of Saturn. Suppose one of your friends wanted a picture of Saturn for an astronomy report. Make a list of the blue, underlined links your friend must click in the correct order to find the Saturn graphic. Assume that your friend will begin at the Web Trainer home page.

5. Enter the URL http://www.atour.com to jump to the Adventure Travel Web site. Write a one-page description of this site. In your paper include a description of the information at the site, the number of pages the site contains, and a diagram of the links it contains.

6. Chris Thomson is a student at UVI and has his own Web pages. In Explore, look at the information Chris has included on his pages. Suppose you could create your own Web page. What would you include? Use word-processing software to design your own Web pages. Make sure you indicate the graphics and links you would use.

QUICK | CHECK ANSWERS

Session 2.1

1. False

2. True

3. home page; start page

4. hypermedia or media

5. Any three of these: Candidate's name and party affiliation; list of qualifications; biography; position statements on campaign issues; list of endorsements with hyperlinks to the Web pages of individuals and organizations that support her candidacy; audio or video clips of speeches and interviews; address and telephone number of the campaign office

6. A computer's IP address is a unique identifying number; its domain name is a unique name associated with the IP address on the Internet host computer responsible for that computer's domain.

7. "http://" indicates use of the hypertext transfer protocol; "www.savethetrees.org" is the domain name and suggests a charitable or not-for-profit organization that is probably devoted to forest ecology; "main.html" is the name of the HTML file on the Web server

8. A Web directory contains a hierarchical list of Web page categories; each category contains hyperlinks to individual Web pages. A Web search engine is a Web site that accepts words or expressions you enter and finds Web pages that include those words or expressions.

Session 2.2

1. You can hide its toolbars or click the Full Screen command on the View menu.
2. History
3. Search
4. East Coast Ensembles, West Coast Ensembles
5. Shift
6. True
7. press F1, click Help on the menu bar

Session 2.3

1. Any three of these: Type the URL in the location field; click a hyperlink on a Web page; click the Back button; click the Forward button; click the Bookmarks button and select a page; click Task on the menu bar, point to Tools, click History, and then click the entry for the site you want to visit
2. history list (or the Back or Forward button)
3. When you want the browser to check to see if the Web page has changed since you last visited it
4. Navigator loads the page that is specified in the Home page section of the Preferences dialog box (which you can open from the Edit menu).
5. encrypt
6. True
7. Navigator feature that enables you to store and organize a list of Web pages that you have visited

In this tutorial you will:

- Learn about e-mail and how it works

- Configure and use two popular e-mail programs and a popular Web-based e-mail service

- Send and receive e-mail messages

- Print an e-mail message

- Forward and reply to e-mail messages

- Create folders for saving e-mail messages

- File and delete e-mail messages and folders

- Create and maintain an electronic address book

E-MAIL BASICS

Evaluating Integrated Browser E-Mail Programs and a Web-Based E-Mail Service

Kikukawa Air

Since 1994, Sharon and Don Kikukawa have operated an air charter service in Maui, Hawaii. At first, Kikukawa Air employed only Sharon, who managed the office, reservations, and the company's financial details; and her husband Don, who flew their twin-engine, six-passenger plane between Maui and Oahu. After many successful years in business, Sharon and Don expanded their business to include scenic tours and charter service to all of the Hawaiian Islands. As a result of their expansion, Kikukawa Air now boasts six twin-engine planes, two turbo prop planes, and a growing staff of over 30 people.

Because Kikukawa Air has a ticket counter at airports on all of the Hawaiian Islands, many miles now separate the company's employees. Originally employees used the telephone and conference calling to coordinate the business's day-to-day operations, such as schedule and reservation changes, new airport procedures, and maintenance requests. Sharon soon realized that the long-distance rates and the fees associated with conference calling services made these forms of communication too expensive to continue using. In addition to these expenses, Sharon was overwhelmed by the effort required to manage the busy schedules of many ground-service agents and pilots and to find convenient times to meet. Sharon believes that Kikukawa Air could benefit from an alternate form of communication. Sharon has hired you to investigate the use of e-mail for the different Kikukawa Air offices and ticket counter facilities. Your job includes evaluating available e-mail systems and overseeing the software's installation. Eventually you will train the staff so they can use the new e-mail system efficiently and effectively.

In this session, you will learn what e-mail is, how it travels to its destination, and what are the parts of a typical e-mail message. You will learn about signature files and how to use them. You will learn how to use an e-mail program to send, receive, print, delete, file, forward, reply to, and respond to e-mail messages. Finally, you will learn how to use an electronic address book to store and manage e-mail addresses.

What Is E-Mail and How Does It Work?

Electronic mail, or **e-mail**, is one of the most popular forms of business communication, and for many people it is their primary use of the Internet. In fact, many people view the Internet as an electronic highway that transports e-mail messages, without realizing that the Internet provides a wide variety of services. E-mail travels across the Internet to its destination and is deposited in the recipient's electronic mailbox. Although similar to other forms of correspondence, including letters and memos, e-mail has the added advantage of being fast and inexpensive. Instead of traveling through a complicated, expensive, and often slow mail delivery service such as a postal system, e-mail travels quickly, efficiently, and inexpensively to its destination down the hall or around the world. You can send a message any time you want, without worrying about when the mail is collected and delivered or adding any postage. For many personal and business reasons, people rely on e-mail as an indispensable form of communication.

E-mail travels across the Internet like other forms of information—that is, in small packets that are reassembled at the destination and delivered to the recipient, whose address you specify in the message. When you send an e-mail message, the message is sent to a **mail server**, which is a hardware and software system that determines from the recipient's address one of several electronic routes on which to send the message. The message is routed from one computer to another and is passed through several mail servers. Each mail server determines the next leg of the message's journey until it finally arrives at the recipient's electronic mailbox.

Sending e-mail uses one of many Internet technologies. Special **protocols**, or rules that determine how the Internet handles message packets flowing on it, are used to interpret and transmit e-mail. **SMTP (Simple Mail Transfer Protocol)** decides which paths your e-mail message takes on the Internet. SMTP handles outgoing messages; another protocol called **POP (Post Office Protocol)** handles incoming messages. POP is a standard, extensively used protocol that is part of the Internet suite of recognized protocols. Other protocols used to deliver mail include **IMAP (Internet Message Access Protocol)** and **MIME (Multipurpose Internet Mail Extensions)**. IMAP is a protocol for retrieving mail messages from a server, and the MIME protocol specifies how to encode nontext data, such as graphics and sound, so they can travel over the Internet.

When an e-mail message arrives at its destination mail server, the mail server's software handles the details of distributing the message locally, in the same way that a mailroom worker unbundles a mailbag and places letters and packages into individual mail slots. When the server receives a new message, it is not saved directly on the recipient's computer, but rather, the message is held on the mail server. When you check for new e-mail messages, you use a program stored on your personal computer (PC) to request the mail server to deliver any stored mail to your PC. The software that requests mail delivery from the mail server to your PC is known as **mail client software**, or an **e-mail program**. You will learn about two popular e-mail programs—Microsoft Outlook Express and Netscape Mail—in Sessions 3.2 and 3.3, respectively.

Common Features of an E-Mail Message

An e-mail message consists of two major parts: the message header and the message body. The **message header** contains all the information about the message, and the **message body** contains the actual message. A message header contains the recipient's e-mail address (To), the sender's e-mail address (From), and a subject line (Subject) indicating the message's topic. In addition, the message header can contain a carbon copy (or courtesy copy) address (Cc), a blind carbon copy (or blind courtesy copy) address (Bcc), and optional attachment filename(s). Your name automatically appears on the From line when you send a message. When you receive an e-mail message, the date and time it was sent and other information is added to the message header automatically.

Figure 3-1 shows a message that Sharon Kikukawa wrote to Bob Merrell, the company's ground service agent at the Honolulu, Oahu airport. The message contains an attached file named MaintenanceSchedule.xls. Sharon created this file using a spreadsheet program, saved it, and then attached it to the message. Notice that Bob's e-mail address appears on the To line. When Bob receives Sharon's message, Sharon's name and e-mail address will appear on the From line. Following good e-mail etiquette, Sharon included a short subject so Bob can quickly determine the content of the message. The Cc line includes an abbreviated address for the maintenance department; each member of this department will receive a copy of the message. Don Kikukawa will also receive a copy of the message, but Sharon entered Don's e-mail address on the Bcc line, so neither Bob nor the maintenance department will know that Don also received a copy of the message. Each of the message parts is described in the next sections.

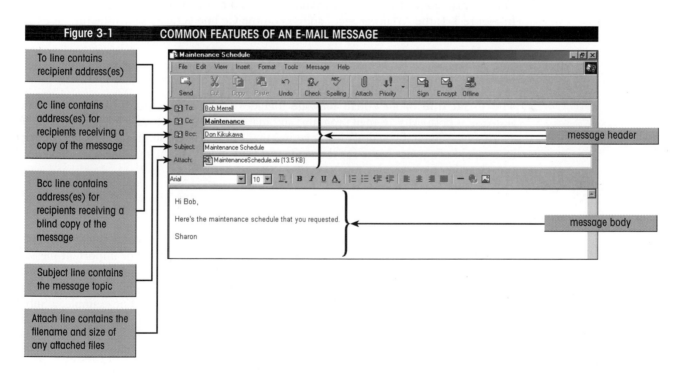

Figure 3-1   **COMMON FEATURES OF AN E-MAIL MESSAGE**

To line contains recipient address(es)

Cc line contains address(es) for recipients receiving a copy of the message

Bcc line contains address(es) for recipients receiving a blind copy of the message

Subject line contains the message topic

Attach line contains the filename and size of any attached files

message header

message body

To

You type the recipient's full e-mail address in the **To line** of an e-mail header. Make sure that you type the e-mail addresses correctly because mistakes can lead to undeliverable messages or messages sent to the wrong recipients. You can send the same message to multiple recipients by typing a comma or semicolon between the recipients' e-mail addresses in the To line. There is no real limit on the number of addresses you can type in the To line or in the other parts of the message header that require an address. Figure 3-2 shows the message header for a message that Sharon is sending to three people.

Figure 3-2	E-MAIL MESSAGE ADDRESSED TO MULTIPLE RECIPIENTS

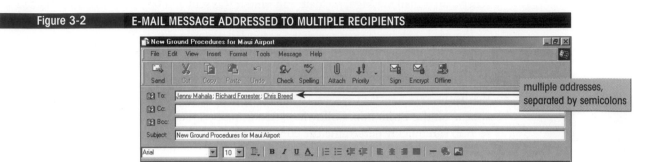

Sometimes the To address contains one physical mailing address that is not one person's address, but rather, a message to a special address called a mailing list. In a mailing list, a single e-mail address can contain several or even thousands of individual e-mail addresses. In Figure 3-1, the "Maintenance" address on the Cc line actually sends the message to the three e-mail addresses contained within it, and not to a "Maintenance" address.

From

The **From line** of an e-mail message includes the sender's name, the sender's e-mail address, or both. Most e-mail programs automatically insert the sender's e-mail address into all messages. Even if you don't insert your e-mail address in an outgoing message, the recipient should *always* be able to see the sender's e-mail address in the message—in other words, you should not send anonymous e-mail.

Subject

The content of the **Subject line** is very important. Often the recipient will scan an abbreviated display of incoming messages, looking for the most interesting or important messages based on the content of the Subject line. If the Subject line is blank, then the recipient might not read the associated message immediately. It is always best to include a message subject so the reader can determine the message's content and importance. For example, a Subject line such as "Just checking" is far less informative and certainly less interesting than "Urgent: new staff meeting time." The e-mail message shown in Figure 3-1, for example, contains the subject "Maintenance Schedule" and thus indicates that the message concerns maintenance.

Cc and Bcc

You can use the optional **carbon copy (Cc)** and the **blind carbon copy (Bcc)** header lines to send mail to people who should be aware of the e-mail message, but who are not the message's main addressees. When an e-mail message is delivered, every recipient can see the addresses of other recipients, except for those recipients who receive a blind carbon copy. Neither the primary recipient (in the To line) nor Cc recipients can view the list of Bcc recipients because Bcc addresses are excluded from messages sent to addresses on the To and Cc lines. Bcc recipients are unaware of other Bcc recipients. For example, if you send a thank-you message to a salesperson for performing a task especially well, you might consider sending a blind carbon copy to that person's supervisor. That way, the supervisor knows a customer is happy and that the praise was unsolicited.

Attachments

Because of the way the messaging system is set up, you can send only text messages using SMTP—the protocol that handles outgoing e-mail. When you need to send a more complex document, such as a Word document or an Excel worksheet, you send it along as an attachment. An **attachment** is encoded so that it can be carried safely over the Internet, to "tag along" with the message. Frequently, the attached file is the most important part of the e-mail message, and the message body contains only a brief statement, such as "Here's the maintenance schedule that you requested." Sharon's e-mail message (see Figure 3-1) contains an attached file, whose filename and size in kilobytes (a **kilobyte** is approximately 1,000 characters and abbreviated as KB) appear in the Attach line in the message header. You can attach more than one file to an e-mail message; if you include multiple recipients in the To, Cc, and Bcc lines of the message header, each recipient will receive the message and the attached files. E-mail attachments provide a simple and convenient way of transmitting electronic documents to one or more people.

When you receive an e-mail message with an attached file, you can view and save the file. E-mail programs differ in how they handle and display attachments. Several e-mail programs identify an attached file with an icon that represents the program associated with the attachment's file type. In addition to an icon, several programs also display an attached file's size in kilobytes and indicate the attached file's name. Other e-mail programs display an attached file in a preview window when they recognize the attached file's format and can start a program to open the file.

Some people refer to the process of saving an e-mail attachment as **detaching** the file. An icon representing an attached file usually accompanies the file. If a worksheet is attached to an e-mail message, for example, a spreadsheet program on your computer starts and opens the worksheet. Similarly, a Word document opens in the Word program window when you double-click the icon representing the Word document inside your e-mail message. When you detach a file, you indicate the disk and folder in which to save it. You won't always need to save an e-mail attachment; sometimes you can view it and then delete it.

Message Body and Signature Files

Most often, people use e-mail to write short, quick messages. However, e-mail messages can be dozens or hundreds of pages long, although the term "pages" has little meaning in the e-mail world. Few people using e-mail think of a message in terms of page-sized chunks; e-mail is more like an unbroken scroll with no physical page boundaries.

Frequently, an e-mail message includes an optional signature that identifies the sender. You can sign a message by typing your name and other information at the end of each message you send, or you can create a signature file. A **signature**, or **signature file**, contains the standard information you routinely type at the end of your e-mail messages. You can set your e-mail program to insert a signature file into every message automatically so you don't have to type it. A signature usually contains the sender's name, title, and company name. Signature files often contain a complete nonelectronic address, facsimile telephone number, a voice phone number, and a Web site address. Some signature files might also include graphics, such as a company logo. Including a signature file in an e-mail message ensures that e-mail recipients can contact you in a variety of ways.

Signatures can be formal, informal, or a combination of both. A **formal signature** usually includes the sender's name, title, company name, company address, telephone and fax numbers, and e-mail address. **Informal signatures** can include nicknames and graphics or quotations that express a more casual style found in correspondence between friends and acquaintances. Most e-mail programs have an option that lets you automatically include a signature at the end of each e-mail message you send. You can easily modify your signature or choose not to include it in selected messages. Most e-mail programs allow you to create multiple signature files so you can choose which one to include when sending a message.

When you create a signature, don't overdo it. A signature that is extremely long is in bad taste—especially if it is much longer than the message. It is best to keep a signature to a few lines that identify ways to contact you. Figure 3-3 shows two examples of signatures. The first signature is informal and typical of one Sharon might send with her internal business correspondence. The second signature is formal and one that Sharon uses for all external business correspondence to identify herself, her title, and her contact information.

Figure 3-3	SAMPLE SIGNATURES

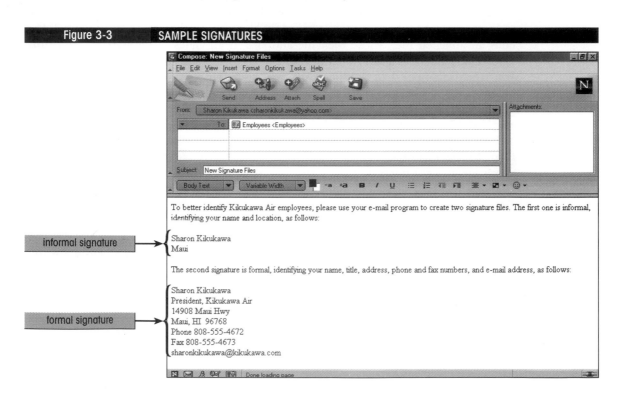

E-Mail Addresses

E-mail addresses, also called Internet addresses, uniquely identify an individual or organization that is connected to the Internet. They are like telephone numbers—when you want to call a friend or business, you dial a series of numbers that route your call through a series of switchboards until your call reaches its destination. For example, calling a friend in San Diego from another country requires you to dial the country code for the United States (the country code varies according to the country from which you are calling). Next, you must dial the three-digit area code for the part of San Diego in which your friend lives. Finally, you must dial your friend's seven-digit local number. Like telephone numbers, e-mail addresses consist of a series of numbers. An address can consist of three or four groups of numbers that are separated by periods. For instance, the number 127.0.0.1 is an **Internet Protocol address**, or more commonly an **IP address**, which corresponds to a single computer connected to the Internet. The IP address uniquely identifies the computer at the organization you want to contact. To route an e-mail message to an *individual* whose mail is stored on a particular computer, you must identify that person by his or her account name, or **user name**, and also by the computer on which mail is stored. The two parts of an e-mail address—the user name and the computer name—are separated by an "at" sign (@). Sharon Kikukawa, for example, uses the user name *sharonkikukawa* for her e-mail. If her account were stored on a computer whose address is 127.0.0.1, then one form of her e-mail address would be sharonkikukawa@127.0.0.1.

Fortunately, you will rarely have to use IP addresses when addressing e-mail messages. Instead, you can purchase and use a **host name**, which is a unique name that is equivalent to an IP address from an Internet Web site that registers and sells them. Sharon Kikukawa's address using a host name is simply sharonkikukawa@kikukawa.com, which is much easier to remember and type. A full e-mail address consists of a user name, followed by @ and the host name (or address). A user name usually specifies a person within an organization, although a user name can also refer to an entire group. In some instances you can select your own user name, but usually an organization through which you obtain an e-mail account has rules about acceptable user names. Some organizations set standards so user names consist of a person's first initial followed by up to seven characters of the person's last name. Other institutions prefer that user names contain a person's first and last names separated by an underscore character (for example, Sharon_Kikukawa). Occasionally, you can pick a nickname such as "ziggy" as your user name. Most e-mail addresses aren't case-sensitive; in other words, the addresses sharonkikukawa@kikukawa.com and SharonKikukawa@Kikukawa.com are the same. It is important for you to enter a recipient's address carefully; if you omit or mistype even one character, your message could be undeliverable or sent to the wrong recipient. When mail cannot be delivered, the electronic postmaster sends the mail back to you and indicates the addressee is unknown—just like conventional mail.

The host name is the second part of an e-mail address. The host name specifies the computer to which the mail is to be delivered on the Internet. Host names contain periods, which are usually pronounced "dot," to divide the host name. The most specific part of the host name appears first in the host address followed by more general destination names. Sharon's host name, kikukawa.com (and pronounced "kikukawa dot com"), contains only two names separated by a period. The *com* in the address indicates that this company falls into the large, general class of commercial locations.

E-Mail Programs

Because no single program works on all computers, there are many choices for receiving, sending, and managing e-mail messages. The good news is that you can use any e-mail program to send mail to people using the same or different e-mail programs. Regardless of which e-mail program you use to send e-mail, recipients can read your messages. If you have an Internet service provider (ISP) with a PPP or SLIP connection, then you can select one of many e-mail programs to use to manage your mail. On the other hand, you might have to use the e-mail program provided by your college or university if you have a dial-up connection that does not provide access to the Internet. Some e-mail programs—called **shareware**—are free or very inexpensive, and others are not. Some e-mail programs are software clients that run on your personal computer (PC) and receive mail from the mail server. Other e-mail programs run strictly on a server that you access from your PC, which acts as a dumb terminal. A **dumb terminal** is an otherwise "smart" computer that passes all your keystrokes to another computer to which you are connected and does not attempt to do anything else during the e-mail session. Examples of popular e-mail programs operating in the Windows environment are Microsoft Outlook Express, Netscape Mail, and Eudora. A widely used e-mail program running on larger, multiuser computers is Pine. Especially popular on university campuses, Pine is a simple system that accepts and displays only plain-text messages. In your future personal and professional life, chances are good that you will encounter a different e-mail program from the one you are currently using, so learning about different e-mail programs is a good idea.

Web-Based E-Mail Services

Many Internet Web sites provide free e-mail addresses and accounts for registered users along with the capability to use any Web browser with Internet access to send and receive e-mail messages. Many people rely on Web-based e-mail as their primary e-mail address; others use Web-based e-mail accounts to set up a separate, personal address when their employer or other owner of their primary e-mail address restricts use of personal e-mail. Some popular choices for free Web-based e-mail services are Yahoo! Mail, ExciteMail, and Hotmail. Figure 3-4 shows how a user views an e-mail message using Yahoo! Mail.

Figure 3-4   **WEB-BASED E-MAIL MESSAGE**

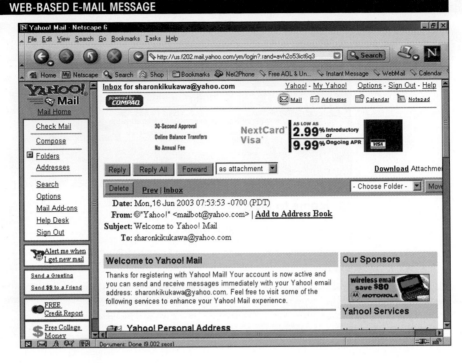

To get your free e-mail address, use your Web browser to visit the sponsor's Web site. After locating the link to the site's e-mail service, you'll need to provide some basic information about yourself, such as your name, address, and phone number. Then you choose a user name and password. If e-mail service verifies that your user name is not in use, you are immediately enrolled in the e-mail service. However, if the user name you selected is in use, the service will ask you to submit a new user name or to change the one you chose slightly by adding digits to the end of it. Web-based e-mail provides a means for people who do not have their own ISP accounts to use e-mail. You can use your Web-based e-mail service from anywhere in the world where there's an Internet connection. None of the messages that you send and receive are stored on the computer that you use; everything happens on the Web-based mail servers. The e-mail messages you send and receive are protected by your password and function just like e-mail messages sent from an e-mail program running on a PC.

You might wonder how these companies can provide free e-mail—after all, nothing is free. The answer is advertising. When you use a Web-based mail service, you will see advertising, such as the **banner** at the top of the page shown in Figure 3-5. You'll also see links to other services offered by the Web-based mail service—in Figure 3-5, you can link to sites that sell airline tickets or let you shop online.

Figure 3-5   ADS SHOWN IN HOTMAIL

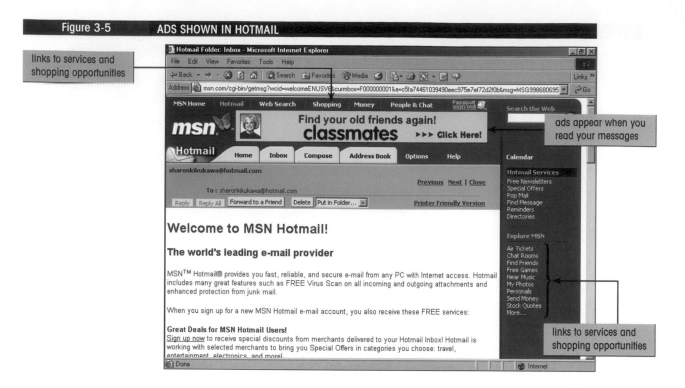

In addition to showing its account holders advertising messages and providing links to additional services, e-mail messages sent from Web-based mail accounts might also contain some sort of advertisement, such as a promotional message or a link to the Web-based mail service. Advertising revenues pay for free e-mail, so you must decide whether you are willing to endure a little advertising in exchange for use of the free e-mail service. Most users of these free services agree that seeing some ads is a small price to pay for the great convenience e-mail provides.

The only real drawback of Web-based e-mail services, other than the advertising messages that pay for it, is that your mailbox size might be limited to a specified amount of file space in which to store your messages. Yahoo! Mail limits the free mailbox to six megabytes; Hotmail limits it to three megabytes. Some Web-based e-mail services offer an option to purchase additional space for a fee. As long as you delete old messages and messages with large file attachments, you shouldn't encounter any space problems in your free mailbox. Most e-mail messages are small in file size.

Setting Up and Using An E-Mail Program

Many ISPs support POP or SMTP, whereby the mail server receives mail and stores it until you use your e-mail program to request delivery of your mail from the mail server to your computer. Similarly, when you send e-mail from your computer, that mail is forwarded across the Internet until the message reaches its destination. Once e-mail reaches the mail server at the recipient's location, the message is stored. Subsequently, e-mail is downloaded from the server to a user on request. In either case—sending or receiving—an e-mail program must notify the mail server to deliver the outgoing mail or accept incoming mail.

Your message might not be sent to the mail server immediately, depending on how the e-mail program is configured on your computer. A message can be **queued**, or temporarily held with other messages, and then sent when you either exit the program or check to see if you received any new e-mail.

Remember, e-mail correspondence can be formal or informal, but you should still follow the rules of good writing and grammar. After typing the content of your message—even a short message—you should check your spelling and grammar. Most mail systems do not allow you to retract mail after you send it, so you should examine your messages carefully before sending them. Always exercise politeness and courtesy in your messages. Don't write anything in an e-mail message that you wouldn't want someone else to post on a public bulletin board.

Receiving Mail

The mail server is always ready to process mail; in theory, the mail server never sleeps. That means that when you receive e-mail, it is held on the mail server until you start an e-mail program on your PC and ask the server to retrieve your mail. Most clients allow you to save delivered mail in any of several standard or custom mailboxes or folders on your PC. However, the mail server is a completely different story. Once the mail is delivered to your PC, one of two things can happen to it on the server: either the server's copy of your mail is deleted, or it is preserved and marked as delivered or read. Marking mail as delivered or read is the server's way of identifying new mail from mail that you have read. For example, when Sharon receives mail on the Kikukawa mail server, she might decide to save her accumulated mail—even after she reads it—so she has an archive of e-mail messages she has received. On the other hand, Sharon might want to delete old mail to save space on the mail server. Both methods have advantages. Saving old mail on the server lets you access your mail from any PC that can connect to your mail server. On the other hand, if you automatically delete mail after reading it, you don't have to worry about storing and organizing messages that you don't need, which requires less effort. In a Web-based mail service, the service might impose limits on the amount of material you can store, so that you must occasionally delete mail from your account to avoid interruption of service. In fact, with most Web-based e-mail services, once you exceed your storage space limit, you cannot receive any messages until you delete existing messages from the server.

Printing a Message

Reading mail on the computer is fine, but there are times when you'll need to print some or all of your messages. Other times, you need to file a message in an appropriate folder and deal with it later or simply file it for safekeeping. You also might find that you don't need to keep or file certain messages, so you can read and immediately delete them. Most e-mail programs provide these capabilities to help you manage your electronic correspondence.

The majority of e-mail programs let you print a message you are composing or that you have received at any time. The Print command usually appears on the File menu, or as a Print button on the toolbar. In a character-based program, the Print command is usually a key combination, such as Ctrl + P.

Filing a Message

Most clients let you create separate mailboxes or folders in which to store related messages. You can create new mailboxes or folders when needed, rename existing mailboxes and folders, or delete mailboxes and folders and their contents when you no longer need them. You can move mail from the incoming mailbox or folder to any other mailbox or folder to file it. Some programs let you use a **filter** to move incoming mail into one or several mailboxes or folders automatically based on the content of the message. Filters are especially useful for moving messages from certain senders into designated folders, and for moving junk mail to a trash folder. If your e-mail program does not provide filters, you can filter the messages manually by reading them and filing them in the appropriate folders.

Forwarding a Message

You can forward any message that you receive to one or more recipients. When you **forward** a message to another recipient, a copy of the original message is sent to the new recipient you specify, without the original sender's knowledge. You might forward a misdirected message to another recipient or to someone who was not included in the original message routing list.

For example, suppose you receive a message intended for someone else, or the message requests information that you do not have but you know a colleague who can provide it. In either case, you can forward the message you received to the person who can best deal with the request. When you forward a message, your e-mail address and name appear automatically on the From line; most e-mail programs amend the Subject line with the text "Fwd," "Forward," or something similar to indicate that the message has been forwarded. You simply fill in the To line and then send the message. Sometimes a forwarded message is sent as an attached file; sometimes it is sent as quoted text. A **quoted** message is a copy of the sender's original message with your inserted comments. A special mark (usually the greater than symbol, >) or a solid, colored vertical line, sometimes precedes each line of the quoted message. Figure 3-6 shows a quoted message; notice the > symbol to the left of each line of the original message and the "Fwd:" text in the Subject line, indicating a forwarded message.

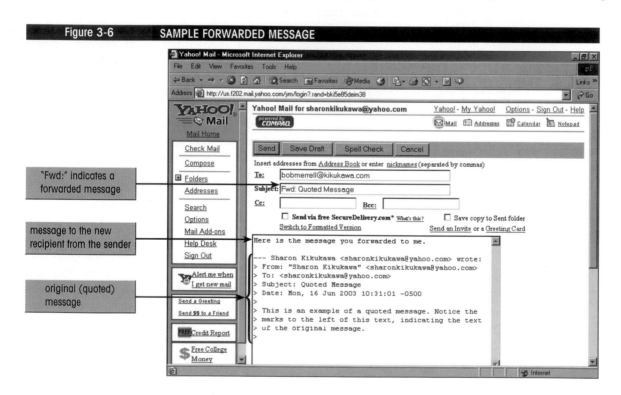

Figure 3-6   SAMPLE FORWARDED MESSAGE

Replying to a Message

When you **reply** to a message, the e-mail program creates a new message and automatically addresses it to the sender. Replying to a message is a quick way of sending a response to someone who sent a message to you. Most e-mail programs will copy the contents of the original message and place it in the message body. Usually, a special mark appears at the beginning of each line to indicate the text of the original message. When you are responding to more than one question, you might type your responses below the original questions. That way, the recipient can better understand the context of your responses. When you respond to a message that has been sent to several people—perhaps some people received the message as a carbon copy—be careful about responding. You can choose to respond to all the original recipients or only to the sender.

Deleting a Message

In most e-mail programs, deleting a message is a two-step process to prevent accidentally deleting important messages. First, you temporarily delete a message by placing it in a "trash" folder or by marking it for deletion. Then you permanently delete the trash or marked messages by emptying the trash or by indicating to the client to delete the messages. It is a good idea to delete mail you no longer need because it takes a lot of space on the drive or server on which your e-mail messages are stored.

Maintaining an Address Book

E-mail addresses are sometimes difficult to remember and type, especially when you send many e-mail messages to the same recipients. You use an **address book** to save e-mail addresses and to associate those addresses with nicknames that are easy to remember.

The features of an e-mail address book vary by e-mail program. Usually, you can organize information about individuals and groups. Each entry in the address book can contain an individual's full e-mail address (or a group e-mail address that represents several individual addresses), full name, and complete contact information. In addition, some e-mail programs allow you to include notes for each contact. You can assign a unique nickname to each entry so it is easier to remember and use e-mail addresses.

After saving entries in your address book, you can refer to them at any point while you are composing, replying to, or forwarding a message. You can review your address book and sort the entries in alphabetical order by nickname, or you can view them in last name order.

Creating a Group Mailing List

What happens if you frequently need to send the same messages to different recipients? You could send the message to all recipients by typing their nicknames in the To line and separating them with a comma. But what if you need to send a message to an entire department or the entire sales staff? You can create a handy address entry called a distribution list. A **distribution list**, or a **group mailing list**, is a single nickname that represents two or more individual e-mail address. For example, you might use the nickname "Web Site" to save the e-mail addresses of your partners on a Web site project. When you need to send a message to your partners, you just type "Web Site" in the To line, and then the client will send the same message to each individual's e-mail address.

Session 3.1 QUICK CHECK

1. True or False: E-mail travels across the Internet in small packets that are reassembled at the destination and delivered to the recipient.

2. The special rules governing how information is handled on the Internet are collectively called _____.

3. An e-mail message consists of two parts: the message _____ and the message _____.

4. When sending the same message to more than one recipient, how do you separate the recipients' addresses on the To line?

5. True or False: Bcc recipients of an e-mail message are aware of other Bcc recipients of the same e-mail message.

6. Can you send a Word document over the Internet? If so, how?

7. What are the two parts of an e-mail address and what information do they provide?

8. Why is it important to delete mail messages that you no longer need?

9. What is a group mailing list?

Now that you understand some basic information about e-mail and e-mail program software, you are ready to start using your e-mail program. If you are using Microsoft Outlook Express, your instructor will assign Session 3.2; if you are using Netscape Mail, your instructor will assign Session 3.3. If you are using Hotmail, your instructor will assign Session 3.4. The authors recommend, however, that you read all sessions to familiarize yourself with the different e-mail programs. In the future, you might encounter a different e-mail program on a public or employer's computer, so it is important to be familiar with many e-mail programs. Fortunately, most e-mail programs work the same, so it is easy to use other programs once you master the basics.

SESSION 3.2	In this session, you will learn how to use Microsoft Outlook Express to send and receive e-mail. You will use this e-mail program to print, file, save, delete, respond to, and forward e-mail messages. Finally, you will organize e-mail addresses in an address book.

Microsoft Outlook Express

Microsoft Outlook Express, or simply **Outlook Express**, is an e-mail program that you use to send and receive e-mail. Outlook Express is installed with Internet Explorer. Outlook Express starts when you click a hyperlink in a Web page to an e-mail address or when you start it using the Start menu.

You are eager to begin your evaluation of e-mail software for Sharon. You start Outlook Express by clicking its icon on the Quick Launch toolbar or by using the Start menu. Figure 3-7 shows the Outlook Express Inbox window.

Figure 3-7	OUTLOOK EXPRESS INBOX WINDOW

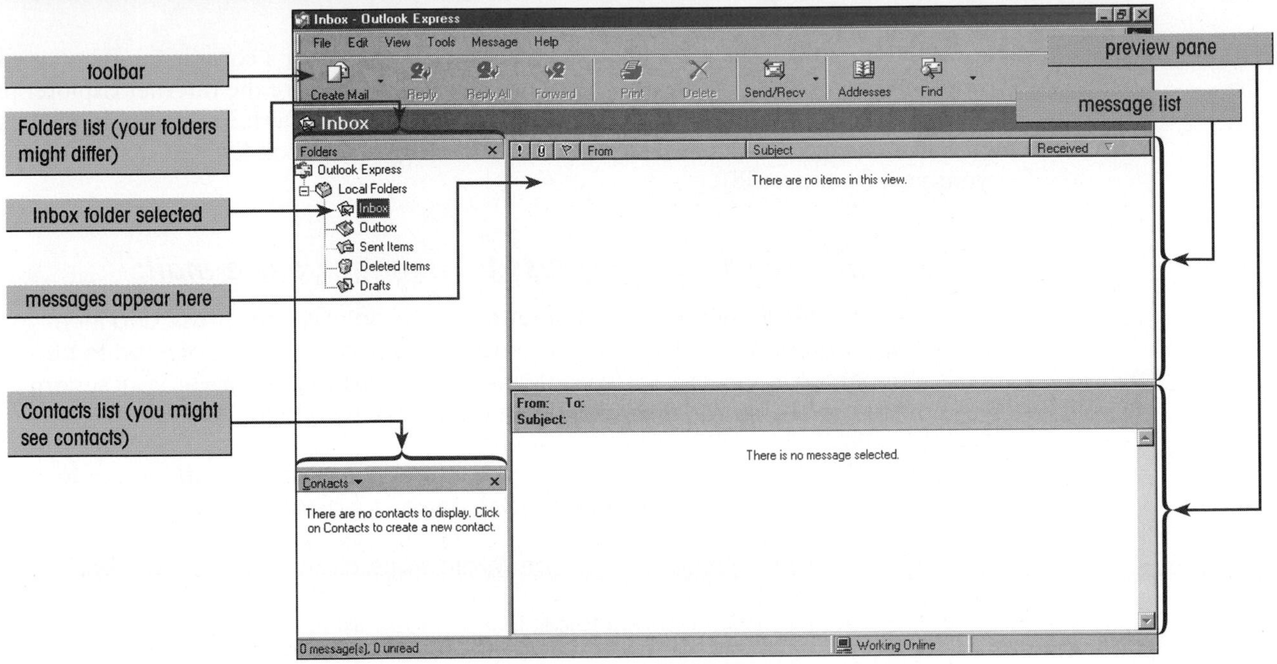

toolbar

Folders list (your folders might differ)

Inbox folder selected

messages appear here

Contacts list (you might see contacts)

preview pane

message list

The Inbox window contains four panes: the Folders list, the Contacts list, the message list, and the preview pane. The **Folders list** displays a list of folders for receiving, saving, and deleting mail messages. You might see different folders from those shown in Figure 3-7, but you should see five default folders. The **Inbox folder** stores messages you have received, the **Outbox folder** stores outgoing messages that have not been sent, the **Sent Items folder** stores copies of messages you have sent, and the **Deleted Items folder** stores messages you have deleted. The **Drafts folder** stores messages that you have written but have not sent. Your copy of Outlook Express may also contain folders you've created, such as a folder in which you store all messages from a certain recipient.

The **Contacts list**, which may be hidden, contains information about the information stored in your address book. You can click a contact in the Contacts list to quickly address a new message to an individual or group.

The **message list** contains summary information for each message that you have received. The first three columns on the left might display none or all of three e-mail message icons for each message. The first column indicates the message's priority; you might see an exclamation point to indicate a message with high priority, a blue down arrow icon to indicate a message with low priority, or nothing, which indicates normal priority. The sender indicates a message's priority before sending it; most messages have no specified priority. The second column displays a paperclip icon when a message contains an attachment. Finally, if you click the third column of a message you have received, a red flag will appear. Usually you use the flags to remind yourself to follow up on the message later.

The message list also displays the sender's name in the From column, the message's subject in the Subject column, and the date and time the message was received in the Received column. You can sort messages by clicking any column in the message list.

The message that is selected in the message list appears in the preview pane. The preview pane appears below the message list and displays the content of the selected message in the message list. You can use the horizontal scroll bar to scroll the message, if necessary. You can customize Outlook Express in many ways by resizing, hiding, and displaying different windows and their individual elements, so your screen might look different from Figure 3-7.

Setting Up E-Mail

You are eager to get started using Outlook Express. Cost is not a consideration because the Outlook Express program is free when you download it as part of the Internet Explorer program from Microsoft's Web site. These steps assume that Outlook Express 6 is already installed on your computer. First, you need to configure Outlook Express so it will retrieve your mail from your ISP.

To configure Outlook Express to manage your e-mail:

1. Click the **Start** button on the Windows taskbar, point to **Programs**, and then click **Outlook Express** to start the program. You normally do not need to be connected to the Internet to configure Outlook Express; however, your system might be configured differently. If necessary, connect to the Internet.

   TROUBLE? If you cannot find the Outlook Express program on your computer, ask your instructor or technical support person for assistance.

   TROUBLE? If the Internet Connection Wizard starts, click the Cancel button.

2. If necessary, click the **Inbox** folder in the Folders list to open it. (See Figure 3-7.)

3. Click **Tools** on the menu bar, click **Accounts**, and then if necessary, click the **Mail** tab so you can set up your mail account settings.

   TROUBLE? If you have already set up your mail account (or if someone has set up another for you), click the Close button in the Internet Accounts dialog box and skip the remaining steps. If you are unsure about any existing account, ask your instructor or technical support person for help.

4. Click the **Add** button in the Internet Accounts dialog box, and then click **Mail**. The Internet Connection Wizard starts. You use this wizard to identify yourself, your user name, and the settings for your mail server. See Figure 3-8.

| Figure 3-8 | INTERNET CONNECTION WIZARD DIALOG BOX |

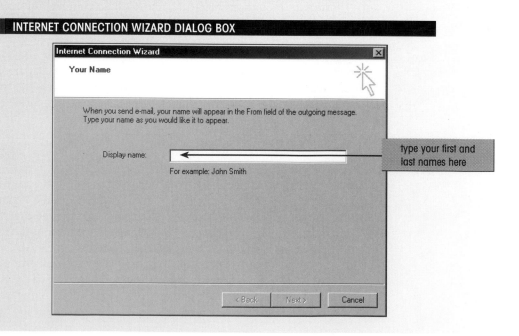

5. Type your first and last names in the Display name text box, and then click the **Next** button to open the next dialog box, where you enter your e-mail address.

6. Type your full e-mail address (such as student@university.edu) in the E-mail address text box, and then click the **Next** button. The next dialog box asks you for your incoming and outgoing mail server names.

7. Enter the name of your incoming and outgoing mail servers in the text boxes where indicated. Your instructor or technical support person will provide this information for you. Usually, your incoming mail server name is POP, POP3, or IMAP followed by a host name. Your outgoing mail server name is either SMTP or MAIL followed by a host name. When you are finished, click the **Next** button to continue.

8. In the Account name text box, type your Internet mail user name, as supplied by your instructor or technical support person. Make sure that you type only your user name and not your host name.

9. Press the **Tab** key, and then type your password in the Password text box. To protect your password's identity, Outlook Express displays asterisks instead of the characters you type. To prevent other users from being able to access your mail account, you will clear the Remember password check box. When you access your mail account, Outlook Express will prompt you for your password. If you are working on a computer on which you have sole access, you might want to set Outlook Express to remember your password, so you don't have to type it every time you access your e-mail.

10. Click the **Remember password** check box to clear it, and then click the **Next** button.

11. Click the **Finish** button to save the mail account information and close the Internet Connection Wizard. The Internet Accounts dialog box reappears, and your account is listed on the Mail tab. Figure 3-9 shows Sharon Kikukawa's information.

| Figure 3-9 | MAIL ACCOUNT CREATED FOR SHARON KIKUKAWA |

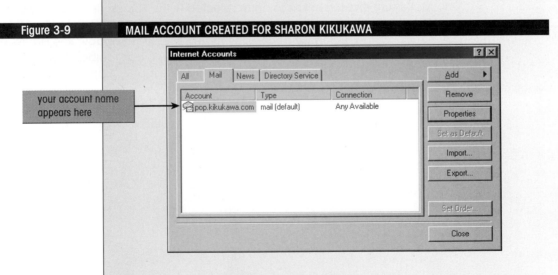

your account name appears here

12. Click the **Close** button in the Internet Accounts dialog box to close it.

Now Outlook Express is set up to send and receive messages, so you are ready to send a message to Sharon. *Note:* In this tutorial, you will send messages to a real mailbox with the address sharonkikukawa@yahoo.com. Follow the instructions carefully and use the correct address. Messages sent to this mailbox are deleted without being opened or read.

Sending a Message Using Outlook Express

You are ready to use Outlook Express to send a message with an attached file to Sharon. You will send a carbon copy of the message to your own e-mail address to make sure that the message and attached file are sent correctly.

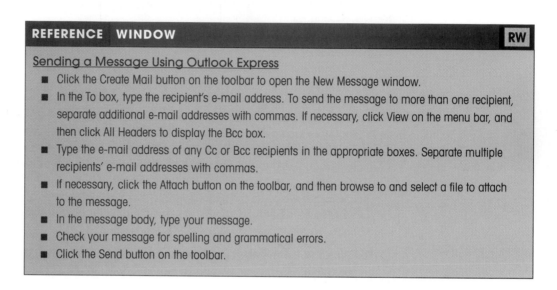

REFERENCE WINDOW | **RW**

Sending a Message Using Outlook Express

- Click the Create Mail button on the toolbar to open the New Message window.
- In the To box, type the recipient's e-mail address. To send the message to more than one recipient, separate additional e-mail addresses with commas. If necessary, click View on the menu bar, and then click All Headers to display the Bcc box.
- Type the e-mail address of any Cc or Bcc recipients in the appropriate boxes. Separate multiple recipients' e-mail addresses with commas.
- If necessary, click the Attach button on the toolbar, and then browse to and select a file to attach to the message.
- In the message body, type your message.
- Check your message for spelling and grammatical errors.
- Click the Send button on the toolbar.

To send a message with an attachment:

1. Make sure that the **Inbox** folder is selected in the Folders list, and then click the **Create Mail** button on the toolbar to open the New Message window. If necessary, click the **Maximize** button on the New Message window. See Figure 3-10. The New Message window contains its own menu bar, toolbar, message display area, and boxes in which you enter address and subject information. The insertion point is positioned in the To box when you open a new message.

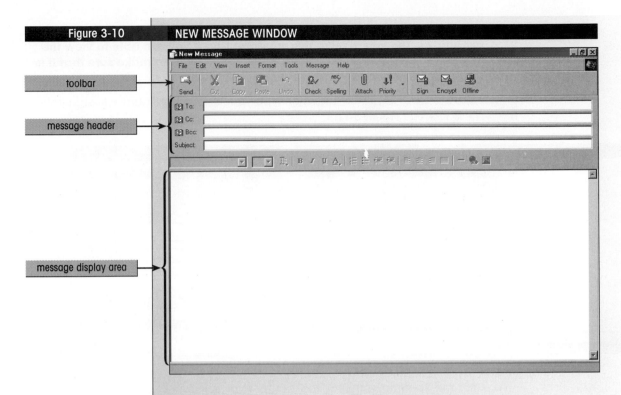

Figure 3-10   NEW MESSAGE WINDOW

toolbar

message header

message display area

TROUBLE? If you do not see the Bcc box, click View on the menu bar, and then click All Headers.

2. In the To box, type **sharonkikukawa@yahoo.com**, and then press the **Tab** key to move to the Cc box.

TROUBLE? Make sure that you use the address sharonkikukawa@yahoo.com, instead of sharonkikukawa@kikukawa.com. If you type Sharon's e-mail address incorrectly, your message will be returned as undeliverable.

3. Type your full e-mail address in the Cc box. When you send this message, you and Sharon will both receive copies.

TROUBLE? If you make a typing mistake on a previous line, use the arrow keys or click the insertion point to return to a previous line so you can correct your mistake. If the arrow keys do not move the insertion point backward or forward in the message header, press Shift + Tab or the Tab key to move backward or forward, respectively.

4. Press the **Tab** key twice to move the insertion point to the Subject box, and then type **Test**. Notice that the title bar now displays "Test" as the window title.

5. Click the **Attach** button on the toolbar. The Insert Attachment dialog box opens.

6. Make sure your Data Disk is in the appropriate drive, click the **Look in** list arrow, and then click the appropriate drive to display the contents of your Data Disk.

7. Double-click the **Tutorial.03** folder, and then double-click **Physicals**. The Insert Attachment dialog box closes, and the attached file's icon, filename, and file size appear in the Attach box.

8. Click the insertion point in the message display area, and then type **Please let me know when you receive this message and if you are able to view the attached file. I'm testing Outlook Express and want to make sure that it is working properly.**

9. Press the **Enter** key twice, and then type your first and last names to sign your message. See Figure 3-11.

| Figure 3-11 | SENDING AN E-MAIL MESSAGE |

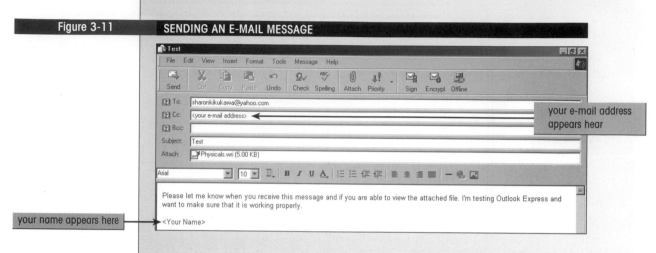

10. Click the **Spelling** button on the toolbar to check your spelling before sending the message. If necessary, correct any typing errors. When you are finished, click the **OK** button to close the Spelling dialog box.

11. Click the **Send** button on the toolbar to mail the message. The Test window closes and the message is stored in the Outbox folder, as indicated by the "(1)" notation next to the Outbox folder name.

    TROUBLE? If a Send Mail dialog box opens and tells you that the message will be sent the next time you click the Send/Recv button, click the OK button to continue.

Depending on your system configuration, Outlook Express might not send your messages immediately. It might queue (hold) messages until you connect to your ISP or click the Send/Recv button on the toolbar. If you want to examine the setting and change it, click Tools on the menu bar, click Options, and then click the Send tab. If the Send messages immediately check box contains a check mark, then Outlook Express sends messages when you click the Send button on the toolbar. Otherwise, Outlook Express holds messages until you click the Send/Recv button.

Receiving and Reading a Message

When you receive new mail, messages that you have not opened have a closed envelope icon to their left in the message list, and messages that you have opened have an open envelope icon next to them. You will check for new mail next.

REFERENCE WINDOW   RW

Using Outlook Express to Send and Receive Messages
- If necessary, connect to your ISP.
- Click the Send/Recv button on the toolbar.

To check for incoming mail:

1. Click the **Send/Recv** button on the toolbar, enter your password in the Password text box of the Logon dialog box, and then click the **OK** button. Depending on your system configuration, you might not have to connect to your ISP and enter your password to get your new mail. Within a few moments, your mail server transfers all new mail to your Inbox. The Test message is sent to Sharon and also to your e-mail address, which you entered in the Cc box. Notice that the Inbox folder in the Folders list is bold, but other folders are not. A bold folder indicates that it contains unread mail; the "(1)" next to the Inbox folder indicates that you have received one new message. Unread mail messages have closed envelope icons in the message list, whereas read messages have open envelope icons.

   TROUBLE? If an Outlook Express message box opens, indicating that it could not find your host, click the Hide button to close the message box, click Tools on the menu bar, click Accounts, and then click the Properties button. Verify that your incoming and outgoing server names are correct, and then repeat Step 1. If you still have problems, ask your instructor or technical support person for help.

   TROUBLE? If you do not see any messages in your Inbox, then either you did not receive any new mail, or you might be looking in the wrong folder. If necessary, click the Inbox folder in the Folders list. If you still don't have any mail messages, wait a few moments, and then repeat Step 1 until you receive a message.

2. If necessary, click the **Test** message in the message list to open the message in the preview pane. See Figure 3-12.

Figure 3-12 | **RECEIVING AN E-MAIL MESSAGE**

Send/Recv button

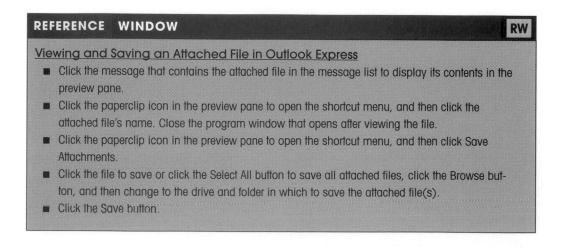

paperclip icon indicates that this message contains an attached file

after a few seconds, this icon changes from "unread" to "read" status

3. Double-click the **Test** message in the message list to open the Test window with the full message content. If necessary, click the **Maximize** button to maximize the Test window.

4. Click the **Close** button on the Test window title bar to close it. You return to the Inbox window.

You received your copy of the test message that you sent to Sharon. The paperclip icon indicates that you received an attachment with the message. When you receive a message with one or more attachments, you can open the attachment or save it.

Viewing and Saving an Attached File

You want to make sure that your attached file was sent properly, so you decide to open it. Then you will save the file on your Data Disk.

REFERENCE WINDOW   **RW**

Viewing and Saving an Attached File in Outlook Express

- Click the message that contains the attached file in the message list to display its contents in the preview pane.
- Click the paperclip icon in the preview pane to open the shortcut menu, and then click the attached file's name. Close the program window that opens after viewing the file.
- Click the paperclip icon in the preview pane to open the shortcut menu, and then click Save Attachments.
- Click the file to save or click the Select All button to save all attached files, click the Browse button, and then change to the drive and folder in which to save the attached file(s).
- Click the Save button.

To view and save the attached file:

1. If necessary, click the **Test** message in the message list. The message appears in the preview pane.

2. Click the **paperclip icon** on the preview pane to open the shortcut menu. See Figure 3-13.

Figure 3-13   VIEWING AN ATTACHED FILE

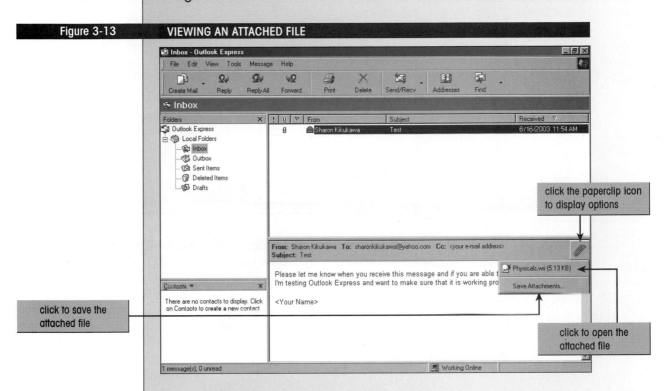

click the paperclip icon to display options

click to save the attached file

click to open the attached file

The shortcut menu shows that a file named Physicals.wri, with a file size of 5.13 KB, is attached to the message. If this message contained other attachments, they would appear on the shortcut menu as well. Clicking Physicals.wri starts a program on your computer that can open the file. Clicking Save Attachments lets you save the file to the drive and folder that you specify.

3. Click **Physicals.wri** on the shortcut menu. WordPad or another text editor program on your computer starts and opens the attached file. If necessary, maximize the program window that opens.

TROUBLE? If an Open Attachment Warning dialog box opens warning you that the file might contain viruses, click the Open it option button, and then click the OK button.

4. Click the **Close** button on the program window. Now that you have viewed the attachment, you can save it on your Data Disk.

5. Click the **paperclip icon** on the preview pane, and then click **Save Attachments** on the shortcut menu. The Save Attachments dialog box opens. The Physicals.wri file is already selected for you.

6. Click the **Browse** button. The Browse for Folder dialog box opens and lists all of the drives on your computer.

7. Scrolling as necessary, open the drive that contains your Data Disk, click the **Tutorial.03** folder to select it, and then click the **OK** button. The Save Attachments dialog box appears again. The Save To location indicates that you will save the attached file to the Tutorial.03 folder. See Figure 3-14.

| Figure 3-14 | SAVE ATTACHMENTS DIALOG BOX |

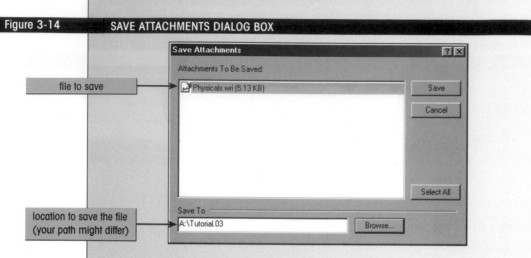

file to save

location to save the file
(your path might differ)

8. Click the **Save** button to save the attached file, and then click the **Yes** button to overwrite the file with the same name on your Data Disk.

When you receive a message with an attached file, you can view and save the attachment for as long as you store the message. When you delete the message, you will delete the file attached to the message. However, because you saved the attachment on your Data Disk, the file exists there for as long as you need it.

Replying to and Forwarding Messages

You can forward any message you receive to one or more e-mail addresses. Similarly, you can respond to the sender of a message quickly and efficiently by replying to a message. Replying to and forwarding messages are common tasks for e-mail users.

Replying to an E-Mail Message

To reply to a message, select the message in the message list, and then click the Reply button on the toolbar to reply only to the sender, or click the Reply All button to reply to the sender and other people who received the original message (those e-mail addresses listed in the To and Cc boxes). Outlook Express will open a new "Re:" message window and place the original sender's address in the To box; other e-mail addresses that received the original message will appear in the To and Cc boxes as appropriate. You can leave the Subject box as is or modify it. Most programs, including Outlook Express, will copy the original message and place it in the response window. Usually, a special mark to the left of the response indicates the text of the original message. Figure 3-15 shows a reply to the Test message.

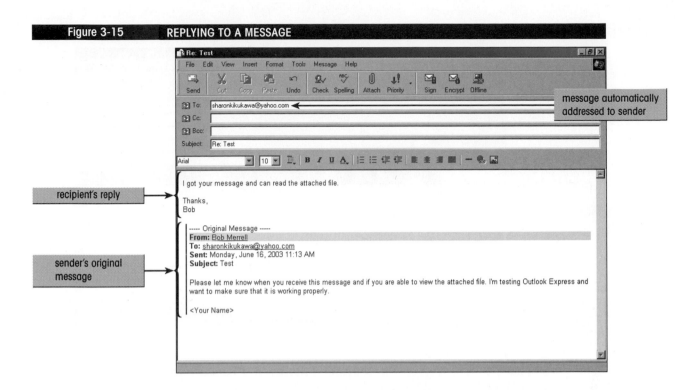

Figure 3-15   REPLYING TO A MESSAGE

recipient's reply

sender's original
message

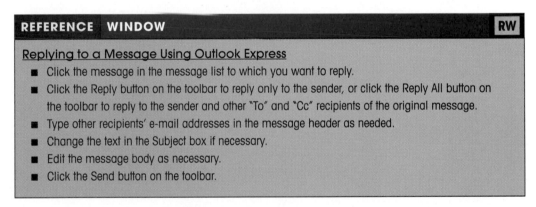

REFERENCE   WINDOW   RW

Replying to a Message Using Outlook Express

■ Click the message in the message list to which you want to reply.

■ Click the Reply button on the toolbar to reply only to the sender, or click the Reply All button on
the toolbar to reply to the sender and other "To" and "Cc" recipients of the original message.

■ Type other recipients' e-mail addresses in the message header as needed.

■ Change the text in the Subject box if necessary.

■ Edit the message body as necessary.

■ Click the Send button on the toolbar.

Forwarding an E-Mail Message

When you forward a message, you are sending a copy of your message to one or more recipients who were not included in the original message. To forward an existing mail message to another user, open the folder containing the message you want to forward, select it in the message list, and then click the Forward button on the toolbar. The "Fw:" window opens, where you can type the address of the recipient in the To box. If you want to forward the message to several people, type their addresses, separated by commas (or semicolons), in the To box (or Cc or Bcc boxes). Outlook Express inserts a copy of the original message in the message display area (as it does when you reply to a message). However, no special mark appears in the left margin to indicate the original message. Figure 3-16 shows a forwarded copy of the Test message.

| Figure 3-16 | FORWARDING A MESSAGE |

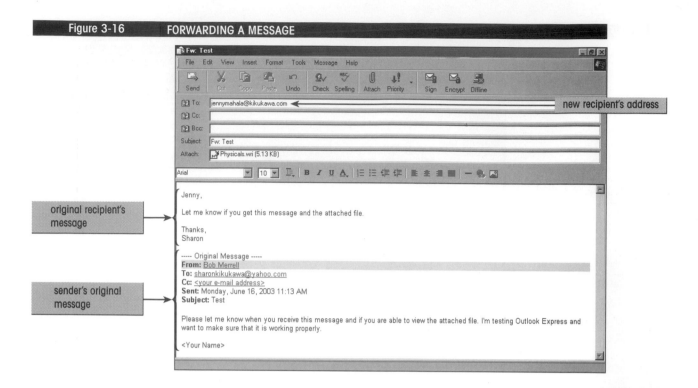

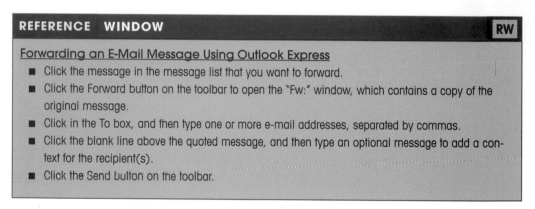

Occasionally, you will receive important messages, so you want to make sure that you can print and file them as needed.

Filing and Printing an E-Mail Message

You can use the Outlook Express mail folders to file your e-mail messages by category. When you file a message, you move it from the Inbox to another folder. You can also make a *copy* of a message in the Inbox and save it in another folder by right-clicking the message in the message list, clicking Copy to Folder on the shortcut menu, and then selecting the folder to store the copy. You will file Sharon's message in a new folder named "FAA" for safekeeping. Later, you can create other folders to suit your style and working situation.

To create a new folder:

1. Right-click the **Inbox** folder in the Folders list to open the shortcut menu, and then click **New Folder**. The Create Folder dialog box opens. When you create a new folder, you first must select the folder at the level above which to create the new folder. Because the Inbox folder is selected, the new folder that you will create will be a subfolder of the Inbox folder.

2. Type **FAA** in the Folder name text box. See Figure 3-17.

Figure 3-17	CREATING A NEW FOLDER

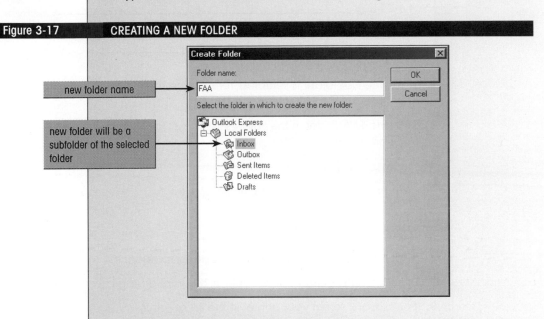

new folder name

new folder will be a subfolder of the selected folder

3. Click the **OK** button to create the new folder and to close the Create Folder dialog box. The new FAA folder appears in the Folders list below the Inbox folder.

After you create the FAA folder, you can transfer messages to it. Besides copying or transferring mail from the Inbox folder, you can select messages in any other folder and then transfer them to another folder.

To file the Test message:

1. Click the **Test** message in the message list to select it.

2. Drag the **Test** message from the message list to the FAA folder in the Folders list. See Figure 3-18.

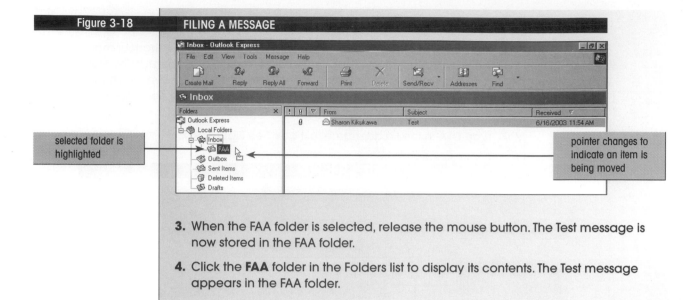

Figure 3-18   FILING A MESSAGE

selected folder is highlighted

pointer changes to indicate an item is being moved

3. When the FAA folder is selected, release the mouse button. The Test message is now stored in the FAA folder.

4. Click the **FAA** folder in the Folders list to display its contents. The Test message appears in the FAA folder.

You will print the message before deleting it.

To print the e-mail message:

1. Click the **Test** message in the message list to select it.

2. Click the **Print** button on the toolbar. The Print dialog box opens.

3. If necessary, select your printer in the list of printers.

4. Click the **Print** button. The message is printed.

You can print a message at any time—when you receive it, before you send it, or after you file it.

Deleting an E-Mail Message and Folder

When you don't need a message any longer, select the message in the message list, and then click the Delete button on the toolbar. You can select multiple messages by pressing and holding the Ctrl key, clicking each message in the message list, and then releasing the Ctrl key. When you click the Delete button on the toolbar, each selected message is deleted. You can select folders and delete them using these same steps. When you delete a message, you are simply moving it to the Deleted Items folder; when you delete a folder you send the folder and its contents to the Deleted Items folder. To remove items permanently, use the same steps to delete the items from the Deleted Items folder. If you are using a public PC in a university computer lab, it is always a good idea to delete all of your messages from the Inbox and then to delete them again from the Deleted Items folder when you finish your session. Otherwise, the next person who uses Outlook Express will be able to access and read your messages.

<u>Deleting an E-Mail Message or a Folder in Outlook Express</u>

■ Click the message in the message list you want to delete. If you are deleting a folder, click the folder to be deleted in the Folders list.

■ Click the Delete button on the toolbar.

■ To delete items permanently, click the Deleted Items folder to open it, click the message or folder that you want to delete permanently, click the Delete button on the toolbar, and then click the Yes button.

or

■ Right-click the Deleted Items folder to open the shortcut menu, click Empty 'Deleted Items' Folder, and then click the Yes button.

To delete the message:

1. If necessary, select the **Test** message in the message list.

2. Click the **Delete** button on the toolbar. The message is deleted from the FAA folder and is moved to the Deleted Items folder.

3. Click the **Deleted Items** folder in the Folder list to display the contents of the folder.

4. Click the **Test** message to select it, and then click the **Delete** button on the tool-bar. A dialog box opens and asks you to confirm the deletion. See Figure 3-19.

| Figure 3-19 | DELETING A MESSAGE |

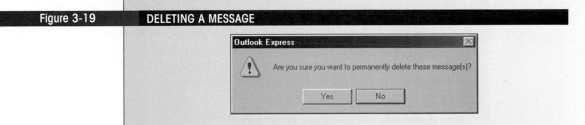

5. Click the **Yes** button. The Test message is deleted from the Deleted Items folder.

To delete the FAA folder, you follow the same steps.

To delete the FAA folder:

1. Click the **FAA** folder in the Folders list to select it. Because this folder doesn't contain any messages, the message list is empty.

2. Click the **Delete** button on the toolbar. A dialog box opens and asks you to confirm moving the folder to the Deleted Items folder.

3. Click the **Yes** button. The FAA folder moves to the Deleted Items folder. The Deleted Items folder contains a plus box to its left, indicating that this folder contains another folder.

4. Click the **plus box** to the left of the Deleted Items folder to display its contents, and then click the **FAA** folder to select it.

5. Click the **Delete** button on the toolbar, and then click the **Yes** button to permanently delete the FAA folder.

6. Click the **Inbox** folder in the Folders list.

Maintaining an Address Book

As you use e-mail to communicate with business associates and friends, you will want to save their addresses in an address book to make it easier to address your messages.

Adding a Contact to the Address Book

You can open the Outlook Express address book by clicking the Addresses button on the toolbar. To create a new address, you open the address book, click the New button on the toolbar, click New Contact from the drop-down list, and then enter information into the Properties dialog box for that contact. On the Name tab, you can enter a contact's names and e-mail address; you use the other tabs to enter optional address, business, personal, and other information about that contact. If you enter a short name in the Nickname text box, then you can type the nickname instead of a person's full name when you address a new message.

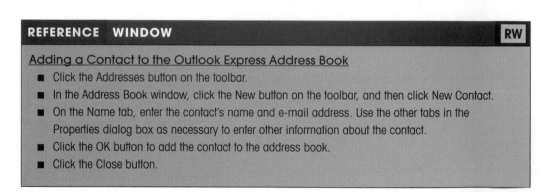

REFERENCE WINDOW **RW**

Adding a Contact to the Outlook Express Address Book
- Click the Addresses button on the toolbar.
- In the Address Book window, click the New button on the toolbar, and then click New Contact.
- On the Name tab, enter the contact's name and e-mail address. Use the other tabs in the Properties dialog box as necessary to enter other information about the contact.
- Click the OK button to add the contact to the address book.
- Click the Close button.

You are eager to add information to your address book. You'll begin by adding Sharon Kikukawa's contact information to your address book.

To add a contact to your address book:

1. Click the **Addresses** button on the toolbar. The Address Book window opens. If necessary, maximize the Address Book window.

2. Click the **New** button on the toolbar, and then click **New Contact**. The Properties dialog box opens with the insertion point positioned in the First text box.

3. Type **Sharon** in the First text box. As you type the contact's first name (and eventually the last name), the name of the Properties dialog box changes to indicate that the properties set in this dialog box belong to the specified contact.

4. Press the **Tab** key twice to move the insertion point to the Last text box, type **Kikukawa** in the Last text box, and then press the **Tab** key three times to move the insertion point to the Nickname text box.

5. Type **Sharon** in the Nickname text box, and then press the **Tab** key to move the insertion point to the E-mail Addresses text box.

6. Type **sharonkikukawa@yahoo.com** in the E-mail Addresses text box, and then click the **Add** button. Sharon's contact is complete. See Figure 3-20.

Figure 3-20	ADDING A CONTACT TO THE ADDRESS BOOK

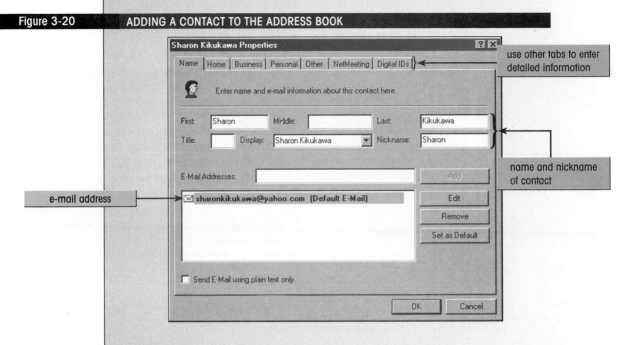

7. Click the **OK** button. The Properties dialog box closes and you return to the Address Book window. Sharon's contact now appears in the Address Book window.

8. Repeat Steps 2 through 7 to create new contacts for the following Kikukawa Air employees:

First Name	Last Name	Nickname	E-mail Address
Chris	**Breed**	**Chris**	**chrisbreed@kikukawa.com**
Jenny	**Mahala**	**Jen**	**jennymahala@kikukawa.com**
Richard	**Forrester**	**Rich**	**richardforrester@kikukawa.com**

9. When you are finished entering the contacts, click the **Close** button on the Address Book window title bar to close it. Now the Contacts list shows the entries you just added to your address book.

Now that these e-mail addresses are stored in the address book, when you start entering a first few letters of a nickname or first name, Outlook Express will complete the entry for you. Clicking the Check button on the toolbar in the New Message window changes the names you typed to their matching entries in the address book. If you need to change an address, click to select it and then press the Delete key.

When you receive mail from someone who is not in your address book, double-click the message to open it, right-click the "From" name to open the shortcut menu, and then click Add to Address Book. This process adds the sender's name and e-mail address to your address book, where you can open his or her information as a contact and edit and add information as necessary.

Adding a Group of Contacts to the Address Book

You can use Outlook Express to create a **group of contacts**, or a mailing list, which is an address book entry consisting of more than one e-mail address in a single group. Usually you create a group of contacts when you regularly send messages to a group of people.

Sharon frequently sends messages to each member of the maintenance department. She asks you to create a group of contacts in her address book so she can type one nickname for the group of e-mail addresses, instead of having to type each address separately.

REFERENCE WINDOW   **RW**

Adding a Group of Contacts to the Address Book

- Click the Addresses button on the toolbar.
- In the Address Book window, click the New button on the toolbar, and then click New Group.
- Type a nickname for the group in the Group Name text box.
- Click the Select Members button.
- Click a name to add to the group, and then click the Select button. Continue adding names to the group until you have selected all group members.
- Click the OK button twice.

To add a group of contacts to your address book:

1. Click the **Addresses** button on the toolbar, and maximize the Address Book window.

2. Click the **New** button on the toolbar, and then click **New Group**. The Properties dialog box opens and displays tabs related to group settings.

3. With the insertion point positioned in the Group Name text box, type **Maintenance**. This nickname will represent the individual e-mail addresses of members of the maintenance department.

4. Click the **Select Members** button. The Select Group Members window opens, with existing contacts appearing on the left side of the window.

5. On the left side of the window, click **Chris Breed**, and then click the **Select** button. A copy of Chris's contact is added to the Members list box.

6. Repeat Step 5 to add the contacts for **Jenny Mahala** and **Richard Forrester** to the group. Figure 3-21 shows the completed group.

Figure 3-21   CREATING A GROUP OF CONTACTS

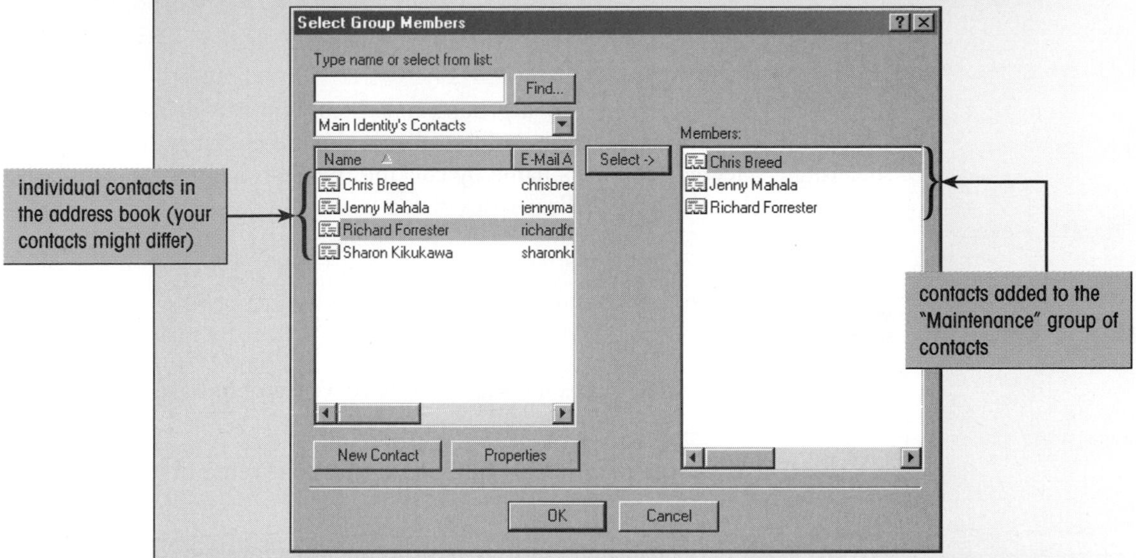

individual contacts in the address book (your contacts might differ)

contacts added to the "Maintenance" group of contacts

7. Click the **OK** button to close the Select Group Members dialog box. The Properties dialog box for the Maintenance group now displays three group members.

8. Click the **OK** button to close the Maintenance Properties dialog box. The nickname of the new group, Maintenance, appears in the address book on the left side of the window and the members of the group are listed in the window on the right.

9. Close the Address Book window by clicking the **Close** button on its title bar. The Maintenance group appears in the Contacts list.

Now, test the new group of contacts by creating a new message.

To address a message to a group of contacts and close Outlook Express:

1. Click the **Create Mail** button on the toolbar. The New Message window opens.

2. Type **Maintenance** in the To box. As you type the first two or three letters, Outlook Express might complete your entry for you by selecting the Maintenance group.

3. Press the **Tab** key.

4. Click the **Check** button on the toolbar, right-click **Maintenance** in the To box to open the shortcut menu, and then click **Properties**. The Properties dialog box shows the three group members who will receive messages sent to the Maintenance group. Now, when Sharon sends mail to the maintenance department members, she can type the group name "Maintenance" in any of a message's boxes (To, Cc, or Bcc) instead of typing each address individually.

5. Click the **OK** button to close the Properties dialog box, click the **Close** button on the New Message window title bar, and then click the **No** button to close the message without saving it.

6. Click **File** on the menu bar, and then click **Exit**. Outlook Express closes.

7. If necessary, log off your Internet connection.

When you need to modify a group's members, you can delete one or more members from the group by opening the address book, double-clicking the group name, and then deleting a selected member's name by clicking the Remove button. Similarly, you can add members using the group's Properties dialog box.

Session 3.2 QUICK CHECK

1. The folder that stores messages you have written but have not yet sent is the _____ folder.

2. True or False: You can set Outlook Express so it remembers your e-mail account password.

3. What happens when Outlook Express queues a message?

4. When you receive a message with an attachment, what two options are available for the attached file?

5. When you delete a message from the Inbox folder, can you recover that message? Why or why not?

6. What information can you store about a person in a contact?

If your instructor assigned Session 3.3, continue reading. If your instructor assigned Session 3.4, proceed to that session. Otherwise, complete the Review Assignments at the end of this tutorial.

SESSION 3.3

In this session, you will learn how to use Netscape Mail to send and receive e-mail. You will use this e-mail program to print, file, save, delete, respond to, and forward e-mail messages. Finally, you will organize e-mail addresses in an address book.

Netscape Mail

Netscape Mail, or simply **Mail**, is the e-mail program that you use to send and receive e-mail. Mail is installed with Netscape Communicator. Mail starts when you click a hyperlink in a Web page to an e-mail address or when you start it using the Start menu.

You are eager to begin your evaluation of e-mail software for Sharon. You start Mail using the Start menu. Figure 3-22 shows the Mail window.

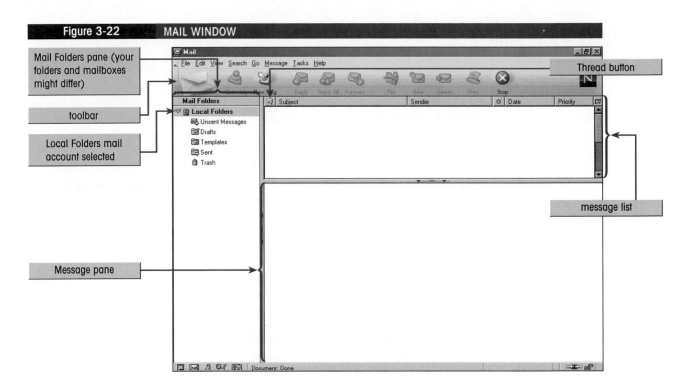

Figure 3-22   MAIL WINDOW

Mail Folders pane (your folders and mailboxes might differ)

toolbar

Local Folders mail account selected

Message pane

Thread button

message list

The Mail window contains three panes: the Mail Folders pane, the message list, and the Message pane. The **Mail Folders pane** displays a list of mailboxes and folders for receiving, saving, and storing mail messages. You might see different folders from those shown in Figure 3-22, but you should see six default mailboxes and folders. The **Inbox** is a mailbox that receives your downloaded messages (this mailbox isn't shown in Figure 3-22 because Mail hasn't been configured for any user yet). The **Unsent Messages mailbox** stores outgoing messages that have not been sent. The **Drafts folder** stores messages that you are composing, but are not yet ready to send. The **Templates folder** contains any template files that you have created for your messages. The **Sent folder** stores copies of each message that you send (note that you can disable this feature). Finally, the **Trash folder** stores messages you have deleted. Your copy of Mail may also contain folders and mailboxes you've created, such as a folder in which you store all messages from a certain recipient.

The **message list** contains summary information for each message that you have received. Clicking the Thread button in the message list groups messages by their threads, or common topics, so you can quickly find all messages you have received based on a specific subject. Messages appearing in bold type are ones that you haven't opened or read yet; other messages appear without bold formatting to indicate that you have reviewed them. To change a message's status from read to unread, click the green dot in the fourth column. The Date column indicates when you received the message, and the Priority column indicates a priority from highest to lowest. If this column's entry is blank, then the sender did not choose a priority. The sender indicates a message's priority before sending it; most messages have no priority specified. Figure 3-22 shows the default configuration for Mail's message list; you might also see other columns if you or another user has used the arrows on the column headings row to display or hide additional columns. You can sort messages by clicking any column in the message list.

The message that is selected in the message list appears in the **Message pane**. The Message pane appears below the message list and displays the message's contents. You use the horizontal scroll bar to scroll the message, if necessary. You can customize Mail in many ways by resizing, hiding, and displaying different panes and their individual elements, so your screen might look different from Figure 3-22.

Setting Up E-Mail

You are eager to get started using Mail. Cost is not a consideration because the Mail program is free when you download it as part of the Netscape Communicator suite from Netscape's Web site. These steps assume that Mail 6.1 is already installed on your computer. First, you need to configure Mail so it will retrieve your mail from your ISP.

To configure Mail to manage your e-mail:

1. Click the **Start** button on the Windows taskbar, point to **Programs**, point to **Netscape 6**, and then click **Mail** to start the program.

   TROUBLE? If you cannot find the Mail program on your computer, ask your instructor or technical support person for assistance.

   TROUBLE? You can configure Mail to open in different ways and to display a Web page in the Message pane when it starts. These screen differences should cause no problems.

2. Click **Edit** on the menu bar, and then click **Mail/News Account Settings**. The Account Settings window opens. You use this window to set up your mail account and to change settings in Mail.

   TROUBLE? If you have already set up your mail account (or if someone else has set up your mail account), click the OK button in the Account Settings window and skip to the next set of steps. If you are unsure about any existing account, ask your instructor or technical support person for help.

3. In the text box on the left, click **Local Folders**, and then click the **New Account** button. The Account Wizard starts so you can set up a new mail account. See Figure 3-23.

Figure 3-23	ACCOUNT WIZARD

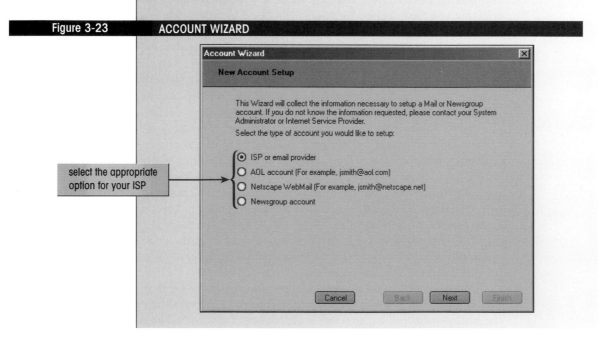

select the appropriate option for your ISP

4. Click the option button for the type of service that you have, and then click the **Next** button. The Account Wizard opens the Identity page, which asks for your full name and e-mail address. Mail will insert this information in the From field when you send messages.

   TROUBLE? If you are unsure of which option to choose, ask your instructor or technical support person for help.

5. Click in the **Your Name** text box, type your first and last names, click in the **Email Address** text box, type your full e-mail address, and then click the **Next** button. The Account Wizard opens the Server Information page, which requests the name of your incoming and outgoing mail servers.

6. Click the POP or IMAP option button to indicate your ISP's incoming server type.

7. In the Server Name text box, type the name of your incoming mail server. Your instructor or technical support person will provide this information for you. Usually, your incoming mail server name is POP, POP3, or IMAP followed by a host name.

8. Press the **Tab** key, type the name of your ISP's outgoing mail server in the Server Name text box, and then click the **Next** button. The Account Wizard opens the User Name page, where you enter the user name given to you by your ISP.

9. Click in the **User Name** text box, and then type your user name, as specified by your instructor or technical support person. Make sure that you type only your user name and not your host name.

10. Click the **Next** button, click the **Next** button again to accept the default account name, confirm the information in the Congratulations! page, and then click the **Finish** button when you are sure that your settings are correct. If you need to make any changes, use the Back button to return to a previous page.

11. Click the **OK** button to close the Account Settings window, and then click **Inbox** for your account in the Mail Folders pane.

Now Mail is set up to send and receive messages, so you are ready to send a message to Sharon. *Note:* In this tutorial, you will send messages to a real mailbox with the address sharonkikukawa@yahoo.com. Follow the instructions carefully and use the correct address. Messages sent to this mailbox are deleted without being opened or read.

Sending a Message Using Mail

You are ready to use Mail to send a message with an attached file to Sharon. You will send a carbon copy of the message to your own e-mail address to make sure that the message and attached file are sent correctly.

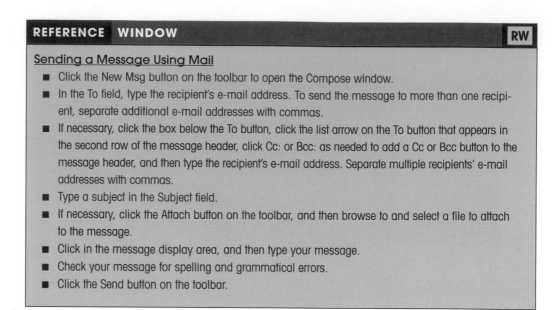

REFERENCE WINDOW   **RW**

<u>Sending a Message Using Mail</u>

- Click the New Msg button on the toolbar to open the Compose window.
- In the To field, type the recipient's e-mail address. To send the message to more than one recipient, separate additional e-mail addresses with commas.
- If necessary, click the box below the To button, click the list arrow on the To button that appears in the second row of the message header, click Cc: or Bcc: as needed to add a Cc or Bcc button to the message header, and then type the recipient's e-mail address. Separate multiple recipients' e-mail addresses with commas.
- Type a subject in the Subject field.
- If necessary, click the Attach button on the toolbar, and then browse to and select a file to attach to the message.
- Click in the message display area, and then type your message.
- Check your message for spelling and grammatical errors.
- Click the Send button on the toolbar.

To send a message with an attachment:

1. Click the **New Msg** button on the toolbar. The Compose window opens. If necessary, click the **Maximize** button on the Compose window to maximize it. See Figure 3-24. The Compose window contains a menu bar, toolbar, message display area, and fields in which to enter addresses and subject information. The insertion point is positioned in the To field when you create a new message.

| Figure 3-24 | COMPOSE WINDOW |

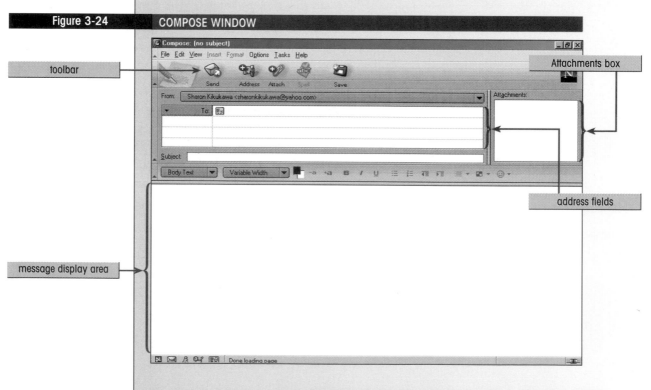

2. In the To field, type **sharonkikukawa@yahoo.com**, and then press the **Enter** key. A To button is added to the second row of the message header.

TROUBLE? Make sure that you use the address sharonkikukawa@yahoo.com, instead of sharonkikukawa@kikukawa.com. If you type Sharon's e-mail address incorrectly, your message will be returned as undeliverable.

3. Click the **list arrow** on the second To button in the message header, and then click **Cc:** in the list. A Cc button replaces the To button on the second row of the message header and the insertion point is positioned in the message header.

4. Type your e-mail address in the Cc field. When you send this message, you and Sharon will both receive copies.

   TROUBLE? If you make a typing mistake on a previous line, use the arrow keys or click the insertion point to return to a previous line so you can correct your mistake. If the arrow keys do not move the insertion point backward or forward in the address fields, then press Shift + Tab or press the Tab key to move backward or forward, respectively.

5. Click in the **Subject** field, and then type **Test**.

6. Click the **Attach** button on the toolbar. The Enter file to attach dialog box opens.

7. Make sure your Data Disk is in the appropriate drive, click the **Look in** list arrow, and then click the appropriate drive to display the contents of your Data Disk.

8. Double-click the **Tutorial.03** folder, and then double-click **Physicals**. The Enter file to attach dialog box closes, and the Attachments box now displays the Physicals.wri file.

9. Click the insertion point in the message body, and then type **Please let me know when you receive this message and if you are able to view the attached file. I'm testing Netscape Mail and want to make sure that it is working properly.**

10. Press the **Enter** key twice, and then type your first and last names to sign your message. See Figure 3-25.

Figure 3-25	SENDING AN E-MAIL MESSAGE

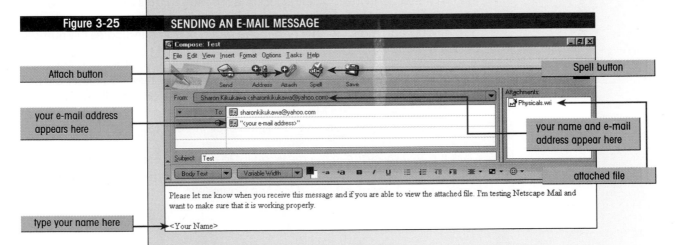

11. Click the **Spell** button on the toolbar to check your spelling before sending the message. If necessary, correct any typing errors. When you are finished, click the **Close** button to close the Check Spelling dialog box.

12. Click the **Send** button on the toolbar to send the message. The Compose window closes, and the message is sent to the mail server for delivery to Sharon.

TROUBLE? If a dialog box opens and tells you that Netscape cannot locate your mail server, click the OK button, connect to your ISP or log on to the network, and then repeat Step 12.

Receiving and Reading a Message

When you receive new mail, messages that you have not opened have closed envelope icons in the message list, and messages that you have opened have open envelope icons. You will check for new mail next.

REFERENCE WINDOW   **RW**

Using Mail to Receive Messages
- Click the Get Msg button on the toolbar.
- If necessary, type your password in the Password Entry Dialog dialog box, and then click the OK button.

To check for incoming mail:

1. Click the **Get Msg** button on the toolbar. The Password Entry Dialog dialog box opens.

2. Type your password in the text box, and then click the **OK** button. Within a few moments, your mail server transfers all new mail to your Inbox. You should see the Test message in the Inbox. The Inbox in the Mail Folders pane is bold, but other folders and mailboxes are not. A bold folder or mailbox indicates that it contains unread mail; the "(1)" next to the mailbox name indicates the number of new messages.

TROUBLE? If you do not see any messages in your Inbox, then you either did not receive any new mail or you might be looking in the wrong mailbox. If necessary, click the Inbox in the Mail Folders pane. If you still don't have any mail messages, wait a few moments, and then click the Get Msg button again.

3. Click the **Test** message in the message list to open the message in the Message pane. The Attachments box in the Message pane indicates that the message contains an attached file. See Figure 3-26.

Figure 3-26	RECEIVING AN E-MAIL MESSAGE

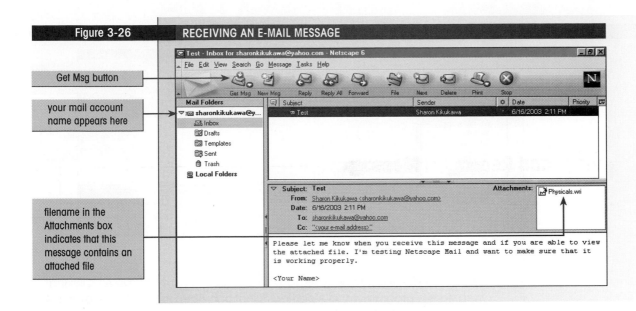

Get Msg button

your mail account name appears here

filename in the Attachments box indicates that this message contains an attached file

You received a copy of the test message that you sent to Sharon. The Attachments box shows the name of the attached file that you received with the message. When you receive a message with one or more attachments, you can open the attachment or save it.

Viewing and Saving an Attached File

You want to make sure that your attached file was sent properly, so you decide to open it. After you are finished viewing the contents of an attached file, you can save or delete it.

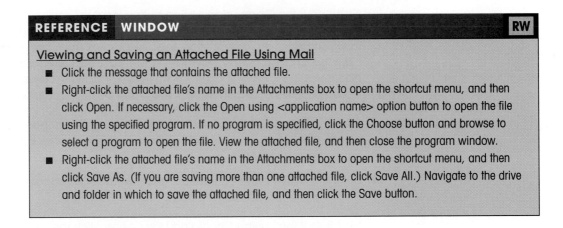

REFERENCE WINDOW **RW**

Viewing and Saving an Attached File Using Mail
- Click the message that contains the attached file.
- Right-click the attached file's name in the Attachments box to open the shortcut menu, and then click Open. If necessary, click the Open using <application name> option button to open the file using the specified program. If no program is specified, click the Choose button and browse to select a program to open the file. View the attached file, and then close the program window.
- Right-click the attached file's name in the Attachments box to open the shortcut menu, and then click Save As. (If you are saving more than one attached file, click Save All.) Navigate to the drive and folder in which to save the attached file, and then click the Save button.

To view and save the attached file:

1. Right-click Physicals.wri to open the shortcut menu. See Figure 3-27.

Figure 3-27   VIEWING AN ATTACHED FILE

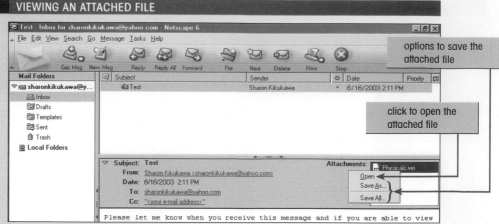

The shortcut menu contains three options: Open, Save As, and Save All. Clicking Open starts a program on your computer that can open the file. Clicking Save As lets you save the file to the drive and folder that you specify. Clicking Save All lets you simultaneously save more than one attachment to the drive and folder that you specify.

2. Click **Open** on the shortcut menu. The Downloading dialog box opens and displays the option of opening the file using a specified program (or one that you choose) or saving the file to disk. The default editor for a file with the .wri extension is WordPad, so the Open using option button is "Open using wordpad.exe."

   TROUBLE? If you can't see the entire Downloading dialog box, drag it to another location.

   TROUBLE? If the Open using option button is set to Word, Notepad, or another text editor, no special action is necessary. If the Open using option button is set to Open using <no application specified>, click the Open using option button, click the Choose button, navigate to the wordpad.exe file on your computer (the default directory is C:\Program Files\Windows\Accessories\), click the wordpad.exe file, and then click the Open button. Continue with Step 3.

3. Click the **Open using** option button if necessary, and then click the **OK** button. WordPad or another text editor starts and opens the file. If necessary, maximize the program window.

4. Click the **Close** button on the program window. Now that you have viewed the attachment, you can save it on your Data Disk.

   TROUBLE? If the Saving File dialog box opens, click the Close button.

5. Right-click **Physicals.wri** in the Attachments box, and then click **Save As** on the shortcut menu. The Save Attachment dialog box opens. The Physicals file is already selected for you in the File name text box.

6. If necessary, click the **Save in** list arrow, browse to and select the drive that contains your Data Disk, and then double-click the **Tutorial.03** folder to open it.

7. Click the **Save** button, and then click the **Yes** button to overwrite the file with the same name on your Data Disk.

When you receive a message with an attached file, you can view and save the attachment for as long as you store the message. When you delete the message, you will delete the file attached to the message. However, because you saved the attachment on your Data Disk, the file exists there for as long as you need it.

Replying **to and Forwarding Messages**

You can forward any message you receive to one or more e-mail addresses. Similarly, you can respond to the sender of a message quickly and efficiently by replying to a message. Replying to and forwarding messages are common tasks for e-mail users.

Replying to an E-Mail Message

To reply to a message, select the message in the message list, and then click the Reply button on the toolbar to reply only to the sender, or click the Reply All button on the toolbar to reply to the sender and to other people who received the original message (those e-mail addresses listed in the To and Cc fields). Mail will open a new Compose window and place the original sender's address in the To field; other e-mail addresses that received the original message will appear in the To and Cc fields as appropriate. You can leave the Subject field as is or modify it. In Mail, when you reply to a message the original message has a blue line to the left of its content to indicate the original message text. Figure 3-28 shows a reply to the Test message.

Figure 3-28   REPLYING TO A MESSAGE

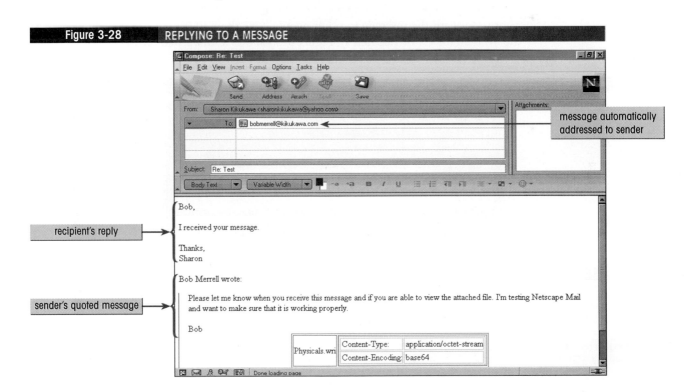

Forwarding an E-Mail Message

When you forward a message, you are sending a copy of the message to one or more recipients who were not included in the original message. To forward an existing mail message to another user, open the folder or mailbox containing the message you want to forward, select it in the message list, and then click the Forward button on the toolbar. In Mail, the default setting is to send a forwarded message as inline text, where an "Original Message" separator separates the current and forwarded messages. You can also send a forwarded message as an attachment, where the forwarded message is sent as an attached file, by clicking Message on the menu bar of the Inbox window, pointing to Forward As, and then clicking Attachment. After the Compose window opens, type the address of the recipient in the To field. If you want to forward the message to other people, type their addresses, separated by commas, in the To field (or Cc or Bcc fields). Figure 3-29 shows a forwarded message.

| Figure 3-29 | FORWARDING A MESSAGE |

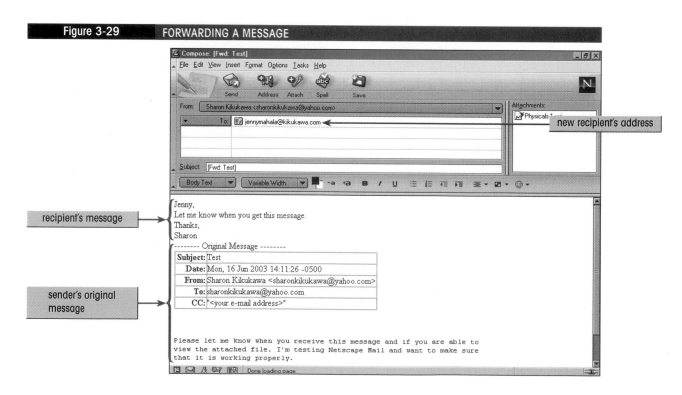

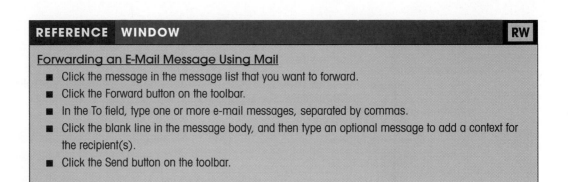

Forwarding an E-Mail Message Using Mail
- Click the message in the message list that you want to forward.
- Click the Forward button on the toolbar.
- In the To field, type one or more e-mail messages, separated by commas.
- Click the blank line in the message body, and then type an optional message to add a context for the recipient(s).
- Click the Send button on the toolbar.

Occasionally, you will receive important messages, so you want to make sure that you print them and then file them in a safe place.

Filing and Printing an E-Mail Message

You can use the folders and mailboxes in Mail to file your e-mail messages by category. When you file a message, you move it from the Inbox to another folder. You can also make a *copy* of a message in the Inbox and save it in another folder by right-clicking the message in the message list, pointing to Copy To on the shortcut menu, and then clicking the mailbox or folder in which to store the copy. You will file Sharon's message in a new folder named "FAA" for safekeeping. Later you can create other folders to suit your style and working situation.

To create the new folder:

1. Right-click **Inbox** in the Mail Folders pane to open the shortcut menu, and then click **New Folder**. The New Folder dialog box opens.

2. In the Name text box, type **FAA**. See Figure 3-30.

Figure 3-30   CREATING A NEW FOLDER

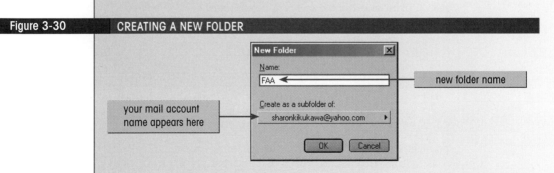

3. Click the **OK** button. The new FAA folder appears in the Mail Folders pane.

After you create the FAA folder, you can transfer messages to it. Besides copying or transferring mail from the Inbox, you can select messages in any other folder and then transfer them to another folder.

To file the message:

1. Click the **Test** message in the message list to select it.

2. Drag the **Test** message from the message list to the FAA folder in the Mail Folders pane. See Figure 3-31.

| Figure 3-31 | FILING A MESSAGE |

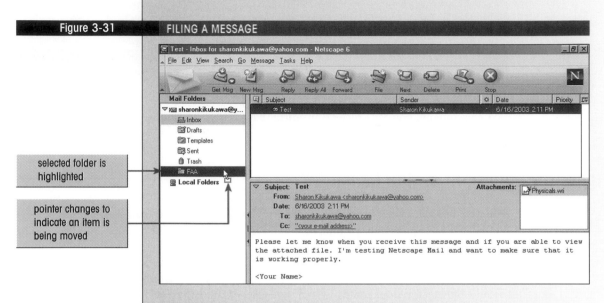

selected folder is highlighted

pointer changes to indicate an item is being moved

3. When the FAA folder is selected, release the mouse button. The Test message is now stored in the FAA folder.

4. Click the **FAA** folder in the Mail Folders pane to display its contents. The Test message appears in the FAA folder.

You might need to print important messages in the future, so you want to make sure that you can print and file messages in a safe place.

To print an e-mail message:

1. Click the **Test** message in the message list to select it.

2. Click the **Print** button on the toolbar. The Print dialog box opens.

3. If necessary, select your printer in the Printer section.

4. Click the **OK** button. The message is printed.

You can print a message at any time—when you receive it, before you send it, or after you file it.

Deleting an E-Mail Message and Folder

When you don't need a message any longer, select the message in the message list, and then click the Delete button on the toolbar. You can select multiple messages by pressing and holding the Ctrl key, clicking each message in the message list, and then releasing the Ctrl key.

When you click the Delete button on the toolbar, each selected message is deleted. You can select folders and delete them using these same steps. When you delete a message, you are really moving it to the Trash folder; when you delete a folder you send the folder and its contents to the Trash folder. To remove items permanently, you need to empty the Trash folder. If you are using a public PC in a university computer lab, it is always a good idea to delete all of your messages from the Inbox and then empty the Trash folder when you finish your session. Otherwise, the next person who uses Mail will be able to access and read your messages.

REFERENCE WINDOW **RW**

<u>Deleting an E-Mail Message or a Folder Using Mail</u>
- Click the message in the message list to delete. If you are deleting a folder, click the folder to delete in the Mail Folders pane.
- Click the Delete button on the toolbar.
- To delete items permanently, click the Trash folder in the Mail Folders pane to open it, click the message or folder that you want to delete permanently, and then click the Delete button on the toolbar.

or

- Right-click the Trash folder in the Mail Folders pane to open the shortcut menu, and then click Empty Trash Can.

To delete the message:

1. If necessary, click the **Test** message in the message list.

2. Click the **Delete** button on the toolbar. The message is deleted from the FAA folder and is moved to the Trash folder.

3. Click the **Trash** folder in the Mail Folders pane to open it.

4. Click the **Test** message to select it, and then click the **Delete** button on the toolbar. The message is deleted from the Trash folder.

To delete a folder, you follow the same steps.

To delete a folder:

1. Click the **FAA** folder in the Mail Folders pane to select it. Because this folder doesn't contain any messages, the message list is empty.

2. Click the **Delete** button on the toolbar. A dialog box opens and asks you to confirm moving the folder to the Trash folder. See Figure 3-32.

| Figure 3-32 | DELETING A MESSAGE |

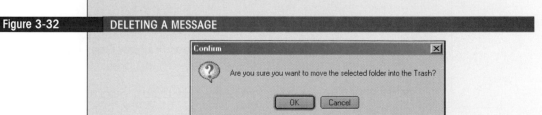

3. Click the **OK** button. The FAA folder moves to the Trash folder. The Trash folder contains an arrow to its left, indicating that this folder contains another folder.

4. Right-click the **Trash** folder in the Mail Folders pane to open the shortcut menu, and then click the **Empty Trash Can**. Mail deletes all items in the Trash folder, which permanently deletes the items from your computer.

Maintaining **an Address Book**

As you use e-mail to communicate with business associates and friends, you will want to save their addresses in an address book to make it easier to address your messages.

Adding a Card to the Address Book

You can open the address book in Mail by clicking Tasks on the menu bar, and then clicking Address Book. To create a new address, you open the address book, click the New Card button on the toolbar, and then enter information into the New Card dialog box that opens. On the Name tab, you can enter a person's name, e-mail address, and various phone numbers. If you enter a short name in the Nickname text box, then you can type the nickname instead of a person's full name when you address a new message.

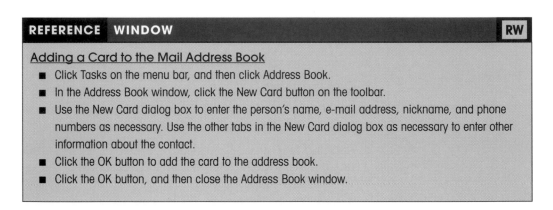

REFERENCE WINDOW   **RW**

Adding a Card to the Mail Address Book
- Click Tasks on the menu bar, and then click Address Book.
- In the Address Book window, click the New Card button on the toolbar.
- Use the New Card dialog box to enter the person's name, e-mail address, nickname, and phone numbers as necessary. Use the other tabs in the New Card dialog box as necessary to enter other information about the contact.
- Click the OK button to add the card to the address book.
- Click the OK button, and then close the Address Book window.

You are eager to add information to your address book. You'll begin by adding Sharon Kikukawa's contact information to your address book.

To add a card to the address book:

1. Click **Tasks** on the menu bar, and then click **Address Book**. The Address Book window opens. If necessary, maximize the Address Book window.

    TROUBLE? If an Instant Messenger Setup dialog box opens, click the Cancel button.

2. Click the **New Card** button on the toolbar. The New Card dialog box opens with the insertion point positioned in the First text box.

    TROUBLE? If you cannot see all of the New Card dialog box, move it so the entire dialog box is visible on the screen.

3. Type **Sharon** in the First text box, and then press the **Tab** key to move the insertion point to the Last text box.

4. Type **Kikukawa** and then press the **Tab** key twice to move the insertion point to the Nickname text box.

5. Type **Sharon** in the Nickname text box, press the **Tab** key to move the insertion point to the Email text box, and then type **sharonkikukawa@yahoo.com**. Your New Card dialog box looks like Figure 3-33.

Figure 3-33   ADDING A CARD TO THE ADDRESS BOOK

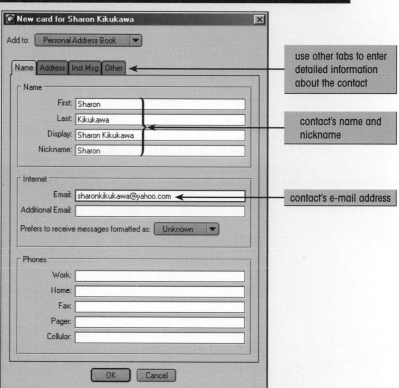

6. Click the **OK** button. The New Card dialog box closes and you return to the Address Book window. Sharon's card information now appears in the Address Book window.

7. Repeat Steps 2 through 6 to create new cards for the following Kikukawa Air employees:

First	Last	Nickname	E-mail
Chris	**Breed**	**Chris**	**chrisbreed@kikukawa.com**
Jenny	**Mahala**	**Jen**	**jennymahala@kikukawa.com**
Richard	**Forrester**	**Rich**	**richardforrester@kikukawa.com**

8. When you are finished adding the addresses, click the **Close** button on the Address Book window title bar to close it.

Now that these e-mail addresses are stored in the address book, when you start entering the first few letters of a nickname or first name, Mail will complete the entries for you. Clicking the Address button on the toolbar in the Compose window lets you select names from the address book instead of typing them. If you need to delete an address, click it to select it, and then click the Remove button.

When you receive mail from someone who is not in your address book, double-click the message in the message list to open it, right-click the "From" name to open the shortcut menu, and then click Add to Address Book. This process adds the sender's name and e-mail address to your address book, where you can open his or her information as a card and edit and add information as necessary.

Creating a Mailing List

You can use Mail to create a mailing list, which is an address entry consisting of more than one e-mail address in a single group. Usually you create a mailing list when you regularly send messages to a group of people.

Sharon frequently sends messages to each member of the maintenance department. She asks you to create a mailing list in her address book so she can type one nickname for the mailing list, instead of typing each address separately.

REFERENCE WINDOW   RW

Creating a Mailing List In Netscape Mail

- Click Tasks on the menu bar, and then click Address Book.
- In the Address Book window, click the New List button on the toolbar.
- In the Mailing List dialog box, type a name for the mailing list in the List Name text box. Type a nickname for the mailing list in the List Nickname text box, and then type an optional description for the mailing list in the Description text box.
- Click the Type names or drag addresses into the mailing list below box, and then type the first e-mail address to store in the mailing list. Continue adding names to the mailing list until you have added all mailing list members.
- Click the OK button, and then close the Address Book window.

To add a mailing list to the address book:

1. Click **Tasks** on the menu bar, and then click **Address Book**. The Address Book window opens. If necessary, maximize the Address Book window.

2. Click the **New List** button on the toolbar. The Mailing List dialog box opens.

3. Click in the List Name text box, type **Maintenance List**, and then press the **Tab** key to move the insertion point to the List Nickname text box.

4. Type **Maintenance** in the List Nickname text box. This nickname will represent the group.

5. Press the **Tab** key twice to move the insertion point to the Type names or drag addresses into the mailing list below box, and then type **C**. A menu of e-mail addresses in your address book and beginning with the letter "C" opens. You can click an address in the list or continue typing.

6. Click the entry for **Chris Breed**. Mail adds Chris's card to the mailing list and creates a new entry for the next name.

7. Press the **Tab** key to enter Chris's name, and then type **J**. Mail opens a list of addresses in the address book that begin with the letter "J."

8. Click the entry for **Jenny Mahala**, press the **Tab** key, and then add Richard Forrester's address to the mailing list. See Figure 3-34.

Figure 3-34   **CREATING A MAILING LIST**

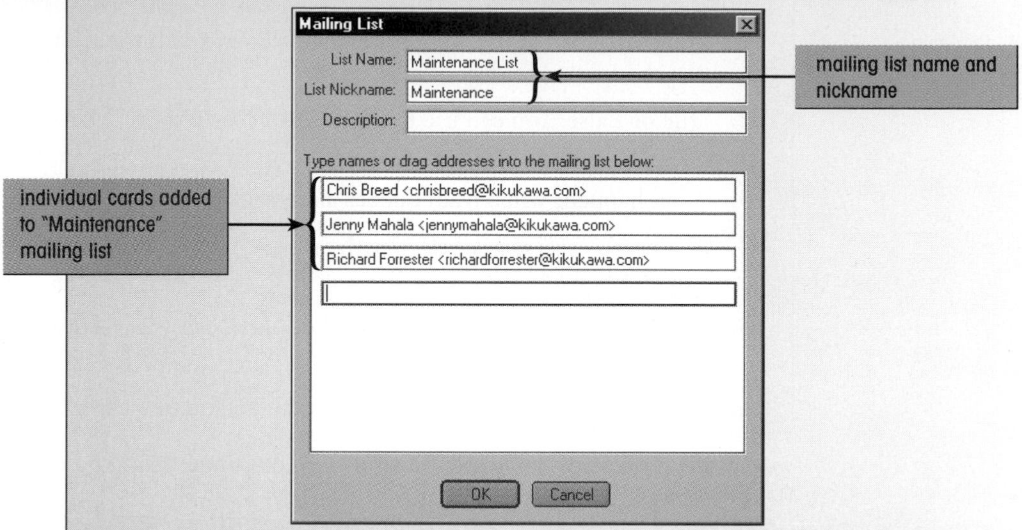

9. Click the **OK** button to close the Mailing List dialog box. The Maintenance List entry appears in the Address Book.

10. Click the **Close** button on the Address Book window title bar to close it.

Now, test the mailing list by creating a new message.

To address a message to a mailing list and close Mail:

1. Click the **New Msg** button on the toolbar. The Compose window opens. If necessary, maximize the Compose window.

2. Type **Maintenance** in the To field. As you type the first two or three letters, Mail's autocompletion feature might complete your entry for you by selecting the Maintenance mailing list.

3. Press the **Tab** key to enter the Maintenance list in the To field. Now when Sharon sends mail to the maintenance department members, she can type the group name "Maintenance" in any of the message's fields (To, Cc, or Bcc) instead of typing each address individually.

4. Click the **Close** button on the Compose window title bar to close the new message.

5. Click **File** on the menu bar, and then click **Exit**. Mail closes.

6. If necessary, log off your Internet connection.

When you need to modify a mailing list's members, you can delete one or more cards from the mailing list by opening the address book, double-clicking the mailing list entry, selecting the card to delete, and then clicking the Remove button. Similarly, you can add cards to the mailing list by entering new names in the Mailing List dialog box.

Session 3.3 QUICK CHECK

1. The folder that stores messages you have written but have not yet sent is the _____ folder.

2. True or False: You can use the Account Wizard to set Mail so it remembers your e-mail account password.

3. What happens when Mail queues a message?

4. When you receive a message with an attachment, what three options are available for the attached file?

5. When you delete a message from the Inbox, can you recover that message? Why or why not?

6. What information can you store about a person in a card?

If your instructor assigned Session 3.4, continue reading. Otherwise, complete the Review Assignments at the end of this tutorial.

SESSION 3.4

In this session, you will learn how to use Hotmail to send and receive e-mail. You will use Hotmail to print, file, save, delete, respond to, and forward e-mail messages. Finally, you will organize e-mail addresses in an address book.

Hotmail

Hotmail is a Web-based e-mail service powered by MSN.com that you use to send and receive e-mail. To use Hotmail, you must use a Web browser, such as Microsoft Internet Explorer or Netscape Navigator, to make a connection to the Internet. Then you navigate to the Hotmail home page, where your e-mail messages are stored.

Most people who use Hotmail and other Web-based e-mail services have Internet access from their employer, school, public library, or a friend. The Hotmail service is free, but you must have a way to access it using a Web browser and an existing Internet connection, which someone else might supply for you. Many public and school libraries provide free Internet access where you can access your Hotmail account. No matter where you are in the world, if you can connect to the Internet, you can access your Hotmail account. This portability makes Web-based e-mail a valuable resource for people who travel or who do not have their own computers.

You are eager to begin your evaluation of e-mail service for Sharon. To begin using Hotmail, you need to use your Web browser to connect to the Hotmail Web site. Then you will create a user account and send and receive messages.

Setting Up a Hotmail User Account

Cost is not a consideration because Hotmail is a free service. The steps in this session assume that you have a Web browser and can make an Internet connection. Before you can use Hotmail, you'll need to establish a user account. A user account establishes your name and Hotmail e-mail address so that you can use Hotmail to send and receive e-mail messages.

To begin setting up a Hotmail user account:

1. Start your Web browser and if necessary, log on to your Internet account.

> TROUBLE? You must have an Internet connection to set up a Hotmail user account. If you cannot connect to the Internet, ask your instructor or technical support person for help.

2. Select any text in your browser's Address bar, type **www.msn.com**, press the **Enter** key, and then click the **Hotmail** link on the MSN.com home page. The home page for Hotmail opens in your browser. See Figure 3-35.

| Figure 3-35 | HOTMAIL SIGN-IN PAGE |

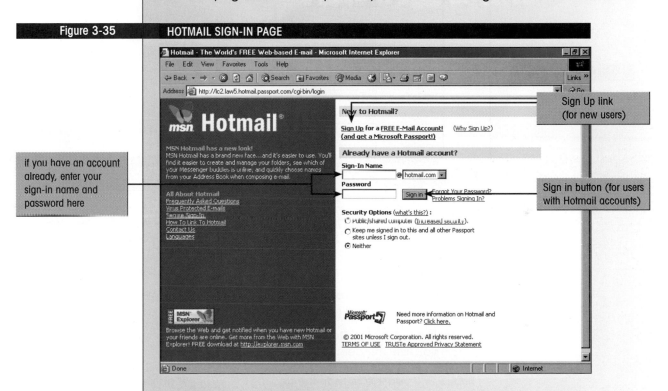

> TROUBLE? If you already have a Hotmail account, log on to your account, and then skip to the next set of steps.

3. In the New to Hotmail? section, click the **Sign Up** link. The Hotmail Registration page shown in Figure 3-36 opens. This page changes occasionally, so your page might look different. However, you will need to supply the same information identified in the steps to create your Hotmail user account.

Figure 3-36   **HOTMAIL REGISTRATION PAGE**

complete this form

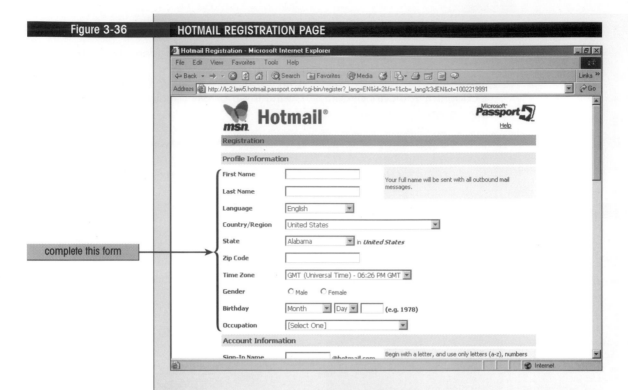

4. With the insertion point in the First Name text box, type your first name, press the **Tab** key to move to the Last Name text box, and then type your last name. The note to the right of the First Name and Last Name text boxes indicates that your full name will appear in all Hotmail messages that you send.

5. If necessary, click the **Language** list arrow and select your preferred language setting. The default setting is English.

6. If necessary, click the **Country/Region** list arrow, and select the country in which you live. The default setting is United States.

TROUBLE? If you live outside the United States, a new page might open in which you select an individual state, province, or other location in your country. Follow the on-screen instructions.

7. If you live in the United States, click the **State** list arrow, and then click the state in which you live. The default setting is Alabama because this state appears first in the alphabetical list of states.

8. Click in the **Zip Code** text box, and then type your zip code. Hotmail will use this information to provide you with additional services, such as local weather forecasts, that you might request in the future.

9. If necessary, click the **Time Zone** list arrow, and then click the time zone in which you live. Hotmail will use this setting to provide accurate date and time information in your e-mail messages.

10. Click the Male or Female option button in the Gender section.

11. Use the **Month** and **Day** list arrows in the Birthday section to indicate the month and date of your birth, click in the **text box** to the left of the Day list box, and then type the four-digit year of your birth.

12. Click the **Occupation** list arrow, and then click an appropriate choice in the list. If you are a student, click **Student**.

Now that you have provided some personal information to Hotmail, you need to create your user name, which Hotmail calls a sign-in name. Your sign-in name must begin with a letter. A sign-in name can contain letters, numbers, and underscore characters (_), but it cannot contain any spaces. After creating a sign-in name, you must create a password containing letters and/or numbers, but no spaces. You'll enter your password twice to ensure that you typed it correctly. Finally, to help you remember your password in the event that you forget it, you'll enter a secret question and its answer so the Hotmail server can verify your identity in the future as necessary.

To finish setting up a Hotmail user account:

1. Scroll down the Hotmail Registration Web page so the "Account Information" heading appears at the top of the browser window. See Figure 3-37.

Figure 3-37	SELECTING A SIGN-IN NAME

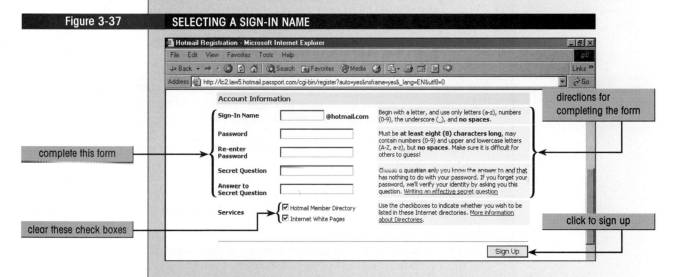

2. Click in the **Sign-In Name** text box, and then type a user name. You can use any sign-in name that you like, but it must be unique. You can try your first and last names, separated by an underscore character, followed optionally by your birth date or year of birth, such as sharon_kikukawa or sharon_kikukawa0922.

3. Press the **Tab** key, and then type a password. Make sure that your password contains at least eight characters. The most effective passwords are ones that aren't easily guessed and that contain letters and numbers. As you type your password, asterisks appear in the Password text box to protect your password from being seen by other users.

4. Press the **Tab** key, and then type your password again. Make sure to type letters in the same case; for example, media3456 and Media3456 are different passwords.

5. Press the **Tab** key, and then type a secret question. Try to ask a question to which only you know the answer, so another user couldn't easily answer your question.

6. Press the **Tab** key, and then type the answer to your secret question. Your answer must contain at least five characters.

7. In the Services section, click the **Hotmail Member Directory** and **Internet White Pages** check boxes to clear them.

8. Click the **Sign Up** button. If you selected a unique sign-in name, the Hotmail Sign Up Successful! page shown in Figure 3-38 opens.

Figure 3-38   HOTMAIL SIGN UP SUCCESSFUL! PAGE

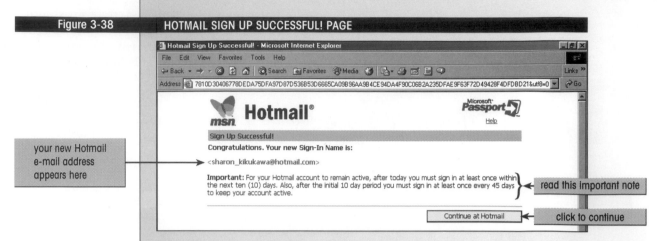

your new Hotmail
e-mail address
appears here

TROUBLE? If a page opens and tells you that the sign-in name that you selected is in use, click one of the suggested sign-in names or type another one in the text box, and then click the Submit New Sign-In Name button.

TROUBLE? If a Confirm dialog box opens and asks if you want to remember your logon, click the No button.

9. Read the information in the page before continuing, and then click the **Continue at Hotmail** button. A page opens describing the terms of use for a Hotmail account.

10. Read the Terms of Use page, and then click the **I Accept** button at the bottom of the page to agree to the terms of use. A Hotmail WebCourier Free Subscriptions page opens.

11. Without making any selections, scroll to the bottom of the page, and then click the **Continue** button. A Hotmail Special Offer Newsletters page opens.

12. Without making any selections, scroll to the bottom of the page, and then click the **Continue to E-mail** button. The Hotmail Home page opens. See Figure 3-39.

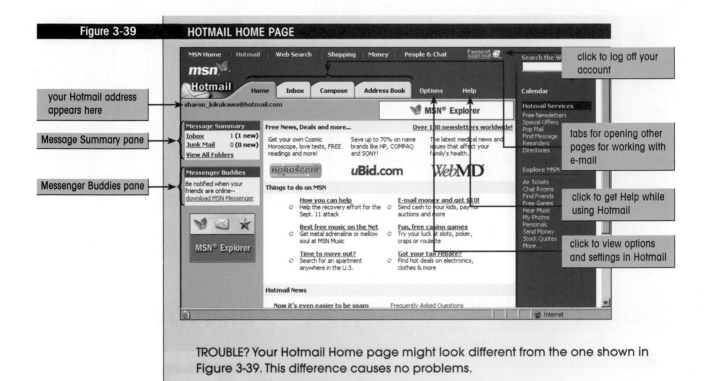

Figure 3-39 | HOTMAIL HOME PAGE

TROUBLE? Your Hotmail Home page might look different from the one shown in Figure 3-39. This difference causes no problems.

The Hotmail Home page shown in Figure 3-39 displays the Home, Inbox, Compose, and Address Book tabs. The **Home tab** shows a page with links to news, shopping opportunities, and general links to other MSN sites. In addition, the Home tab displays a **Message Summary pane**, which shows you how many messages are stored in the specified folders. Clicking a folder name or the View All Folders link opens that folder and displays its contents. The **Messenger Buddies pane** contains a link to download MSN Messenger, a service that alerts you when a specific Internet user name has logged on, so you can send an instant message to that user. When you download and use this service, you can send a message to a friend when he logs on to the Internet, and the message appears on his screen in a special window. This service lets you "chat" in real time, with the help of e-mail.

The **Inbox tab** displays a list of messages that you have received. "Hotmail Staff" will send a message to you with the subject "Welcome New Hotmail User!" or a similarly worded subject when you first access your Hotmail account. The **Compose tab** contains options for creating a new message by displaying the message header options (To, Cc, Bcc, and Subject). The **Address Book tab** contains options for managing your address book of contacts. You can click the Options and Help links to open pages containing program options and help for Hotmail users, respectively.

Now that you have created a Hotmail user account, you are ready to send a message to Sharon. *Note:* In this tutorial, you will send messages to a real mailbox with the address sharonkikukawa@yahoo.com. Follow the instructions carefully and use the correct address. Messages sent to this mailbox are deleted without being opened or read.

Sending a Message Using Hotmail

You are ready to use Hotmail to send a message with an attached file to Sharon. You will send a carbon copy of the message to your own e-mail address to make sure that the message and attached file are sent correctly.

REFERENCE WINDOW **RW**

Sending a Message Using Hotmail
- Open the Hotmail Home page, log on to your account, and then click the Compose tab.
- In the To text box, type the recipient's e-mail address. To send the message to more than one recipient, separate additional e-mail addresses with commas.
- Type the e-mail address of any Cc of Bcc recipients in the appropriate text boxes. Separate multiple recipients' e-mail addresses with commas.
- If necessary, click the Add/Edit Attachments button, click the Browse button to locate the file to attach, click the Attach button, and then click the OK button.
- In the message body, type your message.
- Check your message for spelling and grammatical errors.
- Click the Send button.

To send a message with an attachment:

1. Click the **Compose** tab. A blank message opens. See Figure 3-40.

Figure 3-40   HOTMAIL COMPOSE PAGE

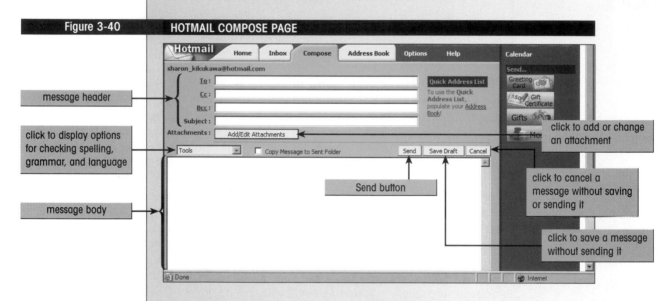

TROUBLE? Depending on the speed on your Internet connection, it might take a few seconds to open new pages. Check your browser's status bar to make sure that pages have fully loaded before using them.

2. In the To text box, type **sharonkikukawa@yahoo.com**, and then press the **Tab** key to move to the Cc text box.

TROUBLE? Make sure that you use the address sharonkikukawa@yahoo.com, instead of sharonkikukawa@kikukawa.com. If you type Sharon's e-mail address incorrectly, your message will be returned as undeliverable.

3. Type your full e-mail address in the Cc text box. When you send this message, you and Sharon will both receive copies.

TROUBLE? If you make a typing mistake on a previous line, use the arrow keys or click the insertion point to return to a previous line so you can correct your mistake. If the arrow keys do not move the insertion point backward or forward in the message header, press Shift + Tab or the Tab key to move backward or forward, respectively.

4. Press the **Tab** key twice to move the insertion point to the Subject text box, and then type **Test**.

5. Click the **Add/Edit Attachments** button. The Hotmail Attachments page opens. You can use Hotmail to send file attachments, but you are limited to a maximum file size of 1024 KB per message.

6. Make sure your Data Disk is in the appropriate drive, click the **Browse** button, and then use the **Look in** list arrow in the Choose file dialog box and select the drive that contains your Data Disk.

7. Double-click the **Tutorial.03** folder, double-click **Physicals**, click the **Attach** button and wait for the Physicals.wri file to appear in the Attachments box, and then click the **OK** button. The Hotmail Compose page now shows the attached file's name in the Attachments section.

8. Click the insertion point in the message display area, and then type **Please let me know when you receive this message and if you are able to view the attached file. I'm testing Hotmail and want to make sure that it is working properly.**

9. Press the **Enter** key twice, and then type your first and last names to sign your message. See Figure 3-41.

Figure 3-41	COMPLETED TEST MESSAGE

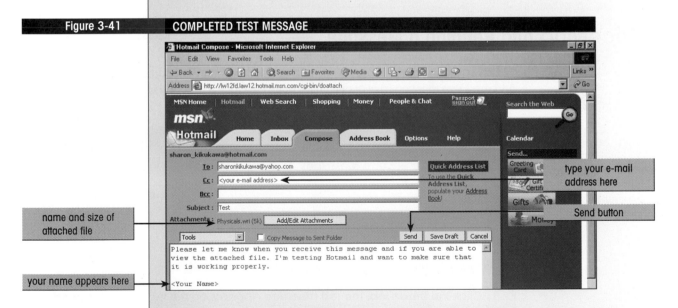

10. Click the **Tools** list arrow, and then click **Spell Check**. If necessary, correct any errors. If your message is free of spelling errors, no dialog box or other indicator will appear.

11. Click the **Send** button to mail the message. The Hotmail Sent Message Confirmation page opens and shows that your message has been sent. See Figure 3-42. Note that the delivery of the message that you sent to yourself might also appear on this screen, depending on how fast the delivery of your Hotmail is.

Figure 3-42   HOTMAIL SENT MESSAGE CONFIRMATION PAGE

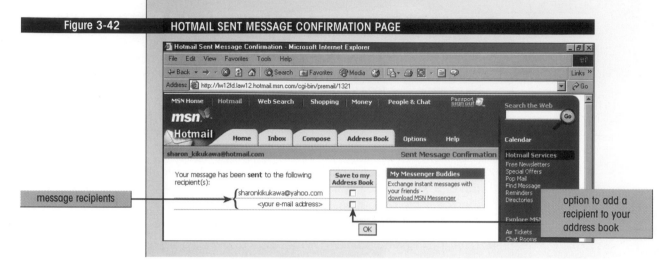

message recipients

option to add a recipient to your address book

Because the e-mail addresses that you used in your Test message do not appear in your Hotmail address book, Hotmail provides an option for you to add these addresses by selecting the check box(es) in the Save to my Address Book column. You will add addresses to the address book later, so no action is necessary now.

Receiving and Reading a Message

When you receive new mail, messages that you have not opened have closed envelope icons, and messages that you have opened have open envelope icons. You will check for new mail next.

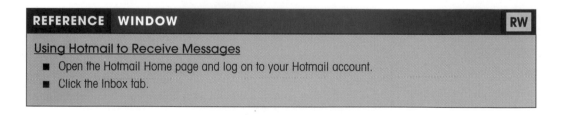

REFERENCE   WINDOW   RW

Using Hotmail to Receive Messages
- Open the Hotmail Home page and log on to your Hotmail account.
- Click the Inbox tab.

To check for incoming mail:

1. Click the **Inbox** tab. The Test message appears on the Inbox tab. The sender's name is formatted as a hyperlink. To read the message, you click the hyperlink.

2. Click the sender's name for the **Test** message. The Hotmail Folder: Inbox page opens and displays the Test message. See Figure 3-43.

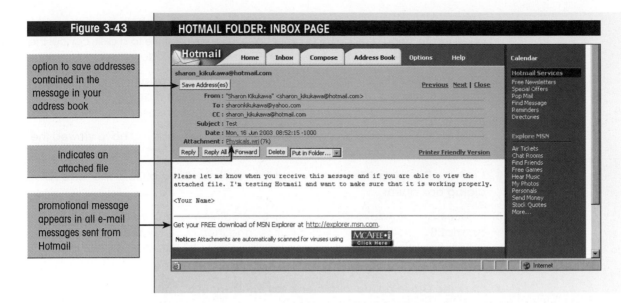

Figure 3-43   HOTMAIL FOLDER: INBOX PAGE

option to save addresses contained in the message in your address book

indicates an attached file

promotional message appears in all e-mail messages sent from Hotmail

You received your copy of the test message that you sent to Sharon. The filename in the Attachment section indicates that you received an attached file with the message. When you receive a message with one or more attachments, you can open the attachment or save it.

Viewing and Saving an Attached File

You want to make sure that your attached file was sent properly, so you decide to open it. Then you will save the file on your Data Disk.

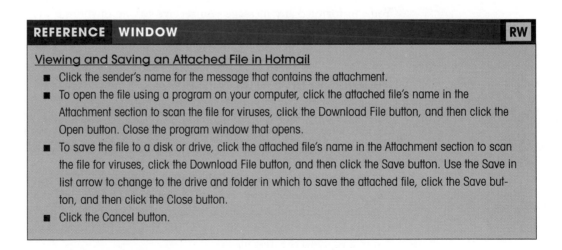

REFERENCE WINDOW   RW

Viewing and Saving an Attached File in Hotmail
- Click the sender's name for the message that contains the attachment.
- To open the file using a program on your computer, click the attached file's name in the Attachment section to scan the file for viruses, click the Download File button, and then click the Open button. Close the program window that opens.
- To save the file to a disk or drive, click the attached file's name in the Attachment section to scan the file for viruses, click the Download File button, and then click the Save button. Use the Save in list arrow to change to the drive and folder in which to save the attached file, click the Save button, and then click the Close button.
- Click the Cancel button.

To view and save the attached file:

1. Click the **Physicals.wri** link in the Attachment section. Hotmail automatically scans the file for viruses to protect your computer. A message appears indicating that no virus was found in the file.

   TROUBLE? If Hotmail finds a virus in the file, follow the instructions on the screen to continue.

2. Click the **Download File** button. The File Download dialog box opens. You can open the file using a program on your computer, save the file to a disk, cancel the download, or click the More Info button to open a Help window for your browser.

3. Click the **Open** button, and then click the **Open** button again. WordPad or another text editor program on your computer starts and opens the attached file. If necessary, maximize the program window that opens.

4. Click the **Close** button on the program window. Now that you have viewed the attachment, you can save it on your Data Disk.

5. Click the **Download File** button, and then click the **Save** button. The Save As dialog box opens.

6. If necessary, browse to locate the drive containing your Data Disk, open the **Tutorial.03** folder, click the **Save** button, and then click the **Yes** button to over-write the existing file with the same name on your Data Disk. The Download complete dialog box opens when the file has been transferred.

7. Click the **Close** button, and then click the **Cancel** button.

When you receive a message with an attached file, you can view and save the attachment for as long as you store the message. When you delete the message, you will delete the file attached to the message. However, because you saved the attachment on your Data Disk, the file exists there for as long as you need it.

Replying to and Forwarding Messages

You can forward any message you receive to one or more e-mail addresses. Similarly, you can respond to the sender of a message quickly and efficiently by replying to a message. Replying to and forwarding messages are common tasks for e-mail users.

Replying to an E-Mail Message

To reply to a message, click the Reply button to reply only to the sender, or click the Reply All button to reply to the sender and other people who received the original message (those e-mail addresses listed in the To and Cc text boxes). Hotmail will open the Hotmail Reply page and place the original sender's address in the To text box; other e-mail addresses that received the original message will appear in the To and Cc text boxes as appropriate. You can leave the Subject text box as is or modify it. Most programs, including Hotmail, will copy the original message and place it in the response window. A > (greater than) symbol appears to the left of the response to indicate the text of the original message. Figure 3-44 shows a reply to the Test message.

| Figure 3-44 | **REPLYING TO A MESSAGE** |

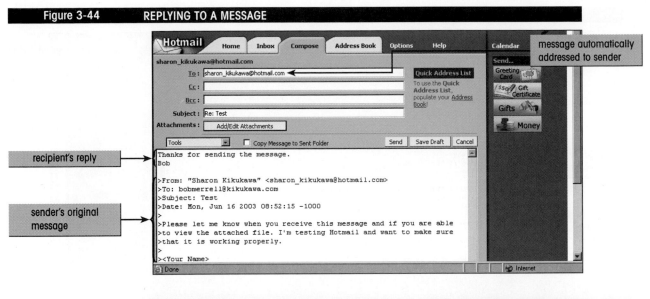

recipient's reply

sender's original message

REFERENCE WINDOW   **RW**

Replying to a Message Using Hotmail

- Open the message to which you want to reply.
- Click the Reply button to reply only to the sender, or click the Reply All button to reply to the sender and other "To" and "Cc" recipients of the original message.
- Type other recipients' e-mail addresses in the message header as needed.
- Change the text in the Subject box if necessary.
- Edit the message body as necessary.
- Click the Send button.

Forwarding an E-Mail Message

When you forward a message, you are sending a copy of your message to one or more recipients who were not included in the original message. To forward an existing mail message to another user, open the message you want to forward, and then click the Forward button. The Hotmail Forward page opens, where you can type the address of the recipient in the To text box. If you want to forward the message to several people, type their addresses, separated by commas, in the To text box (or Cc or Bcc text boxes). Hotmail inserts a copy of the original message in the message display area (as it does when you reply to a message) with a > mark to its left. Figure 3-45 shows a forwarded copy of the Test message.

Figure 3-45   FORWARDING A MESSAGE

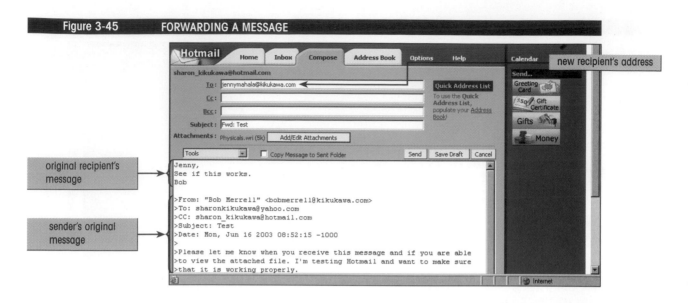

original recipient's message

sender's original message

new recipient's address

REFERENCE WINDOW   RW

Forwarding an E-Mail Message Using Hotmail
- Open the message that you want to forward.
- Click the Forward button.
- Click in the To text box, and then type one or more e-mail addresses, separated by commas. Add Cc and Bcc e-mail addresses as necessary.
- Click the blank line above the quoted message, and then type an optional message to add a context for the recipient(s).
- Click the Send button.

Occasionally, you will receive important messages, so you want to make sure that you can print and file them as needed.

Filing and Printing an E-Mail Message

You can use the Hotmail folders to file your e-mail messages by category. When you file a message, you move it to another folder. You will file Sharon's message in a new folder named "FAA" for safekeeping. Later, you can create other folders to suit your style and working situation.

To create the new folder:

1. Click the **Home** tab, and then click the **View All Folders** link in the Message Summary pane. The Hotmail Folders page opens. See Figure 3-46.

| Figure 3-46 | HOTMAIL FOLDERS PAGE |

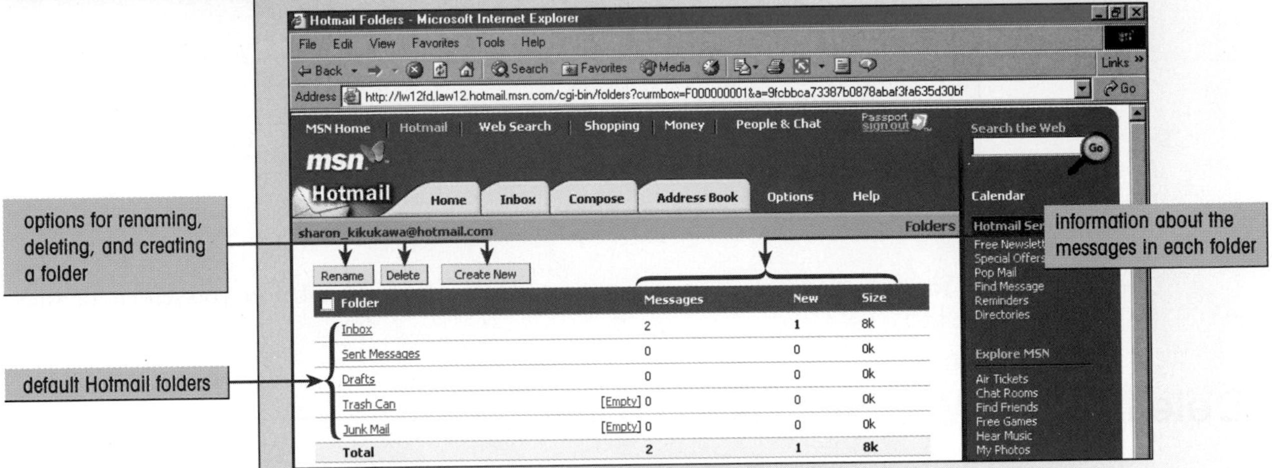

options for renaming, deleting, and creating a folder

information about the messages in each folder

default Hotmail folders

By default, Hotmail includes five folders: Inbox stores your new messages, Sent Messages stores messages that you have sent when you set it to do so, Drafts stores messages that you have written and saved but have not yet sent, Trash Can stores messages that you have deleted, and Junk Mail stores e-mail messages from senders that you specify as bulk mailers, advertisers, or any site from which you don't want to receive mail.

2. Click the **Create New** button. The Hotmail Create New Folder page opens.

3. With the insertion point in the New Folder Name text box, type **FAA**, and then click the **OK** button. The FAA folder appears in the list of folders.

4. Click the **Inbox** tab.

After you create the FAA folder, you can transfer messages to it. Besides transferring mail from the Inbox folder, you can select messages in any other folder and then transfer them to another folder.

To file the Test message:

1. Click the sender's name for the **Test** message to open it.

2. Click the **Put in Folder** list arrow, and then click **FAA**. After a moment, the message is transferred to the FAA folder.

3. Click the **Inbox** tab, and then click the **FAA** folder in the list of folders. The Test message is transferred to the FAA folder.

You will print the message before deleting it.

To print the e-mail message:

1. Click the **Inbox** tab, click the **FAA** folder in the list of folders, and then click the sender's name for the **Test** message to open it.

> **2.** Click the **Printer Friendly Version** link. A new page opens, displaying only the message.
>
> **3.** Click the **Print** button on the browser's toolbar. The message is printed.
>
> TROUBLE? Depending on how your printer is set up, a Print dialog box might open. If so, click the OK or Print button to print the message.
>
> **4.** Click the **Inbox** link to return to the Inbox tab.

You can print a message at any time—when you receive it, before you send it, or after you file it.

Deleting an E-Mail Message and Folder

When you don't need a message any longer, you can delete it by opening the message and clicking the Delete button. You can delete a folder by selecting it on the Hotmail Folders page and then clicking the Delete button. When you delete a message, you are simply moving it to the Trash Can folder; when you delete a folder you send the folder and its contents to the Trash Can folder. To remove items permanently, you must also delete them from the Trash Can folder.

REFERENCE WINDOW   **RW**

Deleting an E-Mail Message Using Hotmail
- Open the folder that contains the message you want to delete, click the check box to the left of the message to select it, and then click the Delete button.
- To delete items permanently, open the Trash Can folder, click the Empty Folder button, and then click the OK button.

To delete the message:

1. Click the **FAA** folder in the list of folders.

2. Click the **check box** to the left of the Test message. This action selects the message.

3. Click the **Delete** button. The message is deleted from the FAA folder and is moved to the Trash Can folder.

4. Click the **Trash Can** folder in the list of folders. The Test message appears in the folder.

5. Click the **Empty Folder** button, and then click the **OK** button. All messages are deleted from the Trash Can folder.

To delete the FAA folder, you must open the Hotmail Folders page.

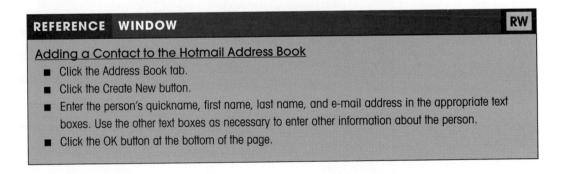

REFERENCE WINDOW   **RW**

Deleting a Hotmail Folder
■ Click the Manage Folders button on the Inbox tab.
■ Click the check box to the left of the folder that you want to delete.
■ Click the Delete button twice.

To delete the FAA folder:

1. Click the **Manage Folders** button to open the Hotmail Folders page. The values of zero in the Messages, New, and Size columns all indicate that this folder is empty.

2. Click the **check box** to the left of the FAA folder to select it, click the **Delete** button, and then click the **Delete** button again. The FAA folder is permanently deleted from Hotmail.

Maintaining an Address Book

As you use e-mail to communicate with business associates and friends, you will want to save their addresses in an address book to make it easier to address your messages.

Adding a Contact to the Address Book

You can open the Hotmail address book by clicking the Address Book tab. To create a new address, you open the address book, click the Create New button, and then use the text boxes to enter a person's information. Each individual address must have a quickname (nickname), a first and last name, and an e-mail address; the rest of the information is optional.

REFERENCE WINDOW   **RW**

Adding a Contact to the Hotmail Address Book
■ Click the Address Book tab.
■ Click the Create New button.
■ Enter the person's quickname, first name, last name, and e-mail address in the appropriate text boxes. Use the other text boxes as necessary to enter other information about the person.
■ Click the OK button at the bottom of the page.

You are eager to add information to your address book. You'll begin by adding Sharon Kikukawa's contact information to your address book.

To add a contact to your address book:

1. Click the **Address Book** tab. The Hotmail Address Book page opens.

2. Click the **Create New** button. The Hotmail Create New Individual page opens. At a minimum, you need to enter a quickname for the person, as well as the person's first and last names and e-mail address. Other information on this page is optional.

3. With the insertion point in the Quickname text box, type **Sharon**.

4. Press the **Tab** key to move the insertion point to the First text box, type **Sharon**, press the **Tab** key to move the insertion point to the Last text box, and then type **Kikukawa**.

5. Click the **Business** option button in the E-mail Address section, press the **Tab** key, and then type **sharonkikukawa@yahoo.com**. Sharon's contact is complete. See Figure 3-47.

Figure 3-47   **HOTMAIL CREATE NEW INDIVIDUAL PAGE**

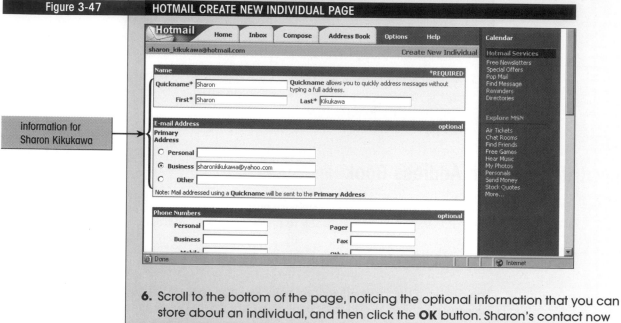

information for
Sharon Kikukawa

6. Scroll to the bottom of the page, noticing the optional information that you can store about an individual, and then click the **OK** button. Sharon's contact now appears in the address book.

7. Repeat Steps 2 through 6 to create new contacts for the following Kikukawa Air employees:

Quickname	First	Last	Business e-mail address
Chris	**Chris**	**Breed**	**chrisbreed@kikukawa.com**
Jen	**Jenny**	**Mahala**	**jennymahala@kikukawa.com**
Rich	**Richard**	**Forrester**	**richardforrester@kikukawa.com**

8. When you are finished entering the contacts, click the **Compose** tab. The quicknames for contacts stored in the address book appear in the Quick Address List.

Now that these e-mail addresses are stored in the address book, you can click a quickname in the Quick Address List to enter it into a text box in the message header.

When you send mail to someone who is not in your address book, the Hotmail Sent Message Confirmation page will include a Save to my Address Book check box for that address. Clicking the check box for a new contact and then clicking the OK button opens the Hotmail Save Address page, where you can add the person's quickname and first and last names to the address book.

Adding a Group to the Address Book

You can use Hotmail to create a **group**, or a mailing list, which is an address book entry consisting of more than one e-mail address. Usually you create a group when you regularly send messages to a group of people.

Sharon frequently sends messages to each member of the maintenance department. She asks you to create a group of contacts in her address book so she can type one quickname for the group of e-mail addresses, instead of having to type each address separately.

REFERENCE WINDOW **RW**

Adding a Group to the Hotmail Address Book

- Click the Address Book tab.
- Click the Groups tab, and then click the Create New button.
- Type a group name for the group in the Group Name text box.
- Click in the Group Members list box, type the e-mail address for the first group member, type a comma, and continue adding names to the group until you have entered the e-mail addresses for all group members.
- Click the OK button.

To add a group to your address book:

1. Click the **Address Book** tab, and then click the **Groups** tab.

2. Click the **Create New** button. The Hotmail Create New Group page opens. On this page, you enter the group name and enter the individual e-mail addresses for members of the group. To separate individual e-mail addresses, press the spacebar or type a comma.

3. Click in the **Group Name** text box, and then type **Maintenance**. This quickname will represent the individual e-mail addresses of members of the maintenance department.

4. Press the **Tab** key to move the insertion point to the Group Members list box, and then type **chrisbreed@kikukawa.com**. Chris is the first member of the group.

5. Type a **comma**, press the **spacebar**, and then type **jennymahala@kikukawa.com**.

6. Type a **comma**, press the **spacebar**, and then type **richardforrester@kikukawa.com**. The group now contains three e-mail addresses.

7. Click the **OK** button. The Hotmail Address Book page now shows the quickname for the group and the e-mail addresses of its group members. See Figure 3-48.

Figure 3-48   **HOTMAIL ADDRESS BOOK PAGE**

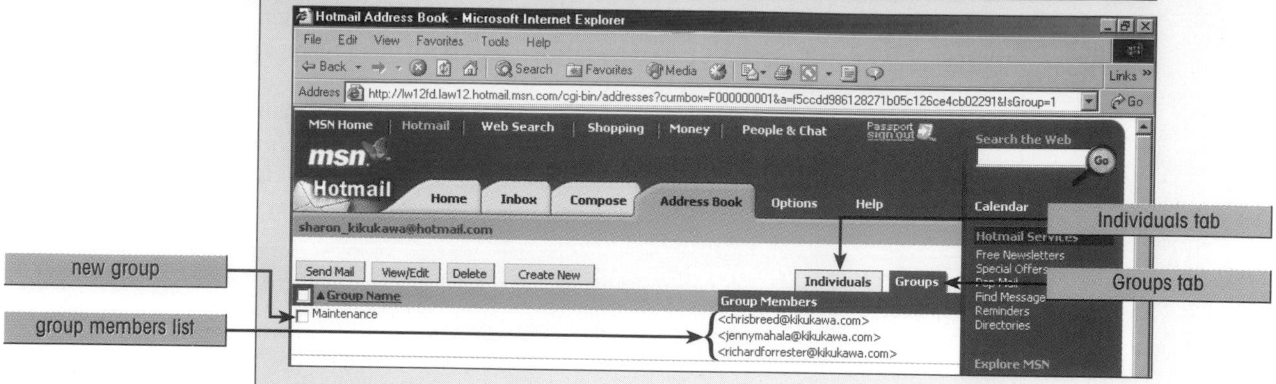

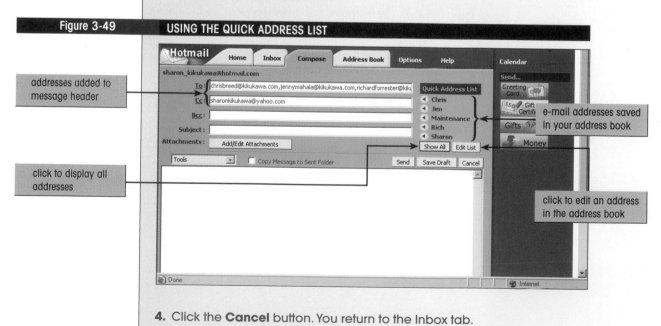

new group

group members list

Individuals tab

Groups tab

8. Click the **Compose** tab. The Maintenance group appears in the Quick Address List.

Now, test the new group by creating a new message.

To address a message to a group:

1. Click in the **To** text box to select it, and then click the **Maintenance** entry in the Quick Address List. Hotmail adds the individual e-mail addresses from the Maintenance group to the To text box.

When your Quick Address List contains many names, you'll need to use the Show All button to view the entire list.

2. Click the **Show All** button below the Quick Address List. The Insert Addresses window opens.

3. Click the **Cc** check box for Sharon, and then click the **OK** button. Hotmail closes the Insert Addresses window and adds Sharon's e-mail address to the Cc text box. See Figure 3-49.

Figure 3-49   **USING THE QUICK ADDRESS LIST**

addresses added to message header

click to display all addresses

e-mail addresses saved in your address book

click to edit an address in the address book

4. Click the **Cancel** button. You return to the Inbox tab.

When you need to modify a group's members, you can delete one or more members from the group by opening the address book, clicking the check box to the left of the group name, and then clicking the View/Edit button, which opens the Hotmail View/Edit Group page, where you can make changes to the group.

You are finished evaluating Hotmail, so you need to log off your Hotmail account and close your browser. It is important that you log off before closing the browser to ensure the security of your e-mail and to prevent unauthorized access.

To log off Hotmail and close your browser:

1. Click the **Passport sign out** link at the top of the page. A Hotmail page opens while your account is logged off, and then the MSN.com home page opens. To log back onto your Hotmail account, click the Hotmail link on the MSN.com home page, type your hotmail sign-in name in the Sign-In Name text box, type your password in the Password text box, and then click the Sign in button.

2. Click the **Close** button on your browser's title bar to close the browser.

3. If necessary, log off your Internet connection.

Session 3.4 QUICK CHECK

1. To set up a Hotmail account, what information must you provide to MSN.com?

2. True or False: If you are using a computer in a public library to access your Hotmail, you should log off your account when you are finished viewing your messages to protect your privacy.

3. Does Hotmail queue a message or send it right away?

4. When you receive a message with an attachment, what two options are available for the attached file?

5. When you delete a message from the Inbox, can you recover that message? Why or why not?

6. What information can you store about a person using the Hotmail address book?

Now you are ready to complete the Review Assignments using the e-mail program of your choice.

REVIEW ASSIGNMENT

Now that you have learned about different types of e-mail programs, Sharon asks you to submit a recommendation about which program to use for Kikukawa Air. Sharon also wants to see how graphics are sent over the Internet, so she asks you to send her the Kikukawa Air logo to simulate how it will appear when sent by Kikukawa employees. To evaluate e-mail alternatives for Sharon, complete the following steps.

1. Start your e-mail program or log on to your Hotmail account.

2. Add your instructor's full name and e-mail address to the address book. Create an appropriate nickname that will be easy for you to remember.

3. Add a mailing list to the address book using the full names and e-mail addresses of three of your classmates. Create appropriate nicknames for each person.

4. Create a new message. Use nicknames to send the message to Sharon and to your instructor. Send a carbon copy of the message to yourself, and use the mailing list address you created to send a blind carbon copy of the message to your classmates. Use the subject "E-mail Recommendation" for the message.

Explore

5. In the message body, type three or more sentences describing your overall impressions about the different e-mail alternatives you have explored. Recommend the program that Kikukawa Air should use based on the program's features, ease of use, and other important considerations that you determine.

6. In the message body, press the Enter key twice, and then type your full name and e-mail address on separate lines.

7. Attach the file named **KAir.gif** from the Tutorial.03 folder on your Data Disk to the message.

8. Check your spelling before you send the message and correct any mistakes. Proofread your message and verify that you have created it correctly, and then send the message.

9. Wait about 30 seconds, check for new mail (and enter your password, if necessary), and then open the message you sent to Sharon and your instructor. Print the message.

Explore

10. In a new message addressed only to your instructor, describe the appearance of the file you attached to the message. Use the subject "Attached Graphics File" and in the message body, explain your findings in terms of attaching a graphic to an e-mail message. Send the message.

Explore

11. Permanently delete the messages you received and *sent* from your e-mail program. (*Hint:* Delete messages from the folder where you receive messages and also from the folder that stores a copy of all sent messages. Make sure to delete messages from the folder that stores your deleted messages, as well.)

12. Exit your e-mail program. If necessary, log off your Internet connection.

CASE PROBLEMS

Case 1. Grand American Appraisal Company You are the office manager for Grand American Appraisal Company, which is a national real-estate appraisal company with its corporate headquarters in Los Angeles. Grand American handles real-estate appraisal requests from all over the United States and maintains a large list of approved real-estate appraisers located throughout the country. When an appraisal request is phoned into any regional office, an office staff member phones or faxes the national office to start the appraisal process. The appraisal order desk in Los Angeles receives the request and is responsible for locating a real-estate appraiser in the community in which the property to be appraised is located. After the Los Angeles office identifies and contacts an appraiser by phone, the appraiser has two days to perform the appraisal and either phone or fax the regional office with a preliminary estimate of value for the property. The entire process of phoning the regional office and then phoning or faxing the national office is both cumbersome and expensive.

Your supervisor asks you to use your e-mail program to set up an account for yourself so you can use e-mail for the appraisal requests instead of the current fax system. You will create a signature file to attach to your messages to identify your name, city, e-mail address, and appraiser license number by completing the following steps.

1. Start your e-mail program or log on to your Hotmail account.

2. Obtain the e-mail address of a classmate, who will assume the role of the Los Angeles order desk. Add your classmate's full name, nickname, and e-mail address to the address book.

3. If necessary, add your instructor's full name, nickname, and e-mail address to the address book.

4. Use your classmate's nickname to address a new message to him or her. Type your e-mail address and your instructor's nickname on the Cc line, and then type "Request for appraisal" on the Subject line.

5. Type a short message that requests the assignment of an appraiser. Include your street address and the request date in the message.

Explore ▶ 6. Use the Help system to learn how to create a signature file with your first and last names on the first line, your city and state on the second line, your e-mail address on the third line, and "License number" plus any six-digit number on the fourth line. (*Hint:* If you are using Outlook Express, search Help using the Index tab for "signatures, personal" and then follow the directions. Do not select the option to attach your signature to all outgoing messages. If you are using Mail, use WordPad or another text editor to create a signature file, and then save the file as **signature.txt** (make sure that you save it as a text file) in the Tutorial.03 folder on your Data Disk. Use the Account Settings dialog box to attach your signature file to outgoing messages. If you are using Hotmail, click the Options link to learn how to create a signature file.)

Explore ▶ 7. Include your signature file in the new message. (*Hint:* In Outlook Express, click Insert on the menu bar, and then click Signature. Mail and Hotmail will attach your signature file automatically.)

8. Send the message, wait a few seconds, and then retrieve your messages from the server. Print the message you sent to your classmate.

Explore ▶ 9. Permanently delete the message you received and *sent* from your e-mail program. (*Hint:* Delete the message from the folder where you receive messages and also from the folder that stores a copy of all sent messages. Make sure to delete messages from the folder that stores your deleted messages, as well.)

Explore ▶ 10. If you are using Outlook Express or Mail, delete your signature file. (*Hint:* In Outlook Express, select your signature on the Signatures tab in the Options dialog box, and then click the Remove button. In Mail, use the Account Settings dialog box to remove the path to your signature file.)

11. Exit your e-mail program. If necessary, log off your Internet connection.

Case 2. Bridgefield Engineering Company Bridgefield Engineering Company (BECO) is a small engineering firm in Somerville, New Jersey, that manufactures and distributes heavy industrial machinery for factories worldwide. Because BECO has difficulties reaching its customers around the world in different time zones, the company has installed an e-mail system to facilitate contact between BECO employees and their customers. As the president's assistant, your first task is to send a test message to several managers to ensure that the new system is working correctly. You will create and send the message by completing the following steps.

1. Start your e-mail program or log on to your Hotmail account.

2. Add to your address book the full name, nickname, and e-mail address of your instructor and two classmates.

3. Create a mailing list for the two classmates you added to the address book in Step 2 using the nickname "managers."

4. Create a new message addressed to your instructor. On the Cc line, enter the mailing list nickname you added to the address book in Step 3. On the Bcc line, enter your e-mail address. Use the subject "Testing new BECO e-mail system."

5. In the message display area, type a short note telling the recipients that you are conducting a test of the new e-mail system and asking them to respond to you when they receive your message. Sign your message with your first and last names.

6. Send the message, wait a few seconds, and then retrieve your messages from the server. Print the message you sent to your instructor.

Explore ▶ 7. If you are using Outlook Express or Mail, save the message in the Tutorial.03 folder on your Data Disk, using the message's subject as the filename. Choose the option to save the file in HTML format.

8. Create a mail folder or mailbox named BECO, and then file the message you received in the BECO folder.

Explore ▶ 9. Permanently delete the message you received and *sent* from your e-mail program and the BECO folder. (*Hint:* Delete the folder and message, delete the message you sent from the folder that stores sent messages, and then empty the folder that stores deleted items.)

10. Exit your e-mail program. If necessary, log off your Internet connection.

Case 3. Recycling Awareness Campaign You are an assistant in the Mayor's office in Cleveland, Ohio. The mayor has asked you to help with the recycling awareness campaign. Your job is to use e-mail to increase awareness of the recycling centers throughout the city and to encourage Cleveland's citizens and businesses to participate in the program. You will send an e-mail message to members of the city's chamber of commerce with an invitation to help increase awareness of the program by forwarding your message and its attached file to their employees and colleagues by completing the following steps.

1. Start your e-mail program or log on to your Hotmail account.

2. Add the full names, e-mail addresses, and nicknames of five classmates to your address book to act as chamber of commerce members. After creating individual entries in the address book for your classmates, add them to a mailing list named "Chamber" in your address book. Then add the full name, e-mail address, and nickname of your instructor to your address book.

3. Create a new message and address it to the Chamber mailing list. Add your instructor's nickname to the Cc line and your e-mail address to the Bcc line. Use the subject "Recycling campaign for businesses—please get the word out!"

Explore ▶ 4. Write a two- or three-line message urging the chamber members to promote the city's new business recycling campaign by forwarding your message and the attached file to local businesses. Make sure to thank them for their efforts on behalf of the Mayor's office.

5. Attach the file named **Recycle.wri** located in the Tutorial.03 folder on your Data Disk to the message.

Explore 6. Use the Help system in your e-mail program to learn how to create and use a signature file. Your signature should include your full name on the first line, the title "Assistant to the Mayor" on the second line, and your e-mail address on the third line. (*Hint:* If you are using Outlook Express, search Help using the Index tab for "signatures, personal" and then follow the directions. Do not select the option to attach your signature to all outgoing messages. If you are using Mail, use WordPad or another text editor to create a signature file, and then save the file as **signature.txt** (make sure that you save it as a text file) in the Tutorial.03 folder on your Data Disk. Use the Account Settings dialog box to attach your signature file to outgoing messages. If you are using Hotmail, click the Options link to learn how to create a signature file.)

Explore 7. Include your signature file in the new message. (*Hint:* In Outlook Express, click Insert on the menu bar, and then click Signature. Mail and Hotmail will attach your signature file automatically.)

8. Proofread and spell check your message, and then send your message. After a few moments, retrieve your e-mail message from the server and print it.

9. Forward the message to one of the classmates in your address book. Add a short message to the forwarded message that asks the recipient to forward the message to appropriate business leaders per your program objectives.

Explore 10. Save a *copy* of your message in a new subfolder of the Inbox named Recycling, and then delete the message from the Inbox.

Explore 11. Permanently delete the message you received and *sent* from your e-mail program and the Recycling folder. (*Hint:* Delete the folder and message, delete the message you sent from the folder that stores sent messages, and then empty the folder that stores deleted items.)

Explore 12. If you are using Outlook Express or Mail, delete your signature file. (*Hint:* In Outlook Express, select your signature on the Signatures tab in the Options dialog box, and then click the Remove button. In Mail, use the Account Settings dialog box to remove the path to your signature file.)

13. Exit your e-mail program. If necessary, log off your Internet connection.

Case 4. Student Study Group In two weeks, you have a final exam, and you want to organize a study group with your classmates. Everyone in your class has an e-mail account on the university's computer. You want to contact some classmates to find out when they might be available to get together in the next week to study for the exam. To create a study group, you'll complete the following steps.

1. Start your e-mail program or log on to your Hotmail account.

2. Obtain the e-mail addresses of at least four classmates, and then enter them on the To line of a new message. On the Cc line, enter your e-mail address, and then on the Bcc line, enter your instructor's e-mail address. Do *not* add these names to your address book.

3. Use the subject "Study Group" for the message. In the message body, tell your classmates about the study group by providing possible meeting times and locations. Ask recipients to respond to you through e-mail by a specified date if they are interested. Sign the message with your full name and e-mail address.

4. Proofread and spell check your message, and then send your message. After a few moments, retrieve your e-mail message from the server and open it.

Explore 5. Add each address on the To and Bcc lines to your address book.

Explore 6. Create a new "study group" mailing list using the addresses you added to your address book in Step 5. Then forward a copy of your message to the study group mailing list.

7. Send your message. After a few moments, retrieve your e-mail message from the server and print it.

Explore   8. Permanently delete the messages you received and *sent* from your e-mail program. (*Hint:* Delete the messages from the Inbox, delete the message you sent from the folder that stores sent messages, and then empty the folder that stores deleted items.)

9. Exit your e-mail program. If necessary, log off your Internet connection.

Case 5. Murphy's Market Research Services You work part-time for Murphy's Market Research Services, a company that surveys students about various topics of interest to college students. A local music store, CD Rocks, wants you to send a short survey via e-mail to students at your university to learn more about student-buying habits for music CDs. You need to find out the names of three of their favorite music CDs, where they prefer to shop for music CDs, and how much time they spend each day listening to music. You will create the survey using any word-processing program, such as Microsoft Word, WordPad, or WordPerfect, and then you'll attach the survey to your e-mail message. You need to receive the survey results within three weeks, so you'll ask the respondents to return the survey via e-mail within that time period. You will create and send the survey by completing the following steps.

1. Using any word-processing program, create a new document named **Survey** with the program's default filename extension in the Tutorial.03 folder on your Data Disk.

2. Create the survey by typing the following questions (separate each question with two blank lines) in the new document:
   a. What are the titles of your three favorite music CDs?
   b. Where is the best place (online or bricks-and-mortar) to shop for music CDs?
   c. Approximately how much time per day do you spend listening to music?

3. At the bottom of the document, type a sentence that thanks respondents for their time, and then on a new line, type your first and last names. Save the document, and then close your word-processing program.

4. Start your e-mail program or log on to your Hotmail account.

5. Obtain the e-mail addresses of three classmates, and then enter them on the To line of a new message. On the Cc line, enter your e-mail address, and then on the Bcc line, enter your instructor's e-mail address. Do *not* add these names to your address book.

6. Use the subject "Music Survey" for the message. In the message body, ask recipients to open the attached file and to complete the survey by typing their responses into the document. Make sure that recipients understand that you need them to return the survey within three weeks. As an incentive for completing the survey, ask recipients to return the survey via e-mail but to print their completed survey and bring it to their local CD Rocks outlet for a $2 discount on any purchase. Sign the message with your full name, the company name (Murphy's Market Research Services), and your e-mail address.

7. Attach the survey to your e-mail message, and then send the message. After a few moments, retrieve your e-mail message from the server.

Explore   8. Open the attached file, and then complete the survey. Before saving the file, use your word-processing program's Print command to print the document.

Explore   9. In your word-processing program, click File on the menu bar, and then click Save As. Navigate to the Tutorial.03 folder on your Data Disk, and then save the file as **Completed Survey**, using the program's default filename extension. Close your word-processing program.

10. Forward the message to your instructor, attach the **Completed Survey** file to the message, make sure that the original message text appears in the message body, type a short introduction (such as "Here is my completed survey."), sign your message with your full name and e-mail address, and then send the message.

Explore

11. Permanently delete the messages you received and *sent* from your e-mail program. (*Hint:* Delete the messages from the Inbox, delete the message you sent from the folder that stores sent messages, and then empty the folder that stores deleted items.)

12. Exit your e-mail program. If necessary, log off your Internet connection.

E-mail

LAB ASSIGNMENTS

E-Mail E-mail that originates on a local area network with a mail gateway can travel all over the world. That's why it is so important to learn how to use it. In this Lab, you will use an e-mail simulator, so even if your school's computers don't provide you with e-mail service, you will learn the basics of reading, sending, and replying to electronic mail. See the Read This Before You Begin page for information on installing and starting this Lab.

1. Click the Steps button to learn how to work with e-mail. As you proceed through the Steps, answer all of the Quick Check questions that appear. After you complete the Steps, you will see a Quick Check summary report. Follow the instructions on the screen to print this report.

2. Click the Explore button. Write a message to re@films.org. The subject of the message is "Picks and Pans." In the body of your message, describe a movie you have recently seen. Include the name of the movie, briefly summarize the plot, and give it a thumbs up or a thumbs down. Print the message before you send it.

3. Look in your In Basket for a message from jb@music.org. Read the message, then compose a reply indicating that you will attend. Carbon copy mciccone@music.org. Print your reply, including the text of JB's original message before you send it.

4. Look in your In Basket for a message from leo@sports.org. Reply to the message by adding your rating to the text of the original message as follows:

Equipment:	Your rating:
Rollerblades	2
Skis	3
Bicycle	1
Scuba gear	4
Snowmobile	5

Print your reply before you send it.

5. Go into the lab with a partner. You should each log on to the E-mail Lab on different computers. Look at the Addresses list to find the user ID for your partner. You should each send a short e-mail message to your partner. Then, you should check your mail message from your partner. Read the message and compose a reply. Print your reply before you send it. *Note:* Unlike a full-featured mail system, the e-mail simulator does not save mail in mailboxes after you log off.

QUICK | CHECK ANSWERS

Session 3.1

1. True

2. protocols

3. header, body

4. Type a comma or semicolon between e-mail addresses.

5. False

6. Yes; you can attach the Word document file to an e-mail message.

7. The account name (or user name) identifies a specific individual and a computer name (or host name) identifies the computer on which that individual's account is stored.

8. By deleting unnecessary messages, you clear space on the drive or server on which your e-mail messages are stored.

9. A group mailing list is a single nickname that represents two or more individual e-mail addresses.

Session 3.2

1. Drafts

2. True

3. Outlook Express holds messages that are queued until you connect to your ISP and click the Send/Recv button on the toolbar.

4. You can view the attached file if your computer has a program that can open it, or you can save the attached file on your computer.

5. Yes, you can recover the message because it is stored in the Deleted Items folder.

6. name, e-mail address, nickname, address, business information, personal information, and so on.

Session 3.3

1. Drafts

2. False

3. Mail holds messages that are queued until you connect to your ISP and click the Send button on the toolbar.

4. You can view the attached file if your computer has a program that can open it, you can save the attached file on your computer, and you can save all attached files on your computer at once.

5. Yes, you can recover the message because it is stored in the Trash folder.

6. name, e-mail address, nickname, address, phone numbers, notes, and so on

Session 3.4

1. Your name, preferred language, country, state, zip code, time zone, gender, birthday, and occupation; you must also submit a unique sign-in name, a password, and a secret question and answer.

2. True

3. Hotmail sends messages right away because all work is completed with a live Internet connection.

4. You can view the attached file if your computer has a program that can open it, or you can save the attached file on your computer.

5. Yes, you can recover the message because it is stored in the Trash Can folder.

6. name, e-mail address, quickname, address, business information, personal information, and so on.

New Perspectives on

THE
INTERNET

3rd Edition

Read This Before You Begin

To the Student

Data Disks

To complete the Level II tutorials, Review Assignments, and Case Problems in this book, you need one Data Disk. Your instructor will either provide you with a Data Disk or ask you to make your own. You will also need to create a Tutorial.06 folder on your computer's hard drive or a personal network drive. In Tutorial 6, you will download several files and programs to your folder. Because the size of these files exceeds the amount of space on a floppy disk, you must download the files to another drive.

If you are making your own Data Disk, you will need **one** blank, formatted, high-density disk. You will need to copy a set of files and/or folders from a file server, a standalone computer, or the Web onto your disk. Your instructor will tell you which computer, drive letter, and folders contain the files you need. You could also download the files by going to **www.course.com** and following the instructions on the screen.

The information below shows you which folders go on your disks, so that you will have enough disk space to complete all the tutorials, Review Assignments, and Case Problems:

Data Disk 3

Write this on the disk label:
Data Disk 3: Tutorial 6

Put this folder on the disk:
Tutorial.06

Refer to the "File Finder" chart at the back of this text for more detailed information on which files are used in the tutorials. See the inside front or inside back cover of this book for more information on Data Disk files, or ask your instructor or technical support person for assistance.

Using Your Own Computer

If you are going to work through this book using your own computer, you need:

■ **Computer System** Netscape Navigator 4.0 or higher or Microsoft Internet Explorer 4.0 or higher and Windows 95 or higher must be installed on your computer. This book assumes a complete installation of the Web browser software and its components, and that you have an existing e-mail account and an Internet connection. Because your Web browser may be different from the ones used in the figures or the book, your screens may differ slightly at times.

■ **Data Disks** You will not be able to complete the tutorials or exercises in this book using your own computer until you have a Data Disk.

Visit Our World Wide Web Site

Additional materials designed especially for you are available on the World Wide Web.
Go to www.course.com/NewPerspectives.

To the Instructor

The Data Disk files are available on the Instructor's Resource Kit for this title. Follow the instructions in the Help file on the CD-ROM to install the programs to your network or standalone computer. For information on creating Data Disks, see the "To the Student" section above. To complete the tutorials in this book, students must have a Web browser, an e-mail account, and an Internet connection.

You are granted a license to copy the Data files to any computer or computer network used by students who have purchased this book.

OBJECTIVES

In this tutorial you will:

- Determine whether a research question is specific or exploratory
- Learn how to formulate an effective Web search strategy to answer research questions
- Learn about Web search tools and how they work
- Create various kinds of search expressions
- Find information using search engines, directories, and other Web research tools

SEARCHING THE WEB

Using Search Engines and Directories Effectively

CASE

Midland News Business Section

The *Midland News* is a top-rated daily newspaper that serves the Midland metropolitan area. The *News* is especially proud of its business section, which has won a number of awards for business reporting and analysis over the years. Anne Hill is the business editor at the *News* and has recruited an excellent staff of editors, reporters, and columnists, who each specialize in different areas of business. Anne has hired you to fill an intern position as her staff assistant. The writers in the business section offices use computers to write and edit the newspaper. Recently, each writer gained access to the Internet on his or her computer. Anne would like you to work with Dave Burton, who is the paper's international news reporter, and Ranjit Singh, who writes a syndicated column on current economic trends. Dave and Ranjit are busy and do not have time to learn how to use the Internet for the quick, reliable research that they need to create and support their writing.

Anne expects you to begin by doing most of the Web searching for Ranjit and Dave yourself; eventually, she wants you to train them to use the Web. You tell Anne that you are just learning to use the Web yourself, but she explains that this will be your full-time job during your internship and she is counting on you to become skilled in Web searching. Anne also reassures you by telling you that she has been working with the Web quite a bit herself and would be happy to help you with questions you might have as you find your way around the Web.

SESSION 4.1

In this session, you will learn about two types of search questions, how to create search expressions, and how to use Web search engines and directories. Also, you will use other Web resources to find answers to your questions or information related to topics in which you are interested.

Types of Search Questions

Anne is present at your first meeting with Dave and Ranjit. Dave asks about what kinds of Web information can help him do his job better. You reply that Dave's Internet connection provides him with information about every country in the world and on most major businesses and industries. No matter what type of story he is writing, you probably can find relevant facts that he can use. Dave mentions that his stories always can use more facts. Anne agrees and says that one of the most frequent editor comments on reporters' stories is to "get the facts."

Ranjit says that his columns do not rely as much on current events and facts—they are longer, more thought-provoking pieces about broad economic and business issues. Quick access to facts is not nearly as important to him as it is to a business news reporter like Dave. Ranjit hopes that the Web can provide him with new ideas that he could explore in his columns. So, instead of fast answers to specific questions, Ranjit explains that he wants to use the Web as a resource for interesting concepts and ideas. He knows that the Web is a good way to find unusual and interesting views on the economy and general business practices. Ranjit is always looking for new angles on old ideas, so he is optimistic that you can find many useful Web resources for him.

Both writers were happy to have an eager assistant "working the Web" for them. Anne explained to you that the writers will need different kinds of help because of their different writing goals. Dave will need quick answers to specific questions. For example, he might need to know the population of Bolivia or the languages spoken in Thailand. Ranjit will need to find Web sites that contain, for example, collected research papers that discuss the causes of the Great Depression.

You can use the Web to obtain answers to both of these question types—specific and exploratory—but each question type requires a different search strategy. A **specific question** is a question that you can phrase easily and one for which you will recognize the answer when you find it. In other words, you will know when to end your search. The search process for a specific question is one of narrowing the field down to the answer you seek. An **exploratory question** is an open-ended question that can be harder to phrase; it also is difficult to determine when you find a good answer. The search process for an exploratory question requires you to fan out in a number of directions to find relevant information. You can use the Web to find answers to both kinds of questions, but each requires a different search strategy.

Specific questions require you to start with broad categories of information and gradually narrow the search until you find the answer to your question. Figure 4-1 shows this process of sequential, increasingly focused questions.

Figure 4-1   **SPECIFIC RESEARCH QUESTION SEARCH PROCESS**

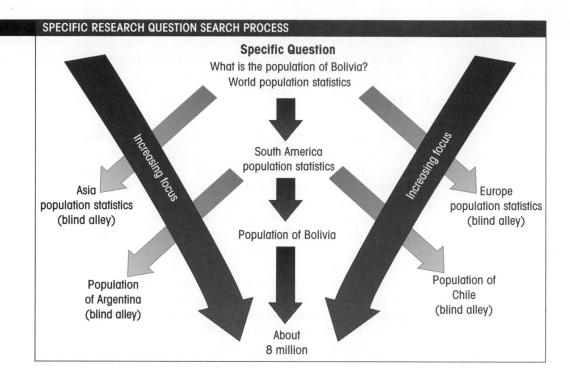

As you narrow your search, you might find that you are heading in the wrong direction, or down a blind alley. In that case, you need to move back up the funnel shown in Figure 4-1 and try another path.

Exploratory questions start with general questions that lead to other, less-general questions. The answers to the questions at each level should lead you to more information about the topic in which you are interested. This information then leads you to more questions. Figure 4-2 shows how this questioning process leads to a broadening scope as you gather information pertinent to the exploratory question.

Figure 4-2   **EXPLORATORY RESEARCH QUESTION SEARCH PROCESS**

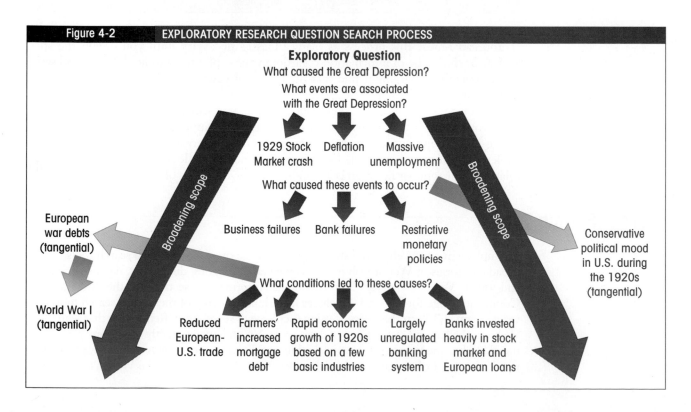

As your search expands, you might find yourself collecting tangential information that is somewhat related to your topic but does not help answer your exploratory question. The boundary between useful and tangential information is often difficult to identify precisely.

Web Search Strategy

Now that you understand the different types of questions that Ranjit and Dave will ask as you begin to work for them, Anne suggests that you learn something about searching the Web. You tell her that you know the Web is a collection of interconnected HTML documents and that you know how to use Web browser software to navigate the hyperlinks that connect these documents. Anne explains that the search tools available on the Web are an integral part of these linked HTML documents, or Web pages.

To search the Web effectively, you should first decide whether your question is specific or exploratory. The steps are the same for each type of question, but the determination of when your search process is completed is different for the two types of questions.

The Web search process includes four steps. First, you should carefully formulate and state your question. The second step is to select the appropriate tool or tools to use in your search. After obtaining your results from a Web search tool, you need to evaluate these results to determine if they answer your question. To continue the search, you can refine or redefine your question and then select a different search tool to see if you get a different result. Figure 4-3 shows the search process.

Figure 4-3	WEB SEARCH PROCESS
1. Formulate and state the question.	
2. Select the appropriate Web search tool.	
3. Evaluate the search results.	
4. Repeat the previous steps until you find the answer (for a specific question) or until you have gathered enough information about the topic (for an exploratory question).	

You can repeat this process as many times as necessary until you obtain the specific answer or the range of information regarding your exploratory topic that you find satisfactory. Sometimes, you might find that the nature of your original question is different than you had originally thought. You also might find that you need to reformulate, or more clearly state, your question. As you restate your question, you should try to think of synonyms for each word. Unfortunately, many words in the English language have multiple meanings. If you use a word in your search that is common and has many meanings, you can be buried in irrelevant information or be led down many blind alleys. Identifying unique phrases that relate to your topic or question is a helpful way to avoid some of these problems.

Web Search Tools

To implement any Web search strategy, you will use one or more Web search tools. The four broad categories of Web search tools include search engines, directories, meta-search engines, and other Web resources. The Additional Information section of the Student Online Companion page for Tutorial 4 includes hyperlinks to many of these Web search tools. In this section, you will learn the basics of using each type of search tool. Remember that searching the Web is a challenging task for any of these tools. No one knows exactly how many pages exist on the Web, but the number is now in the billions. Each of these pages might have thousands of words, images, or links to downloadable files. Thus, the content of the Web is far greater than any library. Unlike the content of a library, however, the content of the Web is not indexed in any standardized way. Fortunately, the tools you have to search the Web are powerful.

Using Search Engines

A Web **search engine** is a special kind of Web site that finds other Web pages that match a word or phrase you enter. The word or phrase you enter, called a **search expression** or a **query**, might include instructions that tell the search engine how to search. A search engine does not search the Web to find a match; it only searches its *own* database of information about Web pages that it has collected, indexed, and stored. This information includes the URL of the Web page (recall from Tutorial 2 that a Web page's URL, or uniform resource locator, is its address). If you enter the same search expression into different search engines, you will get different results because each search engine has collected a different set of information in its database and each search engine uses different procedures to search its database. Most search engines report the number of hits they find. A **hit** is a Web page that is indexed in the search engine's database and contains text that matches your search expression. All search engines provide a series of **results pages**, which are Web pages that contain hyperlinks to the Web pages that contain text that matches your search expression.

Each search engine uses a Web robot to build its database. A **Web robot**, also called a **bot** or a **spider**, is a program that automatically searches the Web to find new Web sites and update information about old Web sites that already are in the database. One of a Web robot's more important tasks is to delete information in the database when a Web site no longer exists. The main advantage of using an automated searching tool is that it can examine far more Web sites than an army of people ever could. However, the Web changes every day, and even the best search engine sites cannot keep their databases completely updated. When you click hyperlinks on a search engine results page, you will find that some of the Web pages no longer exist.

Most search engines allow Web page creators to submit the URLs of their pages to search engine databases. This gives search engine sites another way to add Web pages to their databases. Most search engine operators screen such Web page submissions to prevent a Web page creator from submitting a large number of duplicate or similar Web pages. When the search engine receives a submission, it sends its Web robot out to visit the submitted URL and the robot performs its usual data gathering tasks.

The business firms and other organizations that operate search engines often sell advertising space on the search engine Web page and on the results pages to sponsors. An increasing number of search engine operators also sell paid placement rights on results pages. For example, Toyota may want to purchase rights to the search term "car." When you enter a search expression that includes the word "car," the search engine creates a results page that will have a link to Toyota's Web site at or near the top of the results page. Most, but not all, search engines label these paid placement links as "sponsored."

Search engine sites use the advertising revenue to generate profit after covering the costs of maintaining the computer hardware and software required to search the Web and to create and search the database. The only price you pay for access to these excellent tools is that you will see advertising banners on many of the pages, and you might have to scroll through some sponsored links at the top of results pages; otherwise, your usage is free.

You just received an e-mail message from Dave with your first research assignment. He wants to mention the amount of average rainfall in Belize to make a point in a story that he is writing. This search question is a specific question, not an exploratory question, because you are looking for a fact and you will know when you have found that fact. You can use the four steps from Figure 4-3 as follows:

1. Formulate and state the question. You have identified key search terms in the question that you can use in your search expression: *Belize*, *rainfall*, and *annual*. You will use these terms because they should each appear on any Web page that

includes the answer to Dave's question. None of these terms are articles, prepositions, or other common words. None of the words have multiple meanings. The term *Belize* should be especially useful in narrowing the search to relevant Web pages.

2. Because the question is very specific but could require a search of many categories in a directory, you decide that a search engine might return the answer more efficiently than a search of directories.

3. When you obtain the results, you will review and evaluate them and then decide whether they provide an acceptable answer to your question.

4. If the results do not answer the question to your satisfaction, you will redefine or reformulate the question so it is more specific or exploratory and then conduct a second search using a different tool, question, or search expression.

To find the average annual rainfall in Belize:

1. Start your Web browser, open the Student Online Companion page at **www.course.com/newperspectives/internet3**, click the hyperlink for your book, click the **Tutorial 4** link, and then click the **Session 4.1** link. Click the **AltaVista** link and wait while the browser opens the AltaVista Web page.

2. Type **Belize annual rainfall** in the Search for text box, as shown in Figure 4-4.

| Figure 4-4 | TYPING THE SEARCH EXPRESSION INTO THE ALTAVISTA SEARCH ENGINE |

click here to begin search

search expression

3. Click the **Search** button to start the search. The search results appear on a new page—the page that appears in your browser should state that there are millions of Web pages that might contain the answer to your question.

4. Scroll down the results page and examine your search results. Click some of the links until you find a page or several pages that provide annual rainfall information for Belize. If you do not find any useful links on the first page of search results, click the numbers at the bottom of the page identified as links to more **Result Pages**. Click the **Back** button on your Web browser to return to the results page after going to each hyperlink. You should find that Belize has several climate zones and that the annual rainfall ranges from 50 to 170 inches, or 130 to 430 centimeters.

Dave had expected that you would find one rainfall amount that would be representative for the entire country, which is not the case. Web searches often disclose information that helps you adjust the assumptions you made when you formulated the original research question. Remember that the Web changes constantly and information is updated continuously, so you might find somewhat different information than the results shown here. Dave wants you to check another source to confirm your results, so you decide to search for the same information in HotBot, which is another search engine.

To conduct the same search using the HotBot search engine:

1. Return to the Student Online Companion page for Session 4.1, and then click the **HotBot** link to open the HotBot search engine page.

2. Type **Belize annual rainfall** in the Search Smarter text box, as shown in Figure 4-5.

| Figure 4-5 | TYPING THE SEARCH EXPRESSION INTO THE HOTBOT SEARCH ENGINE |

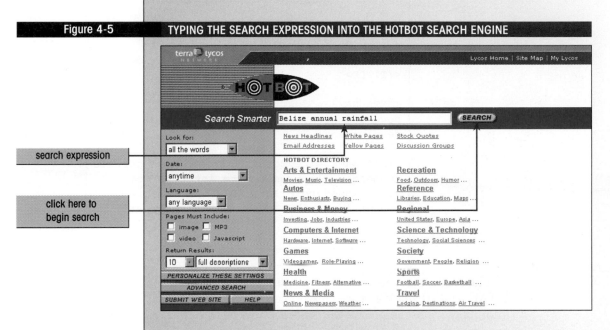

search expression

click here to begin search

3. Click the **SEARCH** button to start the search. The search results appear on a new page, and this time, your search returns a few thousand hits. The HotBot results page may not show this number on the first results page, but the total number of hits at the top of the second and subsequent results pages.

4. Scroll down the results page and examine your search results, and then click some of the links until you find a page that provides the average annual rainfall for Belize. Return to the results page after going to each hyperlink. Once again, you should find that Belize has several climate zones and that the annual rainfall ranges from 50 to 170 inches, or 130 to 430 centimeters.

HotBot returned substantially fewer Web pages than the AltaVista search engine for two reasons: First, each search engine includes different Web pages in its database; second, the HotBot search engine, by default, only returns hits for pages that include *all* of the words you enter in a search expression. The AltaVista search engine's default is to return hits for pages that include *any* of the words. You found the same information after running both searches, so you can give Dave an answer with the second confirmation he requested.

You may have noticed that many of the links on the results pages led to Web sites that had no information about Belize rainfall at all. That is why most researchers routinely use several search engines. Answers that are difficult to find using one search engine are often easy to find with another.

Search engines databases store different collections of information about the pages that exist on the Web at any given time. Many search engine robots do not search all of the Web pages at a particular site. Further, each search engine database indexes the information it has collected from the Web differently. Some search engine robots only collect information from a Web page's title, description, keywords, or HTML tags; others only read a certain amount of the HTML code in each Web page. Figure 4-6 shows the HTML code from a Web page that contains information about electronic commerce.

Figure 4-6	META TAGS FOR A WEB PAGE

```
<HEAD>

<TITLE>
Current Developments in Electronic Commerce
</TITLE>

<META NAME ="description" CONTENT="Current
news and reports about electronic commerce
developments.">

<META NAME ="keywords" CONTENT ="electronic
commerce, electronic data interchange,
value added reseller, EDI, VAR, secure
socket layer, business on the internet">

</HEAD>
```

The description and keywords tags are examples of HTML META tags. A **META tag** is HTML code that a Web page creator places in the page header for the specific purpose of informing Web robots about the content of the page. META tags do not cause any text to appear on the page when a Web browser loads it; rather, they exist solely for the use of search engine robots.

The information contained in META tags can become an important part of a search engine's database. For example, the keywords META tag shown in Figure 4-6 includes the phrase "electronic data interchange." These keywords could be a very important phrase in a search engine's database because the three individual words *electronic*, *data*, and *interchange*, are common terms that often are used in search expressions that have nothing to do with electronic commerce. The word *data* is so common that many search engines might be programmed to ignore it. A search engine that includes the full phrase "electronic data interchange" in its database will greatly increase the chances that a user interested in that topic will find this particular page.

If the terms you use in your search expression are not in the part of the Web page that a search engine stores in its database, the search engine will not return a hit for that page. Some search engines store the entire content of every Web page they place in their databases. This practice is called **full text indexing**. Many search engines, even those that claim to be full text indexed search engines, omit common words such as *and*, *the*, *it*, and *by* from their databases. These are called **stop words**. You can find out if a particular search engine omits stop words by examining the Help pages provided by the search engine Web site. Many search engine sites include information about their search engines, robots, and databases on their Help or About pages. You will learn more about several of the major search engines in Session 4.2.

One recent advance in search engine technology is page ranking. **Page ranking** is a way of grading Web pages by the number of other Web pages that link to them. A page that has more Web pages linking into it is given a higher ranking than a page that has fewer pages linking into it. In complex page ranking schemes, the value of each link varies with the linking page's rank.

For example, a Web page with many inbound links might have a lower ranking than another Web page that has fewer inbound links if the second page's inbound links are from Web pages that, in turn, each have a large number of inbound links themselves. As you can imagine, calculating page ranks can be very complex! The URLs of Web pages with high rankings are presented first on the search results page. One search engine that has been a leader in the use of page ranking is Google. You decide to see how page ranking might affect your search results and run your query about Belize rainfall on the Google search engine.

To examine page ranking effects at Google:

1. Return to the Student Online Companion page for Session 4.1, and then click the **Google** link and wait while your browser opens the Google search engine page.

2. Type **Belize annual rainfall** in the search text box, as shown in Figure 4-7.

Figure 4-7	TYPING THE SEARCH EXPRESSION INTO THE GOOGLE SEARCH ENGINE

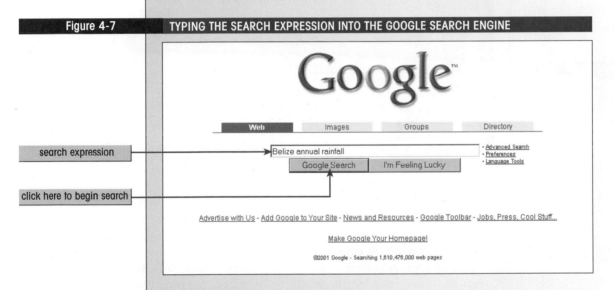

3. Click the **Google Search** button to start the search. The search results appear on a new page and should include a few thousand hits.

4. Scroll down the results page to examine your search results, and then click some of the links to determine whether Google's page ranking approach has provided a better set of search results. Return to the results page after going to each hyperlink.

Another feature that search engine sites are including in their pages is natural language querying. A **natural language query interface** allows users to enter a question exactly as they would ask a person that question. The search engine then analyzes the question using knowledge it has been given about the grammatical structure of questions and uses that knowledge to convert the natural language question into a search query. This procedure of converting a natural language question into a search expression is sometimes called **parsing**. One of the first search engines to offer a natural language query interface was Ask Jeeves. You decide to see how Ask Jeeves handles the Belize rainfall question.

To examine the natural language query interface at Ask Jeeves:

1. Return to the Student Online Companion page for Session 4.1, and then click the **Ask Jeeves** link to open the Ask Jeeves search engine page.

2. Type **What is the annual rainfall in Belize?** in the Ask text box, as shown in Figure 4-8.

Figure 4-8   TYPING THE NATURAL LANGUAGE QUESTION INTO THE ASK JEEVES SEARCH ENGINE

natural language question

click here to begin search

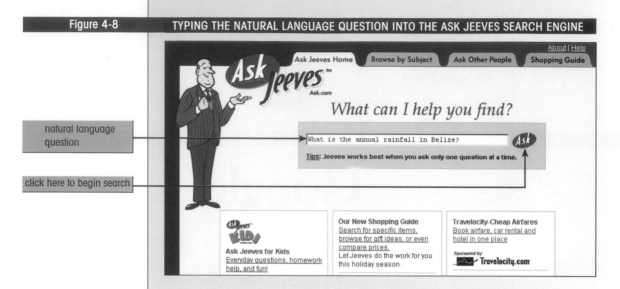

3. Click the **Ask** button to run the search. The search results appear on a new page, and should include a few hundred hits.

4. Scroll down the results page and examine your search results, and then click some of the links to determine whether Ask Jeeves' natural language query interface has provided a good list of search results. Note that the first page contains several alternative reformulations of your natural language query. You can click these to see if any of these reformulated search queries offers better results than your original question. Return to the results page after going to each hyperlink.

Using Directories and Hybrid Search Engine Directories

Search engines provide a powerful tool for executing keyword searches of the Web. However, because most search engine URL databases are built by computers running programs that perform the search automatically, they can miss important classification details that you would notice instantly. For example, if a search engine's robot found a Web page with the title "Test Data: Do Not Use," it would probably include content from the page in the search engine database. If you were to read such a warning in a Web page title, *you* would know not to include the page's contents. However, keep in mind that with billions of Web pages on the Web, the volume of data that a search engine robot obtains as it travels the Web makes it impossible to have people screen every Web page.

Web directories use a completely different approach from search engines to build useful indexes of information on the Web. A **Web directory** is a listing of hyperlinks to Web pages that is organized into hierarchical categories. The difference between a search engine and a Web directory is that *people* select the Web pages to include in a Web directory. These people, who are knowledgeable experts in one or more subject areas and skilled in various classification techniques, review candidate Web pages for inclusion in the directory. When the experts decide that a Web page is worth listing in the directory, they determine the appropriate category in which to store the hyperlink to that page. Many directories allow a Web page to be indexed in several different categories. The main weakness of a directory is that you must know which category is likely to yield the information you desire. If you begin searching in the wrong category, you might follow many hyperlinks before you realize that the information you seek is not in that category. Some directories overcome this limitation by including hyperlinks in category levels that link to lower levels in other categories.

One of the oldest and most respected directories on the Web is **Yahoo!** (see Figure 4-9). Two Stanford doctoral students, David Filo and Jerry Yang, who wanted a way to keep track of interesting sites they found on the Internet, started Yahoo! in 1994. Since 1994, Yahoo! has grown to become one of the most widely used resources on the Web. Yahoo! currently lists hundreds of thousands of Web pages in its categories—a sizable collection, but only a small portion of the billions of pages on the Web. Although Yahoo! does use some automated programs for checking and classifying its entries, it relies on human experts to do most of the selection and classification work.

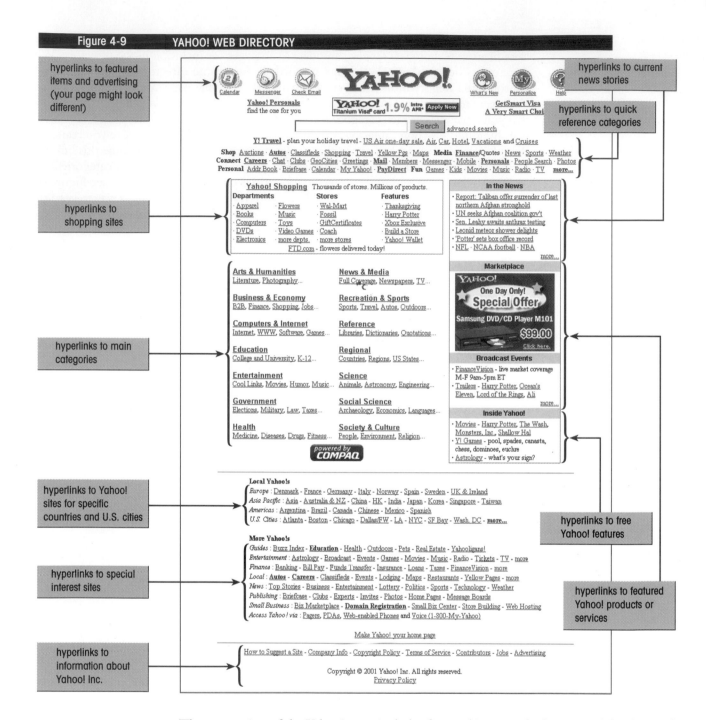

Figure 4-9   YAHOO! WEB DIRECTORY

The top section of the Yahoo! page includes featured items and advertising. The featured items change regularly and usually highlight timely topics that the Yahoo! editors believe will interest many of the site's visitors.

The search tool that appears below the advertising banner is a search engine within the Yahoo! directory. You can enter search terms into this tool, and Yahoo! will search its listings to find a match. This combination of search engine and directory is sometimes called a **hybrid search engine directory**; however, most directories today include a search engine function, so many people just call these sites directories. No matter what it is called, the combination of search engine and directory provides a powerful and effective tool for searching the Web. Using a hybrid search engine directory can help you identify which category in the directory is likely to contain the information you need. After you enter a category, the search engine is useful for narrowing a search even further; you can enter a search expression and limit the search to that category.

The next section of the Yahoo! page includes quick reference categories, which are commonly used categories that might otherwise be hard to find because they would be buried several layers under a main category heading. Also, users might find it difficult to guess which main categories might include these items. For example, "weather" might be classified under the main category headings "News & Media" or "Science." The quick reference section makes often-sought information categories easier to find.

The Yahoo! Shopping section includes hyperlinks to sites that offer goods and services for sale on the Web. Some of these sites are operated by Yahoo!, which rents the space to businesses. Others are independent sites operated by major companies that have paid Yahoo! for this hyperlink space on the Yahoo! page.

The main categories section of the Yahoo! page is the primary tool for searching the directory's listings. Under each of the 14 main categories, Yahoo! lists several subcategories. These are not the only subcategories; they are just a sample of those that are the largest or most used. You can click a main category hyperlink to see all of the subcategories under that category.

The right side of the page includes four sections. The first includes hyperlinks to current news stories. The second includes hyperlinks to featured Yahoo! products or services. The third includes hyperlinks to radio, television, and other multimedia features. The fourth includes links to free Yahoo! features designed to encourage you to return to the site frequently.

The lower section of the Yahoo! main page includes hyperlinks to Yahoo! directories for other countries and large U.S. cities. The lower section also has a collection of hyperlinks to other parts of the directory that contain Yahoo! specialized categories of hyperlinks, such as the Yahooligans! site, which is a version of Yahoo! designed for children. The very bottom of the page includes links to Yahoo! Inc., the company that operates the site.

Just as you are becoming familiar with the layout of the Yahoo! directory, Dave calls you. He is up against a deadline and needs some background information on an organization that does research on business issues named The Conference Board. You tell Dave that you will call him back as quickly as possible. Following your guidelines for searching on the Web, you decide that Dave's question is about a specific fact and:

1. Identify key search terms—Conference Board, business, and organization—that you will use in your search.

2. Use a Web directory to find the answer, so you can search in the business directory instead of searching the entire Web.

3. Examine the results and decide whether a second search using a different category or search terms is necessary.

4. Plan to repeat the first three steps until you determine whether The Conference Board provides any information about itself on the Web.

To find The Conference Board on the Web:

1. Return to the Student Online Companion page for Session 4.1, and then click the **Yahoo!** link and wait while your browser opens the Yahoo! home page.

   You consider the main categories on the Yahoo! page and determine that you could probably find your information in the Business & Economy category.

2. Click the **Business & Economy** category hyperlink, and wait while your browser opens the Yahoo! Business and Economy page shown in Figure 4-10. This page includes hyperlinks to lower levels in the hierarchy and to other points in the

hierarchies of other categories. The hyperlinks to lower-levels in this hierarchy include numbers in parentheses that indicate the number of Web pages included in each lower-level category. The hyperlinks that include the "@" symbol are links to other points in the hierarchies of other categories. New categories and categories that include new Web pages are indicated by a "NEW!" icon.

Figure 4-10   YAHOO! BUSINESS AND ECONOMY CATEGORIES PAGE

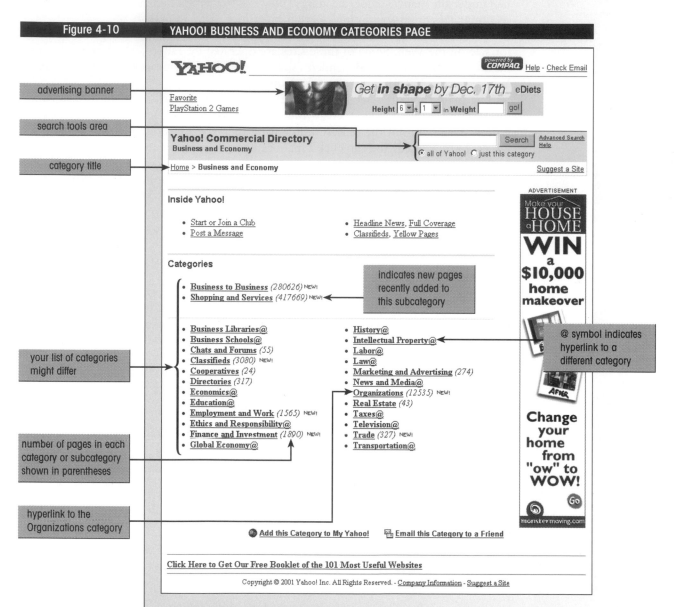

3. Click the **Organizations** category link, and wait while your browser opens the Organizations page.

4. Type **Conference Board** in the search text box, click the **just this category** option button, and then click the **Search** button.

5. The results page opens and lists the hits. See Figure 4-11. The results include a small number of category and Web page hits. Using the search tools within the directory lets you complete your search faster and more efficiently.

Figure 4-11	SEARCH RESULTS PAGE

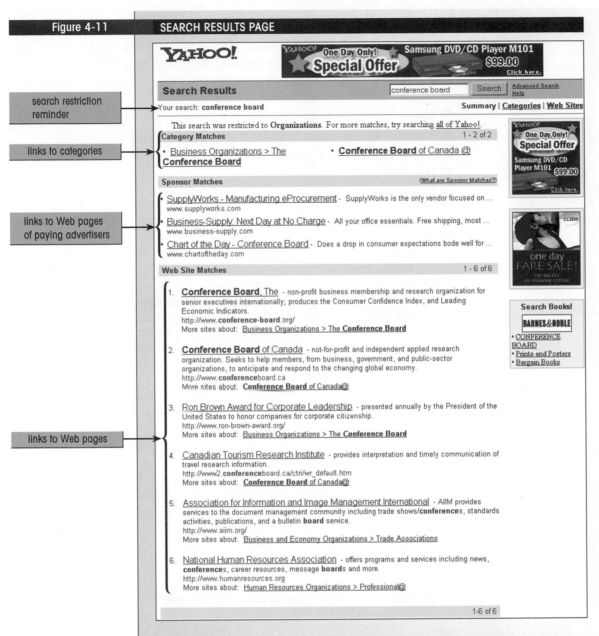

5. Click one or more of the links leading to sites sponsored by The Conference Board to determine if any of them provide background information on the organization.

You should find information about The Conference Board at one or more of the sites listed, so you can call Dave back with the information and help him beat his deadline. Now that you have seen how to use a search engine and a hybrid search engine directory, you are ready to use an even more powerful combination of Web research tools: the meta-search engine.

Using Meta-Search Engines

A **meta-search engine** is a tool that combines the power of multiple search engines. Some meta-search tools also include directories. The idea behind meta-search tools is simple. Each search engine on the Web has different strengths and weaknesses because each search engine

- Uses a different Web robot to gather information about Web pages,
- Stores a different amount of Web page text in its database,
- Selects different Web pages to index,
- Has different storage resources,
- Interprets search expressions somewhat differently.

You saw how these differences cause different search engines to return vastly different results for the same search expression. To perform a complete search for a particular question, you might need to use several individual search engines. Using a meta-search engine lets you search several engines at the same time, so you need not conduct the same search many times. A meta-search engine accepts your search expression and transmits it to several search engines, such as the AltaVista and HotBot search tools you used earlier in this session. These search engines run the search expression against their databases of Web page information and return results to the meta-search engine. The meta-search engine reports consolidated results from all of the search engines it queried. Meta-search engines use the same kinds of programs to run their queries, but they do not have their own databases of Web information.

You want to learn how to use meta-search engines so you can access information faster. You decide to test a meta-search engine using Dave's Belize rainfall question. **Dogpile** is one of the more comprehensive meta-search engines available; it forwards your queries to more than a dozen major search engines and directories, including About.com, AltaVista, FindWhat, LookSmart, Open Directory, Overture, Yahoo!, and several others. The list of search engines and directories might be different when you use this tool because newer and better search tools become available and old favorites disappear over time. MetaCrawler reports results from each search engine or directory separately and does not eliminate duplicate hits. The list of hyperlinks returned by each search engine remains in the order that the search engine reports them to Dogpile. Like most regular search engines, Dogpile now includes a directory feature.

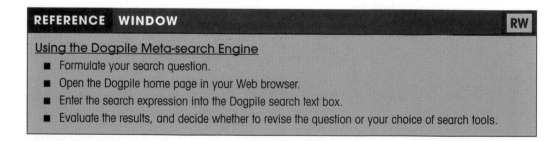

REFERENCE WINDOW **RW**

Using the Dogpile Meta-search Engine
- Formulate your search question.
- Open the Dogpile home page in your Web browser.
- Enter the search expression into the Dogpile search text box.
- Evaluate the results, and decide whether to revise the question or your choice of search tools.

To use the Dogpile meta-search engine:

1. Return to the Student Online Companion page for Session 4.1, and then click the **Dogpile** link and wait while your browser opens the Dogpile Web engine page.

2. Type **Belize annual rainfall** in the Dogpile search text box, as shown in Figure 4-12.

| Figure 4-12 | SEARCHING FOR INFORMATION WITH THE DOGPILE META-SEARCH ENGINE |

search expression

click to begin search

Web directory categories

DOGPILE®
All results, no mess.

Belize annual rainfall   Fetch

Local Search: Select: The Web ▾

🐾 Yellow Pages   🐾 White Pages   🐾 Classifieds

Doggy Daily
Ever get a weather report
from a pooch?

Joke of the Day

Shopping
Go Shopping

Stores
AbtElectronics.com
Amazon.com
Famous Footwear
Spiegel

Departments
Apparel & Accessories
Electronics
Health & Fitness
Home & Garden
Jewelry

Marketplace

$ Pay Bills Online

🐾 Bet on Football

Find Contractors

Request It / Get It

Dogpile References

Favorite Fetches

Autos	Day Trading	Hotels	Options
Casinos/Gambling	Domain Names	Insurance Quotes	Travel
City Maps	Health	Loans	Vacations
Data Recovery	Homes	Mortgages	Further Fetches...

Search Tools

Maps	Photo Personals	City Guides	Classifieds
Weather	Horoscopes	Health Center	Free Games
Low Fares	Singles Pics 🐾	Find Friends	

Web Directory

Auto	Reference	Entertainment	Travel
Food & Wine	Sports	Lifestyle	Work & Money
Health	Computing	Personal	
Home	Connecting	Shopping	

Search the Yellow Pages

⦿ Name of business   ○ Type of business

City   State Choose a State ▾   Find

3. Click the **Fetch** button to run the search. After the search is complete, a Metasearch Results page opens and shows the hits for each search engine.

4. Examine and evaluate your search results.

As you scroll through the search results pages, you can see that there is a wide variation in the number and quality of the results provided by each search engine and directory. You might see many hits but no hyperlinks. You also might notice a number of duplicate hits; however, most of the Web pages returned by one search tool are not returned by any other. You can click the **Next** button that appears at the bottom of the results page to see the hits returned by other search engines.

Using Other Web Resources

A variety of other resources are available for searching the Web that do not fit exactly into the three preceding categories. These search resources are similar to bibliographies, but instead of listing books or journal articles, they contain lists of hyperlinks to Web pages. Just as some bibliographies are annotated, many of these resources include summaries or reviews of Web pages.

These other resources can be very useful when you want to obtain a broad overview or a basic understanding of a complex subject area. A search for such resources that uses a search engine or directory is likely to turn up a narrow list of references that are too detailed and that assume a great deal of prior knowledge. For example, using a search engine or directory to find information about quantum physics will probably give you many references to technical papers and Web pages devoted to current research issues in quantum physics. However, your search probably will yield very few Web pages that provide an introduction to the topic. A Web bibliography page can offer hyperlinks to information regarding a particular subject that is presented at various levels. Many of these resources include annotations and reviews of the sites they list. This information can help you identify Web pages that fit your level of interest.

Some of the names used to identify these Web bibliographies include **resource lists**, **guides**, **clearinghouses**, and **virtual libraries**. Many of these bibliographies are general references, such as the Librarian's Index to the Internet, Information Please, the Scout Report Signpost, and the Argus Clearinghouse. Others are more focused, such as Martindale's The Reference Desk, which emphasizes science-related links. You can visit any of these Web sites by clicking their links on the Tutorial 4 page of the Student Online Companion. The hyperlinks for these resources appear in the Additional Information section of the page under the Other Search Tools and Resources heading.

Ranjit stops by your office and asks for your help. He is planning to write a series of columns on the business and economic effects of current trends in biotechnology. The potential effects of genetic engineering research particularly intrigue him, but he admits that he does not know much about any of these topics. Ranjit wants you to find some Web sites that he could explore to learn more about biotechnology trends in general and genetic engineering research in particular. He mentions that it would be nice, but not essential, to find some recent news summaries about biotechnology and business. You decide to use the Argus Clearinghouse site as a resource to work on the exploratory question that Ranjit has given you. The **Argus Clearinghouse** reviews and provides hyperlinks to subject guides. You determine that Ranjit's request is an exploratory search. You know that biotechnology is a branch of the biological sciences, so you identify three category terms: *biotechnology*, *genetic engineering*, and *biology* to use as your search categories.

REFERENCE WINDOW   RW

Using the Argus Clearinghouse Web Site
- Identify categories and search terms that might lead you to the desired information resources.
- Open the Argus home page in your Web browser.
- Explore the Argus categories that are related to the categories and search terms you identified.
- Follow the category hyperlinks to subcategories and Web pages.
- Evaluate the results and decide whether to revise your categories or choice of Web resources.

To use Argus to conduct an exploratory search:

1. Return to the Student Online Companion page for Session 4.1, and then click the **Argus Clearinghouse** link and wait while the browser opens The Argus Clearinghouse home page.

   As you scan the main categories on the Argus Clearinghouse home page, you do not see any of your search categories listed; however, you know that biology is a science.

2. Click the **Science & Mathematics** link.

3. Click the **biology** link that appears on the Science & Mathematics subcategory page. You see two of your search terms in the keywords list on the biology page and decide to follow both of them.

4. Click the **biotechnology** keyword hyperlink to open the Web page shown in Figure 4-13. The National Biotechnology Information Facility hyperlink is the most highly rated site, as indicated by its five dark check marks, so you decide to open the page.

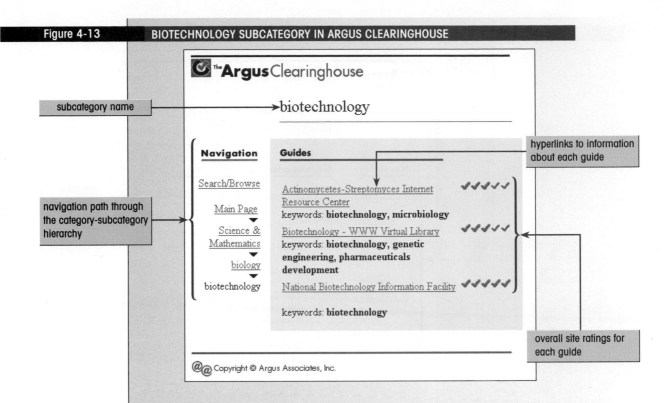

Figure 4-13   BIOTECHNOLOGY SUBCATEGORY IN ARGUS CLEARINGHOUSE

5. Click the **National Biotechnology Information Facility** link to open the Guide Information page for the site shown in Figure 4-14. The Guide Information page includes a hyperlink to the Web site, indexing keywords, information about the author of the site, and detailed ratings on several dimensions. You can follow this site to gather specific information for Ranjit or give him the site's URL and let him explore the site. You might want to gather the URLs of this and other sites that you find and send them all to Ranjit in one e-mail message. You have explored the biotechnology subcategory; next, you will explore the genetic engineering subcategory.

Figure 4-14   INFORMATION ABOUT THE BIOTECH GUIDE WEB SITE

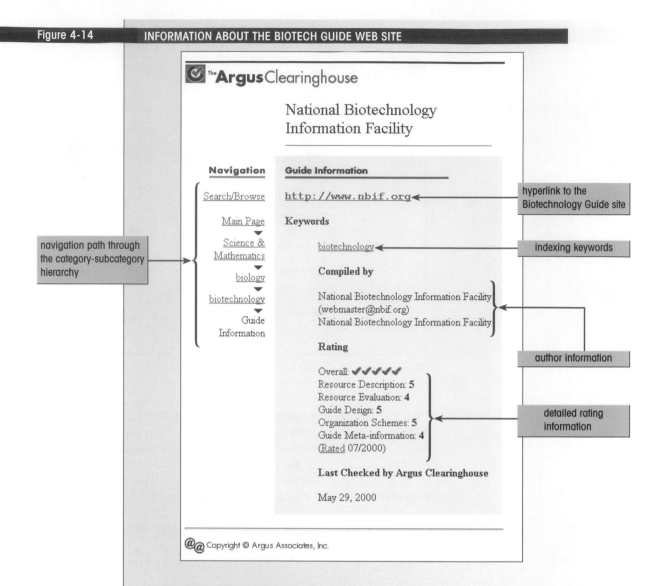

6. Click the **biology** hyperlink that appears in the Navigation path on the left side of the Web page to return to the list of biology keywords.

7. Click the **genetic engineering** hyperlink in the Keywords list to open the genetic engineering page. There are three entries provided in the Guides list. One of these entries is the Biotechnology - WWW Virtual Library page, which also appeared on the biotechnology Guides page shown in Figure 4-13.

8. Click the **Biotechnology – WWW Virtual Library** hyperlink to explore the resources at that site. Remember that Ranjit does not expect you to understand the contents of the Web pages you find; he just wants you to identify resources to help him learn more about trends in this area of scientific research.

9. Examine your search results and determine whether you have gathered sufficient useful information to respond to Ranjit's request.

10. Close your browser, and if necessary, log off your Internet connection.

You have completed your search for Web sites that might help Ranjit. Many of these sites contain hyperlinks to other useful sites that Ranjit might want to explore. You can deliver information from these pages to Ranjit by printing copies of the Web pages, sending the URLs by e-mail, or saving the Web pages and attaching them to an e-mail message. Because your answer to Ranjit's question involves so many pages at different sites, your best approach would be to send an e-mail message with a list of relevant URLs.

Session 4.1 QUICK CHECK

1. What are the key characteristics of an exploratory search question?

2. True or False: Web search engine operators use advertising revenue to cover their expenses and to earn a profit.

3. The part of a search engine site that searches the Web to collect information for the search engine's database is called a(n)_____.

4. A search engine that uses page ranking will list a Web page nearer the top of search results pages if that page has many_____.

5. True or False: Most search engines index all Web page words in their databases.

6. List one advantage and one disadvantage of using a Web directory instead of a Web search engine to locate information.

7. How does a hybrid search engine-directory overcome the disadvantages of using either a search engine or a directory alone?

8. How does a meta-search engine process the search expression you enter into it?

9. What are the key features offered by Web bibliographies?

SESSION 4.2

Although you can find the answers to many research questions on the Web with a simple search using one of the tools described in Session 4.1, some questions are more complex. In this session, you will learn how to use the advanced features of Web search engines, directories, and other Web resources to answer complex questions. Many of these Web search tools use Boolean logic and other filtering mechanisms to select and sort search results; however, many of these search tools implement these mechanisms differently. After learning the basics of Boolean logic and filtering techniques, you will use those techniques in a variety of Web search tools.

Boolean Logic and Filtering Techniques

The most important factor in getting good results from a search engine, a meta-search engine, or a search tool within a hybrid search engine-directory is to select carefully the search terms you use. When the object of your search is straightforward, you can choose one or two words that will work well. More complex search questions require more complex queries, which you can use along with Boolean logic, search expression operators, or filtering techniques, to broaden or narrow your search expression. In the next three sections, you will learn how to use each of these techniques.

Boolean Operators

When you enter a single word into a Web search tool, it searches for matches to that word. When you enter a search expression into a Web search tool that includes more than one word, the search tool makes assumptions about the words that you enter. You learned in Session 4.1 that the AltaVista search engine assumes that you want to match any of the key-words in your search expression, whereas HotBot assumes that you want to match all of the keywords. These different assumptions can make dramatic differences in the number and quality of hits returned. Many search engine operators, realizing that users might want to match all of the keywords on one search and any of the keywords on a different search, have designed their search engines to offer these options. The most common way of implement-ing these options is to offer Boolean operators as part of their search engines.

George Boole was a nineteenth century British mathematician who developed a branch of mathematics and logic that bears his name, **Boolean algebra**. In Boole's algebra, all val-ues are reduced to one of two values. In most practical applications of Boole's work, these two values are *true* and *false*. Although Boole did his work many years before practical elec-trically powered computers became commonplace, his algebra was useful to computer engi-neers and programmers. At the very lowest level of analysis, all computing is a manipulation of a single computer circuit's on and off states. Unlike the algebra you might have learned in your math classes, Boolean algebra does not use numbers or mathematical operators. Instead, Boolean algebra uses words and logical relationships.

Some parts of Boolean algebra are also useful in search expressions. **Boolean operators**, also called **logical operators**, are a key part of Boolean algebra. Boolean operators specify the logical relationship between the elements they join, just as the plus sign arithmetic oper-ator specifies the mathematical relationship between the two elements it joins. Three basic Boolean operators—AND, OR, and NOT—are recognized by most search engines. You can use these operators in many search engines by simply including them with search terms. For example, the search expression "exports AND France" returns hits for pages that con-tain both words, the expression "exports OR France" returns hits for pages that contain either word, and "exports NOT France" returns hits for pages that contain the word *export* but not the word *France*. Some search engines use "AND NOT" to indicate the Boolean NOT operator.

Figure 4-15 shows several ways to use Boolean operators in more complex search expres-sions that contain the words *exports*, *France*, and *Japan*. The figure shows the matches that a search engine will return if it interprets the Boolean operators correctly. Figure 4-15 also describes information-gathering tasks in which you might use these expressions.

Figure 4-15	USING BOOLEAN OPERATORS IN SEARCH EXPRESSIONS	
SEARCH EXPRESSION	**SEARCH RETURNS PAGES THAT INCLUDE**	**USE TO FIND INFORMATION ABOUT**
exports AND France AND Japan	All of the three search terms.	Exports from France to Japan or from Japan to France
exports OR France OR Japan	Any of the three search terms.	Exports from anywhere, including France and Japan, and all kinds of information about France and Japan
exports NOT France NOT Japan	Exports, but not if the page also includes the terms *France* or *Japan*.	Exports to and from any countries other than France or Japan
exports AND France NOT Japan	Exports and France, but not Japan.	Exports to and from France to anywhere else, except exports shipped to Japan

Other Search Expression Operators

When you join three or more search terms with Boolean operators, it is easy to become confused by the expression's complexity. To reduce the confusion, you can use precedence operators, a tool you probably learned in basic algebra, along with the Boolean operators.

A **precedence operator**, also called an **inclusion operator** or a **grouping operator**, clarifies the grouping within a complex expression and is usually indicated by the parentheses symbols. Some search engines use double quotation marks to indicate precedence grouping; however, other search engines use double quotation marks to indicate search terms that must be matched exactly as they appear (that is, search for the exact search phrase) within the double quotation marks. Figure 4-16 shows several ways to use precedence operators with Boolean operators in search expressions.

Figure 4-16	USING BOOLEAN AND PRECEDENCE OPERATORS IN SEARCH EXPRESSIONS	
SEARCH EXPRESSION	**SEARCH RETURNS PAGES THAT INCLUDE**	**USE TO FIND INFORMATION ABOUT**
exports AND (France OR Japan)	Exports and either France or Japan.	Exports from or to either France or Japan.
exports OR (France AND Japan)	Exports or both France and Japan.	Exports from anywhere, including France and Japan, and all kinds of other information about France and Japan.
exports AND (France NOT Japan)	Exports and France, but not if the page also includes Japan.	Exports to and from France, except those going to or from Japan.

Some search engines recognize variants of the Boolean operators, such as "must include" and "must exclude" operators. For example, a search engine that uses the plus sign to indicate "must include" and the minus sign to indicate "must exclude" would respond to the expression "exports + France - Japan" with hits that included anything about exports and France, but only if those pages did not include anything about Japan.

Another useful search expression tool is the location operator. A **location operator**, or **proximity operator**, lets you search for terms that appear close to each other in the text of a Web page. The most common location operator offered in Web search engines is the NEAR operator. If you are interested in French exports, you might want to find only Web pages in which the terms *exports* and *France* are close to each other. Unfortunately, each search engine that implements this operator uses its own definition of how close "NEAR" is. One search engine might define NEAR to mean "within 10 words," whereas another search engine might define NEAR to mean "within 20 words." To use the NEAR operator effectively, you must read the search engine's help file carefully.

Wildcard Characters and Search Filters

Most search engines support some use of a wildcard character in their search expressions. A **wildcard character** allows you to omit part of the search term or terms. Many search engines recognize the asterisk (*) as the wildcard character. For example, the search expression "export*" would return pages containing the terms *exports*, *exporter*, *exporters*, and *exporting* in many search engines. Some search engines let you use a wildcard character in the middle of a search term. For example, the expression "wom*n" would return pages containing both *woman* and *women*.

Many search engines allow you to restrict your search by using search filters. A **search filter** eliminates Web pages from a search. The filter criteria can include such Web page attributes as language, date, domain, host, or page component (URL, hyperlink, image tag, or title tag). For example, many search engines provide a way to search for the term *exports* in Web page titles and ignore pages in which the term appears in other parts of the page.

Advanced Searches

Most search engines implement many of the operators and techniques you have learned about, but search engine syntax varies. Some search engines provide separate advanced search pages for these techniques; others allow you to use advanced techniques such as Boolean operators on their simple search pages. Next, you will learn how to conduct complex searches using the advanced search features of several different search engines.

Advanced Search in AltaVista

Ranjit is working on a series of columns about the role that trade agreements play in limiting the flow of agricultural commodities between countries. This week's column concerns the German economy. He wants you to find some Web page references for him that might provide useful background information for his column. Ranjit is especially interested in learning more about the German perspective on trade issues, but he cannot read German.

You recognize this as an exploratory question and decide to use the advanced query capabilities of the AltaVista search engine to conduct a complex search for Web pages that Ranjit might use for his research. You want to provide Ranjit with a reasonable number of hyperlinks to Web pages, but you do not want to inundate him with thousands of URLs, so you decide to use Boolean and precedence operators to create a search expression that will focus on useful sites. To create a useful search expression, you must identify search terms that might lead you to appropriate Web pages. Some terms you might use are *Germany*, *trade*, *treaty*, and *agriculture*. You decide to use Boolean and precedence operators to combine your search terms. You also decide to use the wildcard character to allow the search to find plural and extended forms of the terms *treaty* (such as *treaties*) and *agriculture* (such as *agricultures*, *agricultural*, and *agriculturally*). Ranjit's primary interest is in trade issues, so you decide to rank the hits returned by *trade*.

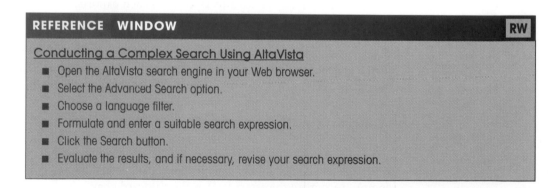

REFERENCE   WINDOW   RW

Conducting a Complex Search Using AltaVista
- Open the AltaVista search engine in your Web browser.
- Select the Advanced Search option.
- Choose a language filter.
- Formulate and enter a suitable search expression.
- Click the Search button.
- Evaluate the results, and if necessary, revise your search expression.

To perform an advanced search using AltaVista:

1. Start your Web browser, open the Student Online Companion page at **www.course.com/newperspectives/internet3**, click the hyperlink for your book, click the **Tutorial 4** link, click the **Session 4.2** link, and then click the **AltaVista** link and wait while the browser opens the AltaVista home page.

2. Click the **Advanced Search** hyperlink on the AltaVista page. Ranjit only reads English, so you need to filter the language.

3. Click the **list arrow** to the right of the box that displays the text "any language," and then click **English**.

4. Click in the **Boolean query** text box, and then type **Germany AND (trade OR treat*) AND agricult***.

5. If necessary, scroll down the page, and then click the **Search** button to start the search. The search settings and results appear in Figure 4-17. The search returns more than 100,000 hits, so you need to refine your search expression. You examine some of the descriptions provided for the first search results listed and find that many of them include information about fertilizer treatments. You decide that narrowing the search to exclude those sites would make the search results more useful to Ranjit.

Figure 4-17	COMPLEX SEARCH USING ALTAVISTA

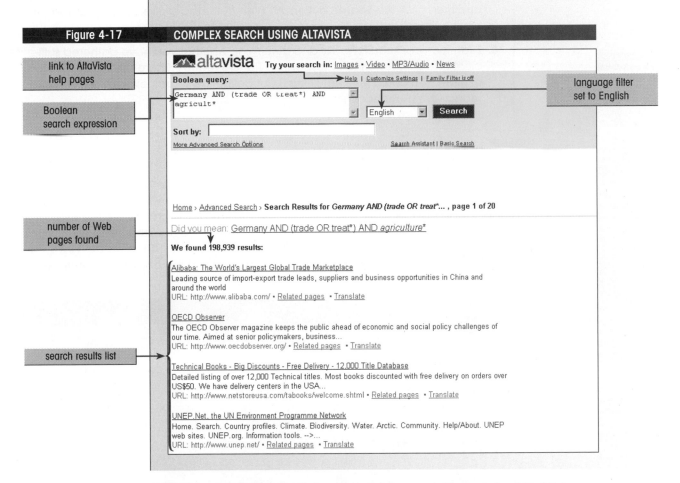

Getting Help and Refining an Advanced Search in AltaVista

Each search engine follows different rules and offers different features. To obtain help for a particular search engine, examine its home page and look for a hyperlink to help pages for that search engine. The AltaVista Advanced Search page includes a hyperlink titled "Help." You decide to exclude the word *treatment* from your Boolean search expression and, to obtain a narrower search that focuses better on the German viewpoint, you decide to restrict the domain to German Web sites.

To obtain help and refine an advanced search in AltaVista:

1. Scroll down the results page, and then click the **Help** hyperlink and wait while the browser opens the AltaVista Advanced Search page.

2. Click the **Advanced Cheat Sheet** link.

3. Scroll down the Web page and look for **domain:***domainname* in the Advanced Search Cheat Sheet table. In AltaVista, the domain filter is "domain:" followed by the name of the domain to which you want to limit your search. Ranjit tells you that the domain name for Germany is "de."

4. Click your browser's **Back** button twice to return to the AltaVista - Advanced Search page.

5. Change your Boolean search expression (at the top of the page) to **Germany AND (trade OR treat*) AND agricult* AND NOT treatment AND domain:de**, and then click the **Search** button. AltaVista returns a much smaller number of hits this time.

6. Examine your search results and determine whether you have gathered sufficient useful information to respond to Ranjit's request. There are many sites to explore. You could give Ranjit this list or define the search expression further to reduce the number of hits.

Advanced Search in HotBot

Dave stops by your office to tell you he is working on a story for tomorrow's edition about the effect of unusual weather patterns and recent rainstorms on Southeast Asian rice crops during the past six months. You decide to use the HotBot search engine to run a complex query for Dave. Although HotBot offers a SuperSearch page with a wide array of search options (to use SuperSearch, click the More Search Options button on the HotBot main page), you can perform Boolean and filtered searches from HotBot's main search page.

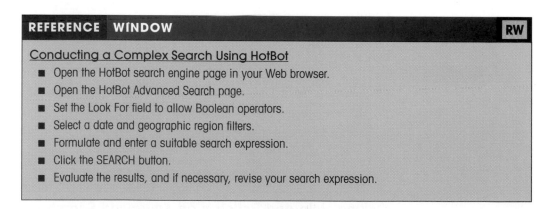

REFERENCE WINDOW   **RW**

Conducting a Complex Search Using HotBot
- Open the HotBot search engine page in your Web browser.
- Open the HotBot Advanced Search page.
- Set the Look For field to allow Boolean operators.
- Select a date and geographic region filters.
- Formulate and enter a suitable search expression.
- Click the SEARCH button.
- Evaluate the results, and if necessary, revise your search expression.

To perform a complex search using HotBot:

1. Return to the Student Online Companion page for Session 4.2, and then click the **HotBot** link and wait while the browser opens the HotBot home page.

2. Click the **ADVANCED SEARCH** button to open the HotBot SuperSearch page that appears in Figure 4-18.

Figure 4-18	ADVANCED SEARCH FEATURES OF THE HOTBOT MAIN SEARCH ENGINE PAGE

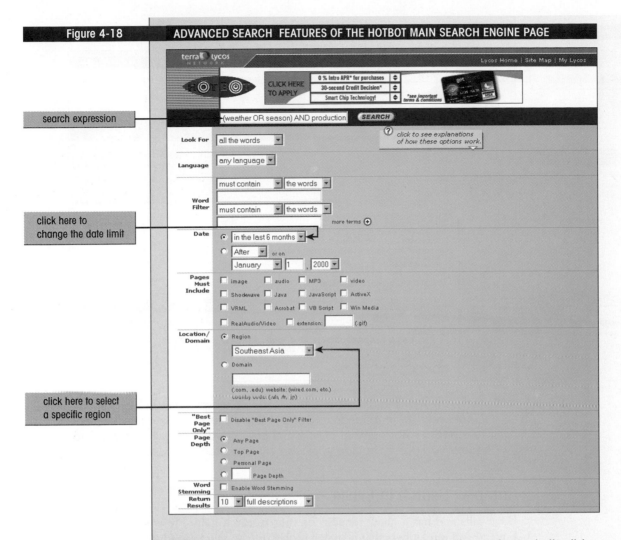

search expression

click here to change the date limit

click here to select a specific region

3. Click the **Look For** list arrow, and then click **boolean phrase** in the list.

4. Click the **Date** list arrow, and then click **in the last 6 months** to change the Date limit from *anytime*.

5. Click the **Location/Domain** list arrow, and click **Southeast Asia** to specify the Region option

   To create a useful search expression, you must identify search terms that might lead you to appropriate Web pages. Some terms you might use are *rice*, *weather*, and *production*. Dave told you that Southeast Asia has a rainy season, so the term *season* might appear instead of *weather* on Web pages that contain information that Dave could use. You decide to use Boolean and precedence operators to combine your search terms. HotBot does not recognize wildcard characters, but it does allow you to set precedence operators.

6. Click in the search text box, and then type **rice AND (weather OR season) AND production**.

7. Click the **SEARCH** button to start the search. Figure 4-19 shows the search results page, where you can see part of the search expression, the filter settings, information about the search, and a partial list of hyperlinks to related Web pages. The description also includes the date each page was last updated.

| Figure 4-19 | HOTBOT SEARCH RESULTS PAGE |

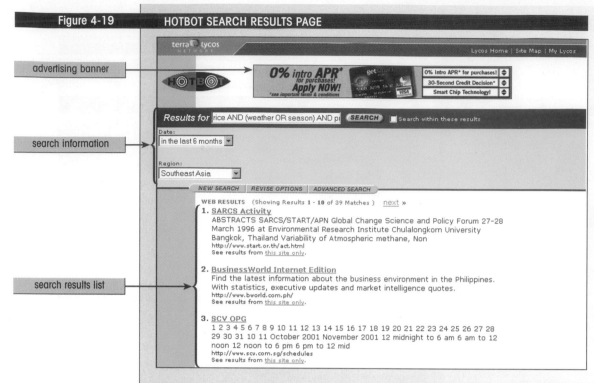

advertising banner

search information

search results list

8. Examine your search results and determine whether you have gathered suffi-cient useful information to respond to Dave's request. Since the search returned a small number of links that contained information relevant to Dave's query, you can conclude your work by forwarding the URLs to Dave.

Complex Search in Excite

Dave calls and has a quick request for your research help. He is working on a story about Finland and remembers that he met a professor who taught graduate business students there. He does not remember the professor's name or the name of the university at which the pro-fessor teaches. Dave is confident that he would recognize the university's name if he saw it again. He would like to interview the professor for his story. Dave asks if you can find some Finnish university names on the Web. After evaluating Dave's request, you decide to use the Excite search engine for this task. To create a useful search expression, you must identify search terms that might lead you to appropriate Web pages. Some terms you might use include *Finland*, *university*, and *business*. You consider that a university with a graduate business program might have an academic unit, "school," so you add that to your search expression as an alternative to "university." Hopeful that someone might have placed a list of universities on the Web, you decide to include *list* as a search term, too. The Excite search engine permits Boolean operators in its main page, so you decide to use that page for your query.

| REFERENCE | WINDOW | RW |

Conducting a Complex Search Using Excite
- Open the Excite search engine page in your Web browser.
- Formulate and enter a suitable search expression.
- Click the Search button.
- Evaluate the results, and if necessary, revise your search expression.

To perform an advanced search using Excite:

1. Return to the Student Online Companion page for Session 4.2, and then click the **Excite** link and wait while the browser opens the Excite home page.

2. Click in the **Search for** text box at the top of the page, and then type **finland AND list AND (university OR school) AND business**.

3. Click the **Search** button to start the search. Figure 4-20 shows the results page.

Figure 4-20	EXCITE SEARCH RESULTS PAGE

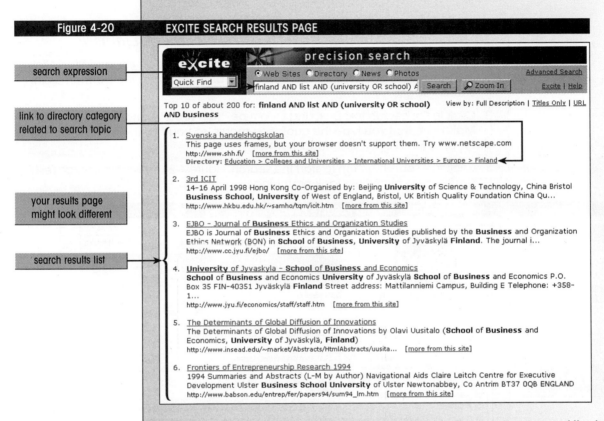

4. Examine your search results and determine whether one or more of the hyperlinks in the search results leads you to a list of Finnish universities that you can give to Dave. Remember that you may need to examine several pages of search results to find exactly what you need.

Complex Search in Northern Light

Ranjit is working on a series about fast-food franchises in various developing countries around the world. He would like to feature this industry's experience in Indonesia in his next column and asks you for help. He mentions that he would like to use industry publications in addition to Web sites for his research on this column. You know that the Northern Light search engine indexes not only the Web, but also a collection of periodicals. Therefore, you decide to run this search for Ranjit on the Northern Light search engine. To create a useful search expression, you must identify search terms that might lead you to appropriate Web pages. Some terms you might use include *fast*, *food*, *franchise*, and *Indonesia*. You are not interested in Web pages that have the individual terms *fast* and *food* as much as you are interested in Web pages that contain the phrase "fast food." The Northern Light search engine does not support full Boolean logic, so you will enter a simple expression and use Northern Light's folders feature to filter your results.

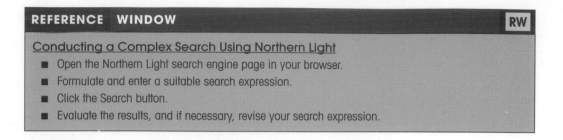

REFERENCE WINDOW   **RW**

Conducting a Complex Search Using Northern Light
- Open the Northern Light search engine page in your browser.
- Formulate and enter a suitable search expression.
- Click the Search button.
- Evaluate the results, and if necessary, revise your search expression.

To perform a complex search using Northern Light:

1. Return to the Student Online Companion page for Session 4.2, and then click the **Northern Light** link and wait while your browser opens the Northern Light Search page.

2. Click in the search text box, and then type **"fast food" franchise Indonesia**. Make sure that you type the quotation marks, so you find the phrase "fast food," instead of the individual terms.

3. Click the **Search** button to start the search. Figure 4-21 shows the search results page; these hyperlinks look promising.

Figure 4-21	NORTHERN LIGHT SEARCH RESULTS PAGE

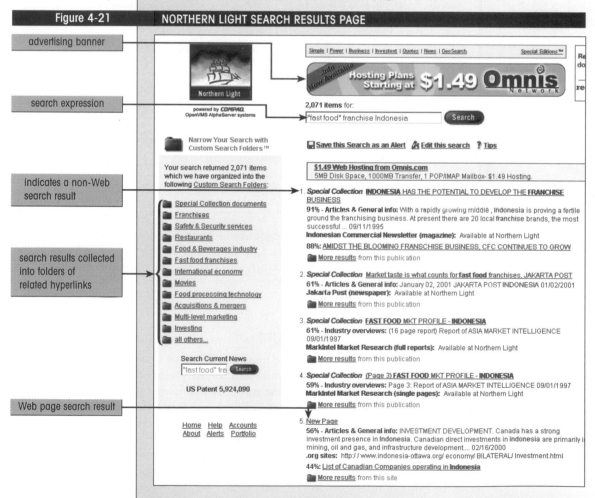

4. In the list of Custom Search Folders links at the left side of the page, click the folders that look promising. Examine your search results from each folder and

Northern Light provides hyperlinks to Web pages and to its own collection of several thousand journals, books, and other print resources. It provides a hyperlink to Web pages it finds and provides a summary of the print resources in its collection. For a fee, you can purchase the right to download and print an item from its collection. However, you can often find the original source in your school or company library if you do not want to purchase the item from Northern Light. Downloading the item would be a nice convenience if you used this search engine frequently.

The first four hyperlinks that appear in the results shown in Figure 4-21 begin with the words "Special Collection" to indicate that they are from Northern Light's own collection. The other hyperlinks are to Web pages.

Another unique feature of Northern Light is that it collects search results into folders, as shown in Figure 4-21. These folders are organized collections of related hyperlinks found in the search. Clicking one of these folders—for example "Food processing technology"—will narrow your results page to include only those hits that fit that category. Your search provides Dave with the information he needs and he congratulates you on a job well done.

Future of Web Search Tools

A number of different companies and organizations are working on ways to make searching the Web easier for the increasing number of people who use the Web. Work on natural language interfaces continues as search engine sites strive to make the job of searching even easier for users. An increasing number of search engines offer natural language querying as an option for entering search expressions. Although it is unlikely that these interfaces will provide the same power as Boolean searches anytime soon, they are much easier for infrequent Internet searchers to use.

One company, **About.com**, hires people with expertise in specific subject areas to create and manage their Web directory entries in those areas. Although Yahoo! uses subject matter experts this way, About.com takes the idea one step further and identifies their experts. Each of the About.com experts, called Guides, hosts a page with hyperlinks to related Web pages, moderates discussion areas, and provides an online newsletter. This creates a community of interested persons from around the world that can participate in maintaining the Web directory. The **Open Directory Project** uses the services of volunteer editors (more than 40,000 of them) who maintain listings in their individual areas of interest.

Dave and Ranjit are pleased with the information that you collected for them. They are anxious to start using search engines, directories, meta-search engines, and other Web resources to help them write their stories. Anne is so impressed with your work that she wants you to conduct some short classes to demonstrate the use of Web search tools to all staff members.

Session 4.2 QUICK CHECK

1. The three basic Boolean operators are_____, _____, and _____.

2. Write a search expression using Boolean and precedence operators that returns Web pages that contain information about wild mustang horses in Wyoming but not information about the Ford Mustang automobile.

3. True or False: The NEAR location operator always returns phrases that contain all keywords within 10 words of each other in a search expression.

4. True or False: In most search engines, the wildcard character is a * symbol.

5. Name three kinds of filters you can include in a HotBot search run from its main search page.

6. In an advanced or Boolean search expression, parentheses are an example of a(n) _____ operator.

7. Name one distinguishing feature of the Northern Light search engine.

REVIEW ASSIGNMENTS

Dave and Ranjit are keeping you busy at the Midland News. Your internship will be over soon, so you would like to leave Anne and the News with hyperlinks to some resources that the international business news section might want to use after you leave. To create those hyperlinks, complete the following steps:

1. Start your Web browser, open to the Student Online Companion page at www.course.comnewperspectives/internet3, click the hyperlink for your book, click the Tutorial 4 link, and then click the Review Assignments link and wait while the browser loads the page. The Review Assignments page contains links to search engines, directories, and meta-search engines.

2. Choose at least one search tool from each category and conduct a search using the search expression "international" and "business."

3. Extend or narrow your search using each tool until you find 10 Web sites that you believe are comprehensive guides or directories that Anne, Dave, and Ranjit should include in their bookmark or favorites lists to help them get information about international business stories.

4. For each Web site, record the URL and write a paragraph that explains why you believe the site would be useful to an international business news writer. Identify each site as a guide, directory, or other resource.

5. When you are finished, close your Web browser, and if necessary, log off your Internet connection

CASE PROBLEMS

Case 1. Key Consulting Group You are a manager at Key Consulting Group, a firm of geological and engineering consultants who specialize in earthquake-damage assessment. When an earthquake strikes, Key Consulting Group sends a team of geologists and structural engineers to the quake's site to examine the damage in buildings and determine what kinds of reconstruction will be needed. In some cases, the buildings must be demolished. An earthquake can occur without warning in many parts of the world, so Key Consulting Group needs quick access to information about local conditions in various parts of the world, including the temperature, rainfall, money exchange rates, demographics, and local customs. It is early July when you receive a call that an earthquake has just occurred in Northern Chile. To obtain information about local mid-winter conditions there so Key Consulting Group can prepare its team, complete the following steps.

1. Start your Web browser, open the Student Online Companion page at www.course.com/newperspectives/internet3, click the hyperlink for your book, click the Tutorial 4 link, and then click the Case Problems link and wait while your browser opens the page. The Case Problems section contains links to search engines, directories, and meta-search engines.

2. Use one of the search tools to conduct searches for information on local conditions in Northern Chile in July.

3. Prepare a short report that includes the daily temperature range, average rainfall, the current exchange rate for U.S. dollars to Chilean pesos, and any information you can obtain about the characteristics of the local population.

4. When you are finished, close your Web browser, and if necessary, log off your Internet connection.

Case 2. *Lightning Electrical Generators, Inc.* You work as a marketing manager for Lightning Electrical Generators, Inc., a firm that has built generators for over 50 years. The generator business is not as profitable as it once was, and John Delaney, the firm's president, has asked you to investigate new markets for the company. One market that John would like to consider is the uninterruptible power supply (UPS) business. A UPS supplies continuing power to a single computer or to an entire computer system if the regular source of power to the computer fails. Most UPSs provide power only long enough to allow an orderly shutdown of the computer. John wants you to study the market for UPSs in the United States. He also wants to know which firms currently make and sell these products. Finally, he would like some idea of what the power ratings and prices are of individual units. To provide John the information he needs, complete the following steps.

1. Start your Web browser, open the Student Online Companion page at www.course.com/newperspectives/internet3, click the hyperlink for your book, click the Tutorial 4 link, and then click the Case Problems link and wait while your browser opens the page. The Case Problems section contains links to search engines, directories, and meta-search engines.

2. Use one of the search tools to conduct searches for information about UPSs for John. You should design your searches to find the manufacturers' names and information about the products that they offer.

3. Prepare a short report that includes the information you have gathered, including the manufacturer's name, model number, product features, and suggested price for at least five UPSs.

4. When you are finished, close your Web browser, and if necessary, log off your Internet connection.

Case 3. *Dunwoody Cams, Inc.* Gunther Dunwoody is the founder of Dunwoody Cams, Inc., a manufacturer of automobile parts. Buyers for the major auto companies frequently visit Dunwoody's factory Web page to obtain quotes on parts. Gunther would like you to find Web pages that contain information about the history of the automobile so he can place hyperlinks to those pages on the Dunwoody Web page, so the site is more interesting to use. He is especially interested in having links to Web sites that have photographs of old autos. To gather the automobile-related information that Gunther wants, complete the following steps.

1. Start your Web browser, open the Student Online Companion page at www.course.com/newperspectives/internet3, click the hyperlink for your book, click the Tutorial 4 link, and then click the Case Problems link and wait while your browser opens the page. The Case Problems section contains links to search engines, directories, and meta-search engines.

2. Use one of the search tools to find Web sites that contain historical information about automobiles and automobile manufacturing.

3. Prepare a list of at least five URLs that Gunther might want to include on the Dunwoody Web page. Be sure that at least one of the URLs is for a Web site that includes photographs of old automobiles.

4. When you are finished, close your Web browser, and if necessary, log off your Internet connection.

Case 4. *Glenwood Employment Agency* You work as a staff assistant at the Glenwood Employment Agency. Eric Steinberg, the agency's owner, wants you to find Web resources for finding open positions in your geographic area. Eric would like this information to gauge whether his own efforts are keeping pace with the competition. He wants to monitor a few good pages but does not want to conduct exhaustive searches of the Web every week. To help Eric find current employment information, complete the following steps.

1. Start your Web browser, open the Student Online Companion page at www.course.com/newperspectives/internet3, click the hyperlink for your book, click the Tutorial 4 link, and then click the Case Problems link and wait while your browser opens the page. The Case Problems section contains links to search engines, directories, and meta-search engines.

2. Use one of the search tools to find Web sites that contain information about job openings in your geographic area. You can use search expressions that include Boolean and precedence operators to limit your searches.

3. Prepare a list of at least five URLs of pages that you believe would be good candidates for Eric's monitoring program.

4. For each URL that you find, write a paragraph that explains why you selected it and then identify any particular strengths or weaknesses of the Web site based on Eric's intended use.

5. When you are finished, close your Web browser, and if necessary, log off your Internet connection.

Case 5. Lynda's Fine Foods For many years, Lynda Reuss has operated a small store that sells specialty foods, such as pickles and mustard, and related gift items. Lynda is thinking about selling her products on the Web because they are small, relatively expensive, and easy to ship. She believes that people who buy her products might appreciate the convenience of ordering via the Web. Lynda would like to find some specialty food store sites on the Web so she can determine what the competition might be and to obtain some ideas that she might use when she creates her own Web site. To research selling specialty food items on the Web, complete the following steps.

1. Start your Web browser, open the Student Online Companion page at www.course.com/newperspectives/internet3, click the hyperlink for your book, click the Tutorial 4 link, and then click the Case Problems link and wait while your browser opens the page. The Case Problems section contains links to search engines, directories, and meta-search engines.

2. Use one of the search engine tools to find Web sites that offer gift items such as pickles or mustard. You can use search expressions that include Boolean and precedence operators to limit your searches.

3. Repeat your search using one of the Web directory tools.

4. Compare the results you obtained using a search engine and using a Web directory. Explain in a memorandum of about 100 words which search tool was more effective for this type of search.

5. When you are finished, close your Web browser, and if necessary, log off your Internet connection.

QUICK | CHECK ANSWERS

Session 4.1

1. open-ended, hard to phrase, difficult to determine when you have found a good answer
2. True
3. Web robot, bot, or spider.
4. many inbound links from other Web pages.
5. False. Most search engines exclude stop words such as *and* or *the*.
6. Advantage: Experts have selected, examined, and classified the entries in a Web directory. Disadvantage: You must know which category to search to find information.
7. The power of the search engine operates on the expert-selected and classified entries in the directory.
8. It forwards the expression a number of other search engines, and then presents and organizes the search results it receives from them.
9. They offer lists of hyperlinks to other Web pages, frequently including summaries or reviews of the Web sites, organized by subject.

Session 4.2

1. AND, OR, NOT
2. One possibility is: (mustang OR horse) AND Wyoming NOT (Ford OR automobile OR auto OR car)
3. False
4. True
5. time period, language, pages that include a specific type of media
6. inclusion, grouping
7. It includes non-Web search results from its special collection and organizes search results into folders of related hyperlinks.

In this tutorial you will:

- Find current news and weather information on the Web

- Obtain maps and city guides

- Use online library resources

- Find and use other Internet research resources

- Evaluate the validity and quality of Internet research resources

- Find graphics, sounds, and video resources

- Learn how copyright affects your use of resources you find on the Web

INFORMATION RESOURCES ON THE WEB

Finding, Evaluating, and Using Web Information Resources

CASE

Cosby Promotions

You just started a new position as the executive assistant to the president of Cosby Promotions, Marti Cosby. Cosby Promotions is a growing booking agency that handles promotion and concert contract negotiations for musicians and bands. Cosby Promotions works with a wide variety of music acts. Their current clients include bands that play pop, Latin, heavy metal, techno, industrial, and urban. The agency does not currently handle many country music acts, but Marti wants to expand their country music business over the next few years. Marti explains that the music business is fast moving—the popularity of musical artists often changes rapidly. The promotion and booking strategies that will work best for a particular client one month might not work well the next month. Promotional tie-ins and sponsorships are also important revenue sources for music acts and the needs of specific sponsors change with shifts in the preferences of their customers.

Your main job is to help Cosby Promotions' staff members stay current on news items and trends that might affect their clients. Marti expects you to use your basic understanding of Web searching techniques to help the firm identify and track important information about the agency's clients and potential sponsors. Your other duties will include updating agency executives and clients about local conditions at travel destinations and working with the firm's Web site design team to develop an effective Web presence for the firm.

In addition to working with Marti and the executive team, you will work closely with Susan Zhu, the firm's research director. Susan has worked at Cosby Promotions for six years in a variety of research jobs. The research department undertakes background investigations related to issues that arise in the firm's dealings with its clients. For example, whenever Marti starts working on a booking for a concert hall or other venue that is new for the firm, she asks Susan to provide background on the venue. Susan is looking forward to having you work with her as part of the Cosby Promotions research team.

SESSION 5.1

In this session, you will search for current news, weather, and travel information. You will find individual and business listings in directories. Finally, you will find multimedia resources and learn about some common Web multimedia formats.

Current Information

In earlier tutorials, you learned how to use search engines, directories, and other resources to find information on the Web. As you begin your new job, Marti explains that many of your assignments will be to find recent news and information about clients, potential sponsors, performance venues, and changes in the music industry.

To help you find current news and information, many search engines and directories include a hyperlink to a "What's new" page. The Yahoo! directory, for example, includes hyperlinks titled "News," "Sports," and "Weather" at the top of its home page. The Excite directory's main page includes a collection of hyperlinks to current events as shown in Figure 5-1.

Figure 5-1	EXCITE'S MAIN SEARCH PAGE

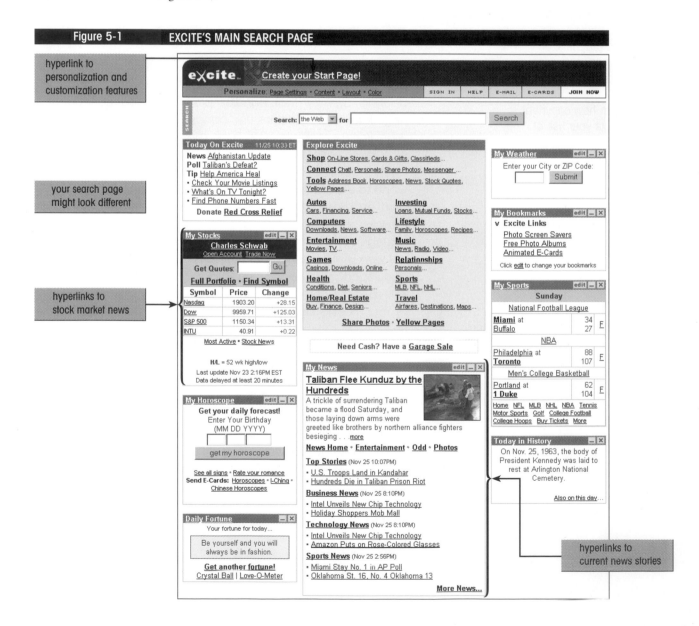

hyperlink to personalization and customization features

your search page might look different

hyperlinks to stock market news

hyperlinks to current news stories

You can see Excite's stock market and current news hyperlinks in Figure 5-1. The page also includes hyperlinks for sports news, weather, and even horoscopes. If you are willing to register with Excite, you can follow the Create your Start Page or Join Now hyperlink (near the top of the Web page) to personalize the page. This personalization feature lets you specify the kind of information that appears on this page when you log on.

Search engines can be useful tools for finding current news stories, too. Many search engines, including HotBot and AltaVista, allow you to choose a date range when you enter a search expression. HotBot provides two ways to do this. On its main page, you can specify one of a range of time options, such as "in the last week" or "in the last 3 months," to limit your search to sites that were last modified within your selected time period. HotBot's Advanced Search page includes the same range of time options as the main page, but it also lets users limit searches to dates before or after a specific date. To open the HotBot Advanced Search page shown in Figure 5-2, click the ADVANCED SEARCH button that appears on the HotBot search engine's main page.

Figure 5-2   **HOTBOT'S SUPERSEARCH PAGE**

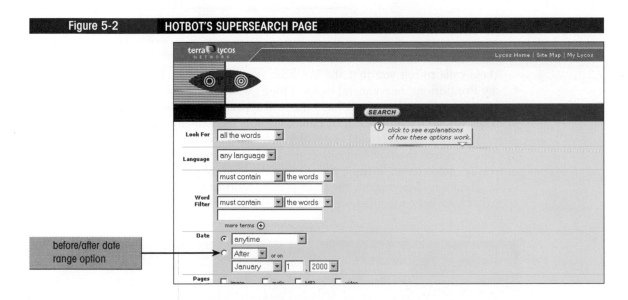

In the section of the HotBot Advanced Search page that is visible in Figure 5-2, you can see the before/after date range option. HotBot, even on its SuperSearch page, does not provide a way to search for sites *within* a specific date range. For example, you could not limit a HotBot search to sites modified between April 24, 2000, and November 11, 2000. As you learned in Tutorial 4, a good Internet researcher will always know how to use more than one search engine. The AltaVista search engine does not have the pre-set range of time options that HotBot offers, but it does allow you to set an exact "between" date range on its advanced search page. Figure 5-3 shows the AltaVista advanced search page with an exact date range set.

Figure 5-3   **DATE RANGE SETTINGS IN AN ALTA VISTA ADVANCED SEARCH**

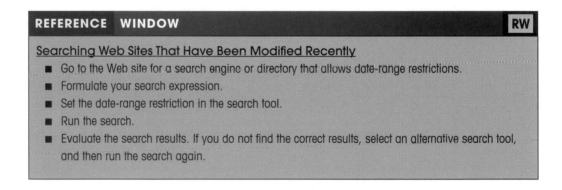

exact "between"
date range settings

Marti calls to tell you that she has been negotiating with Honda on behalf of one of Cosby Promotions' heavy metal bands. Honda wants to increase its appeal to younger drivers and is looking to sponsor a band that will appeal to that market. Marti knows that other agencies will be pitching bands to Honda for this sponsorship, so she wants as much background information on Honda as possible before she meets with them next week. She would like you to search the Web and collect the URLs of any sites that mention Honda and she is especially interested in learning more about the kinds of promotional activities that Honda is already doing. Marti needs the most recent information available, so you will search for sites that have been modified within the last three months.

REFERENCE WINDOW   **RW**

Searching Web Sites That Have Been Modified Recently
- Go to the Web site for a search engine or directory that allows date-range restrictions.
- Formulate your search expression.
- Set the date-range restriction in the search tool.
- Run the search.
- Evaluate the search results. If you do not find the correct results, select an alternative search tool, and then run the search again.

Consider the search tools available. Your search term—Honda—is a brand name, so it is likely that directory builders will collect many useful sites that include that term in their databases. Yahoo! is a directory that includes a date-range restriction option, so you decide to use it for your first search. Remember, if you do not find what you are looking for with one search tool, you can try your search again using different tools until you are satisfied with your results.

To find specific Web pages based on last modified dates:

1. Start your Web browser, and then go to the Student Online Companion page at **http://www.course.com/newperspectives/internet3**, click the hyperlink for your book, click the **Tutorial 5** link, and then click the **Session 5.1** link. Click the **Yahoo!** hyperlink and wait while the browser loads the Yahoo! home page.

2. Click the **advanced search** hyperlink to the right of the Search button to open the Yahoo! Search Options page.

3. Type **Honda** in the search text box.

4. Click the **Find only new listings added during the past** list arrow to open the list of choices (see Figure 5-4), click **3 months**, and then click the **Search** button to start the search.

| Figure 5-4 | SEARCHING THE YAHOO! DIRECTORY USING DATE CRITERIA |

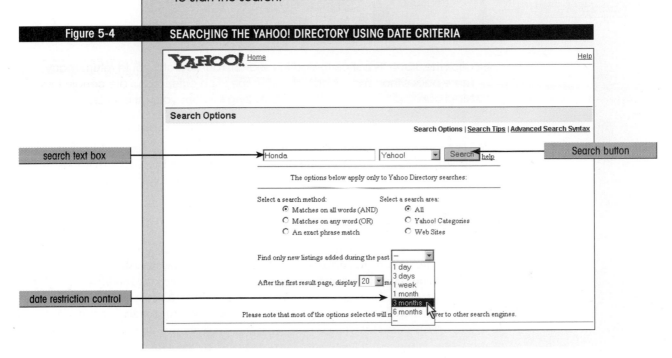

Your search should return fewer than 100 hits and will include the Web pages of Honda motorcycle and automobile dealers. After examining the results, you decide that you did not find what Marti needs. Susan suggests that you try your search again using HotBot because HotBot is a search engine and might return more hits than a directory such as Yahoo!.

To search for last modified dates using HotBot:

1. Use your browser's **Back** button or the history list to return to the Student Online Companion page for Session 5.1, and then click the **HotBot** hyperlink and wait for the HotBot home page to load in your Web browser.

2. Type **Honda AND promotion** in the Search Smarter text box to search for URLs of Web pages that relate to Honda's auto manufacturing operations.

3. Click the **Look for** list arrow, and then click **boolean phrase**.

4. Click the **Date** list arrow, and then click **in the last 3 months** to search for URLs that have been modified in the last three months. The search parameters you have specified appear in the portion of the HotBot search page shown in Figure 5-5.

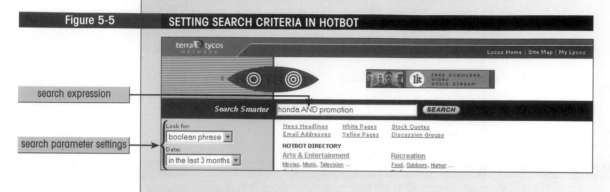

Figure 5-5	SETTING SEARCH CRITERIA IN HOTBOT

5. Click the **SEARCH** button to start the search. Your search should return many more pages than Yahoo! based on the specified criteria. You are certain that Marti can find the information she is looking for from your list of URLs.

You can send the URLs to Marti in an e-mail message, or you can tell her how to obtain the same search results. For now, you decide to cut and paste the URLs that look promising and then send them to her in an e-mail message.

Getting the News

Marti stops by to see you the day after you send her the URLs she requested. She is pleased with many of the recently modified Web pages you found. Now, she asks you to find any recent news stories about Honda that might not appear as part of a recently modified Web page.

Finding current news stories on the Web is an easy task. Almost every search engine and Web directory includes a list of current news hyperlinks to broadcast networks, wire services, and newspapers. A **wire service** (also called press agency or a news service) is an organization that gathers and distributes news to newspapers, magazines, broadcasters, and other organizations that pay a fee to the wire service. Although there are hundreds of wire services in the world, most news comes from the four largest wire services: United Press International (UPI) and the Associated Press (AP) in the United States, Reuters in Great Britain, and Agence France-Presse in France.

All of the major U.S. broadcasters, including ABC, CBS, CNN, Fox, MSNBC (the Microsoft-NBC joint venture), and National Public Radio (NPR) have Web sites that carry news features. Broadcasters in other countries, such as the BBC, also provide news reports on their Web pages. The Reuters Web page includes current news stories in addition to the news services that it sells. Major newspapers, such as *The New York Times*, *The Washington Post*, and the *London Times*, have Web sites that include current news and many other features from their print editions. Many of these broadcast news, wire service, and newspaper Web sites include search features that allow you to search the site for specific news stories. However, not many search tools are available on the Web to search multiple news sources at the same time. You begin to think about the time it will take to do a comprehensive search of just the major news sites for Marti and you begin to worry.

Susan tells you that the **Internet Public Library – Online Newspapers** site includes hyperlinks to hundreds of international and domestic newspapers. Figure 5-6 shows a portion of the Internet Public Library Web site.

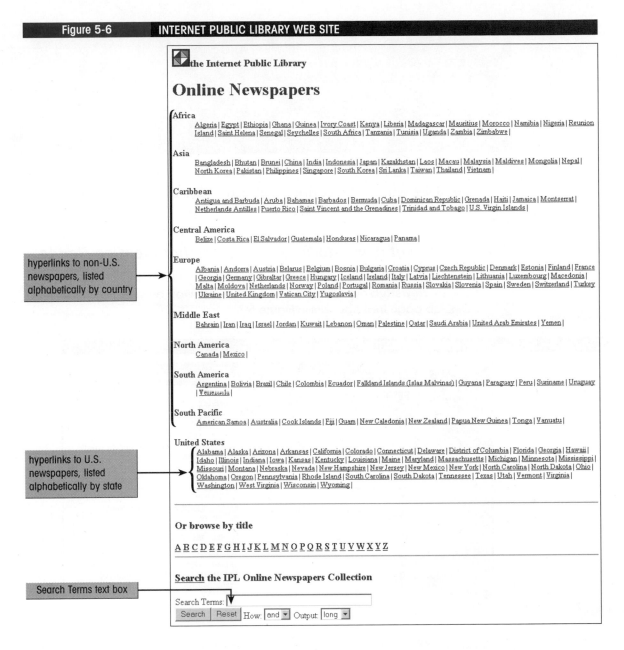

Figure 5-6   INTERNET PUBLIC LIBRARY WEB SITE

As you can see in Figure 5-6, this site has a search field, but it searches only the title and the main entry for each newspaper and does not search the newspaper sites' contents. Therefore, you could use it to identify all of the newspapers in New Jersey or all of the newspapers that had the word *Tribune* in their titles, but you could not use it to find news stories that include the word *Honda*.

Fortunately, several Web sites let you search the content of current news stories in multiple publications and wire services.

Yahoo! News includes the AP and Reuters wire services along with news it purchases from other leading newspapers and magazines. The Northern Light Current News site includes the AP and UPI wire services in its offerings. VPOP Technologies' NewsHub site updates its news database with information from a number of wire services every 15 minutes. To obtain both breadth and currency of coverage, you might want to run the same query using more than one of these search tools.

Searching Current News Stories
- Select a Web site that offers searchable news stories.
- Open the Web site in your Web browser.
- Enter your search expression into the search text box.
- Run the search and evaluate your results.

You would like search coverage that is both current and broad, so you decide to use the NewsHub, Yahoo!, and Northern Light news search tools.

To find recent news stories on the Web that mention Honda:

1. Return to the Student Online Companion Web page for Session 5.1, and then click the **NewsHub** hyperlink and wait while your Web browser loads the NewsHub page that appears in Figure 5-7.

Figure 5-7   NEWSHUB HOME PAGE

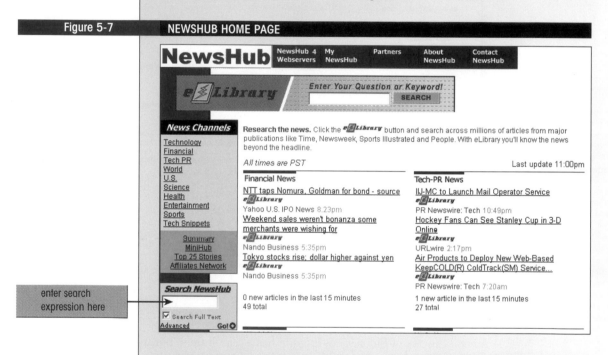

enter search expression here

TROUBLE? If a Privacy dialog box opens about a privacy icon appearing on your taskbar, click OK.

2. Type **Honda** in the **Search NewsHub** text box (do not use the eLibrary search tool at the top of the page), and then click the **Go!** button. Examine the Web pages that NewsHub found, and note the URLs of any pages that might interest Marti. You want to make sure you find enough relevant hits, so you decide to try the other news search tools.

TROUBLE? If your search does not yield many useful results, try using different combinations of words in the search expression. For example, you might find that entering "Honda sponsor" or "Honda promotion" works better than the word "Honda" alone.

3. Return to the Student Online Companion Web page for Session 5.1, and then click the **Yahoo! News** hyperlink to load that page in your Web browser.

4. Type **Honda** in the search text box (you might need to scroll down the page to see the search text box), and then click the **Search** button to start your search. As in Step 2, you can try other words if your search does not yield useful results.

5. Return to the Student Online Companion Web page for Session 5.1, and then click the **Northern Light Current News Search** hyperlink to load the page shown in Figure 5-8.

Figure 5-8	NORTHERN LIGHT CURRENT NEWS SEARCH PAGE

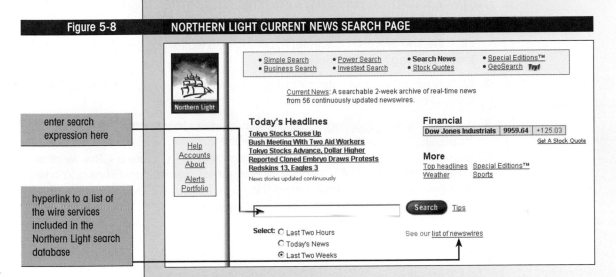

6. Type **Honda** in the search text box, and then click the **Search** button to start your search. The Northern Light results page might include links to its Special Collection pages in addition to Web page results. Also, the search results will be collected in Northern Light's customized folders. Recall that you learned about these two features of the Northern Light search engine in Tutorial 4.

Now you have accumulated a respectable list of URLs about Honda's current promotional and sponsorship activities for Marti. You have gained experience in searching for current topics by examining Web pages that have been modified recently and by using three tools that search the Web specifically for news reports.

Weather Reports

Marti will travel to Nashville later in the week to meet with some new country music artists that she hopes to sign as clients for the agency. Marti already has made her travel plans, and she is interested in the weather forecast for the area. You decide to check two sources for the information because you know that meteorology is not an exact science—forecasts from different sources can differ.

REFERENCE   WINDOW

Finding a Weather Forecast
- Open the weather information Web site you would like to use in a Web browser.
- Locate the weather report for the city or area in which you are interested.
- Repeat the steps to find other weather information in different Web sites.

To find weather forecasts for the Nashville area:

1. Return to the Student Online Companion Web page for Session 5.1, and then click the **The Weather Channel** hyperlink and wait while your Web browser loads the Weather Channel page.

2. Type **Nashville** in the Enter city or US zip code text box, and then click the **GO** button.

3. A page appears showing a number of hyperlinks to U.S. cities named "Nashville." You are interested in weather in Nashville, Tennessee, so click that hyperlink to open a page similar to the one shown in Figure 5-9. The Weather Channel page for Nashville includes a report of current conditions and a ten-day forecast for the Nashville area. The page includes a Doppler radar image and links to many more radar and satellite images.

Figure 5-9	WEATHER CHANNEL NASHVILLE LOCAL FORECAST PAGE

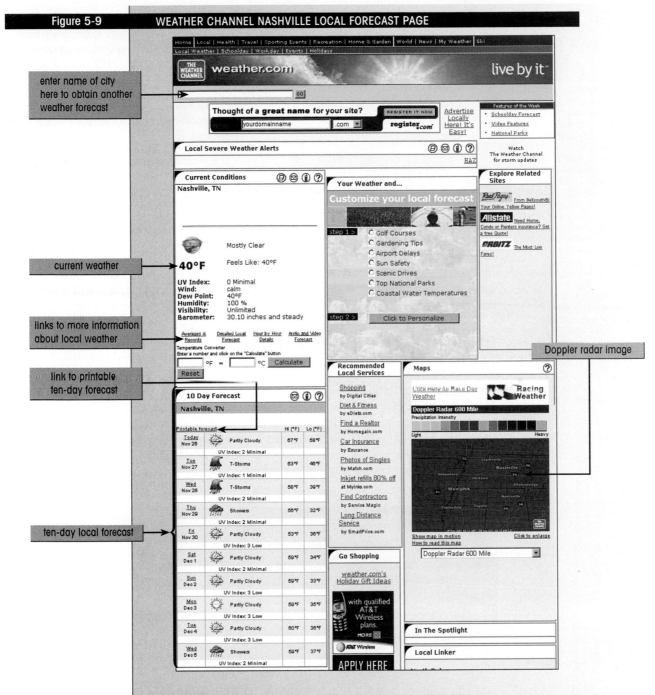

enter name of city here to obtain another weather forecast

current weather

links to more information about local weather

link to printable ten-day forecast

ten-day local forecast

Doppler radar image

TROUBLE? If a small Web page in the form of a dialog box opens, click that page's Close button to dismiss it. The site may also open small Web pages that contain ads. You can click the Close button on those pages also.

TROUBLE? If the Local Weather page for Nashville opens in another window, close the one you used to click the Nashville, Tennessee link.

4. Scroll the page, if necessary, and then click the **Printable forecast** hyperlink to open a page that only shows the ten-day forecast. Later, you can click your browser's **Print** button to print the forecast for Marti. Now, use a different weather source to search for weather conditions in Nashville.

5. Return to the Student Online Companion page for Session 5.1, and then click the **AccuWeather** hyperlink and wait for your Web browser to load the page. The AccuWeather page that opens includes hyperlinks to a variety of weather information, including local forecasts for U.S. cities.

6. Type **Nashville, TN** in the Enter your zip code or city, state text box, and then click the **Go** button to open the AccuWeather local forecast page for Nashville. This page includes a 15-day forecast and hyperlinks to local radar images and a variety of weather maps and other information.

7. Click your browser's **Print** button to print the AccuWeather forecast for Marti.

Usually, weather-forecasting sites will report slightly different (and sometimes completely different) forecasts for the same time period in the same area. Many people who obtain weather forecasts from the Web regularly check two or three sites and compare the forecasts. If you are planning a trip, you might want to check the traveler's forecasts offered by both the Weather Channel *and* the AccuWeather sites. The Weather Channel Web site includes estimates of what the next day's weather-related flight delays will be at domestic and international airports.

Obtaining Maps and City Guides

Marti is excited about her trip to Nashville because this will be her first visit, and she is a country music fan who grew up listening to broadcasts of the Grand Ole Opry on the radio. Marti would like to include a stop at Ryman Auditorium, the original home of the Grand Ole Opry, while she is in Nashville. You offer to find a map of Nashville on the Web that shows the location of Ryman Auditorium. Marti gives you the address, 116 Fifth Avenue North, and you are ready to go to work. You tell Marti that you also will look for some information about restaurants and other things to do in Nashville.

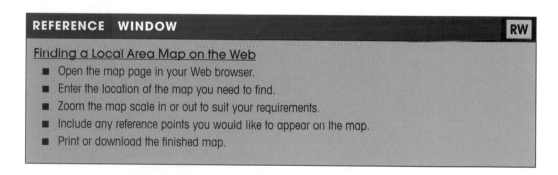

REFERENCE WINDOW   **RW**

Finding a Local Area Map on the Web
- Open the map page in your Web browser.
- Enter the location of the map you need to find.
- Zoom the map scale in or out to suit your requirements.
- Include any reference points you would like to appear on the map.
- Print or download the finished map.

To obtain a map of the Nashville area near Ryman Auditorium:

1. Return to the Student Online Companion Web page for Session 5.1, and then click the **MapQuest Interactive Atlas** hyperlink and wait while your Web browser loads the Web page.

2. Click the **Maps** hyperlink, and then wait for the next page to open, where you can specify the address of the desired map location.

3. Type the address of Ryman Auditorium, **116 Fifth Avenue North**, in the Address or Intersection text box.

4. Press the **Tab** key until you move to the City text box, and then type **Nashville**.

5. Press the **Tab** key, type **TN** in the State text box, and then click the **Get Map** button. Figure 5-10 shows the map for Ryman Auditorium.

| Figure 5-10 | MAPQUEST MAP SHOWING THE LOCATION OF RYMAN AUDITORIUM |

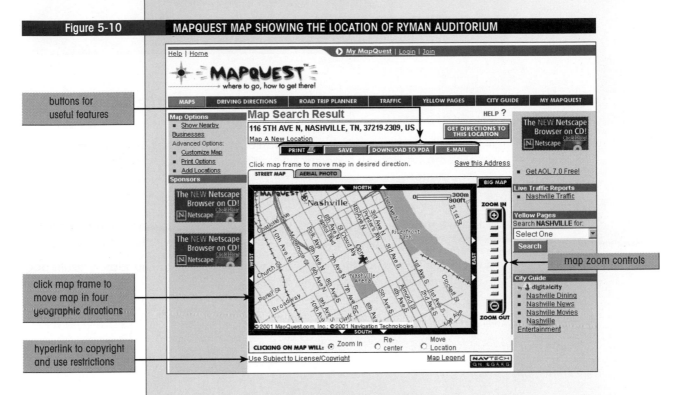

The map identifies the location you requested with a red star, on Fifth Avenue North, just above the intersection with U.S. Route 70. You can adjust the map scale using the controls on the right side of the map. It is often useful to have a street-level version of a map to show detail and a lower-scale version of a map to show more of the surrounding area. You can click the map's frame to move the map within the window in the four geographic directions, the Map Zoom controls to zoom in or out, and the Map Size control to open a larger map in a new browser window. MapQuest provides buttons that let you perform a number of useful functions with the map. You can print or e-mail the map. You can also download the map to a PDA (portable digital assistant, such as a Palm Pilot). You can save the map on the MapQuest server. (You must register as a MapQuest member to use the Save option.) Before you print or download information from a Web page, be sure to check the site for copyright and use restrictions.

6. Click the **All rights reserved. Use Subject to License/Copyright** hyperlink at the bottom of the page and review the terms under which you can use printed or e-mailed maps obtained from this server. After reading the information, close the copyright window.

You have obtained a map that will meet Marti's needs on the Nashville trip. You also would like to find some information about Ryman Auditorium and other things to do in Nashville. The Web offers a number of city guides; hyperlinks to some of these sites appear in the Additional Information section of the Student Online Companion page for Tutorial 5.

Obtaining Travel Destination Information

■ Go to a city guide Web site in your Web browser.
■ Search the site for your destination city, region, or country.
■ Explore the hyperlinks provided by the site for your destination.

To obtain information about Nashville and the Ryman Auditorium:

1. Return to the Student Online Companion Web page for Session 5.1, and then click the **CitySearch** hyperlink and wait while your Web browser loads the Web page.

2. Click the **Nashville** hyperlink in the list of City Guides.

3. Type **Ryman Auditorium** in the Search for ANYTHING text box, and then click the **GO!** Button (the GO! button is to the right of the ANYWHERE search box.)

4. Click the **Ryman Auditorium** hyperlink that appears on the search results page to open the Web page shown in Figure 5-11.

Figure 5-11   CITYSEARCH WEB PAGE

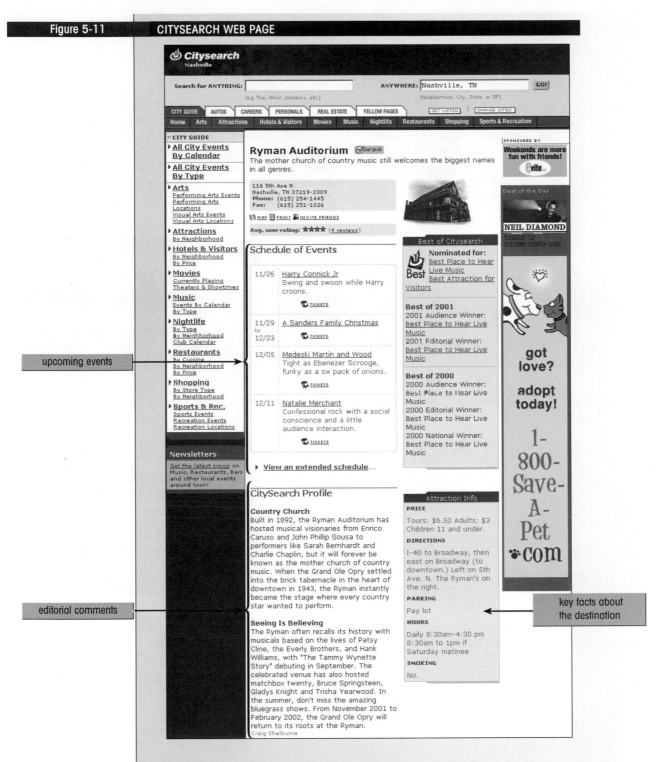

Figure 5-11 shows hyperlinks and other useful information that Marti can use for her trip. The key facts presented include the auditorium's telephone number, hours of operation, and tour prices. The page includes hyperlinks to a map of the local area—provided by MapQuest—and a seating diagram for the venue. The editorial comments provide a short history of the building and its role in the development of country music. The page also includes information about upcoming events scheduled at the auditorium. The hyperlinks at the top of the page link to information about restaurants, nightclubs, bars, theaters, and movies in the area.

You are satisfied that you have found more than enough information to make Marti's Nashville trip memorable and successful.

Finding Businesses

Over the next few years, Marti is interested in developing reciprocal relationships with local booking agencies in Nashville. She would like to make some initial contacts during this trip and asks you to search the Web to find a list of booking agencies in Nashville.

Many search engines on the Web specialize in finding people and businesses. The sites that store only information about businesses are often called **yellow pages** sites. One of these search engines is the **SuperPages.com** site operated by Verizon. You decide to use SuperPages.com to create the booking agency list for Marti.

REFERENCE WINDOW   RW

Finding Business Listings on the Web

- Navigate to a page that provides business listings or a business listing search engine in your Web browser.
- Enter information about the nature and geographic location of the business that you want to find.
- Run the search.
- Examine and evaluate the results to determine whether you should revise your search or try another search engine.

To find Nashville booking agencies on the Web:

1. Return to the Student Online Companion Web page for Session 5.1, and then click the **SuperPages.com** hyperlink and wait while your Web browser loads the Web page.

2. Because you are not sure how booking agents will be listed in the SuperPage.com database, you decide to use a general term to begin your search. Type **Agents** in the Category text box.

3. Press the **Tab** key twice, and then type **Nashville** in the City text box.

4. Click the **State** list arrow, and then click **TN**.

5. Click the **Find It** button to begin the search. The results page includes a list of links to a number of related categories.

6. Click the **Artists, Managers, & Agencies** category link to open a page similar to the one that appears in Figure 5-12.

Figure 5-12   **SUPERPAGES.COM SEARCH RESULTS PAGE**

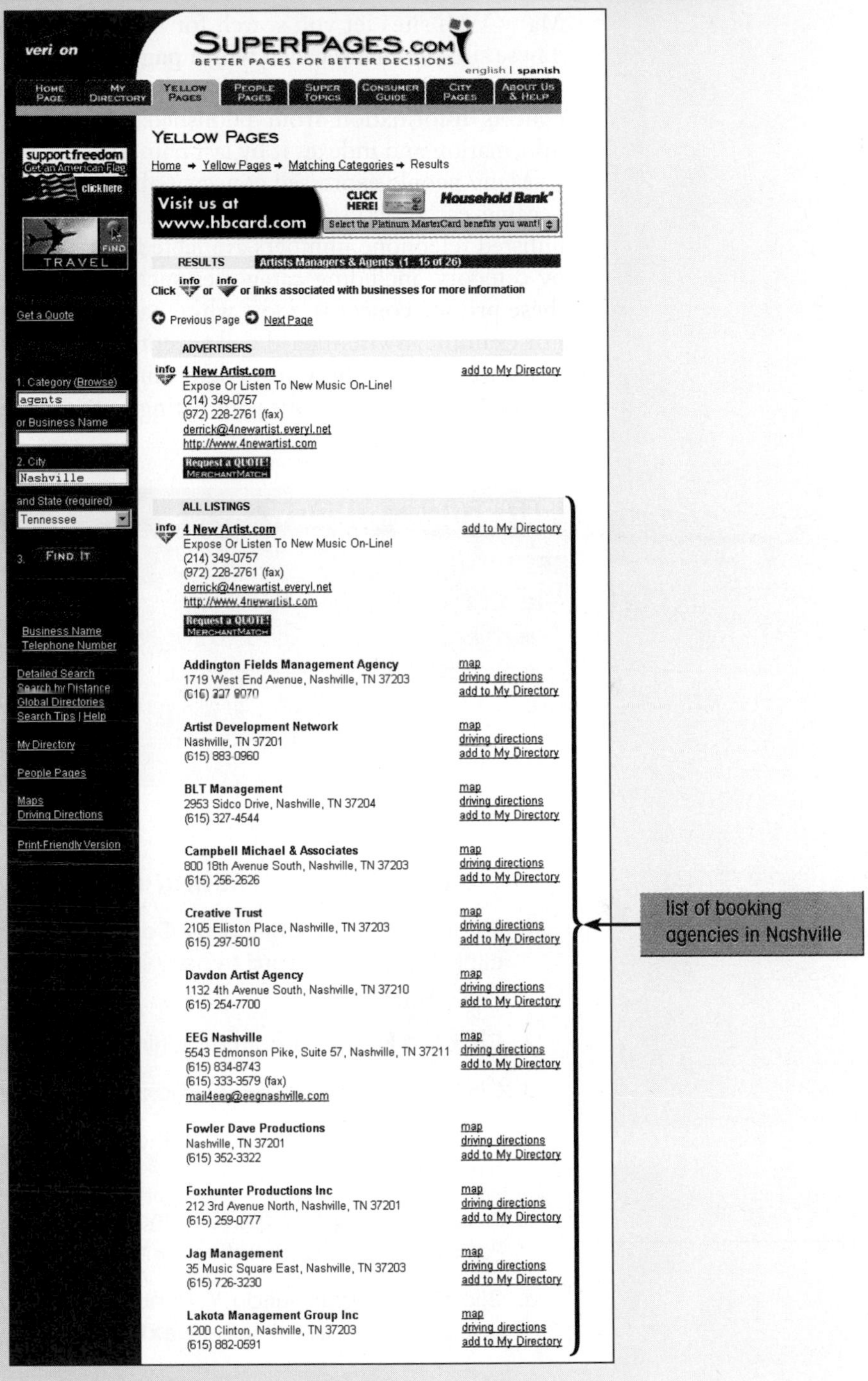

Your search should find booking agencies included in the listings from this SuperPages.com category. The listings include the name, address, telephone number, and a hyperlink to a map for each firm. SuperPages.com also provides a hyperlink to listed firms' Web sites. Some or all of the booking agencies listed in the results pages might not have Web sites and, therefore, your results pages might not include any hyperlinks. Now, you are ready to prepare a report for Marti that contains the agencies' information so she can investigate potential relationships with those agencies.

Finding People and Related Privacy Concerns

Many Web sites let you search for individuals' names, addresses, and telephone numbers. These sites often are called **white pages** sites. One comprehensive site that includes search tools for finding information about businesses and individuals is **Switchboard**. Switchboard collects information from published telephone directories and other publicly available information and indexes it by last name.

Many people expressed concerns about privacy violations when this type of information became easily accessible on the Web. In some cases, Web sites made unpublished and unlisted telephone numbers available for public use. Some sites grouped individual listings by category, including categories such as religious or political affiliations. In response to these privacy concerns, most white pages sites offer people a way to remove their listings. For example, Switchboard will accept a list removal request sent via its Web page, e-mail, or a letter. You might want to determine whether white pages sites have a correct listing for you and whether you want your listing to appear in a white pages site.

REFERENCE WINDOW   **RW**

Searching for Your White Pages Listing
- Open a white pages Web site in your Web browser.
- Enter your name and part of your address.
- Run the search, and then examine the search results.
- Consider repeating the search with various combinations of partial address information or variants of the correct spelling of your name.

To search for your listing on the Switchboard white pages site:

1. Return to the Student Online Companion Web page for Session 5.1, and then click the **Switchboard** hyperlink and wait while your Web browser loads the Web page.

2. Click the **Find a Person** hyperlink to open the Find a Person Web page.

3. Click in the **Last Name** text box, and then type your last name.

4. Press the **Tab** key to move to the City text box, and then type the name of the city in which you live.

5. Press the **Tab** key to move to the State text box, and then type the two-letter U.S. Postal Service abbreviation for the state in which you live.

6. Click the **Search** button. Your name might appear in the first results page. If it does not appear, click the **Next Matches** hyperlink to go to the next page.

   TROUBLE? If your telephone number is listed in another person's name, use that person's name to find your listing.

   TROUBLE? If you do not find your listing, click the Modify Search hyperlink, add more information to the search text boxes, and then search again. If you still cannot find your listing, try searching for a friend's listing or your parents' listing.

7. Close your browser and, if necessary, log off your Internet connection.

You might need to run the search several times using different information to find your listing. If you do not want Switchboard to list your name and information, return to the Switchboard start page, click the My Personal Listing hyperlink near the bottom of the page, and then click the Remove your personal listing hyperlink. Follow the instructions on the page that appears to remove your listing from the Switchboard directory.

The Student Online Companion page for Tutorial 5 contains hyperlinks to other white pages Web sites. You can search those sites for your listing and follow similar steps to remove or change it, if you want.

You have accomplished many tasks and helped Marti quite a bit. You look forward to your meeting with Susan tomorrow morning to discuss the research department's guidelines for evaluating the validity and quality of the information that you obtain during your searches of the Web.

Session 5.1 QUICK | CHECK

1. Reuters is an example of a _____.

2. True or False: NewsHub updates its news stories twice each day.

3. Explain why you might want to consult two or three Web resources for weather information before leaving on an out-of-town trip.

4. List two advantages of using a Web map server instead of a paper map or atlas.

5. Describe three types of information that you might obtain from a city guide Web page.

6. True or False: City guide Web sites are usually created by an agency of the city government.

7. A Web site that helps people find businesses by name or category is often called a _____.

8. A Web site that helps people find the telephone numbers or e-mail addresses of other individuals is often called a _____.

Now that you know more about where to find information on the Web, you need to learn how to evaluate that information. In Session 5.2, you will learn how to assess the validity and quality of the information you find on the Web.

SESSION 5.2

In this session, you will learn how to evaluate the quality of Web research resources based on a site's author, content, and appearance. You will then learn how to use library research resources to find information about a specific topic. You will learn how to find multimedia resources on the Web and how copyright laws affect your ability to use those resources. You also will learn about the future of electronic publishing.

Evaluating the Validity and Quality of Web Research Resources

In your morning meeting with Susan, you reviewed some of the research department's standards and practices for information that the firm collects using the Internet. One of the most important issues in doing Web research is assessing the validity and quality of the information provided on the Internet. Because the Web has made publishing so easy and inexpensive, it allows virtually anyone to create a Web page on almost any subject. Research published in scientific or literary journals is subjected to peer review. Books and research monographs are often reviewed by peers or edited by experts in the appropriate subject area. Information on the Web is seldom subjected to this review and editing process that has become a standard practice in print publishing.

When searching the Web for entertainment, general information, news, or weather information, you are not likely to encounter a site that someone has intentionally created to misinform you. Further, the potential damage caused by a bad weather report or false news is not great. When you are searching the Web for an answer to a serious research question, however, the risks can be significant.

You can reduce your risks by carefully evaluating the quality of any Web resource on which you plan to rely for information related to an important judgment or decision. To develop an opinion about the quality of the resource, you can evaluate three major components of any Web page. These three components are the Web page's authorship, content, and appearance.

Author Identity and Objectivity

The first thing you should try to do when evaluating a Web research resource is to determine who authored the page. If you cannot easily find authorship information on a Web site, you should question the validity of the information included on that site. A Web site that does not identify its author has very little credibility as a research resource. Any Web page that presents empirical research results, logical arguments, theories, or other information that purports to be the result of a research process should identify the author *and* present the author's background information and credentials. The information on the site should be sufficient to establish the author's professional qualifications. You also should check secondary sources for corroborating information. For example, if the author of a Web page indicates that he or she is a member of a university faculty, you can find the university's Web site and see if the author is listed as a faculty member. The Web site should provide author contact information, such as a street, e-mail address, or telephone number, so you can contact the author or consult information directories to verify the addresses or telephone numbers.

In some cases, it can be difficult to determine who owns a specific Web server or provides the space for the Web page. You can make a rough assessment, however, by examining the domain identifier in the URL. If the site claims affiliation with an educational or research institution, the domain should be .edu for educational institution. A not-for-profit organization would most likely have the .org domain, and a government unit or agency would have the .gov domain. These are not hard and fast rules, however. For example, some perfectly legitimate not-for-profit organizations have URLs with a .com domain.

You also should consider whether the qualifications presented by the author pertain to the material that appears on the Web site. For example, the author of a Web site concerned with gene-splicing technology might list a Ph.D. degree as a credential. If the author's Ph.D. is in history or sociology, it would not support the credibility of the gene-splicing technology Web site. If you cannot determine the specific areas of the author's educational background, you can look for other examples of the author's work on the Web. By searching for the author's name and terms related to the subject area, you should be able to find other sites that include the author's work. The fact that a Web site author has written extensively on a subject can add some evidence—though not necessarily conclusive—that the author has expertise in the field.

In addition to identifying the author's identity and qualifications, the author information should include details about the author's affiliations—either as an employee, owner, or consultant—with organizations that might have an interest in the research results or other information included in the Web site. Information about the author's affiliations will help you determine the level of independence and objectivity that the author can bring to bear on the research questions or topics. For example, research results supporting the contention that cigarette smoke is not harmful that are presented in a site authored by a researcher with excellent scientific credentials might be less compelling if you learn that the researcher is the chief scientist at a major tobacco company. By reading the page content carefully, you might be able to identify any bias in the results that is not justified by the evidence presented.

Content

Content is a criterion that is much more difficult to judge than the author's identity and objectivity; after all, you were searching for Web sites so you could learn more about your search topic, which implies that you probably are not an expert in that content area. However, you can look for some things in the Web site's presentation to help determine the quality of information. If the Web page has a clearly stated publication date, you can determine the timeliness of the content. You can read the content critically and evaluate whether the included topics are relevant to the research question at hand. You might be able to determine whether important topics or considerations were omitted. You also might be able to assess the depth of treatment the author gives to the subject.

Form and Appearance

The Web does contain pages full of outright lies and misinformation that are nicely laid out, include tasteful graphics, and have grammatically correct and properly spelled text. However, many pages that contain low-quality or incorrect information are poorly designed and not well edited. For example, a Web page devoted to an analysis of Shakespeare's plays that contains spelling errors indicates a low-quality resource. Loud colors, graphics that serve no purpose, and flashing text are all Web page design elements that often suggest a low-quality resource.

Having explained how these principles of assessing Web page quality are applied to the research team's work at Cosby Promotions, Susan asks you to evaluate a Web page. One of the bands that the agency represents has received a request to perform at a fund-raising concert for an environmental protection group that is concerned about global warming. Susan has been gathering a list of URLs from which she plans to take information to include in a briefing report for the talent manager who will be deciding whether the band should perform at the fund-raising concert. Susan would like you to evaluate the quality of a URL titled "Environmental Health Update" that is on her list.

REFERENCE   WINDOW   **RW**

Evaluating a Web Research Resource
- Open the Web page in your Web browser.
- Identify the author, if possible. If you can identify the author, evaluate his or her credentials and objectivity.
- Examine the content of the Web site.
- Evaluate the site's form and appearance.
- Draw a conclusion about the site's overall quality.

To evaluate the quality of the environmental health update Web page:

1. Start your Web browser, if necessary, and then go to the Student Online Companion page by entering the URL **http://www.course.com/newperspectives/internet3** in the appropriate location in your Web browser. Click the hyperlink for your book, click the **Tutorial 5** link, and then click the **Session 5.2** link. Click the **PSR Program Update** link and wait while the browser loads the Web page that appears in Figure 5-13. Examine the content of the Web page; read the text, examine the titles and headings, and consider the page's appearance.

Figure 5-13	PSR PROGRAM UPDATE WEB PAGE

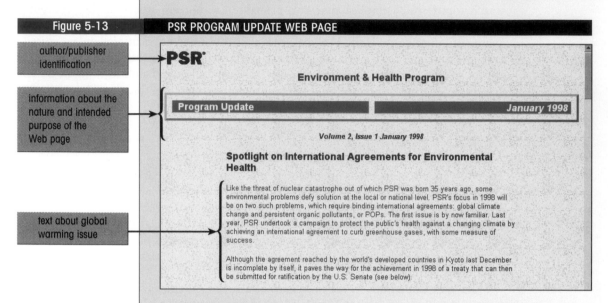

author/publisher identification

information about the nature and intended purpose of the Web page

text about global warming issue

You can see in Figure 5-13 that the author or publisher of the page is identified only as "PSR" and the page has a simple, clear design. The .org domain in the URL tells you that the publisher is a not-for-profit organization. You note that the grammar and spelling are correct, and that the content—although it clearly reflects a strong specific viewpoint on the issue—is not inflammatory or overly argumentative. As you read more of the page, you see that this style of layout and content is consistent in passages related to global warming and other issues discussed on the page. You note that the text cites such authorities as the U.S. National Oceanic and Atmospheric Administration and the *New England Journal of Medicine*. The reputable references and the consistent style of the page suggest that this might be a high-quality site. You also note that the date on the page has been published and kept on the Web for several years. Although this fact alone would not increase your assessment of the page's validity, taken with the other content on the page, it does add help corroborate the quality of the page.

2. Use your browser's scroll bar to scroll to the bottom of the page, which looks like Figure 5-14.

| Figure 5-14 | IDENTIFYING INFORMATION IN THE PSR PROGRAM UPDATE WEB PAGE |

contact information for the national organization

contact information for this program

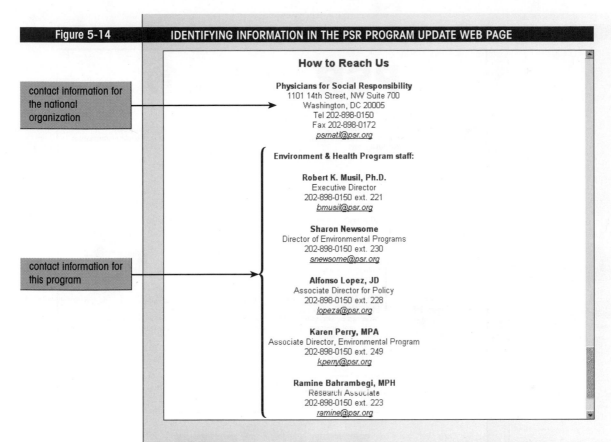

How to Reach Us

Physicians for Social Responsibility
1101 14th Street, NW Suite 700
Washington, DC 20005
Tel 202-898-0150
Fax 202-898-0172
psrnatl@psr.org

Environment & Health Program staff:

Robert K. Musil, Ph.D.
Executive Director
202-898-0150 ext. 221
bmusil@psr.org

Sharon Newsome
Director of Environmental Programs
202-898-0150 ext. 230
snewsome@psr.org

Alfonso Lopez, JD
Associate Director for Policy
202-898-0150 ext. 228
lopeza@psr.org

Karen Perry, MPA
Associate Director, Environmental Program
202-898-0150 ext. 249
kperry@psr.org

Ramine Bahrambegi, MPH
Research Associate
202-898-0150 ext. 223
ramine@psr.org

Now you can see that PSR is an acronym for the Physicians for Social Responsibility organization. Further, you can see that the organization's address, telephone number, and e-mail address are listed along with contact information for key individuals in the PSR's Environment and Health Program. To find more information about PSR, you might want to visit the organization's home page. The Web page shown in Figure 5-14 does not include a home page hyperlink, but you can guess that it might be the first part of the URL for this page.

3. Click in your browser's Location field or Address Bar, and then delete all of the text to the right of the .org/ domain name portion of the URL. Press the **Enter** key to load the Web page shown in Figure 5-15 with the shortened URL.

Figure 5-15 PSR HOME PAGE

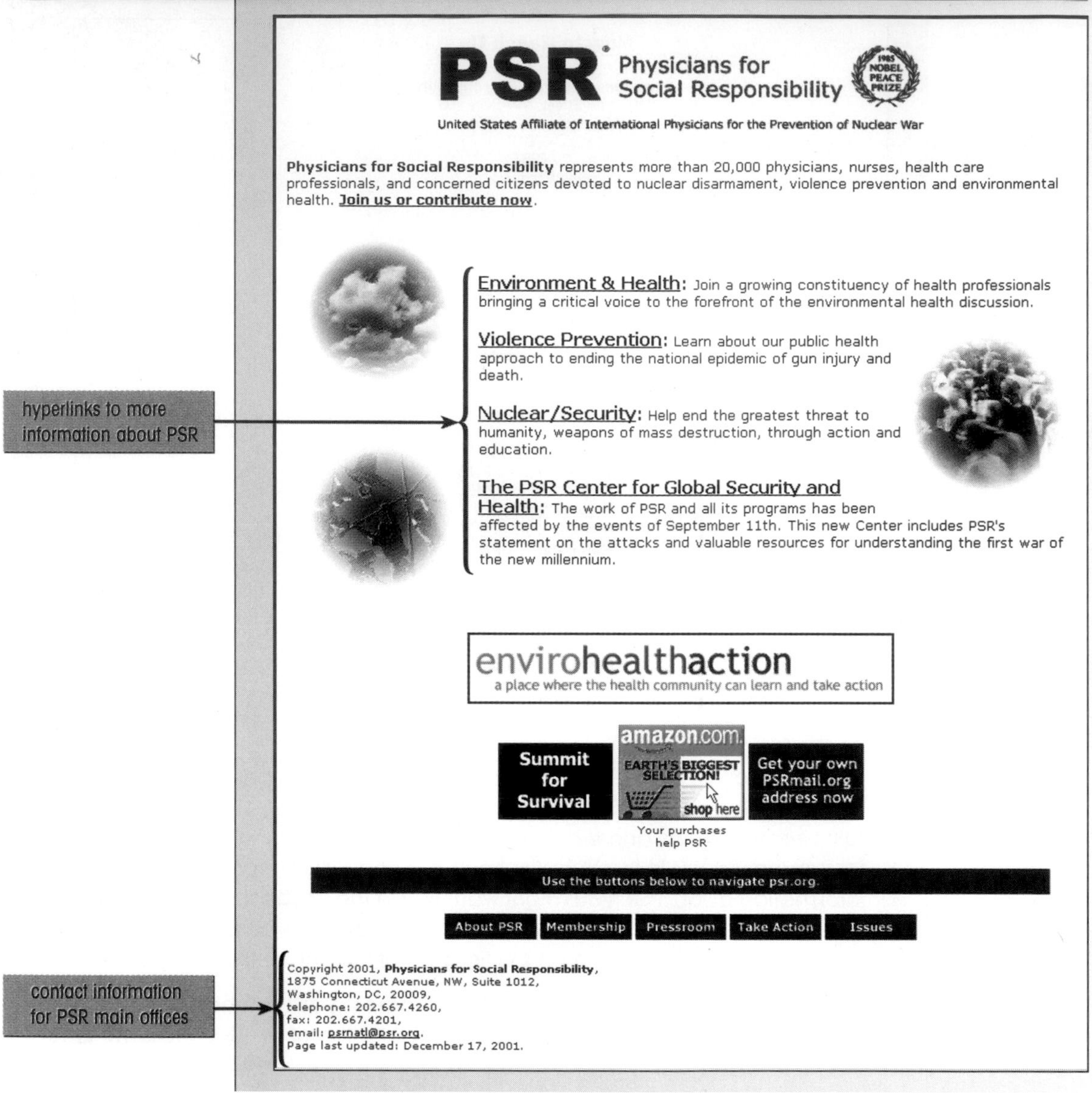

hyperlinks to more information about PSR

contact information for PSR main offices

The Web page shown in Figure 5-15 is, in fact, the U.S. National PSR Office home page that includes hyperlinks to information about the organization, its goals, activities, directors, and membership. The page even indicates that the organization was awarded the Nobel Peace Prize in 1985. This information will allow you to make an accurate evaluation of the site and help Susan to determine how she can use its contents to prepare her report to the Cosby Promotions talent manager.

Library Resources

Susan is very happy with your evaluation of the environmental health update Web page and needs you to do more work for the research department. You ask Susan about the future of traditional libraries, given that so much information is available on the Web. She admits that she might be biased, having worked in a library for several years, but says that libraries will likely be around for a long time. In fact, the Web has made existing libraries more accessible to more people. As traditional libraries and online collections of works that have serious research value begin to recognize each other as complementary rather than as competing, library users should see many new and interesting research resources. One example of this is the **LibrarySpot** Web site, which is a collection of hyperlinks organized in the same general way that a physical library might arrange its collections.

To explore the LibrarySpot Web site:

1. Return to the Student Online Companion Web page for Session 5.2, and then click the **LibrarySpot** hyperlink and wait while your Web browser loads the Web page shown in Figure 5-16.

Figure 5-16	LIBRARYSPOT WEB SITE

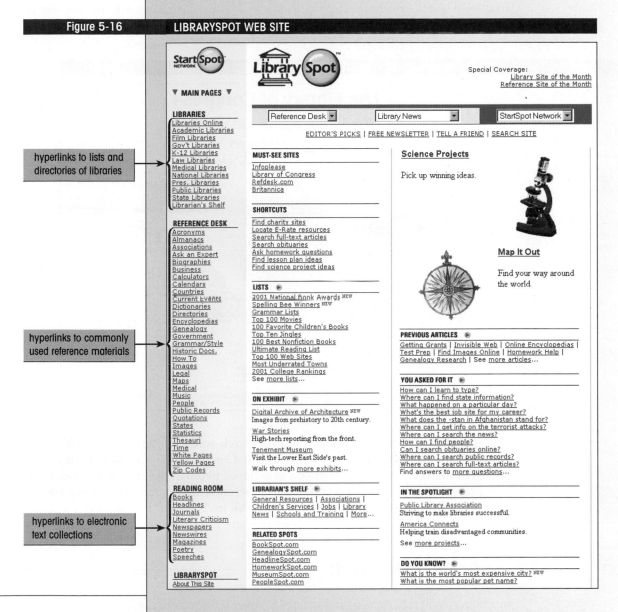

Figure 5-16 shows that the LibrarySpot includes many of the same things you would expect to find in a public or school library. This library is, however, open 24 hours a day and seven days a week. The LibrarySpot site lets you access reference materials, electronic texts, and other library Web sites from one central Web page.

2. Close your browser, and if necessary, log off your Internet connection.

The Student Online Companion page for Tutorial 5 contains many other hyperlinks to useful library and library-related Web sites in the Additional Information section under the "Library Information Sites" heading. Feel free to explore the libraries of the Web the next time you need to complete a research assignment for school or your job.

Figure 5-17 shows the U.S. Library of Congress Web site, which includes links to a huge array of research resources, ranging from the Thomas legislative information site to the Library of Congress archives.

Figure 5-17	LIBRAR.' OF CONGRESS WEB SITE

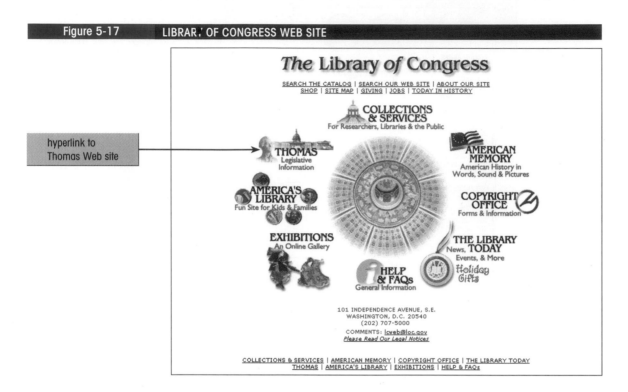

The Thomas Web site provides you with search access to the full text of bills that are before Congress, the *Congressional Record*, and Congressional Committee Reports. The American Memory hyperlinks lead you to archived photographs, sound and video recordings, maps, and collections of everything from seventeenth-century dance instruction manuals to baseball cards. The Exhibitions hyperlink leads you to information about current and past displays sponsored by the Library of Congress.

Text and Other Archives on the Web

In addition to library catalogs and indexes to other information, the Web contains a number of text resources, including dictionaries, thesauri, encyclopedias, glossaries, and other reference works. Many people find reference works easier to use when they have a computerized search interface. For example, when you open a dictionary to find the definition of a specific word, the structure of the bound book actually interferes with your ability to find the answer you seek. A computer interface allows you to enter a search term—in this case, the word to be defined—and saves you the trouble of scanning several pages of text to find the correct entry.

Of course, publishers sell dictionaries and encyclopedias on CDs, but the Web provides many alternatives. These alternatives range in quality from very low to very high. Many of the best resources offered on the Web require you to pay a subscription fee. The free reference works on the Web are worth investigating, however; they are good enough to provide acceptable service for many users. In addition to dictionaries and encyclopedias, the Web includes grammar checkers, thesauri, rhyming dictionaries, and language-translation pages. The Student Online Companion page for Tutorial 5 includes a collection of hyperlinks to a number of these reference resources in the Additional Information section.

The Web also offers a number of full text copies of works that are no longer protected by copyright. Two of the most popular Web sites for full text storage are the **Project Gutenberg** and **Project Bartleby** Web sites. These volunteer efforts have collected the contributions of many people throughout the world who have spent enormous amounts of time entering or converting printed text into electronic form.

The Web itself has become the subject of archivists' attention. The **Internet Archive Wayback Machine** provides researchers a series of snapshots of Web pages as they were at various points in the history of the Web. The Student Online Companion page for Tutorial 5 includes hyperlinks to these and several other Web sites that offer electronic texts and archives in the Additional Information section.

Citing **Web Research Resources**

As you search the Web for research resources, you should collect information about the sites so you can include a proper reference to your sources in any research report you write based on your work. As you collect information, you should record the URL and name of any Web site that you use, either in a word-processor document, as a Navigator bookmark, or as an Internet Explorer favorite. Citation formats are very well-defined for print publications, but formats for electronic resources are still emerging. For academic research, the two most widely followed standards for print citations are those of the **American Psychological Association (APA)** and the **Modern Language Association (MLA).** Various parties have proposed a number of additions to these two styles, but without reaching a consensus. The APA Style information page for Electronic References appears in Figure 5-18.

Figure 5-18	APA ELECTRONIC REFERENCES STYLE PAGE

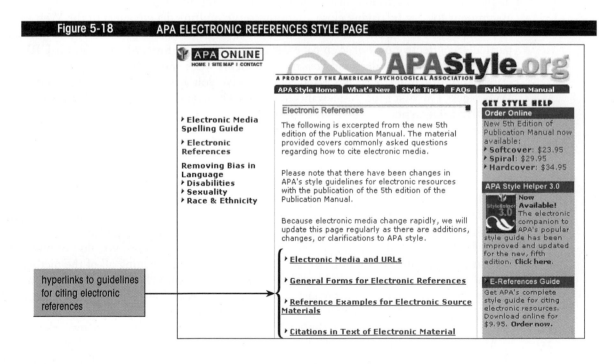

hyperlinks to guidelines for citing electronic references

One of the problems that both standards face is the difficulty of typesetting long URLs in print documents. No clear standards that specify where or how to break long URLs at the end of a print line have emerged. Another typesetting problem is how to distinguish between punctuation that is included in the URL and punctuation that is part of the sentence in which the URL appears. One solution used by some publishers is to enclose the URL with chevron symbols (< >); however, this solution is not generally accepted. The Additional Information section of the Student Online Companion page for Tutorial 5 includes hyperlinks to several citation style and formatting resources on the Web. You can check these Web pages periodically for updates to these changing standards. You also can request specific guidance from your instructor, if your research report is for a course requirement, or from the editor of the publication to which you plan to submit your work.

Any method of citing Web pages faces one serious, yet-unsolved problem—moving and disappearing URLs. The Web is a dynamic medium that changes constantly. The citation systems that academics and librarians use for published books and journals work well because the printed page has a physical existence. A Web page exists only in an HTML document on a Web server computer. If that file's name or location changes, or the Web server is disconnected from the Internet, the page is no longer accessible. Perhaps future innovations in Internet addressing technologies will solve this problem. You thank Susan for providing you with so much information about evaluating and citing Web information resources.

Multimedia Resources

Marti would like to create Web pages for each musical artist that the agency represents. Many of the bands have their own Web pages, but Marti would like to have a page for each band on the Cosby Promotions Web site with a standard set of information (that could include a link to the band's own Web page). She would like you to undertake a long-term assignment for her by paying close attention to the multimedia elements of the Web pages you view as you undertake searches for the agency's staff members. She asks you to note any particularly effective uses of Web page design elements and forward any relevant URLs to her. So that you will understand how these elements work and be better able to gather this information for him, Marti has asked Susan to give you a tour of multimedia elements in Web pages. The first issue Susan wants to discuss with you is how copyright law governs the use of these elements.

Copyright Violation and Plagiarism

Susan explains that when you use your Web browser to see a graphic image, listen to a sound, or view a video clip, your Web browser downloads the multimedia element from the Web server and stores it in a temporary file on your computer's hard drive. This process creates a new, intermediate level of ownership that did not exist before the emergence of the Web. For example, when you go to an art gallery and view a picture, you do not take possession of the picture in any way; in fact, if you went around touching all of the pictures in the gallery, a security guard would probably ask you to leave. When you visit an online art gallery, however, your Web browser takes temporary possession of a copy of the file containing the image. As you have learned in earlier tutorials, it is easy to make a permanent copy of Web page images—even though your copy might violate the image owner's rights.

Making a photocopy of a picture that appears in a book can be a copyright violation. Because computer files are even easier to copy than a picture in a book, the potential for Web copyright violations is much greater. Some Web site owners disclaim liability by storing only hyperlinks to other Web pages that contain copyright-violating multimedia elements; whether this is an effective shield against liability is not clear.

In most cases, scanning a copy of a popular cartoon from a newspaper or magazine and placing it on a Web page is a violation of the owner's copyright. Some cartoonists regularly search the Web, looking for unauthorized copies of their work. They threaten or take legal action when they find Web sites that appear to violate their copyrights.

Some uses of multimedia elements do not present a copyright violation. For example, some sites provide graphics files that are in the **public domain**, which means that you are free to copy the files without requesting permission from the source. Even though you can freely use public domain information, you should check the site carefully for requirements about if and how you acknowledge the source of the material when it is used. Acknowledging a source can be especially important when you use public domain material in papers, reports, or other school projects. Failure to cite the source of material that you use (even though it is in the public domain and not protected by copyright) is called **plagiarism** and can be a serious violation of your school's academic honesty policy.

Other sites offer some files free as samples and offer other files for sale. The free files often carry a restriction against selling or redistributing them, even though you may be able to use them without cost on your own personal Web page. You must carefully examine any site from which you download multimedia files to determine what usage limitations apply. If you cannot find a clear statement of copyright terms or a statement that the files are in the public domain, you should not use them on your Web page or anywhere else.

Images and Graphics

The Student Online Companion page for Session 5.1 contains several hyperlinks to Web pages that offer photographs and images. Some of these sites permit downloading of at least some of the files for personal or commercial use.

Most images on the Web are in one of two file formats, GIF and JPEG. **GIF**, an acronym for **Graphics Interchange Format**, is an older format that does a very good job of compressing small- or medium-sized files. Most GIF files you find on the Web have a .gif extension. This file format can store only up to 256 different colors. The GIF format is widely used on the Internet for images that have only a few distinct colors, such as line drawings, cartoons, simple icons, and screen objects. Some of the more interesting screen objects on the Web are animated GIF files. An **animated GIF file** combines several images into a single GIF file. When a Web browser that recognizes the animated GIF file type loads this type of file, it cycles through the images in the file and gives the appearance of cartoon-like animation. The size and color-depth limitations of the GIF file format prevent animated GIFs from delivering high-quality video, however. **JPEG**, an acronym for **Joint Photographic Experts Group**, is a newer file format that stores many more colors than the GIF format—over 16 million more, in fact—and more colors yields a higher-quality image. The JPEG format is particularly useful for photographs and continuous-tone art; that is, images that do not have sharp edges. Most JPEG files that you find on the Web usually have a .jpg file extension.

Both of these formats offer file compression, which is important on the Web. Uncompressed graphics files containing images of significant size or complexity are too large to transmit efficiently. JPEG file compression is "lossy." Any **lossy compression** procedure erases some elements of the graphic so that when it is displayed, it will not resemble the original image. The greater the level of compression, the more graphic detail is lost.

Graphic images on the Web also use many other file formats—including Windows bitmap file format (.bmp), Tagged Image File Format (or TIFF) format (.tif), PC Paintbrush format (.pcx), and the new Portable Network Graphics (or PNG) format (.png)—but most images you encounter will be in either the JPEG or GIF formats. The Windows bitmap, TIFF, and PC Paintbrush formats are all uncompressed graphics formats. Web page designers usually avoid these formats because a Web browser takes too long to download them. The PNG format is a new format that the World Wide Web Consortium has approved as a standard. Although its promoters hope that it will become the prevailing Web standard, it is not yet widely used.

One of the best Web resources for the fine arts is the **WebMuseum** site, which occasionally features special exhibitions. The WebMuseum's mainstay is its Famous Paintings collection, which includes images of artwork from around the world. Susan wants you to see the museum's portrait of Vincent van Gogh so you can gain experience using and searching for graphics files at a museum Web site.

REFERENCE WINDOW   **RW**

Viewing an Image in an Online Museum
- Open the online museum Web page in your Web browser.
- Follow the directory's hyperlinks or use the site's search engine to find the artist or work in which you are interested.
- Art works are often presented as small images called thumbnails that you can click to open a larger version of the image.

To view Vincent van Gogh's self-portraits at the WebMuseum site:

1. Return to the Student Online Companion Web page for Session 5.2, and then click the **WebMuseum** hyperlink and wait while your Web browser loads the Web page.

2. Scroll down the WebMuseum main page to the General Exhibitions section, and then click the **Famous Paintings** collections hyperlink.

3. Click the **Artist Index** hyperlink.

4. Scroll down the list of artists to find the **Gogh, Vincent van** hyperlink, and then click it.

5. Click the **Self-Portraits** hyperlink to open the page shown in Figure 5-19.

Figure 5-19   **WEBMUSEUM WEB PAGE**

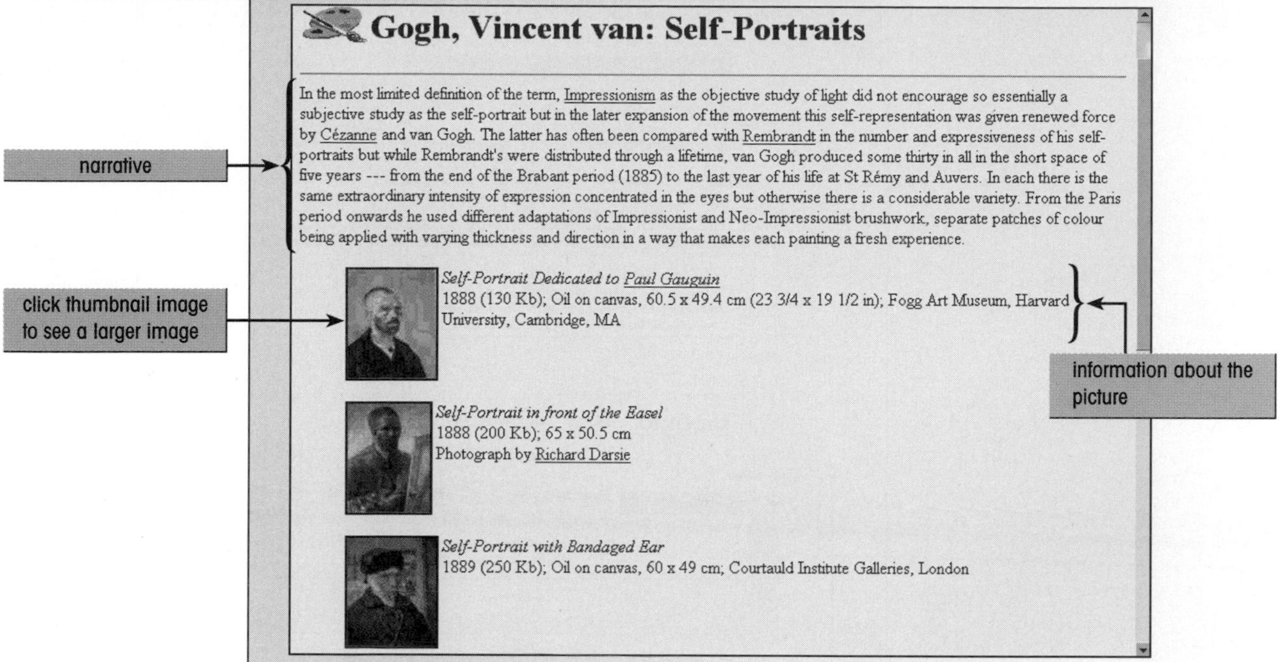

Gogh, Vincent van: Self-Portraits

narrative →

In the most limited definition of the term, _Impressionism_ as the objective study of light did not encourage so essentially a subjective study as the self-portrait but in the later expansion of the movement this self-representation was given renewed force by _Cézanne_ and van Gogh. The latter has often been compared with _Rembrandt_ in the number and expressiveness of his self-portraits but while Rembrandt's were distributed through a lifetime, van Gogh produced some thirty in all in the short space of five years --- from the end of the Brabant period (1885) to the last year of his life at St Rémy and Auvers. In each there is the same extraordinary intensity of expression concentrated in the eyes but otherwise there is a considerable variety. From the Paris period onwards he used different adaptations of Impressionist and Neo-Impressionist brushwork, separate patches of colour being applied with varying thickness and direction in a way that makes each painting a fresh experience.

click thumbnail image to see a larger image →

Self-Portrait Dedicated to Paul Gauguin
1888 (130 Kb); Oil on canvas, 60.5 x 49.4 cm (23 3/4 x 19 1/2 in); Fogg Art Museum, Harvard University, Cambridge, MA

information about the picture

Self-Portrait in front of the Easel
1888 (200 Kb); 65 x 50.5 cm
Photograph by _Richard Darsie_

Self-Portrait with Bandaged Ear
1889 (250 Kb); Oil on canvas, 60 x 49 cm; Courtauld Institute Galleries, London

This page, devoted to van Gogh's self-portraits, includes a narrative about these works; the title, date created, file size, media, size of the original; and information about the work's owner (if it is a public institution). You can click any of the small (or thumbnail) images to view a larger version of the image.

6. Close your Web browser, and if necessary, log off your Internet connection.

Finding image files on the Web can be difficult because the robots that gather information for search engines do not read graphics files to identify their attributes. A search engine, therefore, cannot find all images that contain a particular shade of green, for example. Search engines rely on HTML image tags that Web page builders include in their HTML documents that contain terms that describe the image. One Web site that can help you find clip-art images is the **Clip Art Searcher**, shown in Figure 5-20. The Student Online Companion page for Tutorial 5 contains a link to the Clip Art Searcher Web site in the Additional Information section under the heading "Photographs and Images."

Figure 5-20   SEARCHING FOR CLIP ART

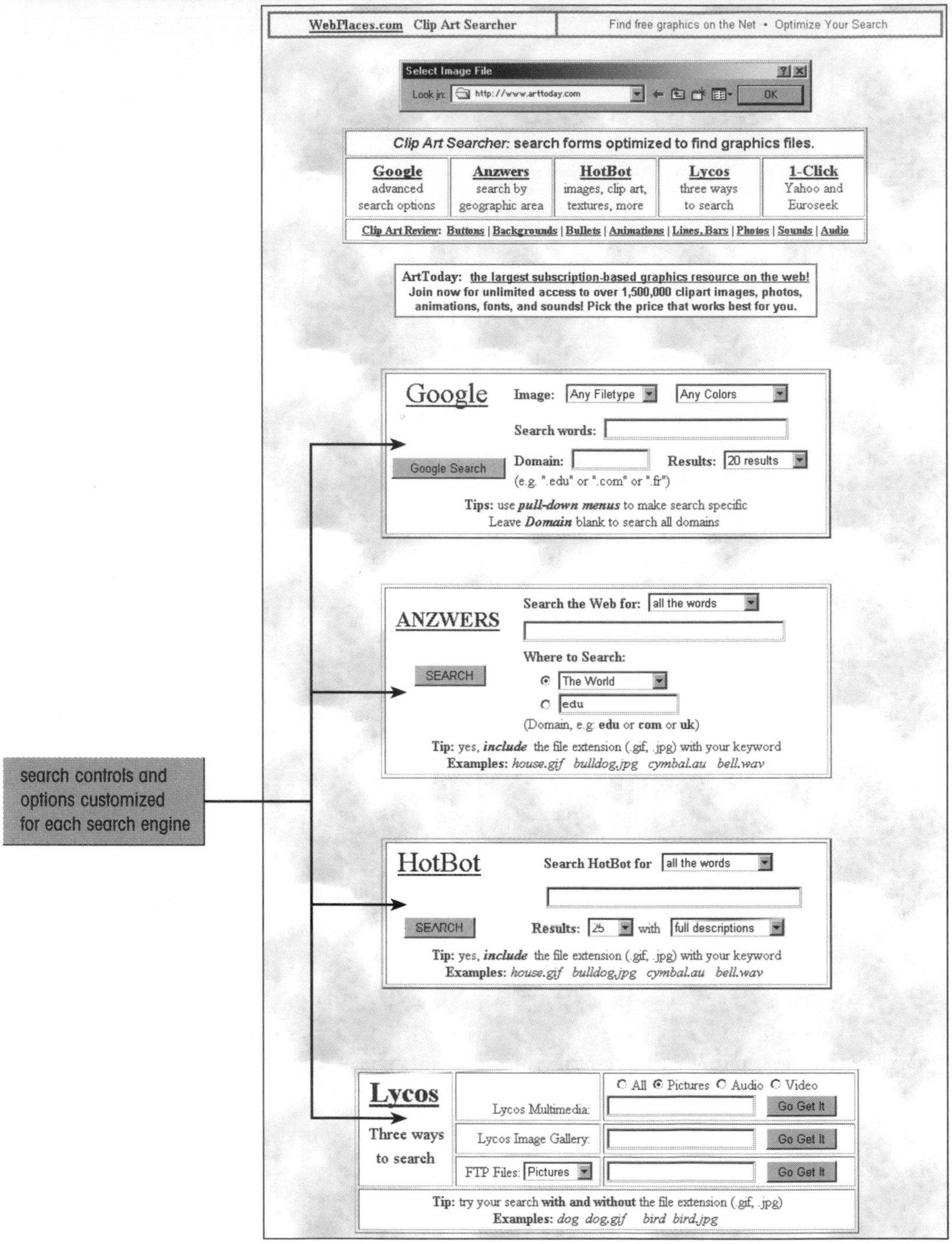

search controls and options customized for each search engine

The Clip Art Searcher Web page is not a search engine, but it includes customized search controls for six search engines and directories. These search controls are optimized for each search engine or directory to help you locate the specific types of graphics files you want to find.

Sounds, Music, and Video Clips

The animated GIF format has only a limited ability to present moving graphics and cannot store audio information along with the video animation. Many Web site designers include sound or video clips to enhance the information on their pages. Unlike graphics files, sound and video files appear on the Web in many different formats and often require that you add software extensions to your Web browser. These software extensions, or **plug-ins**, are usually available as free downloads. The firms that offer media players as free downloads earn their profits by selling encoding software to developers who want to include audio and video files in that format on their Web sites. Each firm that creates a format has an incentive to promote its use, so no clear standards for using audio or video files on the Web have emerged. Another difficulty that you might encounter when playing audio files is that your computer must be equipped with a sound card and either a speaker or earphones. The computers in your school's lab or in your employer's offices might not have a sound card installed; if that's the case, you will not be able to listen to sounds.

One widely used audio file format is the **Wave** format, which was jointly developed by Microsoft and IBM. **Wave (WAV)** files digitize audio waveform information at a user-specified sampling rate and play on any Windows computer that supports sound. WAV files that are recorded at a high sampling rate (the higher the sampling rate, the higher the sound quality) can be very large. A WAV file that stores one minute of CD-quality sound can be over 1 megabyte in size. The size of WAV files limits their use on the Web to situations that require only short, lower-quality audio information. You can recognize a WAV file on the Web by its .wav file extension.

Another commonly used Web file format is the MIDI format. The **MIDI (Musical Instrument Digital Interface)** format is a standard adopted by the music industry for controlling devices that create and read musical information. The MIDI format does not digitize the sound waveform. Instead, it digitally records information about each element of the sound, including its pitch, length, and volume. Most keyboard synthesizers use MIDI so that music recorded on one synthesizer can be played on other synthesizers or on computers that have a MIDI interface. It is much easier to edit music recorded in the MIDI format than music recorded in the WAV format because you can manipulate the individual characteristics of the sound with precision. MIDI files are much smaller than WAV files and are, therefore, often used on the Web. Usually, MIDI files have either a .midi or .mid file extension.

Because the Web originated mostly on computers running the UNIX operating system, that system's audio file format still appears on the Web. Both Navigator and Internet Explorer can read this format, which is known as the AU format because its file extension is normally .au. These files are approximately the same size as WAV files that store the same information.

A very popular technique for transferring both sound and video files on the Web is called streaming transmission. In a **streaming transmission**, the Web server sends the first part of the file to the Web browser, which begins playing the file. While the browser is playing the file, the server is sending the next segment of the file. Streaming transmission allows you to access very large audio or video files in much less time than the download-then-play procedure requires because you start playing the file before you finish downloading. RealNetworks, Inc. has pioneered this technology and developed the RealAudio format for audio files and the RealVideo format for video files. To play these files, which you can recognize by their .ra or .ram file extensions, you must download and install one of the Real file players from the firm's Web site. The RealNetworks formats are compressed to increase further the efficiency with which they can be transferred over the Internet. For example, you can compress a 1-megabyte WAV file into a 30-kilobyte RealAudio file.

Video files are also available in older formats on the Web. Windows computers are able to play Microsoft's **AVI (Audio Video Interleaved)** format files and, with the proper software downloaded and installed, also can play Apple's **QuickTime** format files. One minute of video and sound recorded in either of these formats results in a file that is about 6 megabytes, which is a very large file to transmit over slower types of Internet connections. Because of the larger file sizes, development of better ways to transmit video files over the Internet continues. The International Standards Organization's **Moving Picture Experts Group (MPEG)** has created a series of standards for compressed file formats. As in JPEG graphic files, this compression technique deletes information from the file and can deteriorate quality.

The audio portion of the MPEG file format was responsible for one of the greatest revolutions in online music that has occurred in the history of the Web. The MPEG format's audio track, called **MPEG Audio Layer 3 (MP3)** became wildly popular just as disk storage on personal computers dropped in price and CD writers (also called CD burners) became affordable for home use. Files in the MP3 format are lower in quality than WAV format files, but they are 90 percent smaller. Thus, a CD that might hold 15 popular songs in high quality WAV format (about 40 megabytes per song) could hold 150 popular songs in MP3 format (about four megabytes per song).

Their smaller size made MP3 files easy to send from one person to another through the Internet. File sharing software, such as Napster, became very popular. Companies in the recording industry and the recording artists themselves were not very happy. People could now copy music from CDs that they had purchased and convert that music into MP3 files to exchange with others on the Internet. Recording companies and artists filed suits against Napster and other file-sharing sponsors for violating copyright laws and were generally successful in obtaining court orders or out-of-court settlements that are preventing further copyright violations in many cases. Many individuals, however, still violate the law and share MP3 files that contain copyrighted works.

Sites such as **MP3.com** do offer free downloads of music in MP3 format. The music that is available on such sites is recorded by new or relatively unknown bands (in most cases) and made available to promote the live tours or other recordings of those bands. Many of Cosby Promotions' client bands and musical artists have released MP3 recordings and make them available on their own Web sites and on sites such as MP3.com. The MP3.com Web site appears in Figure 5-21.

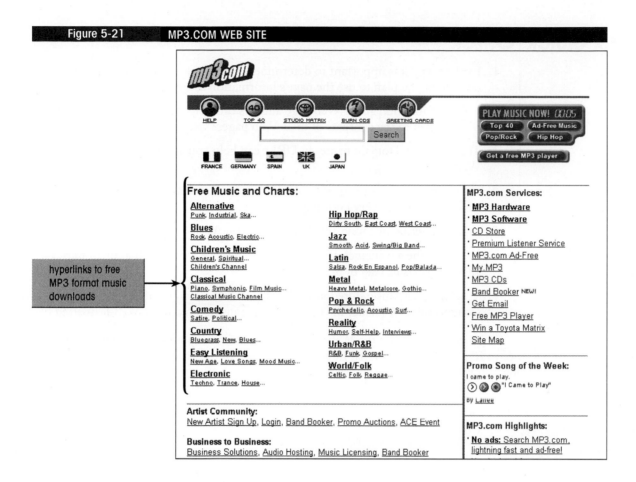

Figure 5-21 | MP3.COM WEB SITE

hyperlinks to free MP3 format music downloads

Future of Electronic Publishing

One of the key changes that the Internet and the Web have brought to the world is that information can now be disseminated more rapidly than ever in large quantities with a low required investment. The impact of this change is that firms in the public relations business—firms that spend great amounts of time and money trying to present their clients through the major media in the best possible light—might be facing a significantly changed business environment. Many industry analysts believe that the ease of publishing electronically on the Web might help reduce the concentration of media control that has been developing over the past three decades as newspapers merged with each other and, along with radio and television stations, were purchased by large media companies.

To be successful in print media publishing—such as a monthly magazine—a publisher must have a large subscription market. The fixed costs of composing and creating the magazine are spread over enough units so that the publisher can earn a profit. The costs of publishing a Web page are very low compared to printing magazines or newspapers. Therefore, the subscription market required for a Web publication to be successful can be very small or even nonexistent. If a Web-based magazine, or an **e-zine**, can attract advertisers, it can be financially successful with no subscribers and a small number of readers. As a result, e-zines are appearing on the Web in increasing numbers. An e-zine does not require a large readership to be successful, so these electronic publications can focus on very specialized, narrow interests. E-zines have become popular places for publishing new fiction and poetry, for example. The Additional Information section of the Student Online Companion page for Tutorial 5 includes hyperlinks to several e-zine Web sites that you might want to explore.

Session 5.2 QUICK CHECK

1. Explain why it is important to determine a Web page author's identity and credentials when you plan to use the page's information as a research resource.

2. What information about Web page authors can help you assess their objectivity with respect to the contents of their Web pages?

3. True or False: Domain names in URLs can help you assess the quality of Web pages.

4. How can you assess the quality of a Web page that deals with a subject area in which you are not very knowledgeable?

5. Briefly describe two ways that libraries use the Web.

6. What are the advantages of using online reference works such as dictionaries or encyclopedias instead of print editions?

7. True or False: Music stored in a WAV file format would be of lower quality and would result in a smaller file than the same music stored in an MP3 formatted file.

When you need to use the Web to find information for your classes or your job, remember to return to the Additional Information section of the Student Online Companion page for Tutorial 5 for a comprehensive list of Web information resources.

REVIEW ASSIGNMENTS

Marti is preparing to visit a new techno band that she would like to sign in Chicago, Illinois. While in Chicago, she would like to visit a number of clubs that feature blues artists.

Do the following:

1. Start your Web browser, go to the Student Online Companion (http://www.course.com/newperspectives/internet3), click the link for your book, click the Tutorial 5 link, and then click the Review Assignments link.

2. Obtain weather forecasts for the Chicago area from the Weather Channel and CNN Weather. Print the forecasts from each site.

3. The band is renting practice space in a warehouse near the corner of West 35th Street and South Morgan Street on the South side of Chicago. Print two maps from the MapQuest site: one street-level map and one higher-level map that shows the surrounding area in Chicago.

4. Use the Trip.com site's Destination Guides to locate information about restaurants in the Chicago area. Prepare a report that lists three restaurants that would be good choices for Marti to entertain clients while in Chicago.

5. Use the Trip.com site's Destination Guides to locate at least two blues clubs that Marti can visit while she is in Chicago.

6. When you are finished, close your Web browser and if necessary, log off your Internet connection.

CASE PROBLEMS

Case 1. Portland Concrete Mixers, Inc.   You are a sales representative for Portland Concrete Mixers, Inc., a company that makes replacement parts for concrete mixing equipment. This equipment is mounted on trucks that deliver ready-mixed concrete to buildings and other job sites. You have been transferred to the Seattle area and would like to plan your first sales trip there. Because you plan to drive to Seattle, you need information about the best route as well as a map of Seattle. You hope to generate some new customers on this trip and, therefore, need to identify sales-lead prospects in the Seattle area. Companies that manufacture concrete are good prospects for you.

Do the following:

1. Start your Web browser, go to the Student Online Companion (http://www.course.com/newperspectives/internet3), click the link for your book, click the Tutorial 5 link, and then click the Case Problems link.

2. Click the MapQuest hyperlink to open the MapQuest Web page.

3. Click the Driving Directions hyperlink to obtain driving directions. Your starting address is Portland, OR, and your destination address is Seattle, WA. Type these city and state names in the appropriate boxes.

4. Click the GET DIRECTIONS button. Print the new Web page that opens.

5. Click the first map on the Web page to zoom in and obtain a more detailed route from Portland to Seattle, and then print it.

6. To obtain a map of Seattle, click the Re-center option button below the map image, and then click Seattle on the map. You can click the plus and minus sign icons in the Map Level settings area to adjust the map to the level of detail you desire.

7. To identify sales leads in Seattle, return to the Student Online Companion and then click the YP.Net hyperlink. Type concrete in the Keywords box, and then click the SEARCH button. Click the View by Business Location button, and then click the link to Washington(WA). On the page that opens, click the link to SEATTLE-BELLE-VUE-EVERETT. On the page that opens, click the link to SEATTLE.

8. The results page contains contact information for a number of companies in the concrete business in Seattle. Copy the names and addresses of at least three sales prospects to a document that you will carry with you on your trip.

9. When you are finished, close your Web browser and, if necessary, log off your Internet connection.

Case 2. Ragtime Tonight   You are the owner of a popular nightclub, Ragtime Tonight, near the convention center. Although you have a good local following with the nightclub's program of stand-up comedy and ragtime piano music, many of your patrons are visitors to the city who stay in hotels near the convention center. You realize that an increasing number of these travelers are making airline, hotel, and car-rental reservations using the Web, and you would like to create a Web site that could help you reach these customers. As you are designing the site, you decide that you would like to add some ragtime audio clips that play when the site is opened using a Web browser. You have heard that single musical instruments, particularly pianos, sound realistic when synthesized in the MIDI format and you would, therefore, like to find some ragtime pieces in that format. Of course, you are willing to locate the composer and performer of any MIDI file you use and obtain the necessary permissions before adding the sound clip to your Web page.

Do the following:

1. Start your Web browser, go to the Student Online Companion (http://www.course.com/newperspectives/internet3), click the link for your book, click the Tutorial 5 link, and then click the Case Problems link.

2. Click one or more of the MIDI music links provided for this Case Problem.

3. Evaluate the files offered on these Web pages or the pages to which they lead. Write a short report summarizing your experience. In your report, describe what copyright restrictions are described on the Web site that offers the file or files that you would like to use.

4. When you are finished, close your Web browser and, if necessary, log off your Internet connection.

Case 3. *Toddle Inn* owns and operates a chain of day-care centers in several Midwestern states from its headquarters in Minneapolis, Minnesota. The directors are interested in undertaking a national expansion program that will require outside financing and an effective public relations program that integrates with their strategic marketing plans. You are an intern in the office of Joan Caruso, a public relations consultant that does work for Toddle Inn. Joan has asked you to help her with some background research as she creates a proposal for the Toddle Inn board of directors next meeting that integrates a Web site into their public relations program.

Do the following:

1. Start your Web browser, go to the Student Online Companion (http://www.course.com/newperspectives/internet3), click the link for your book, click the Tutorial 5 link, and then click the Case Problems link.

2. Use the NewsHub and Northern Light news search engines to find at least three current (within the past three months) news reports about the child-care industry. Write a memo to Joan that summarizes the major issues identified in these reports.

3. Joan would like you to conduct an evaluation of the Child Care Parent/Provider Information Network Web site. Prepare an evaluation of that site that considers the author's or publisher's identity and objectivity, and the site's content, form, and appearance.

4. One of the things that any public relations campaign must consider is the impact of pending legislation. Joan asks you to see if there are any bills pending in the U.S. Congress that will affect the child-care industry. Use the link on the Student Online Companion to open the Thomas legislative information Web site, type "child care" (without quotation marks) in the By Word/Phrase text box and then click the Search button. Read one of the bills listed and prepare a one-paragraph summary for Joan of the bill's likely effects on the child-care industry.

5. When you are finished, close your Web browser and if necessary, log off your Internet connection.

Case 4. *Arnaud for Senate Campaign* You work for the campaign team of Lisa Arnaud, who is running for a seat in the state senate. One issue that promises to play a prominent role in the upcoming election campaign is her opponent's position on privatization of the state prison system. It is important for Lisa to establish a clear position on the issue early in the campaign, and she has asked you to prepare a briefing document for her to consider. Lisa tells you that she has no particular preference on the issue and that she wants you to obtain a balanced set of arguments for each side. Once the campaign takes a position, however, she will need to defend it. Therefore, Lisa wants to have an idea of the quality of the information you gather. You decide to do part of your research on the Web.

Do the following:

1. Start your Web browser, go to the Student Online Companion (http://www.course.com/newperspectives/internet3), click the link for your book, click the Tutorial 5 link, and then click the Case Problems link.

2. Click the AltaVista hyperlink to open that search engine.

3. Type the words "privatization prisons" (without the quotation marks) in the Search for text box, and then click the Search button.

4. Examine your list of search results for authoritative sites that include positions on the issue. You might need to follow a number of results page hyperlinks to find suitable Web pages. In general, you should avoid current news items that appear in the results list.

5. Find one Web page that states a clear position in favor of privatization and another that states a clear position against privatization. Print a copy of each.

6. For each page, prepare a three-paragraph report that evaluates the quality of the page on each of the three criteria: author identity and objectivity, content, and form and appearance.

7. When you are finished, close your Web browser and, if necessary, log off your Internet connection.

Case 5. Dalton Precision Castings You are the office manager for Dalton Precision Castings, a company that makes metal parts for packaging machinery and sells them throughout the world. Two of Dalton's major customers, one from Portugal and one from Italy, are arriving next week for a briefing on new technologies and products. Tom Dalton, the company's president, has asked you to help make these visitors feel welcome. He would like to have a local artist create replicas of the Portuguese and Italian flags as gifts for the visitors. He would like you to find images of the flags from which the artist can create the replicas. You decide to do your research on the Web.

Do the following:

1. Start your Web browser, go to the Student Online Companion (http://www.course.com/newperspectives/internet3), click the link for your book, click the Tutorial 5 link, and then click the Case Problems link.

2. Click the Clip Art Searcher hyperlink to open that Web site.

3. Type the word "flag" (without the quotation marks) in the search text box for the first search engine that appears on the Clip Art Searcher page.

4. Examine your list of search results for sites that might include images of the Portuguese or Italian flags. You might need to follow a number of results page hyperlinks to find suitable Web pages.

5. If you do not find any suitable pages, repeat your search using the search terms "flag Portugal" and "flag Italy" (again, type the terms without the quotation marks). You can also try your search in the Clip Art Searcher search controls for the other search engines on its Web page.

6. When you find a Web page or pages that offer suitable images, examine the Web site to determine what copyright or other restrictions exist regarding your use of the images.

7. Prepare a one-paragraph report for each flag that describes the source you plan to use. Include the URL of the site where you found the flag image and a summary of the restrictions on Dalton's use of that image. If the Web site does not include any description of restrictions, refer to the text and state your opinion regarding what restrictions might exist on Dalton's use of the image.

8. Close your Web browser and, if necessary, log off your Internet connection.

QUICK | CHECK ANSWERS

Session 5.1

1. a major wire service (or press agency or news service) based in Great Britain
2. False. NewsHub updates its stories every 15 minutes.
3. Different meteorologists often predict different weather conditions for the same location; gathering several forecasts provides a range of likely weather conditions.
4. You can change the map's scale, and you can e-mail the map or save it to your PDA.
5. any three of: recommendations and reviews of restaurants, entertainment (or nightlife), sports, shopping, landmarks, and other visitor information
6. False
7. yellow pages site
8. white pages site

Session 5.2

1. Author identity and credentials help establish the credibility of Web page content.
2. their employment or other professional affiliations
3. True
4. timeliness, inclusion of relevant topics, depth of treatment
5. by adding online resources to their collections and by making their collections accessible to remote users and other libraries
6. available 24 hours a day, seven days a week; can be easier and faster to search
7. False

OBJECTIVES

In this tutorial you will:

- Learn what FTP is and how it works

- Learn how to compress and decompress files and to check them for viruses

- Navigate an FTP site using a Web browser

- Download an FTP client program using a Web browser

- Download programs using an FTP client program

- Trace the connection between your computer and a remote computer

- Explore file-based storage options on the Internet

- Use Yahoo! Briefcase to upload and download a file

- Examine the future of subscription software models

FTP
AND DOWNLOADING
AND STORING DATA

*Using FTP and Other Services to
Transfer and Store Data*

CASE

Sound Effects, Inc.

One of the things that Milt Spangler enjoys most about being a musician is being able to manipulate music electronically to create customized sounds. After graduating from the University of Southern California with a degree in business administration, Milt started Sound Effects, Inc., a company that produces sounds and voiceovers for local advertising agencies and other businesses that use digitally produced and created sounds. Soon Milt's business sufficiently expanded so that he could rent a warehouse with a built-in sound studio. As part of the expansion, Milt hired professional actors to do voiceover work and other speaking roles, such as recording characters' voices in CD-ROM games and educational programs for children. Milt soon began receiving contracts from out-of-state businesses, educational software manufacturers, and advertising agencies as his work became nationally recognized. As a result of his success, he needed to expand his pool of actor talent beyond the Los Angeles area.

Sound Effects operates with only a few permanent employees in the Los Angeles area, but many of the actors who provide voiceover work live elsewhere in the United States and in all provinces of Canada. These actors record their material for Milt in studios near their homes. Because their work is produced digitally, Milt needs a way to transfer files from studios in the actors' hometowns to the Los Angeles office, where the files can be edited and finalized for clients. The large file sizes of digitally produced files and the high cost of sending files prohibit Milt from relying on e-mail attachments and overnight delivery services as options for transporting files. He asks you to help him find new ways to send large files using another method.

SESSION 6.1

In this session, you will learn how to use FTP to transmit files between your computer and a computer connected to the Internet. You will learn about the different types of FTP access and the different methods by which you can access an FTP site. You will use a Web browser to navigate an FTP site. Finally, you will learn about file transfer modes, file types and extensions, decompressing files, and checking files for viruses.

Using File Transfer Protocol

You already know that you can use e-mail attachments to send files over the Internet. E-mail is often a good way of transporting a file from one location to another, or even to yourself. For example, if you're in the university computer lab working on a report and forget to bring your disk, you can attach the report to an e-mail message to yourself; when you get home and download your e-mail messages the file arrives on your home computer. This method works for sending files to other people as well. However, many e-mail servers limit the size of files you attach to a single e-mail message. E-mail servers might also limit the types of files you can send. For example, some servers will not accept file attachments that can execute programs for fear that these types of attachments could damage the e-mail server.

To address storage issues and issues related to transmitting large files from one location to another, you can use FTP. **FTP**, or **File Transfer Protocol**, is one of several services built into and supported by the Internet suite of protocols. You can think of FTP as a means of accessing a hard drive to which you connect via the Internet. In some cases, you only can read (view) the files; in other cases you can read and write (edit) the files. FTP is the protocol that transfers files from one computer that is connected to the Internet to another computer that is connected to the Internet. The site to which you are sending files and from which you are receiving files is usually called an **FTP site** or a **remote computer**; when you use your computer to connect to an FTP site it is called the **local computer**. When a file is transferred over the Internet—whether you are viewing it with a Web browser or not—FTP is responsible for sending the file between computers. You can send any file type to an FTP site, including spreadsheet, picture, video, MP3, program, and text files.

When you send a file using FTP, you **upload** a file to send it from your computer to the FTP site. When you receive a file, you **download** the file from an FTP site and send it to your computer. Downloading is more common because people usually receive more files than they send. Whether files are uploaded or downloaded, FTP is the protocol that accomplishes the transfer. FTP can run from a Web browser, with an FTP client program, or through a command-line interface. A **command-line interface** is one in which you enter a command and press the Enter key; the receiving computer then acts on the command you sent. This process continues until you have typed enough single-line commands to complete a task. An **FTP client program** is a Windows program that resides on your PC and transfers files between your computer and an FTP site connected to the Internet. Like other Windows programs, most FTP client programs have menu bars and toolbars with buttons to help you execute commands. Figure 6-1 shows a popular FTP client program, WS_FTP LE, which is communicating with a remote computer.

| Figure 6-1 | FTP CLIENT PROGRAM |

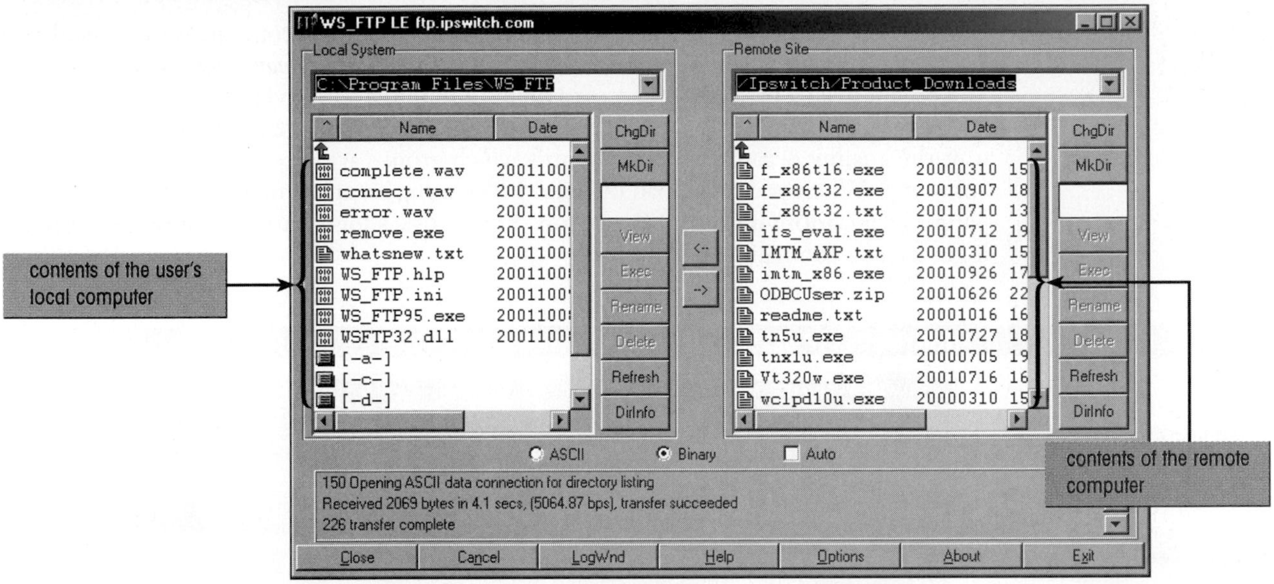

contents of the user's local computer

contents of the remote computer

FTP programs that you execute using a command-line interface are more difficult to use because you have to know the commands, such as *get*, *put*, *cd*, and others, to transfer files. The **Telnet Client** is a Windows program that uses the Telnet protocol and a command-line interface to access a remote computer. To start Telnet, click the Start button on the Windows taskbar, click Run, type Telnet in the Open text box of the Run dialog box, and then click the OK button. Then you can type the commands to request and transfer files between the local and remote computers.

Like other Internet protocols, FTP follows the standard client/server model. When you want to download or upload a file, you connect to a remote computer and request that the FTP site either receive files from your computer or transfer files from the remote computer to your computer. An **FTP server program** receives file transfer requests and then acts on those commands. The FTP server program manages the details of transferring files between your computer and the FTP site. FTP is operating system neutral. For example, your PC might use FTP and Windows XP to communicate with a large minicomputer running the FTP server on a UNIX operating system. It makes no difference that the operating systems are different on each computer; FTP seamlessly transfers files between the computers. Web browsers support FTP and provide a simple and familiar interface for you to locate and download files. In this tutorial, you will learn how to transfer files using an FTP client program and a Web browser.

Accessing an FTP Server

To transfer files between your PC and a remote computer, you must first connect to the remote computer. You can can connect to a remote computer by logging on to it using your Web browser or an FTP client program. Microsoft Internet Explorer and Netscape Navigator both recognize the FTP protocol. To use a remote computer, you must identify yourself, or **log on**, by supplying your user name and a password. Some computer systems provide public access to their computers, which means anyone can connect to the FTP site. When you connect to a public FTP site, your access is restricted to only those files and folders designated for access by public users. Other systems allow restricted access to their computers. To access these computers, you must have an account on the computer.

Anonymous FTP

Logging on to one of the many publicly accessible, remote computers connected to the Internet is known as an **anonymous login** because you type *anonymous* as your user name. You do not need a password to access a public computer. However, it is both customary and polite to enter your full e-mail address when you are prompted for your password. That way, the hosting organization can identify which groups are accessing the public areas of its computer. When you download or upload files using an anonymous login, you are participating in an **anonymous FTP session**. Figure 6-2 shows an example of an anonymous login using a command-line interface.

Figure 6-2   ANONYMOUS FTP SESSION USING THE COMMAND-LINE

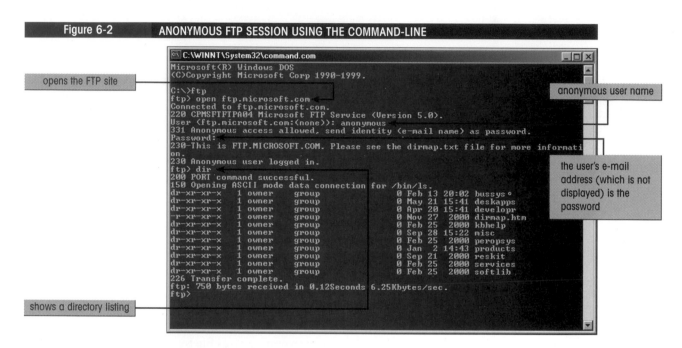

opens the FTP site

anonymous user name

the user's e-mail address (which is not displayed) is the password

shows a directory listing

You can use many of the anonymous FTP computers connected to the Internet to download files to your PC. In most cases, public FTP sites impose limits on uploading files or provide only one publicly accessible directory to which you can upload files. Public FTP sites also limit your access to selected directories and files on their systems. People using FTP sites with anonymous logins cannot open and view all the directories and files on the site. You can determine which directories you can access by experimenting. If you attempt to open directories or examine files that are not accessible to anonymous users, you will receive an error or warning message indicating that you do not have access to the requested file or directory. Experimenting with your access is allowable, but you should obey all rules and regulations regarding anonymous access. Remember that you are using another person's or organization's computer at no cost to download files for your use.

When you connect to a public FTP site using a Web browser, the browser automatically supplies the user name *anonymous* and an appropriate password to access the site and handles all FTP communications with the site. If the site requires you to enter a user name and password, the browser will prompt you for these items. Figure 6-3 shows a browser with a connection to the Netscape FTP site. Notice that the protocol in the site's URL is ftp:// instead of http:// and that the site's URL indicates an FTP site (ftp) instead of a Web site (www).

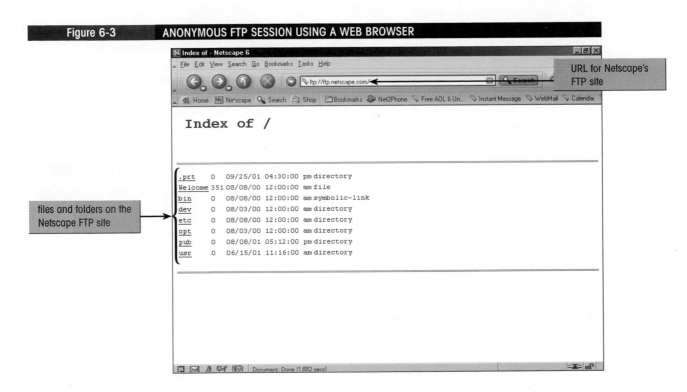

Figure 6-3 ANONYMOUS FTP SESSION USING A WEB BROWSER

Students and other users frequently use FTP to upload group projects to university or other publicly accessible sites so each member of the group can access the project files. Most files must be placed in the public directory, and they often have a maximum life span of a few days or weeks. The site's manager determines how long files can remain in the public directory. Usually, the file-deletion schedule and other policy statements are stored in the readme.txt file in the public directory. If you find a file by that or a similar name, be sure to read it carefully.

Full-Privilege FTP

When you need to access an FTP site that is not public, such as one for your school or employer, you will use **full-privilege FTP**, or **named FTP**, where you have been given full access to its content with a user name and password. Even though you might have an account on a particular FTP site, your access might be limited to transferring files in a specific directory. When you log on to a computer with your user name and password, the system automatically directs you to a particular directory on that computer in which you have full read and write access rights. When you have an account on a computer that is connected to the Internet, you can usually store larger files for longer periods than you can on a public FTP site.

FTP Programs

The choice of FTP program depends on your situation. You can use a command-line FTP program, an FTP client program, or a Web browser to transfer files using FTP.

Command-Line FTP

If you have dial-up access to a computer running the UNIX operating system, then the only choice for transferring files is to use command-line FTP. You use command-line FTP by typing *ftp* at the command prompt and entering a series of one-word commands to establish your FTP session and transfer files. In order to use command-line FTP, you must either have a command-line FTP program installed on your PC (such as the Telnet Client) or access to a host computer that has a command-line FTP program. As you are working, it is important to remember that if you use FTP on a UNIX computer, all commands are case-sensitive; that is, *FTP* and *ftp* are different commands. Figure 6-4 shows some common FTP commands that FTP client programs and browsers issue automatically.

Figure 6-4	COMMON FTP COMMANDS

COMMAND	DESCRIPTION
binary	Sets the transfer mode to binary
cd *directory*	Changes the remote directory to *directory*
close	Disconnects from the current remote computer
get *filename*	Downloads *filename* from the remote computer
help	Displays Help on various FTP topics
lcd *directory*	Changes the current local directory to *directory*
ls or dir	Displays the current folder's filenames and directory names
open *remote*	Connects to a remote FTP site on *remote*
put *filename*	Uploads *filename* to a remote computer
quit	Exits the FTP program and logs off the remote server

REFERENCE WINDOW   RW

Downloading a File Using Command-Line FTP

- Start your FTP program and then type *open ftp address* where *ftp address* is the address of the remote FTP site.
- Log in using *anonymous* as the user name and your e-mail address as the password for public access or using your user name and password for full-privilege FTP.
- Navigate to the file you want to download. Type the *cd* and *dir* commands at the command prompt to change directories and list directory contents, respectively.
- Set the transfer mode to binary by typing the *binary* command at the command prompt, and then press the Enter key.
- Download the file by typing the *get* command and the filename you want to download at the command prompt, and then press the Enter key.
- When the download is complete, disconnect from the remote site by typing the *quit* command, and then press the Enter key.

FTP Client Programs and Web Browsers

Both FTP client programs and Web browsers issue FTP commands automatically so you do not need to learn how to issue commands manually as you would when using command-line FTP. You can use either an FTP client program or a Web browser to download files from an FTP site. FTP client programs usually transfer files faster than Web browsers. When you use a Web browser to transfer a file, the browser automatically determines the file's format and transfers the file in that mode. If the browser determines the file's type incorrectly, the file may become corrupted during the transfer, rendering the file unusable. FTP client programs do not make file type determinations, so *you* must determine a file's type and set its transfer properly.

Web browsers and FTP client programs both allow you to download files from FTP sites, but you can't use a Web browser to upload files to an FTP site. If you need to upload files, you'll need to use an FTP client program.

A Web browser lets you open files by clicking or double-clicking folders and files to open them. The browser handles most simple FTP commands easily, but if you use FTP frequently, you might need the power and additional commands found in an FTP client program. Many FTP client programs are either free or inexpensive. FTP client programs allow you to log on anonymously or with a user name and password. FTP client programs provide many features that vary from one program to another. An FTP client program provides the following desirable features, although some FTP client programs support only a few of these features:

- Provides a multipane display so you can see both the local and remote computer directories simultaneously.
- Allows you to transfer many files in one FTP session.
- Permits drag and drop file transfers so you can use the mouse to drag and drop files between the local and remote computers.
- Simplifies the process of deleting directories and files on local and remote computers.
- Displays an interface similar to that found in Windows Explorer for both the local and remote computers.
- Allows you to set up scheduled file transfers at a future date and time so selected files can be transmitted automatically.
- Recovers interrupted file transfers by continuing the transfer process from the point where it was interrupted.
- Reconnects automatically to sites that disconnect your transfer when your connection exceeds the maximum allotted time.

Now that you have reviewed some basic facts about FTP, Milt asks you to show him how to use a Web browser to navigate an FTP site. Because Microsoft frequently stores program updates on its public FTP site, you will show him this site first.

Using a Web Browser to Navigate an FTP Site

Because most Internet users are adept at using a Web browser and know how hyperlinks work, they will have no difficulty navigating an FTP site in search of files. Using FTP is especially easy when you use a Web browser to log on to a public FTP site because the browser automatically supplies the anonymous login. If you need to upload files to a site requiring full-privilege FTP access rights, then you will need to use an FTP client program.

When you visit an FTP site, your first goal should be to become familiar with its organization. FTP sites are organized hierarchically, much like the folders and files on a computer's hard drive. When you access an FTP site, you usually enter at the site's **root directory**, also called the **home directory** or **top-level directory**. The root directory contains other directories that contain files and other directories, as shown in Figure 6-5. Most sites prevent users with anonymous logins from accessing some files and directories in the root directory. When you enter a root directory for the first time, a message might appear indicating which file contains important information about navigating the site.

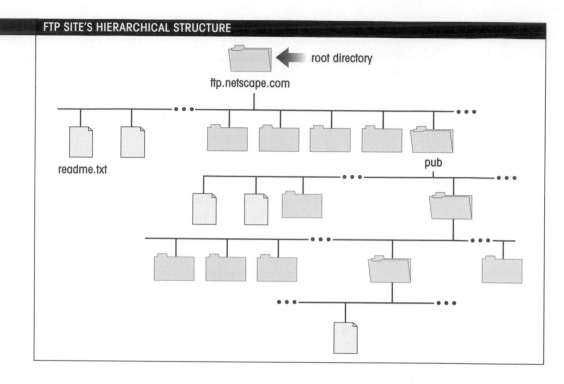

Figure 6-5   FTP SITE'S HIERARCHICAL STRUCTURE

An FTP site usually stores two items—directories (folders) and files—that you either single- or double-click to open. If you use Internet Explorer to access the site, you double-click a directory or file to open it. If you are using Navigator, you will click a link to open a directory or file. Double-clicking a file or clicking a hyperlink to a file either opens the file in a new browser window or a program window so you can view the file or begins downloading it to your computer. Most FTP client programs display directory and file links with different icons or notations so you can distinguish directories from files.

Depending on what software you are using to access an FTP site, you might use a different method for moving up one level in the hierarchy. In Internet Explorer, you click the Up button on the toolbar; in Navigator, you click the set of dots at the top of the page. In both cases, the browser moves up one level and displays that folder's contents. Some FTP client programs display a toolbar button that you can click to move up one level.

Milt asks you to show him how a Web browser opens an FTP site. You'll demonstrate how easy it is to access and navigate an FTP site next.

To open an FTP site using a Web browser:

1. Start your Web browser, open the Student Online Companion page at **www.course.com/newperspectives/internet3**, click the hyperlink for your book, click the **Tutorial 6** link, and then click the **Session 6.1** link. Click the **Microsoft FTP** link and wait while the browser loads the page. Figure 6-6 shows the directories and files in the root directory of Microsoft's FTP site when accessed using Internet Explorer. A yellow folder icon identifies directories; files are identified with a file icon that indicates the file's type. Because the contents of this site change regularly, your screen might look different.

Figure 6-6	MICROSOFT'S FTP SITE ROOT DIRECTORY IN INTERNET EXPLORER

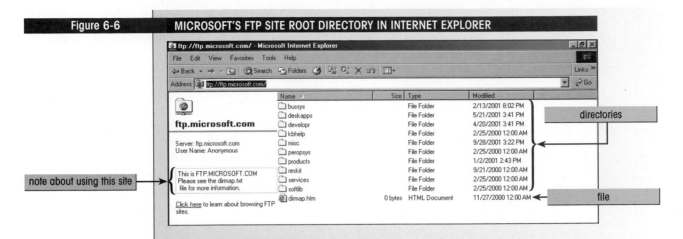

note about using this site

directories

file

If you are using Navigator, directories and files both appear as hyperlinks. Each hyperlink is identified using the word "directory" or "file," as shown in Figure 6-7, to indicate its contents.

Figure 6-7	MICROSOFT'S FTP SITE ROOT DIRECTORY IN NAVIGATOR

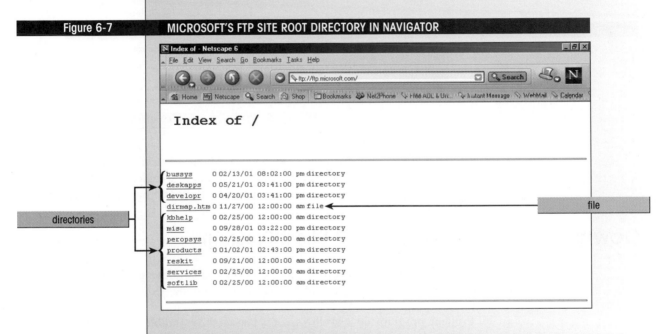

directories

file

2. Locate the **deskapps** directory. If you are using Internet Explorer, double-click **deskapps** to open it; if you are using Navigator, click **deskapps** to open it. The deskapps directory opens and displays several directories and a file. The new page displays directories with familiar names, such as access, excel, and word.

3. Double-click or click the **readme.txt** file and then read the file that opens and describes the files and directories available in the deskapps directory. Sometimes you might find site information in the readme.txt or about.txt file. You might encounter other names, but they all serve the same function—that is, to provide an overview of the site's structure and file locations.

4. If you are using Internet Explorer, click the **Close** button on the title bar to close the readme.txt file; if you are using Navigator, click the **Back** button on the toolbar. You return to the deskapps directory listing.

5. If you are using Internet Explorer, click the **Up** button to move up one level; if you are using Navigator, click the set of dots (**. .**) at the top of the page. You return to the root directory.

6. Close your browser, and if necessary, log off your Internet connection.

If you get lost in an FTP directory structure, there is a simple way to determine your location and get back to the root directory. The URL in your browser's address field lists all the directories that lead to your current location. As you move deeper down the directory hierarchy, a forward slash (/) separates the individual directory names. To move back toward the root directory, click at the end of the URL, press the Backspace key to delete the rightmost (or current) directory name, and then press the Enter key to move up to the previous directory. Figure 6-8 shows a URL indicating that the user is viewing the ie directory, which is a subdirectory of the deskapps directory, which is a directory in the root directory at ftp.microsoft.com. To return to the deskapps directory, you can delete the /ie directory from the URL and then press the Enter key. Using the URL to move up one level is the same as clicking a button or link to move up one level.

Figure 6-8	USING THE URL TO MOVE TO THE ROOT DIRECTORY

Milt now sees that a Web browser easily handles downloading files from an FTP site to a local computer. However, he and his staff frequently will need to upload *and* download files, so he asks you to identify some issues related to using an FTP client program for transferring files.

Downloading Files Using an FTP Client Program

You can use FTP to download programs, data files, and software patches (programs that correct known problems in a particular application) from many different sites. Using either an FTP client program or a Web browser is an easy way to locate and download files. With an FTP client program or a Web browser, you click or double-click items to open and download them.

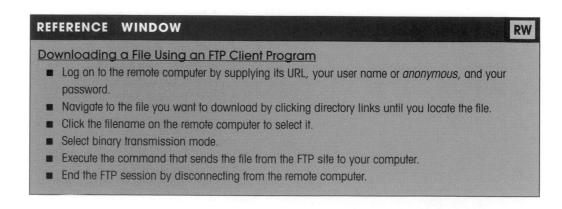

REFERENCE WINDOW   **RW**

Downloading a File Using an FTP Client Program
- Log on to the remote computer by supplying its URL, your user name or *anonymous,* and your password.
- Navigate to the file you want to download by clicking directory links until you locate the file.
- Click the filename on the remote computer to select it.
- Select binary transmission mode.
- Execute the command that sends the file from the FTP site to your computer.
- End the FTP session by disconnecting from the remote computer.

Milt is curious about the transmission modes available for transferring files.

File Transfer Modes

Many files, including Web pages and e-mail messages, consist of ASCII (plain) text. **ASCII text** contains symbols typed from the keyboard but does not include any nonprintable, binary codes. Besides ASCII, many files, such as pictures, movies, sound files, and graphics, are **binary**. Any file created by a word-processing program or a file containing character formatting, such as bold or italics, is binary. FTP can transfer both ASCII and binary files. You select which of the two **file transfer modes**—ASCII or binary—that you want to use before transferring the file. Choose **ASCII mode** to transfer plain-text files; choose **binary mode** for transferring everything else. People usually read plain-text files, whereas computer programs, such as Word or Excel, read binary files. It is important to distinguish between the two types of files, but they are also related. ASCII characters or codes are actually a subset of the larger binary code set. That is, all ASCII characters are also binary characters. The opposite is not true; not all binary representations or codes are ASCII characters. People cannot read many binary codes—only programs can make sense of them. If you download and open a file and it contains a bunch of codes, then you have chosen the wrong transfer mode. Simply execute the FTP operation again using the correct transfer mode.

File Types and Extensions

The decision to transfer a file using binary or ASCII mode is largely determined by noting a file's type, much like Windows programs do. Programs such as Excel, Word, or Internet Explorer determine a file's type by the file extension. A **file extension** is the last three characters following the period in the filename. You can download files with a file extension of .txt in ASCII mode. You should download files with other file extensions in binary mode. It is helpful to understand the relationship between a file's extension and programs that manipulate that file type so you can determine a file's general use and assess your ability to read the file before you download it.

File extensions are added automatically by the program that created them based on a widely agreed-upon convention for associating files with programs. Filenames without periods (called "dots") do not have file extensions. Your PC operating system (Windows, for example) keeps track of most file extension associations and maintains a list of file extensions and programs that can open files with those extensions. Each computer that you use maintains different information about the file types stored on that computer. You can use Windows Explorer to learn about the file associations for your computer.

To view Windows file extension associations:

1. Click the **Start** button on the Windows taskbar, point to **Programs**, point to **Accessories**, and then click **Windows Explorer** to start the program.

2. Click **Tools** on the menu bar, and then click **Folder Options**. The Folder Options dialog box opens.

3. Click the **File Types** tab to see your computer's registered file types and the programs it uses to open those files. Figure 6-9 shows the registered file types for one user's computer; your list will probably differ. The file types are registered each time you install a new software program, so your list of registered file types depends on what programs are installed on your computer. Clicking a registered file type in the list displays more information about that file extension, such as the program that opens the file and a description of the file's purpose.

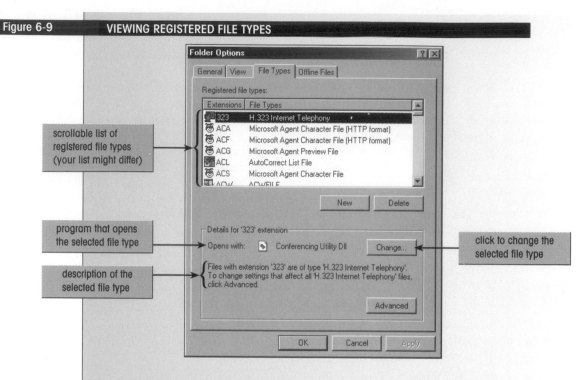

Figure 6-9   VIEWING REGISTERED FILE TYPES

scrollable list of registered file types (your list might differ)

program that opens the selected file type

description of the selected file type

click to change the selected file type

4. Scroll down the list to view all of the registered file types, and then click the **Cancel** button to close the dialog box without making any changes.

5. Close Windows Explorer by clicking its **Close** button.

Figure 6-10 shows several filenames with common file extensions, transfer modes, and programs that open them. Don't worry about remembering all of the different file extensions. In practice, you might encounter only a few of the listed extensions. Most often, you will see files on the Internet with extensions of .doc, .exe, .html, .txt, or .zip.

Figure 6-10   COMMON INTERNET FILE EXTENSIONS, TRANSFER MODES, AND ASSOCIATED PROGRAMS

FILENAME AND EXTENSION	EXTENSION	TRANSFER MODE	TYPE OF FILE
Picture.bmp	.bmp	Binary	Microsoft Paint picture
Readme.doc	.doc	Binary	Word document
Spinner.exe	.exe	Binary	Program
Starship.gif	.gif	Binary	Picture
Index.html or Index.htm	.html or .htm	ASCII	Web page
Employee.mdb	.mdb	Binary	Access database
Help.pdf	.pdf	Binary	Acrobat Portable Document Format
Marketing.ppt	.ppt	Binary	PowerPoint presentation
Readme.txt	.txt	ASCII	Text file
Profit.xls	.xls	Binary	Excel worksheet
File.zip	.zip	Binary	Compressed file

Sometimes you will need to translate the file format of downloaded files into another form before you can read and use them. To translate files, you use a **file utility program**, which is a program that transforms the downloaded file into another format. The most common file type that you find on the Internet is a compressed file. There are many file utility programs that you can use to read compressed files.

Decompressing Downloaded Files

Internet files of all types are frequently stored in compressed form. **Compressed files** use less space when stored, and they take less time to be transferred from one computer to another. For example, you might be able to compress a 1,200 KB file to 400 KB and thereby decrease its download time by over 50%. Compression will be especially important to Milt, because many of his contractors connect to the Internet using dial-up connections with slow upload and download times.

You can use a **file compression program** to decrease the original size of nearly any file. Some widely used file compression programs are WinZip and PKZIP. After you download a compressed file, you must use a program to restore the file to its original state before you can open or execute it. The process of restoring a compressed file to its original state is called **file decompression**, or **file expansion**. FTP recognizes most compressed files by their extensions. The most common extension is .zip, which is why some people refer to compressed files as **zip files** or **zipped files**. The Additional Information section of the Student Online Companion for this tutorial contains links to file compression programs.

Before you install any file or program that you downloaded from another computer, you must first check it for viruses. Milt will want to ensure the health of the computers at Sound Effects, so he wants you to help him locate several options for checking its computers.

Checking Downloaded Files for Viruses

For anyone using the Internet, computer viruses pose a real and potentially costly threat. Computer viruses made their debut shortly after 1985 and have evolved from a nuisance to a hazard for your computer. Computer **viruses** are programs that "infect" your computer and cause harm to your disk or programs. People create viruses by coding programs that invisibly attach themselves to other programs on a computer. Some viruses simply display an annoying or silly message on your screen and then go away, whereas others can cause real harm by reformatting a hard drive or changing all of its file extensions. You have to know how to detect and eradicate viruses if you plan to download anything—including data, programs, or e-mail attachments from either reputable or questionable sources—from the Internet.

Virus detection software, also called **antivirus software**, regularly scans the files on your computer and looks for any infected files by comparing your files to a signature that known viruses carry. A **virus signature** is a sequence (string) of characters that is always present in a particular virus program. A virus detection program can scan a single file or folder or your entire computer to search for infected files. When the virus detection software spots a virus signature, the program warns you. You can either delete the file containing the virus or ask the virus detection program to remove the virus. Most virus detection programs can clean infected files, which removes the virus from the files and renders them "healthy" again. The Additional Information section of the Student Online Companion for this tutorial lists resources for obtaining and using a virus detection program.

Uploading Files

Milt and his associates will need to upload files to remote computers as a means of transporting the files from one location to another. The process of uploading a file is the reverse of downloading one. First, you should check the file for viruses. If your file is large, or if you want to combine several files into one file, then you should compress the files before uploading them to reduce the transfer time and space on the remote computer. With full-privilege access to another computer, you can send the file to a particular folder. Without full-privilege access, you are restricted to uploading a file to the public directory. In any case, you must use an FTP client or command-line program to upload files.

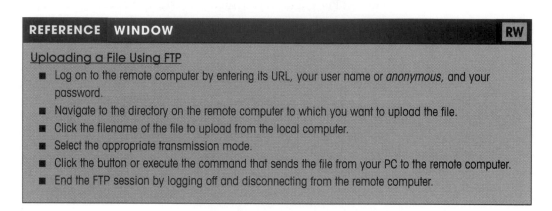

REFERENCE WINDOW   RW

Uploading a File Using FTP
- Log on to the remote computer by entering its URL, your user name or *anonymous,* and your password.
- Navigate to the directory on the remote computer to which you want to upload the file.
- Click the filename of the file to upload from the local computer.
- Select the appropriate transmission mode.
- Click the button or execute the command that sends the file from your PC to the remote computer.
- End the FTP session by logging off and disconnecting from the remote computer.

Using a Public Directory

Milt won't require the use of a public directory because all of the files transmitted to and from Sound Effects will be proprietary in nature. However, some public FTP sites allow users with anonymous FTP access to view only one directory and any files or other directories it contains. That directory is traditionally named *pub* (for public). Besides permitting download access by anonymous users, the site's manager, also referred to as the **webmaster**, might allow users to upload files, making them available to anyone who can connect to the site. Frequently, public directories provide a temporary location for users to upload and share data or programs that they think others might find useful. One problem with sites permitting users with upload privileges is that the webmaster must monitor the files uploaded to a public directory on a regular basis. In addition to worrying about viruses that might be hidden in uploaded files, the webmaster must find and delete any copyrighted files that were illegally uploaded to the site for public use. For example, uploading a program such as Microsoft Word to a public directory is a clear copyright violation because Microsoft's license agreement prohibits you from sharing the program with other users. Many FTP sites have specific policies that force you to acknowledge, before uploading any files, that you are the owner of the material or that its transfer to the FTP site will not violate any copyright or intellectual property restrictions. There are many legitimate uses for public directories, such as sharing data or research with other users. However, it is your responsibility to ensure that someone else does not hold the copyright to the data or research you are sharing.

Most sites have clearly stated rules and policies about the acceptable use of FTP. Be sure to read the site's readme files to learn any rules about acceptable use when you enter an FTP site.

In Session 6.2, you will use the Internet to download an FTP client program that Milt can use to transfer files between his Los Angeles studio and contractors in different areas of the United States and Canada. You will also download a file compression program and a program for reading files saved in the PDF format, investigate the use of a virus detection program, and visit Web sites that provide reviews and information about current releases of different categories of software.

Session 6.1 QUICK CHECK

1. True or False: Only an FTP client program is capable of downloading files from the Internet.

2. When a user logs on to a publicly accessible computer connected to the Internet, what is the customary password that the user should supply?

3. True or False: An FTP client program automatically determines the transfer mode for files that you download.

4. What two types of items might you find in the root directory of an FTP site?

5. What would you type in your browser's address field to open the FTP site at zdnet.com?

6. What type of file uses the .ppt file extension?

7. Programs that reduce a file's size and subsequently its transmission time are known as _____ programs.

SESSION 6.2

In this session, you will visit several Web sites and search for and download software from them. You will use a browser to download and install an FTP client program, and then you will use the FTP client program to download Adobe Acrobat Reader and WinZip. Finally, you will learn how to determine the virtual distance between computers connected to the Internet.

Locating Software Download Sites

Now that Milt understands how FTP works, he is eager to begin using it to transfer files between his Los Angeles studio and its contractors. The computers in the Los Angeles office use Windows 2000 Professional. Because Milt will need to upload and download files, he is most interested in obtaining an FTP client program that can handle both transactions. To help Milt make his decision about an FTP client program, your first goal is to make sure that the software you will download and install is reliable. Cost is not a high-priority issue for Milt at this time, although it is always nice to save money when you can. Perhaps equally important is how various software tools stack up against each other, so you need to find some sort of ratings system that will guide you in making good decisions about which of several software product alternatives to choose.

A good way of locating software on the Internet is to use one or more Internet search engines. If you are searching for FTP client programs, you can look for reviews or comparisons of the software by users or vendors. For example, several popular PC magazines feature articles comparing Internet utility programs and designating one or more programs in a class as the "best of the class" or a "best buy." The criteria these sites use to judge which program is best might be different from your criteria. However, it never hurts to review the ratings when you can. You decide to use a search engine to find information about FTP client programs, so Milt can make an informed choice when selecting an FTP client program.

To use a search engine to find information about FTP client programs:

1. Start your Web browser, open the Student Online Companion page at **www.course.com/newperspectives/internet3**, click the hyperlink for your book, click the **Tutorial 6** link, and then click the **Session 6.2** link. Click the **HotBot** link and wait while the browser opens the HotBot home page.

2. Type **FTP client** in the Search Smarter text box, and then click the **SEARCH** button to start the search. Figure 6-11 shows the first page of search results.

Figure 6-11	FTP CLIENT PROGRAMS RETURNED BY HOTBOT

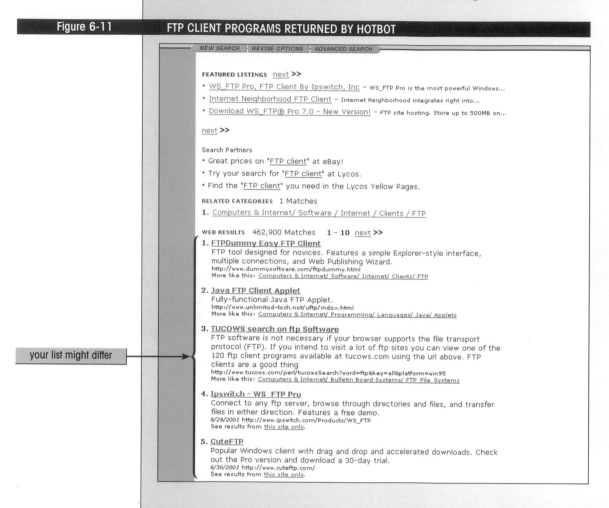

your list might differ

3. Click the first few links on the results page to learn more about FTP client programs.

As you explore some of the links returned by HotBot, you will find that some are relevant and others are not. PC magazines frequently review software using their specially designed software testing laboratories, conduct product comparisons, and report the results. They should not have a vested interest in the outcome, but always view the results with a critical eye to identify any biases. The Additional Information section of the Student Online Companion for this tutorial contains links to publishers of software and hardware product reviews.

You can also try searching for software download sites using the search phrase "software download." The search engine will return a list of sites that contain links to software that you can download from the Internet.

Visiting and Using Popular Download Sites

Several Web sites provide links to freeware and shareware programs; some of these same sites also allow you to download programs directly. To find a list of FTP client programs and reviews about their usage, you decide to visit DOWNLOAD.COM, which contains many freeware and shareware programs organized in different categories.

To browse the DOWNLOAD.COM Web site:

1. Return to the Student Online Companion Web page for Session 6.2, and then click the **DOWNLOAD.COM** hyperlink and wait while your Web browser loads the Web page.

2. Type **FTP client** in the Search text box, as shown in Figure 6-12. Alternatively, you could select a category in which to search, such as Games or Web Authoring. Each category contains subcategories so you can narrow your search.

| Figure 6-12 | SEARCHING FOR FTP CLIENT PROGRAMS USING DOWNLOAD.COM |

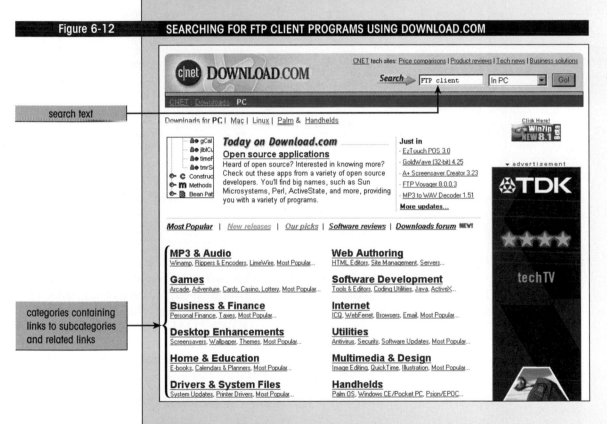

search text

categories containing links to subcategories and related links

3. Click the **Go!** button to search for FTP client programs. Figure 6-13 shows the search results and the different FTP client programs that are available for download from DOWNLOAD.COM. (Your list might differ.) The search returns the date when the files were uploaded to the site and the current number of times each file has been downloaded. Sometimes the download count is a good resource for discovering popular and useful programs because popular programs usually have larger download counts.

Figure 6-13 — FTP CLIENT PROGRAMS RETURNED BY DOWNLOAD.COM

number of programs found

links to information about program use and purchase

click a link for more information about the program

date file was added to DOWNLOAD.COM

program rating provided by current users

number of downloads to date (your number will differ)

file size to download

Found: **118**   Displaying: **1-25**

<Previous 1 2 3 4 5 **Next**>

Re-sort by Name	Purchase info	Date added	User rating	Pick	Downloads Total ‖ Last week	File size
CuteFTP (32-bit) 4.2.4 Transfer files easily with this popular FTP client. OS: Windows 95/98/NT/2000	Demo Register Now	09/07/2001	**86%** 218 votes		9,639,741 *popular*	1.6MB
FTP Voyager 8.0.0.3 Transfer files with ease using this intuitive and powerful FTP client. OS: Windows 95/98/Me/NT/2000	Demo	09/28/2001 *new*	**94%** 2,104 votes	*pick*	3,493,863 *popular*	2.5MB
WS_FTP Pro (32-bit) 7.0 Transfer files over the Internet using this robust FTP client. OS: Windows (all)	Shareware, $40 Check Latest Prices on full version	07/13/2001	**83%** 648 votes		1,577,136 *popular*	4MB
Hotline Connect Client 1.8.5 Connect to a server and chat with other users while you're transferring files. OS: Windows (all)	Freeware	06/25/2001	**91%** 5,172 votes		1,417,373 *popular*	5.5MB
SmartFTP 1.0 build 961 Use a full-featured FTP client with a snazzy interface. OS: Windows 95/98/NT/2000	Freeware	06/05/2001	**92%** 1,477 votes		757,020 *popular*	53.5K
FTP Explorer 1.00.10 Use an FTP client that resembles Windows Explorer. OS: Windows 95	Freeware Register Now	06/16/1997	**93%** 1,375 votes		621,164	661K
LeechFTP 1.3.1.207 Download multiple files at once. OS: Windows 95/98/NT	Freeware	05/20/1999	**93%** 2,765 votes	*pick*	612,235 *popular*	630K
Internet Neighborhood 4.5 Browse FTP sites as if they were folders on your own PC. OS: Windows (all)	Shareware, $30	09/27/2001 *new*	**Submit your opinion**		534,782	3.1MB
CuteFTP Pro 1.0 Take your FTP management to the next level with this sophisticated, professional version of the megapopular FTP client. OS: Windows 95/98/NT/2000	Demo Register Now	03/26/2001	**68%** 978 votes	*pick*	434,546 *popular*	2.5MB

4. Return to the DOWNLOAD.COM home page by clicking your browser's **Back** button.

Another CNET site, Shareware.com, also provides search capabilities for freeware, shareware, and limited edition software. The two sites complement each other, but DOWNLOAD.COM provides more information about downloadable software and advanced search techniques, so that site might provide the best value.

As part of your initial investigation using DOWNLOAD.COM, you find several good FTP client programs for Milt. Before leaving the site, you will explore the category listings to see if they might provide another easy way of searching for downloads.

To browse for Internet software on DOWNLOAD.COM:

1. Click the **Internet** link in the categories list on the DOWNLOAD.COM home page. The Internet category page shown in Figure 6-14 opens and displays a list of Internet software by subcategory. Clicking any of the subcategory links opens a new page that lists related software.

Figure 6-14   DOWNLOAD.COM SUBCATEGORIES

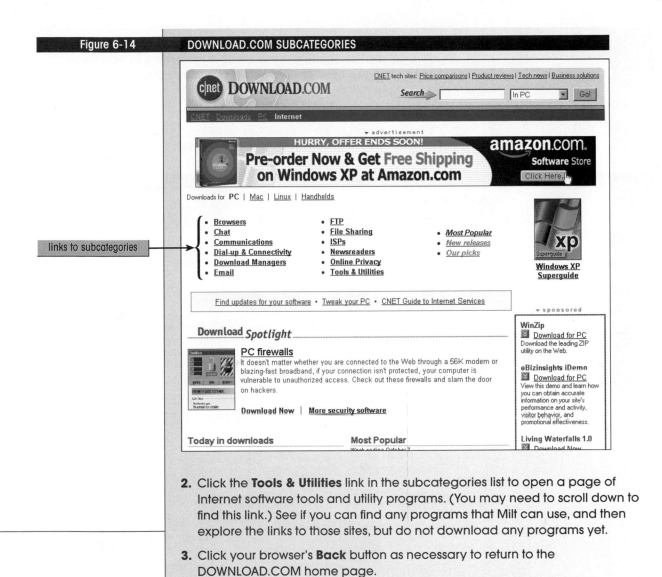

links to subcategories

2. Click the **Tools & Utilities** link in the subcategories list to open a page of Internet software tools and utility programs. (You may need to scroll down to find this link.) See if you can find any programs that Milt can use, and then explore the links to those sites, but do not download any programs yet.

3. Click your browser's **Back** button as necessary to return to the DOWNLOAD.COM home page.

Tucows (which stands for "The Ultimate Collection Of Winsock Software" and is pronounced "two cows") is another popular site that provides quick access to free, inexpensive, and licensed software. Tucows lists its software products by type. You decide to search the Tucows site to see if you can find software that would help Milt.

To browse the Tucows Web site:

1. Return to the Student Online Companion Web page for Session 6.2, and then click the **Tucows** link and wait while your Web browser loads the Web page.

   You can search for software for different operating systems; you will search for Windows 2000 software because that is what Milt and his staff use.

2. Click the **Windows** link. The Choose a Region page opens. Tucows is a busy site with worldwide servers, so you need to click the link for the server closest to you.

3. Click the list arrow for your country, and then select the state, country, or province in which you live. The Choose a Mirror page opens, in which you select the city closest to where you live. You might see only one mirror listed, depending on the location of the country, state, or province in which you live.

4. Click the link of the mirror name in a location close to you. The Welcome to Tucows page shown in Figure 6-15 opens. Because you already selected Windows software, this page lists products for Windows.

Figure 6-15	WELCOME TO TUCOWS PAGE

Internet tab

TROUBLE? You might see more than one link for your location. You can click any entry to open the Welcome to Tucows page. If you cannot open a link, try another state or region until you succeed.

5. Click the **Internet** tab at the top of the page to open a page listing categories of Internet programs, similar to what you viewed using DOWNLOAD.COM.

6. Scroll down the page to examine its contents. Each category contains links that open pages containing more links to detailed information about the individual software programs you can download.

When Milt needs to download files, he might use his browser instead of an FTP client program. You'll need to make sure that he has the most current browser available to ensure the best quality and security available. You'll visit Microsoft's Download Center to investigate new browser programs and updates.

To locate Microsoft Internet Explorer files on Microsoft's Web site:

1. Return to the Student Online Companion Web page for Session 6.2, and then click the **Microsoft Download Center** link and wait while your Web browser loads the Web page shown in Figure 6-16.

Figure 6-16   MICROSOFT DOWNLOAD CENTER PAGE

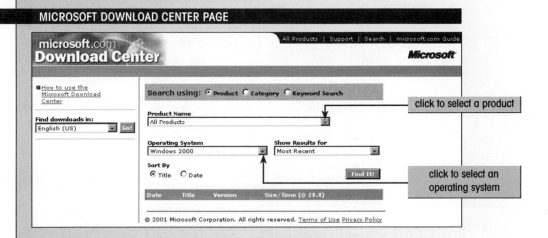

2. Click the **Product Name** list arrow, and then scroll down the list and click **Internet Explorer 6** (or a higher version number if one is available).

3. Click the **Operating System** list arrow, scroll down the list as necessary and click **Windows 2000**, and then click the **Find It!** button. The page that opens lists the files you can download for Internet Explorer version 6 and Windows 2000. Review the links, but do not download any files.

Milt just asked you about another software download site that is maintained by ZDNet. ZDNet tests and reviews information technology products and reports its findings on its Web site. ZDNet issues ratings based on tests and evaluations of users who send their impressions of the software via e-mail to the publisher. Because ZDNet is well regarded for its thorough reviews, you decide to search for antivirus software and use the ratings to identify programs that will provide security for Milt's file transfers.

To search the ZDNet Software Library Web site for antivirus software:

1. Return to the Student Online Companion Web page for Session 6.2, and then click the **ZDNet Downloads** link and wait while your Web browser loads the Web page.

2. Locate the Search For text box near the top of the page, type **antivirus** in the text box, and then click the **GO** button. A search results page opens and returns a list of links to antivirus software programs, as shown in Figure 6-17. Your results might be different from those shown in Figure 6-17, but you should find many antivirus programs in the list.

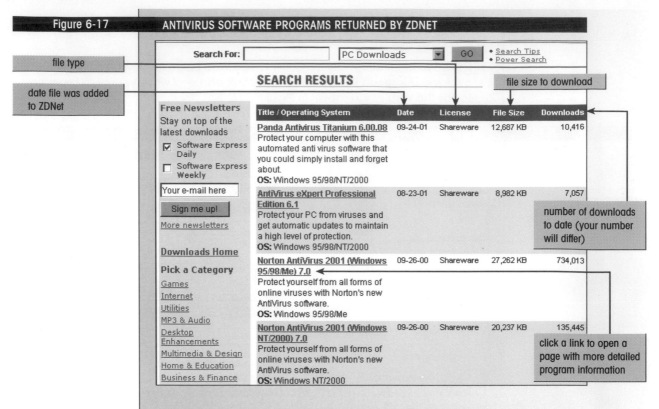

Figure 6-17 **ANTIVIRUS SOFTWARE PROGRAMS RETURNED BY ZDNET**

TROUBLE? If the search results page does not list any files, type "virus" or "antivirus" (without the quotation marks) in the Search For text box, and then click the GO button again. You might need to search several times using different search expressions to find antivirus software.

3. Click the hyperlink for the program named **Norton AntiVirus 2001 (Windows NT/2000) 7.0** to open the page shown in Figure 6-18, which supplies more information about the program, including a detailed description and its compressed file size. You can use this page to download the program by clicking the Download Now link. You can also click the Add to Basket link to place the program in your virtual shopping cart so you can continue selecting programs and download all of them at once.

TROUBLE? If you cannot find the Norton AntiVirus 2001 (Windows NT/2000) 7.0 link, scroll to the bottom of the page, and then click the Hits 27-52 button to view the next group of links.

Figure 6-18   **NORTON ANTIVIRUS 2001 PRODUCT PAGE**

program information

review information

program description

Norton AntiVirus 2001 (Windows NT/2000)

Protect yourself from all forms of online viruses with Norton's new AntiVirus software.

Company: Symantec

Version: v7.0

Date Added: 09-26-00

Size: 19.3 MB

Downloads: 135,219

OS: Windows NT/2000

User Rating: ★★★★
Rate This Title!   **Read User Reviews**
Earn points for writing a review

Requirements: Windows NT/2000

License: Shareware

Norton AntiVirus 2001 automatically keeps virus definitions updated to provide continuous Internet and email protection. Norton AntiVirus 2001 combines virus detection capabilities with updating and scanning technologies to make it easy for users to secure their systems against malicious code. Norton AntiVirus is also an integral component of Symantec s Norton SystemWorks 2001 suite. Norton AntiVirus 2001 guards against malicious code in ActiveX controls and Java applets as well as worms, Trojan Horses, and password-stealers. Key features include:

- Automatic checking for and updating of virus definitions
- Pop-up messages appear if virus definitions become dangerously out-of-date
- Scans program and document files automatically as they are downloaded using browser of choice
- Compressed file scanning
- Automatic scanning of e-mail attachment before the user saves, launches, or otherwise accesses the attachment
- An enhanced interface that integrates an email/Web status panel for easy configuration
- A bootable CD providing easy recovery after virus emergency

Norton AntiVirus 2001 also features an improved LiveUpdate feature, new SmartScan technology, and an improved, easy-to-use interface.

Note: This is a 30-day trial. Registration costs $39.95.

▶ Download Now   ▶ Add to Basket

▶ **Download Now**
▶ **Add to Basket**   ◄ *click to download 30-day trial version*
▶ **Look in Basket**   *click to purchase the full version*

Free Newsletters
Stay on top of the latest downloads
☑ Software Express Daily
☐ Software Express Weekly
[Your e-mail here]
[Sign me up!]
More newsletters

Downloads Home

Pick a Category
Games
Internet
Utilities
MP3 & Audio
Desktop Enhancements
Multimedia & Design
Home & Education
Business & Finance
Web Authoring
Software Development
Drivers & System Files
Windows 9x/Me/NT/2000

See Also
Free Software
Editors' Picks
Macintosh
Palm OS
CE & Pocket PC
Linux

The BEST BUYS
upgrades
software
desktops
scanners
laptops
and more!
COMPUTER SHOPPER.com
Advertisement

Services
Help
Upload a File
Download Basket

See Related Links
» **Hot Clicks**
- Yahoo! Messenger
- What's New
- Today's
- Weekly

SPECIAL OFFERS
from

PC Remote Access & Control
Work on your PC from anywhere. FREE TRIAL

Get Newtella Now
Find and Share MP3s. It's Free!

Get IrfanView
The world's most popular Free image viewer.

GameSpy Arcade
Find, start and join multiplayer games online

✉ E-mail this
🖶 Print this

Now that you have identified several evaluation versions of an FTP client program, browser updates, and an antivirus program, you are ready to locate and download them for Milt so he can begin using them. You begin by using a Web browser to download an FTP client program.

Downloading **Programs**

After downloading anything from the Internet—even files from reputable sources—your first priority is to scan the file for viruses to ensure that installing or opening the program or file will not damage your computer. You can download many high quality antivirus programs from the Internet and install and use them for a limited time to determine their appropriateness for your own security needs. Because most antivirus programs are large in size, you won't download a program in this tutorial, but you can click the links in the Additional Information section of the Student Online Companion page for this tutorial to explore the available antivirus programs for your operating system.

Downloading an FTP Client

One of the most important software tools that you want to locate for Milt is an FTP client program that is user-friendly and contains many features. You conducted your research on FTP client programs by visiting sites that review software searching and read articles about different FTP client programs. In the course of conducting your research, you have found that there are four general classes of downloaded software: freeware, shareware, limited edition, and licensed (or full version).

Internet surfers are often pleasantly surprised to discover that many Internet programs are available for download at little or no cost. Developers often make their software available for free in exchange for user feedback. After collecting user feedback and improving the free software, many developers provide an upgrade of the free version for a nominal fee. Software that is available to users at no cost and with no restrictions is called **freeware**. Freeware users must accept the implicit or explicit warning that the software might contain errors, called **bugs**, which could cause the program to halt or malfunction or even damage the user's computer. The main risk associated with using freeware is that its limited testing often results in a program that contains a lot of bugs, and the software's developer is rarely liable for any damage that the freeware program might cause. On the other hand, a lot of good-quality commercial software started as freeware. Before you use freeware, you should use a Web search engine to locate reviews before you download, install, virus check, and use any freeware program to see what kinds of successes and problems its users have reported.

Shareware is similar to freeware, but it is not entirely free and usually is available only for a short evaluation period. After that evaluation period expires—usually either a specified number of days or a specific number of uses—shareware stops functioning. Shareware users are expected to stop using the shareware after the specified initial trial period and uninstall it from their computers. Otherwise, anyone who likes the program and wants to continue using it can purchase a license. There are three popular ways to turn shareware users into paying customers. The first way is to build a counter into the program that keeps track of the number of times they have used a program. After users have reached a usage limit, the software is disabled. The second way is by inserting an internal date checker as a time-expiration technique that causes the shareware to stop working after a specific time period from the installation date has elapsed, such as 30 days. Third, many shareware developers use a "nag" screen that appears each time you start the program to encourage users who do not purchase a license to stop using the shareware, although the program may continue to work. The screen usually displays a message with the developer's name and Web address and asks you to abide by the licensing agreement and to submit payment for the shareware version of the product.

Shareware is usually slightly more reliable than freeware because the shareware developer is sometimes willing to accept responsibility for the program's operation. Usually, shareware developers have an established way for users to report any bugs and receive free or low-cost software upgrades and bug fixes.

Some developers distribute restricted versions of their software for free to let people use it without risk. A restricted version of a shareware program is called a **limited edition** (or **LE**), and it provides most of the functionality of the full version that is for sale. However, LE software omits one or more useful features of the full version. You can sometimes download an LE version and use it for free. If you really like the LE, then you can purchase the full version. The FTP client program WS_FTP LE is one example of a free limited edition of the full WS_FTP program. The limited edition performs all the standard FTP tasks but omits some of the advanced features that make the full product especially attractive. Because the complete versions of limited edition software are inexpensive, most users of the limited edition will purchase the upgraded, comprehensive version so they can use its additional capabilities.

Regardless of which type of software you use to evaluate a product, most developers provide you with a means of contacting them to purchase a license to use the full version of the evaluation copy. Purchasing a license usually involves paying a fee to get a code to unlock the software and render it fully functional.

From your studies, you conclude that the WS_FTP LE FTP client program is the best choice for Milt, so you will download it next.

To download the WS_FTP LE program:

1. Return to the Student Online Companion Web page for Session 6.2, and then click the **Ipswitch** link and wait while your Web browser loads the Ipswitch home page shown in Figure 6-19.

Figure 6-19	IPSWITCH HOME PAGE

Download Evaluations link

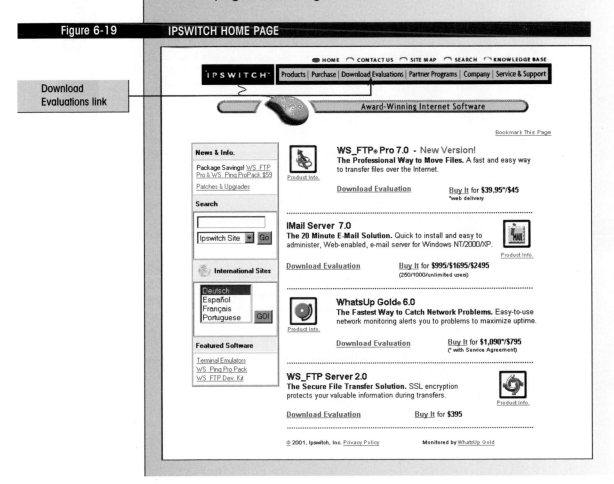

2. Locate and click the **Download Evaluations** link on the link bar that appears at the top of the page. The Download Evaluations page opens.

3. Scroll down the page and locate the WS_FTP LE 5.08 link in the Other Products section.

   TROUBLE? If you see a higher version of the WS_FTP LE program, use that version instead of the one included in Steps 3 and 4.

4. Click the **WS_FTP LE 5.08** link. Your browser opens the page at FTPplanet.com as shown in Figure 6-20. You'll download the WS_FTP LE program from this site.

Figure 6-20 | FTPPLANET.COM HOME PAGE

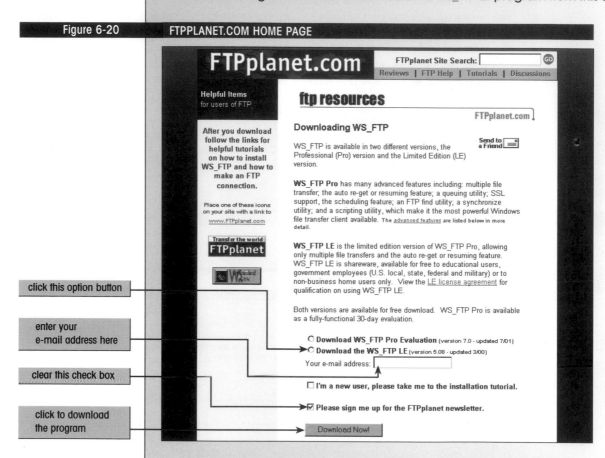

5. Read the page that opens, click the **Download the WS_FTP LE** option button to select it, type your e-mail address in the Your e-mail address text box, clear the check box for signing up to receive the FTPplanet newsletter, and then click the **Download Now!** button.

   TROUBLE? If a dialog box opens and asks if you would like to open or save the file, click the Save button.

6. Make sure your Data Disk is in the appropriate drive, click the **Save in** list arrow and select the appropriate drive, and then double-click the **Tutorial.06** folder to open it. You will accept the default filename of ws_ftple.exe.

7. Click the **Save** button to begin downloading the file to your Data Disk. After a few moments, the compressed file that contains the FTP client program is stored on your Data Disk.

   TROUBLE? If a dialog box opens to indicate that the download is complete, click the Close button.

After you download the program's executable file, you should check it for viruses, and then you must install the program on your computer to use it. You can use Windows Explorer to check the Tutorial.06 folder on your Data Disk to make sure that it contains the ws_ftple.exe file.

Note: If your instructor or technical support person permits you to install and use the program, complete the next set of steps to install the software. If your lab policy prohibits you from installing the program, read the following steps so you know how to install the software, but do *not* complete the steps at the computer.

To install WS_FTP LE on your computer:

1. Make sure that your Data Disk is in the appropriate drive, click the **Start** button on the Windows taskbar, click **Run**, and then type **A:\Tutorial.06\ws_ftple.exe** in the Open list box.

   TROUBLE? If your Data Disk is not in drive A, substitute your drive letter in the Open list box.

2. Click the **OK** or **Open** button (as instructed) to start the installation process. An installation screen appears.

   TROUBLE? If the on-screen instructions for WS_FTP LE differ from those shown in the steps, follow the on-screen instructions.

3. Click the **Continue** button. A second dialog box opens asking you to identify your status.

4. Click the option button to indicate that you are a student, and then click the **Next** button. A dialog box opens and asks how you plan to use the program.

5. Click the **At school** check box to select it, click the **For academic work** check box to select it, and then click the **Next** button. A dialog box opens, displaying the license agreement for using WS_FTP LE. (As a business owner, Milt would choose the appropriate option and follow the license agreement to use the software.)

6. Read the license agreement, and then click the **Accept** button to indicate that you accept the terms of the agreement. (If you do not accept the terms of the license agreement, then the installation process stops.) A WS_FTP LE Installation dialog box opens with a default destination folder for installing the program.

7. Click the **OK** button to accept the default folder in which the program files will be stored, and then click the **OK** button again to accept the default folder for file transfers. (The default directory is C:\Program Files\WS_FTP.) The Program Manager Group dialog box opens.

8. Click the **OK** button to accept the suggested name, WS_FTP LE, for the Program Manager group. (WS_FTP is the name of the Program Manager group folder that will appear on the Programs menu.)

9. Click the **OK** button to complete the installation process. A window opens with the shortcuts for using the WS_FTP LE program.

10. Close the WS_FTP LE window by clicking its **Close** button.

After you are finished installing the program, you may want to read the WS_FTP LE Release Notes file to learn how to use the program, or you can use the program's Help files for program instructions. After installing the product, Milt can use it to send files via FTP to other computers.

Downloading Adobe Acrobat Reader

Sound Effects, Inc. is planning to change the format in which its scripts and other written documents are prepared. **Portable Document Format (PDF)**, developed by Adobe Corporation, provides a convenient, self-contained package for delivering and displaying documents containing text, graphics, charts, and other objects. PDF files and compressed files are both special formats for storing files, but they are not related. PDF files simply provide a universal and convenient way to represent documents, whereas compressed files condense files so they occupy much less space. Compressed files cannot be viewed until you decompress them.

When you download a PDF file, you do not need to use the same program as the file's creator to display, browse, and print the document; you use the **Adobe Acrobat Reader** program to view the document. For example, if you download a PDF file that was created in Microsoft Word, you can use Acrobat Reader to access the document, even if you don't have Word installed on your computer. Most Web browsers can start the Acrobat Reader program so you can use your Web browser to view PDF documents without downloading them first, or you can download the Acrobat Reader program separately to read files that you have already downloaded.

Acrobat Reader is a free, simple to install program. You will use DOWNLOAD.COM's site to search for and download Acrobat Reader so Milt will have it on his computer for testing purposes when he begins using PDF files to prepare scripts and other communications.

Note: You cannot download the Acrobat Reader program to a floppy disk because the program's size (approximately eight megabytes) exceeds the disk's storage capacity. Your instructor might ask you to download the program to your hard drive or to simply read the following steps without actually downloading the file.

To download the Acrobat Reader from DOWNLOAD.COM:

1. Return to the Student Online Companion Web page for Session 6.2, and then click the **DOWNLOAD.COM** link and wait while your Web browser loads the Web page.

2. Type **Acrobat Reader** in the Search text box, and then click the **Go!** button. Your search results page should look similar to Figure 6-21.

Figure 6-21	ADOBE ACROBAT READER LINKS RETURNED BY DOWNLOAD.COM

Found: **7**   Displaying: **1-7**

Re-sort by Name	Purchase info	Date added	User rating	Pick	Downloads Total I Last week	File size
Adobe Acrobat Reader (32-bit) 5.0 Read Adobe PDF files from the Web. **OS:** Windows (all)	Freeware Check Latest Prices on full version	04/19/2001	**92%** 5,596 votes	*pick*	6,096,749 *popular*	8.6MB
Adobe Acrobat 4.05 Update 2 Update your version of Acrobat 4.05. **OS:** Windows 95/98/NT	Freeware	07/26/2000	**97%** 1,708 votes		544,551 *popular*	2.8MB
Adobe Acrobat Reader (16-bit) 3.01 Browse Adobe PDF files for the Web. **OS:** Windows 3.x	Freeware	08/28/1997	**87%** 491 votes		376,516 *popular*	3.7MB
Adobe Acrobat Reader OCX Update 1.0 Fix Adobe Acrobat to work properly with Internet Explorer 4.0. **OS:** Windows 3.x	Freeware	11/18/1997	**91%** 36 votes		62,708 *popular*	1.2MB
Adobe Acrobat Distiller Update 3.02 Fix bugs with a tool included in Adobe Acrobat. **OS:** Windows 95/98/NT/2000	Freeware	10/05/2000	**75%** 36 votes		30,902 *popular*	1MB
Adobe Acrobat Forms Plug-in 3.5 View and print forms created with the Author plug-in. **OS:** Windows 3.x	Freeware	01/29/1998	**76%** 13 votes		23,576 *popular*	2.3MB
Make Accessible Plug-In 5.0 Create tagged PDF files easily with this Acrobat plug-in. **OS:** Windows 95/98/NT/2000	Freeware	04/19/2001	**84%** 25 votes		11,647	1.9MB
Re-sort by Name	Purchase info	Date added	User rating	Pick	Downloads Total I Last week	File size

Found: **7**   Displaying: **1-7**

Filter list by [All OSs ▾] [All categories ▾] [All licenses ▾] [Update]

links to Adobe Acrobat Reader programs (your list might differ)

The Downloads column displays the number of downloads that have occurred to date—a larger number generally indicates that the software is popular and reliable, whereas a smaller number indicates that the software could be relatively new.

TROUBLE? Software vendors update and improve their programs regularly, so your Acrobat Reader program version number might be different. If you see a higher version number than the ones shown in Figure 6-21, download that program in Step 3, which is a more current version.

3. Click the **Adobe Acrobat Reader (32-bit) 5.0** link (or the link for the latest version of Windows) to open the page shown in Figure 6-22. This page provides details about the program and a link to download it.

Figure 6-22   PRODUCT PAGE FOR ADOBE ACROBAT READER

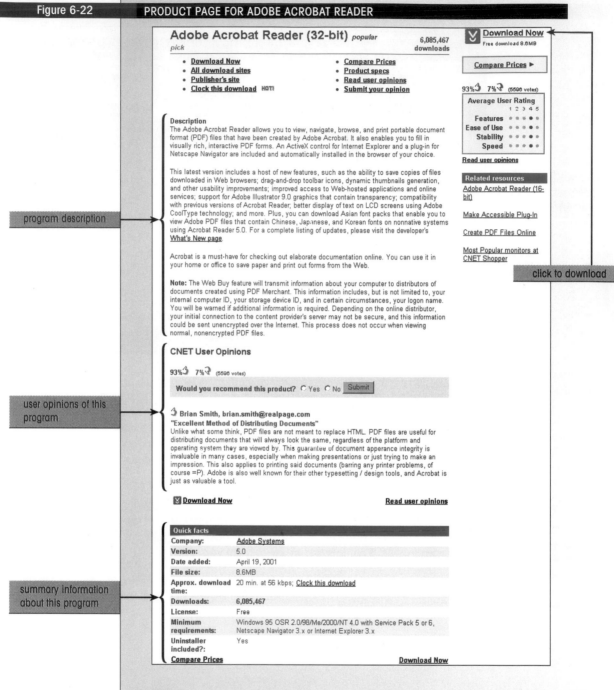

program description

user opinions of this program

summary information about this program

4. Read the program description and the summary of its requirements, and then click the **Download Now** link. DOWNLOAD.COM will select a download site for you automatically.

5. If a dialog box opens and asks if you want to open or save the file, click the **Save** button. If this dialog box does not open, then your browser will automatically choose to save the file to disk.

TROUBLE? Ask your instructor or technical support person if you can download the file to your hard drive. If you cannot download the file, or if you are unsure about downloading the file, then click the Cancel button now and read the rest of the steps without completing them at the computer.

6. In the Save As dialog box, click the **Save in** list arrow, click the drive and folder in which to save the file, and then click the **Save** button. Figure 6-23 shows the dialog box that Internet Explorer displays while it downloads the file. (Navigator displays a different dialog box.)

Figure 6-23   FILE DOWNLOAD DIALOG BOX IN INTERNET EXPLORER

7. After the download is complete, click the **Close** button (if necessary) to close the dialog box that opens.

8. Close your browser, but do not disconnect from your Internet connection.

The time it takes to transfer the program file varies based on the speed of your Internet connection. If you are on a local area network (LAN) with a T1 Internet connection, then the transfer time is a few seconds. If you are using a modem and a dial-up connection, then the transfer time could take several minutes. Another factor in the download time is the amount of traffic at the FTP site. Many simultaneous users (more than 4,000 for example) can directly affect the download process. If you encounter problems while downloading a file, stop the process by clicking the Cancel button and try again later.

Now the downloaded Acrobat Reader file is saved on your hard drive. You can install the program by double-clicking its filename in Windows Explorer and then following the on-screen steps. After installing the Acrobat Reader program, you can delete the downloaded executable file from the drive and folder to which you downloaded it, or you can keep it in case you need to reinstall the program.

Downloading WinZip

Milt is very interested in compressing files to decrease the amount of space they require on an FTP site and also to decrease the time it takes to upload and download files. Many file compression programs available on the Internet are reliable and easy to use. One popular program is WinZip, which is available for free during your evaluation. WinZip has been downloaded millions of times and has received many awards from computing magazines and other sources.

To test the FTP client program that you downloaded earlier, you will use it to connect to the WinZip FTP site so you can download an evaluation copy of the program. When you establish a connection to an FTP site, you can save the site's host address and your user name and password so you can easily return to the site later. When you use an FTP client program to save this information, you are creating an **FTP session profile**.

Note: In the following steps, you will use the WS_FTP LE program to download the WinZip program. If you do not have an FTP client or cannot install one on your school's computer, then read the steps without completing them at the computer.

To establish and save an FTP session profile:

1. Click the **Start** button on the Windows taskbar, point to **Programs**, point to **WS_FTP**, and then click **WS_FTP95 LE** to start the WS_FTP LE program. The Session Properties dialog box opens.

   TROUBLE? If you do not see WS_FTP on the Programs menu, make sure that you downloaded and installed the WS_FTP LE program earlier in this session.

2. Click the **New** button in the Session Properties dialog box to create a new FTP session profile.

3. In the Profile Name text box, type **WinZip** to name the new FTP session profile so you can easily recognize it later.

4. Press the **Tab** key to move to the Host Name/Address text box, and then type **ftp.winzip.com**. This address is the URL to the FTP site for WinZip. You can usually find the FTP address for an FTP site by replacing the "www" in a site's Web address with "ftp". Some companies list their FTP site addresses on their Internet Web pages, as well.

5. Click the **Anonymous** check box to select it. WS_FTP LE automatically adds the anonymous logon to the User ID text box and a default password to the Password text box. You'll change the default password to your e-mail address as is customary on the Internet to identify your use of the site.

6. Select the default password in the Password text box, and then type your full e-mail address. Figure 6-24 shows the Session Properties dialog box settings to establish an anonymous login to the WinZip FTP site.

Figure 6-24	SESSION PROPERTIES DIALOG BOX FOR WINZIP

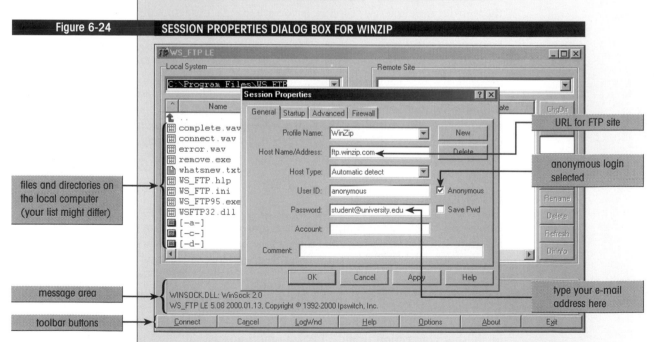

7. Click the **Apply** button to save the WinZip session profile without connecting to the WinZip FTP site.

Now you can easily visit the WinZip FTP site the next time by clicking the Profile Name list arrow in the Session Properties dialog box and then clicking WinZip. With the URL and user information entered, you are ready to log on to the FTP site anonymously and download the WinZip program.

Note: You cannot download the WinZip 8.0 program to a floppy disk because the program's file size (approximately two megabytes) exceeds the disk's storage capacity. Your instructor might ask you to download the program to your hard drive or to simply read the following steps without actually downloading the file.

To log on anonymously and download the file:

1. Click the **OK** button to log on to the WinZip FTP site. Several messages scroll in the message area at the bottom of the WS_FTP LE window. You can use the scroll arrows to view the messages passed between your client and the FTP server.

2. If necessary, click the **Maximize** button to maximize the program window. The Local System pane displays the drives and folders on your computer (the local computer) and the Remote Site pane displays the contents of the WinZip FTP site (the remote computer). You use the buttons to the right of each directory listing to change, make, view, rename, delete, and refresh the directories and files.

3. Click the **ChgDir** button in the Local System pane. The Input dialog box opens and requests the local folder name that you would like to display. See Figure 6-25.

| Figure 6-25 | CHANGING THE LOCAL DIRECTORY |

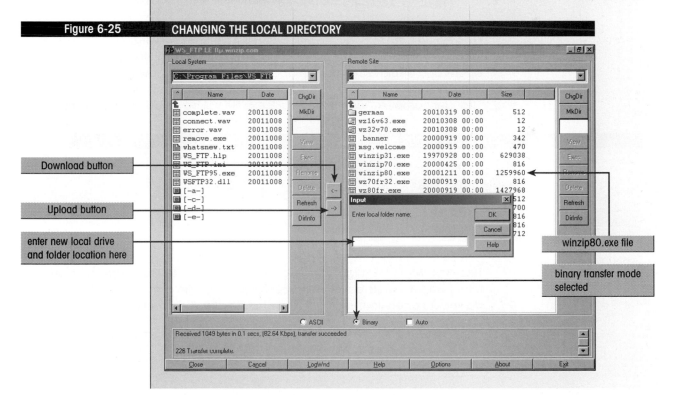

4. Type the drive letter and folder for the location to which you will download the file in the text box (see Figure 6-25), and then click the **OK** button. The Local System pane changes and displays the files and folders on the drive you selected. By changing the drive and folder on the local computer, files you download will be stored in that location.

TROUBLE? If you cannot establish a connection with the WinZip FTP server, then click the Close button at the bottom of the window, click the Connect button to open the Session Properties dialog box, click the Profile Name list arrow, and then click WinZip. Make sure you entered ftp.winzip.com in the Host Name/Address text box. Click the OK button to connect, and then follow the steps.

TROUBLE? If you tried more than once to connect to the WinZip site without success, the site might be busy. When the number of anonymous logins exceeds a large number, the WinZip site rejects all subsequent anonymous FTP sessions. Try again later, or just read the steps so you understand how to use an FTP client to download files.

The file you want to download, winzip80.exe, appears in the Remote Site pane.

5. If necessary, click the **Binary** option button to ensure that the program file is transferred correctly.

6. In the Remote Site pane, locate and then click **winzip80.exe** to select it.

7. Click the **Download** button between the Local System and Remote Site panes (see Figure 6-25) to begin downloading the file from the WinZip FTP site to the location you specified. As shown in Figure 6-26, a Transfer Status dialog box opens and displays information about the status of the download. When the Transfer Status dialog box closes, the message window will display the message "Transfer complete," and the winzip80.exe file will be saved on your computer.

Figure 6-26	TRANSFER STATUS DIALOG BOX

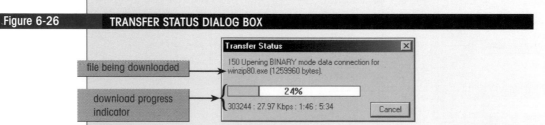

TROUBLE? WS_FTP LE might save a log file named WS_FTP.LOG on the drive and folder where you saved the winzip80.exe file. A log file indicates the status of the download operation; you can delete this file after the download is complete.

8. Click the **Exit** button at the bottom of the window to log off the WinZip FTP site and to close the WS_FTP LE program.

If you are allowed to install the WinZip program, open Windows Explorer, change to the drive and folder to which you downloaded the winzip80.exe file, double-click winzip80.exe, and then follow the on-screen instructions. (Ask your instructor or technical support person first before installing the program.) The WinZip file that you downloaded is an **evaluation version**, which means that you can use it to evaluate the software at no charge. Each time you start the program, it will remind you about your use of an evaluation copy that has not yet been registered. If you continue using the software, you can click a button in the reminder screen to purchase a license to use the full version.

Tracing an Internet Route

In this session, you have encountered Web sites that have asked you to select a download location, also known as a mirror site, from which to download a file. A **mirror site** is a replica of an existing server that provides an alternate location for downloading files. When you select a mirror site, you will usually begin by selecting a site close to you; for example, if you live in Tallahassee, Florida, you might choose a mirror site in Atlanta, Georgia rather than a site in Seattle, Washington. Because the Internet makes it feel as though you are accessing sites from very long distances in just a few seconds, you might think that the physical difference between you and another Internet site is unimportant, but it is. The Internet is a complex network of interconnected computers. Just as the distance between your PC and a remote computer might be measured in miles, the distance between your PC and a remote computer on the Internet is measured in hops. A **hop** is a connection between two computers. If a file travels through 15 computers before arriving at your PC, then the file has made 14 hops (the number of computers in the path minus one). Minimizing the number of hops between a remote computer and your PC reduces the total download time to transfer files between computers.

You can count the hops and identify the computers between your PC and a remote computer using the Windows **tracert** (for *trace route*) program. You can use the tracert program to make an informed choice between alternative download sites. Tracert will show you up to 30 hops and indicate the response time, the site name, and the IP address of each hop along the route. (If you do not have tracert installed on your computer, use a Web search engine to search for **ping**, or **Packet Internet Groper**, which is a program that tests a computer to determine if it is connected to the Internet. You can find several freeware and shareware ping programs that accomplish the same thing as tracert. In addition, the Additional Information section of the Student Online Companion for this tutorial includes links to other programs that trace routes.)

As Milt reviews additional software programs he might be given a list of mirror sites from which to download files; he can use tracert to determine if one mirror site might provide a more direct connection over others. Because many of the actors who provide voiceovers live in New York City, Milt asks you to use tracert to view the hops between your PC and the FTP site at New York University.

To view the hops between your PC and a remote computer:

1. Click the **Start** button on the Windows taskbar, click **Run**, type **command** in the Open list box, and then click the **OK** button. A DOS program window opens. If necessary, click the **Maximize** button on the program window's title bar to maximize it.

2. Type **tracert ftp.nyu.edu** at the command prompt, and then press the **Enter** key to list the hops between your PC and the server at the New York University in New York. Tracert produces a list of each computer's IP address on the path between your PC and the specified URL. When the trace is complete, the "Trace complete" message appears at the bottom of the site trace list. Figure 6-27 shows the hops from a user located in Texas; your trace will be different.

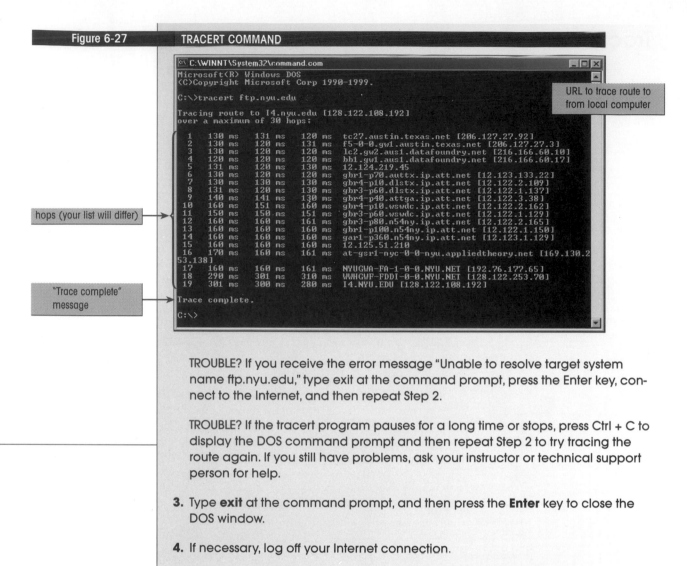

Figure 6-27   TRACERT COMMAND

URL to trace route to from local computer

hops (your list will differ)

"Trace complete" message

TROUBLE? If you receive the error message "Unable to resolve target system name ftp.nyu.edu," type exit at the command prompt, press the Enter key, connect to the Internet, and then repeat Step 2.

TROUBLE? If the tracert program pauses for a long time or stops, press Ctrl + C to display the DOS command prompt and then repeat Step 2 to try tracing the route again. If you still have problems, ask your instructor or technical support person for help.

3. Type **exit** at the command prompt, and then press the **Enter** key to close the DOS window.

4. If necessary, log off your Internet connection.

When you are downloading very large program files, you can use the tracert program any time—even while your browser is running—to find the path with the fewest hops, because that path might reduce your download time significantly. To trace a route while your browser is running, write down or copy the URL to the target site, click the Start button on the Windows taskbar, click Run, and then type *tracert* followed by the URL of the target site. Click the OK button to trace the route. Once the trace is complete, the tracert window closes immediately, so look quickly!

Milt is pleased with the programs that you have found. After testing the programs to make sure that they will satisfy the requirements at Sound Effects, Inc., Milt will fulfill any licensing agreements so he can install the full versions of the programs you downloaded on the office computers.

You successfully downloaded many programs from the Internet. In addition to its utility in transferring files between computers, FTP is an excellent way to share files with other users and to temporarily and permanently store files. In Session 6.3, you'll learn about online storage providers of these services.

Session 6.2 QUICK CHECK

1. What is freeware, shareware, and limited edition software?

2. After downloading a program from the Internet, what should you do prior to installing it?

3. What is the file format that is used for storing documents on the Internet so users can print them without accessing the program used to create the documents?

4. What is the general name for a program that reduces the size of one or more files and that saves multiple files using a single filename?

5. What is a hop?

6. What Windows program determines the distance between computers connected to the Internet?

SESSION 6.3

In this session, you will visit the Web sites of some online storage providers and learn more about the services they provide. You will use Yahoo! Briefcase to upload and download a file and to send a link to a file in an e-mail message. Finally, you will examine the future of subscription models for delivering software products to end users.

Using Online Storage Services

Now that you've provided Milt with the tools he needs to transfer files on the Internet, where is he going to send those files? He can't upload his proprietary data and other sensitive information to a public directory on a publicly accessible FTP site, nor can he ask his contractors to do the same. Milt needs access to an FTP site that is both secure and password protected, with enough storage space so that files can remain on the site for as long as necessary. He also needs to provide access to this site to his contractors so they can upload and download files.

When you use an ISP for your Internet connection and e-mail services, you might also receive some free space to use to store a Web site or files. This space is useful to you, but your user name and password control access to the site. You probably won't want to share this space with other users, because by doing so you will need to give those other users full access to your account, including your e-mail messages. You would have no way of controlling access to the site or securing important data from other users.

Because FTP is easy to use and an efficient way of transferring files across the Internet, many services have evolved to meet the increased need for ways to store and share files. FTP sites are one way of sharing and storing files, but not everyone has full-privilege access to an FTP site. From this need, the creation of a new business model formed, where ISPs and other entities started providing 10 to 50 megabytes of storage space on their servers, either for free or for a fee. This space is secured with an account name and password and permits the sharing of files by many users. As the space sizes increased, so did the possibilities. Many businesses rely on these online storage services to send and receive large files while employees are traveling or as a normal course of business. In addition, the proliferation of large data files moving across the Internet has the potential to overload many networks and e-mail servers when these files are attached to e-mail messages, so these online storage providers provide an alternate to consuming a company's network resources.

At first, many of these services provided up to 50 megabytes of free storage space to registered users. As more registered users started accessing the sites, and as those users started storing large files and increasing the number of daily transfers, many sites experienced conflicts with users competing for the company's resources, so that the free model was in direct conflict with the paid model. As a result of bandwidth problems, many online storage providers changed their policies to limit the number of transfers and amount of space, charge a small monthly fee for the use of the space, or a combination of both. Most services provide additional space and transfers for an additional fee.

Using an online storage provider might be a good opportunity for Milt. As he reviews his requirements, he decides that he needs at least 50 to 100 megabytes of space and the capability to allow restricted and full access, depending on the user. Because the cost of maintaining his own FTP server would be an impediment to his overall operating budget, Milt is willing to pay a monthly fee for use of whichever provider matches his needs best. In addition, because Milt works with only a few contractors at a time, his space will not have a high number of transfers each day. Because Milt will require upload and download transfers, he will need to use an FTP client program or an easy-to-use Web page interface to execute the transfers. Being able to use any FTP client program or a Web browser to log on to the site—and not requiring any proprietary software from the online storage provider—will make it easier for Milt and his contractors to access and use the site. Finally, Milt wants to make sure that the provider will ensure the security of his data from unauthorized use.

You'll use the Internet to conduct your research to help Milt identify some potential providers for his online data storage needs. In the following sections, you will learn about some companies that provide online storage services.

Xdrive

Xdrive Technologies produces several versions of its online storage space for users in many categories, from large corporations to individuals. Many individuals use Xdrive Plus to store and share large files, such as MP3 files, that would otherwise be difficult to transfer across the Internet. Corporations use Xdrive to reduce the amount of traffic generated by large e-mail attachments on their network servers. Xdrive is also a simple way for people employed in satellite and home offices to transfer files to people working in corporate offices. Windows XP, which was released in late 2001, offers an integrated interface with Xdrive, making it very easy to transfer files to Xdrive and share them with other users. The optional Xdrive service, which costs less than $5 a month for most users, is available via the Windows XP Publishing Wizard for those users who purchase it.

Because Xdrive has been a popular service, you decide to investigate its Web site to determine if it might be a candidate for Milt.

To visit the Xdrive Web site:

1. Start your Web browser, open the Student Online Companion page at **www.course.com/newperspectives/internet3**, click the hyperlink for your book, click the **Tutorial 6** link, and then click the **Session 6.3** link. Click the **Xdrive** link and wait while the browser opens the Xdrive Technologies home page.

2. Point to **Products** in the link bar on the left, and then click **Products** in the menu that opens. The Products & Services page shown in Figure 6-28 opens.

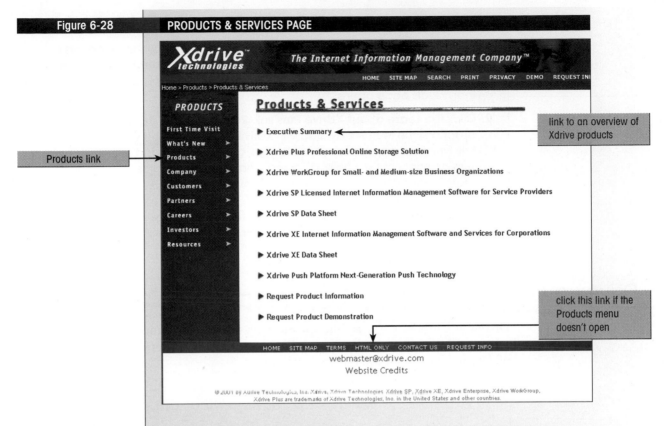

Figure 6-28   PRODUCTS & SERVICES PAGE

TROUBLE? If a menu doesn't open, your browser might not support Java applet code. Scroll to the bottom of the page, and then click the HTML Only link to disable the Java applets so you can display and click links as you would in other Web pages.

Xdrive offers online storage in a variety of formats to address the needs of corporations, service providers, small- and medium-sized businesses, and individuals. You'll examine the Xdrive WorkGroup option, which is geared toward small- and medium-sized businesses, first.

3. Click the **Xdrive WorkGroup for Small- and Medium-size Business Organizations** link. A page opens and offers options for logging into Xdrive WorkGroup and for obtaining information about Xdrive WorkGroup.

4. Click the **Learn about Xdrive WorkGroup** link. Read the page that opens and describes this option. So far, this option might work well for Milt. It includes security features, individualized accounts, and file storage capabilities.

5. At the bottom of the page, click the **Benefits to Employees and Partners** link. Read the page that opens and describes how Xdrive WorkGroup might be used in a business.

Xdrive WorkGroup is a very powerful product and probably would deliver more features than Milt will ever need. You decide to investigate the option for individuals, Xdrive Plus.

To learn more about Xdrive Plus:

1. Click your browser's **Back** button as necessary to return to the Products & Services page, and then click the **Xdrive Plus Professional Online Storage Solution** link. The Xdrive Plus Online File Storage and Collaboration Solution for Individuals page opens.

2. Click the **Learn about Xdrive Plus** link. Read the page that opens and describes the features available in Xdrive Plus. This option would work well for Milt because it provides online storage, group access, and security features with a variety of storage limits at reasonable monthly rates.

Xdrive Plus appears to be a strong candidate for Milt's storage needs. He asks you to continue your search for an online storage provider so you can report back to him about other available options.

Driveway

Driveway Corporation is another provider of solutions for storing and transferring data across the Internet. Similar to Xdrive, Driveway offers several options based on the amount of data and type of storage required by its users.

To examine Driveway's file management options:

1. Return to the Student Online Companion Web page for Session 6.3, and then click the **Driveway** link and wait while your Web browser loads the Driveway Corporation home page shown in Figure 6-29.

Figure 6-29   **DRIVEWAY CORPORATION HOME PAGE**

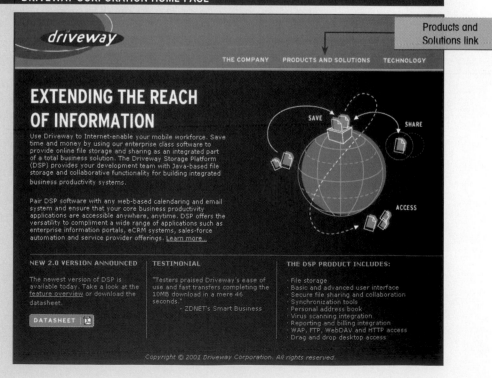

2. Click the **Products and Solutions** link at the top of the page. Read the page that opens and describes the Driveway storage platform service.

3. On the left side of the page, click the **Pricing and Services** link to open the Pricing and Services page. Read the page that opens. Because this service has a minimum fee requirement, it is probably not the best option for Milt.

4. Click the **Product Features** link on the left side of the page and read the page that opens and describes the file management features for Driveway. Notice that Driveway also requires users to download a program to access it.

Driveway is a powerful product, but it is probably too expensive for Milt to use. You'll look at another online storage provider, FreeDrive, next.

FreeDrive

FreeDrive was one of the first Web sites to offer free storage space to registered users. FreeDrive offers different levels of service, based on your usage and storage requirements. Membership is free and you must use a Web browser to transfer files. Although Milt's preference is to use an FTP client program or Web browser to transfer files, he wants you to find out more information about FreeDrive, especially because its basic membership and service are free.

To explore options at FreeDrive:

1. Return to the Student Online Companion Web page for Session 6.3, and then click the **FreeDrive** link and wait while your Web browser loads the FreeDrive home page.

2. On the left side of the page, click the **why sign up?** link and read the page that opens and describes how to use FreeDrive. See Figure 6-30.

Figure 6-30	FREEDRIVE INFORMATION PAGE

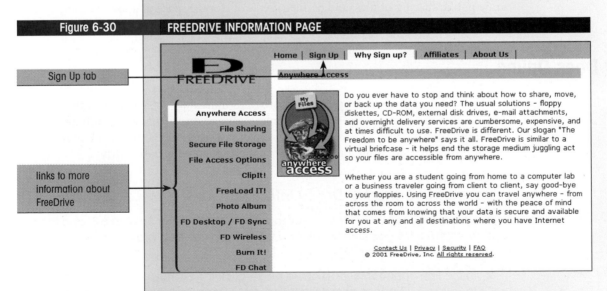

3. On the left side of the page, click the **Secure File Storage** link and read the page that opens. This service provides security features.

4. At the top of the page, click the **Sign Up** tab. The page shown in Figure 6-31 opens, describing the different membership plans for FreeDrive users. Scroll down the page to examine the membership plans for FreeDrive users.

Figure 6-31	FREEDRIVE MEMBERSHIP PLAN INFORMATION

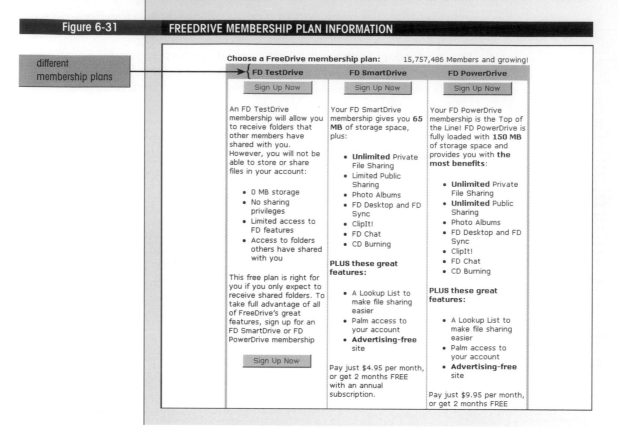

The SmartDrive option is a good candidate for Milt. It provides unlimited transfers, some public sharing of files, and 65 megabytes of storage space at a low monthly fee. You'll present this option to Milt for his storage needs and continue your research.

My Docs Online

My Docs Online is another service that provides individual accounts for transferring files. This service also permits access to your online storage drive from any computer connected to the Internet and also to wireless devices, such as a pager or Palm Pilot. For an additional charge, you can send, print, or fax your documents from your online drive.

To examine the My Docs Online services:

1. Return to the Student Online Companion Web page for Session 6.3, and then click the **My Docs Online** link and wait while your Web browser loads the My Docs Online home page.

2. In the link bar near the top of the page, click the **Features** link. The page shown in Figure 6-32 opens and describes the My Docs Online services. Scroll down the page to view the options.

Figure 6-32   MY DOCS ONLINE SERVICES INFORMATION

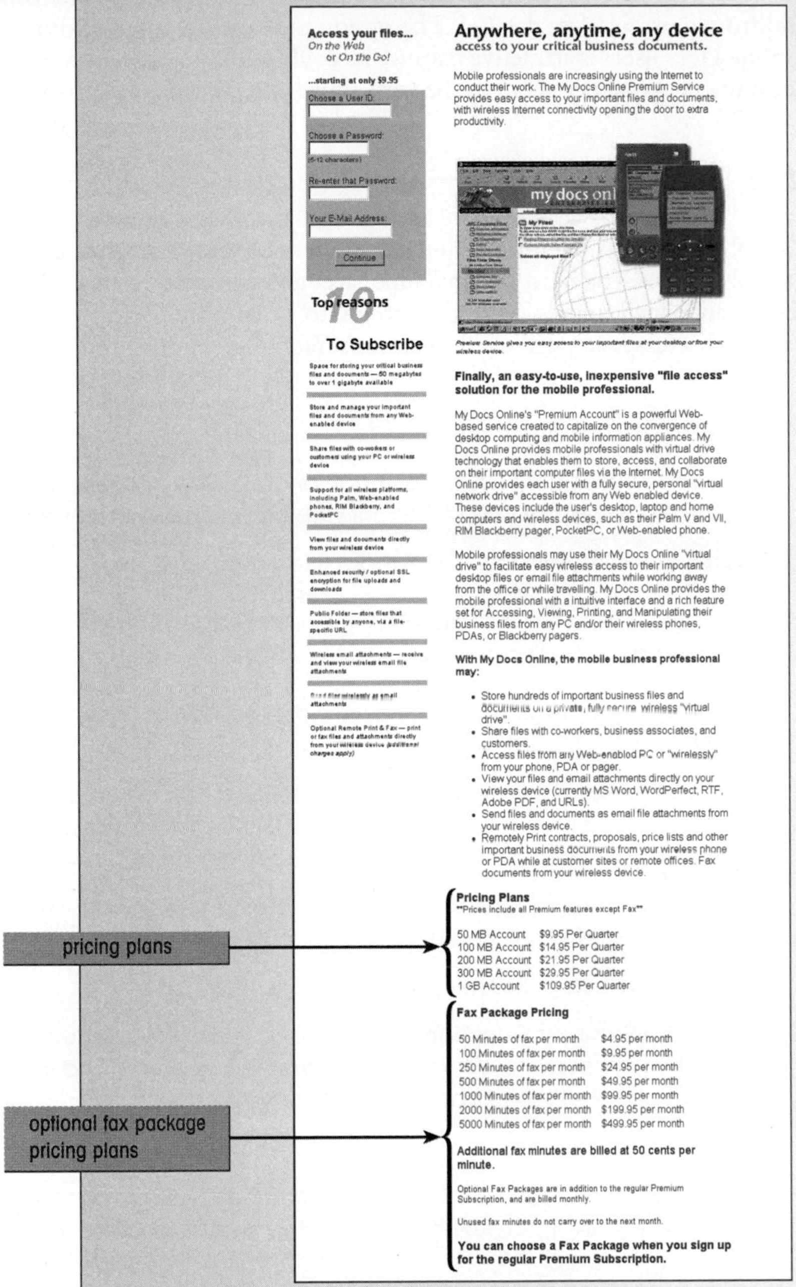

3. In the link bar near the top of the page, click the **FAQ** link. Click the hyperlinks to view some answers to frequently asked questions about the services. Make sure to view answers to questions that Milt may ask, such as "Why is using My Docs Online better than using e-mail attachments?", "How do I login to my account?", "How do I give files to others?", and "Can I give files to people who may not be My Docs Online users?"

My Docs Online provides many of the features that Milt has requested. It does not support use with an FTP client program, but the service is accessible from any Web browser and from most wireless devices. The option to share documents with users who are not My Online Docs users is attractive because he could still transfer files to people who do not have accounts. This service seems to be very affordable, as well.

Yahoo! Briefcase

Yahoo! Briefcase is the final online storage service that you will investigate for Milt. To use Yahoo! services, you must have a Yahoo! account. By creating an account at Yahoo!, you will set up an e-mail address and gain access to other Yahoo! services. To learn more about Yahoo! Briefcase, you will need to create a Yahoo! account.

To create a Yahoo! account:

1. Return to the Student Online Companion Web page for Session 6.3, and then click the **Yahoo!** link and wait while your Web browser loads the Yahoo! home page.

2. Click the **Briefcase** link. The Yahoo! Briefcase page opens.

   TROUBLE? If you already have a Yahoo! account, enter your Yahoo! ID and password on the Yahoo! Briefcase page, and then skip to the next set of steps.

3. Click the **Sign me up!** link in the New User section. A page opens and requests some basic information.

4. Click in the **Yahoo! ID** text box, and then type a user name, such as milt_spangler. If you have a common name, you might try using your name plus some digits (such as your year of birth), such as milt_spangler1980.

5. Press the **Tab** key, and then type a password. Yahoo! passwords are case-sensitive, so be sure and type letters using the correct case.

6. Press the **Tab** key, and then type your password again.

7. Click the **Security Question** list arrow, and then click a question in the list. If you forget your password, Yahoo! will ask you this question and if you respond correctly, Yahoo! will send your password to you via e-mail.

8. Type the answer to your secret question in the Answer text box.

9. Enter your birthday in the text boxes, and then type an alternate e-mail address in the Alternate Email text box (if you don't have an alternate e-mail address, skip this text box).

   TROUBLE? If you enter an alternate e-mail address, Yahoo! will send a confirmation message to that account.

10. Scroll down the page as necessary to the Customizing Yahoo! section, and then select your language, enter your zip or postal code, select your gender, select **college/graduate student** as your occupation, and select **education, research** as your industry.

11. Deselect the **Contact me occasionally** check box so you will not receive special offers from Yahoo!.

12. Scroll down the page to the Word Verification section, and then follow the instructions to enter the word you see in the box.

13. Click the **Submit This Form** button at the bottom of the page. If your Yahoo! ID is not in use, the page shown in Figure 6-33 opens and indicates that your registration is complete. Make sure to write down your Yahoo! ID so you won't forget it.

| Figure 6-33 | YAHOO! BRIEFCASE REGISTRATION COMPLETE PAGE |

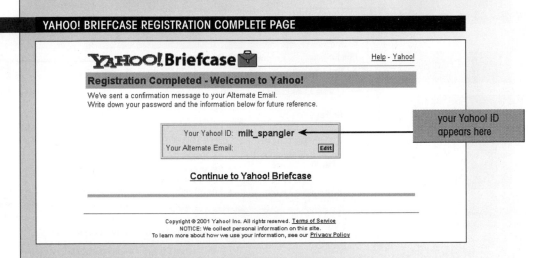

TROUBLE? If your Yahoo! ID is being used, follow the instructions on the screen to create a new ID, and keep resubmitting your application until you receive your Yahoo! ID.

Now that you have a Yahoo! ID, you can use it to send and receive e-mail messages; your e-mail address is your Yahoo! ID followed by @yahoo.com. You'll continue to the Briefcase next.

To set up your Yahoo! Briefcase:

1. Click the **Continue to Yahoo! Briefcase** link. The Yahoo! Briefcase – Account Setup page opens. You use this page to create your Briefcase and to indicate your preferences and the folders you would like it to contain.

2. In the Create Folders section, make sure that the **My Documents** check box is selected, that the other check boxes are not selected, and that the **Yahoo! Specials** check box is deselected. You will accept the default settings in the second section (Select View Preferences).

3. In the Enter Confirmation Code section, follow the instructions to enter your code, and then click the **Submit** button at the bottom of the page. The Yahoo! Briefcase home page shown in Figure 6-34 opens.

Figure 6-34   YAHOO! BRIEFCASE HOME PAGE

TROUBLE? If a dialog box opens and asks if you want to install and run a Flash program, ask your instructor or technical support person for assistance. If you are in a public computer lab, do not install any programs or plug-ins without permission.

Now that you've set up your account and Briefcase, you can upload a file.

Uploading a File to Yahoo! Briefcase

You can upload one file or multiple files to the default folders in your Briefcase, or you can use Briefcase to create new folders. After creating a new folder, you can change the folder's properties to public (so that all users can access it), private (so no other users can access it), or friends (so that only those users you specify can access it). Setting a folder's properties lets you control access to your Briefcase for other users.

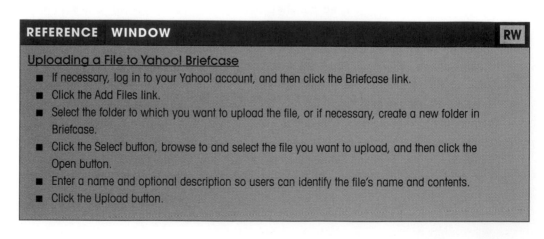

REFERENCE   WINDOW   RW

Uploading a File to Yahoo! Briefcase
- If necessary, log in to your Yahoo! account, and then click the Briefcase link.
- Click the Add Files link.
- Select the folder to which you want to upload the file, or if necessary, create a new folder in Briefcase.
- Click the Select button, browse to and select the file you want to upload, and then click the Open button.
- Enter a name and optional description so users can identify the file's name and contents.
- Click the Upload button.

You'll upload a file from your Data Disk to test the interface and its ease of use.

To upload a file to Yahoo! Briefcase:

1. Click the **Add Files** link. The Select Folder page opens, where you select the Briefcase destination for your files. You can also create a new folder using this page. See Figure 6-35.

| Figure 6-35 | SELECT FOLDER PAGE |

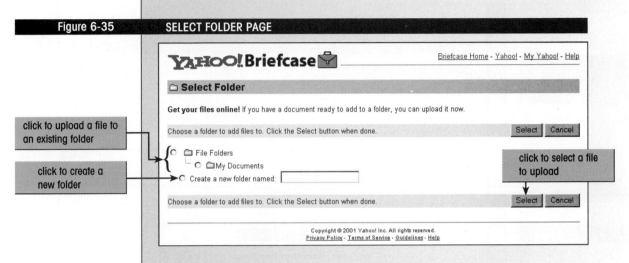

2. Click the **My Documents** option button to select this folder, and then click the **Select** button below the option button. The Add a File page opens. You'll upload a file from your Data Disk to the My Documents folder. You upload files one at a time or as a group; notice that the maximum file size for any single file is five megabytes.

3. Click the **Browse** button in the first section on the page. The Choose file dialog box opens.

4. Use the Look in list arrow to open to the **Tutorial.06** folder on your Data Disk, click the **Memorandum** file to select it, and then click the **Open** button. The path to the Memorandum.doc file on your Data Disk appears in the On your computer text box, as shown in Figure 6-36. (Your path might be different.)

Figure 6-36   ADD A FILE PAGE

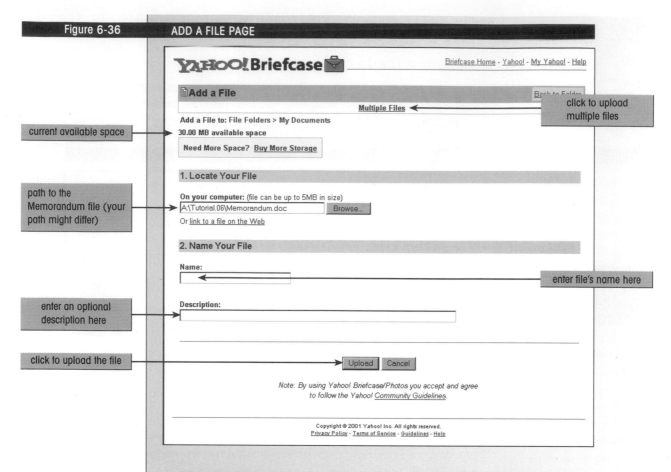

After selecting the file to upload, you need to give it a name and an optional description. By doing so you make it easier for you and other users to identify the file and its contents.

5. Click in the **Name** text box, type **Memorandum**, press the **Tab** key, and then type **Memo to contractors about online storage.**

6. Click the **Upload** button at the bottom of the page. Depending on the speed of your Internet connection, it could take several moments to upload the file. After the file has been uploaded, the confirmation page shown in Figure 6-37 opens and tells you that the transfer is complete.

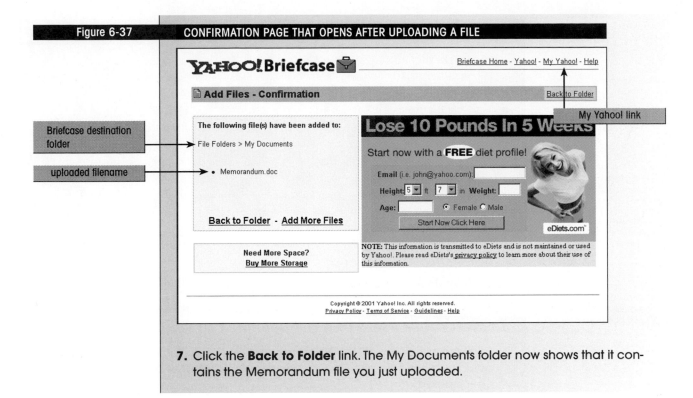

Figure 6-37   CONFIRMATION PAGE THAT OPENS AFTER UPLOADING A FILE

Briefcase destination folder

uploaded filename

7. Click the **Back to Folder** link. The My Documents folder now shows that it contains the Memorandum file you just uploaded.

Now that you've uploaded the file, you need to learn how to make other users aware of it and how to access it.

Sending an E-Mail Message to a File in the Briefcase

When you upload a file to the Briefcase, you make other users aware of the file by selecting it and then sending an e-mail message from Briefcase to the users' e-mail addresses. You can select more than one file per message and up to 10 e-mail addresses at a time to which to send the message. You can also include a personal note in the message; Yahoo! adds the name and description of the file in the message, along with the URL to download it.

Before you can send a message to your Yahoo! e-mail address, you'll need to activate it.

To activate your Yahoo! mailbox:

1. Click the **My Yahoo!** link in the upper-right corner of the page. Your My Yahoo! page opens. Notice that your Yahoo! ID appears on the page, indicating that your account is active.

2. Find the Message Center pane on the My Yahoo! page, and then click the **Check Email** link.

3. Type your first and last names in the appropriate text boxes, and then click the **Set me up** button. A page opens and welcomes you to Yahoo! Mail.

4. Click the **Continue to Yahoo! Mail** button (if there are two buttons on the page, click either one). Your Yahoo! mailbox opens.

Now you can return to Briefcase and send an e-mail message.

Sending an E-Mail Message Linked to a File in Briefcase
- Click the check box for the files that you want to include in the e-mail message.
- Click the Email button.
- Type your return e-mail address in the From text box.
- Type the e-mail address of the recipient in the To text box. If you are sending the message to multiple recipients, separate their addresses with commas or spaces.
- Type an optional message in the Message text box to identify the purpose of the message for the recipients.
- If necessary, click an option button in the Expiration Date section to set an expiration date for downloading the files.
- Click the Send Email button.

You will send the message to yourself to simulate how it will work for another user.

To alert other users of a file uploaded to your Briefcase:

1. Click the check box for the **Memorandum** file to select it. When your Briefcase contains more than one file, you can select multiple files by clicking their check boxes.

2. Click the **Email** button. The Email File Links page opens. You use this page to specify the address to use in the From text box, up to 10 e-mail addresses for the recipients, and an optional message. You can also set an expiration date for the users to have access to the file.

3. If necessary, type your Yahoo! e-mail address in the From text box.

4. Press the **Tab** key, and then type your Yahoo! e-mail address in the To text box. When you send the message to more than one recipient, separate the addresses with commas or spaces.

5. Press the **Tab** key twice, and then type **I am sending a link to a memo that I uploaded to Briefcase.** The completed page is shown in Figure 6-38.

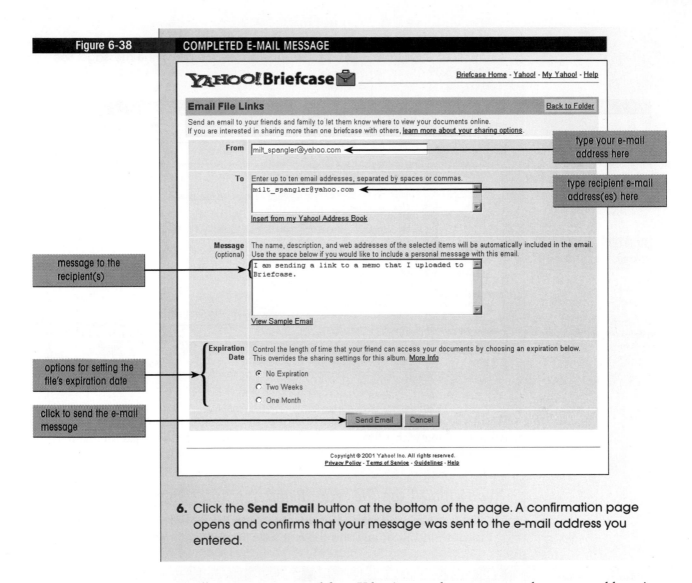

Figure 6-38   COMPLETED E-MAIL MESSAGE

6. Click the **Send Email** button at the bottom of the page. A confirmation page opens and confirms that your message was sent to the e-mail address you entered.

You'll retrieve your e-mail from Yahoo! to see the message another user would receive.

To view the e-mail message you sent:

1. Click the **My Yahoo!** link in the upper-right corner of the confirmation page. Your personalized Yahoo! page opens.

2. Scroll down the page so you can see the Message Center pane, which usually appears on the left side of the page. A new mail icon appears to indicate that you have new mail.

3. Click the **Check Email** link. Your Inbox opens and displays the message you received. Because you just signed up for Yahoo! Mail, you will also have a welcome message from Yahoo! in your mailbox.

4. Click the **Check Mail** link on the left side of the page to open your Inbox. Your message appears in the list.

5. Click the **Yahoo! Briefcase: <your name>'s file(s)** link to open your message, and then scroll down the page so you can see the text of the message. See Figure 6-39.

| Figure 6-39 | E-MAIL MESSAGE SENT FROM BRIEFCASE |

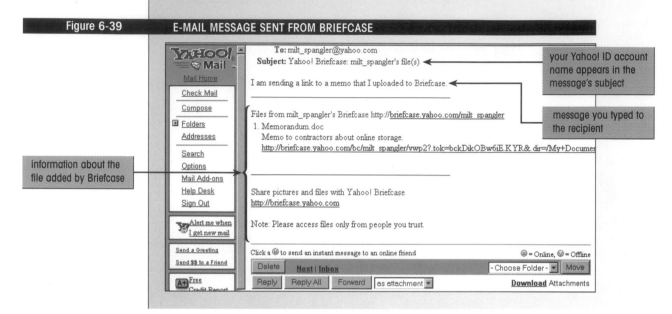

When you send a message from Briefcase, the message contains your message (if you added one), along with a link to the file you uploaded. You'll download the file next to see how it works.

To download the file from Briefcase and open it:

1. Click the link to the **Memorandum.doc** file in the e-mail message. A new browser window opens and shows the file in your Briefcase. See Figure 6-40.

| Figure 6-40 | LINK TO UPLOADED MESSAGE |

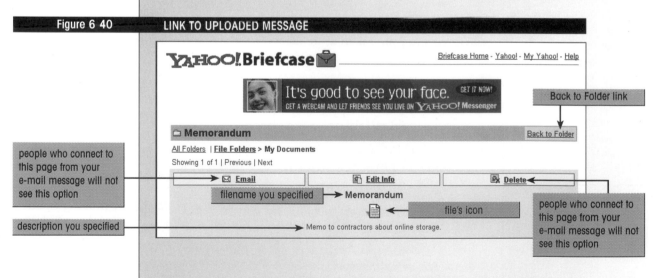

2. Click the file icon for the Memorandum file. Depending on which browser you are using, you might see a dialog box that asks if you would like to open or save the file. If you see this dialog box, click the **Save** button. The Save As dialog box opens.

3. If necessary, use the Save in list arrow to open the **Tutorial.06** folder on your Data Disk, change the filename to **Memorandum1**, and then click the **Save** button. A dialog box opens while the file is being downloaded. If necessary, close this dialog box when the "download complete" message appears.

4. Start Windows Explorer, open the **Tutorial.06** folder on your Data Disk, and then double-click the **Memorandum1** file to start Word or another program and view the file. The file opens.

5. After reading the memo, close Word.

After all users have downloaded the file or when you no longer require its storage in your Briefcase, you can delete the file.

Deleting a File from Briefcase

You downloaded and viewed the file. Now you can delete it.

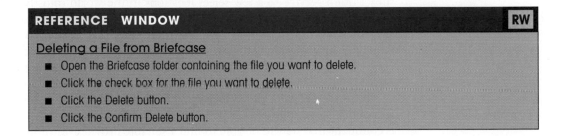

REFERENCE WINDOW **RW**

Deleting a File from Briefcase
- Open the Briefcase folder containing the file you want to delete.
- Click the check box for the file you want to delete.
- Click the Delete button.
- Click the Confirm Delete button.

Because you logged on to your Yahoo! account, you'll be able to delete the file from the screen that you are currently viewing. Other users will not have this option unless you specifically give them permission to change the files in your folder.

To delete the file from your Briefcase and log off:

1. Click the **Back to Folder** link. The contents of the My Documents folder appear.

2. Click the check box for the **Memorandum** file to select it.

3. Click the **Delete** button. A page opens and asks you to confirm the file's deletion.

4. Click the **Confirm Delete** button. The file is deleted and the My Documents folder no longer contains any files.

5. Click the **Sign Off** link near the top of the page. A page opens indicating that you have signed out of your Yahoo! account.

6. Close your browser, and if necessary, log off your Internet connection.

When you need to log back on to your Yahoo! account, return to the Yahoo! Web site at www.yahoo.com, click the link for the page or service that you want to open (Briefcase or Check Email), and then enter your Yahoo! ID and password. Always be sure to log off your account when you are finished using it, especially if you are using a public computer.

The last thing that you'll investigate for Milt is obtaining software updates online.

Subscription Services

For many years, computer manufacturers such as IBM, Hewlett-Packard, and Compaq have offered leases and other incentives to corporations in an effort to make replacing outdated hardware products with newer models more affordable. Recently this idea was carried forward to software programs, as well. When Microsoft announced the release of its Office XP product, its business and marketing plans included a new method of selling the software. A **subscription model**, also called a **subscription service**, is a method of selling software over the Internet in lieu of the traditional boxed product with CD-ROMs that you might purchase in a retail outlet. The software publisher has the advantage of controlling the number of unlicensed copies of the software—for example, when you borrow a friend's CD-ROM disc to install a program—and has a guaranteed source of revenue when new software versions are released. Regardless of the impact of the new software version—major or minor— the publisher is guaranteed that users will use it, because the decision to purchase and install the new software has already been made by way of the subscription. To the end user, a software subscription ensures an up-to-date product because product updates, enhancements, and patches are installed automatically over the Internet.

After careful analysis of the delivery system, Microsoft ultimately decided to offer its new subscription service to a few select locations in the world (mostly in Australia) in order to perfect its delivery system of products over the Internet. However, other software producers are following suit in an effort to offer the same subscription models to their customers. Some industry analysts estimate that by the year 2006, all Microsoft products will be delivered via the Internet. For now, however, you can still purchase your favorite product in a box at the local computer store.

Milt is pleased with the information that you have provided. His goal of finding the perfect online storage provider will be much easier now that he has your research in hand. He is confident that he will be able to find a suitable provider for him and his contractors.

Session 6.3 QUICK CHECK

1. How might an online storage provider help a company to reduce its network activity and increase its productivity?

2. True or False: Some online storage providers offer free online storage for registered users.

3. True or False: Some online storage providers offer the ability to share files between registered and unregistered users.

4. Before using Yahoo! Briefcase, what must the Briefcase owner do?

5. Which folder is created by default in Yahoo! Briefcase?

6. True or False: You can use Yahoo! Briefcase to upload only one file at a time.

7. True or False: Microsoft offers a subscription license for Office XP products sold in the United States.

REVIEW ASSIGNMENTS

Milt has asked you to investigate the use of a new e-mail program, Eudora Pro, which is produced by Qualcomm. Your research reveals that you can download an evaluation copy of Eudora to evaluate the program. If Milt likes this program, he can inquire about purchasing licenses to the more powerful, commercial version of Eudora Pro for his staff. Before downloading the evaluation copy, you would like to read the user's manual to learn more about the program. Fortunately, you can download the user's manual in PDF. You will complete the following steps to download the user's manual.

1. Place your Data Disk in the appropriate drive.

2. Start the WS_FTP LE FTP client program on your computer. (*Note:* The Review Assignments are written for the WS_FTP LE FTP client program you downloaded in this tutorial. However, you can use any FTP client program or a browser to complete these steps by executing the equivalent steps in that program.)

3. Use the Profile Name list arrow to select the Eudora FTP session, or create a new session profile named Eudora. The host name or address is ftp.qualcomm.com. You will log on using an anonymous login and your full e-mail address as the password.

4. Connect and log on to the Qualcomm FTP server. (*Hint*: If necessary, make a dial-up connection before connecting to the Qualcomm server.)

5. If necessary, change the directory on the remote site to /eudora/eudoralight/windows/english.

6. Select the file named eul3manl.pdf on the remote site, and then download that file to your computer. This file contains the user's manual in PDF format.

7. After the download is complete, disconnect from the remote site, close your FTP client program, and then log off your Internet connection if necessary.

Explore ▶ 8. If you have an antivirus program installed on your computer, use it to scan the files you downloaded in this tutorial for viruses.

9. If necessary, install the Adobe Acrobat Reader program you downloaded in Session 6.2. (*Note:* Check with your instructor or technical support person before installing any program on your computer's hard drive.)

10. Open Windows Explorer, and then locate and double-click the eul3manl.pdf file that you just downloaded. Acrobat Reader will start and open the file.

Explore ▶ 11. Locate the pages that describe "Using a Signature" found somewhere in the first 30 pages. (*Hint:* In Acrobat Reader, use the Find command on the Edit menu to search for the three-word term. You'll find an entry in the Contents first, so you'll need to use Find again to locate the heading for this section.) The description of signature files may span more than one page. Print up to two pages describing signature files. (*Hint:* Use the Acrobat Reader's Help system to learn more about using the program to read Eudora's program documentation.)

12. Close Acrobat Reader.

CASE PROBLEMS

Case 1. County Assessor's Office Herb Merrell is the County Assessor for Lancaster County in eastern Nebraska. The county assessor's property office has a large database of information stored on an FTP site that the public can access for a small fee. Realtors and real-estate appraisers are the primary users of this information. However, many other businesses are taking advantage of this online access to Lancaster County property records. Herb has received complaints from customers in the southern part of the county about long delays in accessing the system. You are Herb's chief architect of the information system that supports the entire county assessor's online database. Herb wants you to investigate the system's processing delays. You realize that because the Lancaster system is stored on a network server, some delays are caused by general Internet traffic and, therefore, are unresolvable. Herb wants you to see if the problem is with one of the computer systems that is connected to the main computer that stores the county assessor's files.

You decide to begin your research by installing an Internet ping program to test the Internet connections for delays. You will complete the following steps to research and find programs that can identify processing problems, and then you will download the program.

1. Start your Web browser, open the Student Online Companion page at www.course.com/newperspectives/internet3, click the hyperlink for your book, click the Tutorial 6 link, and then click the Case Problems link. Click the Excite link for Case Problem 1 and wait while the browser loads the page.

Explore
2. Search for information about ping programs using the search phrase "Packet Internet Groper." Follow some of the hits, and then use your browser's Print button to print at least one page of a definition that you think is correct.

3. Return to the Student Online Companion page, and then click the Tucows link for Case Problem 1 to open that page. Use the links to connect to a server for your operating system and in a region or state that is the closest to your location.

4. Click the Internet tab to display a page of Internet categories, and then click the Finger and Ping link in the Network Protocols section.

Explore
5. Explore the links to programs in the Finger and Ping category to learn more about the programs you can download. Use the links in the Additional Information section of the Student Online Companion for Tutorial 6 to see if you can find a review of any of the programs. If you find a review, use your browser's Print button to print one or two pages.

6. Based on your research, locate a program on the Tucows Web site that will help Herb with his problem as described in the case problem description. Use your browser's Print button to print the page that describes the program you are recommending.

7. If you have permission to do so, download to the Tutorial.06 folder on your Data Disk or a hard drive the ping program you are recommending. (*Note:* Check with your instructor before downloading any files from the Internet. Before downloading the file, make sure that you have enough disk space to save it in the location you specify.)

Explore
8. If you are able to do so, scan the file you downloaded for viruses.

9. Close your browser, and if necessary, log off your Internet connection.

Explore
10. On a separate piece of paper, write a short memo to Herb that explains why you have chosen this program and list some advantages it has over other shareware programs available on the Tucows Web site.

Case 2. *Internet Adventures* Internet Adventures is a consulting company providing a variety of services to small- and medium-sized companies. Roxanna Kubovich, owner of Internet Adventures, charges an hourly rate to research and download information on the Internet. Roxanna is currently working with a large CPA firm that wants her to create bookmarks to Web sites that are of interest to tax preparers so the accountants can give them to their clients on disk. Because the firm's clients use Internet Explorer and Navigator to browse the Web, she needs to find a way to convert an existing set of Internet Explorer favorites to Navigator bookmarks. Roxanna remembers reading a review about several shareware products that might be able to maintain a library of common bookmarks that Internet Explorer and Navigator can share. To help Roxanna with her research, you'll complete the following steps.

1. Start your Web browser, open the Student Online Companion page at www.course.com/newperspectives/internet3, click the hyperlink for your book, click the Tutorial 6 link, and then click the Case Problems link. Click the Tucows link for Case Problem 2 and wait while the browser loads the page.

2. Click the link for your operating system, click the Internet tab, scroll down to the Web Browsers & Tools category, and then click the Bookmark Utilities link.

3. Use the links on the page that opens to find three programs that convert Internet Explorer favorites to Navigator bookmarks and vice versa. Review and print the documentation information for each program. Use the links in the Additional Information section of the Student Online Companion for Tutorial 6 to see if you can find a review of any of the programs. If you find a review, use your browser's Print button to print one or two pages.

4. If you have permission to do so, download to the Tutorial.06 folder on your Data Disk or a hard drive the converter program you are recommending for Roxanna. (*Note:* Check with your instructor before downloading any files from the Internet. Before downloading the file, make sure that you have enough disk space to save it in the location you specify.)

Explore ▷ 5. If you are able to do so, scan the file you downloaded for viruses.

6. Close your browser, and if necessary, log off your Internet connection.

Explore ▷ 7. On a separate piece of paper, write a short memo to Roxanna that explains why you have chosen this program and list some advantages it has over other shareware programs available on the Tucows Web site.

Case 3. *Midwestern University* Marco Lozario is director of computing at Midwestern University. He and his staff of three people ensure that the school's computer lab of 45 Windows-based computers function properly. Last week, a virus infected every computer in the lab, and Marco had to close the lab to prevent the virus from spreading to students' disks and to other computers. Some of the lab computers have McAfee Virus Scan software installed and others have Norton Antivirus, but the installed versions of both programs do not recognize and cannot eradicate the new virus pattern. Complete the following steps to locate the latest virus data files from McAfee and Symantec (the company that produces Norton Antivirus) so Marco can clean the infected computers.

1. Start your Web browser, open the Student Online Companion page at www.course.com/newperspectives/internet3, click the hyperlink for your book, click the Tutorial 6 link, and then click the Case Problems link. Click the McAfee link for Case Problem 3 and wait while the browser loads the page.

2. Use your browser to navigate to the readme.txt file at ftp.mcafee.com/pub/antivirus/datfiles/4.x.

3. Open the readme.txt file in this folder and review its contents. Use your browser or the program that opens to print the first page of this document, and then close the browser window or program that opened the file.

Explore ▶ 4. Use your browser's address field to return to the root directory, and then open the licensed folder. What happens?

5. Return to the Student Online Companion page, and then click the Symantec link and wait while your browser loads the page.

6. Use your browser to navigate to the update.txt file at ftp.symantec.com/public/english_us_canada/antivirus_definitions/norton_antivirus.

7. Open the update.txt file in this folder and review its contents. Use your browser or the program that opens to print the first page of this document, and then close the browser window or program that opened the file.

Explore ▶ 8. Marco needs some information about the Live Update product from Symantec so he can look into installing it on the lab's computers. He asks if you can find a text file that describes the Live Update setup. Browse the FTP site at ftp.symantec.com to find this file, and then save the file in the Tutorial.06 folder on your Data Disk. (*Hint:* Use the Save As command on your browser's File menu to save the file.)

9. Close your browser, and if necessary, log off your Internet connection.

Case 4. Englewood Health Club John Rowe owns the Englewood Health Club in Englewood, Colorado. His business transmits all of its employer data on tape to the Internal Revenue Service (IRS) and uses a wire transfer to deposit its employees' federal tax payments into the correct accounts. John just received a letter from the IRS indicating that the tape with his company's federal unemployment data for the third quarter of the year 2000 was lost or damaged in transmit, and that he needs to file submit this form again manually. Because this error was due to an IRS error, neither John nor the club will incur any penalty. John needs to download the correct form to use from the IRS FTP site. He asks you to help him find it and the instructions for its completion. To help John, you'll complete the following steps.

1. Start your Web browser, open the Student Online Companion page at www.course.com/newperspectives/internet3, click the hyperlink for your book, click the Tutorial 6 link, and then click the Case Problems link. Click the Internal Revenue Service link for Case Problem 4 and wait while the browser loads the page.

Explore ▶ 2. The IRS indicates on the site that the file 00-index.txt lists the descriptions of all files in each directory. Open this file in the pub directory and review its contents to learn the location of the directory that contains tax forms in PDF format for the year 2000.

Explore ▶ 3. Open the directory that you found in Step 2, and then open the file 00-index.txt in that directory to learn about the files it contains. Scan through the file to locate and write down the filenames for three files: Form 940 (Employer's Annual Federal Unemployment (FUTA) Tax Return), Form 940EZ (Employer's Annual Federal Unemployment (FUTA) Tax Return), and Form 941 (Employers Quarterly Federal Tax Return). (*Hint:* Use the Find command on the Edit menu or the Find in This Page command on the Search menu in the browser to find your search text in this file.)

Explore ▶ 4. Close the text file, and then locate the three PDF files that you noted in Step 3. Save these three files in the Tutorial.06 folder on your Data Disk. (*Hint:* In Internet Explorer, press and hold the Ctrl key, click each file, release the Ctrl key, click File on the menu bar, and then click Save As to save the files. In Navigator, right-click a file and click Save As on the shortcut menu to save each file individually.)

5. Open the PDF file for Form 941 in the browser. (*Note:* You must have Adobe Acrobat Reader to view this file. If your browser cannot open the file, try double-clicking the file you saved in the Tutorial.06 folder on your Data Disk to open it.) Use your browser's Print dialog box to print page 1 of the PDF file.

6. Close your browser, and if necessary, log off your Internet connection.

Case 5. Seaworthy Engineering Seaworthy Engineering is an engineering consulting group based in San Antonio, Texas. Judy Seaworthy, the company's chief technical officer, oversees the consultants' computer needs. Among her many duties, she is responsible for supplying each consultant with a notebook computer. Because the consultants spend up to 75% of their time in the field with engineering clients, the consultants must carry their computers with them to make appointments for service calls, produce reports to send to the main office, schedule travel between client locations, and access e-mail and Web sites. Most computers have Netscape Navigator 4.76 installed on them. Judy is considering upgrading to a newer version of Netscape. However, before she upgrades the computers, Judy asks you to learn more about a new browser, Opera, which is highly regarded by many of its users. She wants you to find some information about Opera and print a few pages of product information and ratings, if available, so she can investigate it further. To help Judy evaluate Opera, you'll complete the following steps.

1. Start your Web browser, open the Student Online Companion page at www.course.com/newperspectives/internet3, click the hyperlink for your book, click the Tutorial 6 link, and then click the Case Problems link. Click the ZDNet link for Case Problem 5 and wait while the browser loads the page.

2. Use the search text box on the ZDNet home page using the term "Opera." Click the link to Reviews, and then click the link to Opera. Print the page that opens (the Opera product review).

3. Return to the Student Online Companion page for Tutorial 6, and then click the PC World link and wait while the browser opens the page.

4. Use the search text box to search using the term "Opera," and then sort the results page with the most recent matches listed first. Locate and click a link that provides a product review of Opera, and then print the page that opens.

5. Return to the Student Online Companion page for Tutorial 6, and then click the DOWNLOAD.COM link and wait while the browser loads the page.

6. Search for an Opera product page, and then open and print it.

7. On the page that opens, locate and then click the link to the company's Web site (Opera Software). When the Opera Software home page opens, click the Buy Opera link and then print the page that describes the pricing options for Opera.

8. Click the Windows link at the top of the page, click the Features link to open a page listing the Opera browser's features, and then print this page.

9. Close your browser, and if necessary, log off your Internet connection.

Explore 10. In a memo addressed to Judy, make a recommendation about Opera. In your memo, be sure to include data from the research you conducted on the Web sites you visited. Make your recommendation based on a comparison of the features in your current Web browser and those you learned about using the Opera Software Web site. Make sure that you support your recommendation with facts, and consider ease of use, file sizes, download times, and cost.

QUICK | CHECK ANSWERS

Session 6.1

1. False
2. their e-mail addresses
3. False
4. directories (folders) and files
5. ftp://ftp.zdnet.com
6. PowerPoint
7. file compression

Session 6.2

1. Freeware is free software that has no restrictions on its use or guarantees for its performance; shareware is free or for-fee software that usually is operable for a limited time period; limited edition software is a limited version of a complete program that either functions for a limited time or includes only core features.
2. scan it for viruses
3. Portable Document Format (PDF)
4. file compression program
5. A hop is a connection between two computers.
6. tracert

Session 6.3

1. A company can reduce its network activity by encouraging its employees to use an online storage provider instead of e-mail attachments to transport large files. A company can increase its productivity by offering online storage for traveling employees or those employees in satellite offices.
2. True
3. True
4. The user must register with Yahoo! and obtain a Yahoo! ID.
5. My Documents
6. False
7. False

New Perspectives on

THE INTERNET

3ʳᵈ Edition

Read This Before You Begin

To the Student

To complete the Level III tutorials, Review Assignments, and Case Problems in this book, you will need to create a Tutorial.09 folder on a floppy disk or other drive. In Tutorial 9, you will download a program to your folder. There are no starting Data Files for the Level III tutorials.

See the inside back cover of this book for more information on Data Disk files, or ask your instructor or technical support person for assistance.

Course Labs

The tutorials in this book feature one interactive Course Lab to help you understand multimedia concepts. There are Lab Assignments at the end of Tutorial 9 that relate to this Lab.

To start a Lab, click the **Start** button on the Windows taskbar, point to **Programs**, point to **Course Labs**, point to **New Perspectives Course Labs**, and click the name of the Lab you want to use.

Using Your Own Computer

If you are going to work through this book using your own computer, you need:

■ **Computer System** Netscape Navigator 4.0 or higher or Microsoft Internet Explorer 4.0 or higher and Windows 95 or higher must be installed on your computer. This book assumes a complete installation of the Web browser software and its components, and that you have an existing e-mail account and an Internet connection. Because your Web browser may be different from the ones used in the figures or the book, your screens may differ slightly at times.

■ **Data Disks** You must create a Tutorial.09 folder on a floppy disk or other drive to complete Tutorial 9. There are no starting Data Files for the Level III tutorials.

■ **Course Labs** See your instructor or technical support person to obtain the Course Lab software for use on your own computer.

Visit Our World Wide Web Site

Additional materials designed especially for you are available on the World Wide Web.

Go to www.course.com/NewPerspectives.

To the Instructor

The Course Lab is available on the Instructor's Resource Kit for this title. Follow the instructions in the Help file on the CD-ROM to install the program to your network or stand-alone computer. For information about the Data Disk, see the "To the Student" section above. To complete the tutorials in this book, students must have a Web browser, an e-mail account, and an Internet connection.

You are granted a license to copy the Course Lab to any computer or computer network used by students who have purchased this book.

In this tutorial you will:

- Learn about different types of mailing lists
- Join and leave a mailing list
- Post messages to a mailing list
- Locate mailing lists
- Retrieve and read a mailing list's archived files
- Explore the history of the wireless Internet
- Learn about different wireless networks
- Locate products that provide wireless e-mail delivery

ADVANCED E-MAIL

Using Mailing Lists and Exploring Wireless E-Mail Options

CASE

Lincoln Art Glass Company

Lincoln Art Glass Company (LAG) is a small art glass company located in Lincoln, Nebraska. From its combined showroom and studio, LAG sells stained glass, glass supplies, and books to the public. LAG also produces beveled glass that it sells to both wholesale and retail customers, although almost all of its beveled glass sales are to wholesale customers throughout the United States and Canada. In addition to beveled glass, LAG sells glass-beveling machinery to wholesale customers. Mike DeMaine, LAG's owner, has heard some members of the Lincoln Chamber of Commerce discussing the effectiveness of the Internet as a marketing and information tool. For example, several members said that the Internet provides a means for customers and potential customers to contact their businesses, learn about their product lines, and even receive helpful tips about various topics. Mike wants you to investigate how he could use the Internet to expand his business to reach additional customers.

One potential lead is for Mike to use mailing lists as a way to reach interested customers. Because Mike is going to rely on e-mail for a large part of his business with people around and outside of Lincoln, he'll need to make sure that he's always in touch via e-mail. He asks you to learn more about the "wireless" Internet to see if he can still access his e-mail and the Internet without having to make a dial-up connection to his local Internet service provider (ISP) in Lincoln. Having a wireless solution to keeping in touch will be especially important when Mike is traveling to shows and meeting with clients in different states.

When you have completed your research, you will be able to make several recommendations about how Mike can use e-mail to more effectively run his business.

SESSION 7.1

In this session, you will learn how to find, subscribe to, and leave a mailing list. You will also learn how to search, review, and post messages in a mailing list.

What Is a Mailing List?

Besides providing information on the Web, the Internet stores information on a wide variety of topics that you can access using e-mail. A popular way of sharing information is to join, or **subscribe** to, a mailing list. A **mailing list** is a list of names and e-mail addresses for a group of people who share a common interest in a subject or topic and exchange information by subscribing to the list. These mailing lists are not like the ones you created in Tutorial 3, in which you grouped related individuals in your e-mail program's address book for convenience. Mailing lists and the groups they represent (sometimes known as **discussion groups**) do not require you to enter any individual addresses into your e-mail program's address book. You send your information and opinions to a mailing list through e-mail by **posting** (or sending) a message to the list. When you post a message to a mailing list, the e-mail list software running on the server automatically forwards your message to *everyone* on the mailing list. Some different types of e-mail list software are LISTSERV, ListProc, and Majordomo; these programs usually run on large computers running the UNIX operating system. The server that runs the e-mail list software is sometimes called a **list server** because it runs the list. The list server automatically manages users' requests to join or leave a list and receives and reroutes mail messages posted to the list.

You can think of an Internet mailing list just like a mailing list that you might receive in printed form. When you subscribe to a printed newsletter, the newsletter's manager automatically sends newsletters to you as they become available. Postings to mailing lists work in much the same way: They arrive at the list server, which then automatically sends the new messages to every e-mail address on the list. In other words, mailing lists are named collections of e-mail addresses that can receive mail from other members of the same mailing list. The list server and its list of e-mail addresses together provide a simple and convenient way of sending a single message to many people to create a large electronic distribution list. Each person who wants to join a mailing list is responsible for subscribing to the list. Figure 7-1 illustrates how a single message that is sent to a mailing list is forwarded to every list member.

| Figure 7-1 | INFORMATION FLOW IN A MAILING LIST |

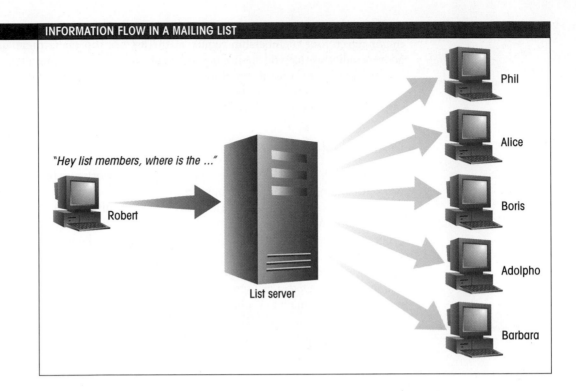

Mailing lists exist for many topics. For example, users of Microsoft Office products can join any of several mailing lists devoted to Word, Excel, Access, PowerPoint, FrontPage, Internet Explorer, and Outlook Express. Mailing lists also exist for hobby topics, such as woodcarving, tennis, or aviation. You can even find college courses conducted through mailing lists. Students enroll in the course by joining the mailing list, and then the instructor delivers "lectures" by sending documents, reading assignments, and quizzes to students who have subscribed to the mailing list.

You also can find examples of **commercial mailing lists**, in which advertisers send promotional materials for specific products or categories of products to customers based on their expressed preferences. For example, a commercial mailing list might send a list of shareware programs, their ratings, and the URLs where customers can locate and download the shareware programs to recipients on a mailing list who have expressed an interest in receiving information about new shareware programs.

Moderated and Unmoderated Lists

Sometimes one person, known as the **list moderator**, moderates a mailing list to ensure that the list always receives and sends appropriate and relevant information to its members. When a list moderator is responsible for discarding any messages that are inappropriate for or irrelevant to the list's members, the list is known as a **moderated list**. If a moderated list receives many postings, managing it can require a lot of time. When an individual does not moderate the list and postings are sent to list members automatically, the list is an **unmoderated list**. Because of the nature of unmoderated lists, you might receive irrelevant or inappropriate messages. However, when you subscribe to a moderated list, the moderator serves as a censor because he or she passes judgment on which messages to send to the list's members. Most mailing lists are unmoderated because of the time it takes to read and evaluate the content of the many messages posted each day to a mailing list by its members.

Mailing lists are either closed or open. A **closed list** is one in which membership is *not* automatic. The **list administrator**, who is a person assigned to oversee one or more mailing lists, can either reject or accept your request to become a list member. The list administrator might reject your membership request if the list has too many members or if your e-mail address indicates that you are not part of the group's specified community. For example, if you try to subscribe to a list devoted to accounting professors, then your subscription might be rejected if you do not have the .edu domain in your e-mail address. However, most lists are **open lists** that automatically accept all members.

Mailing Lists and Usenet

Usenet (User's News Network) is an information network to which people can post and read messages and opinions. **Usenet newsgroups** group postings by topic. Although newsgroups seem similar to mailing lists, there are three important differences. First, you need to know how to use your e-mail program to participate in a mailing list, whereas you must use a newsreader program to access a newsgroup. The second difference is the way you receive information: Any information sent to a mailing list is delivered automatically to every e-mail address on the list; however, in a newsgroup, *you* must retrieve the information. The third difference is that when you send a message to a newsgroup, *anyone* with Internet access and a newsreader can read it. A message sent to a mailing list has limited circulation in that only the list's members can read it.

Warnings About Mailing Lists

Mailing lists can be essential tools for receiving current and useful information in one or more subject areas, but you should be aware of some of their potential problems. Depending on the mailing list's activity, you might receive many messages every day. If you subscribe to many mailing lists, you might find that the mail volume is more than you can read; it is not uncommon to receive hundreds of messages within a couple of days of joining a particularly active list. L-Soft International, Inc., an e-mail list software publisher, reports that one of the largest LISTSERV mailing lists has over 275,000 members on a single list. Another LISTSERV customer's list delivers over 18 million messages per day!

Another potential problem that is often encountered by new list members is repeating questions that have been previously posted on the mailing list. If you are new to a list, you should monitor the list's content for a while before sending messages to it, so you do not comment on topics that other subscribers already have discussed. The best advice is to "listen" first on any list you join. When you are confident that your messages won't repeat recent information, then you can share your ideas with list members. Another resource containing answers is the frequently asked questions (FAQ) list, which contains answers to common questions that users ask. If the list has a FAQ list, view it first before sending a question to list members.

Subscribing to a Mailing List

When you find a mailing list whose members share your interests, you need to subscribe to the list so you can exchange ideas and information with the list's members. You subscribe to a mailing list by sending an e-mail message to the list server with a request to join the list's membership. If you are subscribing to a moderated list, then the list's moderator must approve your membership; if you are subscribing to an unmoderated list, your acceptance is automatic as long as you have formatted the e-mail request properly. Some mailing lists provide an option for receiving **message digests** in which several postings are grouped in a single e-mail message to help reduce the number of messages you receive from the list. Other subscribe options that are available with some lists are options to temporarily stop receiving messages (such as when you are on vacation) and to resume service at a later date.

E-mail list software programs manage messages and commands. **Messages** are simply e-mail messages that express ideas or ask questions that each member of the mailing list receives. **Commands** request the list server to take a prescribed action. Commands are sent as e-mail messages that contain content that is intercepted and processed by the e-mail list program; commands are not forwarded to other list members. To subscribe to and withdraw from a mailing list, you must send the appropriate command to the e-mail list program. Figure 7-2 illustrates how a command flows to the list server; other list members do not receive copies of the command message.

Figure 7-2	COMMAND FLOW IN A MAILING LIST

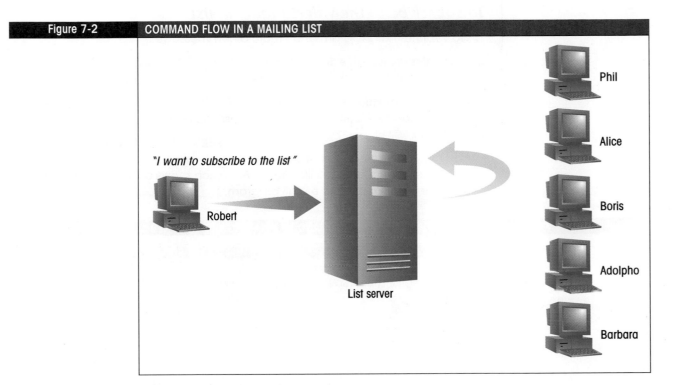

The different programs that run mailing lists send messages from the originator to every list member. The only difference between e-mail list software programs lies in the *commands* they recognize. Fortunately, most e-mail list software programs process the same commands, so once you have learned the commands for one program, you will have learned the basic command set for several programs.

The list server receives many requests every hour. Because of the large volume of messages and requests that a list server must process, the clerical functions are automated. List servers respond to requests in preprogrammed ways. Subscribing to a list is one of those requests to which a list server responds automatically.

REFERENCE WINDOW	RW

Subscribing to a Mailing List
- Use your e-mail program to create a new message.
- Enter the mailing list's administrative e-mail address in the To field.
- Leave the Cc, Bcc, and Subject fields blank.
- Type *subscribe listname yourname* on one line in the message area as your subscription request.
- If necessary, disable your signature file.
- Send the message and wait for the list server's response.

You want to learn more about mailing lists by joining one so that you can report back to Mike on their ease of use and potential effcctiveness to LAG. Mike asks you to join a mailing list that discusses computer viruses, which are a potential concern for any business that is using e-mail as a means of communication. Mike has given you the list's name and address. A group at Lehigh University administers the valert-l mailing list.

To subscribe to the valert-l mailing list:

1. Start your e-mail program and create a new message.

2. Type **listserv@lehigh.edu** in the To field. This is the e-mail address of the list server to which you send command messages for the valert-l mailing list.

3. Leave the remaining message header fields (Cc, Bcc, and Subject) blank, and then position the insertion point in the message area.

4. Type the following command on one line: **SUBSCRIBE VALERT-L** *yourname*, and replace *yourname* with your first and last names, separated by a space. Your message should look like Figure 7-3, which shows a subscription request using the Outlook Express e-mail program.

Figure 7-3	SENDING THE SUBSCRIBE COMMAND TO A MAILING LIST

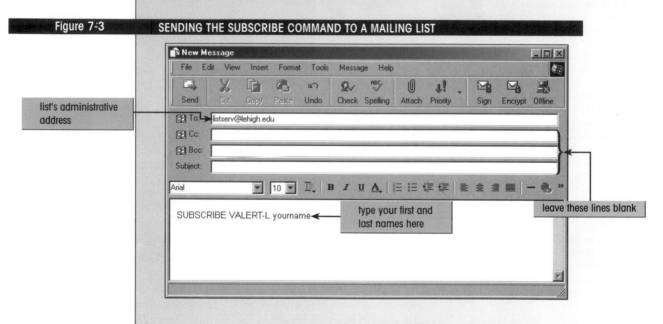

list's administrative address

type your first and last names here

leave these lines blank

5. If necessary, disable your signature file so that the message contains only the subscribe command, and then send the message.

TROUBLE? If your e-mail program warns you that the Subject field is blank, click the OK button to continue.

When you subscribe to a mailing list, you provide your first and last names, but not your e-mail address, because the list server identifies your e-mail address in the From field of your message. When you type your first and last names in the message area of your subscribe message, the list server posts it in the membership log along with your e-mail address so that other list members can identify you using your name and e-mail address. (You will learn how to list members' names later in this session.)

Usually, your subscription request reaches the list server quickly, but the time it takes to confirm your membership in the list can vary from several minutes to several hours, depending on the list's popularity. If you do not receive a confirmation message from the list server within 24 to 36 hours, you should resend the subscription request.

If you submit an incorrect subscription request, the list server returns it without processing it. If this occurs, make sure that you spelled the word *subscribe* correctly, that you typed your first and last names, and that you did not include a signature file. If you type additional information in a subscribe message, the list server will interpret it as another command set that it cannot process.

On high-volume lists, the list server might send you a confirmation message that you must return so it can confirm your e-mail address before you are officially added to the list. If the list server does not receive your reply message within a particular time period (usually 48 hours), then it automatically cancels your request.

Once the list server has accepted and processed your subscription request, you will receive a message confirming your membership in the list. The confirmation message contains valuable information about how to leave the mailing list, special features of the list, and other list details, so you should file the confirmation message in a safe place. Keeping the confirmation message also is a good way to remember which lists you have joined.

To retrieve the confirmation message from the mailing list:

1. Retrieve your new mail messages from your mail server. You should receive a confirmation message from the valert-l mailing list. Figure 7-4 shows the confirmation message for Mike DeMaine in Outlook Express.

| Figure 7-4 | CONFIRMATION MESSAGE RECEIVED FROM LIST SERVER |

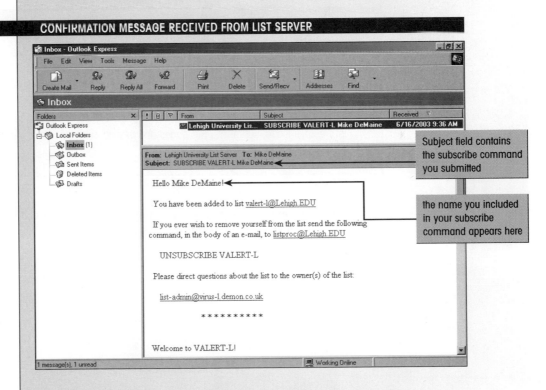

2. Read the message, which confirms your membership and provides information about the list's contents, posting guidelines, and administrator.

TROUBLE? If you do not receive the confirmation message, wait a few minutes and then retrieve your e-mail messages again. Depending on Internet traffic, it might take several minutes for the list server to respond.

The confirmation message doesn't specify that you need to reply to the message, so you are now a member of the list.

Posting a Message to a Mailing List

People interact with mailing lists by posting messages. When you post a message, the list server receives the message, sends it to the list administrator for approval (if necessary), and then forwards the message to every e-mail address on the mailing list. However, before you post a message to a mailing list, you should "lurk before you leap." **Lurking** is the activity of silently observing the postings other list members make to the list and reading the FAQ list to learn about the list's nature and purpose so messages that you post are consistent with other list members' interests.

When you send a message to a mailing list, you send it to the list address; when you send a command (such as subscribe) to a mailing list, you send it to the administrative address. The **list address**, or the **list name**, is the name of the list, such as valert-l@lehigh.edu. The **administrative address** is the e-mail address to which you send commands, such as the address that you use to subscribe to a list (for example, listserv@lehigh.edu). If you inadvertently send a message with a command to the list address instead of to the administrative address, everyone on the mailing list sees your mistake—except for the list server—and the list server will not process your command.

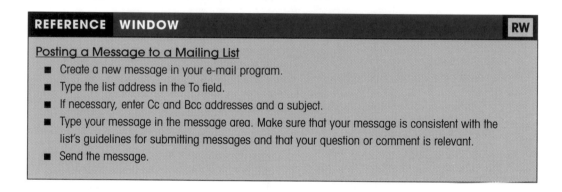

REFERENCE WINDOW **RW**

Posting a Message to a Mailing List
- Create a new message in your e-mail program.
- Type the list address in the To field.
- If necessary, enter Cc and Bcc addresses and a subject.
- Type your message in the message area. Make sure that your message is consistent with the list's guidelines for submitting messages and that your question or comment is relevant.
- Send the message.

Figure 7-5 shows a message that Mike might post to the valert-l mailing list to ask the list members about a virus that has infected his computer.

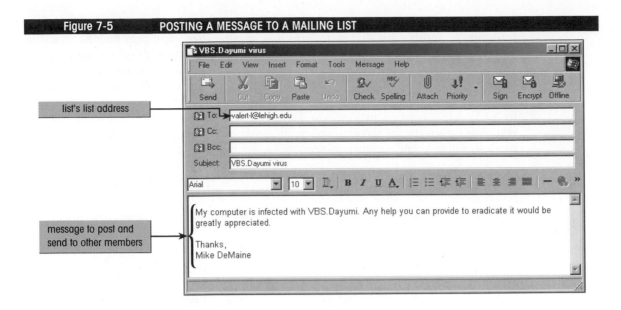

Figure 7-5   POSTING A MESSAGE TO A MAILING LIST

Reading a Mailing List's Archived Files

Many list servers file every message received by the list in an **archive**, although the list server might delete the messages periodically to recover disk space. When you join a new mailing list, you might want to view past messages to find messages of interest. To access the archive, you can send a request for the messages from a particular time frame to the list server, or you can use special functions to search the archive for relevant messages and then ask the list server to send them to you. The first method is simpler; however, using the search functions might make it easier for you to find the messages you need. Sometimes the confirmation message you receive from the list server might include a link to a Web page that contains the mailing list's archive files so you can view and download them in a browser instead of receiving them in an e-mail message.

Whichever method you use, you must retrieve a list of available archive filenames and data. You then request the list server to send you one or more of the named files. You send the **index** command to the mailing list's administrative address to get a list of available archive files.

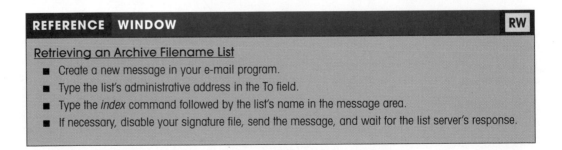

REFERENCE WINDOW   **RW**

Retrieving an Archive Filename List
- Create a new message in your e-mail program.
- Type the list's administrative address in the To field.
- Type the *index* command followed by the list's name in the message area.
- If necessary, disable your signature file, send the message, and wait for the list server's response.

The list server will process the command and send you an e-mail message that contains the archive filename information. You then can select which files you would like to receive and send a **get** command to the list's administrative address. After the list server processes your command, it returns the requested file(s) to you by e-mail. The list server might also send a message to you acknowledging receipt of your command.

Mike wants to learn more about the glass industry outside of Lincoln, so he asks you to subscribe to another list that announces new mailing lists when they become available to find mailing lists related to the glass industry or mailing lists with related interests. First, you will join the list, and then you will search the list's archives and download at least one archive file and read it. The list, called Gleason Sackmann's NEW-LIST, is housed at listserv@listserv.classroom.com, which is maintained by Classroom Connect, Inc. Subscribing to NEW-LIST is a two-step process: First, you must send a subscription request, and then you must return the list server's confirmation message. After you complete the subscription process, you can send a request to retrieve an archive.

To subscribe to the NEW-LIST mailing list:

1. Create a new e-mail message, and then type the list's administrative address **listserv@listserv.classroom.com** in the To field.

2. In the message area, type **SUBSCRIBE NEW-LIST *yourname***, replacing *yourname* with your first and last names, separated by a space.

3. If necessary, disable your signature file, and then send the message.

4. Wait a few minutes, and then retrieve your new messages. You should receive an e-mail request from the list server to which you will reply to confirm your intent to join the list. Read this message carefully, and then continue with Step 5.

5. Use your e-mail program's **Reply** button to reply to the message.

6. Delete the original message from the list server in the message area, and then type **ok**.

7. Send the message. Within a few minutes, the list server responds with a message confirming the receipt of your message and a confirmation message indicating that you have been added to the list.

8. Read the confirmation message so you are aware of the policies and commands available for the NEW-LIST mailing list.

Now that you are a full member of Gleason Sackmann's NEW-LIST mailing list, you can send a request to the list server for a list of past e-mail messages that it has saved in its monthly archives. You will send an *index* command to the list server to get this information.

To get a list of archive filenames:

1. Create a new message in your e-mail program.

2. Type **listserv@listserv.classroom.com** in the To field.

3. In the message area, type **INDEX NEW-LIST**.

4. If necessary, disable your signature file, and then send the message.

5. Wait a few minutes, and then retrieve your new e-mail messages. The list server sends a list of archive filenames in one message and an "Output of your job" message, confirming receipt of the message in which you requested the archive filenames.

6. Open the **File: "NEW-LIST FILELIST"** message. Figure 7-6 shows the archive list; your filenames might be different.

Figure 7-6	LIST OF AVAILABLE ARCHIVE FILES

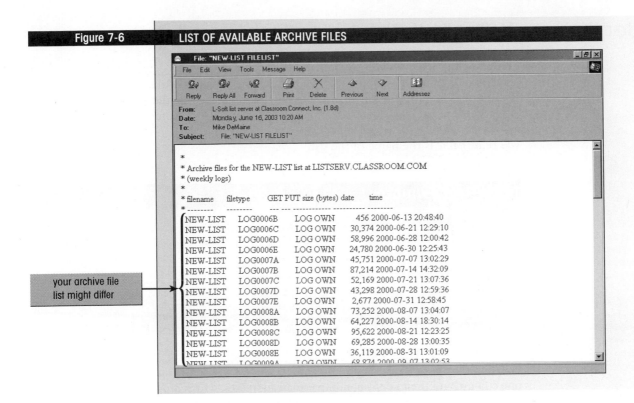

your archive file
list might differ

The NEW-LIST administrator keeps monthly archives of all the e-mail messages sent to the list. You will retrieve the messages sent to the list during October, 2001. If you scroll down the archive list, you will find that the filename corresponding to that month's archive is LOG0110C. To retrieve the file, you use the *get* command followed by the filename.

To retrieve an archive file:

1. Create a new message in your e-mail program.

2. Type **listserv@listserv.classroom.com** in the To field.

3. Type **GET NEW-LIST LOG0110C** in the message area, disable your signature file (if necessary), and then send the message. (The "0" characters in the get command are zeroes, and not the capital letter "O.")

4. After a few minutes, retrieve your new e-mail messages. You will receive an e-mail message that contains the text of all messages sent to the list during October, 2001.

5. Scroll down the message and view its contents. The file contains information about new mailing lists added during the specified time frame and how to subscribe to them. See if you can find any mailing lists that might be of interest to Mike.

Mike is curious to learn more about identifying the members of a mailing list. He asks you to find out how to get a list's membership information.

Identifying a Mailing List's Members

Some mailing lists provide a command that you can use to receive the names and e-mail addresses of other list members. The administrator who controls the list, known as the **list owner**, has the option of making the mailing list members' information available when you use the **review** command. To obtain a listing of members' names and e-mail addresses, you send the command *review listname* to the list's administrative address, where *listname* is the name of the list.

REFERENCE WINDOW   **RW**

Retrieving Member Information from a Mailing List
- Create a new message in your e-mail program, and type the list's administrative address in the To field. Leave the Cc, Bcc, and Subject fields blank.
- Type the *review listname* command in the message area, replacing *listname* with the name of the list.
- If necessary, disable your signature file, and then send the message and wait for the list server's response.

Upon receipt of the review command, the server will send you a list with users' names in one column and their corresponding e-mail addresses, which are usually sorted in alphabetical order by domain name, in the second column. If you want to review members' listings by name, you can send the *review listname by name* command, which sorts the list by name instead of by e-mail address. If the list owner hasn't made list member information available, you might receive a message with some general information about the mailing list or a message indicating that you are not permitted to access the list.

To send the review command to the NEW-LIST list:

1. Create a new message in your e-mail program, and then type **listserv@listserv.classroom.com** in the To field.

2. In the message area, type **REVIEW NEW-LIST**.

3. If necessary, disable your signature file, and then send the message.

4. Wait a few minutes and then retrieve your new e-mail messages. The "Output of your job" message indicates that you are not authorized to review the list. In a separate message, you will receive a header file that provides general information about the list's owner and membership.

5. Open the **File: "NEW-LIST LIST"** message, and then scroll to the bottom of the message to view the number of users and concealed users in the list. See Figure 7-7.

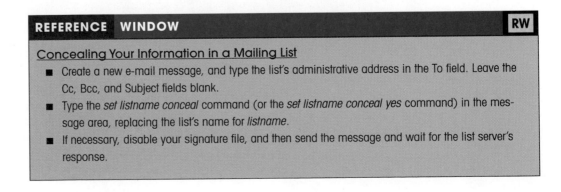

Figure 7-7   **REVIEWING A MAILING LIST'S MEMBERS**

If you submit a review command to the valert-l mailing list, the list server will send you a list of its members. If you scroll to the end of the list of current subscribers, you will find the total number of members, such as "Total number of subscribers: 12913 (12890 shown here)," which means that the list has nearly 13,000 members. The difference between the two numbers in the total, if any, is the number of members' names that are concealed. *Note:* Depending on your e-mail program and your Internet connection speed, it could take a long time to download and display the membership list from the valert-l mailing list, so you won't request it from the list server.

Concealing Your Information from a Mailing List

If you want to be a member of a list, but do not want other members to have access to your name and e-mail address, you can conceal your membership. By default, your name and e-mail address are available and can be listed by any list member who sends the review command to a list server that is configured to reveal members by name and e-mail address. A list's owner can review all members' names and e-mail addresses, regardless of whether list members have concealed their individual names and e-mail addresses.

REFERENCE WINDOW   **RW**

Concealing Your Information in a Mailing List
- Create a new e-mail message, and type the list's administrative address in the To field. Leave the Cc, Bcc, and Subject fields blank.
- Type the *set listname conceal* command (or the *set listname conceal yes* command) in the message area, replacing the list's name for *listname*.
- If necessary, disable your signature file, and then send the message and wait for the list server's response.

Mike asks you to conceal his name from the valert-l mailing list.

To conceal a name on the valert-l list:

1. Create a new message in your e-mail program, and then type **listserv@lehigh.edu** in the To text box. This address is the list's administrative address.

2. In the message area, type **SET VALERT-L CONCEAL**.

3. If necessary, disable your signature file, and then send the message.

4. Wait a few minutes, and then retrieve your new e-mail messages. You should receive a message from the list server indicating that your user name has been concealed ("CONCEAL set to NO for user" plus your user name).

If you decide that you want your name to appear again on a LISTSERV list, follow the same steps but substitute *noconceal* in place of *conceal* in the *set* command.

ListProc list server software has slightly different commands to hide and reveal list-member information. You issue the command *set listname conceal yes* to hide your information and issue the command *set listname conceal no* to reveal your information.

Leaving a Mailing List

When you leave a mailing list, or **drop** the mailing list or **unsubscribe** from the mailing list, you will stop receiving messages. You send your unsubscribe message to the list's administrative address and include the *unsubscribe* (or *signoff*) command, followed by the list's name.

Mike asks you to unsubscribe him from the valert-l and NEW-LIST mailing lists to reduce the amount of mail he receives each day. He might choose to subscribe to these lists again when he is ready to begin receiving messages again.

REFERENCE WINDOW | RW

Leaving a Mailing List

- Create a new message in your e-mail program.
- Type the list's administrative address in the To field. Leave the Cc, Bcc, and Subject fields blank.
- Make sure to send your unsubscribe message using the same e-mail address that you used when you joined the list. If necessary, check the confirmation message you received when you joined the list to confirm your e-mail address on the list.
- Type the *unsubscribe listname* or *signoff listname* command in the message area, replacing *listname* for the list's name. If you are unsure of which command to use, check the confirmation message.
- If necessary, disable your signature file, and then send the message and wait for the list server's response.

Before dropping a mailing list, check the mailing list's confirmation message to determine the proper command to use. For the valert-l mailing list, you'll send the unsubscribe command. You'll send the signoff command to the NEW-LIST mailing list.

To unsubscribe from the mailing lists:

1. Create a new message in your e-mail program, and then type **listserv@lehigh.edu** in the To text box. This address is the list's administrative address.

2. In the message area, type **UNSUBSCRIBE VALERT-L**.

3. If necessary, disable your signature file, and then send the message.

4. Create a new message in your e-mail program, and then type **listserv@listserv.classroom.com** in the To field. This address is the list's administrative address.

5. In the message area, type the single-line message **SIGNOFF NEW-LIST**.

6. If necessary, disable your signature file, and then send the message.

7. Wait a few minutes, and then retrieve your new e-mail messages. You should receive messages from both mailing lists confirming your removal.

   TROUBLE? If a mailing list returns an error message, then you were not removed from the list. Check your unsubscribe message carefully and make sure you used the correct command to leave the list (*unsubscribe* or *signoff*), that you spelled the command and list name correctly, and that you did not include your name or signature file in the message. Correct any problems, and then resend the corrected message to remove your information from the list.

   TROUBLE? If the list is experiencing high traffic, it might take several minutes to return a confirmation message. If you do not receive an error message or a confirmation message, recheck your mail later.

   TROUBLE? If you continue to receive e-mail messages from a list, send another message to drop the list.

8. If you are working on a public computer, permanently delete the e-mail messages that you sent and received during this session.

9. Close your e-mail program, but do not log off your Internet connection.

As soon as you receive confirmation messages from the list servers, you should stop receiving messages from the lists.

Now that Mike knows how to subscribe to and use a mailing list, he needs to know how to find other mailing lists. The NEW-LIST mailing list is a good source of information about new lists that have been created, but he needs a way to find existing lists related to a specific topic. You will show him how to search for mailing lists next.

Searching for Existing Mailing Lists

The Internet provides access to thousands of mailing lists on many different topics—the difficulty is locating them. You can begin your search for lists on your own campus. Frequently, colleges and universities, such as Lehigh University, sponsor several mailing lists. To discover which lists are locally housed at your college or university, send an e-mail message to the administrative address (it usually begins with *listserv* or *listproc*, followed by the host name). In the message body, type the **lists** command and then send the message.

The list server will return an e-mail message containing a list of locally hosted mailing lists. Then you can use the commands you learned in the previous sections to subscribe to and investigate lists that interest you.

You can also use the Internet itself and a Web browser to search for sites that list mailing lists based on keywords or categories. There are several "lists of lists" sites that you can visit to start your search. Mike wants you to search for sites that feature content important to his business. You'll search using the keywords "stained glass" and see what lists are available for Mike to join. Topica is a Web site that identifies and hosts mailing lists by category and name. You'll check that site first.

To use Topica to search for mailing lists:

1. Start your Web browser, open the Student Online Companion page at **www.course.com/newperspectives/internet3**, click the hyperlink for your book, click the **Tutorial 7** link, and then click the **Session 7.1** link. Click the **Topica** link and wait while the browser opens the page shown in Figure 7-8.

Figure 7-8	TOPICA HOME PAGE

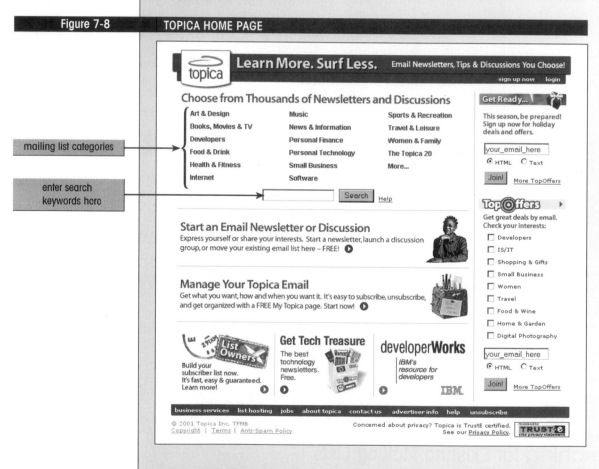

2. Type **stained glass** in the search text box, and then click the **Search** button. Figure 7-9 shows a page containing mailing list categories and mailing lists that match your search criteria. Web pages and mailing lists change so your search might find fewer or more lists. You can click a category to identify the mailing lists in it, or you can click a mailing list to get more information about its contents. If you don't find what you are looking for, try searching the lists in the categories, or return to the home page and try your search again using different keywords.

| Figure 7-9 | RESULTS OF "STAINED GLASS" SEARCH |

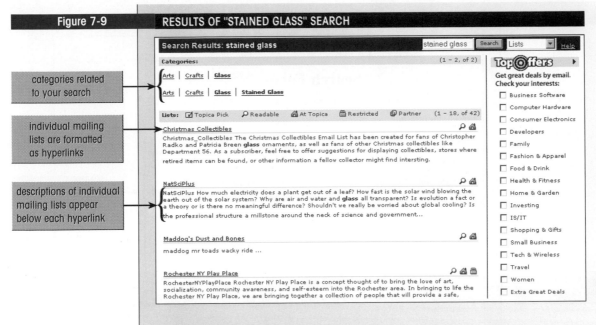

categories related
to your search

individual mailing
lists are formatted
as hyperlinks

descriptions of individual
mailing lists appear
below each hyperlink

3. Scroll down the page and click the **Stained Glass America** link. (If you don't
   see this link, look for another link that includes "stained glass" in its title.) The
   page that opens should provide you with the list's name, where it is stored, and
   instructions for subscribing to and dropping the list.

4. See if you can find other interesting lists for Mike, but for now do not subscribe
   to any of them.

Just as with search engines, different mailing-list sites store information about different
lists. Sometimes, you might find more or better lists by searching different sites. PAML,
which is an acronym for Publicly Accessible Mailing Lists, is a Web site that lists mailing
lists by category and by name.

To use PAML to search for mailing lists:

1. Use your browser's **Back** button to return to the Student Online Companion
   page for Session 7.1, and then click the **PAML** link to open the site.

2. Scroll to the bottom of the Web page, and then click the **Index** link. The PAML - Lists
   by Subject and Name page opens. You can use this page to search for mailing
   lists by name (such as "smallbiztools") or by subject (such as "glass").

3. Scroll to the bottom of the Web page, and then click the **Search** link. The
   Search Form page opens, as shown in Figure 7-10.

Figure 7-10   PAML'S SEARCH FORM

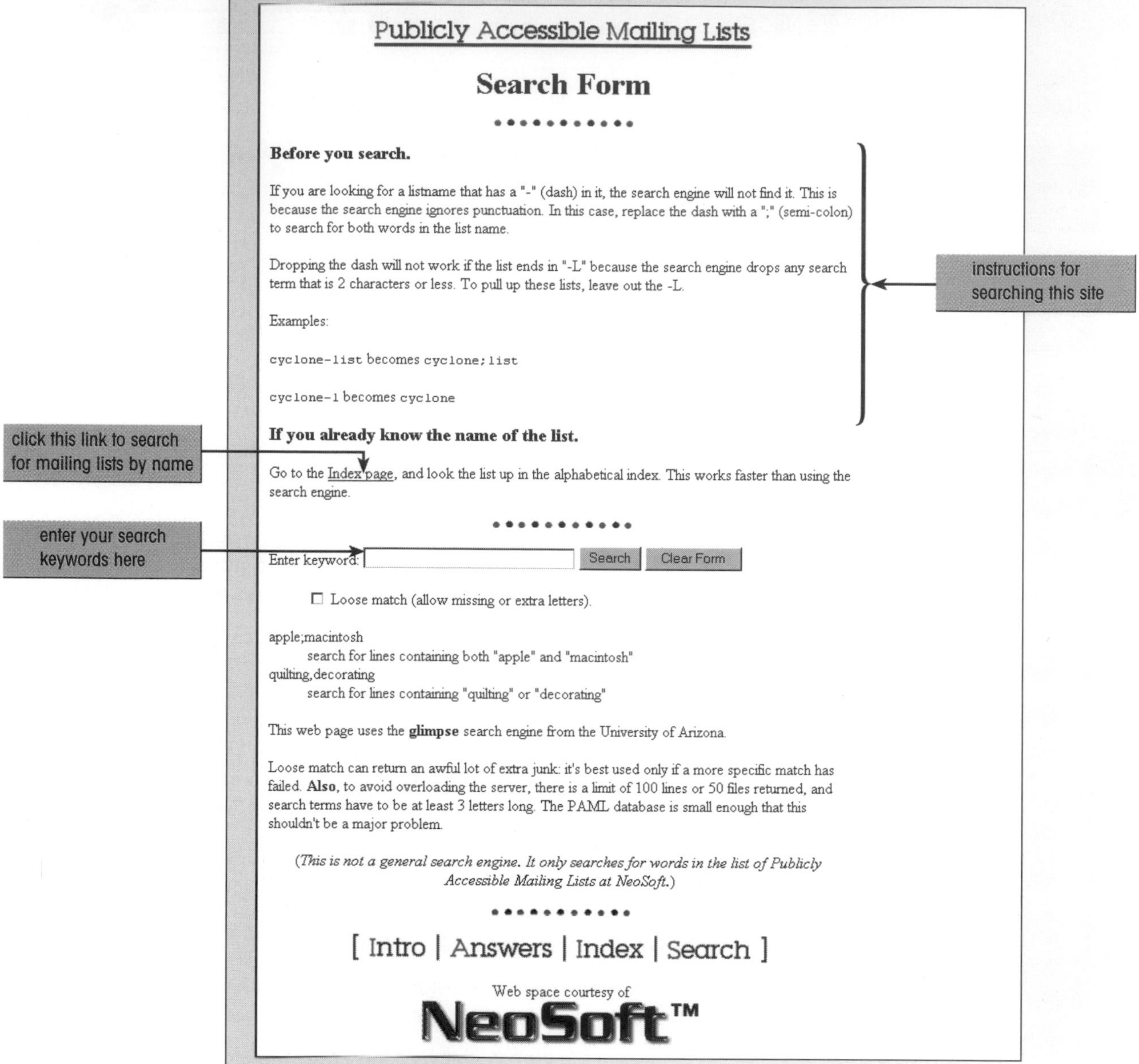

Publicly Accessible Mailing Lists

Search Form

· · · · · · · · · · ·

Before you search.

If you are looking for a listname that has a "-" (dash) in it, the search engine will not find it. This is because the search engine ignores punctuation. In this case, replace the dash with a ";" (semi-colon) to search for both words in the list name.

Dropping the dash will not work if the list ends in "-L" because the search engine drops any search term that is 2 characters or less. To pull up these lists, leave out the -L.

Examples:

`cyclone-list` becomes `cyclone;list`

`cyclone-l` becomes `cyclone`

If you already know the name of the list.

Go to the Index page, and look the list up in the alphabetical index. This works faster than using the search engine.

· · · · · · · · · · ·

Enter keyword: [   ] [Search] [Clear Form]

☐ Loose match (allow missing or extra letters).

apple;macintosh
    search for lines containing both "apple" and "macintosh"
quilting,decorating
    search for lines containing "quilting" or "decorating"

This web page uses the **glimpse** search engine from the University of Arizona.

Loose match can return an awful lot of extra junk: it's best used only if a more specific match has failed. **Also**, to avoid overloading the server, there is a limit of 100 lines or 50 files returned, and search terms have to be at least 3 letters long. The PAML database is small enough that this shouldn't be a major problem.

(This is not a general search engine. It only searches for words in the list of Publicly Accessible Mailing Lists at NeoSoft.)

· · · · · · · · · · ·

[Intro | Answers | Index | Search]

Web space courtesy of

NeoSoft™

(margin annotations:)

instructions for searching this site

click this link to search for mailing lists by name

enter your search keywords here

4. Read the instructions in the Search Form page to learn how to use it. You need to search for entries that contain the words "art" and "glass," so you will separate these keywords with a semicolon.

5. Type **art;glass** in the Enter keyword text box, and then click the **Search** button. After a few moments, the results page opens and lists mailing lists related to art and glass. You can scroll down the list and click the links to mailing lists that might interest Mike. If you do not find any matches when searching for lists, you can refine your search expression or try searching another site for lists.

6. Close your browser, and if necessary, log off your Internet connection.

You are sure Mike will want to subscribe to one or more mailing lists to keep up with the latest art and glass industry information. The Additional Information section of the Student Online Companion for Tutorial 7 contains links to other sites that you can use to search for mailing lists.

Session 7.1 QUICK CHECK

1. What are three types of e-mail list software?

2. What is the difference between a moderated and an unmoderated list?

3. Who is assigned the task of overseeing one or more mailing lists and accepts or rejects a potential member's membership in the lists?

4. What is a message digest?

5. True or False: To join a mailing list, send a subscribe message to the list's list address.

6. What kinds of messages would you send to a list address? How do these messages differ from ones that you might send to the administrative address?

7. Monitoring a mailing list's messages for a sufficient time before posting your first message is called _____.

8. To add your name to a mailing list named EXERCISE-L, what command would you send to the administrative address?

9. The two commands that you can use to remove your name from a list are _____ and _____.

SESSION 7.2

In this session, you will learn about wireless network standards and services for sending and receiving e-mail messages and using the Internet on handheld devices, notebook computers, and wireless telephones. You will also learn about the different types of wireless networks that you can create for business and personal use.

Wireless Technologies

The first wireless technology has its roots in 1978, when a voice-only network started in Chicago and operated on an analog cellular network capable of sending data at a rate of up to 9.6 Kbps (kilobytes per second). These analog cellular networks were the first generation of wireless systems. In 1994, carriers created digital networks, or **Personal Communication Service (PCS)**, where data was carried in bits and at a rate of up to 14.4 Kbps. The year 1999 saw the introduction of the first "wireless" connections to the Internet. At first, the technology was expensive and slow, with poor user interfaces and compatibility problems between mobile devices such as personal digital assistants (PDAs) and cellular phones. Gradually, the **wireless Internet**, as it is called, has expanded to include different hardware devices, networks, and other options. As new technologies emerge, many industry analysts expect wireless Internet devices and services to increase dramatically by the year 2004 or 2005 in North America alone to well over 125 million users.

When you connect to your Internet service provider—whether it's using a dial-up connection via a phone line, a cable modem, a network connection, or a satellite uplink—you're creating a **wired connection**. Cell phones are one of the first wireless technologies. They transferred data—your voice—to another location, often to another cell phone. Eventually cell phone manufacturers figured out a way to support and send text data over the same connection. Chances are good that your cell or wireless phone supports some kind of text messaging service where you can receive very short text-only e-mail messages and read them using your phone's display area. This kind of data transfer occurs over **second-generation wireless systems**, or **2G wireless** for short. The 2G standard allows data transfers of up to 14.4 Kbps. As a point of comparison, a dial-up modem might transfer data at a rate of up to 56.6 Kbps, so 2G wireless systems are very slow for transferring the large amounts of data you can receive over the Internet and in your mailbox. The 2G wireless data transfer rate is fine for chatting with a friend, but it's extremely slow when you're trying to receive formatted information. **Short Message Service (SMS)** lets you send text messages of up to 160 characters over a 2G wireless network to a wireless phone. SMS is slow and you must have a connection to receive the data. If you're out of range of your wireless network, you can't receive the data.

Around the same time that cell phone carriers were converting their old analog cellular networks to digital (in other words, from first generation to second generation wireless), PDAs and other handheld computers were growing in popularity for businesspersons. A PDA is a handheld computer that can send and receive wireless telephone and fax calls, act as a personal organizer, perform calculations, and store your notes. Palm Pilots, Handspring Visors, and other handheld computers use Infrared technology to "beam" information from one source to another. The Infrared technology requires that both devices are compatible and share a direct line of sight. In other words, you can beam information from your Palm Pilot to your co-worker's Palm Pilot only if the devices are pointed at each other and have compatible technology. The Infrared technology eliminated the need for wired connections to share data between devices and increased the need to take wireless to the next level.

In 1999, when wireless devices, such as digital pagers, digital phones, and PDAs became more popular and affordable, carriers started looking for ways to deliver more data faster and to better hardware devices with increased memory, display area, and functionality. The primary impediment to moving forward has been the variety of network standards used by the different carriers providing wireless services. The services you can purchase depend on which carrier's network you use, such as AT&T or PCS Sprint, and your wireless device must support the carrier's network standards. Figure 7-11 describes the different network standards currently in use by the major carriers of 2G wireless systems in the United States.

Figure 7-11	2G WIRELESS NETWORK STANDARDS	
NETWORK STANDARD	**CARRIER**	**FREQUENCY AND DATA TRANSFER RATE**
Time Division Multiple Access (TDMA)	AT&T Wireless, Cingular Wireless	1,900 MHz and 850 MHz; up to 14.4 Kbps
Global System for Mobile Communications (GSM)	Pacific Bell, VoiceStream Wireless	1,900 MHz; up to 14.4 Kbps
Code Division Multiple Access (CDMA)	Sprint PCS, Verizon Wireless	800-900 MHz; up to 14.4 Kbps

These 2G wireless systems already exist in the United States and provide digital voice services and SMS. Japan and South Korea have new 3G wireless systems in place, and some European countries are building and licensing the next phase of wireless systems. Expected in the United States in 2004 or 2005, **third-generation wireless systems (3G wireless** for short) offer data transfers of up to 2 Mbps (megabits per second) and constant connections. This data transfer rate means that you can receive Web pages, play MP3 files, watch a video, and make videophone calls from a single 3G device. The network doesn't require a dial-up connection like 2G wireless systems, so your device is always connected and always available.

There are two major obstacles for getting 3G wireless systems going in the United States. The first is bandwidth—3G wireless must operate in a spectrum where radio frequencies can carry data, and the U.S. federal government has to authorize the use of the spectrum on which 3G wireless systems operate. The second obstacle is cost. Carriers of 3G wireless signals must purchase spectrum licenses to operate 3G wireless systems and then they must build cellular transmitters and radio towers to carry the signals. The conversion from 2G to 3G wireless is similar to the conversion from analog to digital cellular networks in the 1990s—the carriers must invest in technology to make the change. In Europe, the licenses alone have cost carriers over $95 billion and the estimated cost of building the 3G wireless networks is over $125 billion. Much like the early days of cell phones, the technology is only as good as the network and its coverage area.

Between 2G and 3G wireless, many carriers are beginning to transform and upgrade their existing networks, creating **2.5G wireless systems**, which promise to deliver faster transfer speeds of up to 144 to 384 Kbps. The United States already has some 2.5G wireless systems in limited metropolitan areas, including Seattle and New York City. Carriers that are expected to upgrade their existing networks to support faster data transfer rates in a move toward 3G wireless are AT&T, Pacific Bell, Cingular, and Verizon Wireless. In October, 2001, DoCoMo successfully established 3G wireless service in limited areas of Japan with transfer speeds of up to 384 Kbps. The United States might see limited 3G wireless services in 2002 or 2003, with many national 3G wireless systems in place in 2004. Many industry analysts and companies manufacturing hardware devices that operate on 3G wireless systems expect full coverage of the United States by 2005. Figure 7-12 shows how existing 2G network standards will evolve into 2.5G and 3G wireless systems and the maximum data transfer speeds expected with each new generation of wireless systems.

| Figure 7-12 | EVOLUTION OF 3G WIRELESS SYSTEMS IN THE UNITED STATES |

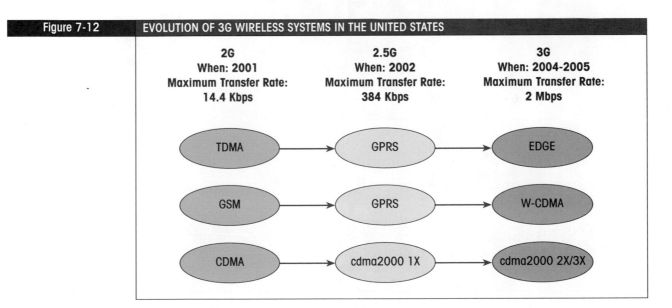

With the number of wireless Internet users expected to increase in the next several years, more devices are being manufactured to support wireless technology, but there isn't a single standard on which to transmit information. The future of 3G wireless systems is not certain, but two standards—cdma2000 and W-CDMA—are expected to be the competing standards.

Generally, you can classify wireless networking into three categories: wireless local area networking, wireless personal area networking, and wireless wide area networking. Some of these wireless options provide opportunities for Mike to reach his customers and stay in touch with them regardless of the location from which he is conducting his business. He asks you to investigate how the different wireless networks and devices can help him stay in touch with customers, suppliers, and his office staff.

Wireless Local Area Networking

Chances are good that the new laptop computer Mike just purchased has been equipped with **Wi-Fi**, or **wireless fidelity**, which is a trademarked name of the Wireless Ethernet Compatibility Alliance (WECA) that specifies the interface between a wireless client and a base station or between two wireless clients. WECA is a not-for-profit organization that certifies interoperability of Wi-Fi wireless local area network products and promotes Wi-Fi as the standard for wireless local area networks. A **WLAN**, or **wireless local area network**, is a network in which devices use high frequency radio waves instead of wires to communicate. Wi-Fi operates in the 2.4 GHz (gigahertz) radio spectrum, which is the same spectrum used by cordless phones and microwave ovens. Because this spectrum is unlicensed, it is free; remember that the 3G wireless spectrum needs to be licensed for huge fees. Figure 7-13 compares a traditional wired local area network to a wireless local area network.

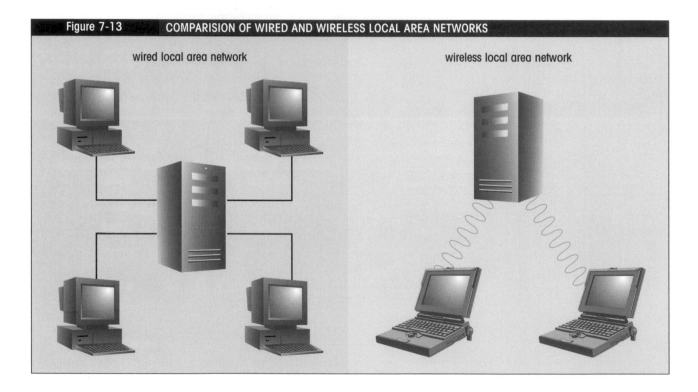

Figure 7-13   COMPARISION OF WIRED AND WIRELESS LOCAL AREA NETWORKS

wired local area network   wireless local area network

Wi-Fi is also known by its technical specification, **802.11b** (pronounced "eight-oh-two dot eleven B"), given to it by the Institute of Electrical and Electronic Engineers (IEEE). Wi-Fi is often used as an alternative in an office building or other area in which you might find a traditional wired local area network (LAN); in cases where wiring cannot be installed, wireless networks might be the only way to connect computers to the network. Computers are still connected to the LAN, but they use radio waves instead of wires for the connections. Laptop computers and other devices that support Wi-Fi must have a separate PC card, or the board, integrated antenna, and software already built into the device to send and receive data to and from the network.

Once you have a Wi-Fi card or other compatible device, you can connect to the WLAN via any Wi-Fi device when it is within the area covered by the network. Because Wi-Fi certified cards and devices must meet WECA requirements for 802.11b wireless standards, any Wi-Fi card can connect to any 802.11b certified access point. An **access point** connects wired and wireless networks to each other and lets the wireless clients send and receive data with the wired network. A hardware device or a computer running specialized software serves as a central point for wireless clients and provides a connection to a wired LAN. These access points already exist in certain hotels, airports, convention centers, and public locations across the United States. As long as you are using WECA-compliant technology, you can connect to the WLAN when you are within the established range of the network. In most cases, network connections are possible within 200 feet of the access point, depending on the surrounding architecture and other obstacles to the radio waves. If you connect enough access points to each other, the network can grow to cover an entire office complex or geographic area. For example, a movement in Seattle called for people to put 802.11b access points in their homes and offices, creating a network of access points and an expanded wireless network in Seattle. You can take your laptop all over town and still connect to the network. But if you need to go to Baton Rouge, Louisiana, you'll need your dial-up connection to connect to the network because you'll be out of range of the wireless network in Seattle.

3Com manufactures a wireless LAN product that provides data transfer rates of up to 11 Mbps. As Mike's business continues to grow and acquire new clients, he might want to investigate installing a wireless LAN to connect the computers in his Lincoln studio and offices. You'll investigate this option for LAG next.

To view the 3Com wireless demo:

1. Start your Web browser, open the Student Online Companion page at **www.course.com/newperspectives/internet3**, click the hyperlink for your book, click the **Tutorial 7** link, and then click the **Session 7.2** link. Click the **3Com Wireless** link and wait while the browser opens the page.

2. If necessary, select a continent and your country.

3. Point to the **Solutions & Professional Services** link on the left side of the page. A menu opens.

4. Click **Wireless & Mobility** in the menu and wait for the 3Com Wireless and Mobility Solutions Index page to open.

5. Click the **Wireless and Mobility Demo** link on the right side of the page. A new browser window opens. See Figure 7-14.

Figure 7-14   3COM WIRELESS LAN DEMO

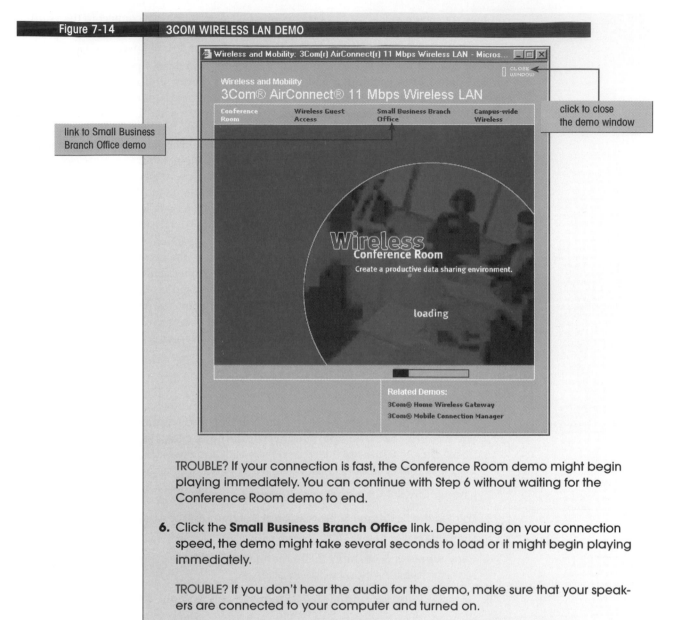

link to Small Business
Branch Office demo

click to close
the demo window

TROUBLE? If your connection is fast, the Conference Room demo might begin
playing immediately. You can continue with Step 6 without waiting for the
Conference Room demo to end.

6. Click the **Small Business Branch Office** link. Depending on your connection
   speed, the demo might take several seconds to load or it might begin playing
   immediately.

   TROUBLE? If you don't hear the audio for the demo, make sure that your speak-
   ers are connected to your computer and turned on.

7. After the demo has finished, click the **Close Window** button to close the demo
   window. You return to the 3Com Wireless and Mobility Solutions Index page.

The wireless LAN option from 3Com might be a good solution for giving employees
some flexibility in where they do their work. Another thing Mike asks you to consider is a
way of sharing devices and peripherals without having to install a network.

Personal Area Networking

Personal area networking refers to the wireless network that you use to connect your personal devices to each other, such as a connection between a PDA and a notebook computer
or connecting a notebook computer to a printer. There are two major types of personal area
networks: Infrared and Bluetooth.

Infrared Technology

The **Infrared Data Association (IrDA)** is a group dedicated to developing low-cost, high-speed wireless connectivity solutions. Using **Infrared** technology, you can wirelessly beam information from one device to another compatible device using Infrared light waves. This technology is popular with PDAs but you can also find it in use for notebook computers, printers, phones, and other peripheral devices. Infrared provides convenient wireless connections, but there are some limitations. The devices must be compatible and in a direct line of site with each other for the waves to reach their destinations. In other words, you can't beam information across a room, through a wall, or around a corner. If you want to print an e-mail message you received on your PDA using your Infrared-compatible printer, you need to move the PDA to the Infrared port on the printer. Infrared transfers data quickly at up to 4 Mbps. Because Infrared uses light waves to carry data, it doesn't interfere with technologies that use radio waves.

Another disadvantage is the lack of software products that can handle the transfer. Not only must devices be compatible with each other, the software that runs them must also be compatible.

Bluetooth

Another technology in personal area networking lets you connect your compatible devices using radio waves instead of wiring devices through a LAN or to each other. **Bluetooth**, named after a 10th century Danish king, is a technology that provides short-range radio links between personal computers, handheld devices such as PDAs, wireless phones, headsets, printers, and other electronic devices. Bluetooth isn't really "owned" by any specific manufacturer or group; according to the official Bluetooth Web site, the goal of the Bluetooth SIG (Special Interest Group) is "to develop, publish and promote the preferred short-range wireless specification for connecting mobile products, and to administer a qualification program that fosters interoperability for a positive user experience." The Bluetooth SIG promoters include 3Com, Agere, Ericsson, IBM, Intel, Microsoft, Motorola, Nokia, and Toshiba, and more than 2500 associate and adopter member companies; these companies are actively creating new ways to use Bluetooth technology and manufacturing products that support it. Because all Bluetooth devices must be certified and tested to meet current product specifications (currently version 1.1), Bluetooth devices are compatible with each other regardless of the type of device or its manufacturer. Figure 7-15 shows how you might use Bluetooth to create a wireless office to connect your electronic devices. When you have visitors to your office, their Bluetooth wireless devices can connect to your devices, as well.

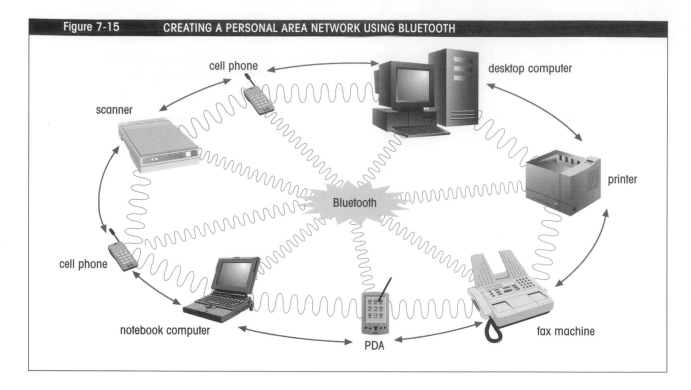

Figure 7-15   CREATING A PERSONAL AREA NETWORK USING BLUETOOTH

Using Bluetooth technology, you can synchronize and share data between as many as eight Bluetooth compatible devices within the specified range, usually about 30 feet, at a rate of up to 1 Mbps. A collection of devices connected via Bluetooth technology is called a piconet. A **piconet** can connect two to eight devices at a time. However, all devices connected in a piconet must have identical configurations. In a piconet, one device acts as a master and the other devices act as slaves during the connection. You can also connect piconets with up to eight devices to each other, allowing you to share information between the master devices. You can use Bluetooth-enabled devices to transfer files, listen to music playing on a computer through a headset, print documents from your office or from another office with a Bluetooth compatible printer, or connect your notebook computer to the Internet using a wireless phone that is in your desk drawer or briefcase. Because Bluetooth uses radio waves, the devices have to be located within the specified range of approximately 30 feet, but the waves can send data around the corner, down the hall, or from your briefcase, without requiring a direct line of site. Bluetooth might seem similar to Wi-Fi, but it's not. Figure 7-16 compares these two standards.

Figure 7-16   COMPARING WI-FI AND BLUETOOTH

	WI-FI (802.11B)	**BLUETOOTH**
Used in	Home or office	Home or office
Range	Up to 200 feet	Up to 30 feet
Connections	128 devices per network	8 devices per piconet
Data transfer rate	Up to 11 Mbps	Up to 1 Mbps

Bluetooth SIG member Ericsson has a simulation on its Web site that shows how you can use Bluetooth technology to enhance communication. You'll view the demo next.

To view the Ericsson Bluetooth demo:

1. Return to the Student Online Companion Web page for Session 7.2, and then click the **Bluetooth Demo** link and wait while your Web browser loads the Web page shown in Figure 7-17.

Figure 7-17	ERICSSON BLUETOOTH USAGE MODELS PAGE

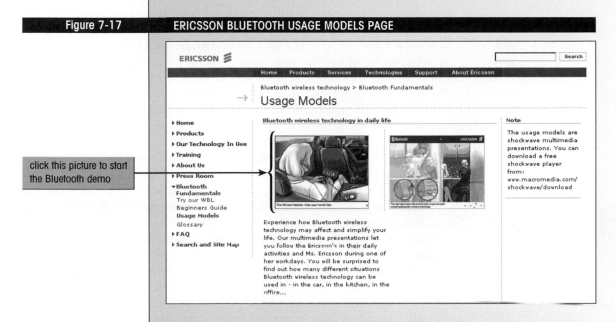

click this picture to start the Bluetooth demo

2. Click the demo on the left (showing a woman sitting in a car and using a PDA) and wait while a new browser window opens and loads the demo. The demo will begin and advance to the next screen automatically. The demo—which includes audio and text captions—runs for approximately four minutes.

TROUBLE? You will need Shockwave to view the demo. If you need to download Shockwave, your browser might automatically begin installing it; in this case, follow the on-screen instructions and then click the Close option when the download is complete. If your browser doesn't begin playing the demo automatically, click the link on the Ericsson Web page to download a free shockwave player and follow the on-screen instructions to install it. Before installing any software on a lab or other public computer, ask your instructor or technical support person for permission to do so.

The demo will loop to the beginning after it finishes.

3. To close the window, click its **Close** button.

Because of the large number of manufacturers creating products that are certified for Bluetooth applications and the unlimited possibilities that this technology brings forth, it is likely that Bluetooth will become a popular wireless alternative in the future, making it very easy for multiple users to share devices without requiring any cables to connect them. Bluetooth sends signals using radio waves that could potentially interfere with other devices, but its power output and range are low so as to minimize interference. As technology improves, Bluetooth might be a way to connect devices to the Internet without requiring separate networks for different devices. Bluetooth will be a technology that Mike will watch carefully in the future.

Wireless Wide Area Networking

As technology changes, so does the need for better, faster ways of getting the Internet and e-mail messages to individuals. On this new horizon are wireless connections, where you can receive e-mail messages and access the Internet on a PDA, wireless phone, or notebook computer from anywhere in the world without a wired connection to a network or phone line. Many devices have been handling the wireless Internet since 1999, but they have been plagued by slow data-transfer speeds, limited interactivity, poor user interfaces, and reliance on only those networks for which they were manufactured. For doctors awaiting lab results or attorneys awaiting court decisions, these devices have given them some freedom to move around locally while waiting for data to arrive. For businesspersons traveling throughout the world, however, the different network standards and limited coverage have made this technology too slow to be useful in the day-to-day operations of an office.

A wireless LAN provides a wireless connection to a network, but devices must be within the stated boundary of the wireless LAN. You can use your notebook computer to make a wireless network connection in your office, the conference room, or anywhere else where you are within the WLAN's range. However, when you're waiting for a plane at the airport or sitting in a hotel room in another state or country, you must use a phone line to connect to the network. You can connect your notebook computer to a wireless phone and reach the network, but this process requires a cable connection between your wireless phone and notebook computer.

With the introduction of 2.5G and 3G wireless systems, **wireless wide area networking (WWAN)** will make it possible to access e-mail and the Internet from anywhere within the boundaries of the wireless network to which you are connected. Wide area networks (WANs) are usually connected using telephone lines or satellites. The Internet itself is an example of a WAN because it is a connection of other networks. Figure 7-18 shows a basic way of connecting a corporate server to a wireless network, to which wireless devices are connected. The wireless devices can communicate over the wireless network, which is connected to the corporate server, allowing businesspersons to connect to the corporate server to retrieve and send e-mail messages and browse the Internet. If the wireless network is global, businesspersons can connect to the corporate server, which is connected to the Internet, from anywhere in the world. The wireless connection provides an Internet connection and a wireless way of sending and receiving e-mail messages on any compatible device.

Figure 7-18	CREATING A WIRELESS WIDE AREA NETWORK

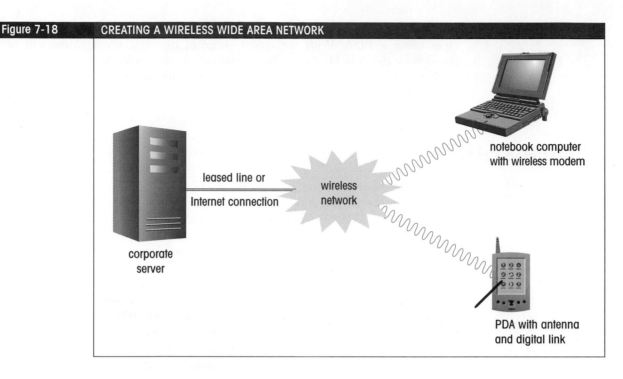

The wireless WAN of the future will use wireless connections and technologies, such as GPRS, to connect networks to each other along a spectrum. Xircom has a small demo of how a WWAN works on its Web site.

To view the Xircom GPRS demo:

1. Return to the Student Online Companion Web page for Session 7.2, and then click the **Xircom** link and wait while your Web browser loads the Web page shown in Figure 7-19. If necessary, scroll down the page to view the animated GPRS demo.

Figure 7-19	XIRCOM "HOW GPRS WORKS" DEMO

The demo plays automatically and shows how a radio tower sends a signal that is received by a notebook computer and a PDA. Notice that the corporate server is connected to the Internet using a wired connection. The connection between the devices and the Internet is wireless using a wireless GPRS network.

The last thing that Mike wants you to investigate is how to send and receive e-mail messages using a PDA. With the recent surge in new customers, Mike will be traveling throughout the year. He'll carry his wireless phone to stay in touch, but he also needs a way to access his e-mail messages without connecting his notebook computer to a phone line. Because PDAs can send and receive e-mail messages using wireless connections, he asks you to investigate some choices for him.

Wireless E-Mail

Because the future of wireless networks is uncertain and expensive, Bluetooth and other technologies are providing opportunities to make the wireless standards today work better and harder to emulate the 3G wireless networks of the future. For example, even though your wireless phone is designed to transmit voice data, your carrier might have a way for you to receive text data. You might enjoy this feature despite its slow transfer and difficulties in reading, receiving, and replying to it.

If you use a PDA, as Mike is planning, you can connect it to a wireless phone to create an Internet connection where you can receive your e-mail messages and download **Web clippings** of preselected content that arrives on your PDA or wireless phone based on your preferences and in a format that increases its transmission speed. The connection between a wireless phone and PDA gives users some freedom to access the Internet and e-mail remotely. For some PDAs, you can install a digital link or other hardware device to connect the PDA to the wireless network on which it operates. The digital link usually includes an antenna that can send and receive data from the network.

As new ways of transmitting data become available, new hardware emerges to make the data easier to read and use. One of those new technologies is a mini, collapsible keyboard that you can connect to certain PDAs and other handheld devices to provide an alternative to typing and tapping messages on a keypad. Different manufacturers have created keyboards that are compatible with their phones; Figure 7-20 shows a product Web page for the Motorola iBoard. Once you connect your wireless phone to the iBoard, you can use it like a regular keyboard to type e-mail messages, notes, and other data into your wireless phone. If your wireless phone's carrier has a network that supports the transmittal of e-mail messages from an e-mail account, you can use your wireless phone to send and receive e-mail messages.

Figure 7-20   **MOTOROLA IBOARD PRODUCT PAGE**

You can also use a portable keyboard to enhance your ability to enter data into a PDA without needing to use a stylus to tap an on-screen keyboard. (A **stylus** is an electronic pen you can use to enter data on a touch screen like the ones in Palm Pilots and Handspring Visors.) Figure 7-21 shows a portable keyboard that you can use with certain Palm Pilot PDAs.

Figure 7-21   **PALM PORTABLE KEYBOARD PAGE**

Mike asks you to investigate his options for using a PDA and a wireless phone to send and receive e-mail messages from anywhere in North America. You'll explore options from Palm, Nextel, and Handspring next.

To view wireless e-mail solutions from Palm:

1. Return to the Student Online Companion Web page for Session 7.2, and then click the **Palm Wireless E-Mail** link and wait while your Web browser loads the Web page shown in Figure 7-22.

Figure 7-22   WIRELESS E-MAIL SOLUTIONS FROM PALM

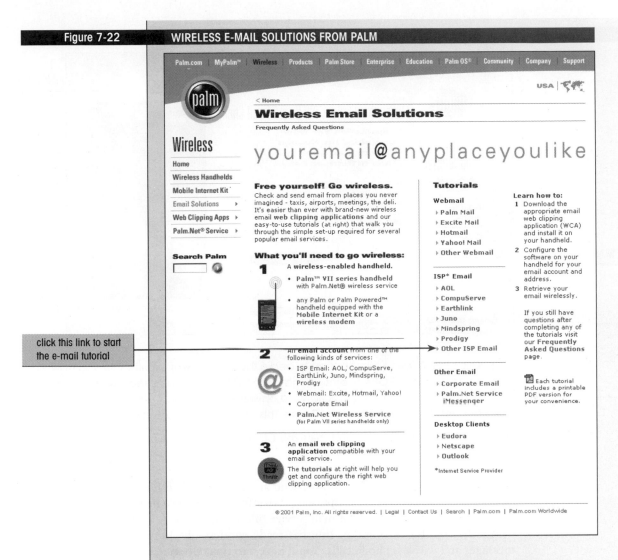

click this link to start the e-mail tutorial

2. Click the **Other ISP Email** link in the Tutorials section. A new browser window opens and starts a tutorial for setting up a compatible Palm Pilot to send and receive e-mail messages from an ISP. See Figure 7-23.

Figure 7-23   PALM EMAIL TUTORIAL WINDOW

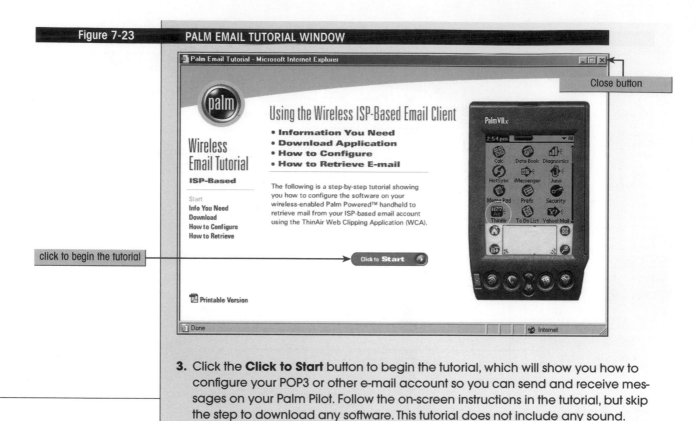

click to begin the tutorial

3. Click the **Click to Start** button to begin the tutorial, which will show you how to configure your POP3 or other e-mail account so you can send and receive messages on your Palm Pilot. Follow the on-screen instructions in the tutorial, but skip the step to download any software. This tutorial does not include any sound.

4. When the tutorial is finished, click the **Close** button on the tutorial window's title bar.

Mike can program a Palm Pilot to send and receive e-mail messages using his LAG or any other e-mail address. This option is very attractive because he wouldn't need a separate e-mail address from a specific e-mail service offered by Palm.

Another option is to use an Internet-ready wireless phone to send and receive e-mail messages and wireless phone calls. You'll look into this option next.

To view the wireless e-mail solutions from Nextel:

1. Return to the Student Online Companion Web page for Session 7.2, and then click the **Nextel** link and wait while your Web browser loads the Web page shown in Figure 7-24.

Figure 7-24	WIRELESS WEB SERVICES FROM NEXTEL

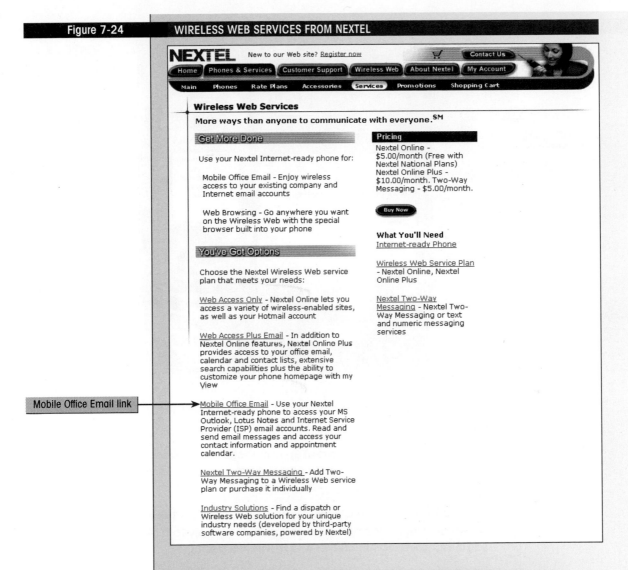

Mobile Office Email link →

2. Scroll down the page, and then click the **Mobile Office Email** link.

3. On the page that opens, click the **View Demo** link near the top of the page.

4. After the page has fully loaded, click the **GO** button. A new browser window opens and offers the chance to view product demonstrations for several Nextel wireless products. See Figure 7-25.

Figure 7-25   **NEXTEL OFFICE EMAIL DEMO WINDOW**

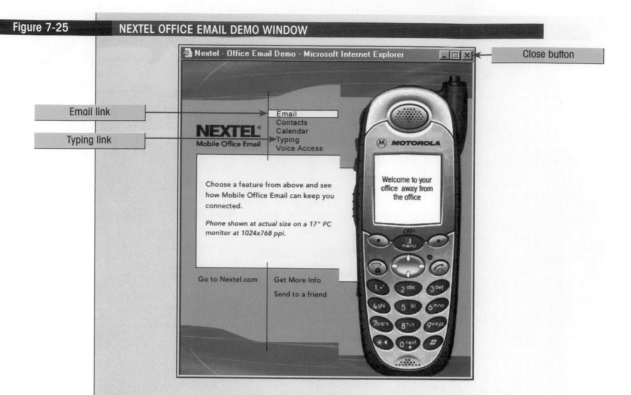

5. Click the **Email** link to start the demo and then follow the on-screen instructions to interact with the simulated phone.

TROUBLE? If you are using a dial-up connection, the pages in the demo might load slowly. Make sure that the pages have fully loaded before continuing to the next page.

6. When you are finished with the Email demo, click the **Typing** link to begin this demo and follow the on-screen instructions to reply to a simulated e-mail message received on the Internet-ready wireless phone.

7. When you are finished with the Typing demo, click the **Close** button on the demo's title bar to close the window.

If you use a wireless phone to send and receive e-mail messages, the wireless phone transmits and receives messages using the wireless network of the wireless phone's carrier. If you're using a PDA to send and receive e-mail messages, you'll need a way to connect the PDA to a network. New products are being developed to provide a wireless connection via the carrier's network. One of these new products is the Handspring Treo. Handspring has a product demonstration on its Web site that you'll view next.

To view the Treo demo:

1. Return to the Student Online Companion Web page for Session 7.2, and then click the **Handspring** link and wait while your Web browser loads the Web page shown in Figure 7-26.

Figure 7-26 HANDSPRING HOME PAGE

Treo link

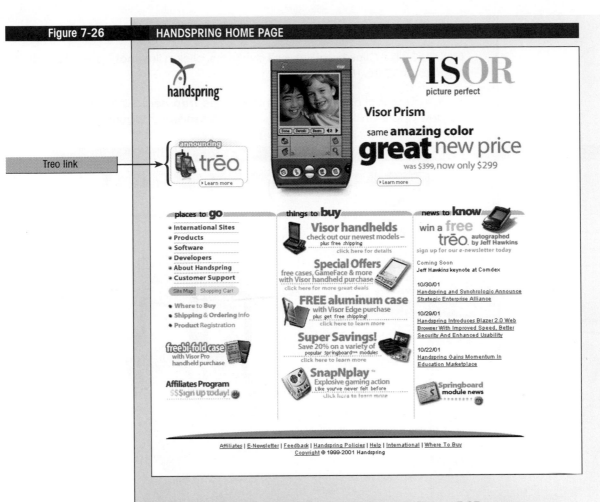

2. Click the **Treo** link. The Web page shown in Figure 7-27 opens.

Figure 7-27 TREO PRODUCT PAGE

click this link to start the demo

3. Click the **Click here!** link.

TROUBLE? If the Clink here! link isn't available, click a link that opens a product page for the Treo 180.

4. On the page that opens, locate and click the **Treo demo** link. A new browser window opens and loads the demo program shown in Figure 7-28.

Figure 7-28	TREO DEMO WINDOW

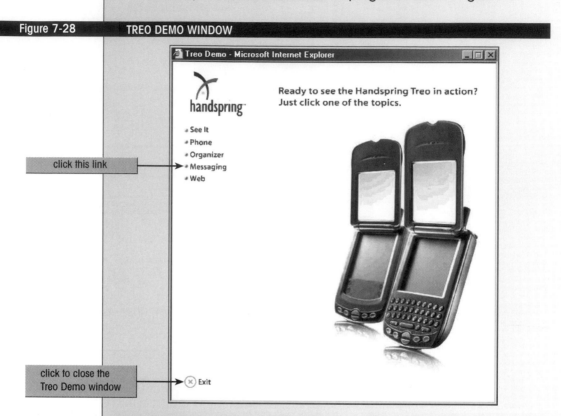

click this link

click to close the
Treo Demo window

5. Click the **Messaging** link, click the **SMS** link, and then watch the demo, which advances automatically. (This demo doesn't include any sound.) Notice that the Treo has a built-in keyboard on which you can type messages.

6. When the **Next** button in the lower-right corner of the window starts blinking, click it to view the Email demo. You can use a Treo to send and receive messages along the network with a wireless phone or other connection.

7. Click the **Next** button again to view the Instant Messenger demo. Instant Messenger is a service that lets you "talk" with other connected users to have a conversation in real-time without the use of e-mail.

8. When you are finished, click the **Exit** button in the lower-left corner of the window to close it.

9. Close your browser, and if necessary, log off your Internet connection.

Mike is excited about the possibilities for creating a mobile office while he travels to visit new clients. With the single purchase of the right PDA or Internet-ready wireless phone, he is confident that he will be reachable via phone and e-mail from almost anywhere he visits in the future.

Session 7.2 QUICK CHECK

1. What is the maximum data transfer rate for an analog cellular network?

2. What is SMS?

3. What are the three primary 2G wireless network standards in the United States?

4. What are the two primary obstacles for installing 3G wireless networks in the United States?

5. Wireless fidelity is also known by the names _____ and _____.

6. True or False: You can connect any 802.11b compatible device to any 802.11b compliant access point.

7. True or False: Bluetooth and Wi-Fi use the same technology to send and receive data.

8. What is a piconet?

Now that you've learned about mailing lists and wireless connections for sending and receiving e-mail from different locations, you're ready to prepare your final report for Mike.

REVIEW ASSIGNMENTS

After viewing the product demos for different types of wireless networks, Mike is eager to begin searching for ways to implement this new technology. He asks you for a list of carriers serving the Lincoln area with digital wireless phone service. In addition, he is traveling to Atlanta, Georgia for a convention next month and wants you to find out if this area has any hotels with wireless access points to which he can connect his notebook computer so he can send and receive e-mail messages. You'll conduct your research and summarize its results in an e-mail message to Mike by completing the following steps.

1. Start your Web browser, open the Student Online Companion page at www.course.com/newperspectives/internet3, click the hyperlink for your book, click the Tutorial 7 link, and then click the Review Assignments link. Click the Wireless Advisor link and wait while the browser loads the page.

Explore

2. On the Wireless Advisor home page, type the zip code 68526, and then click the Search button to display a list of wireless carriers for Lancaster County, Nebraska. In an e-mail message addressed to your instructor, identify two wireless carriers that would provide Mike with wireless calling and text messaging services using a wireless phone.

3. Return to the Student Online Companion page for the Review Assignments, and then click the WLANA link and wait while the browser loads the page for the Wireless LAN Association.

4. Click the link in the photo on the home page with the text beginning "Learn how high speed wireless networking..." (this link opens the page spotlite.htm; if you cannot find this page, type the URL www.wlana.com/spotlite.htm in your browser's address bar and then press the Enter key).

5. Scroll down the page that opens, and then click the Public Access link. A page opens providing a way of locating access points for wireless networks using a city or zip code. Read the text on this page before continuing.

6. Click in the City text box, type "Atlanta," press the Tab key, and then type "G." The City and State text boxes should be set to Atlanta and GA. Click the Search button to start the search.

7. Each location with wireless LAN service appears as a hyperlink. Click a hotel name, locate the URL for the Web site of the wireless carrier in the page that opens and right-click it to open a shortcut menu, and then click Open in New Window to open a new browser window and load the home page for the wireless network.

Explore ▶ 8. On the home page that opens, use the links to locate a page that describes the services offered by that wireless service provider and its rates for individual memberships. When you find this information, use your browser to print it and then close your browser.

Explore ▶ 9. In a new paragraph in the e-mail message you started in Step 2, provide information for Mike about the hotel in Atlanta and the cost and services provided by the wireless service provider for that hotel.

10. When you have finished your report, send the e-mail message to your instructor, close your e-mail program, and then if necessary, log off your Internet connection.

CASE PROBLEMS

Case 1. Join a Mailing List Based on a friend's recommendation, you decide to join a mailing list. First, you will locate one that looks interesting to you. You will then lurk for a while and listen to the messages. To locate and join a mailing list of your choice, you'll complete the following steps.

1. Start your Web browser, open the Student Online Companion page at www.course.com/newperspectives/internet3, click the hyperlink for your book, click the Tutorial 7 link, and then click the Case Problems link. Click the L-Soft CataList link and wait while the browser loads the page.

2. Scroll down the page as necessary, and then click the View lists with 10,000 subscribers or more link in the List information section. (If there are links with the same name, click either one to continue.)

Explore ▶ 3. Scroll the list of mailing lists and locate one that interests you. Click the list's name to open a page containing detailed information about the list, and then print the page. Examine the page's contents and find a hyperlink that you can click to start a new e-mail message to the list's administrative address. If you cannot find a link to the list's administrative address, write down the address, start your e-mail program, and then create a new message.

4. Compose the message to subscribe to the list using the command you located on the list's Web page, and then send the message.

5. When the list server sends you a confirmation message, forward it to your instructor. Make sure to read the confirmation message and reply to it if you are asked to do so.

6. Read the messages on the list for a few days. After you have read several messages, unsubscribe from the list.

7. When you receive a confirmation message about your removal from the list, forward it to your instructor.

8. Close your browser and your e-mail program, and if necessary, log off your Internet connection.

Case 2. Cotton Producers of Hutto Many of the locally owned and operated farms in Hutto, Texas produce and sell cotton. Henry Vanguard is president of the local cotton industry and has started using the Internet to gather information about new research and production methods that he can share with other cotton producers. Henry has asked you to locate mailing lists related to the cotton industry so he can subscribe to and evaluate them. If the lists provide relevant and detailed information, he will recommend them to other producers. To identify potential mailing lists for Henry, you'll complete the following steps.

1. Start your Web browser, open the Student Online Companion page at www.course.com/newperspectives/internet3, click the hyperlink for your book, click the Tutorial 7 link, and then click the Case Problems link. Click the L-Soft CataList link and wait while the browser loads the page.

2. Scroll down the page as necessary, and then click the Search for a mailing list of interest link in the List information section.

3. In the Look for text box, type "cotton." Make sure that the List name and List title check boxes are selected, and then click the Start the search! button. The server returns a list of mailing lists related to cotton.

4. Print the page that displays the search results.

Explore 5. Click the links to open a page containing detailed information about each list that you locate. For two of the mailing lists, print the pages that contain information about subscribing to the lists.

Explore 6. For at least one of the lists, use the Web interface archive link to open a Web site for the list. Open the most recent month's archives and then print the first page of the archive file.

Explore 7. For the site that you located and that contains a Web interface archive, what is the command that you would send to the list server to receive the same archive file via an e-mail message? (Do not send this command to the list.)

Explore 8. Who owns the two lists that you printed in Step 5?

9. Close your browser, and if necessary, log off your Internet connection.

Case 3. Court Reporting Specialists Ginny Rodriguez is the president of Court Reporting Specialists, a local group of over 100 court reporters. At a recent meeting, some of the reporters expressed an interest in creating a mailing list to facilitate communication between members. The purpose of the mailing list is to allow reporters to ask specific questions and receive answers from veteran court reporters, learn about the latest court reporting software, and exchange ideas. Ginny is curious to see if she can easily administer and fund a closed mailing list for Court Reporting Specialists members. She has enlisted your help to locate information about mailing list software. Your task is to locate the major mailing list software programs, determine the cost of each one, and summarize each program's features. You'll report to Ginny by completing the following steps.

1. Start your Web browser, open the Student Online Companion page at www.course.com/newperspectives/internet3, click the hyperlink for your book, click the Tutorial 7 link, and then click the Case Problems link. Click the L-Soft International link and wait while the browser loads the page.

Explore 2. Examine the L-Soft International home page and use its links to find a page with pricing information or a complete description of LISTSERV. Print the page that describes different price plans, and then print a page that describe the software's features.

Explore ▶ 3. Use the ListProc, Majordomo, and Petidomo links on the Student Online Companion page to locate and print pages for each software package that include the software's price and features.

4. When you complete your research, close your browser, and if necessary, log off your Internet connection.

Explore ▶ 5. In an e-mail message to your instructor, use the information in your printouts to recommend a mailing list program for Ginny. Make sure to support your recommendation with facts, compare the programs to each other, and consider the information provided in the Case Problem description.

Case 4. Creating a Personal Area Network for Jack Campbell Jack Campbell is an attorney in Montgomery, Alabama, where he has practiced criminal law for over three decades. Last year, Jack's assistant, Jillian Hately, purchased a wireless phone for Jack and programmed his calendar and other important phone numbers into the phone and also into a PDA. Jack carries the PDA with him to the courthouse, but when working from home, he uses his notebook computer. As a result of his use of different devices, none of them are synchronized and he often misses appointments because they are scheduled on one device but not the others. Jillian thinks that the solution for Jack's problems might be to set up a Bluetooth wireless personal area network in Jack's office, so his devices are automatically synchronized when he walks through the door, leaving Jack free to concentrate on his court trials instead of synchronizing his devices. Jack is skeptical about purchasing new compatible devices because he's not convinced that Bluetooth really has universal standards and is available for purchase. You'll help Jillian convince Jack that Bluetooth might be worth the investment by completing the following steps.

1. Start your Web browser, open the Student Online Companion page at www.course.com/newperspectives/internet3, click the hyperlink for your book, click the Tutorial 7 link, and then click the Case Problems link. Click the Bluetooth link and wait while the browser loads the page.

2. Scroll to the bottom of the Bluetooth home page, and then click the Search for Qualified Products link on the Bluetooth home page. A new browser window opens and displays the Bluetooth Qualification Website home page.

Explore ▶ 3. Click the FAQs link in the navigation bar near the top of the page. A page opens, containing a list of frequently asked questions about qualifying Bluetooth products. Use the list of FAQs to answer the following questions in an e-mail message addressed to your instructor:

a. What is a BQTF and what does it do?

b. What is a BQB and what does it do?

c. Are all Bluetooth products licensed? If so, who or what licenses the products? Is the license a guarantee of the product's compliance?

d. What is the current Bluetooth System Specification?

4. Return to the Bluetooth Qualification Website page, and then search for qualified file transfer products that use the latest Bluetooth spec version. Sort the list by company name and print the first page of results. Close the browser window.

5. Return to the Student Online Companion page for Case Problem 4, and then click the eShop link and wait while the browser loads the page.

6. Click in the Search For text box, type "Bluetooth," and then click the Go button. Click the Personal digital assistants link in the PDAs section to open a page containing Bluetooth PDA devices.

7. Examine the PDA products and use the links for each product to recommend a PDA for Jack to use. When you locate an acceptable choice, print the product page, and then close your browser.

Explore 8. Start a new paragraph in the e-mail message you started in Step 3, write an argument for or against using Bluetooth in Jack's office. Remember that Jack is concerned about the compatibility between devices and the cost and availability of new technology. Support your recommendation with information you found on the Web sites you visited.

9. When you have finished your report, send the e-mail message to your instructor, close your e-mail program, and then if necessary, log off your Internet connection.

Case 5. Finding a Hideaway for Abby London Abby London is the pen name of Patty Newfenbaum. For over 10 years, Patty has been an author in a series of paperback romance novels. She is also a well-known researcher in the area of genetics. Because she must keep her two careers separate, she writes her romance novels in secluded areas. She is considering investing in a small garden home or townhouse in Boca Raton, Florida or San Jose, California. Because being around people inspires her to write her romance novels, she asks you to find out what kind of wireless LAN coverage exists in the local coffeehouses and other public places in these two areas so she'll always have access to her e-mail and other Internet services. You'll help Patty by completing the following steps.

1. Start your Web browser, open the Student Online Companion page at www.course.com/newperspectives/internet3, click the hyperlink for your book, click the Tutorial 7 link, and then click the Case Problems link. Click the Wayport link and wait while the browser loads the page.

Explore 2. Use the links on the home page to identify public places where Wayport locations exist in Boca Raton and San Jose. Print the first page of the list of the Wayport locations for each city.

Explore 3. Return to the Student Online Companion page for Case Problem 5, and then click the MobileStar link. Use the links on the home page to identify public places where MobileStar locations exist in Boca Raton and San Jose. Print the first page of the list of MobileStar locations for each city.

Explore 4. Use the links on the Wayport and MobileStar Web sites to find out what type of wireless connections are available. Print the pages identifying the types of connections.

Explore 5. For each wireless service, print a page that explains the rates for an individual.

6. Close your browser, and if necessary, log off your Internet connection.

Explore 7. In an e-mail message addressed to your instructor, recommend a wireless provider for Patty to use. Be sure to base your recommendation on the type of service Patty needs, the cost, and the availability of access points in the two cities. Based on the availability of access points in Boca Raton and San Jose, which city should Patty consider for her writing? Support your recommendation with information you found on the Wayport and MobileStar Web sites.

QUICK CHECK ANSWERS

Session 7.1

1. LISTSERV, ListProc, and Majordomo

2. A moderated list has a list moderator who is responsible for discarding any messages that are inappropriate for or irrelevant to the list's members. An unmoderated list is one in which no individual is assigned the task of managing the content of the list.

3. list administrator

4. A single message that includes several postings from the mailing list, thereby reducing the total number of messages received from the list.

5. False

6. You can send questions about the list's main topics or you can answer another list member's questions by sending a message to the list address. You send commands to the administrative address.

7. lurking

8. SUBSCRIBE EXERCISE-L *yourname*

9. unsubscribe, signoff

Session 7.2

1. 9.6 Kbps

2. SMS, which stands for Short Message Service, lets you send text messages of up to 160 characters over a 2G wireless network.

3. TDMA, GSM, and CDMA

4. The cost of purchasing spectrum licenses in which to operate the networks and the cost of building cellular transmitters and radio towers to send and receive the signals, and getting the necessary authorization from the U.S. government to use the spectrum.

5. 802.11b, Wi-Fi

6. True

7. False

8. A connection of two to eight Bluetooth compatible devices to each other, in which one device acts as a master and the other devices act as slaves.

In this tutorial you will:

- Learn about and use Internet chat facilities

- Explore Web sites that let you create your own chat rooms and virtual worlds

- Explore virtual worlds that offer entertainment and learning opportunities

- Use the Web to find useful information in Usenet newsgroups

- Reply to and post original articles to Usenet newsgroups

ADVANCED COMMUNICATION TOOLS

Using Chat, Virtual Worlds, and Newsgroups

CASE

MFact Marketing Research

MFact Marketing Research helps clients gather and evaluate information about the marketability of products and services it develops. Founded by Isaac Shores 10 years ago, MFact has grown rapidly. The firm's many satisfied customers include manufacturers of household goods, food products, consumer electronics products, and software. Recently, MFact has started working with clients in the retail merchandising business. Isaac hopes to obtain more service-industry clients, such as law firms, real-estate brokers, and investment advisors. You started working at MFact last year and are impressed with the wide variety of clients that the firm serves.

Market researchers use different approaches to gather their data. For some MFact projects, researchers survey potential buyers of products and services by mail or telephone. In other research projects, MFact gathers a few potential customers and asks them to discuss product features with a trained moderator. These discussion sessions, called focus groups, can be expensive and difficult to arrange because all participants must meet at the same place and time. To obtain a good cross-section of the market for a particular product or service, MFact must conduct focus groups in many different cities. The sales team at MFact learns many details about a product, market, or industry from the focus groups, and the team uses this information to prepare presentations to new clients. Because selling opportunities often arise on short notice, MFact account executives need to obtain marketing information quickly.

During a conversation one morning, Isaac mentions that he is concerned about two issues: the cost of conducting focus groups and the need to gather in-depth information quickly about potential new clients and their products. Isaac tells you he has discussed these issues with Denise Allen, who has held various positions in the computer software industry. Denise told Isaac that he might want to use the Internet to lower the cost of gathering market research data. She mentioned a number of possibilities that use advanced communication tools on the Internet. Denise will serve as a consultant to MFact to help identify ways in which the Internet's advanced communication tools might reduce costs and increase the quality of the marketing research services that MFact offers its clients. Isaac has asked you to work with Denise to explore the potential that these tools might offer.

SESSION 8.1

In this session, you will learn how to communicate "live" with individuals or groups of people using the chat facilities that exist on the Internet and the Web. You will learn how to use the Web to create and host your own chat room. Finally, you will learn about virtual worlds that people have created on the Internet.

What Is Chat?

In Tutorials 2 and 7, you learned how to use Internet e-mail to communicate with one or more people. You also learned how to use mailing lists to communicate with a group of people. When you use e-mail, you must send your message and then wait for a response (or responses). E-mail does not permit real-time conversations, such as those you might conduct using the telephone.

During your first meeting with Denise, she suggests that chat technology might offer a way to conduct focus groups without requiring participants to meet in a common physical location. Denise explains that **chat** is a general term for real-time communication on the Internet or the Web. Originally, the term *chat* described the act of users exchanging typed messages. Today, however, chats can involve exchanging pictures, animations, sounds, and other multimedia files.

A **private chat** occurs between two individuals. Often, the two individuals participating in a private chat meet while chatting among others in a group chat area, or **public chat**. Chats can be continuous, with participants entering and leaving ongoing discussions, or they can be planned for a specific time and to last for a specific duration. Some chats are open to discussions of any topic, whereas others are focused on a specific topic or category of participants. Some chats feature participation by a celebrity or an authority on the chat topic. These chats give worldwide users an opportunity to join discussions with people they would never have the chance to meet otherwise. Most chat tools allow users to save a transcript of the chat session for future reference, which can be especially valuable for chats that focus on highly technical or detailed topics.

Denise notes that chat session transcripts would provide documentation similar to the video and audio recordings that MFact makes of its in-person focus group sessions. Denise explains that you can join public chat sites and simply read the messages sent by other members; you do not need to send messages to the group. This practice of reading messages and not contributing to the discussion is called **lurking**.

In recent years, the Web has offered expanded chat facilities that provide a richer interactive experience than the simple text interchanges that the original Internet chat servers allowed. For example, Web chat sites enable users to send graphic images that are displayed for all chat participants to see. Web chat sites that use the browser client software interface to create combined text and graphic environments for chat participants are called **chat rooms**.

Chatting requires participants to type quickly, even in the enhanced graphical environment of the Web. Therefore, chat participants often omit capitalization and do not worry about proper spelling and grammar. Chat participants use the same **emoticons** (or smileys) that e-mail users find helpful to display humor and emotions in their messages. In addition, chat participants use some of the acronyms shown in Figure 8-1 for common expressions.

Although the acronyms in Figure 8-1 appear in all capital letters, remember that most chat participants type everything—including these acronyms—in lowercase letters because typing in all capital letters usually is interpreted as shouting.

Figure 8-1	COMMONLY USED CHAT ACRONYMS

ACRONYM	MEANING
AFK	Away from keyboard
ATM	At the moment
BBL	Be back later
BFN	Bye for now
BRB	Be right back
BTW	By the way
C U L8R	See you later
C Ya	See you
EG	Evil grin
F2F	Face to face (meeting in person)
FWIW	For what it's worth
G	Grin
IAE	In any event
IMHO	In my humble opinion
IRL	In real life (contrasted with one's online existence)
JK	Just kidding
LOL	Laughing out loud
NP	No problem
OIC	Oh, I see
PMJI	Pardon me, jumping in (when interrupting a conversation)
ROTFL	Rolling on the floor laughing
RTFM	Read the fine manual (usually a suggestion to read a program's documentation)
TTFN	Ta-ta (goodbye) for now
WB	Welcome back

In addition to avoiding all capital letters, most chat participants frown on **flaming**, in which a participant insults or ridicules another participant. Another unwanted practice is **spamming**, in which someone or an organization sends unsolicited commercial messages to a newsgroup, just as an organization might send you e-mail **spam**, or unwanted and unsolicited e-mail messages. Although many chat rooms don't enforce the rules of the Internet, or **netiquette** (short for Internet etiquette), as you use the Internet to communicate, you should exercise common courtesy and decency as you would when speaking in person with other people.

Some chat systems use one server site as a repository for the messages typed by people at different locations. Other chat systems use a series of connected servers that pass messages from user to user so quickly that the messages appear to be stored in one place.

Internet Relay Chat

The early networks that became the Internet included many computers that used the UNIX operating system. Many of these UNIX computers included a program called **Talk** that allowed users to exchange short text messages. In 1988, Jarkko Oikarinen wrote a communications program that extended the capabilities of the Talk program for his employer, the University of Oulu in Finland. He called his multiuser program **Internet Relay Chat (IRC)**. By 1991, IRC was running on over 100 servers throughout the world. IRC became popular among scientists and academicians for conducting informal discussions of experiments and theories with colleagues at other universities and research institutes.

Commercial use of IRC soon followed, with firms using it for virtual meetings with clients and employees at worldwide branch offices. Using IRC in business saves travel costs and is less expensive than long-distance conference calling. Businesses that sell computer software have used IRC to provide customer support and to host user group meetings. News-gathering organizations have used IRC to enhance live coverage of breaking news events. For example, many news reports from the 1991 Gulf War were based on information that came from the war area through IRC and the Internet. By the mid-1990s, hundreds of IRC servers connected thousands of IRC clients.

How IRC Works

IRC uses a client-server network model: IRC servers are connected through the Internet to form an IRC network. Individual chat participants use IRC clients that connect to the servers in the network. Many IRC networks operate independently of each other. The original network was **EFNet**, which is still one of the largest IRC networks today. Other major IRC networks include **IRCNet**, **Undernet**, **DALnet**, and **NewNet**. Although the servers in each of these IRC networks are connected to each other as part of the Internet, IRC traffic is segregated by network. For example, a person using an EFNet client can chat only with another person who also is using an EFNet client—even though the message packets might travel through DALnet and IRCNet servers that are part of the Internet. Figure 8-2 shows this simultaneous interconnection and segregation of IRC network traffic.

| Figure 8-2 | INDEPENDENT IRC NETWORKS ON THE INTERNET |

Chat participants usually run special IRC client software on their computers, although some IRC networks allow clients to connect to their servers using Telnet. IRC client programs often include features such as scripts for common chat commands that can make using IRC easier.

IRC networks organize their chats by topic. Each topic area is called a **channel**, and participants who connect to an IRC network join specific channels in which they conduct their chats. Most IRC networks allow participants to join and participate in several chats simultaneously using *one* connection. Users who have joined a channel receive all messages sent to that channel. Each channel has a name, or a **channel heading**, that uses the pound sign (#) to indicate the chat's topic. For example, a channel in which participants discuss current political issues might have a channel heading of #politics. Most IRC networks maintain lists of their channels, but these lists are never current because chat participants can create new channels at any time. When the last participant leaves, the channel is closed.

When a participant creates a new channel, he or she becomes responsible for managing the channel and is called the **channel operator**, **channel op**, or **IRCop**. The channel operator has rights that other participants who join the channel later do not have. For example, a channel operator can change the channel's topic and heading at any time. The channel operator determines which users may participate in the channel and can change whether the channel is public or private. IRC networks give these powers to channel operators so that each channel can operate smoothly and stay focused on a specific topic. Channel operators can expel users from a channel temporarily or ban them permanently. The authority that channel operators are granted also conveys a responsibility. IRC networks expect channel operators to assist participants who experience problems accessing or using their channels.

IRC participants select nicknames when they log on to an IRC server. The nickname must be unique and cannot be in use anywhere else on that IRC network. A channel operator's nickname is preceded by an "at" symbol (@). IRC servers run automated programs, called **IRC robots** or **bots**, that perform routine services on the IRC system. For example, a bot might announce a new channel participant's entry or respond to participants' help requests. Other bots perform more sophisticated functions, such as detecting banned participants who try to rejoin a channel. Some bots can even detect behavior that violates channel rules (such as profane language or excessive repetition of the same phrase to jam the channel) and automatically expel the offending participant.

Using IRC

Most people connect to an IRC server by using IRC client software on their computer. Many IRC programs are inexpensive shareware programs that you can download from Web pages. Hyperlinks to some of those Web pages appear in the Additional Information section of the Student Online Companion for this tutorial. The computers at your school might already have an IRC client program installed; ask your instructor or technical support person for more information. No matter which IRC client program you use, the commands listed in Figure 8-3 will be helpful as you use IRC.

Figure 8-3	COMMONLY USED IRC COMMANDS
COMMAND	**EFFECT**
/away	Tells other channel participants that you have left your computer temporarily
/help	Presents a list of commands for which the IRC server maintains a Help file
/ignore *nickname*	Suppresses the display of messages from the user with *nickname*
/invite *nickname #channelname*	Sends a message to the user with *nickname* asking him or her to join you on the *channelname* channel
/join *#channelname*	Adds you to the *channelname* channel; if such a channel does not exist, this command creates one
/leave *#channelname* /part *#channelname*	Removes you from the *channelname* channel
/msg *nickname*	Sends a private message to the user with *nickname*
/names *#channelname*	Displays a list of participants in the *channelname* channel
/nick *newname*	Changes your nickname to *newname*
/quit	Closes your connection to the IRC server
/who *#channelname*	Displays the e-mail addresses of participants in the *channelname* channel
/whois *#nickname*	Displays information about *nickname*

Internet Chat

In addition to IRC, other programs use the Internet for chat communication links but do not connect to IRC servers. These Internet chat client programs require each person in the chat to have a copy of the program and a connection to the Internet. **ICQ** (pronounced "I seek you") is one of the most popular Internet chat clients available, with over 117 million worldwide users. The software was created by a small Israeli company, Mirabilis, in 1996. America Online (AOL) purchased the software in 1998 and has continued to offer it as freeware.

To find ICQ client software on the Web:

1. Start your Web browser, open the Student Online Companion page at **www.course.com/newperspectives/internet3**, click the hyperlink for your book, click the **Tutorial 8** link, and then click the **Session 8.1** link. Click the **CNET** link and wait while the browser opens the CNET home page. CNET includes information about different Internet chat client programs and offers downloads for many of them.

2. Click in the **Search** text box that appears near the top of the CNET home page, type **ICQ**, and then click the **Go!** button.

3. One hyperlink that appears on the search results page should be titled "ICQ Tips & Tricks." Click the **ICQ Tips & Tricks** hyperlink to open the page shown in Figure 8-4.

Figure 8-4	ICQ TIPS & TRICKS WEB PAGE

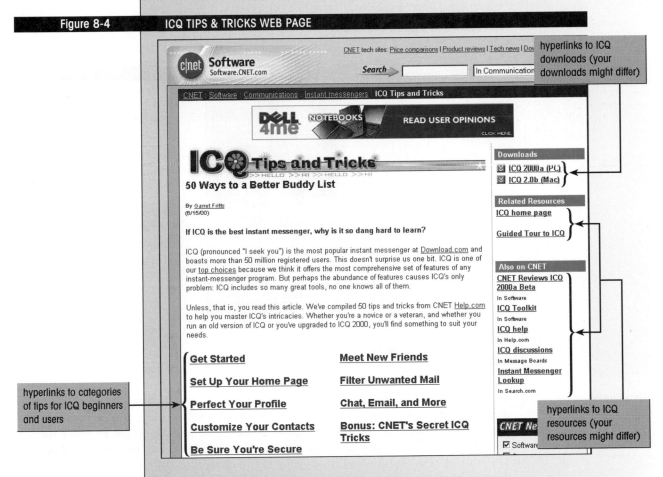

hyperlinks to ICQ downloads (your downloads might differ)

hyperlinks to categories of tips for ICQ beginners and users

hyperlinks to ICQ resources (your resources might differ)

4. You can follow the links on CNET's ICQ Tips & Tricks page to learn more about the ICQ chat client program. Do not download any software unless you are using your own computer or your instructor or lab supervisor gives you permission to download and install software. When you have finished examining this page and its links, use your browser's **Back** button to return to the Student Online Companion page.

5. Click the **ICQ** hyperlink on the Student Online Companion page to open ICQ home page. You can explore the hyperlinks on the home page to find out more about ICQ. When you have finished browsing this site, use your browser's **Back** button to return to the Student Online Companion page.

Instant Messenger

AOL created its own chat software program called **Instant Messenger (IM)**. AOL originally created IM to allow its members to chat with each other, but now AOL has made IM available to anyone for use on the Web. To use IM to talk to other Internet users, you need to download an IM chat client. If you are using Netscape as your browser, a link to download the AOL Instant Messenger appears on the Personal toolbar. If you need to download an IM client, you can use the links on the Yahoo!, MSN, and other Web sites to locate and download an IM client. After installing the IM software from Netscape, the Sign On dialog box shown in Figure 8-5 opens.

Figure 8-5   INSTANT MESSENGER SIGN ON DIALOG BOX

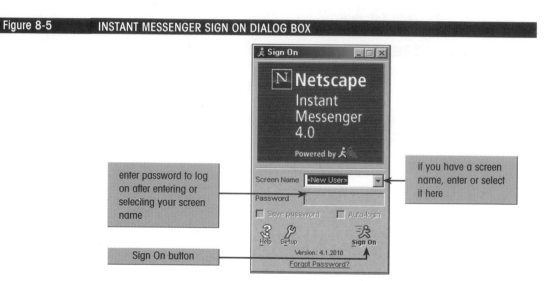

Click the Sign On button to select your screen name. If you use AOL as your Internet service provider, your AOL screen name is your Instant Messenger screen name. Otherwise, you must select and register a unique screen name to use in your IM sessions. After selecting a screen name, you might be prompted to download a newer version of IM if one is available. After downloading and installing any necessary software, you can use IM by signing on with your screen name and password. Use the List Setup tab to enter the screen names of your friends and family members, use the Online tab to see if they are online and available by selecting the buddy or group that you want to talk to, and then click the Send Instant Message button. If the requested person or group is online, they see an Instant Message window like the one shown in Figure 8-6.

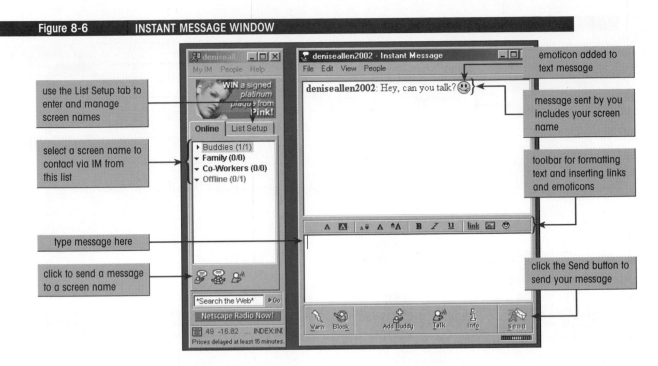

Figure 8-6   INSTANT MESSAGE WINDOW

use the List Setup tab to enter and manage screen names

select a screen name to contact via IM from this list

type message here

click to send a message to a screen name

emoticon added to text message

message sent by you includes your screen name

toolbar for formatting text and inserting links and emoticons

click the Send button to send your message

To reply to the message, the recipient would type a message in the message area and then click the Send button. You can also send hyperlinks and graphics such as smiling faces to express your emotions.

When you sign up for AOL IM or a different version of IM, such as Yahoo! Messenger or MSN Messenger, the provider might send you information via e-mail or provide links to pages about using the service as well as a list of rules and controls that you can use to protect your online privacy and to block specific senders from contacting you. If you receive e-mail messages, be sure to file them in a safe place so you can refer to them as necessary as you are learning to use the software.

Links to the AOL Instant Messenger, Yahoo! Messenger, and MSN Messenger appear in the Additional Information section of the Student Online Companion page for Tutorial 8. (Check with your technical support person or instructor before installing any software on a lab or other public computer.) The Messengers for Yahoo! and MSN require all users to have Yahoo! and Hotmail screen names, respectively.

Denise explains that IRC and Internet chat both continue to be popular with many users. AOL's Instant Messenger service has also grown in popularity as an informal way for friends and family members to keep in touch with an easy-to-use program that lets them talk informally in real time. However, as more people have access to Web browsers, a new kind of chat has emerged. Web sites that offer chat sessions do not need the IRC network, special IRC client software, Internet chat client software, or IM software to function. You agree with Denise that Web chat might be a good alternative to IRC for many of MFact's intended uses.

Web-Based Chat

Web-based chat sites offer the same capabilities as text-based IRC chat networks and more. Further, Web-based chat is often easier to use. The Web's graphical user interface (GUI) environment provides helpful visual cues to the user that text-based IRC does not offer, even for participants using IRC client software. In addition to making chats more accessible to users, Web chat sites allow participants to include multimedia elements and hyperlinks in their messages. These multimedia elements can include pictures, audio clips, and video clips. Figure 8-7 shows a Web chat session in progress that includes multimedia elements.

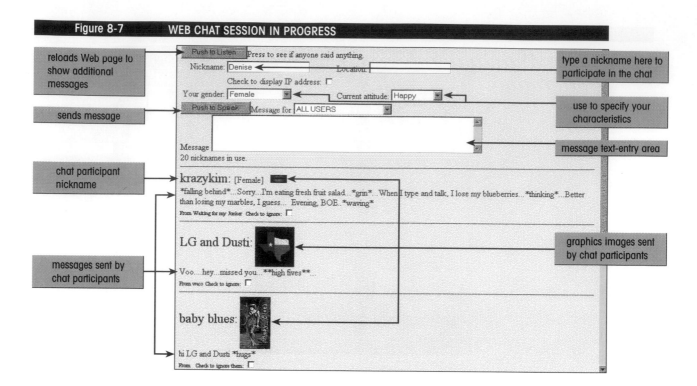

Figure 8-7   WEB CHAT SESSION IN PROGRESS

Figure 8-7 shows messages from three of the 20 participants in the chat. These three participants have chosen images to represent themselves graphically. This chat page also permits users to identify their genders and describe their attitudes by selecting text from the list boxes at the top of the page. You also can use these controls to specify a nickname, identify your location, and reload the Web page to see messages posted after you have initially loaded the page in your browser. You type a message in the large message text-entry area, and use the controls immediately above the text-entry area to send your message to all or specific chat participants. Note that the participants indicate actions or feelings by enclosing the text that describes them in asterisks (such as *grin*), which is a common practice on most Web chat sites.

MFact often conducts focus groups that discuss the package design of a new or improved product. You tell Denise that you can see how MFact might use Web chat's multimedia facilities to send pictures of the new package design to focus group participants in a chat session. Denise explains that she has worked with many businesses that send pictures of products and design drawings during private Web chat sessions with customers.

How Web Chat Works

Denise explains that a Web chat page loads into your Web browser just like any other Web page does. The page is constructed and reconstructed continually by Web chat server software in response to the messages that the site accepts from chat participants. The chat server software re-creates the page every time the server accepts a message.

The operation of a Web chat server differs from that of an IRC network. A Web browser loads the chat site page from a Web server when you connect to it and then waits for your next command. When you connect to an IRC channel, you access a continuous flow of messages from the participants on that channel. If you leave your computer for a minute or two, you will find that your last message has scrolled off the screen of your IRC or Telnet client. To follow a Web chat, you must reload the Web chat page periodically from the Web server that is hosting the chat. You can reload the Web chat page by clicking your browser's Reload or Refresh button. (If a message opens and asks if you want to repost from data, click the No button.) Many Web chat sites include reload options on the Web page itself; some Web chat sites periodically reload the page for you.

Web chat servers accept messages and instructions from participants' Web browsers and convert those messages and instructions to HTML. The Web chat server then uses this HTML code to update the chat page and save it to a publicly accessible area on the Web chat server computer. Web chat site administrators can write instructions for accomplishing these tasks in one of several scripting languages or the Java programming language.

Using Web Chat

Denise suggests that you join a Web chat site to see how it works. Many Web sites offer chats, but most sites require you to register before using their Web chat facilities. Some sites ask you to identify yourself on a registration page before admitting you to the Web chat pages. You should consider carefully whether to provide detailed personal information when you register because most current laws do not require a Web site administrator to maintain the confidentiality of your information. If one Web chat site requires information that you do not want to disclose, simply look for another site with a less intrusive registration page. One Web chat site that has a simple log-on procedure is the Lycos chat site.

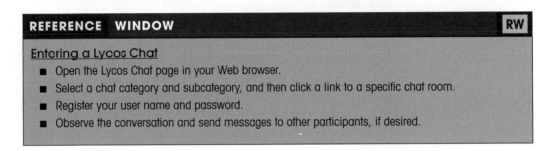

REFERENCE WINDOW **RW**

Entering a Lycos Chat
- Open the Lycos Chat page in your Web browser.
- Select a chat category and subcategory, and then click a link to a specific chat room.
- Register your user name and password.
- Observe the conversation and send messages to other participants, if desired.

Because MFact is working with a retail client that sells dog food and dog supplies, you'll see if you can find a chat room related to pet topics.

To enter a Lycos Web chat:

1. Click the **Lycos Chat** hyperlink on the Student Online Companion page for Session 8.1 and wait while your Web browser loads the Web page shown in Figure 8-8. Your Web page will show different Weekly Chat Events from those that appear in Figure 8-8.

Figure 8-8   LYCOS CHAT WEB PAGE

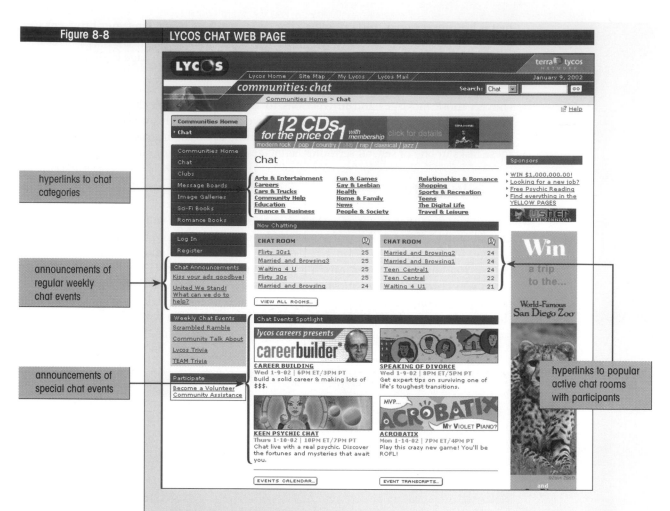

hyperlinks to chat categories

announcements of regular weekly chat events

announcements of special chat events

hyperlinks to popular active chat rooms with participants

2. Click the **Home & Family** category hyperlink. A page opens and lists subcategories related to the home and families.

3. Click the **Pets** category hyperlink to open a page listing chat rooms related to topics about pets. The Chat Room section lists chat rooms in this subcategory and the number of participants currently in each discussion.

4. Choose one of the chat rooms by clicking its name. A new browser window opens and asks you to log on or register to use this site. Because you are a new Lycos user, you'll register to become a member of Lycos Communities.

5. Click the **Register Now** hyperlink.

6. On the page that opens, type the name you would like to use in the Member Name text box. Lycos does not permit duplicate names in its registry, so you should choose a name that includes numbers or is otherwise unusual. Press the **Tab** key to type a password, press the **Tab** key, and then type the password again to confirm it.

7. Enter your information in the second section, including your title, first name, last name, zip/postal code, country, birthday, e-mail address, education, and occupation (choose Student if that is the correct choice). Clear any selected check boxes in the third section so you will not receive any promotional offers from any Lycos sponsors.

8. Click the **Sign Me Up!** button to open the Lycos chat welcome page.

TROUBLE? If Lycos sends a message that you have selected an existing user name, select a different user name in the list of options that Lycos provides or enter a new name. Resubmit the form until you receive a message that Lycos has approved your member name.

9. Click the **Go to Communities!** link. A new browser window opens the Lycos Community Chat page and displays the chat in progress for the chat room that you selected in Step 4. If there are participants in the chat room, you will see their conversation. Figure 8-9 shows the Pet Lovers chat room.

Figure 8-9	PET LOVERS CHAT ROOM

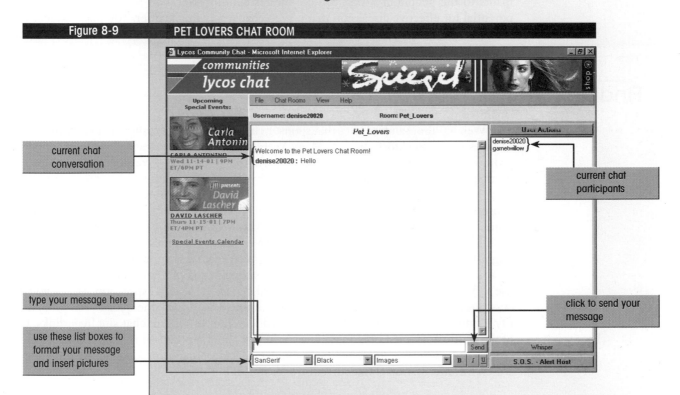

TROUBLE? If a dialog box opens requesting that you download components, such as the Java virtual machine, check with your instructor or technical support person to make sure you are allowed to download the software. If not, read the rest of the instructions without performing the steps.

TROUBLE? Depending on your Internet connection speed, it might take several minutes to load the page. Wait until the page has been fully loaded before continuing.

A list of the chat participants appears in the right frame of the Chat window. To participate in the chat, type the text of your message in the text box below the chat message frame and then click the Send button. In a few moments, you will see your message appear at the top of the chat message frame. Remember that most chats are not censored, so the text that you read might be offensive to you. If you find a chat room to be offensive, try clicking Chat Rooms on the menu bar, click Leave Current Room, and then use the Join a New Room command on the Chat Rooms menu to follow a link to another chat room until you find one that you prefer.

10. When you have chatted enough to experience a Web chat server, click **File** on the menu bar, and then click **Exit Lycos Communities** to return to the main Lycos Chat page.

Denise explains that in a public Web chat site, such as Lycos, you cannot limit the participants to the people in which you are interested. However, you begin to understand the potential for effective discussion that a Web chat server might offer. You plan to meet with Isaac to describe how Web chat might be a useful tool for conducting focus groups and strategy meetings with clients.

Finding Web Chat Sites

The Web has thousands of sites that sponsor chats on topics that range from current movies to investing in the stock market. Many Web chat sites run separate chats for specific age groups. You are convinced that Web chat might be a good way to conduct focus groups with participants who cannot meet because of physical distance limitations, but you are also intrigued by the potential of Web chats as a resource for obtaining a sense of new trends in consumer preferences. Many of MFact's clients need to stay aware of changes in their customers' needs and interests. These clients look to MFact as their marketing research expert for help in this area. You believe that visiting Web chats on topics related to client concerns might be a good way to sense how consumer preferences might be changing.

You suspect that one way to find Web chat sites devoted to a particular topic would be to use a Web search engine and include the word *chat* in the search expression. When you discuss this idea with Denise, she explains that although search engine queries can often identify useful chat sites, several directories provide organized lists of chat site hyperlinks. One of these directories is LookSmart. Isaac told you about a potential new client that is in the fitness and exercise equipment business. You decide to try the LookSmart directory to search for information about current trends in this business.

To use the LookSmart directory to identify fitness Web chat sites:

1. Return to the Student Online Companion Web page for Session 8.1, and then click the **LookSmart Web Directory** hyperlink and wait while your Web browser loads the Web page.

2. Find the People & Chat section of the Web page, and then click the **Chat** hyperlink. The Chat Web page opens, where you can search for chat categories or different types of chats, such as IRC.

3. Click the **Chat by Subject** link. At this point, your screen should resemble Figure 8-10. (Your list of links might differ from those shown.)

Figure 8-10	USING THE LOOKSMART WEB DIRECTORY TO FIND WEB CHATS ON FITNESS TOPICS

hyperlinks to chat subjects

4. Click the **Health & Fitness** hyperlink in the Directory Topics list to open a page of hyperlinks that lead to Web chat sites on related topics.

5. Click the **Fitness & Exercise** hyperlink in the Directory Topics list. A page opens, containing hyperlinks to different chats related to fitness and exercise topics.

The descriptions for each hyperlink tell you more about the nature of the chat to which it leads. Some of the links you see might describe Web chats scheduled for the near future with fitness and health experts. You can follow some of the links and read more about the chat sites or even participate in one or two of the chats, if you wish.

You can find other directories of Web chat sites by subject. Most Web directories offer some kind of chat site list. However, chat site lists sorted by subject often include hyperlinks to general information Web pages for IRC networks along with actual Web chat sites, which can make such lists difficult to use. You will use a Yahoo! chat site list next.

To use lists of Web chat sites:

1. Return to the Student Online Companion Web page for Session 8.1, and then click the **Yahoo! Chat by Subject** hyperlink and wait while your Web browser loads the Web page.

2. Follow some of the category and chat list links on the page. You will find many Web pages that are not chat sites. These Web pages either provide descriptions of IRC channels or require you to download and install software before you can use the site's Web chat pages. However, some of the links do lead to Web chat sites that use HTML pages or Java programs and thus do not require you to download and install additional software.

3. Click your browser's **Back** button to return to the Student Online Companion, and then click the **Yahoo! Web Chat** hyperlink and wait while your browser loads the page. To find chats on subjects in which you are interested, you must follow the links and evaluate each chat site by exploring the categories or the site listings.

Finding Web chat sites that are devoted to specific topics on which MFact requires participants might be a difficult task. After all, many of the chat topics and participants are for entertainment or informal purposes. After discussing this with Denise, you realize that MFact will need to create its own Web chat rooms to make chat an effective tool for conducting focus groups and virtual meetings with clients in remote locations.

Creating a Chat Room

MFact can use existing Web chat sites when conducting research in particular areas. However, much of the research conducted in chat rooms on sites such as Lycos will be general observation, in which MFact tries to learn about new trends in certain industries. For example, in a chat room about health-related topics, MFact might learn that many people are willing to pay more for prescription drugs to lower their overall health insurance premiums. If MFact is representing a health insurance carrier, the account executive for the client's account might recommend a new focus on this information when advertising its services.

Although the chat rooms could provide valuable information, the primary advantage of using focus groups when conducting consumer research is selecting a representative group to provide information. For example, if MFact needs to learn more about the specific buying habits of college-age females, it should select women ages 18 to 22 from different ethnic groups, geographic regions, and economic groups to represent the overall group. Trying to find geographic, ethnic, and economic data about chat room participants is difficult. After all, many of the chat sites are mostly anonymous and for entertainment purposes only. To gain control over the participants, MFact needs a way to build and host its own chat site and then invite certain individuals to join the chat. One site that hosts chat rooms for professionals is ichat.

To explore the ichat Web site:

1. Return to the Student Online Companion Web page for Session 8.1, and then click the **ichat** hyperlink and wait while your Web browser loads the Web page shown in Figure 8-11.

Figure 8-11	ICHAT HOME PAGE

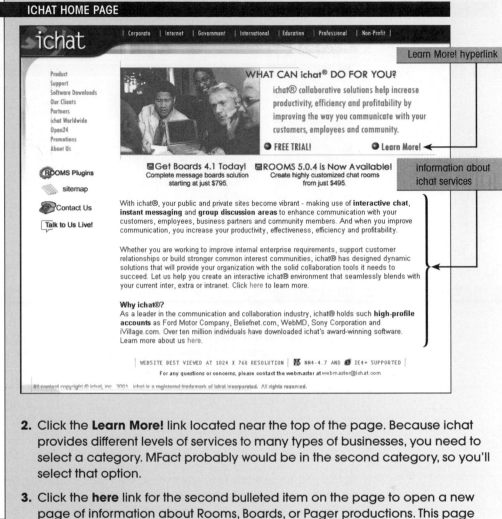

2. Click the **Learn More!** link located near the top of the page. Because ichat provides different levels of services to many types of businesses, you need to select a category. MFact probably would be in the second category, so you'll select that option.

3. Click the **here** link for the second bulleted item on the page to open a new page of information about Rooms, Boards, or Pager productions. This page summarizes three tools offered by ichat: virtual meeting rooms, message boards, and paging services. Denise is interested in the virtual meeting rooms so she can arrange to gather many focus group respondents in one place.

4. Click the **Rooms** link located near the top of the page. The ichat Rooms page opens and describes the interface for using this feature to join a few or many participants in a single place.

MFact could use ichat to bring together focus group respondents and manage the process of adding these respondents to a group. Another Web site that hosts user-created, text-based chat rooms is Talk City. You'll look at that Web site next.

To explore the Talk City Web site:

1. Return to the Student Online Companion Web page for Session 8.1, and then click the **Talk City** hyperlink and wait while your Web browser loads the Web page shown in Figure 8-12.

Figure 8-12 | TALK CITY HOME PAGE

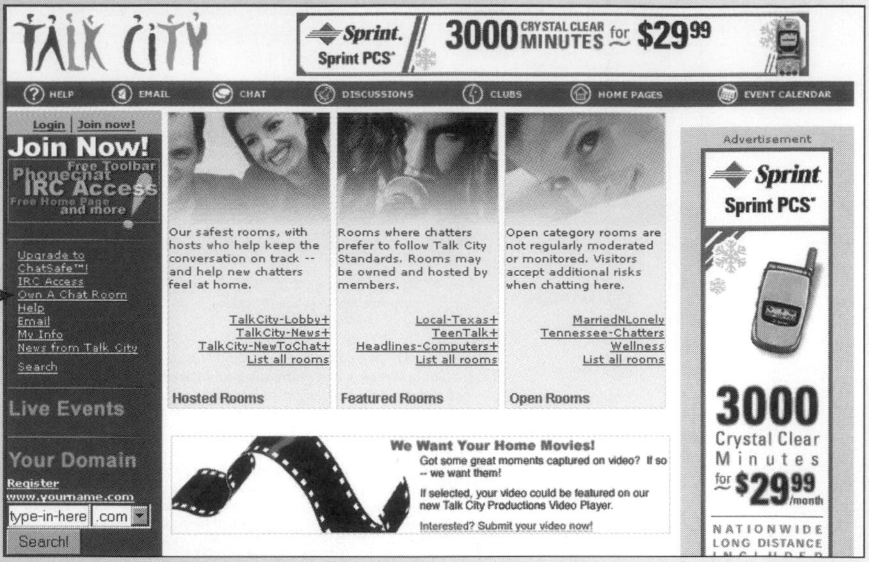

Own A Chat Room hyperlink

2. Click the **Own A Chat Room** link on the left side of the page. The Chat@Talk City page opens. This page describes the free chat room that you can create when you register as a Talk City member. The page also describes the option to create a permanent Talk City chat room, in which you can name and control your chat room for a monthly fee.

3. Click the **Create your club now** link to open the Member Login page. Denise doesn't want to register for a membership yet, but she does want to know more about this service. You'll take the tour to learn more about creating a Club.

4. Click the **Take the Tour** link to start the clubs tour. Click the **Next** button at the bottom of the page after viewing each page. Notice that the Club feature lets you create and name a chat room, invite people to enter it, schedule it for a date and time; it also contains other features that might be important to MFact when it conducts research using chat. The photo feature, where you can post pictures, might be especially helpful when MFact needs to ask its focus group respondents about a particular visual aspect of a product.

5. When you have viewed all of the tour, click the **Finished with Tour!** link at the bottom of the page. You return to the Member Login page.

Denise might try creating a Club room and restrict its access to only focus group respondents. If she and other users find the Club room easy to use, MFact might consider purchasing a permanent chat room to use with marketing research.

Virtual Worlds

Computer games date back to the early days of computing research. Computer scientists amused themselves by creating puzzles and other games that would run on their computers. One of these games, Adventure, became very popular and was widely duplicated, improved, and expanded. In the basic adventure game, the player's goal is to find hidden treasure. The player travels through virtual time and space, gathering clues and tools that will aid in the quest. As adventure games became more sophisticated, the virtual time and space through which the player traveled became more complex. The game programs started including characters that could interact with the game player. Many computer games sold today still use variations of this adventure theme.

MUDs, MOOs, and MUSHs

The creation of the interconnected networks that eventually became the Internet allowed game players to interact with each other across time and space using their computers. Players at multiple sites on the network could participate in the same games and, in some cases, could replace the preprogrammed characters in the games. Other adventure-theme games pitted multiple participants against each other in a race to acquire the game's treasure. In 1979, an Essex University student named Roy Trubshaw wrote a multiuser adventure game program that ran on the university's experimental packet-switched network. He called his program **multiuser dungeon (MUD)**. The university network was connected to the U.S. ARPANET and, later, to the JANET academic network in Great Britain.

In 1980, another Essex student, Richard Bartle, took over and enhanced the program by adding a point system, objectives for players, objects, and better communication. The original MUD program became very popular on these networks during the 1980s. Because many of the players were computer scientists and programmers, some of them worked to improve and modify the program. Most of these MUDs were virtual worlds with fixed rules and features. Each program had dragons to slay, lanterns to carry, inscriptions to decipher, and gold to find. By 1990, new forms of the program were being created that allowed participants to modify the game's structure as they played it. Some of these programs used object-oriented programming techniques, which make programming easier by allowing the reuse of program modules. These programs were called **MUD, object oriented**, or **MOOs**.

The creative and building nature of these programs led to a decreased emphasis on the battles and quests for treasure that had characterized the early MUDs. MOOs that were highly oriented toward creative tasks and programming objectives were called **multiuser shared hallucinations**, or **MUSHs**. In these user-extensible programming environments, many players spend most of their time creating new virtual spaces, objects, and puzzles for other participants to enjoy.

Using a Text-Based Virtual World

Many text-based virtual worlds remain in operation after many years. Some of these virtual worlds have created very formal hierarchies of user authority with titles such as domain master and wizard. At many of these sites, you must apply for permission to build objects. Many of these text-based virtual worlds let you use a common command set to interact with their objects and other participants. Figure 8-13 lists some basic text-based commands.

Figure 8-13   **SOME BASIC MUD/MOO/MUSH COMMANDS**

COMMAND	ACTION
:*action*	Tells other participants that you are engaging in *action*, such as :*smile* to indicate that you are smiling.
help *topicname*	Provides Help on the *topicname* topic; if you omit *topicname*, the command provides a general Help listing.
look *object*	Provides a description of the *object* you specify; if you omit *object*, the command provides a description of the room or other virtual space that you currently occupy.
north, south, east, west, up, down move *location*	Moves your character to other areas in your current virtual space or to another space. Most systems allow you to execute any of these commands by typing its first letter. In a MUSH, use the move *location* command to change positions.
out go *location*	Moves your character through an exit of the room if there is only one exit. If there is more than one exit, use the go *location* command to move to the desired exit or location.
quit QUIT	Exits the virtual world. For MUSHs, the command must be in all capital letters.
say *expression* whisper *username* *expression*	Informs other participants that you have spoken the words in *expression*; the double-quote character (") also issues this command. To speak privately to an individual, use the whisper command.
who who *username*	Lists the names of current participants; when used with *username* the who command lists information about a specific user. The ? character also issues this command.

You type these commands at the screen prompt after you enter a text-based virtual world. Commands that include an "at" sign (@) as the first character change the database. When participants use the say command to communicate with each other, the activity in a virtual world resembles that of an IRC channel. Virtual worlds, however, offer objects with which you can interact. Even if there are no other participants in a virtual world room when you enter it, you still can interact with the objects that exist in that room. Figure 8-14 shows an example of the text-based Lingua MOO, which is hosted by the University of Texas at Dallas.

Figure 8-14   **LINGUA MOO VIRTUAL WORLD**

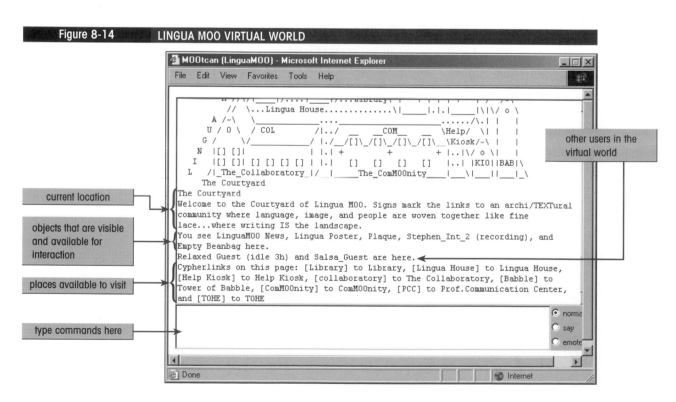

You are intrigued by the possibilities of using text-based virtual worlds for some types of marketing research studies, but you are concerned that the text-based interface might be difficult for some participants to use. Denise explains that newer virtual spaces have been created on the Web that offer more sophisticated interfaces.

GUI Virtual Worlds

A GUI extends the potential of virtual worlds because participants can interact with each other almost as they would in real life. The GUI allows each participant to assume a virtual physical existence and appearance. Such an artificial persona is called an avatar. A participant's **avatar** can be any kind of graphic that the participant would like to use as his or her online representation. Usually, avatars resemble comic-book characters, but other forms are possible. Some firms will, for a fee, create an avatar based on a photo that you provide.

Many of the virtual worlds that incorporate GUIs require that you install special client software on your computer. Some of these programs are standalone programs; your Web browser can run others. However, there are a few Web sites that offer GUI virtual worlds implemented in the Java programming language. Most current Web browsers are Java-enabled and can access these sites without requiring additional software.

Worlds.com lets users create their own virtual, three-dimensional worlds and provides hosting capabilities. You'll explore this option for MFact next.

To examine the Worlds.com virtual world:

1. Use your browser's history list to return to the Student Online Companion Web page for Session 8.1, and then click the **Worlds.com** hyperlink and wait while your Web browser loads the Web page.

2. Scroll down the page and locate the **WorldsShaper** link, and then click it. A new browser window opens and loads the page shown in Figure 8-15, describing the WorldsShaper Web authoring tool. Notice that you can use this software to build your own virtual world. For a small fee, you can purchase software to create your virtual world and host it for one year.

Figure 8-15   WORLDSSHAPER AUTHORING TOOL WEB PAGE

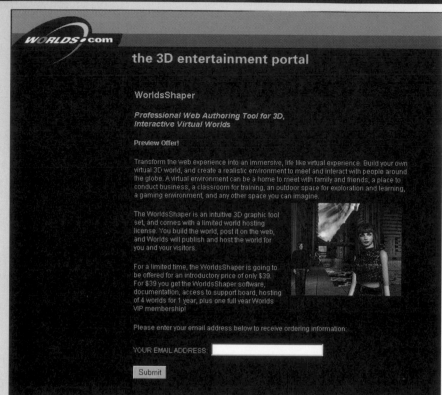

3. Click the **Close** button on the browser's title bar to close it. You return to the Worlds.com home page.

4. Close your browser, and if necessary, log off your Internet connection.

You have gathered a great deal of information about how MFact might be able to incorporate chat facilities and virtual world simulations into its business activities. Before you finish your search activities and prepare your report to Isaac, Denise suggests that you also consider the potential of another Internet-based tool, Usenet newsgroups.

Session 8.1 QUICK CHECK

1. Entering a chat and reading the messages posted by other participants without joining the discussion is called _____.

2. True or False: A data packet from an IRC client on one network might travel through another IRC network server.

3. True or False: The owners of the IRC network appoint IRC channel operators.

4. Name one advantage and one disadvantage of using Web chat instead of IRC.

5. To see the most current messages on a Web chat site, you often must _____ the Web page.

6. The original virtual worlds on computer networks were multiplayer versions of _____-type games.

7. True or False: You can use FTP client software to connect to a text-based MUD, MOO, or MUSH virtual world on the Internet.

8. Virtual worlds on the Web that provide a GUI often allow participants to assume an on-screen persona, or a(n) _____.

SESSION 8.2

In this session, you will learn how to search Usenet newsgroups to gather information and find answers to specific questions. You also will learn how to post newsgroup articles and reply to existing newsgroup articles.

Usenet **Newsgroups**

Denise tells you that the **Usenet News Service**, or **Usenet**, was founded in 1979 at Duke University as a way of collecting information and storing that information by topic category. The original Usenet News Service was devoted to transmitting computing news and facilitating discussions among employees of university computing facilities on topics such as operating systems and programming languages.

The topic categories on Usenet originally were called **newsgroups** or **forums**. Many people still use these terms when they refer to Usenet categories, but another term, **Internet discussion group**, is also becoming popular. Most of these newsgroups are available to the general public; however, some newsgroups are limited to users at a specific site or to those affiliated with a particular organization. Each site that participates in Usenet has the option of selecting which newsgroups it will carry. Therefore, not all newsgroups—even the public ones—are available on every computer system that is connected to Usenet.

Usenet Is Not a Mailing List

Usenet was one of the first large, distributed information databases in the world. A **distributed database** is stored in multiple physical locations, with portions of the database replicated in different locations. Each of these multiple physical locations does not, however, store a complete copy of the database. Usenet is probably the largest decentralized information utility in the world today. There are over 65,000 newsgroups in existence, and messages that total hundreds of megabytes are added to Usenet newsgroups each day. In practice, people use the terms *Usenet*, *Usenet News*, and *newsgroups* interchangeably when referring to this large distributed database.

Newsgroups are similar to mailing lists in that they accept messages from users and make them generally available to other users. However, newsgroups do not use a list server to forward copies of submitted messages to subscribers. Instead, a newsgroup stores messages on an electronic bulletin board as **articles** or **postings** that are sorted by topic. Users who are interested in learning about a particular topic can connect to the bulletin board and read the posted newsgroup articles. Therefore, newsgroups are more suitable for discussions of broad topics that might interest a large audience because they do not require a list server to send a separate e-mail message to each potential reader. Each person reads the same copy of the posted article on the newsgroup bulletin board. This subtle difference between how newsgroups and mailing lists operate was critical in the early days of Usenet because bandwidth and computing power were limited, expensive resources.

When users read Usenet articles to which they would like to respond, they can reply to those articles. If a Usenet article is particularly interesting to many newsgroup readers, it might generate hundreds of responses within a day or two. These responses, in turn, might generate even more responses on the same issue. Most newsgroups have discussions occurring on many different issues simultaneously. A series of postings on a particular issue is called a **thread**. Participants in newsgroups use various types of newsreader software to organize postings by thread within each discussion group.

Some newsgroups have a moderator who reviews all postings before they appear in the newsgroup. These moderated lists tend to focus on technical or specialized topics. Moderators provide a valuable service to Usenet by reducing the number of off-topic postings and messages sent by persons who do not have the necessary qualifications to make a contribution to advanced-level or highly technical discussions.

Usenet Structure

Usenet is a network of computers called **news servers**. This network operates without any central control authority. When a user sends a posting to a particular Usenet newsgroup, it is routed to the news server computer site that has agreed to maintain that newsgroup. The news server stores all of the articles for that newsgroup. News servers share their public newsgroups with each other. Periodically—daily, hourly, or even more frequently—news servers connect to other news servers and compare a list of the articles that each currently is storing. Each newsgroup article has a unique identification number that makes this comparison possible. After this comparison, each news server obtains copies of the articles it does not have. This store-and-forward process is called obtaining a **newsfeed**. Large news servers often maintain a continuous newsfeed connection to other large news servers to maintain the currency of their newsgroup article inventory.

Each news server site employs a **news administrator**, who specifies which other news servers will be newsfeed providers and newsfeed recipients. The news administrator also chooses which newsgroups to carry. Because newsgroups are so large, computer file storage space can be a constraint. Computer sites that operate news servers include most ISPs, universities, large businesses, government units, and other large organizations. In response to the large volume of newsgroup postings, most news servers regularly delete articles after a short period of time. The news administrator is responsible for setting the deletion schedule.

The transmission of newsgroup traffic between news servers originally occurred over leased telephone lines dedicated to that task. Now, however, most newsfeeds occur over the Internet. Newsfeeds use the **Network News Transfer Protocol (NNTP)**, which is part of the TCP/IP protocol suite that is used by all computers connected to the Internet. News servers' universal use of this standard protocol makes it possible for Usenet to function without a central controlling authority.

Newsgroup Hierarchies

Newsgroups are organized into topical hierarchies in which each newsgroup has a unique name that shows its position and classification in the hierarchy. Top-level hierarchies are shown as the first part of a newsgroup's name and then the subcategories follow; these two names are separated from the top-level hierarchy name and each other by periods. For example, one newsgroup that includes discussions of organic chemistry issues is named *sci.chem.organic*. This newsgroup's name shows that it is classified in the top-level category *science* (sci), the science subcategory *chemistry* (chem), and the chemistry subcategory *organic*. The original Usenet News Service included the eight main top-level categories—including one miscellaneous category for alternative topics—that appear in Figure 8-16.

Figure 8-16 | ORIGINAL USENET NEWS SERVICE TOP-LEVEL CATEGORIES

CATEGORY	INCLUDES TOPICS RELATED TO
comp	Computers
rec	Recreation and entertainment
sci	Science
soc	Social issues and socializing
news	Operation and administration of Usenet
talk	Conversations, debates, and arguments
misc	Miscellaneous topics that do not fall within other categories
alt	Alternative and controversial topics

As Usenet grew, the hierarchy of categories that served the original participants—employees of university computing departments—were no longer sufficient to classify the wide range of topics that were being discussed in the newsgroups. Usenet developed a procedure for proposing and voting on the creation of new newsgroups for all categories except the alternative category, which allows users to create new categories at will. Any person can initiate Usenet's official procedure for adding new newsgroups or categories, but all new categories must conform to the existing Usenet hierarchical structure. A portion of the hierarchy under business (biz) appears in Figure 8-17.

Figure 8-17 | PORTION OF THE HIERARCHICAL STRUCTURE OF THE BIZ CATEGORY

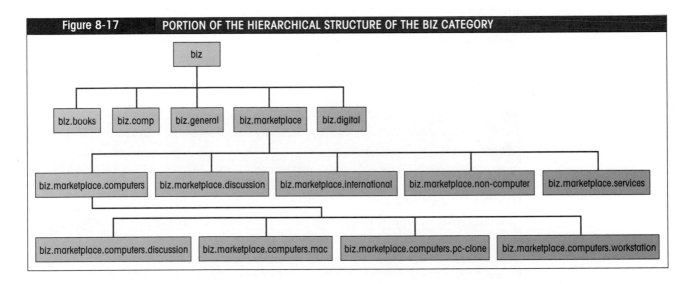

Business (biz) is one of the top-level categories that was added to the original eight categories to accommodate the growing interest of Usenet participants in business matters. The second-level categories include newsgroups devoted to, for example, books about business (biz.books) and about using computers in business (biz.comp). The biz.marketplace category, which includes discussions of how to use newsgroups to conduct business, includes subcategories for newsgroups devoted to buying and selling computers and computer parts through newsgroups (biz.marketplace.computers), conducting international business through newsgroups (biz.marketplace.international), and so on. The biz.marketplace.computers subcategory is further divided into separate subcategories for newsgroups about doing business for specific computer parts, such as the Macintosh (biz.marketplace.computers.mac) or Windows-Intel and similar computers (biz.marketplace.computers.pc-clone).

You tell Denise that newsgroups look as if they might offer a great deal of useful information that MFact could use, but you are concerned about searching through something the size of Usenet. You explain that the hierarchical approach to classifying information makes sense for smaller databases, but for something this large, even the categories might not help. Denise tells you that your fears are well founded and that several businesses have developed tools for searching newsgroups effectively. Two of these firms allow users to read and search newsgroups from their Web sites.

Web **Access to Newsgroups**

Denise explains that when the Usenet News Service began operating in 1979, the only way to read or post to newsgroups was to run newsreader software on your computer. **Newsreaders** were programs designed for the sole purpose of communicating with news server computers. Now, most e-mail programs include newsreader features. (You will learn how to use two e-mail clients to read and post to newsgroups later in this session.) The most recent improvement in Usenet accessibility has been the increase in the number of Web sites that archive newsgroup articles. These Web sites offer search engines that make finding articles on specific topics much easier than was previously possible.

Tile.net Newsgroup Directory

Tile.net is one of many Internet Web sites that maintains a comprehensive list of Usenet newsgroups in its databases. You can browse the hierarchical structure of Usenet or use Tile.net's search engine to find specific articles on topics in which you are interested. You can also search for newsgroups alphabetically. As you recall from your last conversation with Isaac, MFact was working on a proposal to conduct research for a chain of specialty retail-clothing stores. You decide to see what kind of information exists in Usenet about the fashion industry that MFact's account representatives might find useful as they prepare their research proposal.

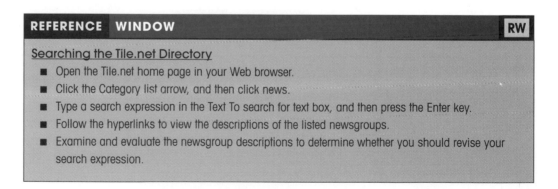

REFERENCE   WINDOW   **RW**

Searching the Tile.net Directory

- Open the Tile.net home page in your Web browser.
- Click the Category list arrow, and then click news.
- Type a search expression in the Text To search for text box, and then press the Enter key.
- Follow the hyperlinks to view the descriptions of the listed newsgroups.
- Examine and evaluate the newsgroup descriptions to determine whether you should revise your search expression.

To search the Tile.net directory for newsgroups related to fashion topics:

1. Start your Web browser, open the Student Online Companion page at **www.course.com/newperspectives/internet3**, click the hyperlink for your book, click the **Tutorial 8** link, and then click the **Session 8.2** link. Click the **Tile.net** link and wait while the browser opens the page shown in Figure 8-18. You can use Tile.net to search for information about Internet mailing lists, Usenet newsgroups, FTP sites, computer products vendors, and Internet and Web design companies.

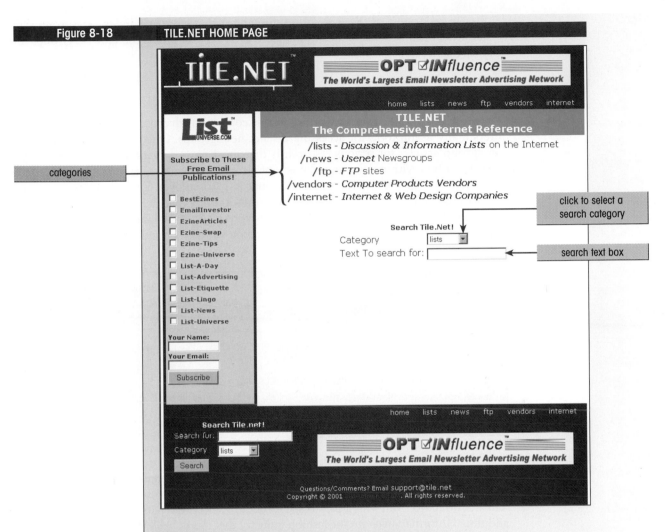

Figure 8-18   TILE.NET HOME PAGE

2. Click the **Category** list arrow, and then click **news**.

3. Type **fashion** in the Text To search for text box, and then press the **Enter** key. After a few moments, the search engine returns a Web page with hyperlinks to newsgroups containing the key term "fashion." One of these hyperlinks is to the newsgroup named alt.fashion.

4. Click the **alt.fashion** hyperlink. A new page opens and provides some information about this newsgroup. The description indicates that this newsgroup contains information about all facets of the fashion industry.

   TROUBLE? If you click the URL "alt.fashion" on this Web page, a newsreader program will open and access this newsgroup. If you accidentally click this link, close the program that opens and click the No button if you are asked to subscribe to the newsgroup. You will learn how to subscribe to a newsgroup in the next section.

5. Click your browser's **Back** button and follow the hyperlinks on the search results page to learn about other fashion related newsgroups. Evaluate the information returned by the search and consider whether you should run a modified search to obtain the information you seek.

Denise tells you that there are other directories that store and index newsgroup articles besides the Tile.net site. One Web site that can be very helpful is the Google Groups directory of Usenet newsgroups.

Google Groups Directory

The Google Groups directory (formerly Deja.com) is an advertiser-supported Web site that offers many useful tools for accessing Usenet newsgroups. One of the drawbacks of using newsgroup articles for serious research is that most news servers delete articles fairly frequently—often within days, and almost always within several weeks. Google Groups does not delete newsgroup articles. Google Groups has stored over 650 million newsgroup articles dating from 1995 in its database. More important is that the Google Groups site has a search engine that allows you to query its newsgroup article database by subject, newsgroup name, or article author. You can limit your search by these criteria and by posting date.

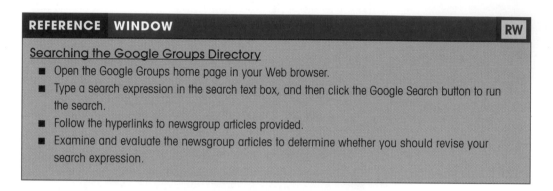

REFERENCE WINDOW   RW

Searching the Google Groups Directory
- Open the Google Groups home page in your Web browser.
- Type a search expression in the search text box, and then click the Google Search button to run the search.
- Follow the hyperlinks to newsgroup articles provided.
- Examine and evaluate the newsgroup articles to determine whether you should revise your search expression.

Because Google Groups lists newsgroups and individual newsgroup articles, you decide to use the Google Groups directory to run a more detailed query from the one you ran using the Tile.net directory. You would like to see if the broader coverage of Google Groups provides additional information about the fashion industry that might help MFact prepare its proposal.

To search Google Groups for newsgroups related to fashion topics:

1. Return to the Student Online Companion Web page for Session 8.2, and then click the **Google Groups** hyperlink and wait while your Web browser loads the Web page shown in Figure 8-19. (Your page might look different.)

Figure 8-19	GOOGLE GROUPS HOME PAGE

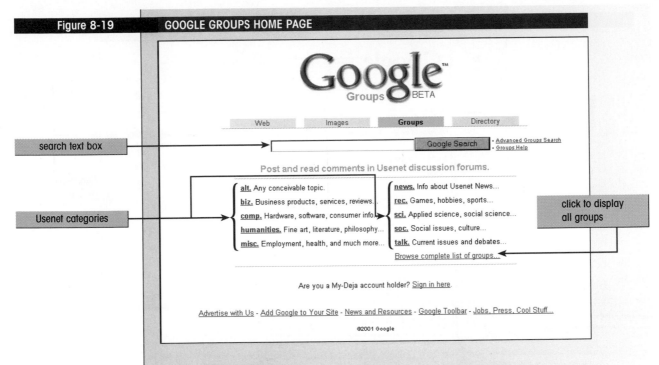

search text box

Usenet categories

click to display all groups

2. Type **fashion industry** in the search text box, and then click the **Google Search** button. After a few moments, the search engine returns a Web page similar to the one shown in Figure 8-20 with hyperlinks to information matching your search expression.

Figure 8-20   GOOGLE SEARCH RESULTS FOR "FASHION INDUSTRY"

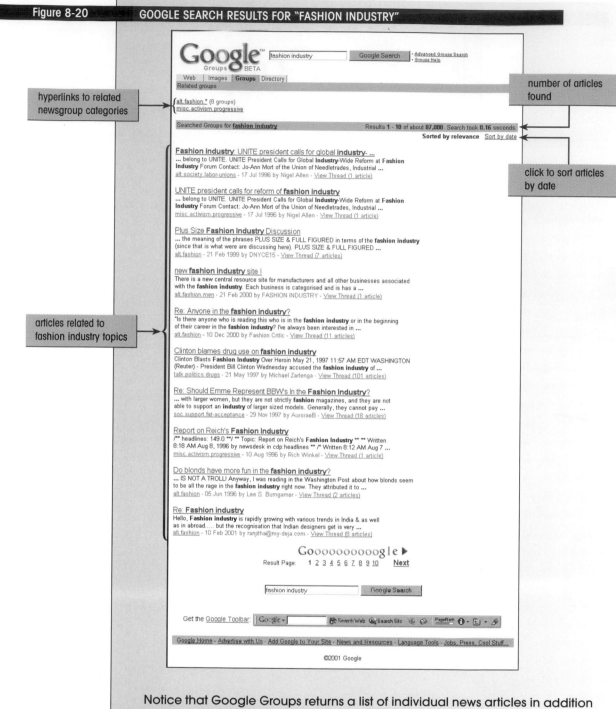

Notice that Google Groups returns a list of individual news articles in addition to the newsgroup names that the Tile.net directory returned. You can click the article hyperlinks to read individual newsgroup postings related to the fashion industry and they will load in your Web browser, instead of using a newsreader program. To obtain a more complete list of discussion groups on topics related to the fashion industry, click a hyperlink in the Related groups section. Evaluate the information returned by the search and consider whether you will need to run a modified search to obtain the information you seek

3. When you have finished examining the newsgroup postings, return to the Student Online Companion page for Session 8.2.

After examining the information provided by the two different searches, you conclude that the Tile.net and the Google Groups directories each offer a different view of the current fashion scene. You found information in both searches that might be helpful to MFact as it prepares the client proposal.

Using a Newsreader

After learning how to find newsgroup articles and reading a few of them, you become interested in finding out how to post articles of your own to newsgroups that you find interesting. Denise explains that you must use some type of newsreader software to reply to articles or to post original messages. The Google Groups Web site includes a built-in newsreader that you can use to view articles. Microsoft and Netscape both include newsreader software in their Web browser suites.

Note: If you are using Microsoft Internet Explorer as your browser, complete the steps in the "Microsoft Outlook Newsreader" section. If you are using Netscape Navigator as your Web browser, complete the steps in the "Netscape Mail" section.

Microsoft Outlook Newsreader

The Microsoft Outlook Newsreader is included as part of the Outlook Express e-mail software, which is part of the Internet Explorer Web browser. There are several ways to start Outlook Express, but because you are already familiar with the Internet Explorer Web browser, it will be easy for you to start Outlook Newsreader from Internet Explorer.

REFERENCE WINDOW   **RW**

Starting Outlook Newsreader
- Start Internet Explorer.
- Click the Mail button on the toolbar, and then click Read News.

To start Outlook Newsreader:

1. Click the **Mail** button on the toolbar. A drop-down list opens, displaying options for reading your e-mail messages, creating a new e-mail message, sending an e-mail message that contains a link to the currently displayed Web page, sending an e-mail message that contains the currently displayed Web page, and reading news articles.

2. Click **Read News** in the drop-down list. The Microsoft Outlook Newsreader program starts.

   TROUBLE? If an Internet Connection Wizard dialog box opens, type your name as you want it to appear in the newsgroup, click the Next button, and then follow the on-screen instructions. Your instructor will provide you with your news server's name (the news server name for most organizations is "news" followed by your ISP's domain name).

   TROUBLE? If a Browse for Folder dialog box opens, accept the default folder and continue.

TROUBLE? If a dialog box opens and asks if you want to make Outlook Express your default newsreader, click the No button.

3. Double-click the **news** entry in the left pane of the Outlook Newsreader window (your news entry will contain your domain name) to expand the list of newsgroups so that your screen looks like Figure 8-21.

Figure 8-21   MICROSOFT OUTLOOK NEWSREADER

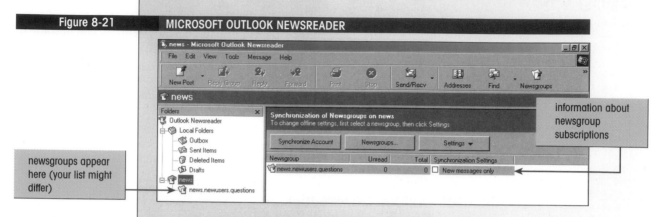

newsgroups appear here (your list might differ)

information about newsgroup subscriptions

TROUBLE? The list of newsgroups on your screen will be different from the list shown in Figure 8-21. Newsgroups that previous users of the computer on which you are working have used will appear in the list. If you or previous users of the computer have not read any newsgroups, a dialog box will open and ask if you would like to view a list of available newsgroups. If this occurs, click the Yes button. Outlook Newsreader will open the Newsgroup Subscriptions dialog box and download a list of newsgroups, which can take several minutes. When the list has finished loading, type news.newusers.questions in the Display newsgroups which contain text box, and then click the news.newusers.questions newsgroup in the search results that appears. Click the Subscribe button, and then click the OK button to close the Newsgroup Subscriptions dialog box.

TROUBLE? If your computer displays the error message "No NNTP server is configured," ask your instructor or technical support person to add the name of your host's news server to the Outlook Newsreader installation on your computer.

You can use Outlook Newsreader to read, reply to, and create your own newsgroup articles. The news.misc newsgroup provides a place where new users can send test messages and otherwise become familiar with the operation of newsreader software.

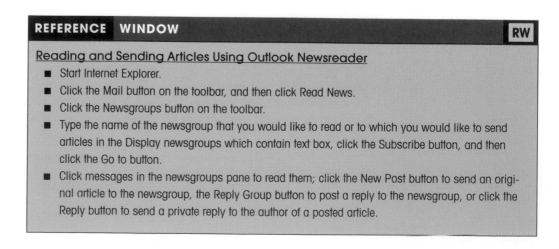

REFERENCE WINDOW   **RW**

Reading and Sending Articles Using Outlook Newsreader
- Start Internet Explorer.
- Click the Mail button on the toolbar, and then click Read News.
- Click the Newsgroups button on the toolbar.
- Type the name of the newsgroup that you would like to read or to which you would like to send articles in the Display newsgroups which contain text box, click the Subscribe button, and then click the Go to button.
- Click messages in the newsgroups pane to read them; click the New Post button to send an original article to the newsgroup, the Reply Group button to post a reply to the newsgroup, or click the Reply button to send a private reply to the author of a posted article.

To read and send articles using Outlook Newsreader:

1. Click the **Newsgroups** button on the toolbar. The Newsgroup Subscriptions dialog box opens.

2. Type **news.misc** in the Display newsgroups which contain text box, and then click the **news.misc** entry in the search results.

3. Click the **Subscribe** button. An icon appears to the left of the news.misc entry, indicating that you have subscribed to this newsgroup.

4. Click the **Go to** button. The newsgroups pane of the window displays message headings and the message text pane displays the contents of the selected message, as shown in Figure 8-22.

| Figure 8-22 | READING AN ARTICLE USING OUTLOOK NEWSREADER |

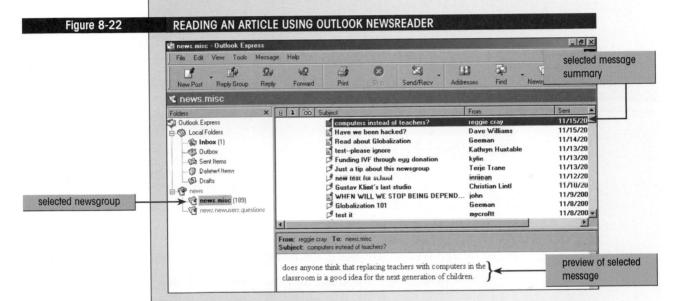

TROUBLE? Depending on your Internet connection speed, it might take up to several minutes to download the newsgroups.

TROUBLE? The messages that appear in the list on your screen will be different from those that appear in Figure 8-22.

5. To read a message, click the message header in the newsgroups pane of the Outlook Newsreader window. The preview pane will display the contents of the message, similar to how you view e-mail messages. Messages that have plus boxes to the left of their summaries have replies to them; recall that these replies are called threads. Clicking a plus box displays the replies to the original message.

6. To reply to a message, click the message header in the newsgroups pane of the message to which you would like to reply, and then click the **Reply Group** button to reply to the group or click the **Reply** button to reply privately to the author of the original article.

7. To post a new article, click the **New Post** button on the toolbar to open the New Message window, where you can type a subject and the content of a new article. To send the article to the newsgroup, click the **Send** button.

8. When you have finished experimenting with reading, replying to, and sending messages to newsgroups, click **File** on the menu bar, and then click **Exit** to close Outlook Newsreader.

9. Close your browser, and if necessary, log off your Internet connection.

Because Outlook Newsreader is a part of Outlook Express, you can apply the skills you learned in Tutorial 3 for sending and replying to e-mail messages to sending and replying to newsgroup articles. You also already know how to save and print newsgroup articles because you performed these tasks for e-mail messages.

Netscape Mail

The Netscape Mail newsreader is included with the Netscape Communicator software suite as part of the Netscape Mail program that you use to send and receive e-mail messages. To use the newsreader, you start Mail. If you are viewing Web pages in Navigator, you can start Mail using the menu bar.

REFERENCE WINDOW   **RW**

Starting Netscape Mail
- Start Navigator.
- Click Tasks on the menu bar, and then click Mail & Newsgroups.

To start Netscape Mail and create a newsgroup account:

1. Click **Tasks** on the menu bar, and then click **Mail & Newsgroups**. Netscape Mail starts.

   TROUBLE? If you see the Mail command on the Tasks menu, click it instead of the Mail & Newsgroups command.

2. Click the **news** folder icon to open a list of newsgroups for your computer, as shown in Figure 8-23.

Figure 8-23	NETSCAPE MAIL

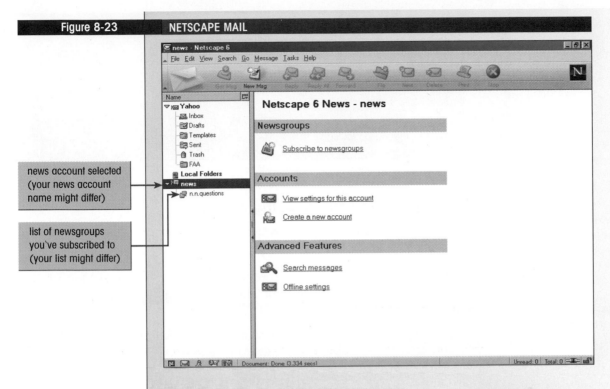

news account selected (your news account name might differ)

list of newsgroups you've subscribed to (your list might differ)

TROUBLE? The list of newsgroups that appears on your screen will be different from the list shown in Figure 8-23, depending on which newsgroups you and other computer users have selected.

TROUBLE? If you don't see the news folder in the Mail Folders pane, click Edit on the menu bar, click Mail & Newsgroups Account Settings (or Mail/News Account Settings), click the New Account button, and then follow the instructions in the Account Wizard dialog boxes to create a news account. The news server name is usually "news" followed by your ISP's domain name. After finishing the Account Wizard, click the news folder in the Mail Folders pane, click the Subscribe to newsgroups link, and then wait while Mail downloads the newsgroups on your news server. When all of the newsgroups have been downloaded, type news.newusers.questions in the Show items that contain text box, and then click the news.newusers.questions newsgroup in the search results that appears. Click the Subscribe button, and then click the OK button to close the Subscriptions dialog box.

TROUBLE? If your computer displays the error message "No NNTP server is configured," ask your instructor or technical support person to add the name of your host's news server to the Netscape installation on your computer.

You can use Mail to read, reply to, and create your own newsgroup articles. The news.misc newsgroup provides a place where new users can send test messages and otherwise become familiar with using newsgroups.

Reading and Sending Articles Using Mail
- Start Navigator.
- Click Tasks on the menu bar, and then click Mail & Newsgroups.
- In the Mail Folders pane, click the newsgroup that you would like to open.
- Click messages in the newsgroups pane to read them, or click the New Msg button on the Navigation toolbar button to send a message to the selected newsgroup.

To read and send articles using Mail:

1. Click the **Subscribe to newsgroups** link in the main window. The Subscribe dialog box opens.

   TROUBLE? If you haven't previously subscribed to any newsgroups, Mail will download them. Depending on your Internet connection speed, it could take up to several minutes to download the list.

   TROUBLE? If you are using Netscape Mail 6.1 or an earlier version, you will not see the "Subscribe to newsgroups" link in the main window. Click Edit on the menu bar, click Mail & Newsgroups Account Settings (or Mail/Newsgroups Account Settings), click the news category, click Server Settings, click the Ask me before downloading more than check box to select it, type 50 in the text box, and then click the OK button. Skip to Step 6.

2. Click in the **Show items that contain** text box, and then type **news.misc**. As you type, the list of newsgroups changes and eventually displays the news.misc newsgroup.

3. Click the **news.misc** newsgroup to select it, click the **Subscribe** button, and then click the **OK** button.

4. If necessary, click the **n.misc** newsgroup to select it. The Download Headers dialog box opens. Mail gives you the opportunity to limit the number of articles to download or to download all of them. To increase download time, you'll set the limit to 50 articles.

5. Make sure that the **Download 500 headers** option button is selected, select **500** (or the value in the text box), type **50**, and then click the **Download** button. The message list displays message summaries. When you click a message in the message list, its preview appears in the Message pane, as shown in Figure 8-24.

Figure 8-24 READING AN ARTCILE USING MAIL

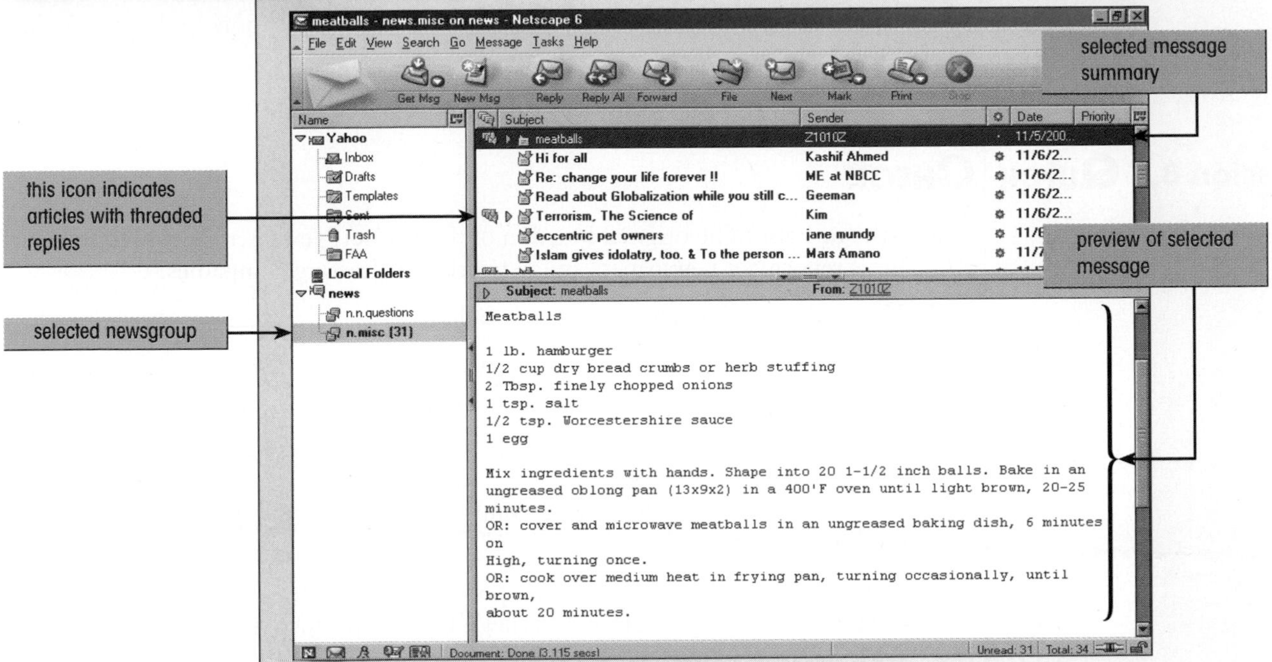

TROUBLE? The messages that appear in the list on your screen will be different from those that appear in Figure 8-24.

6. To reply to a message, click a message summary in the message list, click the **Reply All** button to post your reply to the entire newsgroup, or click the **Reply** button to send a private message to the message's original author. Messages that have icons in the first column of the message list have replies to them; recall that these replies are called threads. Clicking this icon displays the replies to the original message.

7. To post your own original message to the newsgroup, click the **New Msg** button, type a subject and a message, and then click the **Send** button.

8. When you have finished experimenting with reading, replying to, and sending messages to newsgroups, click **File** on the menu bar, and then click **Exit** to close Mail.

9. Close your browser, and if necessary, log off your Internet connection.

Because working with a newsgroup is similar to sending and receiving e-mail messages, you can apply the skills you learned in Tutorial 3 to working with newsgroups. You also already know how to save and print newsgroup articles because you performed these tasks for e-mail messages.

You are convinced that Usenet newsgroups can offer MFact an excellent vehicle for obtaining current information about the business environments in which its clients operate. You also believe that newsgroups will give MFact a way to obtain detailed information about rapidly changing opinions among consumers that will interest MFact's market research staff and MFact's clients. You can see how MFact can use newsgroups and chats to hold discussions among MFact employees and between MFact and its clients when scheduling online chat sessions or conference telephone calls is inconvenient.

Isaac is impressed with the information you gathered about Usenet newsgroups. Now you are ready to continue your work by preparing a report of your findings so Isaac can evaluate the usefulness of the Internet's advanced communication tools for conducting MFact focus groups.

Session 8.2 QUICK CHECK

1. True or False: The original function of the Usenet News Service was to transmit news reports for newspapers and network broadcasting companies.

2. Messages posted to a newsgroup are called _____.

3. A series of messages posted to a newsgroup that discuss the same subject is collectively called a(n) _____.

4. Most newsgroups allow anyone to post messages to the newsgroup. Some newsgroups, however, have a(n) _____ who reviews messages and only posts those messages that are relevant to the newsgroup's topic and/or from credible senders.

5. True or False: The news server computers in the Usenet network send newsfeeds to each other using a part of the Internet's TCP/IP protocol suite called the Network News Transfer Protocol (NNTP).

6. A friend tells you about some messages she read on the rec.autos.makers.honda newsgroup. What do you think is the focus of that newsgroup?

7. True or False: Most news servers in the Usenet network keep newsgroup messages for one year before deleting them.

8. _____ is a Web site that provides a search engine for finding newsgroups and newsgroup messages on specific topics.

9. To create a message or to reply to another user's message and post it to a newsgroup, you must use a(n) _____ program.

REVIEW ASSIGNMENTS

You met with Isaac and briefed him on what you learned about the Internet's communication tools. Isaac is pleased with the work you have done and is interested in learning more about each tool. He realizes that chat, virtual worlds, and newsgroups each offer MFact an opportunity to conduct advanced communications within the firm and with worldwide clients, but Isaac wonders whether the participation in these public forums is truly global. To assess the breadth of participation in chat, virtual worlds, and newsgroups, Isaac asks you to undertake a research project that will provide some measure of breadth of participation. You'll gather the research by completing the following steps.

1. Start your Web browser, open the Student Online Companion page at www.course.com/newperspectives/internet3, click the hyperlink for your book, click the Tutorial 8 link, and then click the Review Assignments link.

2. Click the Lycos Chat hyperlink, log on using the user name and password that you created in Session 8.2, and enter a chat room that you find interesting that has several participants currently logged on.

Explore   3. Join the chat session and ask participants where they are physically located. Write down the name of the country or, if in the United States, the name of the state in which three participants are located.

4. After you have collected some location names, exit the chat.

5. Start your newsreader program from your browser.

6. Open the news.misc newsgroup.

Explore   7. Examine 10 or 20 of the postings to see if you can determine the country of the messages' origins and write down any origins that you can identify.

8. Close your newsreader and your browser, and if necessary, log off your Internet connection.

Explore   9. Prepare a short summary of your findings.

CASE PROBLEMS

Case 1. Rockin' Tees   Laura Jensen is president of Rockin' Tees, a small manufacturer of printed t-shirts that specializes in creating designs using images of popular rock bands and solo artists. Rockin' Tees either must purchase the rights to use band and solo artist names and likenesses or must agree to pay negotiated per-shirt royalties to them. Therefore, Rockin' Tees must estimate the demand for their t-shirt designs before they negotiate with the artists' agents and agree to payment terms. You'll prepare a report for Laura by completing the following steps.

1. Start your Web browser, open the Student Online Companion page at www.course.com/newperspectives/internet3, click the hyperlink for your book, click the Tutorial 8 link, and then click the Case Problems link.

2. Click the Yahoo! Chat link, and then locate and click the link to the Music chat category.

Explore   3. Explore the hyperlinks on the Yahoo! Chat page and examine some of the Web sites to which they lead. Remember that you are collecting information for Laura, so keep focused on her research question.

4. Close your browser, and if necessary, log off your Internet connection.

Explore   5. Write a short memo that explains how Laura might use surveys of Web chat activity on some of the chat sites you found to estimate the popularity of a particular band or solo artist.

Case 2. Southern State University   Del Valerio is a professor of foreign languages at Southern State University (SSU). SSU has been facing budget cuts the past few years, and Del is concerned that the quality of foreign language instruction might be suffering at SSU. He is looking for inexpensive ways to improve students' exposure to written and spoken foreign languages. New audio and video tapes for the language lab have become very expensive, and additional reading materials written in foreign languages have just been cut from the library's budget for next year. You'll use the Internet to find new language resources for Del by completing the following steps.

1. Start your Web browser, open the Student Online Companion page at www.course.com/newperspectives/internet3, click the hyperlink for your book, click the Tutorial 8 link, and then click the Case Problems link.

2. Click the Lingua MOO link, and then examine the contents and links on that Web site.

Explore →   3. Prepare a one-page report describing what a MOO-based virtual world site might offer the SSU foreign languages program. Be sure to address Del's budget concerns in your report.

4. Close your browser, and if necessary, log off your Internet connection.

Case 3. West Park Employment Agency Elaine Tagliaferri is the owner of the West Park Employment Agency. Elaine is always looking for new sources of employment leads and regularly scans the local and regional newspaper help-wanted ads. Unfortunately, most jobs that become available are never advertised. To identify these potential opportunities, Elaine also tries to stay aware of new businesses and larger firms that are moving their operations to the area. You'll help Elaine find new job sources by completing the following steps.

1. Start your Web browser, open the Student Online Companion page at www.course.com/newperspectives/internet3, click the hyperlink for your book, click the Tutorial 8 link, and then click the Case Problems link.

2. Click the Google Groups link.

Explore →   3. Assume that the West Park Employment Agency is located in your city or town. Browse through the newsgroup postings indexed at the Google Groups Web site and identify three articles that provide leads that you would recommend to Elaine.

Explore →   4. For one of the articles you identify, write a short reply to the posting's author or to the newsgroup. Do not send the message, but include it with copies of the three messages in a short report to your instructor.

5. Close your browser, and if necessary, log off your Internet connection.

Case 4. Triangle Research Dan Rivetti is the director of Triangle Research, a small laboratory that tests metal parts and assemblies using physical and computer models. Usually, Dan knows enough about the general design of the parts and assemblies that he can develop the testing procedures. Sometimes, however, he would like to conduct background research and contact experts in the field before designing his testing procedures. Dan has heard that Usenet newsgroups might offer the information and the opportunity to post inquiries that he desires, but he has also heard that some newsgroups are more reliable than others. You'll help Dan evaluate the quality of some newsgroups by completing the following steps.

1. Start your Web browser, open the Student Online Companion page at www.course.com/newperspectives/internet3, click the hyperlink for your book, click the Tutorial 8 link, and then click the Case Problems link.

2. Click the Tile.net Newsgroups link. On the page that opens, click the Newsgroup Hierarchy link. The page that opens displays a bulleted list of numbers and the letters of the alphabet. To examine the science newsgroups, scroll down the page as necessary and then click the S link.

Explore →   3. Examine and follow some of the links beginning with "sci" (for science) on the Web page that opens. You are searching for newsgroups that might be of interest to Dan.

4. Select one moderated and one unmoderated newsgroup that might be of interest to Dan. Click the URL link on the description pages to load the messages in your news-reader program.

5. Examine a sample of messages from each type of newsgroup devoted to your topics.

6. Close your browser, and if necessary, log off your Internet connection.

Explore ▶

7. Prepare a short report describing the differences you found between the postings in the moderated and unmoderated newsgroups. Include an explanation of which type of newsgroup would best serve Dan's needs.

Case 5. NASA Reunion Committee Buck Sherman worked for NASA in Houston, Texas for several years during the Apollo space program. The challenging work and long hours of the tight-knit group of programmers, engineers, and people in other technical specialties produced many friendships that have endured over time and great geographic distances. Many of the Apollo programmers went on to follow careers in the space program, aeronautics, engineering, and computer programming. On several occasions, Buck has tried to arrange for a reunion but it has been difficult arranging a convenient time, date, and location for the group to meet. Buck wonders if the Internet might be an appropriate way for group members to stay in touch on a regular basis, without requiring specific software or meeting times. You'll help Buck investigate the creation of an MSN Community for the Apollo space team by completing the following steps.

1. Start your Web browser, open the Student Online Companion page at www.course.com/newperspectives/internet3, click the hyperlink for your book, click the Tutorial 8 link, and then click the Case Problems link.

2. Click the MSN Communities link.

3. Click the Browse by Category link, which should appear below or close to the Find a Community text box.

Explore ▶

4. Use the Browse Communities Web page to locate a community that might be similar in focus to the community that Buck wants to create. Point to the icons to the left of each community name to learn their meanings. See if you can find two public communities that deal with reunions or professional associations.

Explore ▶

5. Click a link to one of the communities that you located and then explore the community without interacting with it.

6. Click the Help link near the top of the Communities page (it appears with the hyperlinks "Home" and "My Communities" on the left side of the page). The MSN Communities window opens and lists Help topics.

Explore ▶

7. Use the MSN Communities window Help topics to learn more about MSN Communities. Remember that you are trying to determine the effectiveness of a community for the Apollo group.

Explore ▶

8. Using your experience with the community that you explored and resources of the Help system, answer the following questions in a memo:

   a. Explain the way that members access a community. Do they need special software? Do they need to sign in using a user name and/or password?
   b. What is the basic procedure for creating a community?
   c. What is the difference between a private and public community?
   d. How would Buck invite people to join the community?

9. Close your browser, and if necessary, log off your Internet connection.

Explore ▶

10. Using the information you found in Steps 5 and 8, would a community be a good way to continue friendships with the members of the Apollo group? Support your recommendation.

QUICK CHECK ANSWERS

Session 8.1

1. lurking
2. True
3. False
4. Advantages: Do not need Telnet or IRC client software, messages can include multimedia elements and hyperlinks, GUI can be easier to use. Disadvantages: Must reload page to obtain new messages.
5. reload or refresh
6. adventure
7. False
8. avatar

Session 8.2

1. False
2. articles or postings
3. thread
4. moderator
5. True
6. The newsgroup's focus is probably on the features and styling of automobiles made by Honda.
7. False
8. Tile.net or Google Groups
9. newsreader

OBJECTIVES

In this tutorial you will:

- Learn how to enhance your Web browser capabilities with browser extensions

- Discover where to locate popular browser extensions for Microsoft Internet Explorer and Netscape Navigator

- Visit a Web site where you can test a plug-in

- Investigate Internet security and learn about secrecy, integrity, necessity, and privacy

- Identify several ways to defend against security risks

- Learn about copyright and intellectual property rights on the Internet

LABS

Multimedia

ADVANCED WEB TOPICS

Browser Extensions and Internet Security

Remes Video Productions

Remes Video Productions (RVP) is a full-service, video-production company that specializes in producing training and safety videos. RVP also contracts for smaller jobs, such as producing wedding and family-reunion videos and other non-business events. Located In Eagan, Minnesota, RVP's business has grown steadily since Mark Remes, the company's CEO, founded it in 1997. Mark has acquired video cameras and sophisticated editing equipment to create pro-fessional-quality video productions.

Mark wants to expand his business outside the Minneapolis/St. Paul area with the goal of increasing sales by 25% next year. One way to increase video-production sales is to increase RVP's market visibility, especially among potential clients who travel to the Minnesota area for weddings, vacations, and business events to enjoy the moderate summer climate. Mark has used print advertising successfully in the past, but now he needs to reach a larger audience. He is particularly interested in using the Internet to market RVP to all of Minnesota, its surrounding states, and the central provinces of Canada.

Mark has hired you as a consultant, and your first job is to create a plan for a future Web presence with Web pages containing samples of RVP productions. These pages will include graphics, video clips, and sounds to showcase RVP's work and provide sample material for potential clients to examine. At first, Mark only wants you to help him understand the current capabilities of Web browsers to deliver rich and diverse Web content to potential clients. Mark knows that Web browsers can handle graphics, sounds, and movies but he is unsure of what steps potential clients might need to take to access this con-tent. He wants you to research and install the types of browser enhancements needed to view dynamic content. Mark is also inter-ested in visiting Web sites that contain movies and content similar to what he is planning to include on the RVP Web site. If Web site visitors will require any special software to view the content of the RVP Web site, Mark wants to make it easy for them to download it.

Because the RVP Web site will include sample RVP productions, Mark wants to make sure that these productions are protected from illegal use. In addition, Mark is planning to create a Web page that will let clients use a credit card to pay the required 20% down payment to reserve a date and time for their productions. Mark is concerned about the security of his clients' personal information and wants you to research these and other possible threats unique to conducting business over the Internet.

SESSION 9.1

In this session, you will learn about, find, and use browser extensions. You will visit download sites that include downloadable browser plug-ins and other browser accessories. Finally, you will learn about and visit Web sites where you can test your installed browser extensions.

Browser Extensions

Originally, Web browsers displayed only text and simple graphics. Very quickly, developers expressed a desire for more Web page features, such as sound and animation. However, these features were then, and still are, beyond the capabilities of the HTML language that creates Web pages. Because of HTML limitations, companies developed their own software to enhance the capabilities of Web browsers. These enhancements, called **browser extensions**, allow a Web browser to perform tasks it was not originally designed to perform. **Browser extension players** deliver content to an end user. For example, browser extensions might deliver and play audio clips or display movies. Some browser extensions are called **plug-ins**; in this category you'll find programs that a browser starts to display or play a specific file. Other browser extensions are called **helper applications** or **helper apps**, because they "help" a browser to display or play a file.

What Are Plug-ins and Helper Applications?

Plug-ins differ slightly from helper applications in the way they run. Whereas both plug-ins and helper applications enhance browsers and extend their capabilities, helper applications are independent programs that are stored on your computer and are activated automatically when needed. Plug-ins, on the other hand, do their work *inside* the browser and do not activate a standalone program that is stored on your computer. Many plug-ins began as helper applications; in fact, several helper applications have been reissued as plug-ins because they provide seamless activation from inside a browser. Another difference is that unlike helper apps, plug-ins cannot execute by themselves. Plug-ins are not independent programs; they can start only from within a browser. Helper apps, on the other hand, are useful on their own. For example, a spreadsheet program can function as a helper application when a browser starts it to display a spreadsheet. When a browser encounters a MIDI sound file, the browser might start a MIDI player helper application on your computer to play it. Because your computer probably has many helper applications already installed, this tutorial concentrates on plug-ins, which are not always installed on your computer but are useful for displaying a variety of file formats that you will encounter as you browse the Internet.

When you install a Web browser, many popular plug-ins are often installed with it. When you encounter a Web page that requires a plug-in you do not have, you will see a message that the plug-in is required to view the page or specific content on that page. If you do not have the required plug-in, you can download or purchase it. The majority of plug-ins—and all of the plug-ins featured in this tutorial—are free from the plug-ins' developers.

You might wonder why most plug-ins are free. The developers offering free browser plug-ins often charge a fee for the plug-in content-development programs or for their server programs designed to *deliver* multimedia content. Plug-in content-development programs are required to *create* content using that technology so Web browsers have a file they can view or play. For example, Real.com offers a free plug-in named RealPlayer that plays streaming audio files over the Internet. (Remember from Tutorial 5 that streaming is a technology that delivers a continuous flow of information from the server to your browser and allows you to play the information—audio, video, etc.—*before* the entire file has been downloaded to your browser.) Streaming can reduce the time required to play a file from several minutes to several seconds. RealPlayer works with most Web browsers to play video clips, music, and streaming media formats on the Web. Real.com also sells RealOne Player, which includes the basic features found in RealPlayer plus access to additional multimedia features and richer content, including content from major network news and entertainment sources. Real.com also licenses server software that companies can install on their Web servers. The server-side software helps to deliver the streaming information. This arrangement works well because the Web browsing public can download and install free or inexpensive plug-ins that enhance their Web experiences, and developers can include attractive and rich content on their Web sites that will attract and appeal to customers.

How Do Plug-ins Operate?

Each time you start your browser, it checks your computer to see which plug-ins you have installed. As you move from one Web site to another, your browser will encounter links that refer to files whose file extensions are *not* .htm or .html, which are the universal extensions for Web pages. Instead, your browser might encounter .mp3 or .mov files, for example. If your browser cannot interpret a filename that you click, it usually will prompt you to save the file on your computer. If you have a plug-in that can interpret the filename you clicked, the plug-in will execute the appropriate action. For instance, if you click a link with the extension .mov (for a QuickTime movie file), the QuickTime plug-in starts, downloads the file, and plays the movie within the Web page—all automatically. If your browser doesn't have the QuickTime plug-in, you might see instructions for downloading the plug-in or only the file.

How Do You Know When You Need a Plug-in?

When you are browsing the Web, you might encounter Web pages indicating that you need a specific plug-in to view or hear the page's content. If you do not have the required plug-in to play the content, nothing happens; you see only what your Web browser can activate, without hearing a sound or seeing a video. For example, Figure 9-1 shows a Web page that displays animation and three-dimensional views of a scene. The user's browser is missing a required plug-in; a broken link icon appears in an empty frame instead of the scene that a plug-in would display. When you see icons or empty frames similar to the ones that appear in Figure 9-1, you know that you are missing a plug-in.

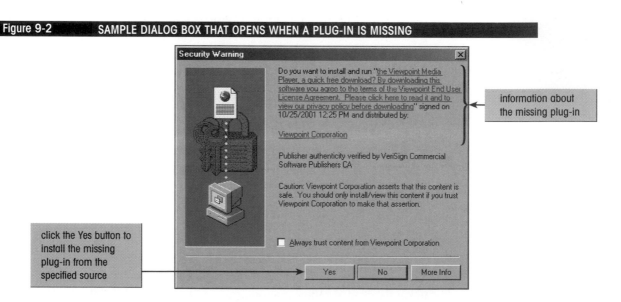

Figure 9-1 — WEB PAGE REQUIRING A PLUG-IN THAT IS NOT CURRENTLY INSTALLED

icon and empty frame indicate that a plug-in needed to display this object is missing

When you click the object shown in Figure 9-1, Figure 9-2 shows the dialog box that opens and provides information about the missing plug-in and where to obtain it. When you view pages requiring plug-ins that your browser does not have, you miss some or all of the richness of the page supplied by the plug-in.

Figure 9-2 — SAMPLE DIALOG BOX THAT OPENS WHEN A PLUG-IN IS MISSING

information about the missing plug-in

click the Yes button to install the missing plug-in from the specified source

Locating Missing Plug-ins

When you encounter a file that your browser cannot execute, it cannot perform the operation required by the file, such as playing an audio file or displaying animation. In some cases, your browser might automatically open a dialog box and then describe where to acquire or how to install the missing plug-in. When this occurs, the browser might open a site where you can download the missing plug-in; usually, this site is the plug-in developer's site. Most Web pages that include content that a plug-in must display or play usually contain a link to the site where you can download the required plug-in. For example, Figure 9-3 shows a Web page that requires the Shockwave Player plug-in. When you click the Shockwave link, your browser will open the Shockwave developer's Web site so you can download the Shockwave Player plug-in. The Shockwave Player plug-in plays movies, animations, interactive games, slide shows, streaming audio, and background music that are required to view the Web page correctly.

Figure 9-3	WEB PAGE THAT REQUIRES SHOCKWAVE

this page might download Shockwave automatically if your browser doesn't have it

link to download the Shockwave Player if you need to install it

When you upgrade your browser to a newer version, you might lose many or all of the plug-ins that you have installed; in some cases, when you upgrade to a new browser version, it might automatically install plug-ins that you previously had to install yourself. For example, recent versions of Netscape Navigator include plug-ins to run Java applets and Macromedia Flash for displaying Web content. As plug-ins become popular and essential for Web browsing, most browser developers change the browser so these plug-ins are installed automatically.

Browser Extension Categories

Mark is interested in examining many browser extension types to locate the right mix to build a professional Web site for RVP. You want to investigate each of the extension categories and see how other Web sites use them to design effective Web presences. Because many browser extensions are available today, it is helpful to group them into the following categories.

- Document and productivity
- Image viewer
- Multimedia
- Sound player
- Video player
- VRML and 3-D

Because RVP is a video-production company, Mark wants its Web site to reflect the same high-quality presentations reflected in its video productions. Mark is particularly interested in evaluating the latest plug-ins that will let potential clients see and hear sample RVP productions of commercial-quality training and safety videos and a variety of private family events.

Document and Productivity Browser Extensions

Document and productivity browser extensions let you use a browser to read documents, such as files saved in PDF format and viewed using Adobe Acrobat Reader. If your browser has Acrobat Reader installed, it can display and print files with .pdf extensions. If your computer has Microsoft Office installed, the browser can start Word, Excel, and other Office programs to display files with Office file extensions, such as .doc and .xls. Other examples of browser extensions in this category are worksheet manipulation and display programs and forms for data entry. For example, Internet Explorer usually uses Excel as a helper application to display worksheet files. Actuate e.Spreadsheets provide an alternative way to handle Web spreadsheets, which are identified with a special secondary name. Accelio Corporation has developed a plug-in that processes electronic forms and automates business processes on the Internet.

Image Viewer Browser Extensions

Web extensions that fall into the **image viewer** category let the browser display graphics, such as interactive road maps or alternative file formats and viewers for GIF and JPEG files. Autodesk developed a plug-in to display line drawings in the proprietary Drawing Web format. iPIX lets you view an area from all angles by panning an image left, right, up, or down to see it from the sky or ground or to turn it in a circle. Real estate agents use iPIX to display a 360-degree view of the rooms in a house they have listed for sale so potential buyers can use the agent's Web site to view a home's interior design and features.

Image viewer plug-ins also display different picture file formats. You can find several different image formats on the Web; no single format is dominant, so you will need more than one graphic viewer on your computer to view the different kinds of pictures you'll encounter in Web sites. You can wait to download each graphic viewer until you encounter Web sites that indicate you need it to enjoy the site.

Multimedia Browser Extensions

Multimedia, perhaps the largest category of browser extensions, contains browser extensions that appeal to most of the senses. Macromedia Shockwave and Flash both provide animation for images, games, and other animated content on the Web. You can use your browser and the Shockwave and Flash Players to play interactive games, view animated interfaces, listen to streaming CD-quality audio music and speech, and view instructional presentations.

Shockwave

Shockwave is a browser plug-in that provides animated interfaces, interactive advertisements and product demonstrations, multiuser games, and streaming CD-quality audio. Some instructors use Shockwave to deliver audio instruction and interact with students as they would in the classroom. Shockwave is a very popular plug-in; according to Macromedia, people download the software at a rate of nearly 200,000 copies per day. Because Shockwave uses streaming technology, you do not have to wait for an entire audio file to download before playing it—the animation or sound plays almost immediately. Figure 9-4 shows an example of a Shockwave-enhanced game. Shockwave provides animation and sound for this game produced by The Groove Alliance.

Figure 9-4	SHOCKWAVE-ENHANCED WEB GAME

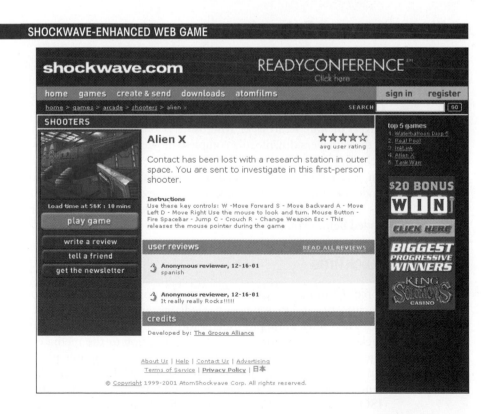

Flash

Flash is another popular plug-in that lets your Web browser display high-impact user interfaces, interactive online advertising, and animation. According to Macromedia, over 414 million Web users rely on Flash to display animated content as they browse the Web. Because of Flash's popularity, it is installed automatically with Internet Explorer and Navigator so you can begin using it immediately.

Sound Player Browser Extensions

Sound player browser extensions, such as Beatnik, Crescendo, and RealPlayer, let your Web browser play sounds. Many extensions, including Crescendo and Beatnik, play CD-quality streaming audio. RealPlayer and RealOne Player are widely distributed and play audio over a variety of slow and fast connections ranging from 56.6K modems to faster cable modems.

Beatnik, Crescendo, and RealPlayer are examples of Web audio players that play sound files stored in various formats. Beatnik and Crescendo deliver high-quality interactive music and sound on the Web, whereas RealPlayer delivers MIDI music in very small file sizes. In addition, Beatnik can embed copyright information in the delivered audio files by using an encrypted character string that is hidden within the music file. The embedded information is similar to a watermark on a sheet of paper.

Besides supporting its native Rich Music Format (RMF) files, Beatnik supports the commonly used Web audio formats of MIDI, WAV, and AIFF. RealPlayer, once known as RealAudio, plays streaming audio and video on the Web, though the music is less than CD quality. RealPlayer provides a feature called **buffered play**, in which music is downloaded and queued for play when the transfer/play rate exceeds your modem's speed.

Video Player Browser Extensions

Video player browser extensions deliver movies to Web browsers over the Internet. When you click a movie link, the movie downloads and begins playing in its own window. QuickTime, which makes video, sound, music, 3-D, and virtual reality come alive on both Macintoshes and PCs, was one of the first movie players developed. Other successful movie players include RealPlayer, Microsoft Windows Media Player, and VivoActive Player. Some of these players download a complete movie before playing it, whereas others use streaming technology to play a movie before it has been completely downloaded. Several video players can play either live downloads or on-demand files, such as movie files. If you are using a modem to play a movie, you'll want to use one of the players that can play the file before it has been completely downloaded, so you don't have to wait for the entire file to be downloaded before you can start viewing it.

QuickTime

Apple Computer's **QuickTime** technology plays video, sound, and music for both Macintoshes and PCs almost immediately after clicking the link containing a sound or video file. The QuickTime proprietary format allows developers to store video frames and audio tracks and also to store a complete description of the media composition. One key advantage of the QuickTime movie format is that it is computer-platform neutral; that is, it works equally well on Windows, Macintosh, and UNIX systems. Another advantage is that the QuickTime format is a widely accepted format. The International Standards Organization (ISO) adopted Apple's QuickTime file format as the starting point for developing an improved and unified digital media storage format for the MPEG-4 specification, which plays audio and visual applications on wireless devices. Figure 9-5 shows links to some sample QuickTime movies; you can click the Movie link in the Additional Information section of the Student Online Companion page for Tutorial 9 to visit this site. (You must install a movie viewer plug-in to see the movies; check with your instructor or technical support person before downloading and installing any plug-in on a public computer.)

| Figure 9-5 | QUICKTIME MOVIES |

clicking a thumbnail downloads the QuickTime movie and plays it if your browser has the required QuickTime plug-in

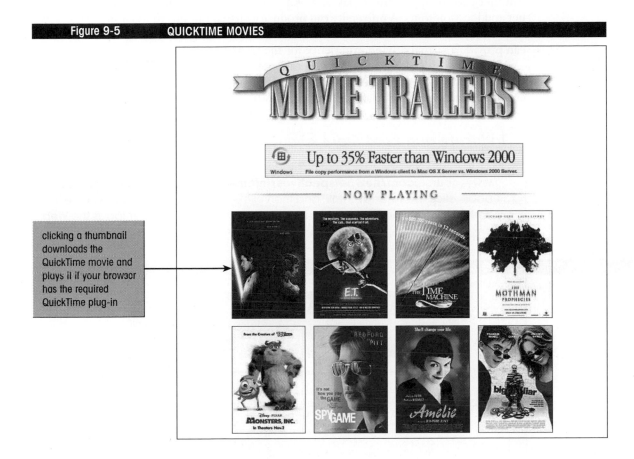

VRML and 3-D Browser Extensions

Virtual Reality Modeling Language or **VRML** (pronounced "ver-muhl") is an Internet programming language that creates three-dimensional environments that can mimic known worlds or define fictional ones. With VRML, you can navigate and interact with a three-dimensional scene. VRML plug-ins permit your Web browser to interact with and move through a scene by opening doors, rotating the view to show the landscape behind you, and then moving ahead. VRML modelers can create fictional planetary environments complete with red skies and harmful vegetation, or a realistic three-dimensional tour of the human brain for medical students. Special VRML browsers work alongside your browser, which reads only HTML documents and not VRML files, to wander through a VRML-enabled site. Your Web browser automatically detects a VRML-enabled site and starts the VRML browser extension required to produce the VRML content. More than display screens, VRML browsers and VRML browser extensions are three-dimensional generating engines containing navigation controls that allow you to explore a three-dimensional landscape and investigate its objects.

Cosmo Player

Cosmo Player is a VRML player from Silicon Graphics that lets you experience three-dimensional Web worlds without having special three-dimensional graphics acceleration hardware installed on your computer. VRML sites are often set up so game players can wander through fictional three-dimensional worlds and interact with objects they encounter. Another class of applications that take advantage of a VRML player's capabilities are product and location tours. A university can produce a virtual campus tour, allowing the observer to turn any direction and walk around and through buildings. An automobile manufacturer can provide a virtual driving experience for the viewer.

Mark asks you to find some Web sites that explain more about VRML technology, as he might explore this technology as a production method in the future. You decide to use a search engine to find sites that explain browsing with VRML and creating virtual-reality sites.

To locate and read more about VRML on the Web:

1. Start your Web browser, open the Student Online Companion page at **www.course.com/newperspectives/internet3**, click the hyperlink for your book, click the **Tutorial 9** link, and then click the **Session 9.1** link. Click the **Web3D Repository** hyperlink and wait while your Web browser loads the Web page shown in Figure 9-6.

Figure 9-6   THE WEB3D REPOSITORY WEB PAGE

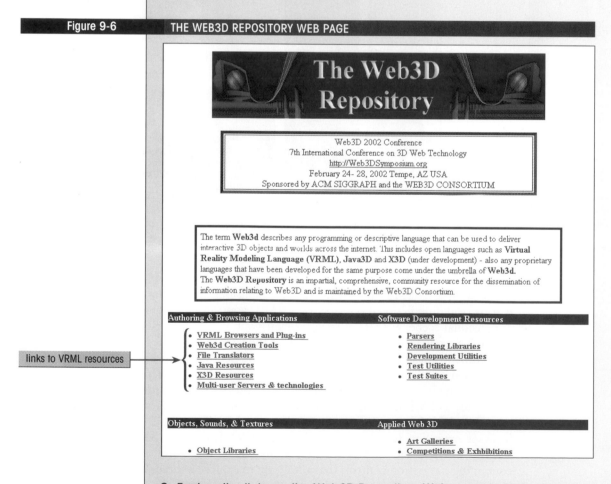

2. Explore the links on the Web3D Repository Web page to find out more about virtual-reality applications.

Mark is impressed with the opportunities offered by virtual-reality sites. He wants to study virtual-reality and VRML browser extensions more before making a decision about whether to use the technology.

Finding Browser Extensions

Now that you know about the general categories of browser extensions, you need a way to locate them. You can find and download browser extensions from different Web sites; in fact, many browser extension developers store extensions on their own Web sites. Some Web sites, such as DOWNLOAD.COM, CNET, and Yahoo!, include searchable collections of links to browser extensions grouped by category or the functions they perform. Some of these sites indicate the number of times people have downloaded each one, which acts as a popularity ranking. Some sites also provide reliability rankings and links to each product. The Additional Information section of the Student Online Companion page for Tutorial 9 contains links to several Web sites containing searchable lists of browser extensions.

Because you want to show Mark the variety of available plug-ins, you decide to locate and examine some of the plug-in download sites. You are especially interested in the audio, video, and multimedia plug-ins and their reliability ratings. You decide to start by visiting the CNET Internet Services page.

To search for plug-ins on the CNET site:

1. Use your browser's **Back** button to return to the Student Online Companion page for Session 9.1, and then click the **CNET Internet Services** link and wait while the browser opens the page.

2. Click in the **Search** text box near the top of the page, type **plug-ins**, and then click the **Go!** button.

3. On the page that opens, click the **Browser plug-ins** link, which appears in the Best Bets section. The Plug-ins page opens and lists plug-ins in descending order by the date the software was added to the list.

4. Click the **Downloads** link in the Plug-in section to sort the list in descending order based on the number of times each item has been downloaded, as shown in Figure 9-7. (Your page might look different because the plug-ins and their statistics change over time.)

Figure 9-7

CNET PLUG-INS SORTED BY DOWNLOAD COUNT

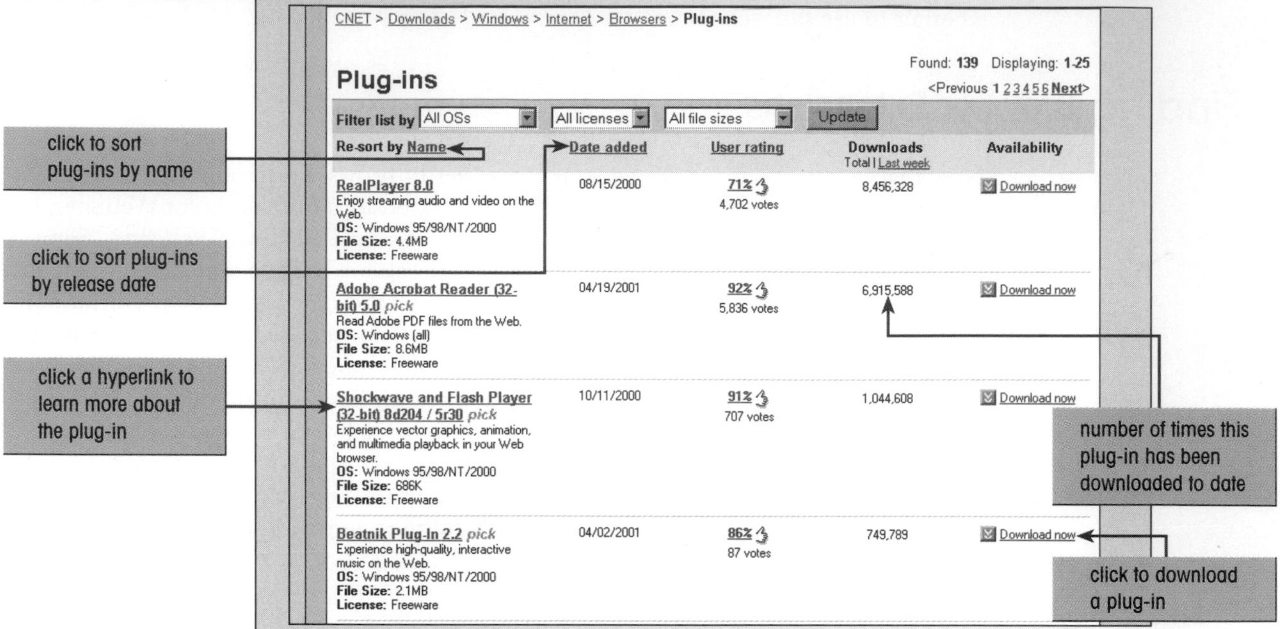

CNET > Downloads > Windows > Internet > Browsers > **Plug-ins**

Plug-ins

Found: **139** Displaying: **1-25**

<Previous 1 2 3 4 5 6 **Next**>

Filter list by All OSs ▼   All licenses ▼   All file sizes ▼   Update

Re-sort by <u>Name</u> ◄ — — ► <u>Date added</u>   <u>User rating</u>   **Downloads**   **Availability**
                                                                Total | <u>Last week</u>

click to sort plug-ins by name

click to sort plug-ins by release date

click a hyperlink to learn more about the plug-in

RealPlayer 8.0 Enjoy streaming audio and video on the Web. **OS:** Windows 95/98/NT/2000 **File Size:** 4.4MB **License:** Freeware	08/15/2000	<u>71%</u> ⬆ 4,702 votes	8,456,328	☑ Download now
Adobe Acrobat Reader (32-bit) 5.0 *pick* Read Adobe PDF files from the Web. **OS:** Windows (all) **File Size:** 8.6MB **License:** Freeware	04/19/2001	<u>92%</u> ⬆ 5,836 votes	6,915,588	☑ Download now
Shockwave and Flash Player (32-bit) 8d204 / 5r30 *pick* Experience vector graphics, animation, and multimedia playback in your Web browser. **OS:** Windows 95/98/NT/2000 **File Size:** 686K **License:** Freeware	10/11/2000	<u>91%</u> ⬆ 707 votes	1,044,608	☑ Download now
Beatnik Plug-In 2.2 *pick* Experience high-quality, interactive music on the Web. **OS:** Windows 95/98/NT/2000 **File Size:** 2.1MB **License:** Freeware	04/02/2001	<u>86%</u> ⬆ 87 votes	749,789	☑ Download now ◄

number of times this plug-in has been downloaded to date

click to download a plug-in

5. As you scroll down the page, notice the number of times that each plug-in has been downloaded. The Date added and Downloads columns indicate each plug-in's release date and popularity, respectively. Clicking a column heading sorts the list based on the contents of the column. If you scroll to the bottom of the page, you can use the list boxes in the Filter list by section to select an operating system, software class (Demo, Free, or Shareware), or file size and to display software filtered using these criteria.

One of the advantages of the CNET Web site is that you can sort the plug-ins list in different orders. If you want to see the most popular plug-ins, sort the plug-ins by download count. If you want to locate a plug-in by name, sort the list in alphabetical order.

You can also search for plug-ins and information about them by using an Internet search engine. Using a search term such as "plug-ins" will yield many sources of plug-ins. You will find it a much simpler task to review and download browser plug-ins and other extensions if you use a site that specializes in them. Another good source for plug-ins is Tucows, which groups plug-ins by the functions they perform.

To search for plug-ins on the Tucows site:

1. Use your browser's **Back** button to return to the Student Online Companion page for Session 9.1, and then click the **Tucows** hyperlink and wait while your browser loads the Web page.

2. Click the **Windows** link to select that operating system.

3. If necessary, use the list box for your country to select the state or region in which you live or the one closest to you.

4. If a list of other regions or states appears, select a site closest to you. The Welcome to Tucows Web page opens and displays featured downloads for the Windows operating system.

5. Click the **Internet** tab near the top of the page. The Tucows Internet Software page opens and displays a list of categories for Internet software, as shown in Figure 9-8.

Figure 9-8   TUCOWS INTERNET SOFTWARE PAGE

Internet tab

Web Browser
Add-ons link

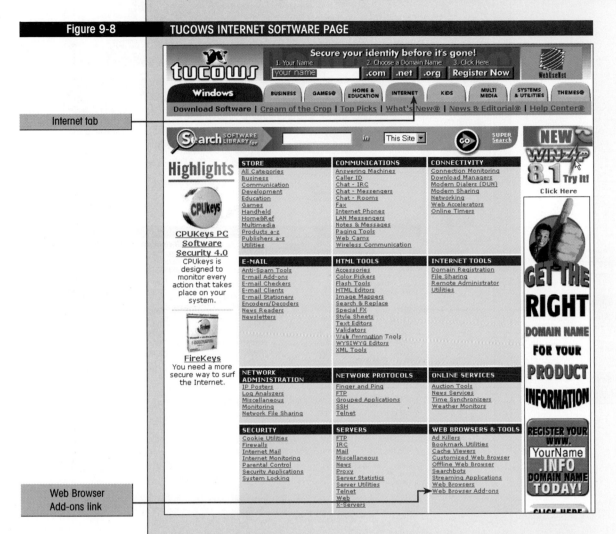

6. Scroll down the page as necessary, locate the Web Browsers & Tools category, and then click the **Web Browser Add-ons** link. A page opens and lists browser plug-ins alphabetically by title, as shown in Figure 9-9. For each plug-in, Tucows lists the title and version number, release date, type of license, rating, and file size.

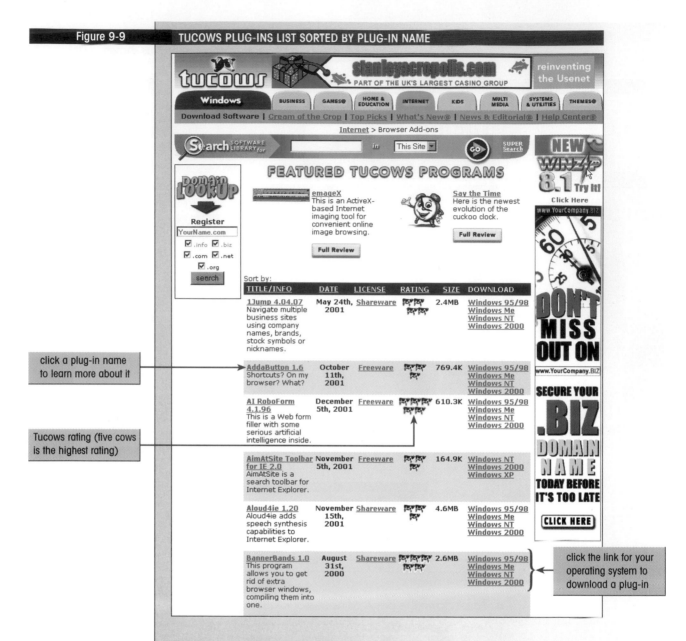

Figure 9-9   TUCOWS PLUG-INS LIST SORTED BY PLUG-IN NAME

click a plug-in name to learn more about it

Tucows rating (five cows is the highest rating)

click the link for your operating system to download a plug-in

7. As you scroll down the page, notice all of the different plug-ins that you can download from Tucows. The last column includes links to download the plug-in for the operating system you are using. (At this time, you will not download any plug-ins.)

Mark is impressed by the variety of plug-ins available on the Tucows Web site. By organizing the plug-ins into categories, it is easy to locate the items he needs. The BrowserWatch Web site organizes its available plug-ins by function, such as multimedia, graphics, sound, document and productivity, and VRML/3-D. The Full List category includes all of the plug-ins available from the entire site. For example, if Mark needs a plug-in that plays a specific audio file format, he can narrow his search quickly by clicking the Sound category. To make sure Mark is familiar with this categorization of plug-ins, you decide to demonstrate the BrowserWatch Web site to him and identify plug-ins in the multimedia category because they will be an integral part of the RVP Web site.

To view multimedia plug-ins on the BrowserWatch Web site:

1. Return to the Student Online Companion Web page for Session 9.1, and then click the **BrowserWatch** hyperlink and wait while your Web browser loads the BrowserWatch home page.

2. On the left side of the page in the Features box, click the **Plug-In Plaza!** link. The BrowserWatch Plug-In Plaza Web page shown in Figure 9-10 opens and groups plug-ins by category and platform.

| Figure 9-10 | BROWSERWATCH PLUG-IN PLAZA WEB PAGE |

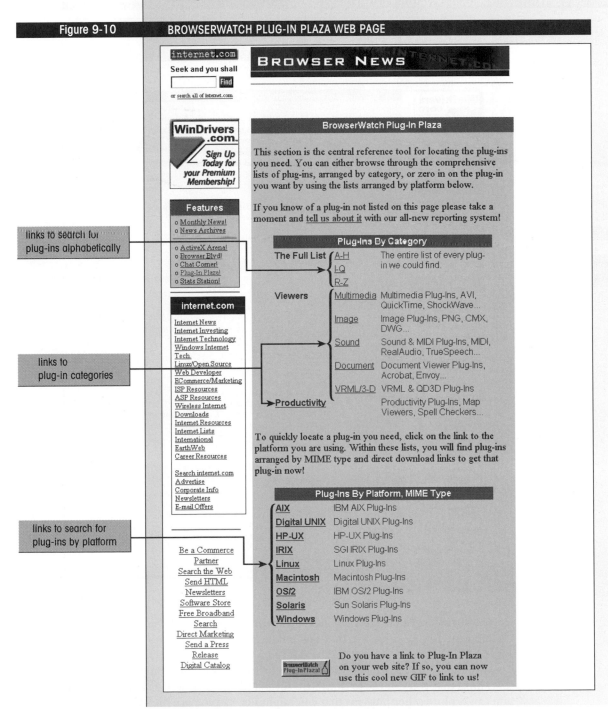

links to search for plug-ins alphabetically

links to plug-in categories

links to search for plug-ins by platform

3. Click the **Multimedia** link in the Plug-Ins By Category list to open a page containing a list of multimedia plug-ins arranged in alphabetical order.

4. As you scroll down the page, notice that each plug-in includes the name, developer, URL, and a link to a page that contains a sample file that the plug-in can play. Figure 9-11 shows an example of several multimedia plug-ins; your list of plug-ins might differ.

Figure 9-11   BROWSERWATCH MULTIMEDIA PLUG-INS

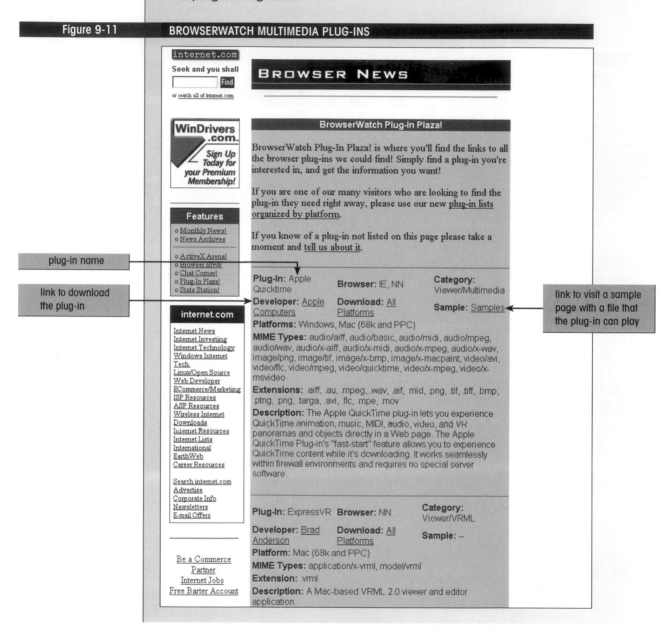

The BrowserWatch Web site lets you narrow your search for plug-ins by clicking a plug-in category. If you know the first few characters of the plug-in's name, you can click The Full List link and scroll down to the desired plug-in.

The Additional Information section of the Student Online Companion for Tutorial 9 contains links that you can use to download several plug-ins, as well as links to download sites, so you can explore other plug-ins that you might need as you use the Web. You are satisfied that you can locate browser extensions using the three download sites you visited. Now that you can find these plug-ins, Mark has identified the ones that he would like for you to download and install.

Installing and Testing Browser Extensions

After you locate browser extensions and download them to your computer, the next step is to install them. When you download a plug-in, you will need to install it by following the instructions provided on the developer's Web site. To install a plug-in, you usually double-click the downloaded file and then follow the on-screen instructions.

Note: If you are using a university or other public computer, you should check with your instructor or technical support person before downloading and installing any software on that computer. This textbook does *not* require you to install plug-in software to understand how to use it. If you are downloading software to your own computer, then you can decide to download and install it. However, you should know that some plug-ins are unreliable and can damage your computer. In the next section, you will learn how to install and test plug-ins, but you should not install the plug-ins on a public computer without proper authorization. Testing to see which plug-ins are installed is always permissible because this activity will not alter the software on the computer you are using. If you cannot install a plug-in, read the material without completing the steps at the computer so you will know about the installation process.

Installing a Browser Extension

The method you use to install a browser extension depends in part on which browser you are using. For example, if you are using Navigator, then you typically install a downloaded extension by double-clicking the extension's filename in Windows Explorer. The same is true for Internet Explorer. However, if you are using Internet Explorer and download an extension from Microsoft's Web site, then the download and installation processes might occur automatically, so you might not need to do anything other than download the file. If there is only one download link available, then the extension usually will work with both browsers.

Mark sees the benefit of using the Shockwave plug-in and wants to consider using it on the RVP Web site, so he asks you to download and install the Shockwave Player. Having a Shockwave-enhanced site will add visual and audio interest to the site and attract the type of viewers that typify RVP's clients. To download and install the Shockwave Player, complete the first set of steps if you are using Internet Explorer; complete the second set of steps if you are using Navigator.

To install the Shockwave Player for Internet Explorer:

1. Return to the Student Online Companion Web page for Session 9.1, and then click the **Macromedia** hyperlink and wait while your Web browser loads the Macromedia Downloads page.

2. Click the **Macromedia Shockwave Player** link in the Macromedia Web Players section and wait for the page to load.

3. Click the **Install Now** link. A Security Warning dialog box opens and asks if you want to install and run the Shockwave Player.

   TROUBLE? Before downloading any software on a public computer, make sure that you are authorized to do so by checking with your instructor or technical support person.

4. Click the **Yes** button in the Security Warning dialog box to continue. Depending on your Internet connection speed, it might take anywhere from a few seconds to several minutes to download the Shockwave Player. The progress indicator will identify the installation progress and then it will install the file.

5. When you see the Welcome to Shockwave Player dialog box, click the **Next** button to continue.

6. Register your copy of the Shockwave Player by indicating your age, name, and e-mail address. You can clear the check boxes to prevent messages about Shockwave updates from being sent to your e-mail address and to avoid receiving automatic updates.

7. Click the **Finish** button, and then click the **Next** button in the Installation Complete dialog box. The Welcome to Shockwave page opens. After this page has been fully loaded, you will hear an audio file and then see links to different Shockwave-enabled games and puzzles.

8. Click the **Close** button on the title bar of the Welcome to Shockwave window to close it.

Use the following steps to install the Shockwave Player for Navigator; if you already installed the Shockwave Player for Internet Explorer, you can skip these steps.

To install the Shockwave Player for Navigator:

1. Return to the Student Online Companion Web page for Session 9.1, and then click the **Macromedia** hyperlink and wait while your Web browser loads the Macromedia Downloads page.

2. Click the **Macromedia Shockwave Player** link in the Macromedia Web Players section and wait for the page to load.

3. Click the **Download Now** button link. The Downloading shockwaveinstaller.exe dialog box opens and asks if you want to open or download the file.

   TROUBLE? If the Downloading shockwaveinstaller.exe dialog box doesn't open, you or another user may have disabled this dialog box. Select the Tutorial.09 folder on your Data Disk, click the Save button, and then continue with Step 6.

4. Click the **Save this file to Disk** option button, click the **OK** button, click the **Save in** list arrow, click the drive that contains your Data Disk, double-click the **Tutorial.09** folder to open it, and then click the **Save** button. The Saving File dialog box opens and identifies the download status for the file. The file has been completely downloaded when the progress indicator shows 100%.

5. If necessary, click the **Close** button to close the Saving File dialog box, and then close Navigator.

   TROUBLE? If necessary, close any other applications that are running on your computer before installing the Shockwave Player.

6. Use Windows Explorer or My Computer to display the contents of the Tutorial.09 folder on your Data Disk, and then double-click the **shockwaveinstaller.exe** file. The Installing Shockwave Player dialog box opens.

7. Click the **Next** button to continue. If necessary, select the version of Netscape that you are using, and then click the **Install** button.

8. Click the **Continue** button. Navigator starts and loads the Macromedia Web Player Download Center page.

9. Wait for the movie to begin playing in the specified area, close Navigator, and then restart Navigator to complete the installation.

Now that you have downloaded and installed the Shockwave Player for your Web browser, you need to test it to make sure that it is working correctly. You'll visit a Web site to test the Shockwave Player.

Testing a Browser Extension

You won't notice that you've installed a browser extension until you visit a Web site that requires it to display or play the site's contents correctly. Audio plug-ins often begin playing music when you visit the audio plug-in developer's site. Movie plug-ins play when you double-click a hyperlink to play a movie. Some Web sites let you test your browser to see which plug-ins are installed on your computer. Next, you will visit a Web site where you can test the Shockwave Player that you just installed.

To test the Shockwave Player:

1. Return to the Student Online Companion Web page for Session 9.1, and then click the **Shockwave Test** hyperlink and wait while your Web browser loads the Web page shown in Figure 9-12.

Figure 9-12	SHOCKWAVE TEST PAGE

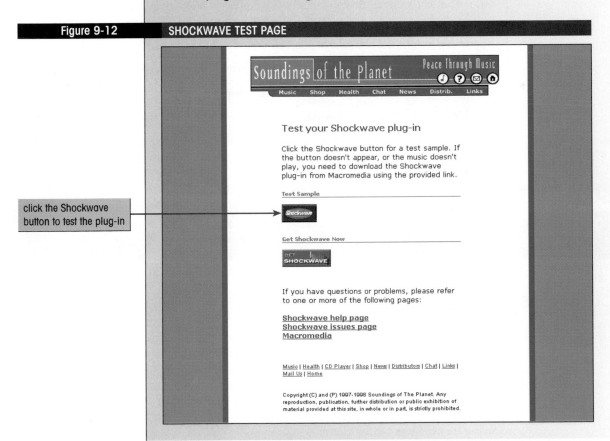

click the Shockwave button to test the plug-in

> **2.** Click the **Shockwave** button below the Test Sample text. If your computer has speakers and they are turned on, you will hear music indicating that the Shockwave Player has been correctly installed on your computer.
>
> **3.** Close your browser, and if necessary, log off your Internet connection.

After you have installed the Shockwave Player, you can use it to play games, music, and animated content. For a list of Shockwave-enabled content, click the Shockwave link in the Additional Information section of the Student Online Companion page for Tutorial 9. You can test your browser for the presence of other plug-ins by visiting the developer's Web site and locating the test feature on one of the site's Web pages.

Mark was pleased to hear of your progress in understanding and using different file formats on the Web. Based on your information, Mark is ready to begin planning the RVP Web site. He's especially excited about the possibility of using animation, sounds, and sample video clips.

In the next session, you'll research Internet security issues related to Mark's goal of providing sample RVP productions on the Web site and a way for clients to make down payments on their productions by using the RVP Web site and a credit card.

Session 9.1 QUICK | CHECK

1. How do plug-in developers earn a profit?

2. What is the main difference between a plug-in and a helper application?

3. True or False: Most Web pages containing content that requires a plug-in also contain a link to the site where you can download the plug-in.

4. What are the six primary categories of browser extensions?

5. What does the acronym "VRML" stand for?

6. How might a bed-and-breakfast inn owner use iPIX on the inn's Web site?

7. List the names of three free sound player plug-ins for Web browsers.

SESSION 9.2

In this session, you will learn about Internet security topics, including secrecy, privacy, integrity, necessity, and fraud. Once you understand the potential security threats on the Internet, you will study ways to protect against them. Finally, you will learn about copyright and intellectual property issues related to the Internet.

Security Overview

Mark is busy planning the content of the RVP Web site using the plug-in information you provided. Mark's next task is to make sure that it is easy for clients to submit a down payment to make a reservation for RVP services. Because most clients will use their credit cards to make this down payment, Mark wants to ensure that all transactions are secure and protected from unauthorized use. He also wants to protect content on the RVP Web site from unauthorized duplication or use. Mark needs to secure what's on the Web site in addition to securing its use by potential clients.

Security is broadly defined as the protection of assets from unauthorized access, use, alteration, or destruction. There are two types of security: physical security and logical security. The security provided by Fort Knox is almost entirely physical security. **Physical security** includes tangible protection devices, such as alarms, fireproof doors, security fences, safes or vaults, and bombproof buildings. Protection of assets using non-physical protections is called **logical security**. Protection of computer assets—both data and procedures to deal with the data—is an example of logical security, which also is broadly called **computer security**. Any act or object that threatens computer assets is known as a **threat**.

Countermeasure is the general name for a procedure, either physical or logical, that recognizes, reduces, or eliminates a threat. Countermeasures vary depending on the importance of the asset at risk. Countermeasures can recognize and manage threats or they can eliminate them. Other threats that are deemed low-risk and less likely to occur can be ignored when the cost to protect against the threat is more than the value of the protected asset. For example, a tornado is a low-risk threat to a computer network located in Southern California, but it is a high-risk threat for a computer network located in Kansas. It would make sense to protect the computer network in Kansas, which has a lot of tornado activity, but not to protect one in Los Angeles, where tornadoes are unlikely to strike. The risk management model shown in Figure 9-13 illustrates four actions that you could take to manage risks based on the impact (cost) and probability of the physical threat. In this model, a tornado in Kansas would be in the quadrant for high probability and high impact, whereas a tornado in Los Angeles would be in the quadrant for low impact and low probability.

Figure 9-13	RISK MANAGEMENT MODEL

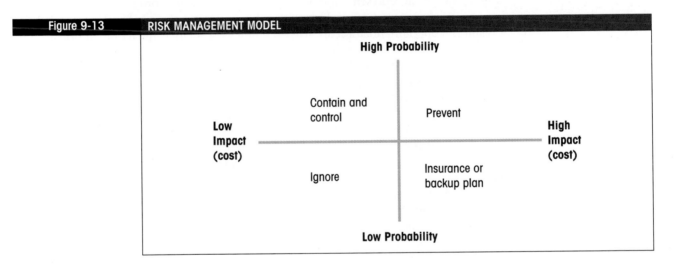

The same sort of risk management model applies to protecting Internet assets from non-physical threats, such as impostors, eavesdroppers, and thieves. To implement a good security scheme, you identify the risk, determine how you will protect the affected asset, and calculate how much you can spend to protect the asset. Your primary focus in risk management protection is not on the protection costs or value of assets; it is on identifying threats and determining ways to protect the assets from those threats.

Computer Security Classification

Computer security experts generally agree that you can classify computer security into three categories. The names of these categories vary, but the widely accepted ones are secrecy, integrity, and necessity. **Secrecy** prevents unauthorized data disclosure and ensures the authenticity of the data's source, **integrity** prevents unauthorized data modification, and **necessity** prevents data delays or denials. Secrecy and threats to secrecy are the best known of the computer security categories. News services frequently report illegal break-ins to governmental computers or unauthorized uses of stolen credit card numbers to order goods and services. Integrity threats tend to be reported less frequently and thus might be less familiar to the public. An example of an integrity violation occurs when a message's or property's shipping address is changed from the intended receiver to another individual's address, thereby stealing the message or property. Instances of necessity violations occur frequently. For example, if you send an important e-mail message to a shipper and ask to cancel an order—and someone prevents the shipper from receiving it—then the message is never delivered and the shipment is sent. Delaying a message can have huge consequences. For example, if you send an e-mail message to your stockbroker and ask him to buy 10,000 shares of company X at 10:00 A.M. and he receives the message after the stock market has closed for the day, the delay could cost you an additional price on the stock.

Copyright and Intellectual Property

Copyright and safeguarding intellectual property rights are also security issues, although they are protected with different countermeasures. **Copyright** is the protection of expression—someone's or some entity's intellectual property—and it typically covers items such as literary and musical works; pantomimes and choreographic works; pictorial, graphic, and sculptural works; motion pictures and other audio-visual works; sound recordings; and architectural works. (**Intellectual property** is the ownership of ideas and control over the tangible or virtual representation of those ideas.) Just like any other security threat, breaching a copyright causes damage. However, unlike computer security breaches, the damages as a result of copyright violation are narrow and have a smaller impact on an organization or individual. The U.S. Copyright Act of 1976 protects items, such as those in any of the preceding categories, for a fixed period. For items published before 1978, the copyright expires 75 years from the item's publication date. For items published after January 1, 1978, the copyright expires 50 years beyond the life of the author for an individual holder or 75 years after the date of the publication for employers of the author. In other words, unless you have received permission to reproduce the item protected by copyright, you are violating the Copyright Act if you illegally reproduce an item in any form before its copyright expires.

On the Internet, there are thousands of examples of copyright violations. You can go to any search engine, type the search term "copyright," and locate hundreds of Web sites that discuss copyright issues. Several of these Web sites document explicit and famous cases of copyright violations.

Mark wants to know more about copyright protection on the Web. He wants to know what is covered to ensure that any video clips he places on the RVP Web site are properly covered by copyright protection. You tell him about an informative site called the Copyright Clearance Center, Inc., and decide that's a good place to start researching copyright issues.

To open the Copyright Clearance Center Web page:

1. Start your Web browser, open the Student Online Companion page at **www.course.com/newperspectives/internet3**, click the hyperlink for your book, click the **Tutorial 9** link, and then click the **Session 9.2** link. Click the **Copyright Clearance Center** link and wait while the browser loads the page shown in Figure 9-14.

| Figure 9-14 | COPYRIGHT CLEARANCE CENTER WEB PAGE |

copyright resources link

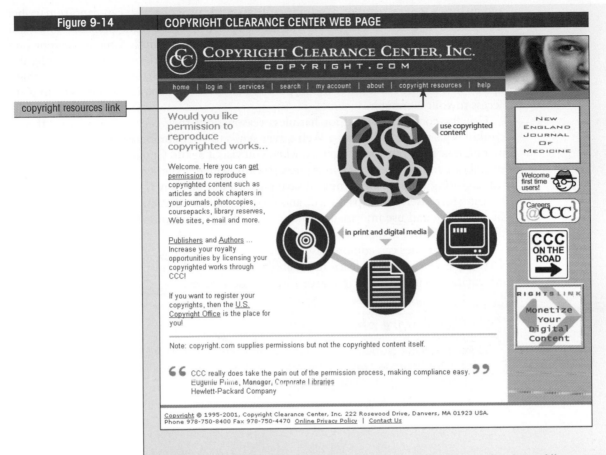

2. Click the **copyright resources** link in the link bar near the top of the page to open a page with information about copyright law on the Web. This page includes information about intellectual property, different types of copyrights and how to secure them, and how to use copyrighted material. In addition, you can click the links to get more information about compliance guidelines, copyright registration, and litigation, and to find a list of links to other Web sites.

With just a quick review of its contents, you are certain that Mark can use this Web site to get useful information about copyrighting the sample RVP materials on his Web site. Now that you can provide Mark with information about how to copyright his material, you need to let him know how to protect his material and his clients' credit card information from unauthorized use.

Security Threats

You can examine security threats by category. Secrecy and privacy threats are the most reported types, but other threats are equally destructive.

Secrecy and Privacy Threats

Many Web site visitors eagerly and regularly conduct business on the Web. The possibility of someone stealing your credit card number in a Web transaction is perhaps the most visible of the secrecy threats, but it represents only one of many. Intelligence gathering or industrial espionage can cause financial damage. For example, a **sniffer program** monitors and analyzes network traffic. Used illegally, a sniffer program also can capture data being transmitted on a network including user names, passwords, and other personal information. **Authentication** is verifying that the source or sender is identified correctly. Anyone on the Internet can pretend to be someone else, which poses a security risk. For example, if you receive a software update from Microsoft and install the update, how do you know that the update is from the real Microsoft Corporation and not from someone interested in gaining access to your computer?

Usually, cookies are used for harmless reasons, but they can pose a security threat. A **cookie** is a small text file that a Web server sends to your computer. A cookie stores information that the Web server can read when you visit it again. Cookies usually store information about your interests and your **click stream**, which is the sequence of links you clicked while visiting the site. Creating and saving cookies in this way is harmless. However, cookies can store user name, password, and credit card information, which allows illicit Web sites to store and use information about you without your knowledge by reading a cookie file stored on your computer.

Because cookies can compromise a client's personal information, Mark wants you to find a Web site where he can learn more about them so RVP can protect its clients' personal information from unauthorized access by outside sources.

To learn more about cookies:

1. Return to the Student Online Companion Web page for Session 9.2, and then click the **Cookie Central** hyperlink and wait while your Web browser loads the Cookie Central Web page shown in Figure 9-15.

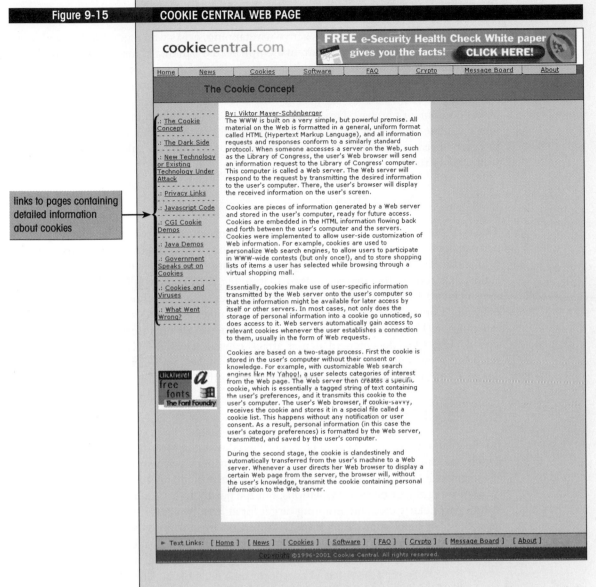

Figure 9-15   **COOKIE CENTRAL WEB PAGE**

links to pages containing detailed information about cookies

TROUBLE? If you are using Internet Explorer and a Security Warning dialog box opens, your browser is missing an ActiveX control required to access the site. Click the Yes button to load the ActiveX control only if you have permission from your instructor or technical support person to do so. If you want to cancel loading the ActiveX control, click the No button. Clicking the No button will not greatly affect your Cookie Central viewing experience.

2. Follow several of the links and read the pages that open so you can learn more about cookies. Mark will be especially interested in the information about cookie security, frequently asked cookie questions, and how to stop Web servers from writing cookies on clients' computers.

Mark is pleased with the cookie resources that you found. However, he is concerned about other types of threats, so you continue your Web research.

Integrity Threats

An integrity threat, also known as active wiretapping, exists when an unauthorized party has the chance to alter a message's contents. Unprotected banking transactions, such as deposits transmitted over a network, are subject to integrity violations. For example, a person could monitor a bank transmission sent over a network to alter a deposit transaction's amount by increasing its real value. By tampering with an electronic shipping address, someone could divert equipment purchased using the Internet to an address other than the intended recipient's. Unlike secrecy or inactive wiretapping, where the viewer simply sees information, integrity threats can change the actions a person or corporation takes because the transmission was altered.

Delay and Denial Threats

The goal of a delay or denial attack is to disrupt normal computer processing or, possibly, to deny processing entirely. A program exhibiting this behavior slows down processing to an intolerably slow speed. For example, if the processing speed of a single ATM machine transaction slows down from two seconds to 30 minutes, then users won't be able to get cash when they need it. Delaying processing can also render a service unusable or unattractive; for example, a newspaper that reports three-day-old news is worthless when you need current information. Denial attacks entirely remove a service or delete information from a transmission or file. One documented denial attack caused selected PCs that have Quicken (an accounting program) installed on them to divert money to a different bank account—the denial attack, in this case, stole money from its rightful owners.

Intellectual Property Threats

Intellectual property threats are a large problem due to the Internet and the relative ease with which one can use existing material without the owner's permission. Actual monetary damage resulting from a copyright violation is more difficult to measure than damage from secrecy, integrity, or necessity violations, but the harm can be just as great. The Internet presents a particularly easy and tempting target for at least two reasons. First, it is very simple to reproduce an exact copy of anything you find on the Internet, regardless of its copyright restrictions. Second, many people are simply naïve or unaware of copyright restrictions that protect intellectual property. Examples of both unwitting and willful copyright infringements are common on the Internet and occur on a daily basis. Although copyright laws were enacted before the creation of the Internet, the Internet itself has complicated the enforcement of copyrights by publishers. Recognizing the unauthorized reprinting of written text is relatively easy; tracing the path of a photograph that has been borrowed, cropped, and illegally used on a Web page is a more difficult task. Most experts agree that copyright infringements on the Web occur because of ignorance of what cannot be copied. Most people do not maliciously copy a protected work and post it on the Web. The most misunderstood part of the U.S. copyright law is that a work is protected when it is created—the work does not require a copyright notice, such as *Copyright © 2003 ABC Company*, to be protected.

Threat Delivery Mechanisms

There are many ways to breach security and threaten a system's integrity. Over the last decade, the most visible computer attacks have come from software. A **hacker**—usually a computer programmer who writes programs that damage computers—uses Trojan horses, viruses, and worms to attack computers and the programs they run.

A **Trojan horse** is a small program hidden inside another program. Taking its name from the legendary battle in which the city of Troy received a gift of a large wooden horse, Trojan horse programs are not what they appear to be. They claim to be legitimate programs that accomplish some task when, in fact, they do harm. They are unleashed when the program in which they are hidden is executed. Trojan horse programs range from prank programs that display a message and then disappear, to destructive programs that reformat hard drives or delete program and data files. A Trojan horse does not replicate itself, nor does it affect other files or programs.

You learned in Tutorial 6 that a computer virus is a computer program that harms your computer and attaches itself to legitimate programs. Besides being destructive, a virus infects other programs on your computer. Because a virus cannot exist alone, it must attach itself to a host program. When a program containing a virus is run, the virus has another opportunity to replicate itself. The term *virus* has come to mean any program that attempts to disguise its true function. Although all viruses are Trojan horses (because they hide within other legitimate programs), not all Trojan horse programs are viruses because Trojan horses cannot infect other programs. Like Trojan horses, viruses range from mildly annoying to extremely destructive.

An organization named **CERT (Computer Emergency Response Team)** has teams around the world to recognize and respond to computer attacks. The CERT Coordination Center studies Internet security issues and responds to security incidents reported to it. CERT publishes various security alerts and develops plans for individual computer sites to improve their security. RVP wants to allow its customers to conduct transactions using the Internet, so Mark should have access to the CERT site in case a security threat occurs.

To visit the CERT Web site:

1. Return to the Student Online Companion Web page for Session 9.2, and then click the **CERT Coordination Center** hyperlink and wait while your Web browser loads the Web page.

2. Scroll down the page to view the headings and links on the CERT home page, as shown in Figure 9-16. Notice that you can get information about improving and evaluating security, reviewing publications by CERT staff members, or learning more about the CERT.

Figure 9-16   **CERT COORDINATION CENTER WEB PAGE**

CarnegieMellon
Software Engineering Institute   **Home   Site Index   Search   Contact   FAQ**
CERT® Coordination Center | *vulnerabilities,* | *security practices* | *survivability* | *training &* |
| *incidents & fixes* | *& evaluations* | *research & analysis* | *education* |

Options

links to different sources of security information →

Vulnerabilities,
Incidents & Fixes

Security Practices
& Evaluations

Survivability
Research &
Analysis

Training &
Education

Related

CERT Contact
Information

CERT Statistics

Meet the CERT/CC

CERT/CC Overview
and Intruder Trends

CERT Annual
Reports

Publications by
CERT Staff

Presentations by
CERT Staff

Press Releases

links to
related information →

Employment
Opportunities

Other Sources of
Security
Information

Messages
comments &
questions
webmaster
@cert.org.

advisories &
summaries
by email
The CERT®
Advisory Mailing
List

new to internet
security?
We have compiled
a set of documents
for new and home
users.

Related Sites

INTERNET
SECURITY
ALLIANCE

welcome

The CERT® Coordination Center (CERT/CC) is a center of Internet security expertise, at the Software Engineering Institute, a federally funded research and development center operated by Carnegie Mellon University. We study Internet security vulnerabilities, handle computer security incidents, publish security alerts, research long-term changes in networked systems, and develop information and training to help you improve security at your site.

What's New

- **CERT Summary CS-2001-04**
  November 20, 2001
  Topics in this regularly scheduled CERT Summary include the W32/Nimda Worm and active exploitation of vulnerabilities in SSH1 CRC-32 Compensation Attack Detector and in Microsoft DNS servers.

- **Trends in Denial of Service Attack Technology**
  October 19, 2001
  This paper (pdf) highlights recent trends in DoS attack technology based on intruder activity and attack tools reported to and analyzed by the CERT/CC.

- **UNIX Security Checklist v2.0**
  October 8, 2001
  This document has been published jointly by The Australian Computer Emergency Response Team (AusCERT) and the CERT® Coordination Center (CERT/CC) and details steps to improve the security of Unix Operating Systems.

  more of What's New ...

For New & Home Users

- **Feature**:
  Attack Scenarios: How to get There from Here

- **Article**:
  Means, Motive, and Opportunity

- **Tech Tip**:
  Home Network Security

- **Article**:
  Security of the Internet

  more home user documents...

Upcoming Events

- **December 18, 2001**
  Creating a Computer Security Incident Response Team

  more Training Courses...

2002
Download: 2002 Course Brochure (pdf, ~36k)

General Documents about Internet Security

- *Infosec Outlook* articles
- *SEI Interactive* articles
- Testimony

  full list of Publications

Search the CERT/CC web site

[   ] [GO]
Customized Search

links to current security threats

React To Today's Problems

Advisories & Incident Notes

- **CA-2001-35**
  Recent Activity Against Secure Shell Daemons

- **CA-2001-34**
  Buffer Overflow in System V Derived Login

- **IN-2001-15**
  W32/Goner Worm

- **CA-2001-33**
  Multiple Vulnerabilities in WU-FTPD

- **IN-2001-14**
  W32/BadTrans Worm

  all advisories | all incident notes

Vulnerability Notes

Browse the Vulnerability Notes Database

Current Activity: Tue Dec 4 18:50:22 EST 2001

- W32/Goner
- W32/Badtrans
- "Kaiten" malicious code installed by exploiting null default passwords in MS-SQL
- Exploitation of vulnerability in SSH1 CRC-32 compensation attack detector
- W32/Nimda
- Scans and Probes

Improve Security with Practices & Evaluations

- **OCTAVE℠ Evaluation Method**
  OCTAVE is a comprehensive risk evaluation that allows you to identify the information assets that are important to the mission of your organization, the threats to those assets, and vulnerabilities that may expose the information assets to the identified threats.

- **SNA Evaluation Method**
  The Survivable Network Analysis method helps you define and implement system improvements to deal with inevitable intrusions in a proactive manner.

- **CERT Security Practices**
  Practical guidance that helps you improve security within your organization. Also available in book form.

Keep Up With Survivability Research

- **Easel Survivability Simulation**
  Easel can be used to simulate the effects of cyber attacks, accidents, and failures, and can be used to predict the survivability attributes of complex systems while they are under development, preventing costly vulnerabilities before the system is built.

- **All Research Papers**

Disclaimers and copyright information | Last updated December 13, 2001 | 🖶 Printable version of this portal

> **3.** Follow some of the links that might interest Mark. When you have reviewed a few pages of content, return to the Student Online Companion page for Session 9.2.

Now that Mark understands more about different types of threats, he is curious to learn how a computer virus spreads from a single "infected" source to other computers. You explain to him that he might download a file from a Web site that contains a virus. When he accesses the file, he deploys the virus, which might attach itself to other files on his hard drive without his knowledge. Meanwhile, Mark might unwittingly attach an infected file to an e-mail message, which transfers the virus to the recipient's computer. A virus's reproduction cycle is fast: Once the program is installed on a computer, it silently infects other programs. Those programs, in turn, can infect other systems when the programs or files are copied and installed there. Without virus detection software, a long time can pass before you see and detect the virus.

Now that you are aware of the different types of computer threats, Mark asks you to investigate ways to prevent them.

Security **Countermeasures**

Security countermeasures are procedures, programs, and hardware that detect and prevent computer security threats. No single countermeasure is effective against all security attacks, but selected countermeasures can provide excellent protection from selected security threats. Countermeasures should, when used together, protect against various secrecy, integrity, and necessity threats. The security countermeasures necessary for Internet transactions should ensure that the transaction or message being sent:

- Cannot be read by anyone except the intended recipient
- Is tamperproof, ensuring that no one was able to modify its contents or delete it entirely
- Is authored by the person who claims to be the sender

Mark is concerned about the security of all transactions on the RVP Web site—especially those involving confidential customer information, such as credit card numbers, names, and addresses. He wants to assure his customers that there will be no security breach of personal information during a transaction. In addition, he wants to enact countermeasures to prevent impostors from ordering services from the RVP Web site. Finally, he wants to ensure that no customer's request for services is delayed or denied.

Identification and Authentication

User identification is the process of identifying yourself to a computer. Most computer systems implement user identification with user names and passwords; the combination of a user name and password is sometimes called a **login** or your **login information**. Similarly, most Web sites require you to establish a user name and password before you can order goods or services. When you revisit the Web site, you can log in with your user name and password and then purchase goods and services. You can create almost any user name and password you like. The issue is not the accuracy of your login information when compared to your real name, but that only *you* know your user name and password. As long as these facts are not compromised, the Web site or other computer system assumes that the person who enters the login information is, in fact, the identified user. The efficacy of the identification system is tied to the strength of the password. A hacker cannot guess a long and/or complicated password. Creating a strong password involves using uncommon strings of letters not found in a dictionary, including numbers and special characters, combinations of uppercase and lowercase letters, and long passwords. Hackers can run programs that create and enter passwords from a dictionary or a list of commonly used passwords to break into a system. Called a **brute force attack**, this type of program tries character combinations until the system accepts one. Some systems will send a warning to the computer's operator or lock out a user name when someone attempts to log in to a system an excessive number of times without succeeding. An intruder who successfully guesses your login is **masquerading** as you.

User authentication is the process of associating a person and his identification with a very high level of assurance. In other words, authentication techniques give a high level of confidence that *you* are correctly identified when *you* log in. Authentication techniques include using biometrics, such as a retina scan or fingerprint scan, or asking a series of questions to which only the authentic user could know the correct answers, such as entering a password code or knowing the answer to a question that you selected when you created your user name.

The system that accepts your newly created user name and password must save your login information securely. Otherwise, an attacker could locate the system file containing user names and passwords and obtain login information for all users. Most systems store passwords (and sometimes user names) in a special, encrypted form. **Encrypted** data are the unreadable, scrambled letters created by an encryption program. (Encryption programs are described later in this session.)

Users connected to the Internet from networked PCs, such as computers in a university computer lab, usually do not have to log in with a user name and password. Starting a Web browser almost never requires you to enter a user name and password. All e-mail client programs require you to log on to the mail system with a user name and password. However, it is possible, but not recommended, to send mail under an assumed name with a fictitious return address.

How can you authenticate an e-mail message's name and address? One way to authenticate users is to use digital certificates, which combine identification and authentication. A **digital certificate** is an encrypted and password-protected file that contains sufficient information to authenticate and prove a sender's identity. Usually, a digital certificate contains the following information:

- The certificate holder's name, address, and e-mail address
- A special key that "unlocks" the digital certificate, thereby verifying the certificate's authenticity
- The certificate's expiration date or validity period
- A trusted third party, called a **certificate authority (CA)**, which verifies the person's identity and issues the digital certificate

A digital certificate is an electronic equivalent of an identification card. By looking at a person's driver's license, you can verify a person's identity by confirming the stated height, weight, and eye color printed on the license. Outlook Express and Netscape Mail provide the technology to send and receive digital certificates with e-mail messages so a recipient can verify your identity. Although individuals can use personal digital certificates, Web servers currently account for the largest percentage of digital certificates. Server-side digital certificates provide you with assurance that the Web site that *looks* like microsoft.com really *is* the Web site for Microsoft Corporation. Internet Explorer and Navigator both automatically receive and process digital certificates from Web sites. Figure 9-17 shows how a server receives and processes a digital certificate.

| Figure 9-17 | SENDING AND PROCESSING A DIGITAL CERTIFICATE |

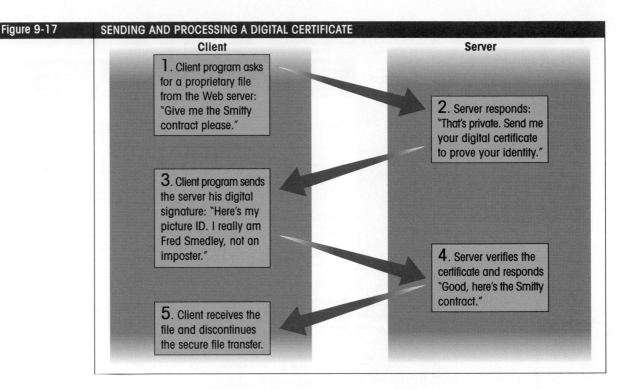

The first and largest commercial certifying authority is VeriSign, Inc. Mark asks you to visit the VeriSign Web site to search for more information about digital certificates, as he may want to secure his e-mail messages and the RVP Web site with certificates in the future.

To open the VeriSign Web site:

1. Click the **VeriSign** hyperlink on the Student Online Companion page for Session 9.2 and wait while your Web browser loads the page shown in Figure 9-18.

Figure 9-18   VERISIGN SECURE E-MAIL WEB PAGE

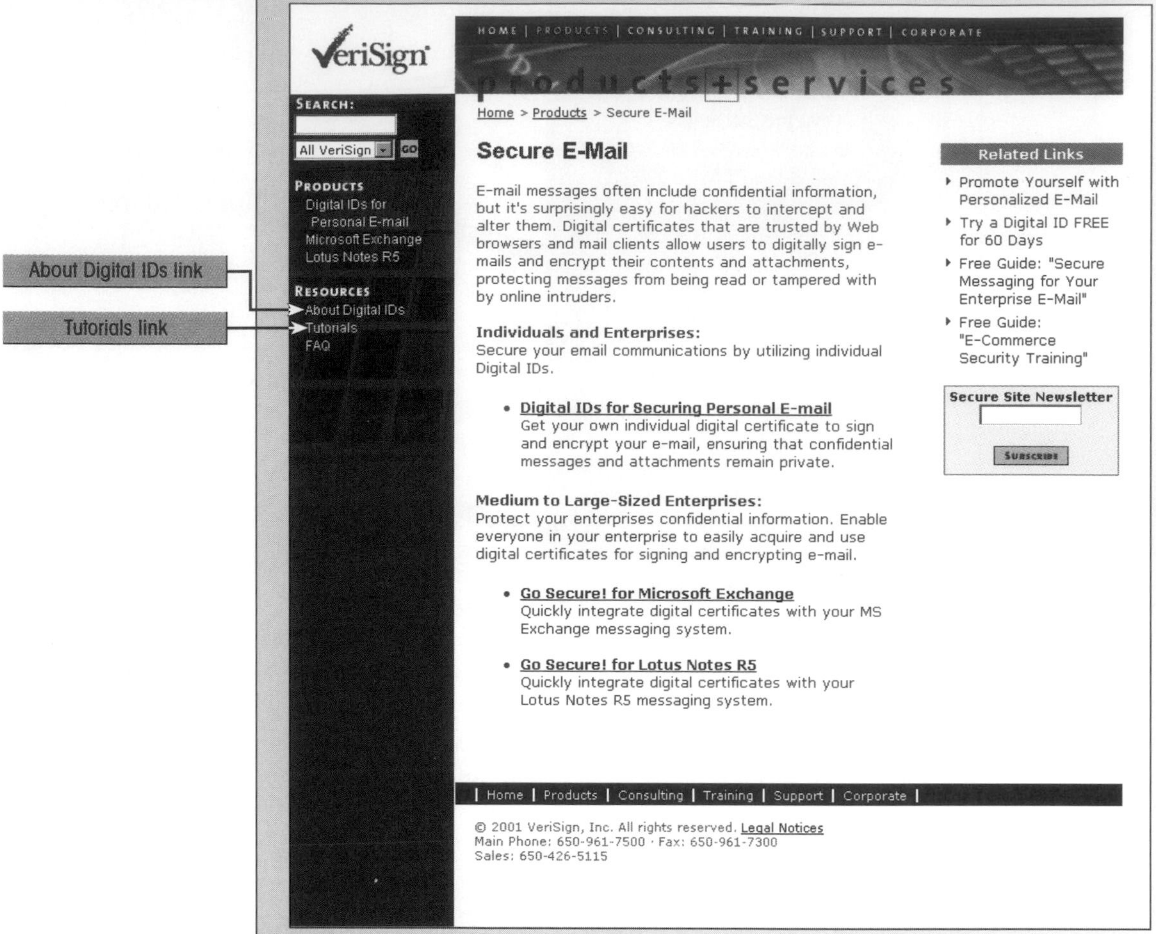

About Digital IDs link

Tutorials link

2. Read the page that opens, and then click the **About Digital IDs** link on the left side of the page. Use the links on the General Information About Digital IDs page to learn more about digital certificates. As you review each page, consider how Mark might use this information to protect his messages.

3. When you are finished exploring several of the links on the General Information About Digital IDs page, return to the Secure E-Mail page and then click the **Tutorials** link on the left side of the page.

4. Use the links on the Tutorials page to learn more about how to implement a digital certificate using the mail program for your browser.

Mark thinks that digital certificates could be a useful resource in the future as he begins to secure the RVP Web site and the e-mail messages sent from and received by the RVP server. He asks you to look into secrecy and privacy issues next.

Secrecy and Privacy

Security measures involve both people procedures and computer processes. For privacy, Mark is interested in computer processes to protect information automatically, but he knows that he also needs administrative procedures for people to follow—one of the most important procedures people can follow is authentication.

Mark understands that sending information on the Internet is subject to alteration, being copied, or being read by an unauthorized individual who is monitoring messages. Protecting business transactions is necessary before you can set up a Web business site. The solution to protecting messages from prying eyes and safeguarding their contents from tampering is to use encryption. Encryption is the process of coding information using a mathematical-based program and a secret key to produce a string of characters that is unreadable. To read the encrypted information, you need a key or password to convert the meaningless characters back into a readable form. The process of reversing encrypted text is called **decryption**. In order to decrypt text, you need a key to "unlock" it. Without the key, the program alone cannot reveal the encrypted message's content. Encrypted information is called **cipher text**, whereas unencrypted information is called **plain text**.

Two types of encryption are used today: symmetric encryption (private-key) and asymmetric encryption (public-key). **Symmetric encryption** uses a single key that is known by the sender and receiver. This method works well in a highly controlled environment in which the sender can safely pass the secret key to the receiver via a human courier or other procedure. Symmetric encryption breaks down when it is used in an uncontrolled environment in which you cannot ensure that the key has been safely sent to the receiver. In addition, exchanging secret keys with people to whom you want to send encrypted messages is nearly impossible. Figure 9-19 shows how a symmetric-encryption system works.

Figure 9-19	SYMMETRIC (PRIVATE-KEY) ENCRYPTION

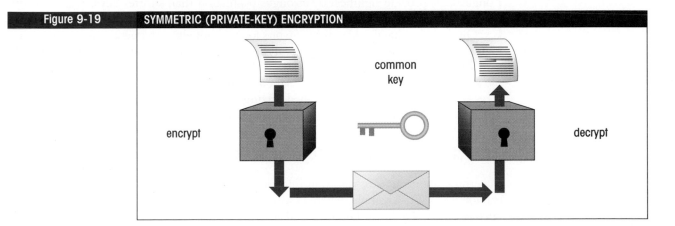

Public-key encryption solves the secret-key distribution problem. **Public-key encryption** is an encryption system that uses two different keys—a **public key** known to everyone and a **private** or **secret key** known only to the person who owns both keys. With a public-key system, each person has a private key that is secret and a public key that is shared with other users. Messages encrypted with a private key must be decrypted with the public key, and vice versa. For example, when an RVP customer sends an encrypted transaction, he or she uses RVP's public key to encrypt the message—that's the only key anyone outside of RVP knows. The RVP site then uses its private key to decrypt the message and process the transaction.

Using a similar scheme, you can verify that the sender is genuine. To send your electronic signature, you encrypt your message with your own, personal private key. The receiver verifies that the message is from you by decrypting the message with the public key you distribute or post on your Web site. If the message decrypts correctly, then the message's recipient can be confident the sender is authentic. In other words, if you try to pretend to be Ralph Nader and send a message to Mark Remes, Mark will try to decrypt the message with Ralph Nader's public key, but the message will consist of random characters after decryption. That is the signal that the pretender who sent you the message is *not* Ralph Nader. Figure 9-20 shows how a public-key encryption system works.

Figure 9-20 ASYMMETRIC (PUBLIC-KEY) ENCRYPTION

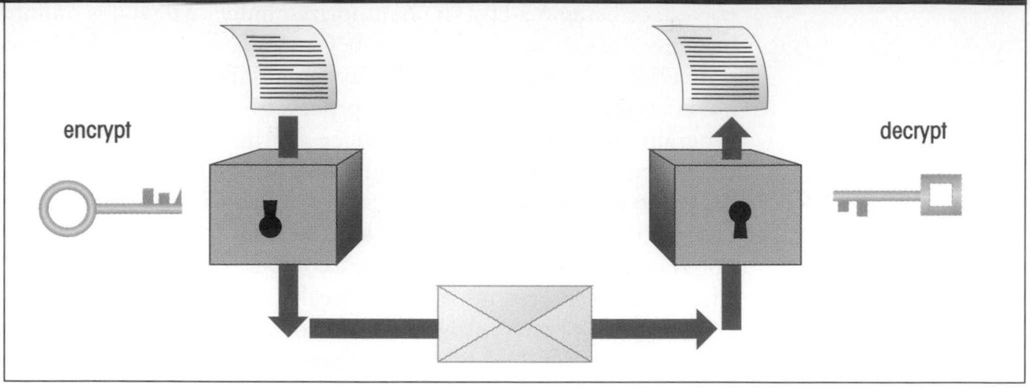

Encryption is considered to be weak or strong based on its algorithm and the length of the encryption key. An **algorithm** is a formula or set of steps to solve a particular problem. Years of research have yielded several secure algorithms with no inherent security weaknesses. The key(s) used to encrypt a message are equally important to the strength of the encryption method. Keys can be any set of characters that are used to encode the text. Longer keys provide significantly stronger protection than shorter keys. Experts estimate that it would take about 30 hours of computation time to decrypt a 40-bit (or six-character) key. On the other hand, a key that is 56 bits long (about eight characters) would take an estimated 228 *years* to discover through analysis of encrypted text. Further, 128-bit keys would take about 1,024 years to untangle. These calculations are all based on the number of possible keys that must be tried to "break" an encrypted message to read the plain-text message. Keys that are 128 bits long are called **strong keys**. Internet Explorer and Navigator use both symmetric- and asymmetric-encryption methods employing 128-bit keys.

Protecting Web Commerce Transactions

In certain circumstances, you want information you enter to be protected so someone else cannot see it. For example, when a customer purchases services from RVP, he or she will need to enter a credit card number and additional identification information. The customer will expect that this information is available to RVP employees only. How will RVP protect transactions between customers and the Web site? The RVP Web site can use the Secure Sockets Layer Internet protocol to handle the transactions. Designed by Netscape, **Secure Sockets Layer (SSL)** is a widely used, nonproprietary protocol that travels as a separate layer or "secure channel" on top of the TCP/IP Internet protocol. SSL provides a security handshake when your browser and the Web page to which you are connected want to conduct a secure communication. Most Web sites automatically switch to a secure state before asking you for sensitive information. Web pages secured by SSL have URLs that begin with *https://* instead of *http://*; the "s" indicates a secure connection. Even if you haven't selected a public- and private-key set, SSL automatically handles the details of obtaining a temporary pair for you. The result is that the client browser and server automatically arrange to encrypt information flowing between them; in this case, your Web browser will display a security icon on the status bar to let you know that you are using a secure site. Figure 9-21 shows the Internet Explorer security icon, and Figure 9-22 shows the Navigator security icon. When you finish your transactions and go to another Web page, the browser and Web server return to a nonsecure state, which is indicated by an open padlock or by the omission of a padlock on the status bar.

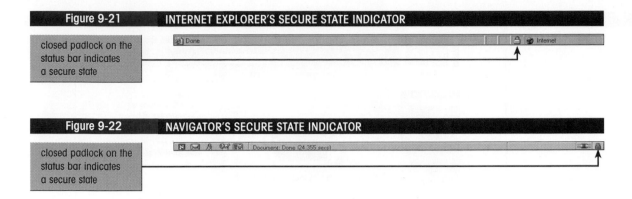

Figure 9-21 — **INTERNET EXPLORER'S SECURE STATE INDICATOR**

closed padlock on the status bar indicates a secure state

Figure 9-22 — **NAVIGATOR'S SECURE STATE INDICATOR**

closed padlock on the status bar indicates a secure state

SSL uses both symmetric and asymmetric encryption and keys to ensure privacy. SSL creates a public-key pair so that it can safely transmit data using a symmetric key. The symmetric key is encrypted using public-key encryption and sent to your browser. Using the symmetric key protects the remainder of the information transfer between your browser and the Web site. Symmetric encryption is faster than asymmetric encryption—that's why the remainder of the session's messages are encrypted with the symmetric key. When the session ends, these temporary keys, or **session keys**, are discarded—session keys exist only during a single, active session between the browser and server.

Protecting E-Mail

Encryption is used to protect e-mail and to authenticate the sender. Encryption protects a message's contents from inadvertent or malicious exposure, much like an envelope shields a letter's contents before it is opened. Two Internet protocols—S/MIME and PGP/MIME—are vying for acceptance as the encryption standard for e-mail. The main difference between these protocols is in the cryptographic programs they use. S/MIME is an e-mail security protocol introduced in 1995 by RSA Data Security. S/MIME uses a "digital envelope" approach, whereby the digital signature and a symmetric key are encrypted with a public key. Most other encryption, including the message, is encrypted with a symmetric key. The symmetric key is encrypted with the digital signature to protect it when it is sent to the receiver. Figure 9-23 shows the RSA home page and some links that you can use to find out more about encryption. You can open the RSA site by clicking the RSA Security link in the Session 9.2 section of the Student Online Companion page for Tutorial 9.

Figure 9-23   RSA SECURITY HOME PAGE

PGP/MIME is an e-mail security protocol invented by Phil Zimmermann. **PGP** stands for **Pretty Good Privacy**. PGP uses the same basic approach to create a protective virtual envelope; the technical details aren't important for this discussion. Network Associates, Inc., a company formed with several others, including McAfee, Network General, PGP, and Helix, has PGP software. You can visit the Network Associates Web page by clicking its link in the Session 9.2 section of the Student Online Companion page for Tutorial 9. Figure 9-24 shows the Network Associates home page. You can click the links to learn more about how to purchase PGP or download free trial versions.

Figure 9-24   NETWORK ASSOCIATES HOME PAGE

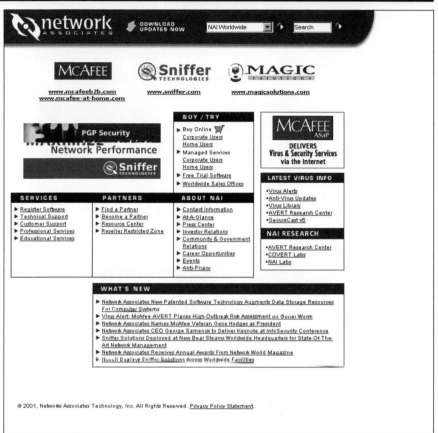

The Massachusetts Institute of Technology (MIT) distributes PGP *free* for noncommercial use in cooperation with Phil Zimmermann and with RSA Data Security, Inc., which licenses patents to the public-key encryption technology on which PGP relies. If you are interested in learning more about PGP and downloading a free version, click the MIT Free PGP link in the Session 9.2 section of the Student Online Companion page for Tutorial 9. Many software vendors, including Netscape Communications, Microsoft, and Lotus Development, support S/MIME in their products. Other vendors, such as Qualcomm, support PGP.

Integrity

Protecting an e-mail message by encrypting it is analogous to sealing a letter in an envelope—if the envelope's seal is broken when you receive it, you can suspect that someone intercepted, and possibly altered, the letter's contents. Sealing an envelope preserves the letter's integrity. To maintain the integrity of an e-mail message, you send the message through a **message digest function program** (or a **hash code function program**) to produce a number called a **message authentication code**, or **MAC**. This scheme works because it is almost impossible for a message and any other altered version of it to have an identical MAC. Figure 9-25 shows how the message digest function produces the MAC "AC2345HJ" for the text message "preserve this message." After it receives the MAC, the e-mail program sends the message and matching MAC together (or you can encrypt both pieces to preserve secrecy) to the recipient. The recipient's e-mail program recomputes the message's MAC and compares the computed MAC to the received MAC. If they match, then the message is unaltered. If they do not match, then the message has been altered and cannot be trusted.

| Figure 9-25 | PRODUCING A MAC FOR A MESSAGE |

There are many ways to encode a message to produce a value. But to be useful, the message digest function must exhibit these characteristics:

■ It must be impossible or costly to reverse the MAC and produce the original message

■ The MAC should be random to prevent creating the original message from the MAC

■ The MAC must be unique to the message so there is an extremely small chance that two messages could ever produce the same MAC

The Additional Information section of the Student Online Companion page for Tutorial 9 includes additional links that you can explore to read more about various security topics and preserving message integrity.

Necessity

A necessity attack can slow down processing, completely remove an item, or deny its use. Although you cannot do much to protect the Web servers you browse from being attacked, you can protect your own browser program and your PC. One of the most dangerous entry points for delay and resource denial threats come from programs that travel with applications to your browser and execute on your PC. These programs are Java, JavaScript, and ActiveX components, all of which run programs on your PC. When you visit Web sites with active content—information that changes because of behind-the-scenes programs driving them—then you run a risk of loading a Trojan horse that can slow down your computer, reformat your hard drive, or perform other destruction.

For example, a destructive **Java applet**, which is a program written in the Java programming language, could execute and consume all your computer's resources. Similarly, a **JavaScript program** can pose an additional problem because its programs can execute directly without being compiled (translated into special codes) before running on your computer. A cleverly written JavaScript program could examine your PC's programs and e-mail a file from your computer back to the Web server. **ActiveX components** are Microsoft's technology for writing small applications that perform some action in Web pages—these components have full access to your PC's file system. For example, a hidden ActiveX component in a Web page could scan your hard drive for PCX and JPEG files and print them on any network printer. Similarly, a renegade ActiveX component could reformat your hard drive.

Although most Java, JavaScript, and ActiveX component are beneficial, you can protect your computer from these delay/denial attacks. Perhaps the simplest strategy is to disallow Web programs from running them. Next, you will disable your Web browser from running Java and JavaScript programs. If you are using Internet Explorer, complete the first set of steps. If you are using Navigator, skip to the next set of steps.

To strengthen security in Internet Explorer:

1. Click **Tools** on the menu bar, and then click **Internet Options**. The Internet Options dialog box opens.

2. Click the **Security** tab to display security settings.

3. If directed to do so by your instructor, select a different zone by clicking the appropriate icon in the top panel. The default zone is Internet, which is all Web sites that are not included in the other zones. The Local intranet zone includes all Web sites that are included on an intranet to which you are connected, the Trusted sites zone includes Web sites that you have specified as being safe, and the Restricted sites zone includes Web sites that you have specified as being potentially hazardous to your computer.

4. Click the **Default Level** button in the Security level for this zone box. A slider appears in the box and the current security level for your browser appears in bold text. A short description of the current security level appears below the bold security setting. The default setting is Medium.

5. Click and drag the slider in the Security level for this zone box to the top position. The security level changes to High, as shown in Figure 9-26. The High setting provides the highest level of security as you are using the Internet. If you are an advanced user and want to customize your security settings, you could click the Custom Level button and set many individual options for allowing ActiveX, Java, and JavaScript commands to execute on your PC.

Figure 9-26	INTERNET EXPLORER INTERNET OPTIONS DIALOG BOX

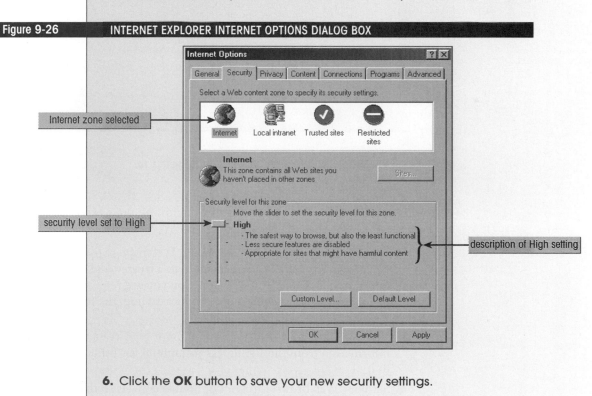

Internet zone selected

security level set to High

description of High setting

6. Click the **OK** button to save your new security settings.

If you are using Navigator, complete the following set of steps. If you are using Internet Explorer, skip to the next section.

To strengthen security in Navigator:

1. Click **Edit** on the menu bar, and then click **Preferences** to open the Preferences dialog box.

2. Click **Advanced** in the Category box to display the advanced settings in the right panel of the Preferences dialog box.

3. If necessary, click the **Enable Java**, **Enable JavaScript for Navigator**, and **Enable JavaScript for Mail & Newsgroups** check boxes to clear them. See Figure 9-27.

Figure 9-27	NAVIGATOR PREFERENCES DIALOG BOX

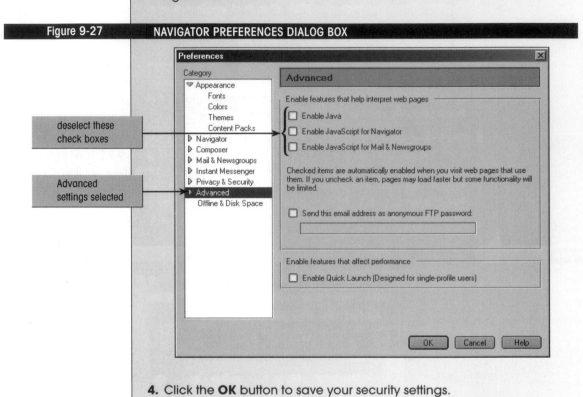

4. Click the **OK** button to save your security settings.

You can apply other defensive strategies to minimize your exposure to security threats, such as:

■ Whenever possible, avoid completing Web page registration forms unless you are sure you are sending material to a trusted and secure site. In addition, carefully consider the information you are required to give. For example, if you are only requesting a product catalog, the form should not ask you to enter a credit card number.

■ If you publish your own Web pages, omit your résumé and other personal information from the site unless you intend for other people to have access to it.

■ Set your Web browser to limit or disable cookies so that various sites cannot record and process your click stream.

- Purchase and use a virus detection program that not only monitors the files on your computer, but also your downloaded e-mail messages and browser activity.

- Download software and files only from known and trustworthy sources. If you are not familiar with a source, search for information about that source and try to determine its credibility before downloading anything.

Now, you are prepared to ensure the safe transaction of customer information over the Web. Mark is impressed with the information you found about security threats and protection measures. He will find these resources to be valuable as he collects his thoughts about the RVP site.

Session 9.2 QUICK CHECK

1. Three widely accepted categories of computer security are _____ _____, and _____.

2. What is the name for the protection of expression?

3. True or False: An Internet cookie is always harmful.

4. What type of threat prevents a message from arriving in a timely fashion?

5. Protecting a message so that only the intended recipient can read it is an example of preserving integrity, necessity, or secrecy?

6. Another term for public-key encryption is _____ encryption.

7. Who invented the PGP (Pretty Good Privacy) protocol?

REVIEW ASSIGNMENTS

Mark wants to learn more about PGP and asks you to locate two browser plug-ins that will let users view movies on a Web page and cause sounds to play based on the user's mouse movements. To find this information for Mark, you'll complete the following steps.

1. Start your Web browser, open the Student Online Companion page at www.course.com/newperspectives/internet3, click the hyperlink for your book, click the Tutorial 9 link, and then click the Review Assignments link. Click the Yahoo! link and wait while the browser loads the page.

2. Click the Computers & Internet category.

3. On the page that opens, click the Security and Encryption link.

4. On the page that opens, click the PGP – Pretty Good Privacy link.

Explore
5. Use the page that opens to locate and click the link to open the MIT distribution site for PGP Web page, which describes how to obtain a freeware version of PGP. If you cannot find this link, use the other links on the page to find another source of information about PGP. Read the page that you found to learn more about PGP and where and how to download it. When you are finished reading the page, print the first page only.

6. Return to the Yahoo! home page, click the Computers & Internet category, and then click the World Wide Web@ link.

7. On the page that opens, click the Browsers@ link, and then click the Plug-Ins link.

Explore 8. In the Categories list, click the Sound and Video link. Use the page that opens to see if you can locate a plug-in that plays movies on a Web page and another plug-in that lets you embed sound files that respond to a user's mouse movements on a Web page. When you locate these plug-ins, click their links to open a page with more information about them, and then print the first page of the page that opens for each plug-in. If you cannot find these exact plug-ins, search for something similar.

Explore 9. In a memo addressed to Mark, describe the general requirements for using the freeware version of PGP and identify whether RVP could use it. Then in a separate paragraph, rate the two plug-ins that you located in terms of how effective they might be for accomplishing their intended goals. Finally, in a third paragraph, evaluate the effectiveness of the Yahoo! Web site in locating the information Mark requested. If necessary, click several links to identify how Yahoo! organizes the material and the ease of which you are able to locate plug-ins and information about security topics.

10. Close your browser, and if necessary, log off your Internet connection.

CASE PROBLEMS

Case 1. Rowing Marvels Rowing Marvels manufactures racing shells, including singles, quads, and eights (eight-seat shells), all of which are used by rowing crews throughout Europe and the United States. Peter Beneski, owner and CEO of Rowing Marvels, wants to expand its marketing efforts with a Web site to sell the various racing shells and also to roll out a new line of accessories, including videos, rowing machines, unisuits, graphite blades ("oars"), and riggers. To make the Web site fun to use, Peter wants to use virtual reality, motion, and sound to create a virtual-reality race on the Web site for entertainment purposes. Because the Web site will accept online orders, Peter asks you to learn more about the Secure Sockets Layer protocol. To help Peter plan the Rowing Marvels Web site, you'll complete the following steps.

1. Start your Web browser, open the Student Online Companion page at www.course.com/newperspectives/internet3, click the hyperlink for your book, click the Tutorial 9 link, and then click the Case Problems link. Click the Netscape link and wait while the browser loads the page.

2. Locate and click the Browser Central link on the home page, and then click the Browser Plug-Ins link. If you cannot find one or either of these links, use the search text box on the home page to search for plug-ins.

Explore 3. Click a link to view information about plug-ins for 3D and animation. On the page that opens, examine two or three plug-ins to find one that might be appropriate for an on-screen simulated race in a Rowing Marvels racing shell. For each plug-in that would be appropriate for this objective, print the first page of information that you found. (Do not download any plug-ins.)

4. Return to the Student Online Companion page for Case Problem 1, and then click the SSL link to open the Secure Sockets Layer page at Netscape.com.

5. Read the page that opens and follow the links to get more information about digital server certificates and to learn more detailed information about how SSL works.

6. Close your browser, and if necessary, log off your Internet connection.

Explore
7. In a memo addressed to Peter, identify some basic information about SSL and how to get a digital certificate.

Case 2. Golden Kennels Ginger Gotcher is a registered breeder and trainer of Golden Retrievers. Because many of Ginger's dogs have reached champion status, puppies bred on her ranch are in high demand from people across the United States. Ginger receives many calls from potential owners of new puppies and from breeders requesting sire services from her champion male dogs. Because Ginger frequently travels to dog shows across the country, it is inconvenient for her to rely on the telephone to conduct business. Ginger has created a Web site to communicate information and also to let potential owners request and purchase puppies. Ginger is concerned about security—both for her site and also for the protection of her clients' personal information. Ginger has heard that many Web sites post their privacy policies on their Web sites so people can examine them and understand how companies collect information about customers and what they do with that information. To help Ginger learn more about privacy policies, you will visit the Web sites of several prominent online stores and report your findings to her by completing the following steps.

1. Start your Web browser, open the Student Online Companion page at www.course.com/newperspectives/internet3, click the hyperlink for your book, click the Tutorial 9 link, and then click the Case Problems link. Click the Amazon.com link and wait while the browser loads the page.

Explore
2. Locate and click the link to Amazon.com's privacy notice. On a sheet of paper, answer the following questions.
   a. What does the policy say about revealing your name and address to other companies?
   b. Does this site use cookies?

3. Return to the Student Online Companion page for Case Problem 2, and then click the Starbucks hyperlink.

Explore
4. Locate and click the link to the Starbucks privacy policy. In a new paragraph, answer the following questions.
   a. Does Starbucks permit Web site visitors to log into the Web site?
   b. How does Starbucks authenticate users?
   c. How might Starbucks use the information you provide without your permission?

5. Return to the Student Online Companion page for Case Problem 2, and then click the BBBOnline hyperlink.

Explore 6. Use the links and pages in the BBBOnline Web site to learn more about the privacy program of the Better Business Bureau (BBB), and then in a new paragraph, answer the following questions.
   a. What is a privacy seal?
   b. How do you obtain a privacy seal?
   c. How does the BBB's privacy program for children differ from the standard commercial version?
   d. Is the children's privacy program voluntary? Why or why not?

7. Close your browser, and if necessary, log off your Internet connection.

Case 3. Apartment Referrals, Inc. Apartment Referrals, Inc. is a student-run service that matches university students with available apartments in the community by storing information in a database. The business is highly competitive, and the main source of communication between the referral service and students is by e-mail. Recently a competing student-run referral service bombarded Apartment Referrals with fictitious requests for referrals. As one of the members of the student advisory board, you are concerned about the lack of security for the e-mail system used by Apartment Referrals. You want to ensure that anything submitted to Apartment Referrals is protected from unauthorized use. To research public-key encryption, you'll complete the following steps.

1. Start your Web browser, open the Student Online Companion page at www.course.com/newperspectives/internet3, click the hyperlink for your book, click the Tutorial 9 link, and then click the Case Problems link. Click the HotBot link and wait while the browser loads the page.

Explore 2. Use the search text box to find information about public-key encryption. (*Hint:* Avoid commercial papers and sales sites.) Locate and read three sources of information about public-key encryption. Your focus should be on securing e-mail messages. For each valuable Web site that you locate, print the first page of information.

3. Return to the Student Online Companion, and then click the AltaVista link and wait while your browser opens the page.

4. Search AltaVista for information about secure e-mail. Use the links to find three sources of information about securing e-mail messages. For each valuable Web site that you locate, print the first page of information.

Explore 5. In a memo addressed to the board of directors of Apartment Referrals, Inc., suggest two viable alternatives for securing the mail server so that it is protected from malicious threats and pranks. Support your recommendations with facts you learned from your research. If necessary, return to the Web sites to search for more information about e-mail security.

6. Close your browser, and if necessary, log off your Internet connection.

Case 4. Bolton Brokerage Services Les Bolton is a prominent real estate broker in upstate New York. Les provides many of the agents working for him with office space, phone and Internet services, and staff support. Les has had trouble lately with hacker attacks on his Web site. Three times in the last six months, attackers have successfully penetrated his system and placed electronic graffiti on the home page. In addition, someone has copied the company's corporate logo and other copyrighted real-estate pictures and information and posted it on another site that is masquerading as Bolton Brokerage Services. Les has hired you to look into the security measures he could take to prevent the break-ins his business is experiencing. Also, Les would like to see if there is a way to protect the company's logo and real-estate photos by encoding them with an imperceptible mark clearly identifying the rightful owner. To help Les protect his business and clients, you'll complete the following steps.

1. Start your Web browser, open the Student Online Companion page at www.course.com/newperspectives/internet3, click the hyperlink for your book, click the Tutorial 9 link, and then click the Case Problems link. Click the Thawte link and wait while the browser loads the page.

Explore ▷ 2. See if Thawte offers any support for a free test of a computer network's vulnerability to hackers. If you find a service, print the first page of information about it.

Explore ▷ 3. Use the Thawte Web site to determine the cost of Secure Sockets Layer certificate. When you find this information, use your browser to print it.

Explore ▷ 4. Return to the Student Online Companion page and use the Digimarc Web site to learn more about protecting copyrighted material and print at least two pages that focus on protecting Les's system and information.

Explore ▷ 5. Use a search engine of your choice to learn about steganography and digital watermarks. Print a Web page for each term. Could Les use both of these methods to protect his Web site? How?

6. Close your browser, and if necessary, log off your Internet connection.

Case 5. Personal Research about Cookies You are writing a research paper on the history, use, and potential abuses of cookies. You need to learn how cookies are stored on a site visitor's computer and what potential security threats they present. To get started on your paper, you'll complete the following steps.

1. Start your Web browser, open the Student Online Companion page at www.course.com/newperspectives/internet3, click the hyperlink for your book, click the Tutorial 9 link, and then click the Case Problems link. Click the Cookie Central FAQ link and wait while the browser loads the page.

2. On a sheet of paper, use the Cookie Central FAQ page to answer the following questions.
   a. Who coined the term "cookie" and what was the term's original use?
   b. What are two popular uses of cookies?
   c. In what file format are cookies stored?
   d. Why are cookies potential privacy threats? What can you do to prevent cookies from becoming threats?
   e. What are the six parameters that can be passed to a cookie?

3. Return to the Student Online Companion page for Case Problem 5, and then click the Kookaburra link and wait while the browser loads the page.

4. In a new paragraph, describe Cookie Pal and give one example of how you might use it.

5. Close your browser, and if necessary, log off your Internet connection.

LAB ASSIGNMENTS

Multimedia brings together text, graphics, sound, animation, video, and photo images. In this Lab, you will learn how to apply multimedia and then have the chance to see what it might be like to design some aspects of multimedia projects. See the Read This Before You Begin page for information on installing and starting the Lab.

1. Click the Steps button to learn about multimedia development. As you proceed through the Steps, answer the Quick Check questions. After you complete the Steps, you will see a Quick Check Report. Follow the instructions on the screen to print this report.

2. In Explore, browse through the STS-79 Multimedia Mission Log. How many videos are included in the Multimedia Mission Log? The image on the Mission Profile page is a vector drawing. What happens when you enlarge it?

3. Listen to the sound track on Day 3. Is this a WAV file or a MIDI file? Why do you think so? Is this a synthesized sound or a digitized sound? Listen to the sound track on page 8. Can you tell if this is a WAV file or a MIDI file?

4. Suppose you were hired as a multimedia designer for a multimedia series targeting fourth- and fifth-grade students. Describe the changes you would make to the Multimedia Mission Log so it would be suitable for these students. Also, include a sketch showing a screen from your revised design.

5. When you view the Mission Log on your computer, do you see palette flash? Why or why not? If you see palette flash, list the images that flash.

6. Multimedia can be effectively applied to projects such as encyclopedias, atlases, and animated storybooks; to computer-based training for foreign languages, first aid, or software applications; for games and sports simulations; for business presentations; for personal albums, scrapbooks, and baby books; for product catalogs and Web pages.

7. Suppose you were hired to create one of these projects. Write a one-paragraph description of the project you would be creating. Describe some of the multimedia elements you would include. For each of the elements, indicate its source and whether you would need to obtain permission for its use. Finally, sketch a screen or two showing your completed project.

QUICK CHECK ANSWERS

Session 9.1

1. Plug-in creators earn profits from licensing their plug-in development software so other Web site developers can create Web pages that deliver content that utilizes the plug-in to their Web site visitors.

2. Plug-ins operate within the browser; helper applications are separate programs that execute when you click a link requiring them.

3. True

4. document and productivity, image viewer, multimedia, sound player, video player, VRML, and 3-D

5. Virtual Reality Modeling Language

6. The inn owner might use iPIX to feature video segments of the inn's bedrooms and common areas so potential clients can tour the inn without visiting it first.

7. Beatnik, Crescendo, and RealPlayer

Session 9.2

1. secrecy, integrity, necessity

2. copyright

3. False

4. necessity

5. secrecy

6. asymmetric

7. Phil Zimmermann

In this tutorial you will:

- Learn about Web portal sites and how to customize them

- Create and customize a Web calendar

- Create and customize a Web address book

- Visit Web sites that conduct electronic commerce

- Understand the basics of electronic commerce

WEB PORTALS AND ELECTRONIC COMMERCE

Doing Business on the Internet

CASE

Network Design and Consulting

Network Design and Consulting (NDC) is a medium-sized consulting firm located in Plano, Texas. Steven Boyce founded the company in 1992 with four employees. Since then, he has hired 32 additional employees and broadened the company's focus to include a variety of computer network design, implementation, and analysis projects. Most of NDC's staff members are computer technicians, network analysts, and project managers. NDC has developed an excellent reputation with customers of all sizes, ranging from small businesses with 15 to 20 computers to much larger companies with hundreds of computers. A number of NDC's best engagements have been helping state and local government agencies upgrade their computer networks. Most of NDC's projects are smaller jobs that require only five or six NDC staff members and that have a duration of less than six months.

NDC identifies business consulting opportunities by reviewing publications that list government projects seeking contractors, such as the *Commerce Business Daily*, a U.S. Department of Commerce publication, and several industry newspapers. Melinda McHenry, vice president of engineering, reads these publications and notes any projects that involve computer networking elements. The NDC sales staff call on potential business customers for direct leads. They also call on computer hardware vendors to identify referral opportunities. When the sales staff obtains a lead, they notify Melinda of the opportunity. When Melinda hears from one of the sales staff or identifies an appropriate government project, she quickly assembles a proposal-writing team to create a proposal. Most of these proposals are quite detailed and are usually between 50 and 100 pages. Often, the team must write and submit the proposal within a few days. If NDC is the successful bidder on the project, Melinda forms a work team to execute the project. The work team creates a workflow structure, which specifies which NDC staff members will be assigned to various parts of the project. Work team members must keep track of each project's contact persons, their mobile and office phones, and the best times to contact them. The NDC staff working on a project meet regularly to keep each other informed about the project's progress.

Because of the number of appointments that the NDC staff must handle, each staff member must carefully schedule client meetings so they do not conflict with internal NDC team meetings. So far, each person has kept his or her appointments and contact information in a Personal Digital Assistant (PDA). That arrangement does not allow staff members on the same project to coordinate their schedules with each other. What they all need is a way to post their individual appointments somewhere that allows other team members to check the group schedule before committing to individual appointments. Steven wants you to learn more about Web technologies that might help his company schedule appointments and store client contact information so that company team members can access a common pool of client information.

SESSION 10.1

In this session, you will learn about Web portals and visit a few popular portal sites. You will customize a portal to deliver just the information that interests you. Then, you will create your own Yahoo! Calendar and enter your appointments and important engagements into it. Finally, you will open your private Yahoo! address book.

Web Portals

Web portals represent a way to supply clients with current, customized information. A **Web portal** (or simply a **portal**) is a doorway to the Web. Some portals allow you to customize their entry page contents. Portals are starting points for Web surfers—they usually include general interest information and can help users of the portal find just about anything on the Web. Examples of portals include the AOL, Excite, InfoSpace, MSN, Netscape, and Yahoo! Web sites. Web portals share some common characteristics, including free e-mail, links to search engines, Web directories, membership services, news headlines and articles, discussion groups, chat rooms, links to virtual shopping malls, calendars, and address books.

One term used by advertisers and webmasters for the number of people (or "eyes") who visit a site or see an advertisement is **eyeballs**. These types of audience size measures are important because sites with a large audience can charge higher advertising rates than a site with a smaller audience. A goal of portals and channel providers is to maximize their audience size. Another way of measuring portal and Web page popularity is a page view. A **page view** measures the number of unique visitors to a Web page; in other words, it measures only the number of people who visit the site, and not the number of total visitors, which includes people who visit it more than once. A page view count is a good measure of a site's popularity. Portals usually have page view counts higher than those for other Web pages. The quality of a portal has a tremendous effect on keeping people coming back to a site.

Steven wants you to find some examples of portal sites. Melinda suggests that you start with Excite, one of the earliest Web portal sites.

To examine the Excite portal site:

1. Start your Web browser, open the Student Online Companion page at **http://www.course.com/newperspectives/internet3**, click the hyperlink for your book, click the **Tutorial 10** link, and then click the **Session 10.1** link. Click the **Excite** link and wait while the browser loads the page shown in Figure 10-1.

Figure 10-1   EXCITE PORTAL SITE

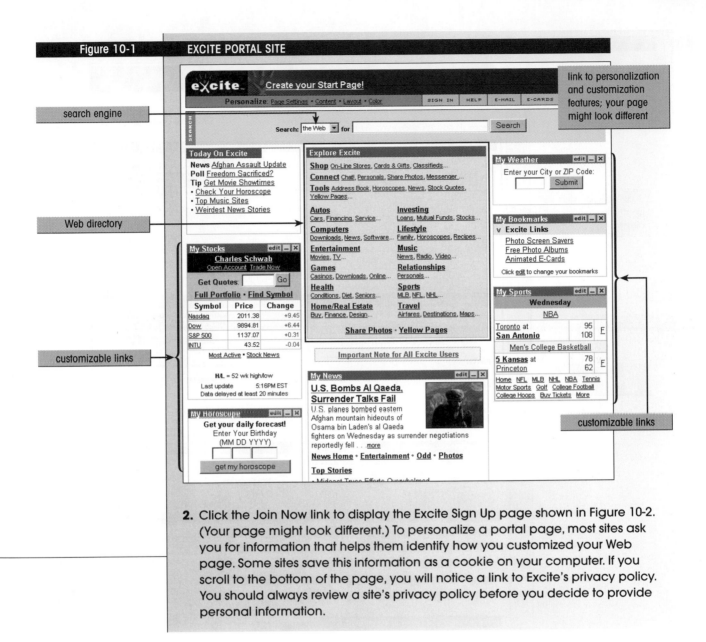

search engine

Web directory

customizable links

link to personalization and customization features; your page might look different

customizable links

2. Click the Join Now link to display the Excite Sign Up page shown in Figure 10-2. (Your page might look different.) To personalize a portal page, most sites ask you for information that helps them identify how you customized your Web page. Some sites save this information as a cookie on your computer. If you scroll to the bottom of the page, you will notice a link to Excite's privacy policy. You should always review a site's privacy policy before you decide to provide personal information.

Figure 10-2   **EXCITE SIGN UP PAGE**

excite **join now!**

Sign Up for Your FREE Excite Membership Fill out the form below for instant access to email, chat, local weather, and other Member-only features on Excite, Webshots, and Blue Mountain Arts. It's quick, easy, and 100% free!

Outside the USA?
Click Here to Sign Up

About You (Required)

First name

Last Name

Birthdate   Month ▾ Day ▾
                                    (e.g. 1968)

Gender   Please Choose ▾

Street Address

ZIP Code   (e.g. 94114)

Primary Email

(your primary email, not your Excite email)

Customize Your Service
Personal information like your ZIP code and birthday lets us customize your experience with features like your local weather, TV listings, and horoscope. It also helps ensure that only you can access your account.

Privacy
We respect your privacy and guarantee to adhere to the policies of TRUSTe.

Choose a Unique Excite Member Name and Password (Required)

Member Name

Password

Repeat Password

Reminder Phrase

Choosing your Excite Member Name
Choose a name to identify yourself with in the Excite Network. Pick a name that nobody else would think of, like i_luv_spinach. If your name is already used, we'll ask you for another name.

Member Name & Password Rules
• 6 to 20 characters
• Use letters (a-z), numbers (1-9), and dashes
• No spaces

Password Reminder Phrase
Pick a phrase to remind you of your password in case you forget it. For example, if your password is your dog's name, you might enter the phrase, "My dog's name".

Your Interests (Optional)

Help us customize your service by selecting areas of interest that are important to you:

☐ Auto   ☐ Entertainment   ☐ Money/Investing   ☐ Sports
☐ Computer/Internet   ☐ Home & Family   ☐ Shopping   ☐ Travel

Great Offers (Optional)

Yes! ☑ I would like to periodically receive email notification of new features and special offers from The Excite Network.

Yes! ☑ Excite may make the information I supplied available to selected companies so that they may contact me regarding products or services that may be of interest to me.

Yes! ☑ Please list my email address, city, state and gender in Excite's free member directories.

[Done]

Privacy Policy and Terms of Agreement

By clicking on the above "Done" button, you are agreeing to our Terms of Use. To get information about the conditions of using Excite, Inc. services, read the Excite, Inc. Terms of Service Agreement.

reviewed by
TRUSTe
site privacy statement

Copyright© 2001 At Home Corporation. All rights reserved. Excite, @Home, and the Excite @Home logos are service marks or registered service marks of At Home in the U.S. and other countries. Disclaimer | Privacy Policy

Submit a Site | Advertise on Excite | Jobs@Excite | Press Releases | Investor Relations | General Excite Help

> Excite requests personal information from members

> account setup information

> link to Excite's privacy policy

3. Click your browser's **Back** button until you return to the Student Online Companion page for Session 10.1.

Next, you decide to look at the Lycos Web portal sites.

To view the Lycos portal site:

1. Return to the Student Online Companion page for Session 10.1, and then click the **Lycos** link to open the Lycos home page shown in Figure 10-3.

Figure 10-3	LYCOS PORTAL SITE

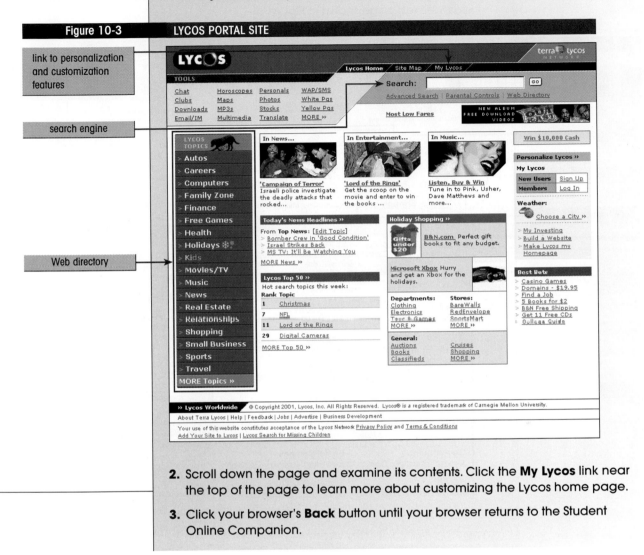

2. Scroll down the page and examine its contents. Click the **My Lycos** link near the top of the page to learn more about customizing the Lycos home page.

3. Click your browser's **Back** button until your browser returns to the Student Online Companion.

Next, you will customize a portal Web page to learn more about the process.

Customizing a Portal

Yahoo! is a busy site that receives a large number of hits each day and thus is a prime location for advertising. Over the years, Yahoo! has grown from a directory-only service to a true portal. Yahoo! offers all of the services and features of a typical portal site. You can use the My Yahoo! feature to save your preferences and deliver current information to your PC each time you visit the Yahoo! site.

Steven wants you to use My Yahoo! to customize a page that he can use to see how a portal works.

To establish your personal Yahoo! ID and password:

1. Return to the Student Online Companion Web page for Session 10.1, if necessary, and then click the **Yahoo!** hyperlink and wait while your Web browser loads the Web page shown in Figure 10-4.

Figure 10-4   YAHOO! SITE BEFORE CUSTOMIZATION

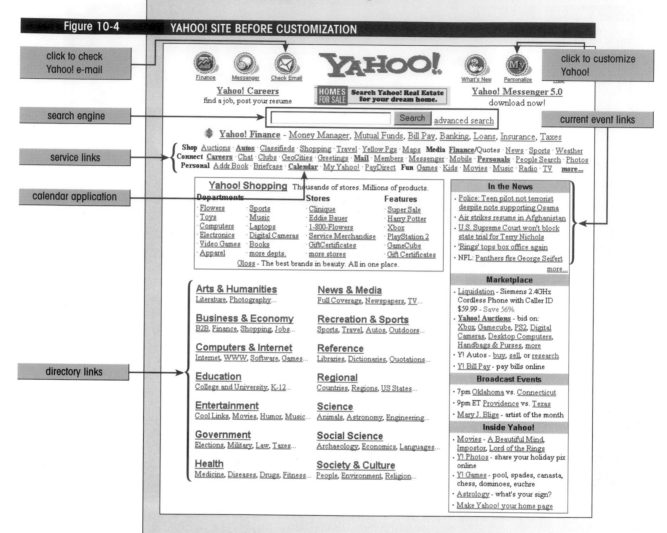

click to check Yahoo! e-mail

click to customize Yahoo!

search engine

service links

calendar application

current event links

directory links

2. Click the **Personalize** button at the top of the Yahoo! home page (see Figure 10-4) to open the Welcome to My Yahoo! page. You must enter and submit a Yahoo! ID and a password, which the Yahoo! server stores as a cookie on your PC, to visit this site. (If you use a different computer the next time you visit Yahoo!, you can ask Yahoo! to find your information on its server.)

   TROUBLE? If you already have a Yahoo! ID, enter your Yahoo! ID and your Yahoo! password in the appropriate text boxes, click the Sign in button, and then skip the remaining steps.

3. Click the **Get Your Own My Yahoo!** link (or the **Sign Up Now** link) in the frame at the left side of the page to open the Welcome to Yahoo! page shown in Figure 10-5.

Figure 10-5	CREATING YOUR YAHOO! ID AND PASSWORD

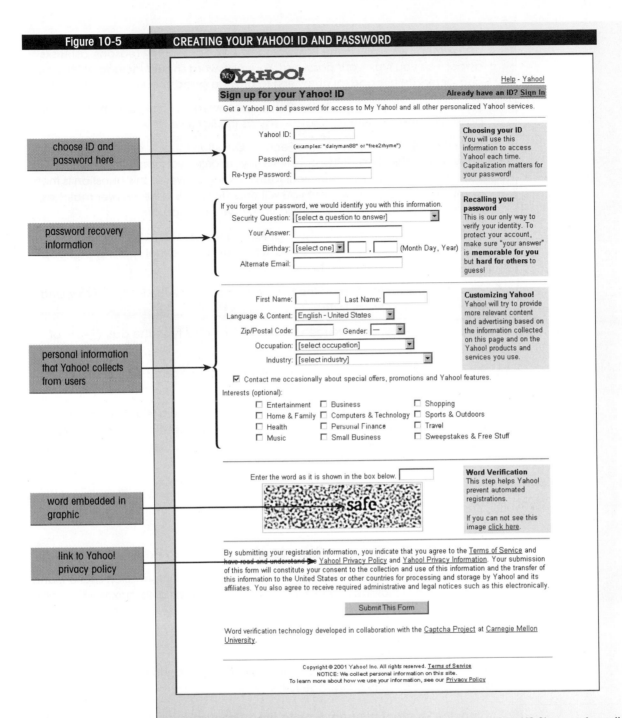

TROUBLE? If you are *not* a U.S. resident, then click the Non-US Sign up form link at the top of the page and enter your information in that form.

4. Click in the **Yahoo! ID** text box, and then type a user ID to identify you. There are several examples below the Yahoo! ID text box on the form. You can use numbers, letters, and the underscore character in your user ID; however, you cannot use any spaces.

5. Press the **Tab** key to move to the Password text box. Type a password that you can remember easily in the Password text box. For security reasons, asterisks appear as you type your password. Your password should include at least six characters (letters and/or numbers) to provide good security.

6. Press the **Tab** key to move to the Retype password text box, and then type your password again exactly the same way as the first time.

7. Press the **Tab** key to move to the Security Question list box, click the list box arrow, and select one of the questions. If you forget your password, Yahoo! will ask you this question to verify your identity. Your answer to this question is then compared to Your Answer that you will enter in Step 8. If the answer matches, Yahoo! will e-mail your password to you so you can log on.

8. Press the **Tab** key to move to the Your Answer text box, and then type the answer to the question you selected. Remember the exact spelling and capitalization in case you need to recover your password.

9. Press the **Tab** key to move to the Birthday list box, click the list box arrow, and click the month of your birth.

10. Press the **Tab** key to move to the next text box and type the day (1–31) of your birth.

11. Press the **Tab** key to move to the last birthday text box and type the four-digit year of your birth.

12. Press the **Tab** key to move to the Alternate Email Address text box, and then type your full e-mail address. Your e-mail address is used only to send your password to you if you request it.

Next, you need to add some additional information about yourself. Then, you can submit your information to Yahoo! and visit your new customized portal site.

To submit your information to Yahoo! and create your page:

1. Scroll down the page to move to the Personal Account Information section, and then enter the following items using the appropriate text or list boxes: your name, your five-digit Zip code, your gender, your occupation (select **college/graduate student** from the list if it applies to you), and your industry (if you are a student, you can select **other**, the last entry in the list).

   TROUBLE? If you are not a U.S. resident, enter the appropriate information in the Country and Primary Language text boxes.

2. Clear the **Contact me from time to time about specials and new products** check box so that you will not receive any unsolicited e-mail from Yahoo! or its affiliates. If you wish, you can click as many check boxes as you have interests that are included in the list.

3. Type the word embedded in the graphic that appears on your page in the text box provided. Yahoo! uses this embedded graphic technique to prevent people from using a computer program to open a large number of accounts very quickly. People that need many e-mail addresses to use when sending junk e-mail could otherwise use Yahoo! as a convenient e-mail address generator.

4. After reviewing the Yahoo! Privacy Policy by following the appropriate links, click the **Submit this Form** button to submit your responses. Yahoo! records your responses and displays a summary of your account ID information and e-mail address, similar to that shown in Figure 10-6.

| Figure 10-6 | YAHOO! ID SUCCESSFUL COMPLETION NOTICE |

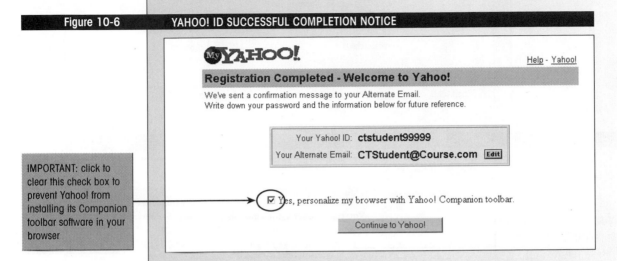

IMPORTANT: click to clear this check box to prevent Yahoo! from installing its Companion toolbar software in your browser

TROUBLE? If you receive an error message that your Yahoo! ID already exists, select a different Yahoo! ID and then resubmit the form. Try using digits after your user name such as the four-digit year of your birth.

TROUBLE? If you receive an error message that you omitted information, correct the omission and then resubmit the form.

5. Clear the check box next to the statement Yes, personalize my browser with Yahoo! Companion toolbar. This prevents Yahoo! from installing its toolbar on your Web browser.

6. Click the **Continue to Yahoo!** link to go to your personalized My Yahoo! page. Notice that your Yahoo! ID appears on the page.

TROUBLE? If a Security Alert dialog opens now or at any other time, click the Yes button and then continue.

The information that you entered is saved as a cookie file on your PC and on the Yahoo! server. If you established a Yahoo! ID on your own computer, then you do not need to worry about someone else using your Yahoo! ID. If you created your account on a public computer (such as a computer in a school computer lab or in an Internet cafe), then the next person who uses a Web browser to visit the Yahoo! Web site will see your Yahoo! customized Web page by default. To avoid this problem, always sign out of your Yahoo! account before closing your Web browser.

To sign out of your Yahoo! account:

1. With the My Yahoo! page displayed, click the **Sign Out** link at the top of the page (see Figure 10-7). When you sign out, Yahoo! displays a screen similar to the one shown in Figure 10-8.

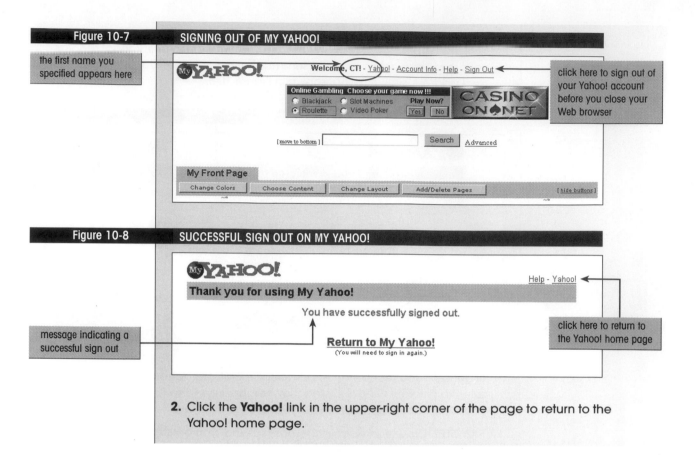

Figure 10-7   SIGNING OUT OF MY YAHOO!

the first name you specified appears here

click here to sign out of your Yahoo! account before you close your Web browser

Figure 10-8   SUCCESSFUL SIGN OUT ON MY YAHOO!

message indicating a successful sign out

click here to return to the Yahoo! home page

2. Click the **Yahoo!** link in the upper-right corner of the page to return to the Yahoo! home page.

Next, you will sign in to your Yahoo! account so you can demonstrate to Steven how he can customize a portal site.

To sign in to your personal Yahoo! account:

1. Return to the Student Online Companion Web page for Session 10.1, and then click the **My Yahoo!** hyperlink and wait while your Web browser loads the Web page.

2. Type your Yahoo! ID in the Yahoo! ID text box, press the **Tab** key to move to the Yahoo! Password text box, and then type your password. Figure 10-9 shows an example of user CTStudent99999 signing in with her user name and password. Notice that the password displays asterisks instead of the actual password for security reasons.

Figure 10-9   **SIGNING IN TO A YAHOO! ACCOUNT**

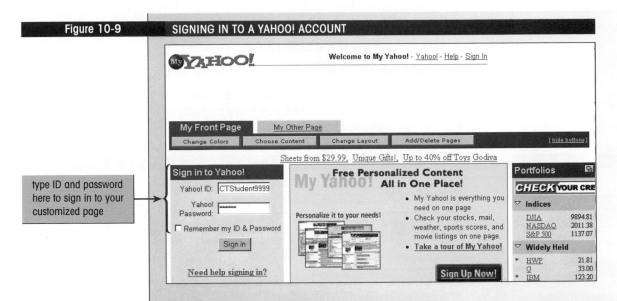

type ID and password here to sign in to your customized page

3. If you are on a public computer, then make sure to clear the **Remember my ID & Password** check box, if it is not already clear, so that your identification and password are not saved on that computer.

4. Click the **Sign in** button below the Yahoo! Password text box to open your Front Page. Once you sign in, your Front Page opens. The My Front Page tab is highlighted, indicating the name of your open Web page. You can add other pages by clicking the Add Page link. If you choose to do that, a tab placed to the right of your Front Page tab represents each page.

Now that you have signed in, you can customize your Yahoo! page in many ways. First, you can customize the general layout of your page by selecting particular modules that you want to see. Second, you can select specific content for each module that you choose. Next, you will customize the general layout of your page.

To personalize your Yahoo! Front Page:

1. Click the **Choose Content** button (see Figure 10-9) to open a Personalize Page Content page. Several categories are listed beneath the Choose Your Content heading. You can select the contents of your Front Page by checking or clearing the contents check boxes. Checked items are included on your Front Page, and unchecked ones are not. You can change the arrangement of the left and right sides of your display by clicking the Change Layout button.

2. Clear all check boxes in every My Yahoo! Category.

3. In the My Yahoo! Essentials list, check the **Headlines** and **Weather** check boxes, and in the **Business & Finance** list, check the **Stock Portfolios** check box.

4. Check the **Best Fares** check box in the Travel category.

5. Click the **Finished** button. (A Finished button is located at both the top and bottom of the page.)

   You return to My Front Page. Next, you will arrange the content you selected on your Front Page.

6. Click the **Change Layout** button.

7. Click **Best Fares** in the Left Side list box.

8. Click the **up arrow** twice to move Best Fares to the top of the list.

9. Click **Weather** and then click the **down arrow** once to move the Weather section to the bottom of the list. When you have completed these steps, your screen should look like Figure 10-10.

Figure 10-10	CUSTOMIZING YOUR FRONT PAGE LAYOUT

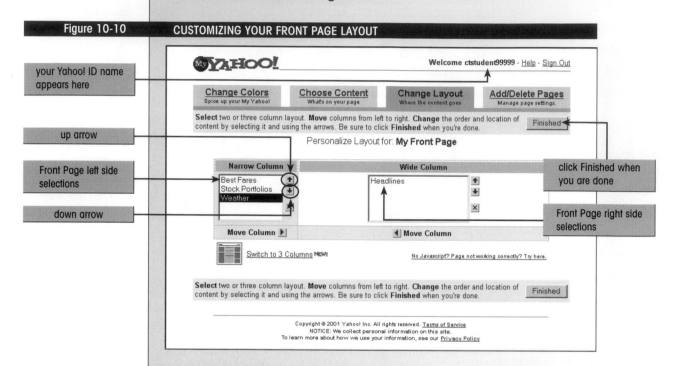

10. Click the **Finished** button to submit your Front Page layout choices. Your newly customized Front Page opens. Notice that the left side displays best airline fares, a module to hold your stock portfolio, and the weather for your city. Yahoo! determines which city's temperature to display based on the Zip code that you entered when you obtained your account. The right side contains news (see Figure 10-11).

Figure 10-11   **CUSTOMIZED YAHOO! FRONT PAGE**

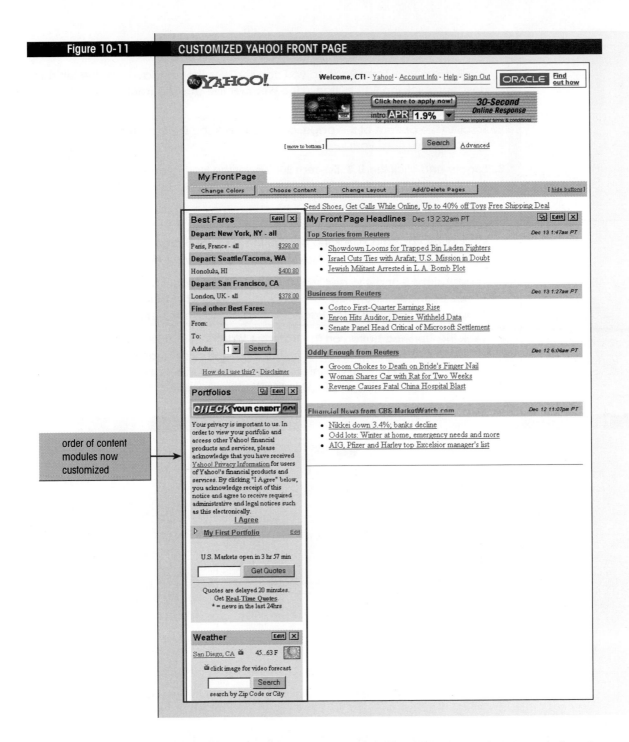

order of content
modules now
customized

You can personalize other pages by clicking the Add/Delete Pages link at the top of your Front Page and then following a similar procedure.

Once you have established the general layout of a page, such as your Front Page, you can fine-tune the contents of each section of a page. You have kept your Front Page simple, but there is still room for further refinement. Steven travels extensively, so you will modify the Weather section of your Front Page to display weather for five cities.

To modify the Weather section of your Front Page:

1. Scroll down your Front Page so you can see Weather displayed on the left side, and then click the **Edit** button in the Weather title bar. The Track the Weather Forecasts page opens.

2. Scroll to the bottom of the page, and then click the **Delete all cities** link to clear all cities from your weather list.

3. Locate and click the **U.S. Eastern** link under the North America heading of the Available Sections list. The Choose your Weather Cities page opens.

4. Scroll down in the Available Cities list until you can click **U.S. Eastern: Boston, MA**. (Cities are arranged alphabetically by country name, then by section of the country, and then by state.) Click the **Add** button to place Boston in the Your Choices column. Click the **Finished** button to return to the Edit your Weather Module.

5. Repeat Steps 3 and 4 to add the following cities to your list: **Paris** (Europe, France), **London Heathrow Airport** (Europe, UK and Ireland), **Tokyo** (Asia, Japan), and **Sydney** (South Pacific, Australia and New Zealand).

6. Click the **Finished** button on the Track the Weather Forecasts page. Your customized Front Page opens showing the list of five cities and their temperatures (see Figure 10-12). If you are interested in learning more about a particular city's weather, click the city's link in the Weather section of your Front Page.

Figure 10-12   WEATHER LIST FOR SELECTED CITIES

7. Click the **Sign Out** link at the top of the My Yahoo! page.

8. Close your browser, and, if necessary, log off your Internet connection.

You can customize other Web pages, such as Excite and Lycos in much the same way you created a customized Yahoo! portal site. You might want to make your customized page at My Yahoo! or another Web portal site your home page that opens when you start your browser. (Review Tutorial 2 to recall how to make a Web page your starting page.)

Now Steven can use the customized Yahoo! site by logging on with your Yahoo! ID and password. An added benefit of a Yahoo! account is that you can create an e-mail address tied to that Yahoo! ID automatically. Just click the Check Email button on the Yahoo! home page and follow the simple e-mail sign-up procedure.

Steven is impressed with his new portal site. He is looking forward to learning how to set up a calendar and address book on the Web.

Creating and Using a Web Calendar

Melinda wants the teams that work on various contracts to be able to enter their appointments and see when the group has scheduled meetings. Although all team members use PDAs to store their own critical data, they cannot share their scheduled appointments very easily. E-mail helps, but sometimes the groups need to check a globally accessible team calendar to keep up to date with appointments. Melinda has read that several portal sites, including Yahoo!, have free calendar services available. She wants you to investigate calendar features, try a test run of the calendar on one project team, and determine if the Web calendars can synchronize their data with the team members' PDAs.

Logging onto the Yahoo! Calendar

You remember seeing a link to a calendar the last time you visited Yahoo!, so you begin your research of Web calendars with that portal.

To log onto the Yahoo! Calendar:

1. Return to the Student Online Companion Web page for Session 10.1, and then click the **Yahoo! Calendar** hyperlink and wait while your Web browser loads the Web page. Alternatively, you can open the Yahoo! home page and click the **Calendar** link located near the top of the Yahoo! home page in the list of links just below the Search text box. Either way, the Yahoo! Calendar Welcome page appears. and displays a login for Existing Yahoo! users.

   TROUBLE? If the Yahoo! Calendar page displays "Welcome" followed by a user name (not yours), then someone who was using the Yahoo! pages on that computer forgot to sign out before closing the Web browser. If this occurs, click the Sign Out link near the top of the page. On the next Yahoo! page that opens, click the Yahoo! link near the top, right side of the page. Then click the Calendar link as directed in Step 1.

2. Type your Yahoo! ID and password in the text boxes and then click the **Sign in** button to open your personal Yahoo! Calendar. The welcome message at the top displays "Welcome" followed by your Yahoo! ID (see Figure 10-13). This page lets you customize the look of your calendar in several ways. In the first section of the page, you can specify the working hours that will appear in your calendar and choose the default view (Day, Week, Month, Year). The other sections of the page provide controls that you can use to set the Time Zone (your calendar is set initially to the time zone for the Zip code you entered when you created your Yahoo! account), reminder options for appointments (including an option to have your calendar e-mailed to you each day), and select items to include in your calendar such as holidays and sports schedules.

| Figure 10-13 | SETTING UP A YAHOO! CALENDAR |

your Yahoo! ID name should appear here

use these tools to customize your calendar

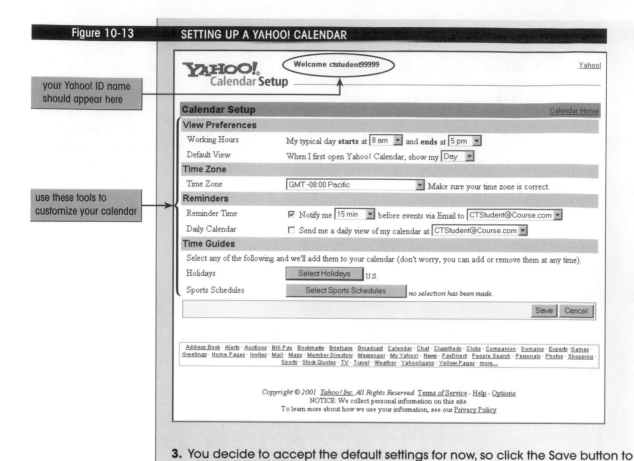

3. You decide to accept the default settings for now, so click the Save button to open the Yahoo! Calendar page shown in Figure 10-14.

Figure 10-14   YAHOO! CALENDAR PAGE

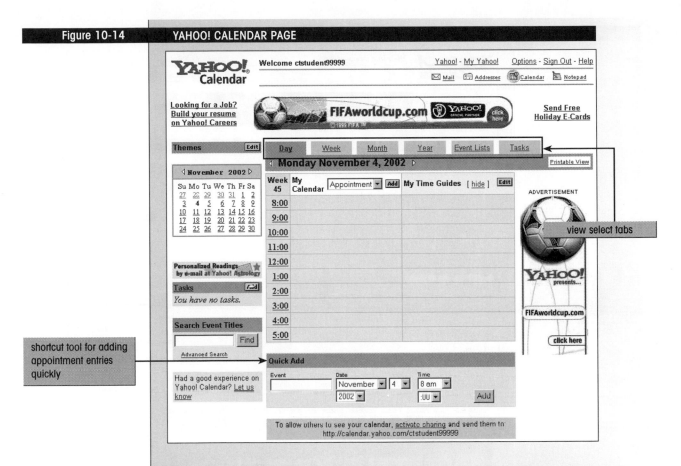

shortcut tool for adding appointment entries quickly

view select tabs

4. Click the **Options** link near the top of the page and then click the **Synchronize** link. You can learn here how to synchronize and upload your team member's schedules from their PDAs. Yahoo! continually updates this page with information about the latest synchronization software available for download. In addition to PDAs, the devices that can be synchronized with a Yahoo! calendar include mobile phones, pagers, and other handheld devices. The Yahoo! calendar can also be synchronized with computers running various software packages for managing contacts and e-mail addresses. You can always check this page (see Figure 10-15) to learn about the latest additions to the Yahoo! calendar's synchronization abilities.

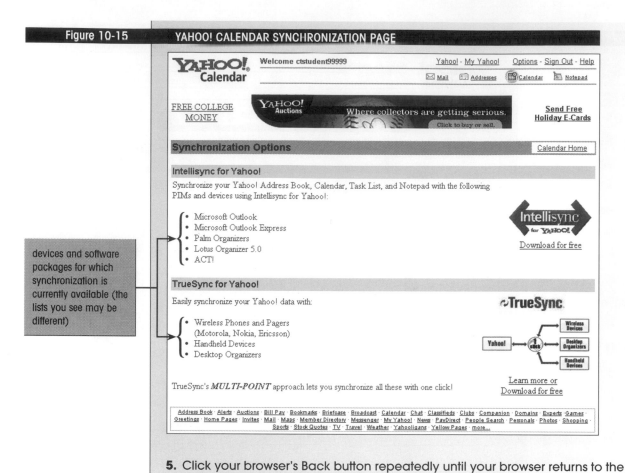

Figure 10-15   YAHOO! CALENDAR SYNCHRONIZATION PAGE

devices and software packages for which synchronization is currently available (the lists you see may be different)

5. Click your browser's Back button repeatedly until your browser returns to the Yahoo! Calendar page. Do not close your browser yet.

Yahoo! Calendar appears to be the answer—or at least one answer—to keeping your teams' schedules coordinated on a Web-accessible calendar system. You are also encouraged to learn that you can download software to provide interaction between your PDA and the Yahoo! calendar. You push ahead in your research.

Entering Appointments

Entering appointments such as a project status review meeting are important to your group and the company. You decide to see how easy that is. A memo arrived today reminding you about your meeting on November 1, 2002, with the LAN Design Team to review their current projects. Although the entry is on your personal calendar, you want everyone to be able to see the details about your appointment—the title, description, and its time—so you will create a **public** entry (later, you will make your personal calendar visible to the public). Yahoo! Calendar also lets you set an event to **Show as Busy**, which indicates you have an event scheduled that day, but the details are private. By default, all calendar events you enter are **private**, and no one except you knows you have an appointment that is marked private.

Entering a Single Appointment

Melinda has asked you to begin adding calendar events to your own calendar to help you evaluate the Yahoo! calendar. The first event you will add is the current project status review meeting with the LAN Design Team on November 1, 2002 at 11:00 AM. You expect that the meeting should last less than three hours. You will create your first Yahoo! Calendar entry to record this meeting.

To enter a single, public appointment:

1. Click the **Year** view select tab at the top of the empty calendar for today.

2. If the year displayed in the bar at the top of the calendar is not 2002, use the scroll arrows to the right and left of the year displayed to change the year displayed to 2002.

3. Scroll down the page if necessary to find November 1 in the calendar display, and then click the digit **1**.

4. Click the **Day** view select tab to open the day's calendar for November 1, 2002.

5. The meeting is scheduled for 11:00 AM, so click the **11:00** link in the calendar to open up a page in which you can enter the appointment details.

6. In the Title text box type **LAN Design Team - Current project status review** and ensure that the Type list box displays Appointment.

7. Click the **Public** option button so that anyone can see the appointment once you publish your calendar (see Figure 10-16).

| Figure 10-16 | RECORDING AN APPOINTMENT |

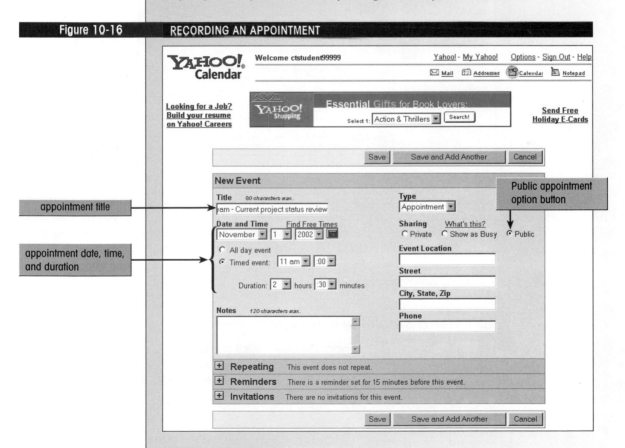

8. Click the Duration **hours** list arrow and select **2**, and click the Duration **minutes** list arrow and select **:30** to indicate that the meeting is scheduled to last 2 hours and 30 minutes.

9. Click the **Save** button to save the new appointment. (You can click the Save button at either the top or bottom of the page.) The new appointment appears in the calendar for November 1, 2002 (see Figure 10-17).

Figure 10-17   A NEW PUBLIC APPOINTMENT

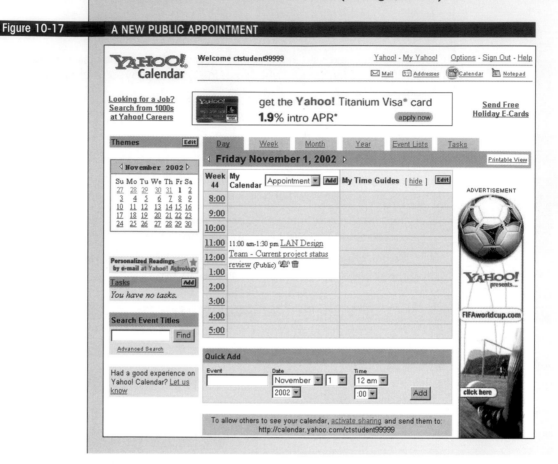

Yahoo! Calendar is easy to use and very convenient. You can create an appointment that others in your group (and anyone else) can see. On November 8, 2002, you have an appointment with your dentist. Because this is a personal appointment and no one else needs to know about it, you will create a private appointment. The dental appointment is 10:00 AM and lasts 45 minutes (you hope). Follow these steps to create a private appointment. The procedure is almost the same as setting up a public appointment.

To enter a single, private appointment:

1. With your Yahoo! Calendar still open, click the **Year** view select tab at the top of the calendar page and click the digit **8** in the November calendar (you might need to scroll down the page to find the November calendar).

2. Click the **Day** view select tab to open the day's calendar for November 8, 2002.

3. Click the **10:00** link in the calendar for the 8th.

4. In the Title text box type **Dental checkup** and ensure that the Type list box displays Appointment. Also check to ensure that the date shown is November 8.

5. Click the **Private** option button, if it is not already selected, in the Sharing category. Nobody needs to know about this appointment.

6. Click the **Timed event** list arrow and select **10 am** if it is not already selected.

7. Click the Duration **hours** list arrow and select **0**, and click the Duration **minutes** list arrow and select **:45** to indicate that the appointment should last 45 minutes.

8. Click the **Save** button to save the new appointment. The new appointment appears in your calendar (see Figure 10-18).

| Figure 10-18 | NOVEMBER APPOINTMENTS |

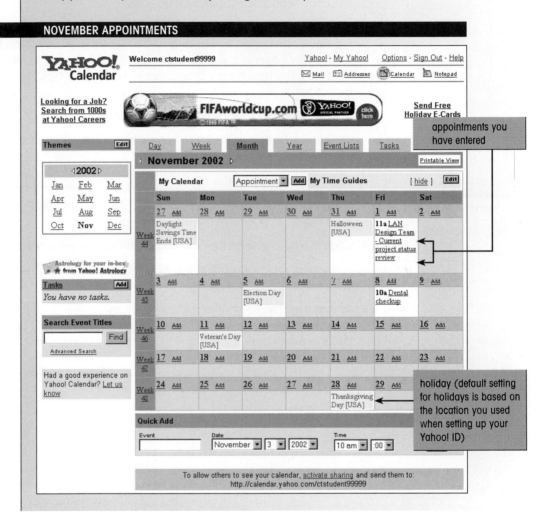

You decide to try entering a recurring appointment. One time when you were experimenting with Yahoo! Calendar, you clicked Help and learned a great deal about recurring appointments. (Yahoo! Calendar has very good help. Simply click the Help link at the bottom of any calendar page.) Recurring events can appear in your calendar daily, weekly, on a certain day every week, every two weeks, every month, and every year. You also control how long the recurring event occurs. Birthday reminders are an example of an annually recurring event that Yahoo! Calendar can record.

Entering a Recurring Appointment

Your group has a staff meeting every Monday morning from 9:00 AM until 10:00 AM to discuss the current week's plans. They plan to have this meeting for three months beginning in November, 2002. You set out to pencil in that appointment. You want your colleagues to know you are busy during that time each week, but they do not need to know the details about the meeting. Thus, you will designate the meeting as "Show as Busy."

To enter a recurring, limited-duration appointment:

1. If necessary, log back into Yahoo! Calendar with your Yahoo! ID.

2. Using the skills you have learned in the previous steps, navigate to the Day view for November 4, 2002.

3. Click the **9:00** link to open that time slot.

4. Click the **Title** text box and type **Staff meeting**, and click the **Type** list box and type **m**. Event names are arranged alphabetically in the Type list. When you type the first few letters of the listed event types, the list scrolls to the event type automatically. The type Meeting appears in the Type list box. The default duration of 1 hour is fine.

5. In the Sharing category, click **Show as Busy**.

6. Click the **+** button, called Edit Details, to the left of "Repeating" to specify more details about the meeting.

7. Click the **Repeat on the** option button.

8. Click the list arrow on the first list box to the right of the "Repeat on the" option button and click **First** in the list, if necessary.

9. Click the list arrow on the day list box and click **Mon** in the list.

10. If necessary, click **month** in the third list box to the right of the "Repeat on the" option button.

11. To limit the duration of the repeating event, click the **Until** option button. To click **January** in the month list box, click **6** in the day list box, and then click **2003** in the year list box. Your completed recurring event information should look like Figure 10-19.

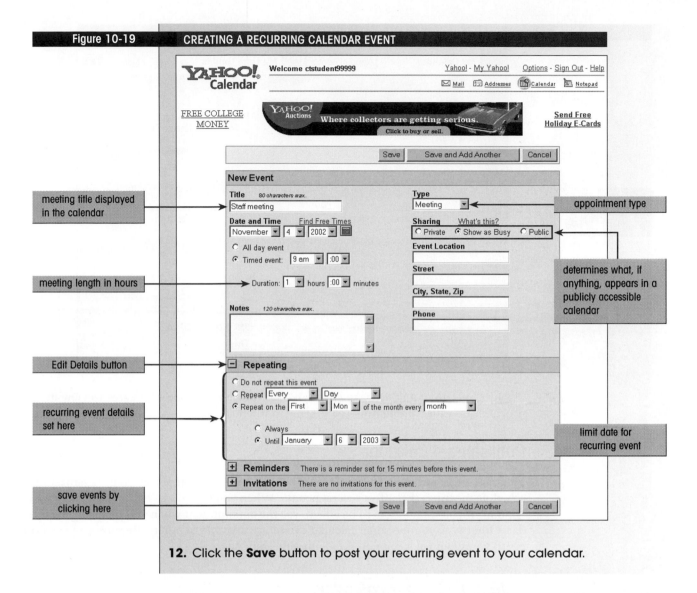

| Figure 10-19 | CREATING A RECURRING CALENDAR EVENT |

meeting title displayed in the calendar

appointment type

meeting length in hours

determines what, if anything, appears in a publicly accessible calendar

Edit Details button

recurring event details set here

limit date for recurring event

save events by clicking here

12. Click the **Save** button to post your recurring event to your calendar.

Scroll through your calendar to verify that the staff meeting occurs the first Monday of November and December of 2002 and January of 2003 Because you are viewing your own calendar, all three of November's appointments appear (see Figure 10-20, which shows the calendar panel portion of the Web page for November in Month view). You have complete control over your own calendar. You can see all of the public, "Show as Busy," and private calendar entries that you have made.

Figure 10-20   STAFF MEETING IN MONTHLY CALENDAR

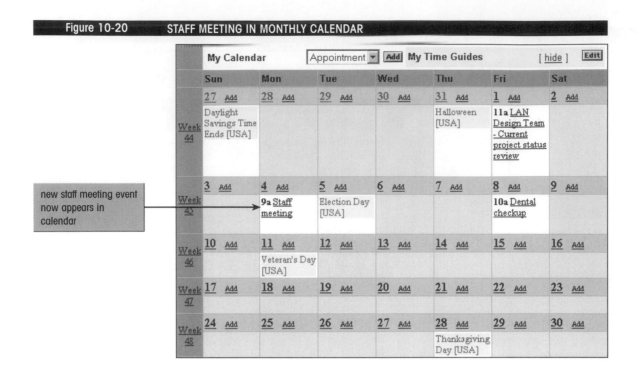

new staff meeting event now appears in calendar

Next, you are going to make your calendar visible to anyone who cares to view it. That procedure is called **publishing** (or **sharing**) a calendar.

Publishing a Calendar

You can use a **published calendar** to make it easier for others in your organization to schedule meetings that affect several people. When you create a calendar event, designate it "public" if you want others to be able to see the appointment when you publish your calendar. Otherwise, your personal calendar events are invisible to others. Because you want others to view your calendar, you decide to publish it.

To publish your calendar:

1. If necessary, log back into the Yahoo! Calendar with your Yahoo! ID.

2. Scroll to the bottom of your calendar page and click **activate sharing** link. A page opens displaying several calendar-sharing options.

3. Click the **Allow anyone to view my calendar** option button in the Activate Sharing section. Doing so opens any public appointments to the public. (If you wanted to share your calendar with a select group, then you could choose the "Allow only people on this list to view my calendar" option; see Figure 10-21).

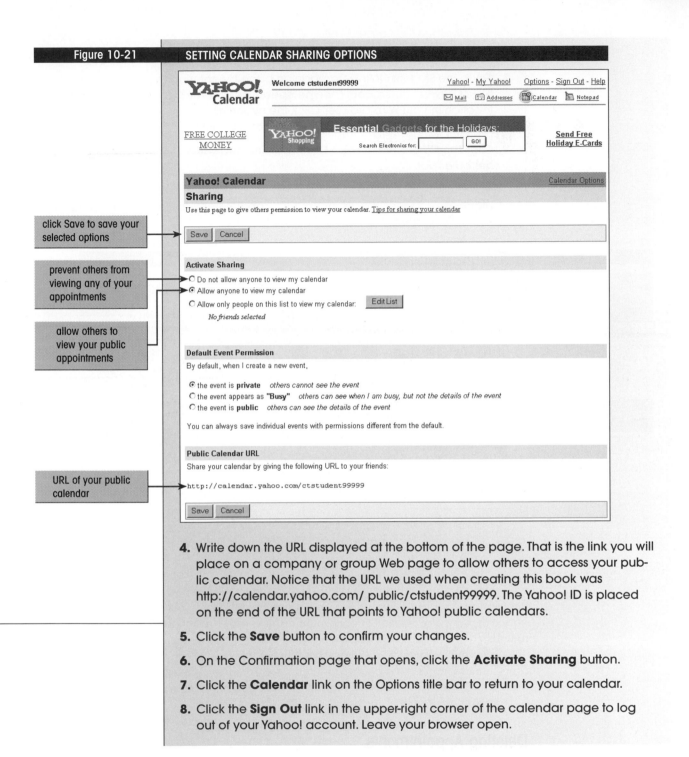

Figure 10-21   SETTING CALENDAR SHARING OPTIONS

click Save to save your selected options

prevent others from viewing any of your appointments

allow others to view your public appointments

URL of your public calendar

4. Write down the URL displayed at the bottom of the page. That is the link you will place on a company or group Web page to allow others to access your public calendar. Notice that the URL we used when creating this book was http://calendar.yahoo.com/ public/ctstudent99999. The Yahoo! ID is placed on the end of the URL that points to Yahoo! public calendars.

5. Click the **Save** button to confirm your changes.

6. On the Confirmation page that opens, click the **Activate Sharing** button.

7. Click the **Calendar** link on the Options title bar to return to your calendar.

8. Click the **Sign Out** link in the upper-right corner of the calendar page to log out of your Yahoo! account. Leave your browser open.

You can navigate to other persons' posted Yahoo! Calendar URLs and view their public appointments. To try it out, you decide to go to the calendar we created for the screen shots in this book. The URL for the account we used appears in the figures and is available in the Student Online Companion for the book.

To view the public events of someone's private Yahoo! Calendar:

1. Go to the Student Online Companion page by entering the URL **http://www.course.com/newperspectives/internet3** in the appropriate location in your Web browser. Click the hyperlink for your book, click the **Tutorial 10** link, and then click the **Session 10.1** link.

2. Click the **CT Student Public Calendar** link and wait while the browser loads her calendar.

3. Navigate to the month of November, 2002, and then display the calendar in Month view to see CT Student's public appointments in November. Figure 10-22 shows CT Student's public appointments.

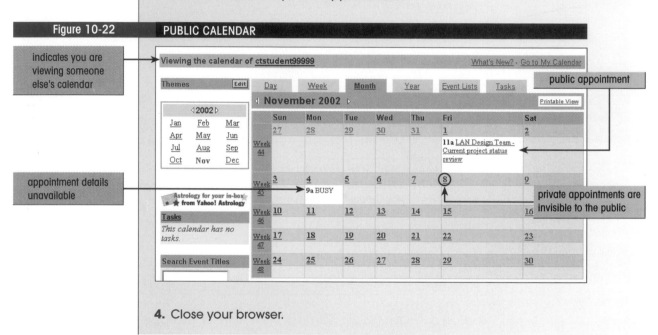

Figure 10-22   PUBLIC CALENDAR

4. Close your browser.

Notice that in CT Student's calendar the November 1 appointment exhibits a complete description. You can click on the link and view details of that public appointment. Also notice that the November 4 appointment displays only the notation "BUSY." This appointment is, in effect, a semi-private appointment. The details of that appointment are not available, but your colleagues will know that you are unavailable for other appointments at that time. Finally, notice that no appointments are listed for November 8, the day when CT Student scheduled a dental appointment. That appointment was designated "Private" to hide it from public view.

Deleting Appointments

Yahoo! Calendar lets you delete appointments easily. You can delete a single appointment, one of several recurring appointments, all appointments of a series of recurring appointments, or even clear the entire calendar.

Deleting One Appointment in a Recurring Set

One of the people who was to present important project information at next Monday's first staff meeting is sick. Rather than trying to find a substitute presenter, Melinda asks you to simply cancel that single meeting. Remembering that the meeting is scheduled for the first Monday of the next three months, you want to be careful not to delete all the meetings. Only the calendar's owner—the person who made the original appointment—can delete any calendar entries. Next you will cancel a single meeting in the recurring set.

To delete an appointment from your Yahoo! Calendar:

1. Start your Web browser, open the Student Online Companion page at **http://www.course.com/newperspectives/internet3**, click the hyperlink for your book, click the **Tutorial 10** link, and then click the **Session 10.1** link.

2. Click the **Yahoo! Calendar** link and wait while the browser loads the Yahoo! Calendar page.

3. Log onto Yahoo by typing your Yahoo! ID and password in the text boxes and clicking the **Sign in** button. Your personal calendar opens.

4. Navigate to the date November 4, 2002 and display your calendar in Month view. Your appointments for November appear.

5. Click the **Staff meeting** link displayed for November 4, 2002. A page opens that displays details of that appointment and that allows you to edit those details.

6. Click the **this date only** option button in the Apply changes to row so that you delete only this particular date, not all recurring dates.

7. Click the **Delete** button to delete the entry. November's appointments reappear, but the November 4 staff meeting is gone. Navigate to the next two months to make sure you did not delete the other two appointments.

When you delete an appointment, you cannot undo the deletion, so be very careful. Double check that you are not deleting *all* appointments whenever an appointment recurs periodically.

Deleting a One-Time Appointment

To delete a one-time appointment—one that does not recur—follow the same steps as above except that you do not need to click the *this date only* option button. In other words, click the appointment to open an appointment details page and click the Delete button.

Clearing the Entire Calendar

When you decide to clear your entire calendar and start over, you can do so almost too easily. Melinda doesn't want you to do this, but she does want to make sure Yahoo! Calendar provides that function. She asks you to look into it. You decide that you can recreate the three appointments and that it would be instructive to make sure you can clear all your appointments. Do the following to clear out *all* appointments in your Yahoo! Calendar. (Yahoo! calls the operation *resetting* your calendar.) **Warning**: If you really do keep appointments in your Yahoo! Calendar and you have entered several that you want to keep, then *do not* do the steps in this section. There is no way to recover calendar entries that you delete.

To clear all appointments from your Yahoo! Calendar:

1. With your personal calendar still available in your browser, click the **Options** link located at the top and the bottom of every Yahoo! Calendar page. The Options page opens (see Figure 10-23). This page includes links that allow you to customize Yahoo! Calendar in many ways.

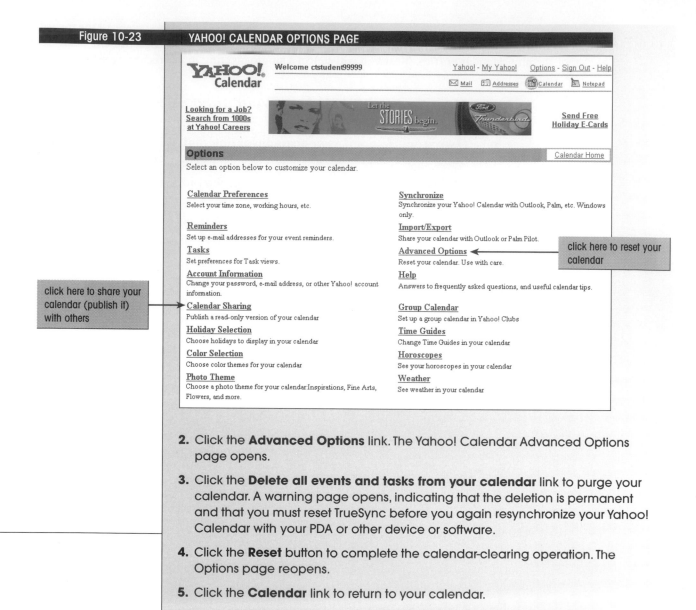

Figure 10-23   YAHOO! CALENDAR OPTIONS PAGE

2. Click the **Advanced Options** link. The Yahoo! Calendar Advanced Options page opens.

3. Click the **Delete all events and tasks from your calendar** link to purge your calendar. A warning page opens, indicating that the deletion is permanent and that you must reset TrueSync before you again resynchronize your Yahoo! Calendar with your PDA or other device or software.

4. Click the **Reset** button to complete the calendar-clearing operation. The Options page reopens.

5. Click the **Calendar** link to return to your calendar.

6. Click the **Sign Out** link to sign out.

7. Close your browser.

Printing a Calendar

Though the primary purpose of a Yahoo! Calendar is online viewing through a browser from anywhere at any time, you can also print a copy of your calendar for a day, a week, a month, or a year. (A year view does not show your appointments and is thus not useful for that purpose.) Display the calendar in the view that you want to print (day, week, month, or year) and then click the Printable View link in the upper-right corner of the calendar. The view opens in a Web page that is more suitable for printing than the default online viewing presentation. You can then use your browser's Print command (in the File menu or on a toolbar button) to print the calendar. When you have finished printing the calendar item, click the Calendar Home link on the right side of the calendar to return to the normal calendar view.

Creating and Using a Web Address Book

Melinda wants you to learn how to store customer contact information in a Web address book so that staff members can access critical telephone numbers and addresses from any location that has a Web browser. Having a Web-based address book relieves employees from remembering to carry their PDAs everywhere they travel. It also serves as a safe backup location for valuable information in case their hand-held organizers should fail. Storing valuable information in two locations makes a lot of sense and provides an electronic insurance policy against loss. You set off to investigate Yahoo! address books.

Entering Address Information

Yahoo!, like other popular portals, provides a convenient way to store name, address, and phone number data—contact information—on the globally accessible Web site. The process of creating and maintaining addresses on the Yahoo! site costs you nothing, and it is sometimes more convenient than always carrying an electronic organizer everywhere you go. You want to store several staff members' addresses on the Yahoo! site, and you are eager to see for yourself if the feature is easy to use.

To add contacts to a Yahoo! Address Book:

1. Start your Web browser, open the Student Online Companion page at http://www.course.com/nowperspectives/internet3, click the hyperlink for your book, click the Tutorial 10 link, and then click the Session 10.1 link.

2. Click the **Yahoo! Calendar** link to open up the Yahoo! Calendar page.

3. Log onto your Yahoo! account: type your Yahoo! ID in the Yahoo! ID text box, type your password in the Password text box, and click the **Sign in** button. Your private calendar showing today's appointments opens.

   TROUBLE? If you are using Internet Explorer and an AutoComplete dialog box pops up asking you if you want it to remember your ID and password, click **No** if you are on a public computer. It is not a good idea to store your password on public computers (your password is saved in a cookie on the computer). If you are on your own, private computer that only you use, then you can click **Yes** to store the password and save some steps the next time.

   TROUBLE? If you logged on correctly, the top of the page should display a personal welcome message. Notice that there are links to Mail, Addresses, Calendar, and Notepad to the right of the message, at the top right of the page.

4. Click the **Addresses** link. The Yahoo! Address Book page opens (see Figure 10-24).

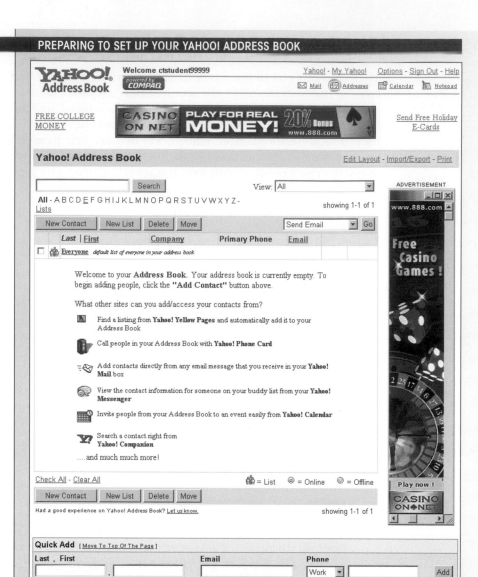

Figure 10-24   PREPARING TO SET UP YOUR YAHOO! ADDRESS BOOK

5. Click the **New Contact** button to open the Add Contact page.

6. Enter the following three names, addresses, and telephone numbers. Set the Category field to **Professional** and click the **Work** Primary Phone option button for each address entry. After you enter each person's information, click the **Save** button to store the information. You may add additional information about each contact in the Work, Home, Internet, and Personal Information sections if you wish. Then click the **Add Contact** button to add the next person. Figure 10-25 shows the Yahoo! Address Book Add Contact page after entering Lin Choong's contact information but before clicking the Save button. After you have added the third contact's information and saved it, your completed address book shows the names you have added (see Figure 10-26).

First	Last	Email	Company	Work Phone
David	Golkin	dgolkin@cavco.com	Cavco Industries Inc.	602.555.6141
James	Garcia	jgarcia@roanoke.com	Roanoke Electric Corp.	703.555.1909
Lin	Choong	choong@lilly.com	Lilly Industries, Inc.	317.555.6762

Figure 10-25 **ADDING A CONTACT TO THE ADDRESS BOOK**

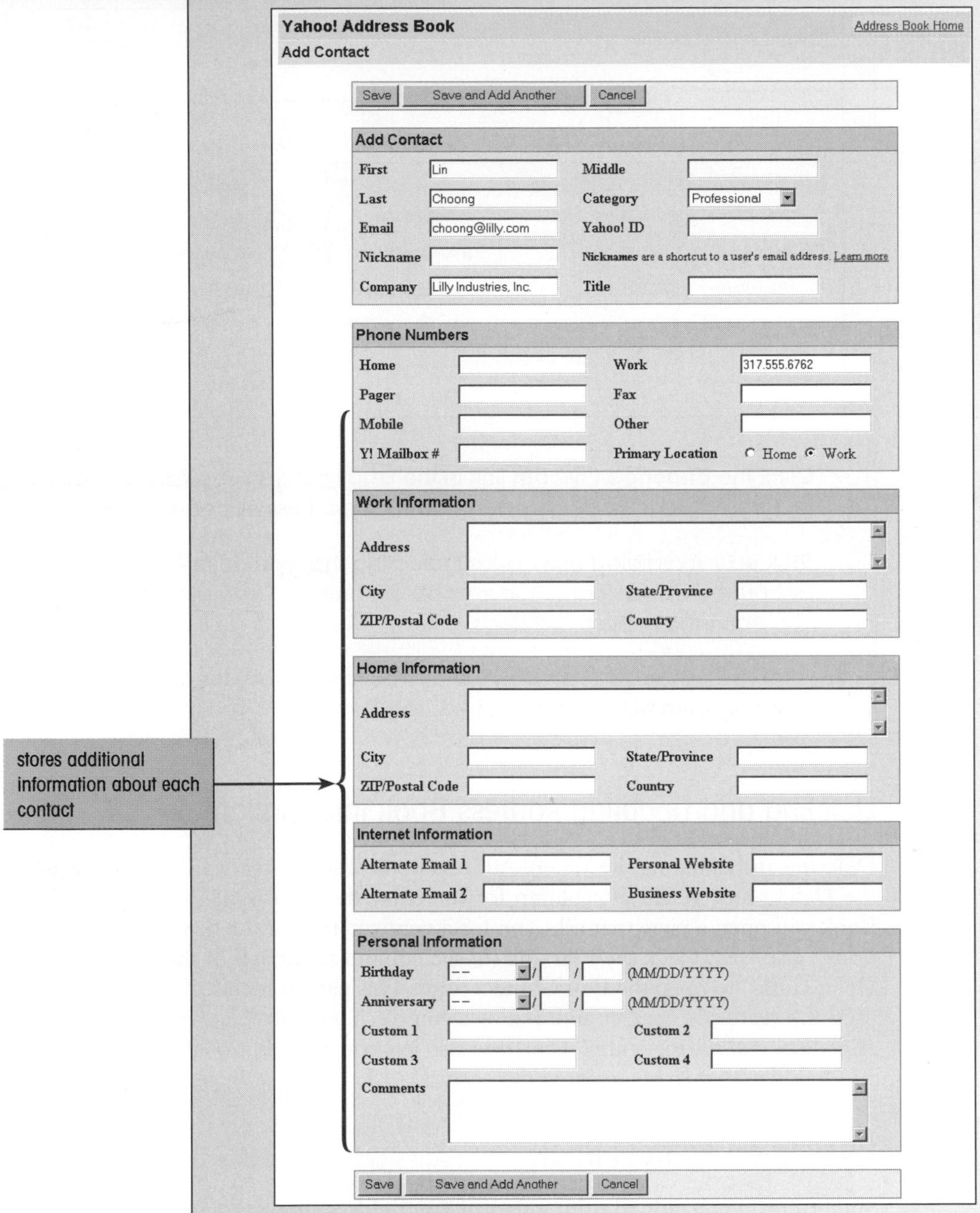

Yahoo! Address Book   Address Book Home
Add Contact

[Save] [Save and Add Another] [Cancel]

Add Contact

First	Lin	Middle	
Last	Choong	Category	Professional
Email	choong@lilly.com	Yahoo! ID	
Nickname			**Nicknames** are a shortcut to a user's email address. Learn more
Company	Lilly Industries, Inc.	Title	

Phone Numbers

Home		Work	317.555.6762
Pager		Fax	
Mobile		Other	
Y! Mailbox #		Primary Location	○ Home ◉ Work

Work Information

Address

| City | | State/Province | |
| ZIP/Postal Code | | Country | |

Home Information

Address

| City | | State/Province | |
| ZIP/Postal Code | | Country | |

Internet Information

| Alternate Email 1 | | Personal Website | |
| Alternate Email 2 | | Business Website | |

Personal Information

Birthday	-- / / (MM/DD/YYYY)
Anniversary	-- / / (MM/DD/YYYY)
Custom 1		Custom 2	
Custom 3		Custom 4	
Comments	

[Save] [Save and Add Another] [Cancel]

stores additional information about each contact

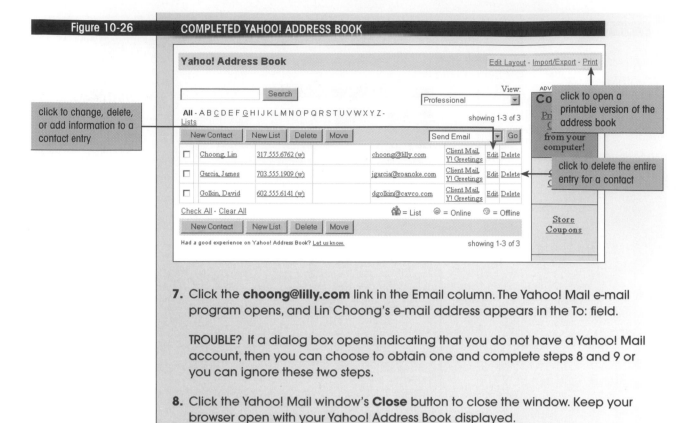

Figure 10-26   COMPLETED YAHOO! ADDRESS BOOK

7. Click the **choong@lilly.com** link in the Email column. The Yahoo! Mail e-mail program opens, and Lin Choong's e-mail address appears in the To: field.

   TROUBLE? If a dialog box opens indicating that you do not have a Yahoo! Mail account, then you can choose to obtain one and complete steps 8 and 9 or you can ignore these two steps.

8. Click the Yahoo! Mail window's **Close** button to close the window. Keep your browser open with your Yahoo! Address Book displayed.

Deleting and Updating Address Book Information

Deleting and updating the Yahoo! Address Book is straightforward. To delete an entry, click the Delete link in the last column for the entry that you want to remove. Yahoo! Address Book will open a page that asks you for a confirmation of the deletion. Updating information is also easy. Click the Edit link (in the column to the left of the column containing the Delete links) to open the Edit Contact page. This page is identical to the Add page that you used to create the contact and it allows you to change or delete any information you have already stored for that entry. This page also lets you add additional information in fields that you left blank when you created the entry.

Printing an Address Book

Sometimes it is handy to print a part of your address book. You may want to share a paper copy of it with co-workers, have a backup copy for emergencies, or take it with you on a trip. Printing a Yahoo! Address Book is straightforward. Do the following to print your three-entry address book.

To print a Yahoo! Address Book:

1. With the Yahoo! Address Book open, click the **Print** link located in the upper-right corner of the Address Book area of the page.

2. Click the **Customized Layout** option button so you can print exactly the portions of your address book entries that you choose.

3. Click the **Clear All** link to clear all checked entries in the Customize Layout Options panel and place a checkmark next to these fields: **First Name**, **Work**, **Last Name**, and **Email**. Your screen should resemble Figure 10-27.

Figure 10-27	SELECTING YAHOO! ADDRESS BOOK FIELDS TO PRINT

click to open a preview of the printed copy of your address book selection

Yahoo! Address Book   Address Book Home
Printable Address Book

| Display for Printing | View Sample | Cancel |

Select a layout and if you are ready to print, click **Display for Printing**. If you wish to view a sample layout or need additional information on how to print click **View Sample**.

○ **Summary Layout**
   Print same fields that are displayed in your address book when viewing "All".
○ **Detailed Layout**
   Print all the fields in your address book excluding Personal Information fields.
◉ **Customized Layout**
   Customize your Printout. Choose from the information below what you wish to print.

Customize Layout Options

General Information

☑ First Name	☐ Middle Name	☐ Home	☑ Work
☑ Last Name	☐ Nickname	☐ Pager	☐ Fax
☐ Company	☐ Title	☐ Mobile	☐ Other
☑ Email	☐ Yahoo! ID	☐ Yahoo!	
☐ Comments			

Phone Numbers

Mailing Addresses   **Internet Information**

| ☑ Work Address | ☑ Home Address | ☐ Alternate Email 1 | ☐ Alternate Email 2 |
| | | ☐ Personal Website | ☐ Business Website |

Check All - Clear All

click to clear all checked fields

| Display for Printing | View Sample | Cancel |

4. Click the **Display for Printing** button to preview the printed address book.

5. Click your browser's **Print** command in the **File** menu and then click **OK** to print your short address book. You can try different settings on the Printable Address Book page and then view them by clicking either the **Display for Printing** button or the **View Sample** button.

6. Click the **Sign Out** link near the top, right of the page to sign out of your Yahoo! account.

7. Close your browser and, if necessary, log off your Internet connection.

Session 10.1 QUICK CHECK

1. What term do Web advertisers sometimes use when they describe the audience size of a Web portal?

2. Usually, portal sites require you to establish a(n) _____ and a(n) _____ before customizing a portal.

3. True or False: You can customize every Web page to display only the information you need.

4. True or False: By marking an appointment in your Yahoo! Calendar as "Public," you ensure that the public can view that entry in your private calendar. Explain.

5. Explain briefly one advantage of using a Web-based calendar compared to a PDA's built-in calendar or calendar software on your desktop computer.

SESSION 10.2

In this session, you will learn about electronic commerce and visit several sites that use electronic commerce effectively to conduct business. You also will explore some of the concerns that consumers have when using electronic commerce sites.

What Is Electronic Commerce?

Steve has heard many people in his industry talk about how electronic commerce is becoming the growth market of the future. He would like you to find out more about electronic commerce and how SSP might use it.

You begin your research by talking with a number of businesspersons that you know. You find that everyone you ask seems to have a different idea of what electronic commerce is. Some people and businesses use the term electronic business (or e-business) when they are discussing electronic commerce in this broader sense. However, most people use the terms electronic commerce and electronic business interchangeably. Many not-for-profit organizations conduct "business" activities; for example, a museum might sell tickets for an upcoming special exhibition on its Web site. In this book, the term electronic commerce (or e-commerce) is used in its broadest sense; that is, the conduct of selling, buying, logistics, or other organization management activities via the Web.

Jeff Bezos, a young financial analyst and fund manager who had become intrigued by the rapid growth of the Internet, founded one of the fastest growing electronic commerce sites in 1994. Bezos listed 20 products that he thought might sell well on the Internet. After some intense analysis, he determined that books were at the top of his list. Bezos had no experience in the book-selling business, but he realized that books were small-ticket commodity items that would be easy and inexpensive to ship. He knew many customers would be willing to buy books without inspecting them in person and that books could be impulse purchase items if properly promoted.

Bezos believed that many people would find buying books from an online seller to be more attractive than visiting the local bookstore. He envisioned his Web site's software tracking customer's purchases and recommending similar titles. He wanted to give his customers the option of requesting notification when a particular author publishes a new book. By paying attention to every process involved in buying, promoting, selling, and shipping books, and by working to improve each process continuously, Bezos and Amazon.com have become one of the first highly visible electronic commerce Web sites.

As it has grown, Amazon.com has continued to expand its business. In 1998, it began selling music CDs, its first non-book item. In subsequent years, Amazon.com has added consumer electronics, toys, camera and photo items, software, computer and video games, health and beauty products, tools and hardware, lawn and patio items, kitchen products, and wireless electronics to its list of offerings. Six years after opening its Web site, Amazon.com had annual sales of over $2 billion.

Some companies, believing that Amazon.com has developed an excellent Web site for selling products to customers, have created partnerships in which they include their Web sites inside the Amazon.com site and have Amazon handle the order-taking and delivery processes for them. Retailers that have done this include Target, Toysrus.com, and Drugstore.com. Amazon also hosts smaller retailers in the section of its site called zShops.

To visit the Amazon.com retail electronic commerce site:

1. Start your Web browser, open the Student Online Companion page at **http://www.course.com/newperspectives/internet3**, click the hyperlink for your book, click the **Tutorial 10** link, and then click the **Session 10.2** link. Click the **Amazon.com** link and wait while your browser loads the Amazon.com home page. Note that Amazon.com has expanded from its beginnings as an online bookstore. The tabs across the top of the home page are hyperlinks to some of the Amazon stores and a complete list of links to Amazon's offerings appear on the left side of the page. See Figure 10-28.

Figure 10-28	AMAZON HOME PAGE

tabs are links to main shopping categories

links to Amazon product categories, services, and hosted stores for other merchants

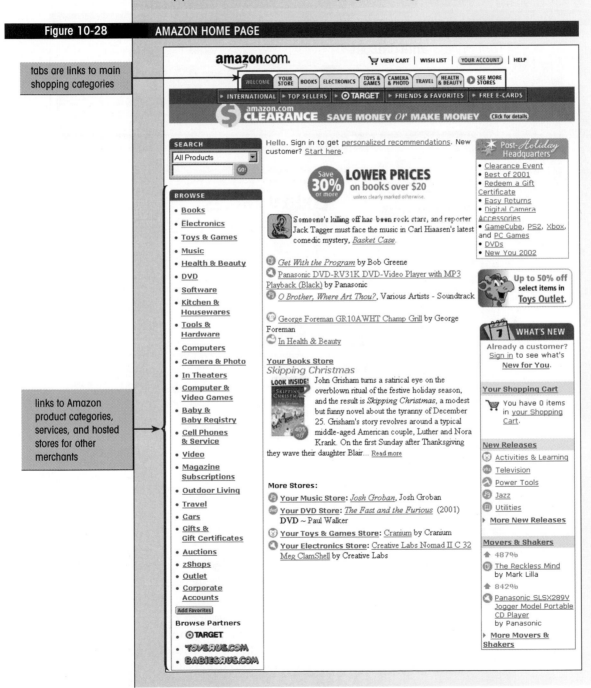

2. Click the **Books** hyperlink on the left side of the page to open the Books Web page shown in Figure 10-29. A new set of hyperlinks appears just under the tabs that let you search for a specific book, browse categories of books, go directly to the week's bestsellers, find a used book, and perform other tasks that site visitors do frequently. Return visitors who have purchased books from the site or who have registered their preferences will find that the ads for books and other items that appear on the home page and the category pages are tailored to match the types of books they have purchased in the past or the preferences they have expressed.

| Figure 10-29 | THE AMAZON BOOKS PAGE |

links to commonly used features and sections of the BOOKS area of the site

links to categories of book products offered for sale

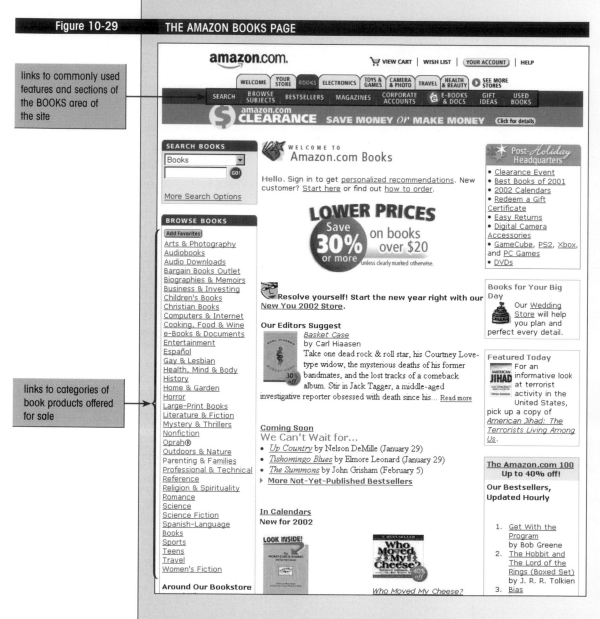

3. Use the links on this page to explore the offerings of Amazon.com. You can click your browser's **Back** button to return to the home page and explore other categories of products offered. Note the way Amazon.com has combined the technologies it uses to generate the Web pages for each product with the business strategies that underlie the way each product is presented on the site.

As you consider this combination of technology and business strategy, you make some notes for your report to Steve. You realize that Amazon.com's Web site provides a blueprint for many different types of business that might be thinking of ways to use the Web:

- Carefully analyze the characteristics of the markets into which you sell and from which you buy
- Consider the different possible ways of delivering your product or service to customers
- Identify ways the Web can help you capitalize on the opportunities that exist in your business

As important as the selling opportunities were, the structure of the supply side of the book business was equally important to Amazon.com's success. When the company started, there were a large number of book publishers, so it would be difficult for a single supplier to restrict Amazon.com's book purchases or enter its market as a competitor. The firm located in Seattle, close to a large pool of programming talent and near one of the largest book distribution warehouses in the world. Once again you see that a combination of business strategy and technology helped Amazon.com become successful.

History of Electronic Commerce

Although the Internet and the Web have made electronic commerce possible for many businesses and individuals, electronic commerce has existed for many years. For decades, banks have been using **electronic funds transfers** (**EFTs**, also called **wire transfers**), which are electronic transmissions of account exchange information over private networks. Businesses also have engaged in a form of electronic commerce known as electronic data interchange for many years. **Electronic data interchange** (**EDI**) occurs when one business transmits computer-readable data in a standard format to another business. The standard formats used in EDI have been designed to contain the same information that businesses would include in standard paper forms, such as invoices, purchase orders, and shipping documents.

For EDI to work, both parties to the transaction must have compatible computer systems, must have some kind of communications link to connect them, and must agree to follow the same set of EDI standards. When two businesses meet these three criteria, they are called **trading partners**. Figure 10-30 compares the paper flow that occurs in a traditional sale purchase transaction with the electronic information flow that occurs when two businesses use EDI.

Figure 10-30	COMPARISON OF TRADITIONAL AND EDI IMPLEMENTATIONS OF SALE-PURCHASE TRANSACTIONS

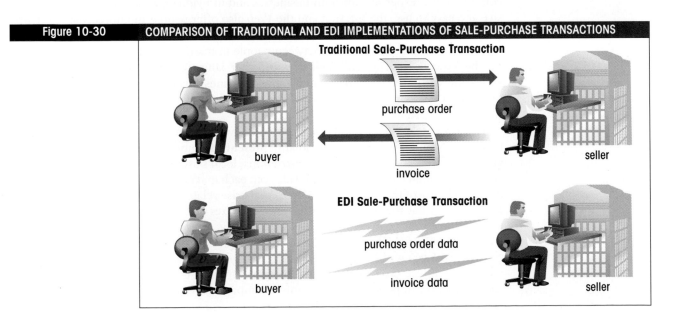

EDI replaces the paper purchase order and invoice with electronic messages. When it was originally introduced, EDI required trading partners to purchase expensive computers and maintain communication links between them. The initial cost of early EDI installations was prohibitive for use by smaller businesses. However, as large businesses realized cost savings from EDI, they began requiring all of their suppliers to use it. Installing EDI systems presented great difficulties for many smaller firms that wanted to sell products to larger firms but could not afford to implement EDI. As the cost of computers decreased and the availability of communications links (including the Internet) increased, more smaller firms were able to participate as EDI trading partners.

The transaction shown in Figure 10-30 is not complete; for example, it does not show the buyer's payment for the goods received. To consummate the traditional transaction, the buyer sends a check to the seller in payment for the goods received. Early EDI implementations used electronic transfer for the transaction information but still handled payments by mailing checks. As EDI became more common, trading partners wanted to handle the payments electronically, too. When EDI includes payment information, it is called **financial EDI**.

Although banks use EFTs to transfer funds for their own accounts and for large customer transactions that require immediate settlement, EFTs are too expensive to use for large volumes of ordinary business transactions. Banks settle most of their customers' business transactions through **automated clearinghouses** (**ACHs**), which are systems created by banks or groups of banks to electronically clear their accounts with each other. Many individuals have their employers make ACH deposits of their paychecks or use ACH withdrawals to make their monthly car payments.

As the number of businesses using EDI has grown, the demand for efficient networking and payment systems has increased. Businesses called **value-added networks** (**VANs**) were created to meet the demands imposed by EDI. A VAN accepts EDI transmissions in a variety of formats, converts the formats as needed, ensures that the EDI transmissions are received and acknowledged, and can forward the financial transaction instructions to the trading partners' banks or ACHs. A VAN is a neutral third party that can offer assurances and dispute-resolution services to both EDI trading partners.

International Nature of Electronic Commerce

Many of the advantages that electronic commerce offers arise from its ability to reduce transaction costs. By making communication quick and inexpensive, technology makes commerce less expensive for both businesses and individuals. In addition to being inexpensive and easy to use, the Internet and the Web also offer people an unprecedented degree of geographic reach. The Internet brings people together from every country in the world because it reduces the distances between people in many ways. The predominant language on the Web is English, although sites in other languages and in multiple languages are appearing with increasing frequency. Once a business overcomes the language barrier, the technology exists for it to conduct electronic commerce with any other business or consumer, anywhere in the world.

Unfortunately, the political structures of the world have not kept up with Internet technology, so doing business internationally presents a number of challenges. Currency conversions, tariffs, import and export restrictions, local business customs, and the laws of each country in which a trading partner resides can each make international electronic commerce difficult. Many of the international issues that arise relate to legal, tax, and privacy concerns. Each country has the right to pass laws and levy taxes on businesses that operate within their jurisdictions. European countries, for example, have very strict laws that limit the collection and use of personal information that companies gather in the course of doing business with consumers. Even within the United States, individual states and counties have the power to levy sales and use taxes on goods and services. In other countries, national sales and value-added taxes are imposed on an even more comprehensive list of business activities.

Future of Electronic Commerce

The Internet has allowed far more businesses, organizations, and individuals to become interconnected by their computers than the pioneers of EDI and EFT ever could have imagined. The Web has given the Internet an easy-to-use interface. The combination of the Web's interface and the Internet's extension of computer networking have opened new opportunities for electronic commerce. Businesses that in the past sold retail goods to consumers through catalogs using mail or telephone orders can now use the Internet to make shopping more convenient. Other retailers, such as booksellers, can use large-volume buying power to provide Internet shoppers with low prices and a wide variety of products. Information providers, such as newspapers, magazines, and newsletters, find that the Internet offers new ways to sell existing products and platforms on which to deliver entirely new products. Software manufacturers see that the Internet is an excellent vehicle for distributing new products, delivering upgrades to existing products, and providing low-cost support to users. The immediacy of the medium offers businesses such as stockbrokerages an attractive way to accept orders from investors. In the following sections, you will learn how some firms have used the Internet and the Web to engage in electronic commerce and how others plan to use it in the near future.

Reducing Transaction Costs

Many researchers and business managers argue that the main contribution of electronic commerce is to reduce transaction costs. Transaction costs are the total of all costs that a buyer and a seller incur as they gather information and negotiate a purchase-sale transaction. Transaction costs include brokerage fees, sales commissions, and the costs of information search and acquisition. Businesses and individuals can use the Web to reduce the transaction costs that occur in virtually every step of commerce.

As you think about how buyers and sellers might use the Web to reduce the cost of each step, you begin to consider how buyers might use the Web to search for products. The Web can help buyers conduct their information searches more cheaply and efficiently than by making telephone calls, sending faxes, or driving from store to store in hopes of finding the right product at the right price. In fact, some firms have started services that help buyers find products. One of these firms is Price Watch. Steven mentions to you that he would like to upgrade the memory on one of the company's desktop computers, but he has been so busy that he has not had time to shop for it. He asks you to give Price Watch a try.

To use price comparison Web sites to search for a specific item:

1. Click your browser's **Back** button or use its history list to return to the Online Companion page for Session 10.2, and then click the **Price Watch** hyperlink and wait while your browser loads the Price Watch home page.

2. Click the **System** hyperlink under the Memory subheading. The page that loads lists some memory chips and includes a search box so you can search within the category. See Figure 10-31.

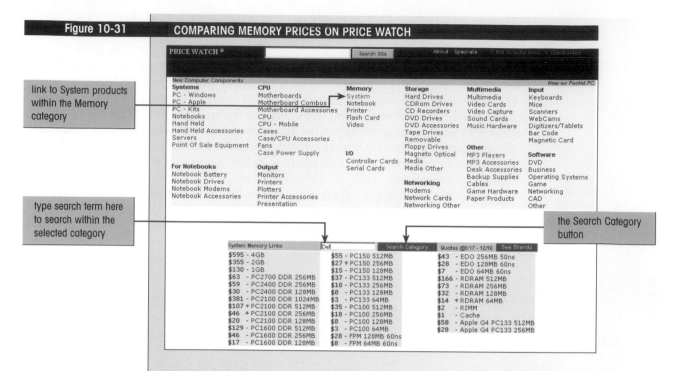

Figure 10-31   COMPARING MEMORY PRICES ON PRICE WATCH

link to System products
within the Memory
category

type search term here
to search within the
selected category

the Search Category
button

Dell manufactured the computer, so you will search for memory products that work in Dell computers.

3. Type **Dell** in the Search Category text box and then click the **Search Category** button. The Price Watch site returns a list of memory chips for Dell computers that are offered for sale by a variety of vendors. The products listed includes the full range of memory types for all kinds of Dell computers, ranging from laptops to the largest server computers that Dell makes. For each item, the search results page shows the brand, product name, description, price, shipping costs, and information about the dealer offering the item. The results page includes a hyperlink to each dealer's site that you can click to make your purchase. The Price Watch site includes information supplied voluntarily by vendors.

Other comparison shopping sites operate their own Web robots (bots) that search the Web and find price information from vendors' Web sites. MySimon is an example of another bot-based comparison shopping site.

4. Click your browser's **Back** button or use its history list to return to the Online Companion page for Session 10.2, and then click the **mySimon** hyperlink and wait while the mySimon home page loads in your Web browser.

5. Click the **Computers & Software** link, and then click the **Memory Upgrades** link on the next Web page that loads.

6. Type **Dell** in the Model or Keyword text box, and then click the **Search** button.

7. Examine the search results page (see Figure 10-32) and compare these results to those you obtained using the Price Watch site. Depending on the available products at the time of your search, you might find many similar entries. The mySimon site allows you to sort the results by attributes of the products such as manufacturer, model, or price. To sort by attribute, click on the sort by links at the top of the attribute columns in the product listings area of the Web page. For example, you could sort by the computer model to make finding the right memory upgrade easier.

Figure 10-32	COMPARING MEMORY PRICES ON mySIMON

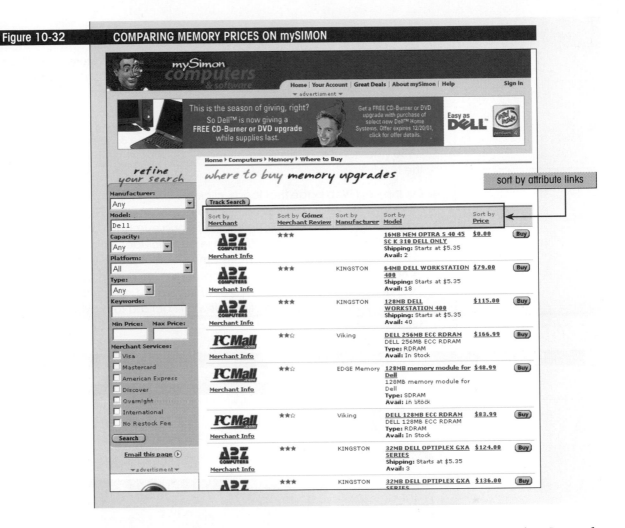

In about 10 minutes, you found several retailers that you can recommend to Steven for the memory upgrade. You are happy to find that this part of electronic commerce is something that you can use easily. You now begin to think about how sellers can use the Web to reduce costs on their side of the purchase transaction. One of the most expensive parts of many sellers' transactions is the provision of after-sale support. After-sale support is especially high for complex technology products such as computers and electronic equipment. For example, many computer printers use software drivers to translate the information a computer sends to them into printing instructions. As computers improve and new software becomes available, printer manufacturers can update their printer driver software to take advantage of new features and capabilities. The traditional method of providing this software on disk to customers who have purchased printers has always been difficult and expensive for printer manufacturers.

You remember that Melinda was complaining this morning that she had just installed some new software on her computer that would not print correctly on her Hewlett-Packard printer. You offer to obtain an updated printer driver for her from Hewlett-Packard's Web site.

To find printer driver software for a Hewlett-Packard printer:

1. Click your browser's **Back** button or use its history list to return to the Online Companion page for Session 10.2, and then click the **Hewlett-Packard** hyperlink and wait while your browser loads the Hewlett-Packard home page.

2. Click the **drivers & downloads** graphic link.

3. In the text box under the text "enter product name & number," type **LaserJet 4000** (the name of Melinda's printer), and then click the arrow button next to the text box.

4. On the next Web page that loads, click the **drivers & downloads** link for the hp LaserJet 4000. After a few moments, the page shown in Figure 10-33 opens. This page provides links to the printer drivers for a number of different operating systems for Melinda's printer. The page also includes links to other information resources that Hewlett-Packard customers can use to help themselves without needing to call a Hewlett-Packard representative during business hours or wait for a disk to arrive in the mail—all of which saves Hewlett-Packard a significant amount of money. The Web allows Hewlett-Packard to provide good customer service at a lower cost.

| Figure 10-33 | DRIVERS AND DOWNLOADS PAGE |

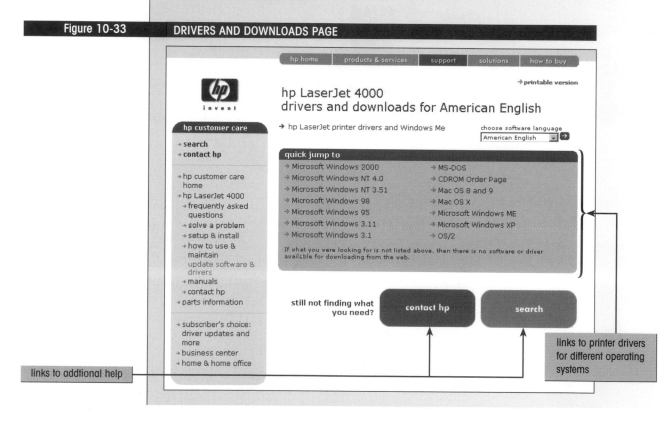

You stop by Melinda's office and show her how to use the Hewlett-Packard site to find the printer driver she needs. A short time later, Melissa has downloaded and installed the updated printer driver and her new software is working with the printer.

Web Catalog Retailing

A number of businesses that have traditionally sold goods through catalogs using mail and telephone orders have established electronic commerce sites on the Web. This is a natural transition because these businesses already have functioning product-delivery systems and know how to anticipate their customers' needs to stock the right merchandise. Lands' End sells over $1 billion of clothing, luggage, domestics, and related products each year through its catalogs. Since 1995, Lands' End also has advertised and sold its products through its Web site. Lands' End has a number of competitors that also have established Web presences for conducting retail electronic commerce. One of those competitors is L.L.Bean, a firm that has used catalogs to sell clothing and outdoor gear for many years.

Melinda is creating a proposal to do some network design work for a new Web clothing retailer and would like some background on the industry. She asks you to visit these two sites and compare their electronic commerce approaches.

To compare the Lands' End and L.L.Bean Web sites:

1. Start your Web browser, open the Student Online Companion page at http://www.course.com/newperspectives/internet3, click the hyperlink for your book, click the Tutorial 10 link, and then click the Session 10.2 link. Click the **Lands' End** link and wait while the browser loads the page.

2. Examine the Lands' End home page shown in Figure 10-34.

| Figure 10-34 | LANDS' END ELECTRONIC COMMERCE SITE |

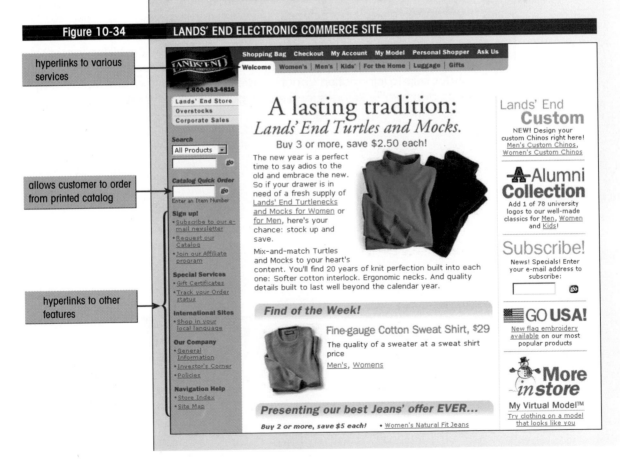

hyperlinks to various services

allows customer to order from printed catalog

hyperlinks to other features

The Lands' End home page is an example of effective Web page design for electronic commerce. The banner across the top of the page includes hyperlinks to the main commercial functions of the site. For example, the Men's link leads to the men's store. The Overstocks link leads to a list of reduced-price items. The left side of the page includes hyperlinks to information and other site features. The Ask Us link provides live help, called *Lands' End Live*, for those who are having difficulty locating merchandise. You can choose between live phone help or using live chat in which Lands' End employees answer your questions in a chat-room setting. Other useful features of this page include the Catalog Quick Order, which lets customers easily order items they have found in the printed catalog, and Store Index, which displays a hierarchical list of links to all the Lands' End departments.

3. After exploring the Lands' End site, use your browser's **Back** button to return to the Student Online Companion page for Session 10.2.

4. Click the **L.L.Bean** hyperlink to open the company's home page.

The L.L.Bean home page is another example of how a catalog retailer can create an effective Web page design for an electronic commerce site. The page gives customers hyperlinks that they can use to conduct business—the Free Catalogs link, for example—and obtain more information about L.L.Bean and the Web site. The page includes links to information about how the firm provides security and privacy for customers who place online orders. The page also includes a Search text box to help site visitors find specific information on the site. Just as the Lands' End site offers free information that is not directly related to its products, the L.L.Bean site includes a series of links under the heading "Explore the Outdoors" that lead to tips for camping, hiking, and other outdoor activities. The Park Search link leads to a page (see Figure 10-35) that includes links to information about hundreds of U.S. National and State Parks, Forests, and Wildlife Refuges; and similar public parks and preserves throughout the world.

| Figure 10-35 | L.L.BEAN ELECTRONIC COMMERCE SITE |

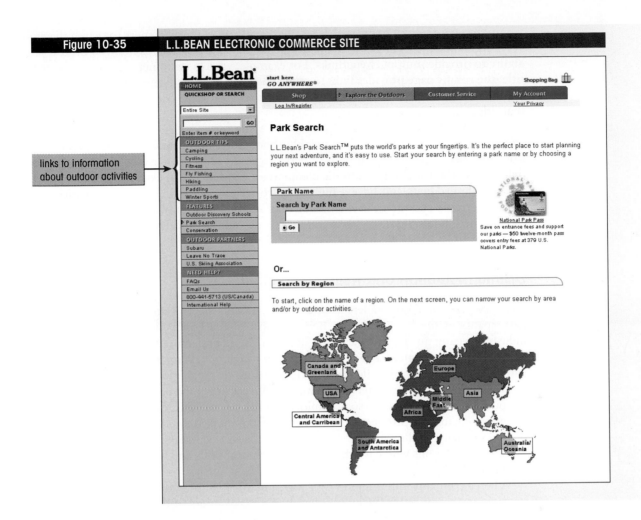

As you examine these two Web sites, you note design features, hyperlinks, and layout ideas that Melinda might find useful in understanding how a Web retailer meets the needs of its visitors. You decide that both Lands' End and L.L.Bean carefully considered their customers' needs, desires, and concerns when they created their Web sites. You note that these will be important considerations for Melinda as she works on her proposal.

Both Lands' End and L.L.Bean have developed successful electronic commerce Web sites for their customers by expanding their existing business models. To convert their catalog retail businesses into Web-based businesses, they only had to replace their printed catalogs and their telephone order-takers with properly designed Web pages. These firms still carry the same inventory and order that inventory the same way they always have. In other words, their basic business models did not change.

In contrast, the retail book business has seen significant transformation over the past 20 years. During this time, the once-predominant small neighborhood bookshop has been replaced by ever-larger book superstores throughout the United States. As you learned earlier in this session, Amazon.com added a new element to the industry: the online bookstore.

One of the main reasons that larger bookstores have been more successful than smaller ones is that they can offer a wider selection. Many bookstore customers want to buy a particular book when they go shopping, whereas other customers know that they want to buy a book with some specific characteristic. For example, a customer might be looking for a book on a particular topic or by a particular author. A larger bookstore has a higher likelihood of having the title or author that a customer wishes to purchase.

Amazon.com set out to create a Web site that would allow customers to search through a very large database of books by topic, title, and author. The firm capitalized on the Web's ability to provide multiple hyperlinks. For example, when a customer searches for a specific title, the results page provides links to other books by that book's author, books on the same or similar topics, and even a list of books that other customers bought when they purchased that title.

Amazon.com uses the Web to provide the same services that customers once obtained from the knowledgeable clerk in a neighborhood bookshop, while offering a greater selection than the largest physical book superstore could offer. Other characteristics of books helped make book-selling electronic commerce a good idea. For example, books are readily identifiable products and have a high value-to-weight ratio. These characteristics helped make electronic commerce in retail book sales successful because a customer does not need to examine a book physically to determine its desirability and books can be shipped cost-effectively.

Disintermediation and Reintermediation

The strategies of Web retailers such as Amazon.com are to remove and replace existing participants in the book industry. Because most of the companies that participate in an industry occupy an intermediate step between the manufacturer and the final consumer, they are called **intermediaries**. The process in which one company removes another company from the industry is called **disintermediation**.

Disintermediation can affect individual employees of companies as well as the companies themselves. For example, persons employed in the sale of autos, travel services, and securities are all facing the prospect of being laid off from their jobs as electronic commerce Web sites offer many of the same services they provide. Of course, these Web sites offer many new jobs for persons who have the necessary technical skills and business knowledge to create and build them.

When a company enters an industry with a new way of providing value to the other participants in that industry (including the ultimate consumers of the product or service created in that industry), it is called **reintermediation**. For example, if Amazon.com displaces sales from neighborhood bookstores and forces the neighborhood bookstores to close, Amazon.com will have disintermediated those bookstores. By taking the place of the bookstores in the industry, Amazon.com will have reintermediated itself into the book industry.

The characteristics of book sales—customers that have specific titles or characteristics in mind, easily identifiable product, high value-to-weight ratio—are also characteristics of music CD sales. Firms such as CDnow have created successful Web sites that sell music CDs. Amazon.com has certainly realized this—the first product category it added to its original books-only offerings was the music CDs category. The main CDnow Web page appears in Figure 10-36.

Figure 10-36 CDNOW ELECTRONIC COMMERCE SITE

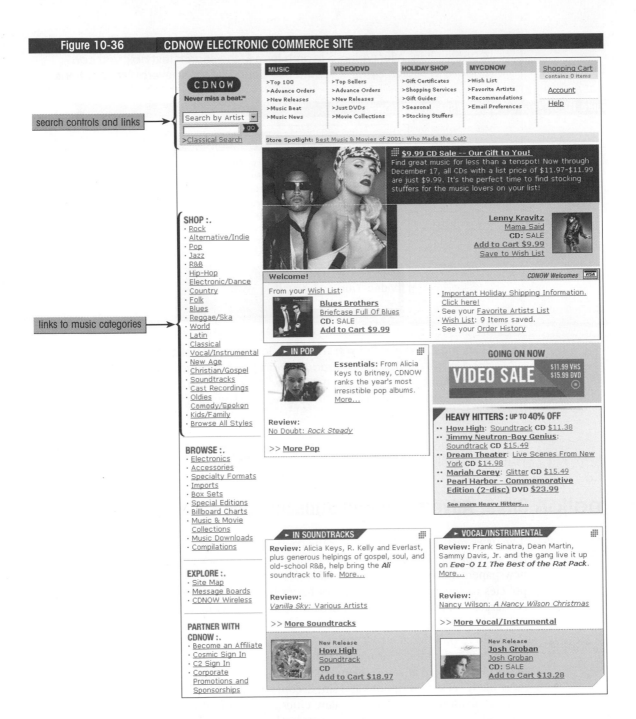

You decide to examine the CDnow site to identify useful features that Melinda should know about.

To explore the CDnow site:

1. Return to the Student Online Companion Web page for Session 10.2, and then click the **CDnow** hyperlink and wait while your Web browser loads the Web page.

2. Click the **CDnow** hyperlink to open its CD music sales Web page.

3. Click the list arrow (See Figure 10-37) to see the different search options that CDnow offers. After typing a search term in the search text box, you can choose to search by Artist, Album Title, Song Title, and several other options.

Figure 10-37	CDNOW SEARCH OPTIONS

4. Click the **Classical Search** link that is located just below the search tool you used in the previous step. Because most people search for classical recordings using different criteria than they use when searching for all other categories of music, CDnow provides this page of search links and tools.

You report to Melinda that the CDnow site also offers a flexible interface that gives site visitors the tools they need to meet their differing needs.

Information Sites: Advertising and Subscriptions

The news media have changed over the course of this century as technology has changed. At the start of the 1900s, improvements in printing presses and distribution methods made newspapers much more widely available. Newspapers changed their editorial and advertising policies to serve their new audiences better by including many more members of low and moderate socioeconomic groups. Broadcast radio, television, and cable television were technological innovations that increased the competition for audience and advertising dollars.

All three traditional media outlets—print, radio, and television—provide their audiences with news and other information. They obtain their revenues by charging a subscription fee, accepting paid advertisements, or by some combination of both. Your local newspaper most likely sells subscriptions and single copies on newsstands, but it also obtains significant revenue from its advertisers. In many cities, you can find weekly newspapers that are distributed free; these newspapers are completely supported by advertising. Similarly, advertising supported broadcast radio and television for many years. The advent of cable television introduced viewer subscription payments to the electronic media.

The online world offers all three payment schemes: advertising supported, subscription supported, and various combinations of the two. Many of the news sites on the Web are completely free to visitors; they display advertising banners to generate revenues sufficient to offset their costs and earn a profit. Other sites, particularly those that offer highly specialized news information, such as earnings forecasts or stock purchase recommendations, require you to pay a subscription fee and obtain a password for access.

An increasingly common revenue model for Web sites is a combination of some free information, sometimes accompanied by advertising, with a more extensive set of information available on a subscription or pay-per-item basis. Two news Web sites that offer this combination are the BusinessWeek Online and The Wall Street Journal Interactive Edition sites that you will explore next. Steven is interested in how electronic commerce information sites earn a profit because he is thinking about placing some technical computer networking information on the NDC Web site. He has not decided whether to charge a subscription fee for this information or make it available free. Steven has asked you to investigate how two of the major Web information sites that use a combination of subscriptions and free information do things on their sites.

To explore the BusinessWeek Online and The Wall Street Journal Interactive Edition sites:

1. Return to the Student Online Companion Web page for Session 10.2, and then click the **BusinessWeek Online** hyperlink and wait while your Web browser loads the Web page.

2. Examine the BusinessWeek Online home page.

   The BusinessWeek site offers an interesting mix of options. Some of the news items are available to all visitors; others require that you register or are accessible only to subscribers of the print edition of *Business Week*. The site offers Web-only subscriptions to persons who want access to the full online content but are not interested in receiving the print edition. The site also offers a separate subscription or pay-per-article access to its archived issues.

3. When you have completed your review of the BusinessWeek Online site, use your browser's **Back** button to return to the Student Online Companion page, and then click the **WSJ.com** hyperlink to open its Web page.

   The Wall Street Journal site provides free access to a more limited set of information than the BusinessWeek Online site provides. The subscribers-only links are on the left side of the page and the free content is listed on the right. Notably, the classified job ads and the annual report service are both included in the free information set. Because advertisers pay to have the widest possible distribution of these features, it is in the site's best interest to offer them to all visitors. Subscribers to the print edition must pay to access the rest of the site, although their fee is lower than the subscription charge for persons who do not subscribe to the print edition.

4. Click the **Careers** hyperlink, located under the WSJ.com NETWORK heading (you might need to scroll the page down in the browser window, to open the CareerJournal.com page, and then click the **Advanced Search** link underneath the Find a Job text box to open the page shown in Figure 10-38. (Your page might differ.)

Figure 10-38   SEARCHING FOR JOBS ON THE CARRERJOURNAL WEB SITE

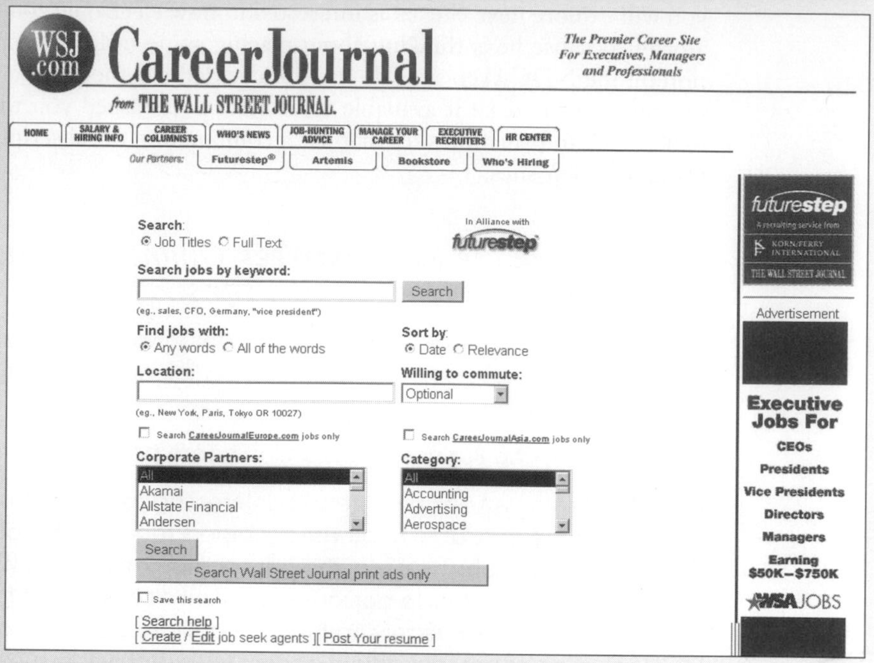

5. The site's search engine allows visitors to select ads for positions by keyword criteria such as company name, industry, job function, and location. This can be a much more efficient way to search the ads than scanning them in the print edition. It also exposes the ads to potential applicants who are not subscribers, which might allow the Journal to charge higher rates for their ads.

Although many members of the Internet community feel that information on the Web should be freely available to the browsing public, an increasing number of firms are offering valuable information and charging for it. One compromise solution, as you have seen in the BusinessWeek and The Wall Street Journal sites, is to offer a combination of free and subscription-charge information on the same Web site.

Fee-for-Transaction Web Sites

Travel agents earn commissions on each airplane ticket, hotel reservation, auto rental, or cruise that they book. The transportation or lodging provider pays these commissions to the travel agent. The travel agency business model involves receiving a fee for facilitating a transaction. The value added by a travel agent is that of information consolidation and filtering. A good travel agent knows a lot about travel destinations and knows enough about the traveler to select the information elements that will be useful and valuable to the traveler. Computers, and particularly computers networked to large databases, are very good at information consolidation and filtering. In fact, travel agents have used networked computers, such as the Sabre Group systems, for many years to make reservations for their customers.

When the Internet emerged as a new way to network computers and then became available to commercial users, many online travel agencies began conducting business using the Web. Existing travel agencies did not, in general, rush to the new medium. They believed that a Web site could not replace the key value they added—personal customer service. Therefore, the first Web-based travel agencies were new entrants. One of these sites,

Travelocity, uses the same Sabre system that traditional travel agents use. Microsoft has entered the online travel agency business with its Expedia site. In 2001, a group of airlines joined together and formed a third major travel site, Orbitz (See Figure 10-39). Your Student Online Companion for this book includes links to these three travel sites in its Additional Information section for Tutorial 10.

| Figure 10-39 | ORBITZ TRAVEL SITE |

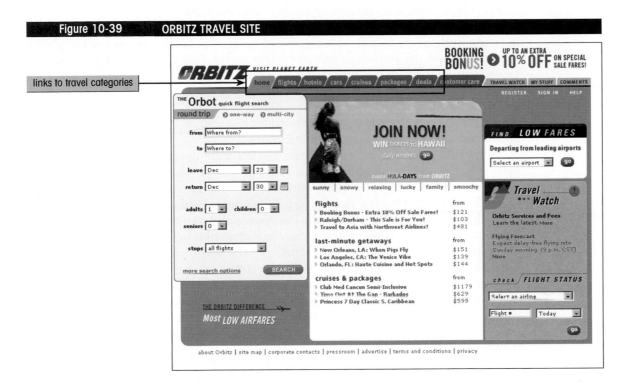

In addition to earning commissions from the transportation and lodging providers, these sites generate advertising revenue from ads placed on their travel information pages. These ads are similar to those on search engine results pages, because they can be targeted without obtaining demographic details about the site visitor.

Auto dealers buy cars from the manufacturer and sell them to consumers. They provide showrooms and salespeople to help customers learn about product features, arrange financing, and make a purchase decision. Autobytel.com and other firms will locate dealers in the buyer's area that are willing to sell cars for a small premium over the dealer's nominal cost. The buyer can purchase the car from the dealer without negotiating its price with a salesperson. Autobytel charges participating dealers a fee for this service. Autobytel is disintermediating the salesperson and reintermediating itself into the value chain. The consumer spends less time buying the car and often pays a lower price; the dealer pays a fee to Autobytel that is lower than the commission it would otherwise pay to its salesperson. Stock brokerage firms also use a fee-for-transaction model. They charge their customers a commission for each trade executed. Online brokers such as E*Trade and Ameritrade are threatening traditional brokerage firms by offering trading over the Web. Your Student Online Companion includes links to auto buying sites and online brokerage firms in its Additional Information section for Tutorial 10.

Online Auctions

One of the more interesting and innovative implementations of electronic commerce is the creation of Web sites that conduct online auctions. Although some of these sites offer merchandise that is the inventory of the Web site owner, most of these sites auction the property of others much as an auctioneer would at a public auction.

Each site establishes its own bidding rules; however, most auctions remain open for a few days or a week. Some sites provide automated agents that bidders can instruct to place bids as needed to win the auction, subject to a maximum limit set by the bidder. Because bidders face a significant risk of buying a misrepresented product in a sight-unseen online auction, some auction sites offer mediation/escrow services that hold the buyer's payment until he or she is satisfied that the item matches the seller's description. The advantages of conducting online auctions include a large pool of potential bidders, 24-hour access, and the ability to auction hundreds of similar items simultaneously.

In 1995, Pierre Omidyar was working as a software developer and, in his spare time, operating a small Web site that provided updates on the Ebola virus. His girlfriend mentioned that she collected Pez candy dispensers but had trouble finding other people who shared her interest. Omidyar decided to help her out by adding a small auction function to his Web site so that people could trade Pez dispensers and other items. Interest in the site's auctions grew so rapidly that within a year, he had quit his job to devote his full energies to the Web auction business he had created. By the end of its second year in operation, Omidyar's Web site, which he called eBay, had auctioned over $95 million worth of goods.

Because eBay was one of the first auction Web sites and because it has pursued an aggressive promotion strategy, it has become the first choice for many people who want to participate in auctions. Both buyers and bidders benefit from the large marketplace that eBay has created. EBay's early advantage in the online auction business will be hard for competitors to overcome.

You decide to take a break from your work for NDC and use the Web to pursue one of your hobbies, collecting guitars. You are especially fond of a series of guitars made for many years by the Gibson Company that were originally designed and played by Les Paul. You decide to search for auctions of Les Paul model guitars on eBay.

To search for auctions on eBay:

1. Return to the Student Online Companion Web page for Session 10.2, and then click the **eBay** hyperlink and wait while your Web browser loads the eBay home page (see Figure 10-40).

Figure 10-40   **EBAY HOME PAGE**

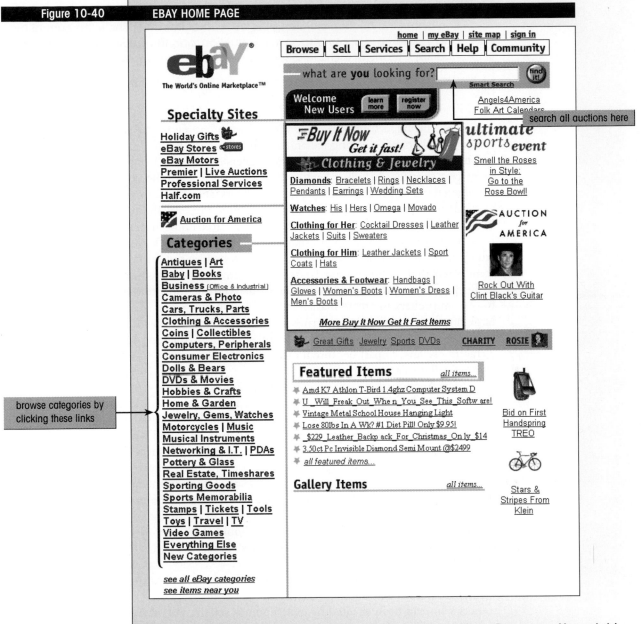

2. Type **Les Paul** in the search text box near the top of the eBay page. You might see a few auctions of old audio recordings made by Les Paul and Mary Ford, but most of the several hundred auctions on the results page should be for Gibson guitars. The first auctions listed might be "featured" auctions—the seller has paid eBay an extra fee to have the auction listed first. The other auctions are listed in the order of the auction expiration date, with the auctions ending soon listed first. You can change the order in which the auctions are listed, which is helpful for a search such as this that returns hundreds of listings.

3. Click the **highest priced** link at the top of the auction listings. This will sort the auctions in descending order of the highest bid made thus far in the auction. If no bids have been made, the price used is the minimum price that the seller has placed on the auction. Any featured auctions will still be listed at the top of the results page.

4. Click the links to several of the auctions. The auction page will show information about the auction including the eBay ID of the seller, show the current bid and the number of bids made in the auction, and the auction's closing date and time. Many of the auctions will include detailed photographs of the guitar.

5. Close your Web browser and, if necessary, log off your Internet connection.

Sellers and buyers must register with eBay and agree to the site's basic terms of doing business. Sellers pay a listing fee and a sliding percentage of the final selling price. Buyers pay nothing. In addition to the basic fees, sellers can choose from a variety of enhanced and extra-cost services, including having their auctions listed in bold type or as included as featured auctions which appear at the top of bidders' search results pages.

In an attempt to address bidder concerns about seller reliability, eBay has instituted a rating system. Buyers can submit ratings of sellers after doing business with them. These ratings are converted into graphics that appear with the seller's nickname on each auction in which that seller participates. Although this system is not without flaws, many eBay customers feel that it affords them some level of protection from unscrupulous sellers.

Because one of the major determinants of Web auction site success is attracting enough buyers and sellers to create markets for enough items, some Web sites that already have a large number of visitors are entering this business. Sites such as Yahoo! Auctions have added auctions similar to those available on eBay. Yahoo! Auctions had some early success in attracting sellers, in part because it offered its auction service to sellers at no charge. It now charges sellers just as eBay does.

Yahoo! Auctions has been less successful in attracting buyers, resulting in less bidding action in each auction than generally occurs on eBay. It is possible that Yahoo! Auctions will be able to convince its visitors to participate in its auctions with more success. In Japan, Yahoo! auctions began operations six months before eBay and now holds more than 90% of the online auction market in that country. The potential for success in the United States and other markets does exist for Yahoo! because it is one of the most-visited sites on the Web.

Amazon.com also operates auctions on its site. Although the number of auctions is small, Amazon is aggressively marketing its auction business. Some industry observers note that Amazon may earn more by charging a commission on the auction of a used book than it could earn by selling the same title as a new book! With over 30 million registered users of its existing book, music, video, and other sales pages, Amazon is truly a potential challenger to eBay.

One of the aggressive marketing positions that Amazon has already taken is its "Auctions Guarantee." This guarantee directly addresses concerns raised in the media by eBay customers who had been cheated by unscrupulous sellers. When Amazon opened its auctions site, it agreed to reimburse any buyer for merchandise purchased in an auction that was not delivered or that was "materially different" from the seller's representations. Amazon limited its guarantee to items costing $250 or less; however, buyers of more expensive items generally protect themselves by using a third party **escrow service**, which holds the buyer's payment until he or she receives and is satisfied with the purchased item. EBay responded immediately by offering its customers the same guarantee; however, this guarantee helped to establish Amazon as a serious competitor in the Web auctions business.

Consumer Concerns

Participants in electronic commerce have two major concerns. Their first concern is for transaction security. Buyers in an electronic marketplace often do not know who is operating a Web site from which they would like to make a purchase. They also desire assurance that the payments they make for goods purchased via the Internet are secure.

Buyers' second major concern is that their privacy not be violated in the course of conducting electronic commerce. Web sites can gather a great deal of information about their customers, even before customers purchase anything from the site. The Web electronic commerce community has made efforts toward ensuring both transaction security and buyer privacy, but these efforts are not yet complete. Many potential consumers are reluctant to make purchases over the Internet because of continuing concerns about these two issues. Several assurance providers have begun operations in recent years. An **assurance provider** is a third party that, for a fee paid by the electronic commerce Web site, will certify that the site meets some criteria for conducting business in a secure and privacy-preserving manner.

Transaction Security and Privacy

Potential customers worry about a number of issues when they consider dealing with a Web-based business. They might wonder whether the firm is a real company that will deliver the merchandise ordered or, if the merchandise is defective, will replace it or refund the purchase price within a reasonable period. Potential customers of any business worry about the same issues; however, the virtual nature of a Web electronic commerce site increases these concerns. In addition, potential customers are concerned about the security of their credit card numbers as those numbers travel over the Internet.

As you learned in Session 9.2, many Web sites use the SSL security protocol to encrypt information flowing between a Web server and a Web client. Many Web sites used in electronic commerce use the SSL protocol to protect sensitive information as it travels over the Internet.

A greater concern is how electronic commerce Web sites store their customer information. Many sites store their customers' credit card numbers so that the customers do not have to type the card numbers every time they visit the site to buy something. Of course, the computer that stores these card numbers is connected (directly or indirectly) to the Internet. Any computer that is connected to the Internet is subject to attack from persons outside the company that have access to the Internet.

There have been a number of widely reported cases in which an intruder has broken into an electronic commerce site's computer and stolen names, addresses, and credit card information. Sometimes, these individuals, called **hackers** or **crackers**, have even posted the credit card information on the Internet.

Many potential customers of Web-based businesses are also concerned about their privacy. Web sites can collect a great deal of information about customers' preferences—even before they place an order. By recording a user's **clickstream**, which is a record of which pages the user visited on a site, the Web server can gather extensive knowledge about that visitor. Many Web sites use clickstream information to display different ad banners to different visitors.

No general standards currently exist in the United States for maintaining confidentiality regarding clickstream information, much less general identifying information about Web site visitors and customers. Many business Web sites include statements of privacy policy directed at concerned customers, but no U.S. laws exist requiring such statements or policies. The European Community (EC) does have laws that restrict companies' use of information collected from customers. These laws apply to U.S. companies that do business with customers in the EC.

Assurance Providers

To fill the need for some kind of assurance over Web site transaction security and privacy policies, several assurance providers have started offering various kinds of certifications. Web sites can purchase these certifications and display the logo or seal of the assurance provider on the Web site for potential customers to examine. Most of these logos are hyperlinks to the assurance provider's site, at which customers can find out more about the nature of the specific assurances given by that provider. Currently, there are five major assurance providers: the Better Business Bureau (BBB), TRUSTe, the International Computer Security Association (ICSA), VeriSign, and WebTrust.

The Better Business Bureau's BBBOnLine certification program grants a Web site the right to use its logo after it has joined the BBB; been in business for at least one year; compiled a satisfactory complaint-handling record; and agreed to follow BBB member guidelines for truthful advertising, prompt response to customer complaints, and binding arbitration of customer disputes. The BBB conducts a site visit during which it verifies the street address, telephone number, and existence of the business.

The TRUSTe program focuses on privacy issues. To earn the right to display the TRUSTe logo, a Web site must explain and summarize its information-gathering policies in a disclosure statement on the site. The site must adhere to its stated policies and several other guidelines concerning the privacy of communications. TRUSTe enforces its program by various methods, including surprise audits that it and two accounting firms conduct.

The ICSA is an independent association that has developed a series of computer security certifications. The goal of ICSA Web certification is to reduce Web site risks and liability for the site and its customers. ICSA conducts an initial on-site evaluation using its certification field guide and uses subsequent remote testing and random spot-checking of site availability, information-protection measures, and data-integrity provisions.

VeriSign provides a range of services to electronic commerce Web sites, including certification of secure server status and EDI certifications. It is also a partner with the American Institute of Certified Public Accountants (AICPA) in the WebTrust program. The WebTrust program is a comprehensive assurance that requires reviews by a licensed CPA (or Chartered Accountant in Canada) before the site is approved. The review includes examination of Web site performance disclosures, such as delivery times and handling of customer complaints. The site is granted a WebTrust logo only after it satisfies a number of criteria relating to business practices, transaction integrity, and information protection. The WebTrust program requires recertification every 90 days. Links to these assurance service providers are included in the Student Online Companion for this tutorial in the Additional Information section.

Web Business Rating Services

Another useful type of service that can help you evaluate an electronic commerce Web site are Web business rating services. These companies evaluate electronic commerce sites and publish ratings for major sites.

The Gómez Consumer Guides (see Figure 10-41) provide rankings for the top sites in a number of categories. BizRate is another site that conducts surveys of electronic commerce site customers and compiles ratings which it reports on its Web site. Links to these rating services are included in the Student Online Companion for this tutorial in the Additional Information section.

Figure 10-41   GÓMEZ CONSUMER GUIDES WEB SITE

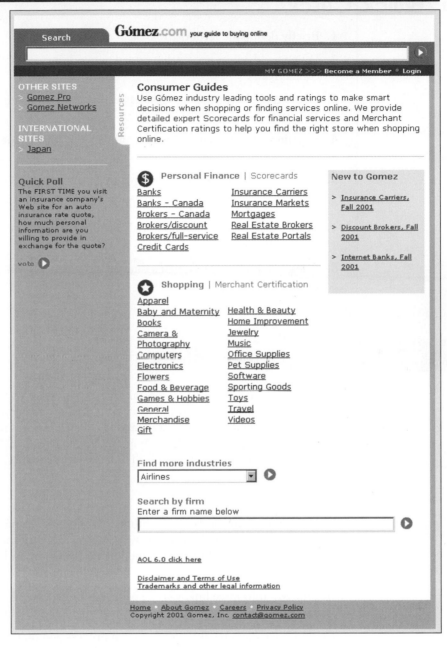

Session 10.2 QUICK CHECK

1. Briefly define the term *electronic data interchange* (EDI).

2. Why would a firm use a value-added network instead of the Internet for electronic commerce?

3. Name three business activities that a software manufacturer might conduct from its Web site.

4. Explain why a firm might include information that is not related to its products on a Web site designed to sell merchandise.

5. Why are music CDs and videotapes good candidates for electronic commerce?

6. Describe three risks that you would face as a successful bidder in an online auction.

7. Name two concerns that potential customers often have about making a purchase from a Web site.

8. Briefly describe the role that assurance providers play in the conduct of electronic commerce.

REVIEW ASSIGNMENTS

Steven liked using your my Yahoo! portal page, and now he would like for you to help him personalize a portal site of his own. He wants to include directories, news, and business information that could be helpful in obtaining critical business information about the software industry in general and software contracting in particular. Then Steven wants you to create customized portals for three of NDC's key sales people so they can stay on top of current industry trends.

Do the following:

1. Start your Web browser, go to the Student Online Companion (http://www.course.com/newperspectives/internet3), click the link for your book, click the Tutorial 10 link, and then click the Review Assignments link in the left frame. Click the InfoSpace custom portal link.

2. Click the My InfoSpace link. On the page that loads, click the Register now link and follow the instructions to create an appropriate member name and a password for Steven.

3. After you have completed the registration process, log on to your new account.

4. Click the My InfoSpace Page link to create the start page for Steven's portal.

5. Click the Edit Content link at the bottom of the My Information Manger section of the page.

6. Clear all of the check boxes in the first column except Stocks, Weather, and My Links.

7. Clear all of the check boxes in the second column except Information Manager, Search Forms, and News.

8. Click the Save Changes button.

9. Click the Edit button at the top of the News section. On the page that opens, clear all of the check boxes except those for US News, Business, and Sci-Tech. Use the drop down arrow to change the number of headlines to display to 5.

10. Click the Save Changes button.

11. In the My Information Manager section, click the Calendar link.

12. Click Add Event and, using the page that opens, create a recurring appointment for the first Monday of each month for Steve's staff meeting at 8:00 AM. *Hint*: You must set the Recurrence value to Monthly by Day of Week and allow the page to reload before you can complete the entry of this event.

13. Use your browser's Back button to return to your main portal page and print it.

14. Sign out of your InfoSpace account.

15. Close your Web browser and, if necessary, log off your Internet connection.

CASE PROBLEMS

Case 1. Sagamore Community College Sagamore Community College (SCC) offers two-year associate degree programs in computer technologies. Because of its impressive array of computer laboratories and its state-of-the-art computer infrastructure, the college attracts students from a community that employs many high-tech workers. Unfortunately, SCC does not currently provide timely course and degree information on its Web site. Ernesto Cervantes, SCC's director of Academic Computing, wants to change the SCC home page so students can customize and use it as a portal site. Ernesto wants the portal to offer class lists, information about instructors, and course information. Ernesto would like to see examples of existing portal sites that can serve as examples for constructing SCC's home page.

Do the following:

1. Start your Web browser, open the Student Online Companion page at www.course.com/newperspectives/internet3, click the hyperlink for your book, click the Tutorial 10 link, and then click the Case Problems link. Click the My Lycos link under the Case Problem 1 heading.

2. Click the SIGN UP link near the top of the page to open that Web page.

3. Enter your information into the required text boxes and then click the Sign Me Up! (or I Agree) button at the bottom of the page.

4. Return to the Lycos home page by entering the URL http://www.lycos.com and then click the My Lycos link.

5. Click the Add & Remove link to open the Add/Remove Boxes tool and then eliminate the information items in which you are not interested. Retain at least the News, Portfolio, and Weather sections.

6. Customize the News, Stocks, and Weather sections to meet your personal needs. Click the I'm Done button when you are finished.

Explore ▶ 7. Click the Change colors button and select a color scheme that you like.

Explore ▶ 8. Change the layout of your page by clicking the Move and Change box size buttons on the My Lycos page to a layout that you like.

Explore 9. Close your Web browser and, if necessary, log off your Internet connection.

Case 2. Dorm Lamps, Inc. Your friend Robin has invented a new high-intensity lamp that is an ideal product for college students who share dorm rooms. You have been selling the lamps for three months through word-of-mouth advertising on your campus. You would like to expand your sales to other college campuses. Robin suggests creating a Web page that will accept orders. The lamps are small and lightweight; therefore, they could be shipped to customers easily using a variety of methods. Because you are both college students with no business experience, you wonder who will trust you or your Web site to deliver quality merchandise. You would like to investigate the terms and conditions of several Web site assurance providers to determine which, if any, Robin should use for the proposed site.

Do the following:

1. Start your Web browser, open the Student Online Companion page at http://www.course.com/newperspectives/internet3, click the hyperlink for your book, click the Tutorial 10 link, and then click the Case Problems link. Click the BBBOnline link to open that page.

2. Examine the Web site assurance criteria presented on this site and determine whether Dorm Lamps would qualify. Be sure to assess the approximate cost of obtaining this assurance.

3. Click the Back button on your browser to return to the Student Online Companion page, and then click the VeriSign hyperlink.

4. Examine the various Web site assurance services listed for this case in the Online Companion, including the WebTrust assurance service, and evaluate the costs and benefits for Dorm Lamps to obtain each service.

5. Write a three-page summary of your findings. Be sure to recommend a specific assurance service or explain why none of the services you identified would be suitable for Dorm Lamps, Inc. Support your recommendation with facts and logical arguments.

6. Close your Web browser and, if necessary, log off your Internet connection.

Case 3. Finding a New VCR on the Web Your VCR has started randomly ejecting the videotape while you are watching your favorite movies, so you decide it is time to buy a new VCR. You want to buy your new VCR on the Web and would like to start by doing some comparison shopping.

Do the following:

1. Start your Web browser, open the Student Online Companion page at http://www.course.com/newperspectives/internet3, click the hyperlink for your book, click the Tutorial 10 link, and then click the Case Problems link. Click the buy.com link.

2. Click the Electronics hyperlink near the top of the buy.com home page to open the Electronics page. Type VCR in the search box at the top of the page and click the Go link.

3. The search results page appears, listing over a dozen VCRs with their part numbers, prices, and information about their current availability for shipment. Some buyers may make their selection using the brief descriptions that appear on this page. However, other buyers may want more information. To provide a customized level of product information on this site, buy.com formatted the name of each VCR as a hyperlink that you can click to learn more about that particular model. Click some of these hyperlinks to learn more about at least three VCRs that are currently for sale.

4. When you have finished examining information about VCRs for sale at the buy.com site, click your browser's Back button until you have returned to the Case Problems section of the Online Companion for Tutorial 10.

5. Click the Amazon.com link and wait while your browser loads the Amazon.com home page. Click the Electronics link in the tab at the top of the page (or the Electronics link on the left side of the page).

6. Type VCR in the Search text box, and then click the GO! button. The first page of search results appears, listing a number of VCRs with their part numbers, prices, and current availability for shipment. The name of each VCR is a hyperlink that you can follow to obtain more details about each VCR. The additional information includes customer reviews of the product and even includes ratings of the reviews (each review has an indicator that states how many people found that review to be helpful). Click some of these hyperlinks to learn more about at least three VCRs that are currently for sale.

7. When you have finished examining information about VCRs for sale at Amazon.com, close your Web browser and, if necessary, log off your Internet connection.

8. For each site, answer the following questions: Was the site easy to use? Why or why not? Did the site offer VCRs in which you would be interested? Did the site display product information that was easy to understand? Why or why not? Would you use these sites to purchase items online? Why or why not? Print one page of information about a particular VCR from each site. On each page, indicate one helpful design feature.

Case 4. Battery World You have been using electronic devices such as calculators, cameras, and portable CD players for years. Recently, you started using laptop computers in your job. One frustration you have experienced using all of these devices is replacing the batteries. You realize that, as more electronic devices need more and different kinds of batteries, a business that offers overnight shipments of batteries might be a good idea. After much research, you have decided to open a Web-based business, Battery World, which will stock a wide variety of batteries ready for overnight delivery. You have worked out many of the details of ordering and stocking your batteries, but you have not yet decided on how you might best ship them.

Do the following:

1. Start your Web browser, open the Student Online Companion page at http://www.course.com/newperspectives/internet3, click the hyperlink for your book, click the Tutorial 10 link, and then click the Case Problems link. Click the FedEx hyperlink to open that page.

2. Examine the services provided on the Federal Express Web site for overnight shipments. Include the elements of package tracking, obtaining rate information, and pickup and delivery services information in your study.

3. Click the Back button on your browser to return to the Student Online Companion page, and then click the United Parcel Service hyperlink.

4. Examine the services provided on the United Parcel Service Web site for overnight shipments. Include the elements of package tracking, obtaining rate information, and pickup and delivery services information in your study.

5. Click the Back button on your browser to return to the Student Online Companion page, and then click the DHL Worldwide hyperlink.

6. Examine the services provided on the DHL Worldwide Web site for overnight shipments. Include the elements of package tracking, obtaining rate information, and pickup and delivery services information in your study.

7. Write a two-page summary that includes a comparison of how easy each company's site was to use as you searched it for the information you needed.

8. Close your Web browser and, if necessary, log off your Internet connection.

Case 5. Flowers on the Web Many firms sell flowers and related gift items on the Web. FTD.com started as the world's first "flowers-by-wire" service in 1910 and moved to the Web in 1994. The 1-800-flowers.com site is an outgrowth of that company's telephone order business. Newer entrants to the online flower industry, such as Proflowers.com, started their businesses on the Web and work with a very different business strategy.

1. Start your Web browser, open the Student Online Companion page at http://www.course.com/newperspectives/internet3, click the hyperlink for your book, click the Tutorial 10 link, and then click the Case Problems link. Click the FTD.com link and wait while your browser loads the FTD.com home page.

2. Click the About Us hyperlink near the bottom of the page to open the About Us page in your browser. This page includes a history of the company and describes many of the details of its operations. Read this page carefully so you understand what FTD.com is, who its customers are, and how it accepts and delivers orders. You might want to explore other pages on the site to learn more about how FTD.com does business.

3. When you have finished exploring the FTD.com site, click your browser's Back button until you have returned to the Case Problems section of the Online Companion for Tutorial 10.5.

4. Click the 1-800-flowers.com hyperlink. When the 1-800-flowers.com home page opens, click the About Us hyperlink near the bottom of the page. When the About 1-800-flowers.com page opens, read it carefully. This page includes a company overview, information about the company's access channels, and a description of the flower shop network that fulfills the company's orders. You might want to explore other pages on the site to learn more about 1-800-flowers.com.

5. When you have finished exploring the 1-800-flowers.com site, click your browser's Back button until you have returned to the Case Problems section of the Online Companion for Tutorial 10.

6. Click the Proflowers.com hyperlink. When the Proflowers.com home page opens, click the About Us hyperlink on the left side of the page. When the About Us page opens, read it carefully. This page includes a mission statement, information about how the company does business, and a section on how they ship and package the flowers. You might want to explore other pages on the site to learn more about Proflowers.com.

7. When you have finished examining the Proflowers.com site, close your browser and log off your Internet connection, if necessary.

8. Each of these three companies uses a different business strategy to sell flowers and related gift items to consumers. Based on your examination of the three Web sites, write one paragraph for each company that describes the key elements in its business strategy, and then write one paragraph in which you compare and contrast the three different business strategies.

QUICK CHECK ANSWERS

Session 10.1

1. Commonly used terms include eyeballs and page views.

2. user name or ID, password

3. False. You can only customize portal Web pages. "Normal" Web pages are fixed by the publisher and cannot be changed.

4. False. In addition, you must publish your calendar to make its public entries available to the public.

5. The main advantage of Web-based calendars is that you can access your calendar from any place that has a browser. Additionally, you can share the calendar with others. Neither of these is possible with a PDA or calendar software running on a desktop computer.

Session 10.2

1. EDI occurs when one business transmits computer-readable data in a standard format to another business.

2. The value added network (VAN) can provide third-party assurances and dispute resolution services.

3. distribute new products, deliver upgrades to existing products, and provide user support

4. to attract potential purchasers to the site

5. Customers often have specific titles or characteristics in mind, the products are easily identifiable, and the products have a high value-to-weight ratio.

6. misrepresented product, damaged product, seller does not deliver product

7. transaction security and buyer privacy

8. They provide some assurance that a Web site meets some criteria for conducting business in a secure manner for years.

New Perspectives on

CREATING WEB PAGES WITH HTML,

2ⁿᵈ Edition

Read This Before You Begin

To the Student

Data Disks

To complete the Level I tutorials, Review Assignments, and Case Problems in this book, you need two Data Disks. Your instructor will either provide you with Data Disks or ask you to make your own.

If you are making your own Data Disks, you will need two blank, formatted high-density disks. You will need to copy a set of folders from a file server or standalone computer or the Web onto your disks. Your instructor will tell you which computer, drive letter, and folders contain the files you need. You could also download the files by going to http://www.course.com, clicking Data Disk Files, and following the instructions on the screen.

The following table shows you which folders go on your disks, so that you will have enough disk space to complete all the tutorials, Review Assignments, and Case Problems:

Data Disk 1

Write this on the disk label:
Data Disk 1: Level 1 Tutorial 1

Put these folders on the disk:
Tutorial.01

Data Disk 2

Write this on the disk label:
Data Disk 2: Level 1 Tutorial 2

Put these folders on the disk:
Tutorial.02

When you begin each tutorial, be sure you are using the correct Data Disk. See the inside front or inside back cover of this book for more information on Data Disk Files, or ask your instructor or technical support person for assistance.

Course Lab

Tutorial 1 features an interactive Course Lab to help you understand Web page concepts. There are Lab Assignments at the end of the tutorial that relate to this Lab. To start the Lab, Click the Start button on the Windows taskbar, point to Programs, point to Course Labs, point to New Perspectives Applications, and click creating Web Pages: HTML.

Using Your Own Computer

If you are going to work through this book using your own computer, you need:

- **Computer System** A text editor and a Web browser (preferably Netscape Navigator or Internet Explorer, versions 3.0 or higher) must be installed on your computer. If you are using a non-standard browser, it must support frames and HTML 3.2 or higher. Most of the tutorials can be completed with just a text editor and a Web browser. However, to complete the last sections of Tutorial 2, you will need an Internet connection and software that connects you to the Internet.

- **Data Disks** Ask your instructor or lab manager for details on how to get the Data Disk. You will not be able to complete the tutorials or exercises in this book using your own computer until you have Data Disks. The Data Disk Files may be obtained electronically over the Internet. See the inside back cover of this book for more details.

Visit Our World Wide Web Site

Additional materials designed especially for you are available on the World Wide Web. Go to http://www.course.com. For example, see our Student Online Companion that contains additional coverage of selected topics in the text. These topics are indicated in the text by an online companion icon located in the left margin.

To the Instructor

The Data Disk Files are available on the Instructor's Resource Kit for this title. Follow the instructions in the Help file on the CD-ROM to install the programs to your network or standalone computer. For information on creating Data Disks, see the "To the Student" section above.

You are granted a license to copy the Data Disk Files to any computer or computer network used by students who have purchased this book.

OBJECTIVES

In this tutorial you will:

- Explore the structure of the World Wide Web

- Learn the basic principles of Web documents

- Get to know the HTML language

- Create an HTML document

- View an HTML file in a Web browser

- Tag text elements, including headings, paragraphs, and lists

- Insert character tags

- Add special characters

- Insert horizontal lines

- Insert an inline graphic image

LAB

Web Pages & HTML

CREATING A WEB PAGE

Web Fundamentals and HTML

CASE

Creating an Online Resume

Mary Taylor just graduated from Colorado State University with a master's degree in telecommunications. Mary wants to explore as many employment avenues as possible, so she decides to post a copy of her resume on the World Wide Web. Creating an online resume offers Mary several advantages. The Web's skyrocketing popularity gives Mary the potential of reaching a large and varied audience. She can continually update an online resume, offering details on her latest projects and jobs. An online resume also gives a prospective employer the opportunity to look at her work history in more detail than is normal with a paper resume, because Mary can include links to other relevant documents. Mary asks you to help her create an online resume. You're happy to do so because it's something you wanted to learn anyway. After all, you'll be creating your own resume soon enough.

Introducing the World Wide Web

The **Internet** is a structure made up of millions of interconnected computers whose users can communicate with each other and share information. The physical structure of the Internet uses fiber-optic cables, satellites, phone lines, and other telecommunications media that send data back and forth, as Figure 1-1 shows. Computers that are linked together form a **network**. Any user whose computer can be linked to a network that has Internet access can join the worldwide Internet community.

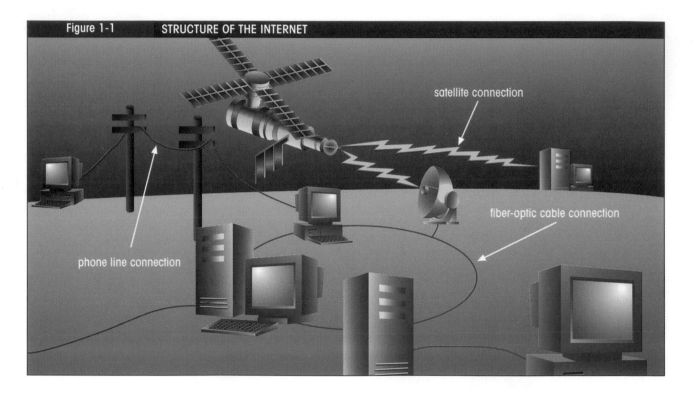

Figure 1-1   STRUCTURE OF THE INTERNET

Before 1989, anyone with Internet access could take advantage of the opportunities the Internet offered, but not without some problems. New users often found their introduction to the Internet an unpleasant one. Many Internet tools required you to master a bewildering array of terms, acronyms, and commands before you could begin navigating the Internet. Navigation itself was a hit-and-miss proposition. A computer in Bethesda might have information on breast cancer, but if you didn't know that computer existed and how to reach it, the Internet offered few tools to help you get there. What Internet users needed was a tool that would be easy to use and would allow quick access to any computer on the Internet, regardless of its location. This tool would prove to be the World Wide Web.

The Development of the World Wide Web

The **World Wide Web** organizes the Internet's vast resources to give you easy access to information. In 1989, Timothy Berners-Lee and other researchers at the CERN nuclear research facility near Geneva, Switzerland, laid the foundation of the World Wide Web, or the Web. They wanted to create an information system that made it easy for researchers to locate and share data and that required minimal training and support. They developed a system of hypertext documents that made it very easy to move from one source of information to another. A **hypertext document** is an electronic file that contains elements that you can select, usually by clicking a mouse, to open another document.

Hypertext offers a new way of progressing through a series of documents. When you read a book, you follow a linear progression, reading one page after another. With hypertext, you progress through pages in whatever way is best suited to your goals. Hypertext lets you skip from one topic to another, following a path of information that interests you. Figure 1-2 shows how topics could be related in a hypertext fashion, as opposed to a linear fashion.

Figure 1-2	LINEAR VS. HYPERTEXT DOCUMENTS

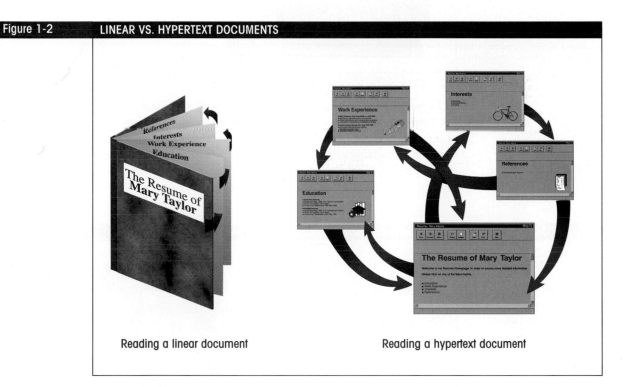

Reading a linear document   Reading a hypertext document

You might already be familiar with two common sources of hypertext: Windows Help files and Macintosh HyperCard stacks. In these programs, you move from one topic to another by clicking or highlighting a phrase or keyword known as a **link**. Clicking a link takes you to another section of the document, or it might take you to another document entirely. Figure 1-3 shows how you might navigate a link in a Help file.

Figure 1-3   **CLICKING A LINK IN A HELP FILE**

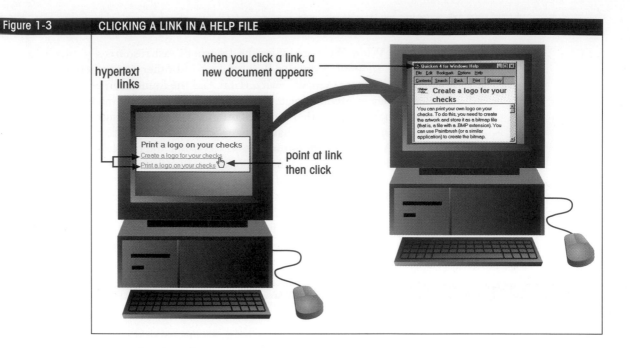

Hypertext as implemented by the CERN group involves jumping from one document to another on computers scattered all over the world. In Figure 1-4, you are working at a computer in Canada that shows a hypertext document on traveling in the United States. This document contains a link to another document located on a computer in Washington, D.C., about the National Park Service. That document in turn contains a link to a document located in California on Yosemite National Park.

Figure 1-4   **NAVIGATING HYPERTEXT DOCUMENTS ON THE WEB**

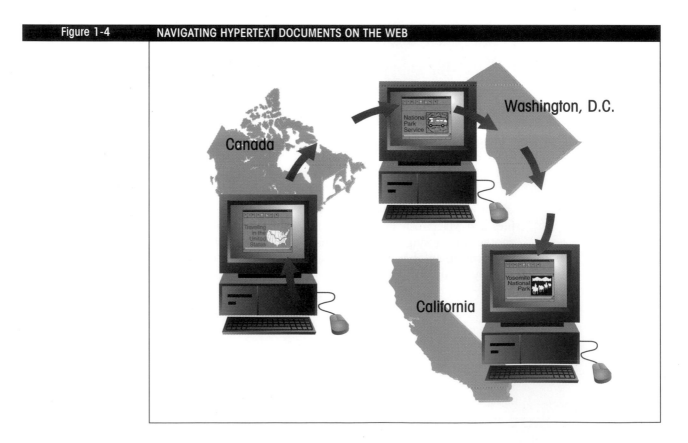

You move from document to document (and computer to computer) by simply clicking links. This approach makes navigating the Internet easy. It frees you from having to know anything about the document's location. The link could open a document on your computer or a document on a computer in South Africa. You might never notice the difference.

Your experience with the Web is not limited to reading text. Web documents, also known as **pages**, can contain graphics, video clips, sound clips, and, more recently, programs that you can run directly from the page. Moreover, as Figure 1-5 shows, Web pages can display text in a wide variety of fonts and formats. A Web page is not only a source of information, it can also be a work of art.

| Figure 1-5 | WEB PAGE FEATURING INTERESTING FONTS, GRAPHICS, AND LAYOUT |

A final feature that contributes to the Web's popularity is that it gives users the ability to easily create their own Web pages. This is in marked contrast to other Internet tools, which often require the expertise of a computer systems manager. Figure 1-6 illustrates the growth of the world online population. In a space of six years, the online population is projected to more than triple in size. Is there any doubt why Mary sees the Web as a worthwhile place to post a resume?

Figure 1-6   GROWTH OF THE WORLD ONLINE POPULATION

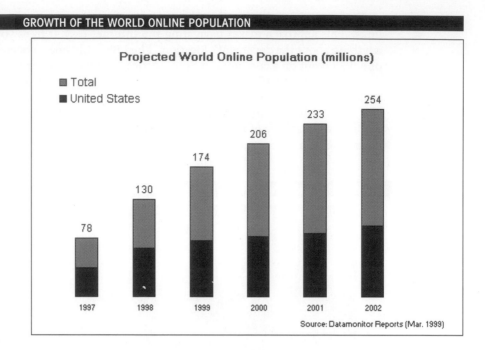

Web Servers and Web Browsers

The World Wide Web has the two components, shown in Figure 1-7. The **Web server** is the computer that stores the Web page that users access. The **Web browser** is the software program that accesses the Web document and displays its contents on the user's computer. The browser can locate a page on a server anywhere in the world and display it for you to see.

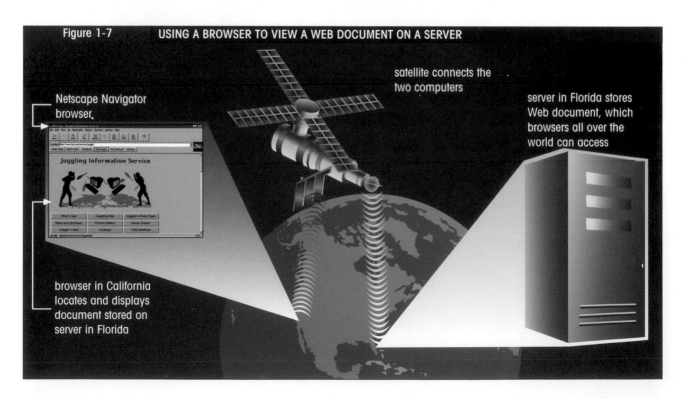

Browsers can either be text-based, like the Lynx browser found on UNIX machines, or graphical, like the popular Internet Explorer and Netscape browsers. With a **text-based browser**, you navigate the Web by typing commands; with a **graphical browser** you can use the mouse to move from page to page. Browsers are available for virtually every computer platform. No matter what kind of computer you have, you can probably use it to navigate the Web.

HTML: The Language of the Web

Web pages are written in a language called the **Hypertext Markup Language** or **HTML**. A **markup language** is a language used to describe the content and format of documents. HTML is only one example of a markup language. HTML has its roots in the **Standard Generalized Markup Language (SGML)**, a language used for large-scale documents. SGML though proved to be too cumbersome and difficult for use on the Internet, and thus HTML was created based on the principles of SGML.

The success of the World Wide Web is due in no small part to HTML. HTML allows Web authors to create documents that can be displayed across different operating systems and the HTML code is straight-forward enough that even non-programmers can learn to use it. Millions of Web sites are based on HTML, and there is every indication that HTML will continue to be the dominant language of the Web for a long time to come.

HTML formats a document in very general way. If you've used a word processor, you know that you control the appearance of text by the font you choose (such as Arial or Times Roman), or by an attribute (such as bold, or italic). Basic HTML doesn't describe how text looks. Instead it uses a **tag** describing the purpose that the text has in the document. Text appearing in the document's heading is marked with a heading tag. Text appearing in a bulleted list is marked with a list tag. A Web browser interprets these tags to determine how it will render the text. One browser might apply a Times Roman font to the text in the document's heading, while another browser might apply an Arial Font. Figure 1-8 shows how the same HTML file might appear on two different browsers.

Figure 1-8	TWO DIFFERENT BROWSERS DISPLAYING THE SAME HTML FILE

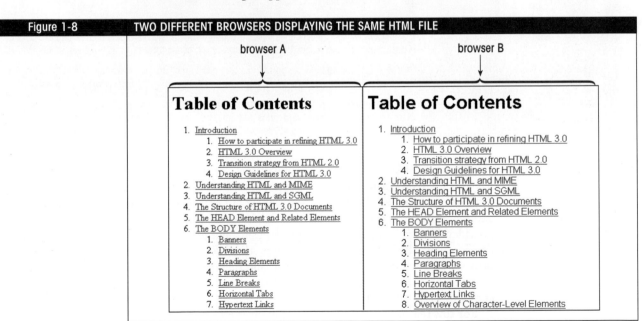

There are a couple of reasons to put the formatting choices in the control of the browser. Web pages must be **portable**, so that they can work well with all kinds of operating systems and applications. Because different operating systems and applications differ in how they code and render information, it would be a daunting task to create a page for all users. Portability frees Web page authors from this concern. HTML can also work with a wide range of devices, from clunky teletypes to high-end workstations. It also works with non-visual medium such as speech software. Web pages can even be rendered in Braille.

Of course portability does limit one's ability to exactly define the Web page's appearance. For this reason, HTML has allowed the use of **style sheets**, in which the Web page author can define the fonts and formats the Web browser should apply to the document's text. Style sheets are a topic that should be mastered only after one has become familiar with basic HTML.

A second reason to put the formatting choices in the browser's control is speed. Specifying the page's exact appearance could dramatically increase both the size of the document file and the time required to retrieve it. It is much quicker to render the document on the user's own computer. The downside of this approach is that you cannot be sure exactly how each browser and browser version will render your document. For this reason, it is important that you test your document code on several different browsers, and if possible, several different operating systems.

Versions of HTML

HTML has a set of rules, called **syntax**, that control how document code is to be written. There must be a consensus among the creators of Web browsers on these rules, or else there would be no guarantee that documents would be rendered correctly. It wouldn't do Mary much good to create a stunning online resume, unreadable by potential employers. This consensus appears as a set of **standards** or **specifications** developed by a consortium of Web developers called the **World Wide Web Consortium**, or more commonly known as the **W3C**. Figure 1-9 describes a history of the various versions of HTML that have been released by the W3C. For more information on the W3C, see their home page at http://www.w3c.org.

Figure 1-9	VERSIONS OF HTML	
VERSION	**DATE**	**DESCRIPTION**
HTML 1.00	1989–1994	The first public version of HTML, which included browser support for inline images and text controls
HTML 2.00	1995	The version supported by all graphical browsers, including Netscape Communicator, Internet Explorer, and Mosaic. It supported interactive form elements such as option buttons and text boxes. A document written to follow 2.0 specifications would be readable by most browsers on the Internet.
HTML 3.20	1997	This version included more support for creating and formatting tables, and expanded the options for interactive form elements. It also allows for the creation of complex mathematical equations.
HTML 4.01	1999	This version adds support for style sheets, to give Web authors greater control over page layout. It adds new features to tables and forms and provides support for international features. This version also expands HTML's scripting ability and support for multimedia elements.

The world of Web browsers is a competitive one however, and over the years each browser has added **extensions** to HTML, supporting new features and tags. Netscape and Internet Explorer have added the most extensions to HTML, and often these extensions have been adopted in the next set of HTML specifications released by the W3C. These extensions have provided Web page authors with more options, but at the expense of fragmenting Web page development. Before using an extension, the Web page author has to determine which browser and browser versions support it, and then the author has to create a workaround for browsers that do not support the extension. All of this complicates Web page development, and betrays the properties of HTML that made it so integral to the success of the Web.

For this reason, future Web development is focusing more on XML and XHTML. **XML (Extensible Markup Language)** is used for developing customized document structures. With XML, Web authors can create their own tags and attributes for their documents. XML combined with style sheets, can provide the same functionality as HTML, with greater flexibility. **XHTML (Extensible HyperText Markup Language)**, is a stricter and cleaner version of HTML, designed to overcome some of the problems of competing HTML standards introduced by the various browsers. Any Web page written in XHTML will be automatically compatible with HTML 4.01.

Tools for Creating HTML Documents

HTML documents are simple text files. The only software package you need to create them is a basic text editor such as the Windows Notepad program. If you want a software package to do some of the work of creating an HTML document, you can use an HTML converter or an HTML editor.

An **HTML converter** takes text in one format and converts it to HTML code. For example, you can create the source document with a word processor such as Microsoft Word, and then have the converter save the document as an HTML file. Converters have several advantages. They free you from the occasionally laborious task of typing HTML code, and, because the conversion is automated, you do not have to worry about typographical errors ruining your code. Finally, you can create the source document using a software package that you might be more familiar with. Be aware that a converter has some limitations. As HTML specifications are updated and new extensions created, you will have to wait for the next version of the converter, to take advantage of these features. Moreover, no converter can support all HTML features, so for anything but the simplest Web page, you still have to work with HTML.

An **HTML editor** helps you create an HTML file by inserting HTML codes for you as you work. HTML editors can save you a lot of work. They have many of the same advantages and limitations as converters. They do let you set up your Web page quickly, but to create the finished document, you often still have to work directly with the HTML code.

Session 1.1 QUICK | CHECK

1. What is hypertext?

2. What is a Web server? A Web browser? Describe how they work together.

3. What is HTML?

4. How do HTML documents differ from documents created with a word processor such as Word or WordPerfect?

5. What are the advantages of letting Web browsers determine the appearance of Web pages?

6. What are HTML extensions? What are some advantages and disadvantages of using extensions?

7. What software program do you need to create an HTML document?

SESSION 1.2

In this session you begin entering the text that will form the basis of your Web page. You will insert the appropriate HTML codes, creating a simple Web page that outlines Mary's work experience and qualifications.

Creating an HTML Document

It's always a good idea to plan the appearance of your Web page before you start writing code. In her final semester, Mary developed a paper resume that she distributed at campus job fairs. Half her work is already done, because she can use the paper resume as her model. Figure 1-10 shows Mary's hardcopy resume.

Figure 1-10   **MARY'S PAPER RESUME**

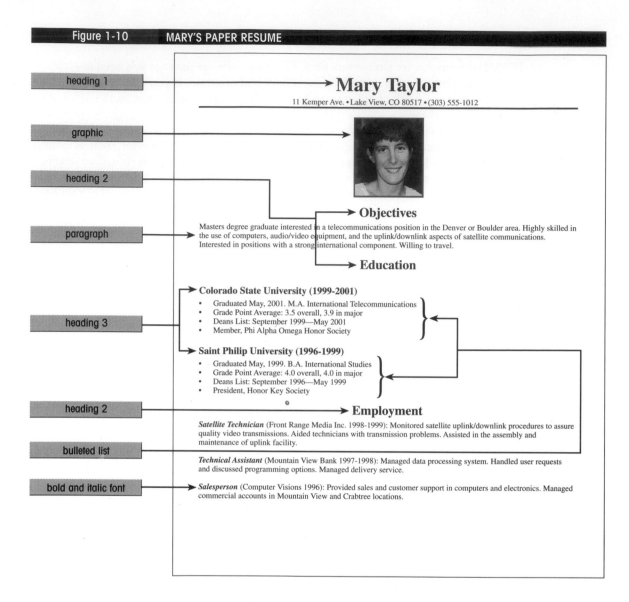

Mary's paper resume includes several features that she would like you to implement in the online version. A heading at the top prominently displays her name in a large font. Beneath the heading is her photo. Mary's resume is divided into three sections: Objectives, Education, and Employment. Within the Objectives section, a paragraph describes Mary's interests and future goals. Within the Education section, two smaller headings name the two universities she attended. Under each of these headings, a bulleted list details her accomplishments. The Employment section describes each position she's held, with the official title in boldface and italics. Mary's paper resume has three heading levels, bulleted lists, formatted characters, and graphics. When she creates her online resume with HTML, she wants to include these features. As you help Mary create this document for the World Wide Web, you will probably want to refer to Figure 1-10 periodically as the page develops.

HTML Syntax

An HTML document has two elements: document content and tags. **Document content** are those parts of the document that you want the user to see, such as text and graphics.

The HTML syntax for creating the kinds of features that Mary wants in her page follows a very basic structure. You apply a tag to document content using the syntax:

```
<Tag Name Properties> Document Content </Tag Name>
```

You can always identify a tag by the brackets (< >) that enclose the tag name. Some tags can include **properties**, or additional information placed within the brackets that controls how the tag is used. Tags usually come in pairs: the **opening tag** is the first tag, which tells the browser to turn on the feature and apply it to the document content that follows. The browser applies the feature until it encounters the **closing tag**, which turns off the feature. Note that closing tags are identified by the slash (/) that precedes the tag name. Not every type of tag has an opening and closing tag. Some tags are known as **one-sided tags** because they require only the opening tag. **Two-sided tags** require both opening and closing tags.

For example, look at the first line of Mary's resume, the name Mary Taylor, in Figure 1-10. You could format this line with the two-sided HTML tag as follows:

```
<H1 ALIGN=CENTER>Mary Taylor</H1>
```

Here the `<H1 ALIGN=CENTER >` opening tag tells the browser that the text that follows, Mary Taylor, should be formatted with the H1 style (H1 stands for Heading 1; you'll learn what this means later). This tag also includes a property, the **alignment property** (ALIGN), which tells the browser how to align the text: in this case, centered. After the opening tag comes the content, Mary Taylor. The `</H1>` tag signals the browser to turn off the H1 style. Remember that each browser determines the exact effect of the H1 tag. One browser might apply a 14-point Times Roman bold font to Mary's text, whereas another browser might use 18 point italic Arial—but in each case, the font would be appropriately larger than the normal font of the document. Figure 1-11 shows how three different browsers might interpret this line of HTML code.

Figure 1-11	EXAMPLES OF HOW DIFFERENT BROWSERS MIGHT INTERPRET THE HTML <H1> TAG
BROWSER INTERPRETING THE H1 TAG	**APPEARANCE OF THE DOCUMENT CONTENT**
Browser A	Mary Taylor
Browser B	**Mary Taylor**
Browser C	*Mary Taylor*

Tags are not case sensitive. That means that typing "<H1>" has the same effect as typing "<h1>". Many Web authors like to use only uppercase for tags, to distinguish tags from document content. We'll follow that convention throughout this book.

Creating Basic Tags

When you create your Web page, you first enter tags that indicate the markup language used in the document, identify the document's key sections, and assign the page a title.

In the steps that follow, type the text exactly as you see it. The text after the steps explains each line. To start entering code, you need a basic text editor such as Notepad or WordPad.

To start creating an HTML file:

1. Place your Data Disk in drive A.

TROUBLE? If you don't have a Data Disk, you need to get one. Your instructor will either give you one or ask you to make your own. See the Read This Before You Begin page at the beginning of the tutorials for instructions.

TROUBLE? If your Data Disk won't fit in drive A, try drive B. If it fits in drive B, substitute drive B for drive A in every tutorial.

2. Open a text editor on your computer, and then open a new document.

TROUBLE? If you don't know how to locate, start, or use the text editor on your system, ask your instructor or technical support person for help.

3. Type the following lines of code into your document. Press the **Enter** key after each line (twice for a blank line).

```
<HTML>
<HEAD>
<TITLE>The Resume of Mary Taylor</TITLE>
</HEAD>

<BODY>
</BODY>

</HTML>
```

4. Save the file as **Resume.htm** in the Tutorial.01 folder on your Data Disk, but do not close your text editor. The text you typed should look something like Figure 1-12.

Figure 1-12 INITIAL HTML TAGS

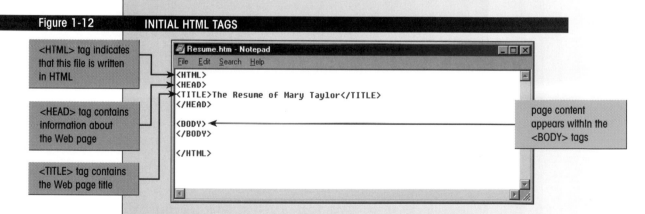

TROUBLE? If you don't know how to save a file on your Data Disk, ask your instructor or technical support person for assistance.

TROUBLE? Don't worry if your screen doesn't look exactly like Figure 1-12. The text editor shown in the figures is the Windows Notepad editor. Your text editor might look very different. Just make sure you entered the text correctly.

> TROUBLE? If you are using the Windows Notepad text editor to create your HTML file, make sure you don't save the file using the text document type (.txt), which Notepad automatically adds to the filename. This renders the file unreadable to the Netscape Navigator browser, which requires an .htm or .html file extension. So make sure you save the file using the All Files (*.*) type, and then add the .htm or .html extension to the filename yourself.

The opening and closing HTML tags bracket all the remaining code you'll enter in the document. This indicates to a browser that the page is written in HTML. While you don't have to include this tag, it is necessary if the file is to be read by another SGML application. Moreover, it is considered good style to include it.

The <HEAD> tag is used where you enter information about the Web page itself. One such piece of information is the title of the page, which appears in the title bar of the Web browser. This information is entered using the <TITLE> tag. The title in this example is "The Resume of Mary Taylor".

Finally, the portion of the document that Web users will see is contained between the <BODY> tags. At this point, the page is blank, with no text or graphics. You'll add those later. The <HEAD> and <BODY> tags are not strictly required, but you should include them to better organize your document and make its code more readable to others. The extra space before and after the BODY tags is also not required, but it will make your code easier to view as you add more features to it.

Displaying Your HTML Files

As you continue adding to Mary's HTML file, you should occasionally display the formatted page with your Web browser to verify that there are no syntax errors or other problems. You might even want to view the results on several browsers to check for differences between one browser and another. In the steps and figures that follow, the Internet Explorer browser is used to display Mary's resume page as it gradually unfolds. If you are using a different browser, ask your instructor how to view local files (those located on your own computer rather than on the Web).

To view the beginning of Mary's resume page:

1. Start your browser. You do not need to be connected to the Internet to view a file loaded on your computer.

   TROUBLE? If you try to start your browser and are not connected to the Internet, you might get a warning message. Netscape Navigator, for example, gives a warning message telling you that it was unable to create a network socket connection. Click OK to ignore the message and continue.

2. After your browser loads its home page, click **File** on the menu bar and then click **Open**.

   TROUBLE? If you're using Netscape Navigator, you will have to use a different command to open the file from your Data Disk. Talk to your instructor or technical support person to find out how to open the file.

3. Locate the **Resume.htm** file that you saved in the Tutorial.01 folder on your Data Disk, and then click Open. Your browser displays Mary's file, as shown in Figure 1-13. Note that the page title, which you typed earlier between the <TITLE> tags, appears in the browser's title bar.

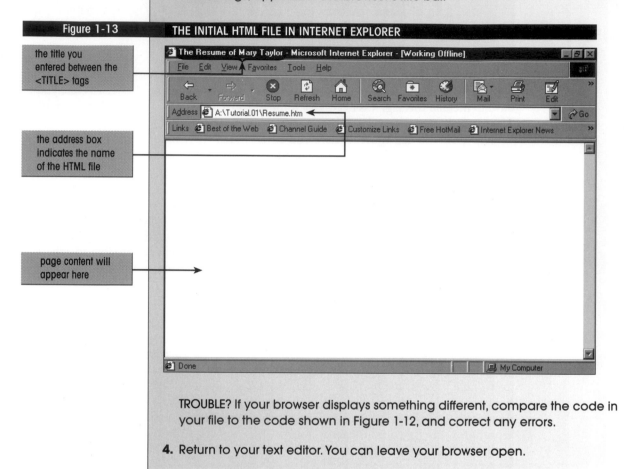

Figure 1-13   THE INITIAL HTML FILE IN INTERNET EXPLORER

the title you entered between the <TITLE> tags

the address box indicates the name of the HTML file

page content will appear here

TROUBLE? If your browser displays something different, compare the code in your file to the code shown in Figure 1-12, and correct any errors.

4. Return to your text editor. You can leave your browser open.

Creating Headers, Paragraphs, and Lists

Now that the basic structure of Mary's page is set, you can start filling in the page content. One place to start is the headers for the various sections of her document. Her document needs a header for the entire page and headers for each of three sections: Objectives, Education, and Employment. The Education section has two additional headers that provide information about the two universities she attended. You can create all these headers using HTML heading tags.

Creating Header Tags

HTML supports six levels of headers, numbered <H1> through <H6>, with <H1> being the largest and most prominent, and <H6> being the smallest. Headers (even the smallest) appear in a larger font than normal text, and some headers are boldface. The general syntax for a header tag is:

```
<Hy>Heading Text</Hy>
```

where y is a header numbered 1 through 6.

Figure 1-14 illustrates the general appearance of the six header styles. Your browser might use slightly different fonts and sizes.

Figure 1-14	SIX HEADER LEVELS

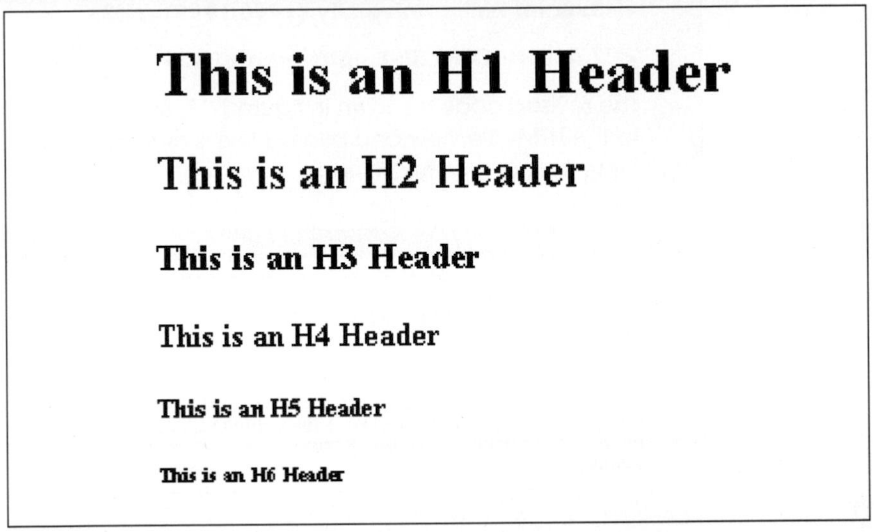

This is an H1 Header

This is an H2 Header

This is an H3 Header

This is an H4 Header

This is an H5 Header

This is an H6 Header

REFERENCE WINDOW   **RW**

Creating a Header Tag
- Open the HTML file with your text editor.
- Type <Hy> where y is the header number you want to use.
- If you want to use a special alignment, specify the alignment property setting after y and before the closing symbol, >.
- Type the text that you want to appear in the header.
- Type </Hy> to turn off the header tag.

Starting with HTML 3.2, the header tag can contain additional properties, one of which is the alignment property. Mary wants some headers centered on the page, so you'll take advantage of this property. Although Mary's address is not really header text, you decide to format it with an <H5> tag, because you want it to stand out a little from normal paragraphed text.

To add headings to the resume file:

1. Return to your text editor, and then open the **Resume.htm** file, if it is not already open.

2. Type the following text between the <BODY> and </BODY> tags (type the address and phone number all on one line, as shown in Figure 1-15):

   <H1 ALIGN=CENTER>Mary Taylor</H1>

   <H5 ALIGN=CENTER>11 Kemper Ave. Lake View, CO 80517 (303) 555-1012</H5>

<H2 ALIGN=CENTER>Objectives</H2>

<H2 ALIGN=CENTER>Education</H2>

<H3>Colorado State University (1999-2001)</H3>

<H3>Saint Philip University (1996-1999)</H3>

<H2 ALIGN=CENTER>Employment</H2>

The revised code is shown in figure 1-15. To make it easier to follow the changes to the HTML file, new and altered text is highlighted in red. This will not be the case in your own text files.

Figure 1-15	ENTERING HEADER TAGS

```
<BODY>
<H1 ALIGN=CENTER>Mary Taylor</H1>
<H5 ALIGN=CENTER>11 Kemper Ave. Lake View, CO 80517 (303) 555-1012</H5>
<H2 ALIGN=CENTER>Objectives</H2>
<H2 ALIGN=CENTER>Education</H2>
<H3>Colorado State University (1999-2001)</H3>
<H3>Saint Philip University (1996-1999)</H3>
<H2 ALIGN=CENTER>Employment</H2>
</BODY>
```

3. Save the revised Resume.htm file in the Tutorial.01 folder on your Data Disk. You can leave your text editor open.

The section headers all use the ALIGN=CENTER property to center the text on the page. The <H3> tags used for the two university headers, however, do not include that property and will be left-justified because that is the default alignment setting. If a browser that displays Mary's page does not support HTML 3.2 (or above) or does not support the alignment property through an extension, the headers will appear, but all of them will be left-justified.

To display the revised Resume.htm file:

1. Return to your Web browser.

2. If the previous version of the file still appears in the browser window, click **View** on the menu bar, and then click **Refresh**. If you are using Netscape, you will need to click **View** and then click **Reload**.

The updated Resume.htm file looks like Figure 1-16.

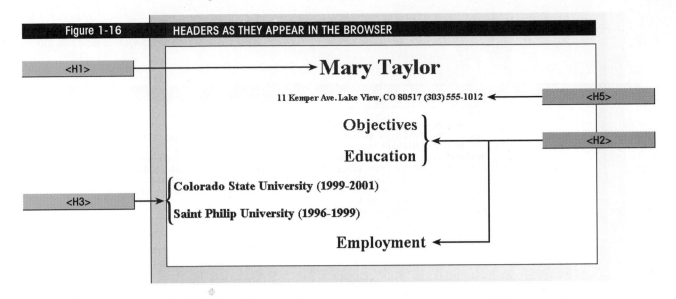

Figure 1-16	HEADERS AS THEY APPEAR IN THE BROWSER

Entering Paragraph Text

The next thing that you have to do is enter information for each section. If your paragraph does not require any formatting, you can enter the text without tags.

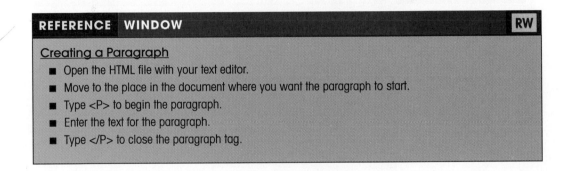

REFERENCE WINDOW   **RW**

<u>Creating a Paragraph</u>
- Open the HTML file with your text editor.
- Move to the place in the document where you want the paragraph to start.
- Type <P> to begin the paragraph.
- Enter the text for the paragraph.
- Type </P> to close the paragraph tag.

Mary's career objective, which appears just below the Objectives heading, does not require formatting, so you can enter that as paragraph text.

To enter paragraph text:

1. Return to your text editor, and then reopen the **Resume.htm** file, if it is not already open.

2. Type the following text directly after the line of code that specifies the Objectives heading:

   Masters degree graduate interested in a telecommunications position in the Denver or Boulder area. Highly skilled in the use of computers, audio/video equipment, and the uplink/downlink aspects of satellite communications. Interested in positions with a strong international component. Willing to travel.

Your text should be placed between the Objectives head and the Education head, as shown in Figure 1-17. Check your work for mistakes, and edit the file as necessary.

Figure 1-17 **ENTERING PARAGRAPH TEXT**

```
<BODY>
<H1 ALIGN=CENTER>Mary Taylor</H1>
<H5 ALIGN=CENTER>11 Kemper Ave. Lake View, CO 80517 (303) 555-1012</H5>
<H2 ALIGN=CENTER>Objectives</H2>
Masters degree graduate interested in a telecommunications position in
the Denver or Boulder area. Highly skilled in the use of computers,
audio/video equipment and the uplink/downlink aspects of satellite
communications. Interested in positions with a strong international
component. Willing to travel.
<H2 ALIGN=CENTER>Education</H2>
```

TROUBLE? If you are using a text editor like Notepad, the text might not wrap to the next line automatically. You might need to select the Word Wrap command on the Edit menu, or a similar command, so you can see all the text on your screen.

3. Save the changes you made to the Resume.htm file.

4. Return to your Web browser, and then reopen the **Resume.htm** file to view the text you've added. See Figure 1-18.

Figure 1-18 **PARAGRAPH TEXT IN THE BROWSER**

Mary Taylor

11 Kemper Ave. Lake View, CO 80517 (303) 555-1012

Objectives

Masters degree graduate interested in a telecommunications position in the Denver or Boulder area. Highly skilled in the use of computers, audio/video equipment, and the uplink/downlink aspects of satellite communications. Interested in positions with a strong international component. Willing to travel.

Education

5. Now enter the Employment paragraph text by returning to your text editor and reopening the **Resume.htm file**, if needed.

6. Go to the end of the file, and, in the line before the final </BODY> tag, type the following text:

Satellite Technician (Front Range Media Inc. 1998-1999): Monitored satellite uplink/downlink procedures to assure quality video transmissions. Aided technicians with transmission problems. Assisted in the assembly and maintenance of uplink facility.

Technical Assistant (Mountain View Bank 1997-1998): Managed data processing system. Handled user requests and discussed programming options. Managed delivery service.

Salesperson (Computer Visions 1996): Sales and customer support in computers and electronics. Managed commercial accounts in Mountain View and Crabtree locations.

Figure 1-19 shows the new code in Mary's resume file.

Figure 1-19	ENTERING EMPLOYMENT TEXT

```
<H2 ALIGN=CENTER>Education</H2>
<H3>Colorado State University (1999-2001)</H3>
<H3>Saint Philip University (1996-1999)</H3>
<H2 ALIGN=CENTER>Employment</H2>
Satellite Technician (Front Range Media Inc. 1998-1999): Monitored
satellite uplink/downlink procedures to assure quality transmissions.
Aided technicians with transmission problems. Assisted in the assembly
and maintenance of uplink facility.

Technical Assistant (Mountain View Bank 1997-1998): Managed data
processing system. Handled user requests and discussed programming
options. Managed delivery service.

Salesperson (Computer Visions 1996): Sales and customer support in
computers and electronics. Managed commercial accounts in Mountain View
and Crabtree locations.
</BODY>
```

employment history

7. Save the changes you've made to the file.

8. Return to your Web browser, and then reopen the **Resume.htm** file.

9. Scroll down to see how the new text looks (see Figure 1-20).

Figure 1-20	THE EMPLOYMENT HISTORY DISPLAYED BY THE BROWSER

Education

Colorado State University (1999-2001)

Saint Philip University (1996-1999)

employment history is not separated into paragraphs

Employment

Satellite Technician (Front Range Media Inc. 1998-1999): Monitored satellite uplink/downlink procedures to assure quality transmissions. Aided technicians with transmission problems. Assisted in the assembly and maintenance of uplink facility. Technical Assistant (Mountain View Bank 1997-1998): Managed data processing system. Handled user requests and discussed programming options. Managed delivery service. Salesperson (Computer Visions 1996): Sales and customer support in computers and electronics. Managed commercial accounts in Mountain View and Crabtree locations.

To your surprise, the text you typed into the HTML file looks nothing like what appeared on the browser, as you can see from Figure 1-20. Instead of being separated by blank lines, the three paragraphs are running together. What went wrong?

The problem here is that HTML formats text only through the use of tags. HTML ignores such things as extra blank spaces, blank lines, or tabs. As far as HTML is concerned, the following three lines of code are identical, so a browser interprets and displays each line just like the others, ignoring the extra spaces and lines:

```
<H1>To be or not to be. That is the question.</H1>
<H1>To be or not to be.   That is the question.</H1>
<H1>To be or not to be.
              That is the question.</H1>
```

At first glance, the Employment section seemed not to need any formatting; however, each paragraph needs to be separated by a blank line. To add this space between paragraphs, you need to use the **paragraph tag**, **<P>**, which adds a blank paragraph (the extra line you need) before text to separate it from any text that precedes it.

To add paragraph tags for blank lines:

1. Return to your text editor and the Resume.htm file.

2. Modify the Employment text, bracketing each paragraph between a **<P>** and **</P>** tag, so that the lines now read:

<P>Satellite Technician (Front Range Media Inc. 1998-1999): Monitored satellite uplink/downlink procedures to assure quality video transmissions. Aided technicians with transmission problems. Assisted in the assembly and maintenance of uplink facility.</P>

<P>Technical Assistant (Mountain View Bank 1997-1998): Managed data processing system. Handled user requests and discussed programming options. Managed delivery service. </P>

<P>Salesperson (Computer Visions 1996): Sales and customer support in computers and electronics. Managed commercial accounts in Mountain View and Crabtree locations.</P>

3. Save the revised text file.

4. Return to your Web browser, and then reopen the **Resume.htm** file. The text in the Employment section is properly separated into distinct paragraphs, as shown in Figure 1-21.

Figure 1-21   **EMPLOYMENT HISTORY SEPARATED INTO PARAGRAPHS**

Colorado State University (1999-2001)

Saint Philip University (1996-1999)

Employment

the text is now separated into paragraphs

Satellite Technician (Front Range Media Inc. 1998-1999): Monitored satellite uplink/downlink procedures to assure quality transmissions. Aided technicians with transmission problems. Assisted in the assembly and maintenance of uplink facility.

Technical Assistant (Mountain View Bank 1997-1998): Managed data processing system. Handled user requests and discussed programming options. Managed delivery service.

Salesperson (Computer Visions 1996): Sales and customer support in computers and electronics. Managed commercial accounts in Mountain View and Crabtree locations.

If you start examining the HTML code for pages that you encounter on the Web, you might notice that the <P> tag is used in different ways on other pages. In the original version of HTML, the <P> tag inserted a blank line into the page. In HTML 1.0, <P> was placed at the end of each paragraph; no </P> tag was required. In versions 2.0 and 3.2, the paragraph tag is two-sided: both the <P> and </P> tags are used. Moreover, the <P> tag is placed at the beginning of the paragraph, not the end. Starting with HTML 3.2, you can specify the alignment property in a paragraph tag, but in HTML 1.0 and 2.0 you cannot; paragraphs are always assumed to be left justified. For the Web documents that you are creating in this book, you should use the style convention shown in the above example.

Creating Lists

You still need to enter the lists describing Mary's achievements at Colorado State University and Saint Philip University. HTML provides tags for such lists. HTML supports three kinds of lists: ordered, unordered, and definition.

An **ordered list** is a list in numeric order. HTML automatically adds the numbers once you display your Web page in a browser. If you remove an item from the list, HTML automatically updates the numbers to reflect the new order. For example, Mary might want to list her scholastic awards in order from the most important to the least important. To do so, you could enter the following code into her HTML document:

```
<H3>Scholastic Awards</H3>
<OL>
<LI>Enos Mills Scholarship
<LI>Physics Expo blue ribbon winner
<LI> Honor Key Award semifinalist
</OL>
```

This example shows the basic structure of an HTML list. The list text is bracketed between the <OL> and </OL> tags, where OL stands for ordered list. This tells the browser to present the text between the tags as an ordered list. Each list item is identified by a single <LI> tag, where LI stands for list item. There is no closing tag for list items.

A Web browser might display this code as:

Scholastic Awards

1. Enos Mills Scholarship

2. Physics Expo blue ribbon winner

3. Honor Key Award semifinalist

You can also specify the symbol used for the ordered list, using the **TYPE** property. The default, as you've seen, is a number. By setting the TYPE property to "a", you can use letters instead of numbers. For example, the code:

```
<OL TYPE=a>
<LI>Enos Mills Scholarship
<LI>Physics Expo blue ribbon winner
<LI> Honor Key Award semifinalist
</OL>
```

yields the following list:

a. Enos Mills Scholarship

b. Physics Expo blue ribbon winner

c. Honor Key Award semifinalist

Other values of the TYPE property are "A" for uppercase letters, "i" for lowercase Roman numerals, and "I" for uppercase Roman numerals. Be aware that the TYPE property is not supported by all browsers. It was not part of the HTML standards prior to HTML 3.0.

You can also create an **unordered list**, in which list items have no particular order. Browsers usually format unordered lists by inserting a bullet symbol before each list item. The entire list is bracketed between the <UL> and </UL> tags, where UL stands for unordered list. If Mary wants to display her awards without regard to their importance, you could enter the following code:

```
<H3>Scholastic Awards</H3>
<UL>
<LI>Enos Mills Scholarship
<LI>Physics Expo blue ribbon winner
<LI>Honor Key Award semifinalist
</UL>
```

A Web browser might display this code as:

Scholastic Awards

- Enos Mills Scholarship
- Physics Expo blue ribbon winner
- Honor Key Award semifinalist

As with the ordered list, you can use the TYPE property to specify the type of symbol used in the list. The default symbol is a bullet or "disc." Other values for the TYPE property are SQUARE for square bullets and CIRCLE for circles. This property was introduced with HTML 3.0, although Netscape has supported it since version 1.0. Internet Explorer does not support this property, although this may change with new versions. If symbol type is an important part of your document, you will probably want to test this feature on several different browsers.

A third type of list that HTML can display is a definition list. A **definition list** is a list of terms, each followed by a definition line, usually indented slightly to the right. The <LI> tag used in ordered and unordered lists for individual items is replaced by two tags: the <DT> tag used for each term in the list and the <DD> tag used for each term's definition. As with the <LI> tag, both of these tags are one-sided. The entire list is bracketed by the <DL> and </DL> tags, indicating to the browser that the list is a definition list. If Mary wants to create a list of her scholastic awards and briefly describe each, she can use a definition list, even though the items are not actually terms and definitions. To create a definition list for her awards, you could enter this code into her HTML file:

```
<H3>Scholastic Awards</H3>
<DL>
<DT>Enos Mills Scholarship<DD>Awarded to the outstanding
student in the senior class
<DT>Physics Expo blue ribbon winner<DD>Awarded for a research
 project on fiber optics
<DT>Honor Key Award semifinalist<DD>Awarded for an essay on
the information age
</DL>
```

A Web browser might display this code as:

Scholastic Awards

Enos Mills Scholarship

　　Awarded to the outstanding student in the senior class

Physics Expo blue ribbon winner

　　Awarded for a research project on fiber optics

Honor Key Award semifinalist

　　Awarded for an essay on the information age

REFERENCE   WINDOW   **RW**

<u>Creating Lists</u>
- Open the HTML file with your text editor.
- Move to the place in the document where you want the list to appear.
- Type <OL> to start an ordered list, <UL> to start an unordered list, and <DL> to start a definition list.
- For each item in an ordered or unordered list, type <LI> followed by the text for the list item. For each item in a definition list, type <DT> before the term and <DD> before the definition.
- To turn off the list, type </OL> for an ordered list, </UL> for an unordered list, and </DL> for a definition list.

On her paper resume (Figure 1-10), Mary's educational accomplishments are in a bulleted list. You can include this feature in Mary's online resume by using the <OL> and <LI> tags.

To add an unordered list to the resume file:

1. Return to your text editor and reopen the **Resume.htm file**, if it is not still open.

2. Type the following code and text between the headers "Colorado State University" and "Saint Philip University":

   <UL>

   <LI>Graduated May, 2001. M.A. International Telecommunications

   <LI>Grade Point Average: 3.5 overall, 3.9 in major

   <LI>Dean's List: September 1999-May 2001

   <LI>Member, Phi Alpha Omega Honor Society

   </UL>

3. Type these lines of code after the heading "Saint Philip University":

   <UL>

   <LI>Graduated May, 1999. B.A. International Studies

   <LI>Grade Point Average: 4.0 overall, 4.0 in major

   <LI>Dean's List: September 1996-May 1999

   <LI>President, Honor Key Society

   </UL>

   The new lines in the resume file should look like Figure 1-22.

Figure 1-22   ENTERING UNORDERED LISTS

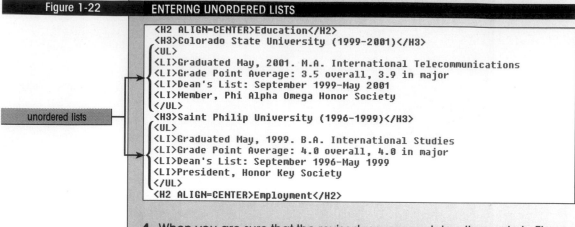

unordered lists

```
<H2 ALIGN=CENTER>Education</H2>
<H3>Colorado State University (1999-2001)</H3>
<UL>
<LI>Graduated May, 2001. M.A. International Telecommunications
<LI>Grade Point Average: 3.5 overall, 3.9 in major
<LI>Dean's List: September 1999-May 2001
<LI>Member, Phi Alpha Omega Honor Society
</UL>
<H3>Saint Philip University (1996-1999)</H3>
<UL>
<LI>Graduated May, 1999. B.A. International Studies
<LI>Grade Point Average: 4.0 overall, 4.0 in major
<LI>Dean's List: September 1996-May 1999
<LI>President, Honor Key Society
</UL>
<H2 ALIGN=CENTER>Employment</H2>
```

4. When you are sure that the revised resume matches the code in Figure 1-22, save the file.

5. Switch to your Web browser and reopen the **Resume.htm file**, shown in Figure 1-23.

Figure 1-23   THE UNORDERED LISTS IN THE BROWSER

Education

Colorado State University (1999-2001)

- Graduated May, 2001. M.A. International Telecommunications
- Grade Point Average: 3.5 overall, 3.9 in major
- Dean's List: September 1999-May 2001
- Member, Phi Alpha Omega Honor Society

Saint Philip University (1996-1999)

- Graduated May, 1999. B.A. International Studies
- Grade Point Average: 4.0 overall, 4.0 in major
- Dean's List: September 1996-May 1999
- President, Honor Key Society

Mary's resume file now includes lists formatted much like those on her paper resume. If your browser does not create a page that looks like Figure 1-23, return to the HTML file, and check for inconsistencies.

Creating Character Tags

Until now you've worked with tags that affect either the entire document or individual lines. HTML also lets you modify the characteristics of individual characters. A tag that you apply to an individual character is called a **character tag**. You can use two kinds of character tags: logical and physical. **Logical character tags** indicate how you want to use text, not necessarily how you want it displayed. Figure 1-24 lists some common logical character tags.

Figure 1-24	COMMON LOGICAL CHARACTER TAGS
TAG	**DESCRIPTION**
<EM>	Indicates that characters should be emphasized in some way. Usually displayed with italics.
<STRONG>	Emphasizes characters more strongly than <EM>. Usually displayed in a bold font.
<CODE>	Indicates a sample of code. Usually displayed in a Courier font or a similar font that allots the same width to each character.
<KBD>	Used to offset text that the user should enter. Often displayed in a Courier font or a similar font that allots the same width to each character.
<VAR>	Indicates a variable. Often displayed in italics or underlined.
<CITE>	Indicates short quotes or citations. Often italicized by browsers.

Figure 1-25 shows examples of how these tags might appear in a browser. Note that you can combine tags, allowing you to create boldface and italics text by using both the <EM> and the <STRONG> tags.

Figure 1-25	LOGICAL CHARACTER TAGS AS THEY APPEAR IN THE BROWSER

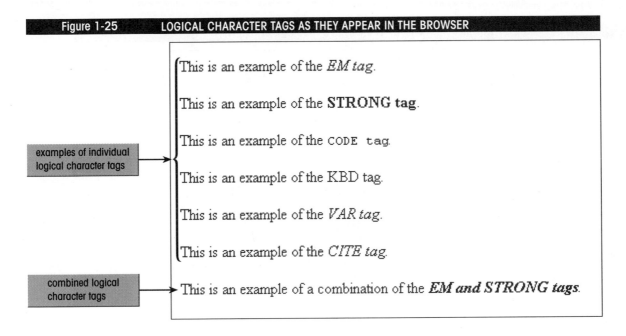

HTML authors can also use **physical character tags** to indicate exactly how characters are to be formatted. Figure 1-26 shows common examples of physical character tags.

Figure 1-26 COMMON PHYSICAL CHARACTER TAGS

TAG	DESCRIPTION
<B>	Indicates that the text should be bold.
<I>	Indicates that the text should be italic.
<TT>	Indicates that the text should be used with a font such as Courier that allots the same width to each character.
<BIG>	Indicates that the text should be displayed in a big font. Available only in HTML 3.0.
<SMALL>	Indicates that the text should be displayed in a small font. Available only in HTML 3.0.
<SUB>	The text should be displayed as a subscript, in a smaller font if possible. Available only in HTML 3.0.
<SUP>	The text should be displayed as a superscript, in a smaller font if possible. Available only in HTML 3.0.

Figure 1-27 shows examples of how these tags might appear in a browser. Some browsers also support the <U> tag for underlining text, but other browsers might not show underlining, so use it cautiously.

Figure 1-27 PHYSICAL CHARACTER TAGS AS THEY APPEAR IN THE BROWSER

This is an example of the **B tag**.

This is an example of the *I tag*.

This is an example of the `TT tag`.

This is an example of the **BIG tag**.

This is an example of the SMALL tag.

This is an example of the SUB tag.

This is an example of the SUP tag.

Given the presence of both logical and physical character tags, which should you use to display some text in an italicized font: <EM> or <I>? Some older versions of browsers are text-based and cannot display italics. These older browsers ignore the <I> tag, so the emphasis you want to place on a certain piece of text is lost. If this a concern, you should use a logical tag. On the other hand, the physical character tags are more commonly used today and are easier to interpret. Some Web page authors believe that the use of logical character tags such as <EM> and <STRONG> is archaic and confusing.

Only one part of Mary's resume requires character tags: the Employment section, where Mary wants to emphasize the title of each job she has held. She decides to use a combination of the <B> and <I> tags to display the titles in boldface and italics.

To add character tags to the resume file:

1. Return to your text editor, and reopen the **Resume.htm** file if necessary.

2. Type the **<I>** and **<B>** tags around the job titles in the Employment section of the resume (just after the <P> tags), so that they read:

   <I><B>Satellite Technician</B></I>

   <I><B>Technical Assistant</B></I>

   <I><B>Salesperson</B></I>

   See Figure 1-28.

Figure 1-28	APPLYING CHARACTER TAGS

use the <B> and <I> tags to display this text in boldface and italics

```
<H2 ALIGN=CENTER>Employment</H2>
<P><I><B>Satellite Technician</B></I> (Front Range Media Inc. 1998–
1999): Monitored satellite uplink/downlink procedures to assure quality
transmissions. Aided technicians with transmission problems. Assisted
in the assembly and maintenance of uplink facility.</P>

<P><I><B>Technical Assistant</B></I> (Mountain View Bank 1997–1998):
Managed data processing system. Handled user requests and discussed
programming options. Managed delivery service.</P>

<P><I><B>Salesperson</B></I> (Computer Visions 1996): Sales and
customer support in computers and electronics. Managed commercial
accounts in Mountain View and Crabtree locations.</P>
</BODY>
```

3. Save the changes to your Resume file.

4. Return to your Web browser, and reopen the Resume file. The updated Employment section of Mary's page should look like Figure 1-29.

Figure 1-29	THE EFFECT OF THE CHARACTER TAGS IN THE BROWSER

boldface and italics

Employment

Satellite Technician (Front Range Media Inc. 1998-1999): Monitored satellite uplink/downlink procedures to assure quality transmissions. Aided technicians with transmission problems. Assisted in the assembly and maintenance of uplink facility.

Technical Assistant (Mountain View Bank 1997-1998): Managed data processing system. Handled user requests and discussed programming options. Managed delivery service.

Salesperson (Computer Visions 1996): Sales and customer support in computers and electronics. Managed commercial accounts in Mountain View and Crabtree locations.

5. If you are continuing to Session 1.3, you can leave your text editor and browser open. Otherwise, close your browser and text editor.

When you apply two character tags to the same text, you should place one set of tags completely within the other. For example, you would combine the <I> and <B> tags like this:

```
<I><B>Satellite Technician</B></I>
```

and not like this:

```
<I><B>Satellite Technician</I></B>
```

Although many browsers interpret both sets of code the same way, nesting tags within each other rather than overlapping them makes your code easier to read and interpret.

You have finished adding text to Mary's online resume. In Session 1.3, you will add special formatting elements such as lines and graphics.

Session 1.2 QUICK CHECK

1. Why should you include the <HTML> tag in your Web document?

2. Describe the syntax for creating a centered heading 1.

3. Describe the syntax for creating a paragraph.

4. If you want to display several paragraphs, why can't you simply type an extra blank line in the HTML file?

5. Describe the syntax for creating an ordered list, an unordered list, and a definition list.

6. Give two ways of italicizing text in your Web document. What are the advantages and disadvantages of each method?

SESSION 1.3

In this session you will insert three special elements into Mary's online resume: a special character, a line separating Mary's name and address from the rest of her resume, and a photograph of Mary.

Adding Special Characters

Occasionally you will want to include special characters in your Web page that do not appear on your keyboard. For example, a math page might require mathematical symbols such as β or μ. As Mary views her resume file, she notices a place where she could use a special symbol. In the address information under her name, she finds that the street address, city, and phone numbers all flow together. She decides to look into special characters that could separate the information.

HTML supports several character symbols that you can insert into your page. Each character symbol is identified by a code number or name. To create a special character, type an ampersand (&) followed either by the code name or the code number, and then a semicolon. Code numbers must be preceded by a pound symbol (#). Figure 1-30 shows some HTML symbols and the corresponding code numbers or names. A fuller list of special characters is included in Appendix B.

Figure 1-30		SPECIAL CHARACTERS AND CODES		
SYMBOL	**CODE**	**CODE NAME**	**DESCRIPTION**	
©	&#169;	&copy;	Copyright symbol	
®	&#174;	&reg;	Registered trademark	
•	&#183;	&middot;	Middle dot	
º	&#186;	&ordm;	Masculine ordinal	
TM	&#153;	&trade;	Trademark symbol	
			Nonbreaking space, useful when you want to insert several blank spaces, one after another	
<	&#60;	&lt;	Less than symbol	
>	&#62;	&gt;	Greater than symbol	
&	&#39;	&amp;	Ampersand	

One solution for Mary's resume is to insert several **nonbreaking spaces** using the   character code. However, Mary decides it would look better to insert a bullet (•) between the street address and the city, and another bullet between the zip code and the phone number.

To add a character code to the resume file:

1. Make sure the **Resume.htm** file is open in your text editor.

2. Revise the address line at the beginning of the file, inserting the code for a middle dot, **·**, between the street address and the city, and between the zip code and the phone number, so that the line reads:

   <H5 ALIGN=CENTER>11 Kemper Ave. · Lake View, CO 80517 · (303) 555-1012</H5>

   TROUBLE? In your text editor this line probably appears as a single line.

3. Save the changes to your Resume file.

4. Return to your Web browser and reopen the Resume file. Figure 1-31 shows Mary's resume with the bullets separating the address elements.

Figure 1-31	SPECIAL CHARACTERS IN THE BROWSER

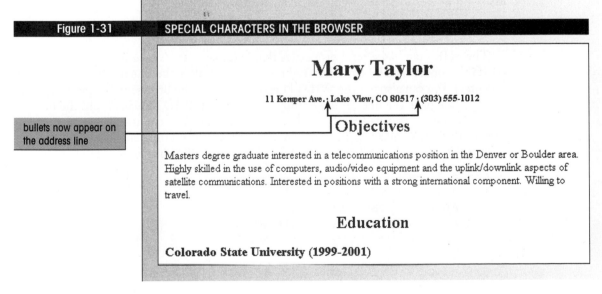

bullets now appear on the address line

Mary Taylor

11 Kemper Ave. · Lake View, CO 80517 · (303) 555-1012

Objectives

Masters degree graduate interested in a telecommunications position in the Denver or Boulder area. Highly skilled in the use of computers, audio/video equipment and the uplink/downlink aspects of satellite communications. Interested in positions with a strong international component. Willing to travel.

Education

Colorado State University (1999-2001)

The next thing Mary wants in her resume is a horizontal line separating the name and address information from the rest of her resume.

Inserting Horizontal Lines

The horizontal line after Mary's name and address in Figure 1-10 lends shape to the appearance of her paper resume. She'd like you to duplicate that in the online version. You use the **<HR>** tag to create a horizontal line, where HR stands for horizontal rule. The <HR> tag is one-sided. When a text-based browser encounters the <HR> tag, it inserts a line by repeating an underline symbol across the width of the page. A graphical browser inserts a graphical line.

> *To add a horizontal line to the Resume file:*
>
> **1.** Return to your text editor and reopen the **Resume.htm** file if necessary.
>
> **2.** At the end of Mary's address line, press the **Enter** key to insert a new blank line.
>
> **3.** In the new line, type **<HR>**.
>
> **4.** Save the changes to your Resume file.
>
> **5.** Return to your Web browser and reopen the Resume file. The Resume file with the new horizontal line appears in Figure 1-32.

Figure 1-32	HORIZONTAL LINE AS IT APPEARS IN THE BROWSER

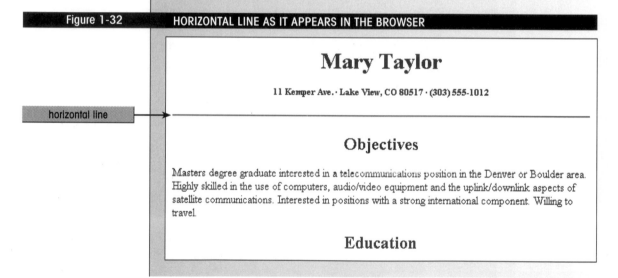

Mary Taylor

11 Kemper Ave. · Lake View, CO 80517 · (303) 555-1012

← horizontal line

Objectives

Masters degree graduate interested in a telecommunications position in the Denver or Boulder area. Highly skilled in the use of computers, audio/video equipment and the uplink/downlink aspects of satellite communications. Interested in positions with a strong international component. Willing to travel.

Education

The <HR> tag has several properties that you may want to use in your Web page. The ALIGN property can be set to left, right, or center to place the line on the page (the default is center). You can also use the WIDTH property to tell the browser what percentage of the width of the page the line should occupy. For example, WIDTH=50% tells the browser to place the line so that its length covers half of the page. You can use the SIZE property to specify the line's thickness in pixels. A pixel, short for picture element, is ½-inch wide. Figure 1-33 shows how a browser would interpret the following lines of HTML code:

```
<HR ALIGN=CENTER SIZE=12 WIDTH=100%>
<HR ALIGN=CENTER SIZE=6 WIDTH=50%>
<HR ALIGN=CENTER SIZE=3 WIDTH=25%>
<HR ALIGN=CENTER SIZE=1 WIDTH=10%>
```

Figure 1-33   **DIFFERENT LINE STYLES**

| SIZE=12 WIDTH=100% |
| SIZE=6 WIDTH=50% |
| SIZE=3 WIDTH=25% |
| SIZE=1 WIDTH=10% |

Netscape Navigator and Internet Explorer also support properties specific to those browsers. As always, you should remember that using browser-specific extensions might produce wildly different results on browsers that do not support the extensions.

Inserting a Graphic

One feature of Web pages that has made the World Wide Web so popular is the ease of displaying a graphic image. The Web supports two methods for displaying a graphic: as an inline image and as an external image.

An **inline image** appears directly on the Web page and is loaded when the page is loaded. Two of the more commonly supported image types are GIF (Graphics Interchange Format) and JPEG (Joint Photographic Experts Group). Before you display a graphic image, you should convert it to one of these two types.

An **external image** is not displayed with the Web page. Instead, the browser must have a **file viewer**, a program that the browser loads automatically, whenever it encounters the image file, and uses to display the image. You can find file viewers at several Internet Web sites. Most browsers make it easy to set up viewers for use with the Web. External images have one disadvantage: you can't actually display them on the Web page. Instead they are represented by an icon that a user clicks to view the image. However, external images are not limited to the GIF or JPEG formats. You can set up virtually any image format as an external image on a Web page, including video clips and sound files.

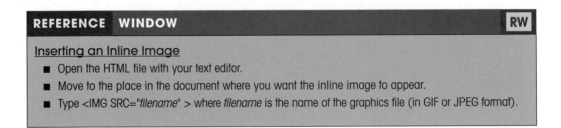

Mary is more interested in using an inline image than an external image. **<IMG>** is the tag used for displaying an inline image. You can place inline images on a separate line in your document, or you can place the image within a line of text (hence the term "inline").

To access the image file, you need to include the filename within the tag. You do this using the SRC property, short for "source." The general syntax for an inline image is:

```
<IMG SRC="filename">
```

If the image file is located in the same folder as the HTML file, you do not need to include any folder information. However, if the image file is located in another folder or on another computer, you need to include the full path with the SRC property. Tutorial 2 discusses directory paths and filenames in more detail. For now, assume that Mary's image file is placed in the same folder as the HTML file. The image file that Mary has created is a photograph of herself in JPEG format. The name of the file is Taylor.jpg.

You'd also like to center the image on the page. There is no property in the <IMG> tag that would allow you to center it on a page, but you can nest the <IMG> tag within a paragraph tag, <P>, and then center the paragraph on the page using the ALIGN=CENTER property for the <P> tag. This has the effect of centering all of the text in the paragraph, including any inline images. Note that the ALIGN property was introduced in HTML 3.2; in browsers that do not support this convention, Mary's image may be left-justified.

To add Mary's photo to the online resume:

1. Look in the Tutorial.01 folder on your Data Disk and verify that both the Resume.htm file and Taylor.jpg file are there.

2. Return to your text editor with the Resume.htm file open.

3. At the end of the line with the <HR> tag that you just typed, press the **Enter** key to create a new line.

4. Type **<P ALIGN=CENTER><IMG SRC="Taylor.jpg"></P>** and then save the changes to the Resume file.

5. Print a copy of your completed Resume.htm file, and then close your text editor, unless you are continuing to the Review Assignments.

6. Return to your Web browser, and reopen the Resume file. Mary's online resume now includes an inline image. See Figure 1-34 for a view of the entire page.

Figure 1-34 | MARY'S COMPLETED RESUME PAGE

Mary Taylor

11 Kemper Ave. · Lake View, CO 80517 · (303) 555-1012

Objectives

Masters degree graduate interested in a telecommunications position in the Denver or Boulder area. Highly skilled in the use of computers audio/video equipment, and the uplink/downlink aspects of satellite communications. Interested in positions with a strong international component. Willing to travel.

Education

Colorado State University (1999-2001)

- Graduated May, 2001. M.A. International Telecommunications
- Grade Point Average: 3.5 overall, 3.9 in major
- Dean's List: September 1999-May 2001
- Member, Phi Alpha Omega Honor Society

Saint Philip University (1996-1999)

- Graduated May, 1999. B.A. International Studies
- Grade Point Average: 4.0 overall, 4.0 in major
- Dean's List: September 1996-May 1999
- President, Honor Key Society

Employment

Satellite Technician (Front Range Media Inc. 1998-1999): Monitored satellite uplink/downlink procedures to assure quality transmissions. Aided technicians with transmission problems. Assisted in the assembly and maintenance of uplink facility.

Technical Assistant (Mountain View Bank 1997-1998): Managed data processing system. Handled user requests and discussed programming options. Managed delivery service.

Salesperson (Computer Visions 1996): Sales and customer support in computers and electronics. Managed commercial accounts in Mountain View and Crabtree locations.

7. Use your browser to print a copy of Mary's online resume.

Compare the printout of the code, shown below, to the online resume on your browser. When you finish, you can exit your browser unless you're continuing to the Review Assignments.

```
<HTML>
<HEAD>
<TITLE>The Resume of Mary Taylor</TITLE>
</HEAD>
<BODY>
<H1 ALIGN=CENTER>Mary Taylor</H1>
<H5 ALIGN=CENTER>11 Kemper Ave. &#183; Lake View, CO 80517
&#183; (303) 555-1012</H5>
<HR>
<P ALIGN=CENTER><IMG SRC="Taylor.jpg"></P>
<H2 ALIGN=CENTER>Objectives</H2>
Masters degree graduate interested in a telecommunications
position in the Denver or Boulder area. Highly skilled in
the use of computers, audio/video equipment, and the uplink/
downlink aspects of satellite communications. Interested in
positions with a strong international component. Willing to
travel.
<H2 ALIGN=CENTER>Education</H2>
<H3>Colorado State University (1999-2001)</H3>
<UL>
<LI>Graduated May, 2001. M.A. International Telecommunications
<LI>Grade Point Average: 3.5 overall, 3.9 in major
<LI>Dean's List: September 1999-May 2001
<LI>Member, Phi Alpha Omega Honor Society
</UL>
<H3>Saint Philip University (1996-1999)</H3>
<UL>
<LI>Graduated May, 1999. B.A. International Studies
<LI>Grade Point Average: 4.0 overall, 4.0 in major
<LI>Dean's List: September 1996-May 1999
<LI>President, Honor Key Society
</UL>
<H2 ALIGN=CENTER>Employment</H2>
<P><I><B>Satellite Technician</B></I> (Front Range Media Inc.
1998-1999): Monitored satellite uplink/downlink procedures
to assure quality video transmissions. Aided technicians
with transmission problems. Assisted in the assembly and
maintenance of uplink facility.</P>
<P><I><B>Technical Assistant</B></I> (Mountain View Bank 1997
-1998): Managed data processing system. Handled user requests
and discussed programming options. Managed delivery
service. </P>
<P><I><B>Salesperson</B></I> (Computer Visions 1996): Sales
and customer support in computers and electronics. Managed
commercial accounts in Mountain View and Crabtree
locations.</P>
</BODY>
</HTML>
```

You show the completed online resume file to Mary; she thinks it looks great. You tell her that the next step is adding hypertext links to other material about herself for interested employers. You take a break while she heads to her desk to start thinking about what material she'd like to add. You'll learn about hypertext links in Tutorial 2.

Session 1.3 QUICK CHECK

1. How would you insert a copyright symbol, ©, into your Web page?

2. What is the syntax for inserting a horizontal line into a page?

3. What is the syntax for creating a horizontal line that is 70% of the display width of the screen and 4 pixels high?

4. What is an inline image?

5. What is an external image?

6. What is the syntax for inserting a graphic named Mouse.jpg into a Web document as an inline image?

7. What are two graphic file formats you can use for inline images?

REVIEW ASSIGNMENTS

After thinking some more about her online resume, Mary Taylor decides that she wants you to add a few more items. In the Education section, she wants you to add that she won the Enos Mills Scholarship contest as a senior at St. Philip University. She also wants to add that she worked as a climbing guide for The Colorado Experience touring company from 1994 to 1995. She would like to add her e-mail address, mtaylor@tt.gr.csu.edu, in italics at the bottom of the page. You tell her that adding a horizontal line to separate it from the rest of the resume might look nice. She agrees, so you get to work.

1. Open the **Resume.htm** file located in the Tutorial.01 folder on your Data Disk. This is the file you created over the course of this tutorial.

2. Save the file on your Data Disk in the Tutorial.01/Review folder with a new name: Resume2.htm, so that you will leave your work from the tutorial intact.

3. After the HTML line reading "President, Honor Key Society," enter a new line, "Winner of the Enos Mills Scholarship."
Use the <LI> tag to format this line as an addition to the existing list.

4. Move to the Employment section of the Resume2.htm file.

5. After the paragraph describing Mary's experience as a salesperson, insert a new paragraph, "Guide (The Colorado Experience 1994-1996): Climbing guide for private groups and schools." Make sure you mark the text with the correct code for a two-sided paragraph tag.

6. Using the <I> and <B> tags, bracket the word "Guide" in the line you just entered to make it both bold and italic.

7. After the paragraph on Mary's climbing guide experience, insert a horizontal line using the <HR> tag. Set the thickness of the line to 6 pixels.

8. After the horizontal line, insert a new line with Mary's e-mail address.

Explore ▶ 9. Use the <CITE> tag to format her e-mail address as a citation:
<CITE>mtaylor@tt.gr.csu.edu</CITE>

10. Save the changes to your Resume2.htm file and print it.

11. View the file with your Web browser.

12. Print a copy of the page as viewed by your browser.

PROJECTS

1. Creating a Web Page at the University Music Department   You are an assistant to a professor in the Music Department who is trying to create Web pages for topics in classical music. He wants to create a page showing the different sections of the fourth movement of Beethoven's Ninth symphony. The page should appear as shown in Figure 1-35.

Figure 1-35

Beethoven's Ninth Symphony

The Fourth Movement

Sonata-Concerto Form

1. Open Ritornello
2. Exposition
   1. Horror/Recitative
   2. Joy Theme
   3. Turkish Music
3. Development
4. Recapitulation
   1. Joy Theme
   2. Awe Theme
5. Coda Nos. 1 2 3

The page needs an inline image, three headings, and a list of the fourth movement's different sections. Several of the sections also have sublists. For example, the Recapitulation section contains both the Joy and Awe themes. You can create lists of this type with HTML by inserting one list tag within another. The HTML code for this is:

```
<OL>
<LI>Recapitulation
        <OL>
        <LI>Joy Theme
        <LI>Awe Theme
        </OL>
</OL>
```

1. Open a text editor program.

2. Type the <HTML>, <HEAD>, and <BODY> tags to identify different sections of the page.

3. Within the HEAD section, insert a <TITLE> tag with the text: "Beethoven's Ninth Symphony, 4th Movement".

4. Within the BODY section, create an <H1> header with the text "Beethoven's Ninth Symphony" and center the heading on the page with the ALIGN property.

5. Below the <H1> header, create an <H2> header with the text "The Fourth Movement" and then center the header on the page.

6. Below the <H2> header, create an <H3> header with the text "Sonata-Concerto Form", but this time do not center the header.

7. Create an ordered list using the <OL> tag, with the list items "Open Ritornello", "Exposition", "Development", "Recapitulation", and "Codas Nos. 1 2 3".

Explore ▷ 8. Within the Exposition list, create an ordered list with the items "Horror/Recitative", "Joy Theme", and "Turkish Music".

Explore ▷ 9. Within the Recapitulation list, create an ordered list with the items "Joy Theme" and "Awe Theme".

10. Before the <H1> header, insert the inline image LVB.jpg (located in the Projects folder of the Tutorial.01 folder on your Data Disk) centered on the page.

11. After the <H2> header, insert a horizontal line that extends the width of the page and is 1 pixel in height.

12. Save the file as Ludwig.htm in the Cases folder of the Tutorial.01 folder on your Data Disk, print it, and then close your text editor.

13. View the file with your Web browser, print it, and then close your browser.

2. Creating a Web Page for the Mathematics Department   Professor Laureen Coe of the Mathematics Department is preparing material for her course on the history of mathematics. As part of the course, she has written short profiles of famous mathematicians. Using content she's already written, Laureen would like you to create several Web pages to be placed on the university's Web server. You'll create the first one in this exercise. A preview of one of the pages about the mathematician Leonhard Euler is shown in Figure 1-36.

Figure 1-36

Euler, Leonhard

(1707-1783)

The greatest mathematician of the eighteenth century, **Leonhard Euler** was born in Basel, Switzerland. There, he studied under another giant of mathematics, **Jean Bernoulli**. In 1731 Euler became a professor of physics and mathematics at St. Petersburg Academy of Sciences. Euler was the most prolific mathematician of all time, publishing over *800 different books and papers*. His influence was felt in physics and astronomy as well. Euler's work on mathematical analysis, <u>Introductio in analysin infinitorum</u> (1748) remained a standard textbook for well over a century. For the princess of Anhalt-Dessau he wrote *Lettres à une princesse d'Allemagne* (1768-1772), giving a clear non-technical outline of the main physical theories of the time.

One can hardly write mathematical equations without copying Euler. Notations still in use today, such as *e* and *π*, were developed by Euler. He is perhaps best known for his research into mathematical analysis. Euler's formula:

$$\cos(x) + i\sin(x) = e^{(ix)}$$

demonstrates the relationship between analysis, trignometry and imaginary numbers, in one beautiful and elegant equation.

Leonhard Euler died in 1783, leaving behind a legacy perhaps unmatched, and certainly unsurpassed, in the annals of mathematics.

Math 895: The History of Mathematics

1. Start your text editor and then open the file **Eulertxt.htm**, located in the Cases folder of the Tutorial.01 folder on your Data Disk, and save it as Euler.htm.

2. Add the opening and closing <HTML>, <HEAD>, and <BODY> tags to the file in the appropriate locations.

3. Insert "Leonhard Euler" as a page title in the Head section of the document.

4. Insert the inline image **Euler.jpg** (located in the Tutorial 1 Projects folder on your Data Disk) at the top of the body of the document.

5. Format the first line of the page's body, "Euler, Leonhard", with the <H1> tag, and format the second line of the page's body, "(1707-1783)", with the <H3> tag.

6. Add the appropriate paragraph tags, <P>, to the document to separate the paragraphs.

7. Within the first paragraph, display the names, "Leonhard Euler" and "Jean Bernoulli" in boldface. Italicize the phrase "800 different books and papers", and underline the publication "Introductio in analysin infinitorum".

8. Replace the one-letter word "a" in "Lettres a une princesse d'Allemagne" with an *à*, using the character code &agrave, and then italicize the entire name of the publication.

9. In the second paragraph, italicize the notation "e" and replace the word "pi" with the inline image "**pi.jpg**" located in the Cases folder on your Data Disk.

Explore 10. Center the equation and italicize the letters "x", "i", and "e" in the equation. Display the term "(*ix*)" as a superscript, using the <SUP> tag.

Explore 11. Format the name of the course at the bottom of the page using the <CITE> tag.

12. Add horizontal lines before and after the biographical information.

13. Save the Euler.htm file, and then print it from your text editor.

14. View the file in your Web browser, and then print a copy of the page as displayed by the browser.

3. Chester the Jester   A friend of yours who performs as a clown named "Chester the Jester" wants to advertise his services on the World Wide Web. He wants his Web page to be bright and colorful. One way of doing this is to create a colorful background for the page. You create a background using a graphic image. Such backgrounds are called tile-image backgrounds because the graphic image is repeated over and over again, like tiles, until it covers the entire page. To create a tile-image background, you must have a graphic image in either GIF or JPEG file format. You insert the file in the background by adding the BACKGROUND property to the <BODY> tag with the syntax:

```
<BODY BACKGROUND= "filename">
```

Your friend gives you a JPEG file named Diamonds.jpg, which contains the pattern he uses in his clown costume. He also has a JPEG file named Chester.jpg, which shows him in his clown outfit. A preview of the page you'll create is shown in Figure 1-37.

Figure 1-37

Chester the Jester

Clown • Juggler • Magician

Hire him for your child's party today!

- Reasonable rates
- 60 minute, 90 minute programs
- Birthday surprises!

Call 555-2312 and ask for "Chester"

1. Start your text editor, open the file **Chestertxt.htm** from the Cases folder of the Tutorial.01 folder on your Data Disk, and save it as Chester.htm.

2. Insert the <HTML>, <HEAD>, and <BODY> tags in the appropriate locations.

3. Insert a <TITLE> tag in the Head section, giving the Web page the title "Chester the Jester".

Explore   4. Modify the <BODY> tag to read:

```
<BODY BACKGROUND="Diamonds.jpg">
```

5. Format the text "Chester the Jester" with the <H1> tag and center it on the Web page.

6. Format the text "Clown Juggler Magician" with the <H3> tag and center it on the page. Insert a middle dot, character symbol •, between each word.

7. Insert the inline image "**Chester.jpg**" (located in the Projects folder of the Tutorial.01 folder on your Data Disk) after the <H3> header. Center it on the page.

8. Format the text "Hire him for your child's party today!" with the <H3> tag, centered on the page.

9. Insert a horizontal line after the <H3> header.

10. Format the next three lines as an unordered list.

11. Format the text in the last line of document text, using the <I> tag.

12. Save the Chester.htm file and then print it from your text editor.

13. View the file in your Web browser and then print it in your browser.

4. Create Your Own Resume   After completing Mary Taylor's resume, you are eager to make your own. Using the techniques from this tutorial, design and create a resume for yourself. Make sure to include these features: section headers, bulleted or numbered lists, bold and/or italic fonts, paragraphs, special characters, inline graphic images, and horizontal lines.

1. Start your text editor, and then create a file called MyResume.htm in the Cases folder of the Tutorial.01 folder on your Data Disk. Type the appropriate HTML code and content.

2. Add any other tags you think will improve your document's appearance.

3. You could take a picture of yourself to your lab or a local office services business and scan it. If you do, save it as a GIF or JPEG file. Then place the graphic file in the Projects folder of the Tutorial.01 folder on your Data Disk. Add the appropriate code in your MyResume.htm file. If you don't have your own graphic file, use the file **Kirk.jpg** located in the Projects folder of the Tutorial.01 folder on your Data Disk.

4. You could use a graphics package that can store images in GIF or JPEG format to create a background image that you could insert as you did in Case Problem 3. If you do, use light colors so the text you place on top is readable. Add the appropriate code to your MyResume.htm file, using the steps in Case Problem 3.

5. Test your code as you develop your resume, by viewing MyResume.htm in your browser.

6. When you finish entering the code, save and print the MyResume.htm file from your text editor.

7. View the final version in your browser, print the Web page, and then close your browser and text editor.

Web Pages & HTML

LAB ASSIGNMENTS

This Lab Assignment is designed to accompany the interactive Course Lab called The Internet World Wide Web. To start the Internet World Wide Web Course Lab, click the Start button on the Windows taskbar, point to Programs, point to Course Labs, point to New Perspectives Applications, and click The Internet World Wide Web. If you do not see Course Labs on your Programs menu, see your instructor or technical support person.

The Internet World Wide Web Lab Assignment   One of the most popular services on the Internet is the World Wide Web. This Lab is a Web simulator that teaches you how to use Web browser software to find information. You can use this Lab whether or not your school provides you with Internet access.

1. Click the Steps button to learn how to use Web browser software. As you proceed through the Steps, answer all of the Quick Check questions that appear. After you complete the Steps, you will see a Quick Check Summary Report. Follow the instructions on the screen to print this report.

2. Click the Explore button on the Welcome screen. Use the Web browser to locate a weather map of the Caribbean Virgin Islands. What is its URL?

3. A scuba diver named Wadson Lachouffe has been searching for the fabled treasure of Greybeard the pirate. A link from the Adventure Travel Web site leads to Wadson's Web page, called "Hidden Treasure". In Explore, locate the Hidden Treasure page and answer the following questions:
   a. What was the name of Greybeard's ship?
   b. What was Greybeard's favorite food?
   c. What does Wadson think happened to Greybeard's ship?

4. In the Steps, you found a graphic of Jupiter from the photo archives of the Jet Propulsion Laboratory. In the Explore section of the Lab, you can also find a graphic of Saturn. Suppose one of your friends wanted a picture of Saturn for an astronomy report. Make a list of the blue, underlined links your friend must click to find the Saturn graphic. Assume that your friend will begin at the Web Trainer home page.

5. Enter the URL *http://www.atour.com* to jump to the Adventure Travel Web site. Write a one-page description of this site. In your paper include a description of the information at the site, the number of pages the site contains, and a diagram of the links it contains.

6. Chris Thomson is a student at UVI and has his own Web pages. In Explore, look at the information Chris has included on his pages. Suppose you could create your own Web page. What would you include? Use word-processing software to design your own Web pages. Make sure you indicate the graphics and links you would use.

QUICK CHECK ANSWERS

Session 1.1

1. Hypertext refers to text that contains points called links that allow the user to move to other places within the document, or to open other documents, by activating the link.

2. A Web server stores the files used in creating World Wide Web documents. The Web browser retrieves the files from the Web server and displays them. The files stored on the Web server are described in a very general way; it is the Web browser that determines how the files will eventually appear to the user.

3. HTML, which stands for Hypertext Markup Language, is used to create Web documents.

4. HTML documents do not exactly specify the appearance of a document; rather they describe the purpose of different elements in the document and leave it to the Web browser to determine the final appearance. A word processor like Word exactly specifies the appearance of each document element.

5. Documents are transferred more quickly over the Internet and are available to a wider range of machines.

6. Extensions are special formats supported by a particular browser, but not generally accepted by all browsers. The advantage is that people who use that browser have a wider range of document elements to work with. The disadvantage is that the document will not work for users who do not have that particular browser.

7. All you need is a simple text editor.

Session 1.2

1. The <HTML> tag identifies the language of the file as HTML to packages that support more than one kind of generalized markup language.

2. <H1 ALIGN=CENTER> *Header text* </H1>

3. <P> *Paragraph text* </P>

4. HTML does not recognize the blank lines as a format element. A Web browser will ignore blank lines and run the paragraphs together on the page.

5. Unordered list:
```
<UL>
    <LI> List item
    <LI> List item
</UL>
```
Ordered list:
```
<OL>
    <LI> List item
    <LI> List item
</OL>
```
Definition list:
```
<DL>
    <DT> List term <DD> Term definition
    <DT> List term <DD> Term definition
</DL>
```

6. <EM> *Italicized text* </EM>
   and
   ```
   <I> Italicized text </I>
   ```
   The advantage of using the <EM> tag is that it will be recognized even by older browsers that do not support italics (such as a terminal connected to a UNIX machine), and those browsers will still emphasize the text in some way. The <I> tag, on the other hand, will be ignored by those machines. Using the <I> tag has the advantage of explicitly describing how you want the text to appear.

Session 1.3

1. ©

2. <HR>

3. <HR WIDTH=70% SIZE=4>

4. An inline image is a GIF or JPEG that appears on a Web document. A browser can display it without a file viewer.

5. An external image is a graphic that requires the use of a software program, called a viewer, to be displayed.

6. <IMG ALIGN=LEFT SRC="Mouse.jpg">

7. GIF's and JPEGs

OBJECTIVES

In this tutorial you will:

- Create hypertext links between elements within a document

- Create hypertext links between one document and another

- Review some basic Web page structures

- Create hypertext links to pages on the Internet

- Understand the difference between and use absolute and relative pathnames

- Learn to create hypertext links to various Internet resources, including FTP servers and newsgroups

ADDING
HYPERTEXT LINKS
TO A WEB PAGE

Developing an Online Resume with Hypertext Links

CASE

Creating an Online Resume, continued

In Tutorial 1 you created the basic structure and content of an online resume for Mary Taylor. Since then Mary has made a few changes to the resume, and she has ideas for more content. The two of you sit down and discuss her plans. Mary notes that although the page contents reflect the paper resume, the online resume has one disadvantage: prospective employers must scroll around the document window to view pertinent facts about Mary. Mary wants to make it as easy to jump from topic to topic in her online resume as it is to scan through topics on a one-page paper resume.

Mary also has a few references and notes of recommendation on file that she wants to make available to interested employers. She didn't include all this information on her paper resume because she wanted to limit that resume to a single page. With an online resume, Mary can still be brief, but at the same time she can make additional material readily available.

SESSION 2.1

In this session you will create anchors on a Web page that let you jump to specific points in the document. After creating those anchors, you will create and then test your first hypertext link to another document.

Creating a Hypertext Document

In Tutorial 1 you learned that a hypertext document contains **hypertext links**, items that you can select, usually by clicking a mouse, to instantly view another topic or document, often called the **destination** of the link. These links can point to another section in the same document, to an entirely different document, to a different Web page, and to a variety of other Web objects, which you'll learn about later in this tutorial.

In addition to making access to other documents easy, hypertext links provide some important organizational benefits. They indicate what points or concepts you think merit special attention or further reading. You can take advantage of these features by adding hypertext links to Mary's online resume.

At the end of Tutorial 1, the resume had three main sections: Objectives, Education, and Employment. You and Mary have made some additions and changes since then, including adding a fourth section, Other Information, which provides additional information about Mary that employers might find helpful in their job searches. However, because of the document window's limited size, the opening screen does not show any of the main sections of Mary's resume. The browser in Figure 2-1 shows Mary's name, address, and photograph, but nothing about her education or employment history. Employers have to scroll through the document to find this information.

Figure 2-1	OPENING SCREEN OF MARY'S ONLINE RESUME

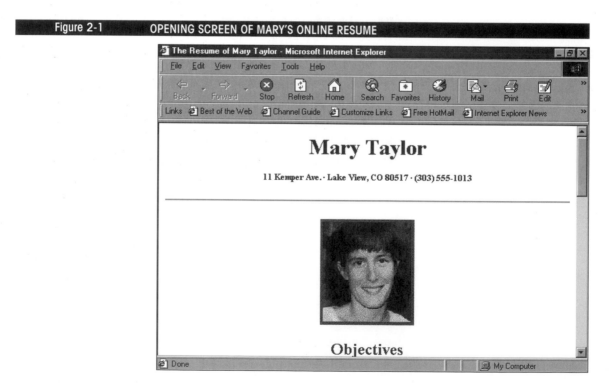

Without using hypertext links, you can do little to show more of Mary's resume in the browser except remove the image file or move it to the end of the resume, which Mary doesn't want you to do. However, you could place text for the four headings (Objectives,

Education, Employment, and Other Information) at the top of the document and then turn these headings into hypertext links. When readers open Mary's resume, they'll see not only her name, address, and photo, but also links to the main parts of her resume. They can then click any of the headings, and they will immediately see that section of the document. The hypertext links that you create here point to sections within the same document. You'll create such hypertext links in Mary's resume using three steps:

1. Type the headings into the HTML file.

2. Mark each section in the HTML file using an anchor. (You'll learn what this is shortly.)

3. Link the text you added in Step 1 to the anchors you added in Step 2.

You can accomplish the first step using techniques you learned in Tutorial 1. You need to open the Resume.htm text file in your text editor and then enter the text. You want the text to appear on the same line as Mary's photo in the browser, as in Figure 2-2.

Figure 2-2	**ADDING TEXT FOR LINKS TO LATER SECTIONS IN THE RESUME**

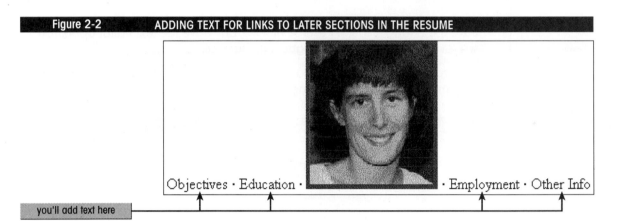

you'll add text here

To achieve this, you place the text within the paragraph tags that already encompass the Taylor.jpg graphics file. You could type all the text into the HTML file on the same line, but to keep the HTML file as legible as possible, add the text in two lines instead. This way, when you add more tags to the text later, it will still be easy to read. Remember that because you format with markup tags in HTML, putting the text on different lines does not affect its appearance in the browser.

To add text to the document, indicating the different sections of the resume:

1. Open your text editor.

2. Open the file **Resumetxt.htm** from the Tutorial.02 folder on your Data Disk, and then save it as **Resume.htm** in the Tutorial.02 folder so you still have a copy of the original.

   TROUBLE? If you can't locate the Resumetxt.htm file in the Tutorial.02 folder in your text editor's Open dialog box, you might need to set the file type to All Files.

3. Before "<IMG SRC="Taylor.jpg">", type **Objectives · Education ·** (be sure to type the semicolons), and then press the **Enter** key so this new entry is on its own line.

4. Create a new line directly after "<IMG SRC="Taylor.jpg">" and then type **· Employment · Other Info** so this new entry is on its own line. See Figure 2-3. The new lines include the special character code · which inserts a bullet into the text to separate section headings.

Figure 2-3	INSERTING NEW TEXT IN THE RESUME PAGE

```
<BODY>
<H1 ALIGN=CENTER>Mary Taylor</H1>
<H5 ALIGN=CENTER>11 Kemper Ave. &#183 Lake View, CO 80517 &#183 (303) 555-
1013</H5>
<HR>

<P ALIGN=CENTER>
Objectives &#183; Education &#183;
<IMG SRC="Taylor.jpg">
&#183; Employment &#183; Other Info
</P>

<H2 ALIGN=CENTER>Objectives</H2>
```

5. Save the changes to the Resume.htm file, but leave the text editor open. You will revise this document throughout this tutorial.

6. Start your Web browser (you do not have to connect to the Internet), and open **Resume.htm** to verify the change. See Figure 2-4.

Figure 2-4	NEW RESUME PAGE TEXT

Mary Taylor

11 Kemper Ave. · Lake View, CO 80517 · (303) 555-1013

Objectives · Education ·   · Employment · Other Info

Creating Anchors

Now that you've created the text describing the resume's different sections, you need to locate each header and mark it in the document, using the <A> tag. The **<A> tag** creates an **anchor**, text that is specially marked so that you can link *to* it from other points in the document. Text that is anchored will become the *destination* of a link; it is *not* the text you click. You assign each anchor its own anchor name, using the NAME property. For example, if you want the text "Employment" to be an anchor, you could assign it the anchor name "EMP":

```
<A NAME="EMP">Employment</A>
```

Later, when you create a link to this anchor from the headings you just inserted at the beginning of Mary's resume, the link will point to this particular place in the document, using the anchor name, EMP. Figure 2-5 illustrates how the anchor you create will work as a reference point to a link.

Figure 2-5   ANCHORING TEXT

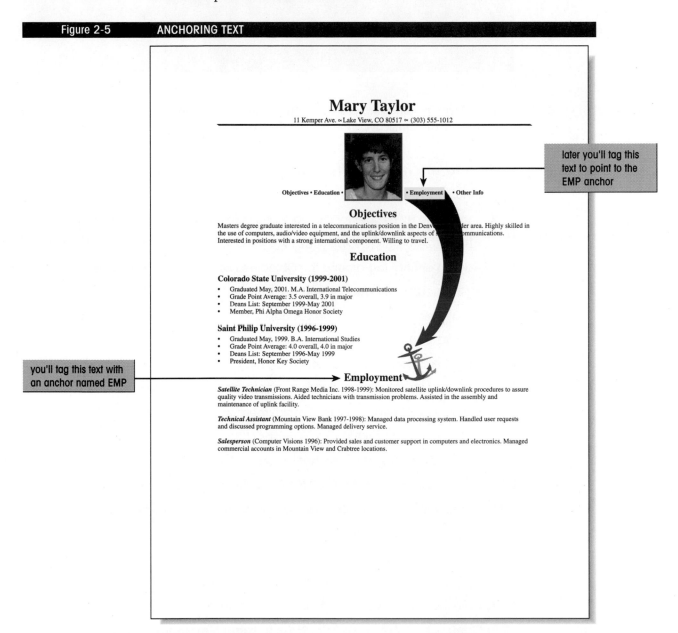

An anchor doesn't have to be just text. You can also mark an inline image using the same syntax:

```
<A NAME="PHOTO"><IMG SRC="Taylor.jpg"></A>
```

In this example, you anchor a photo. You can create a link to this photo from other points in the document by using the anchor name PHOTO. As you'll see, adding an anchor does not change your document's appearance in any way.

REFERENCE WINDOW   **RW**

<u>Creating Anchors</u>
- Locate the text or graphic you want to anchor.
- Before the text or graphic, place the tag
  <A Name="*anchor_name*"> where *anchor_name* is the name you choose for your anchor.
- After the text or graphic, place a closing </A> tag to turn off the anchor.

For Mary's resume file, you decide to create four anchors named OBJ, ED, EMP, and OTHER for the Objectives, Education, Employment, and Other Information sections.

To add anchors to the resume's section headings:

1. Return to your text editor and open the **Resume.htm** file, if it is not already open.

2. Locate the H2 header for the Objectives section. This line currently reads:

   `<H2 ALIGN=CENTER>Objectives</H2>`

3. Add an anchor tag around the Objectives heading so that it reads:

   `<H2 ALIGN=CENTER><A NAME="OBJ">Objectives</A></H2>`

4. Locate the H2 header for the Education section. This line currently reads:

   `<H2 ALIGN=CENTER>Education</H2>`

5. Add an anchor tag around the Education heading so that it reads:

   `<H2 ALIGN=CENTER><A NAME="ED">Education</A></H2>`

6. Locate the H2 header for the Employment section, which reads:

   `<H2 ALIGN=CENTER>Employment</H2>`

   and add an anchor tag so that it reads:

   `<H2 ALIGN=CENTER><A NAME="EMP">Employment</A></H2>`

7. Locate the H2 header for the Other Information section, which reads:

   `<H2>Other Information</H2>`

   and add an anchor tag so that it reads:

   `<H2><A NAME="OTHER"> Other Information</A></H2>`

8. Save the changes you made to the Resume file.

9. Open your Web browser, reload the **Resume.htm** file, then scroll through Resume.htm to confirm that the Resume file appears unchanged. Remember that the marks you placed in the document are reference points and should not change the appearance of the resume in your browser.

   TROUBLE? If you see a change in the document, check to make sure that you used the NAME property of the <A> tag.

You created four anchors in the Web page. The next step is to create links to those anchors from the text you added around Mary's picture.

Creating **Links**

After you anchor the text that will be the destination for your links, you create the links themselves. For Mary's resume, you want to link the text you entered around her photograph to the four sections in her document. Figure 2-6 shows the four links you want to create.

Figure 2-6   LINKS YOU NEED TO CREATE

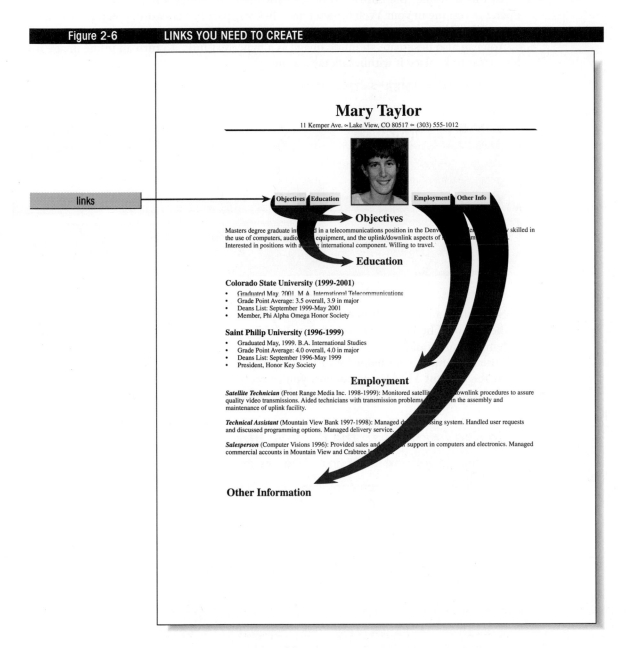

To create a link to an anchor, you use the same [A] tag you used to create the anchor. The difference is that instead of using the NAME property to define the anchor, you use the **HREF** property, short for Hypertext Reference, to indicate the location to jump to. HREF can refer to an anchor that you place in the document, or, as you'll see later, to a different Web page or a resource on the Internet. <A> tags that create links are called **link tags**.

You link to an anchor using the anchor name preceded by a pound (#) symbol. For example, to create a link to the Employment heading in Mary's resume, you use the anchor name EMP and this HTML tag:

```
<A HREF="#EMP">Employment</A>
```

In this example, the entire word "Employment" becomes a hypertext link. When you open the resume in your Web browser and click any part of that word, you jump to the location of the EMP anchor.

You can also designate an inline image as a hypertext link. To turn an inline image into a hypertext link, place it within link tags, as in:

```
<A HREF="#OTHER"><IMG SRC="Taylor.jpg"></A>
```

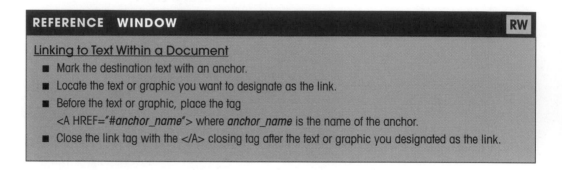

REFERENCE   WINDOW   **RW**

__Linking to Text Within a Document__
- Mark the destination text with an anchor.
- Locate the text or graphic you want to designate as the link.
- Before the text or graphic, place the tag
  <A HREF="*#anchor_name*"> where *anchor_name* is the name of the anchor.
- Close the link tag with the </A> closing tag after the text or graphic you designated as the link.

Sometimes a link does not work as you expect. One common source of trouble is the case of the anchor. The HREF property is case sensitive. The anchor name "EMP" is not the same as "emp". You should also remember to make each anchor name unique within a document. If you use the same anchor name for different text, your links won't go where you expect.

In the current HTML document, you've created four anchors to which you can link. You're ready to place the link tags around the appropriate text in the HTML file.

To add link tags to the Resume.htm file:

1. Return to your text editor and make sure the Resume.htm file is open.

2. Locate the paragraph containing the four section headings and Mary's photograph at the top of the page. Within that paragraph you need to bracket each section heading with a link tag and the HREF property.

3. Change the line reading "Objectives · Education ·" to

   ```
   <A HREF="#OBJ">Objectives</A> &#183;
   <A HREF="#ED">Education</A> &#183;
   ```

4. Change the line reading "· Employment · Other Info" to

   ```
   &#183; <A HREF="#EMP">Employment</A> &#183;
   <A HREF="#OTHER">Other Info</A>
   ```

5. Compare your HTML file to Figure 2-7.

Figure 2-7	ADDING LINK TAGS

```
<BODY>
<H1 ALIGN=CENTER>Mary Taylor</H1>
<H5 ALIGN=CENTER>11 Kemper Ave. &#183 Lake View, CO 80517 &#183 (303) 555-
1013</H5>
<HR>

<P ALIGN=CENTER>
<A HREF="#OBJ">Objectives</A> &#183; <A HREF="#ED">Education</A> &#183;
<IMG SRC="Taylor.jpg">
&#183; <A HREF="#EMP">Employment</A> &#183; <A HREF="#OTHER">Other Info</A>
</P>

<H2 ALIGN=CENTER><A NAME="OBJ">Objectives</A></H2>
```

6. Save the changes you made to Resume.htm.

7. Open your Web browser and reload the **Resume.htm** file. The headings should now be a different color and be underlined—the standard formatting for links in most browsers. See Figure 2-8.

Figure 2-8	TEXT LINKS AS THEY APPEAR IN THE BROWSER

Mary Taylor

11 Kemper Ave. · Lake View, CO 80517 · (303) 555-1013

Objectives · Education · · Employment · Other Info

text links

TROUBLE? If the headings do not appear as text links, check your code and make sure that you are using the <A> tag around the text and the HREF property within the tag.

Before continuing, you should verify that the links work properly. To test a link, you click it.

To test your links:

1. Click one of the links. You should jump to the section of the document indicated by the link. If not, check your code for errors by comparing it to Figure 2-7.

2. Click each of the other links, scrolling back to the top of the page each time.

3. If you are continuing to Session 2.2, you can leave your browser and text editor open. Otherwise, close them.

If you still have problems, make sure you used the correct case and that you coded the anchor and link tags correctly. When you add an anchor to a large section of text, such as a section heading, make sure to place the anchor within the header tags. For example, you should write your tag as:

`<H2><A NAME="EMP">Employment</A></H2>`

not as:

`<A NAME="EMP"><H2>Employment</H2></A>`

The latter could confuse some browsers. The general rule is to always place anchors within other tag elements. Do not insert any tag elements within an anchor, except for tags that create document objects such as inline graphics.

You show the new links to Mary. She is excited to see how they work. She thinks they will quickly inform interested employers about her resume's contents and help them quickly find the information they want. In the next session, you'll create links that jump to other HTML documents.

Session 2.1 QUICK | CHECK

1. What is the HTML code for marking the text "Colorado State University" with the anchor name CSU?

2. What is the HTML code for linking the text "Universities" to an anchor that is named CSU?

3. What is wrong with the following statement?

   `<A NAME="INFO"><H3>For more information</H3></A>`

4. What is the HTML code for marking an inline image, Photo.jpg, with the anchor name PHOTO?

5. What is the HTML code for linking the inline image Button.jpg to an anchor with the name LINKS?

6. True or False: Anchor names are case insensitive.

SESSION 2.2

In Session 2.1 you created hypertext links to other points within the same document. In this session you will create links to other HTML documents.

Mary wants to add two more pages to her online resume: a page of references and a page of comments about her work from former employers and teachers. She then wants to add links on her resume that point to both these pages. Figure 2-9 shows what she has in mind.

Figure 2-9	MARY'S THREE WEB DOCUMENTS

Mary wants you to create links from her resume to her Comments page and her References page

References

View My Resume • Comments

Comments about my work

View My Resume • References

Mary Taylor

11 Kemper Ave. ~ Lake View, CO 80517 ~ (303) 555-1012

Objectives

Masters degree graduate interested in a telecommunications position in the Denver or Boulder area. Highly skilled in the use of computers, audio/video equipment, and the uplink/downlink aspects of satellite communications. Interested in positions with a strong international component. Willing to travel.

Education

Colorado State University (1999-2001)
- Graduated May, 2001. M.A. International Telecommunications
- Grade Point Average: 3.5 overall, 3.9 in major
- Deans List: September 1999-May 2001
- Member, Phi Alpha Omega Honor Society

Saint Philip University (1996-1999)
- Graduated May, 1999. B.A. International Studies
- Grade Point Average: 4.0 overall, 4.0 in major
- Deans List: September 1996-May 1999
- President, Honor Key Society

Employment

Satellite Technician (Front Range Media Inc. 1998-1999): Monitored satellite uplink/downlink procedures to assure quality video transmissions. Aided technicians with transmission problems. Assisted in the assembly and maintenance of uplink facility.

Technical Assistant (Mountain View Bank 1997-1998): Managed data processing system. Handled user requests and discussed programming options. Managed delivery service.

Salesperson (Computer Visions 1996): Provided sales and customer support in computers and electronics. Managed commercial accounts in Mountain View and Crabtree locations.

References page

Comments page

Resume page

You tell Mary that her ideas are good, but that before she starts thinking about how the documents will link to each other, she should understand the basics of Web page structures.

Web Page Structures

The three pages that will make up Mary's online resume—Resume, Comments, and References—are part of a system of Web pages. Before you set up links for navigating a group of Web pages, it's worthwhile to map out exactly how you want the pages to relate, using a technique known as storyboarding. **Storyboarding** your Web pages before you create links helps you determine which structure works best for the type of information you're presenting. You want to make sure readers can navigate easily from page to page without getting lost.

Linear Structures

You'll encounter several Web structures as you navigate the Web. Examining these structures can help you decide how to design your own system of Web pages. Figure 2-10 shows one common structure, the **linear structure**, in which each page is linked to the next and to previous pages, in an ordered chain of pages.

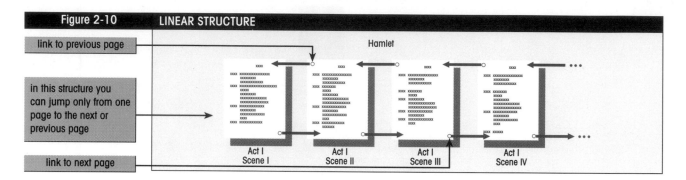

Figure 2-10   LINEAR STRUCTURE

link to previous page

in this structure you can jump only from one page to the next or previous page

link to next page

Hamlet

Act I
Scene I

Act I
Scene II

Act I
Scene III

Act I
Scene IV

You could use this type of structure in Web pages that have a defined order. Suppose that a Web site of Shakespeare's *Hamlet* has a single page for each scene. If you use a linear structure for these pages, you assume that users want to progress through the scenes in order.

You might, however, want to make it easier for users to return immediately to the opening scene, rather than backtrack through several scenes. Figure 2-11 shows an **augmented linear structure**, in which you include a link in each page that jumps directly back to the first page, while keeping the links that allow you to move to the next and previous pages. This kind of storyboarding can reveal approaches to organizing the Web site that otherwise might not be noticed.

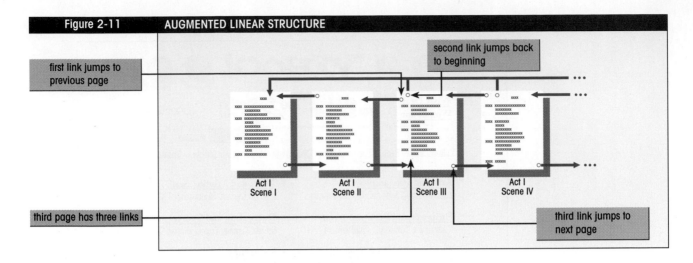

Figure 2-11 AUGMENTED LINEAR STRUCTURE

Hierarchical Structures

Another popular structure is the hierarchical structure of Web pages shown in Figure 2-12. A **hierarchical structure** starts with a general topic that includes links to more specific topics. Each specific topic includes links to yet more specialized topics, and so on. In a hierarchical structure, users can move easily from general to specific and back, but not from specific to specific.

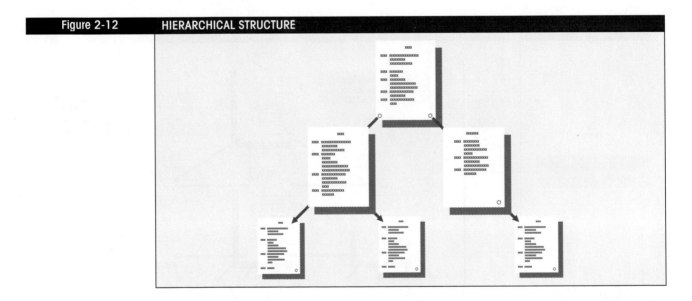

Figure 2-12 HIERARCHICAL STRUCTURE

As with the linear structure, including a link to the top of the structure on each page gives users an easy path back to the beginning. Subject catalogs such as the Yahoo! directory of Web pages often use this structure. Figure 2-13 shows this site, located at *http://www.yahoo.com.*

Figure 2-13   **HIERARCHICAL STRUCTURE ON YAHOO! WEB PAGE**

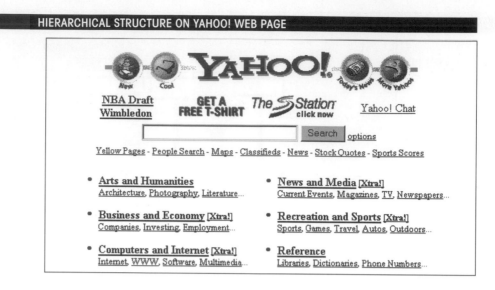

Mixed Structures

You can also combine structures. Figure 2-14 shows a hierarchical structure in which each level of pages is related in a linear structure. You might use this system for the *Hamlet* Web site to let the user move from scene to scene linearly, or from a specific scene to the general act to the overall play.

Figure 2-14   **COMBINATION OF LINEAR AND HIERARCHICAL STRUCTURES**

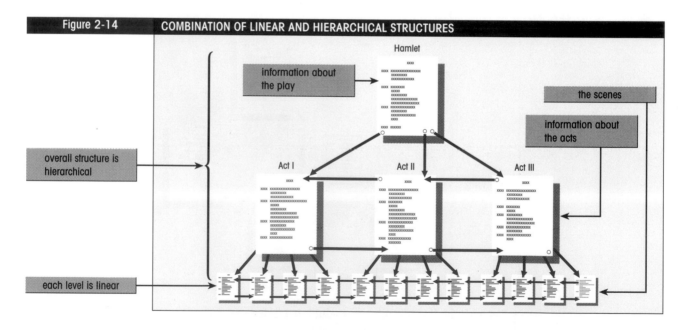

As these examples show, a little foresight can go a long way toward making your Web pages easier to use. The best time to organize a structure is when you first start creating multiple pages and those pages are small and easy to manage. If you're not careful, your structure might look like Figure 2-15.

| Figure 2-15 | MULTIPAGE DOCUMENT WITH NO COHERENT STRUCTURE |

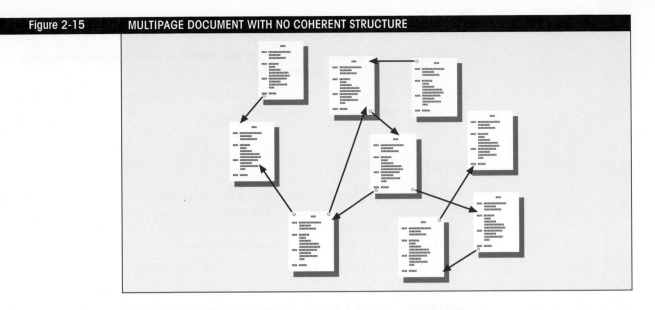

This structure is confusing, and it makes it difficult for readers to grasp the contents of the entire Web site. Moreover, a user who enters this structure at a certain page might not even be aware of the presence of other pages at the far end of the chain.

Creating **Links Between Documents**

Mary and you discuss the type of structure that will work best for her online resume. She wants employers to move effortlessly among the three documents. Because there are only three pages, all focused on the same topic, you decide to include links within each document to the other two. If Mary later adds other pages to her resume, she will need to create a more formal structure involving some principles discussed in the previous sections.

For her simple three-page site, the structure shown in Figure 2-16 works just fine.

| Figure 2-16 | STRUCTURE OF MARY'S WEB PAGES |

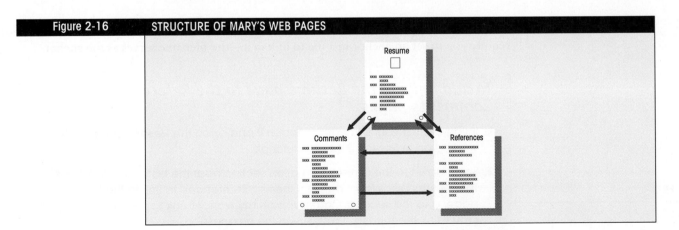

Mary has given you the information to create two additional HTML files: Refertxt.htm, a page with the names and addresses of previous employers and professors; and Comtxt.htm, a page with comments from previous employers and teachers. You suggest that Mary include a graphic—a check mark–on the Comments page. You have just the file for her, Check.jpg. These three files are in the Tutorial.02 folder on your Data Disk. You should save these files with new names: Refer.htm and Comments.htm, to keep the originals intact.

To rename the Refertxt.htm and Comtxt.htm files:

1. Using your text editor, open **Refertxt.htm** from the Tutorial.02 folder on your Data Disk, and save it as **Refer.htm**.

2. With your text editor, open the file **Comtxt.htm** in the Tutorial.02 folder, and save it as **Comments.htm**.

Linking to a Document

You begin by linking Mary's Resume page to the References and Comments pages. You use the same <A> tag that you used earlier. For example, let's say you wanted a user to be able to click the phrase "Comments on my work" to jump to the Comments.htm file. You could enter this HTML command in your current document:

```
<A HREF="Comments.htm">Comments on my work</A>
```

In this example, the entire text "Comments on my work" is linked to the HTML file, Comments.htm. In order for the browser to be able to locate and open the Comments.htm file, it must be in the same folder as the Resume.htm file, the document containing the links.

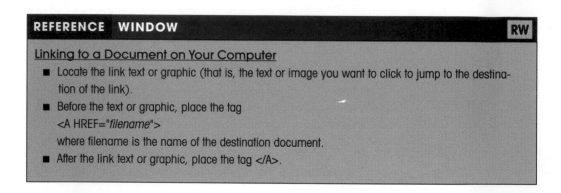

REFERENCE WINDOW   **RW**

Linking to a Document on Your Computer
- Locate the link text or graphic (that is, the text or image you want to click to jump to the destination of the link).
- Before the text or graphic, place the tag
  <A HREF="*filename*">
  where filename is the name of the destination document.
- After the link text or graphic, place the tag </A>.

Unlike creating hypertext links between elements on the same page, this process does not require you to set an anchor in a file to link to it—the filename serves as the anchor.

To add links in the Resume page to the References and Comments pages:

1. If you closed your text editor, reopen it and open the **Resume.htm** file that you worked on in Session 2.1 of this tutorial.

2. Scroll down to the Other Information section near the bottom of the page. Three items are listed; you want the first, References, to link to the References page, and the second, Comments on my work, to link to the Comments page. (You'll link the third to a Web site in the next session.)

3. Change the line reading "<LI>References" to:

   ```
   <LI><A HREF="Refer.htm">References</A>
   ```

4. Change the line reading "<LI> Comments on my work" to read:

   ```
   <LI><A HREF="Comments.htm">Comments on my work</A>
   ```

See Figure 2-17.

Figure 2-17   TEXT LINKED TO OTHER FILES

<A> tag creating a link
to another file

```
<H2><A NAME="OTHER">Other Information</A></H2>
<UL>
<LI><A HREF="Refer.htm">References</A>
<LI><A HREF="Comments.htm">Comments on my work</A>
<LI>Go to Colorado State
</UL>

<H3> Interested? </H3>
Contact Mary Taylor at mtaylor@tt.gr.csu.edu

</BODY>
```

5. Save the changes to the Resume file.

6. Open your Web browser, if it is not open already, and view Resume.htm. The items in the Other Information section now appear as the text links shown in Figure 2-18.

Figure 2-18   NEW LINKS

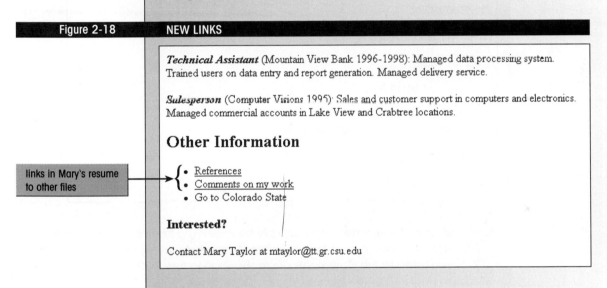

Technical Assistant (Mountain View Bank 1996-1998): Managed data processing system. Trained users on data entry and report generation. Managed delivery service.

Salesperson (Computer Visions 1995): Sales and customer support in computers and electronics. Managed commercial accounts in Lake View and Crabtree locations.

Other Information

links in Mary's resume
to other files

- References
- Comments on my work
- Go to Colorado State

Interested?

Contact Mary Taylor at mtaylor@tt.gr.csu.edu

7. Click the **References** link to verify that you jump to the References page shown in Figure 2-19.

TROUBLE? If the link doesn't work, check to see that Resume.htm and Refer.htm are in the same folder on your Data Disk.

Figure 2-19   REFERENCES PAGE

References

View My Resume · Comments

Lawrence Gale, Telecommunications Manager

Front Range Media Inc.
1000 Black Canyon Drive
Fort Tompkins, CO 80517
(303) 555-0103

Karen Carlson, Manager

Mountain View Bank
2 North Maple St.
Lake View, CO 80517
(303) 555-8792

Trent Wu, Sales Manager

Computer Visions
24 Mall Road
Lake View, CO 80517
(303) 555-1313

Robert Ramirez, Prof. Electrical Engineering

Colorado State University
Kleindist Hall
Fort Collins, CO 80517

8. Go back to the Resume page (usually by clicking a Back button on the toolbar of your browser), and then click the **Comments on my work** link to verify that you jump to the Comments page shown in Figure 2-20.

Figure 2-20   COMMENTS PAGE

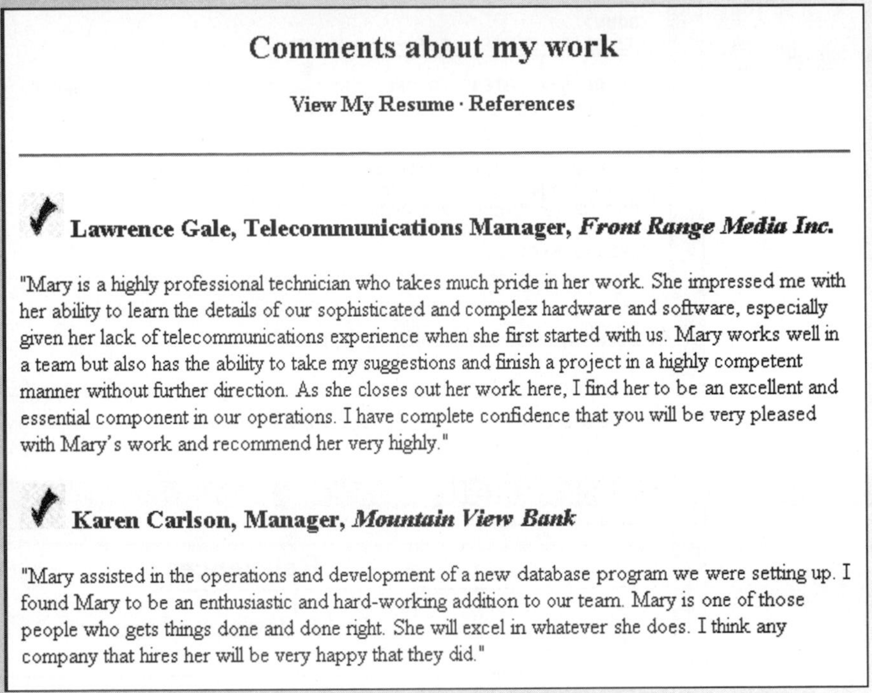

Comments about my work

View My Resume · References

 Lawrence Gale, Telecommunications Manager, *Front Range Media Inc.*

"Mary is a highly professional technician who takes much pride in her work. She impressed me with her ability to learn the details of our sophisticated and complex hardware and software, especially given her lack of telecommunications experience when she first started with us. Mary works well in a team but also has the ability to take my suggestions and finish a project in a highly competent manner without further direction. As she closes out her work here, I find her to be an excellent and essential component in our operations. I have complete confidence that you will be very pleased with Mary's work and recommend her very highly."

 Karen Carlson, Manager, *Mountain View Bank*

"Mary assisted in the operations and development of a new database program we were setting up. I found Mary to be an enthusiastic and hard-working addition to our team. Mary is one of those people who gets things done and done right. She will excel in whatever she does. I think any company that hires her will be very happy that they did."

Next you want to add similar links in the Refer.htm and Comments.htm files that point to the other two pages. Specifically, in Refer.htm, you need to add one link to Resume.htm and another to Comments.htm; in Comments.htm you need one link to Resume.htm and another to Refer.htm. This way, each page will have two links on it that point to the other two pages.

To add links in the References page to the Resume and Comments pages:

1. Return to your text editor and then open the file **Refer.htm** from the Tutorial.02 folder on your Data Disk.

2. Locate the H4 header at the top of the page.

3. Change the text "View My Resume" to:

   ```
   <A HREF="Resume.htm">View My Resume</A>
   ```

4. Locate the text "Comments" on the same line. Change "Comments" to:

   ```
   <A HREF="Comments.htm">Comments</A>
   ```

5. Compare your code to Figure 2-21.

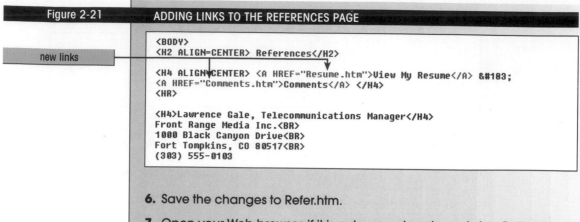

Figure 2-21   ADDING LINKS TO THE REFERENCES PAGE

new links

```
<BODY>
<H2 ALIGN=CENTER> References</H2>

<H4 ALIGN=CENTER> <A HREF="Resume.htm">View My Resume</A> &#183;
<A HREF="Comments.htm">Comments</A> </H4>
<HR>

<H4>Lawrence Gale, Telecommunications Manager</H4>
Front Range Media Inc.<BR>
1000 Black Canyon Drive<BR>
Fort Tompkins, CO 80517<BR>
(303) 555-0103
```

6. Save the changes to Refer.htm.

7. Open your Web browser, if it is not open already, and view Refer.htm. Your links should now look like Figure 2-22.

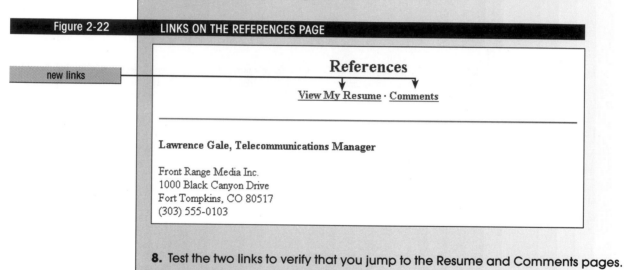

Figure 2-22   LINKS ON THE REFERENCES PAGE

new links

References

View My Resume · Comments

Lawrence Gale, Telecommunications Manager

Front Range Media Inc.
1000 Black Canyon Drive
Fort Tompkins, CO 80517
(303) 555-0103

8. Test the two links to verify that you jump to the Resume and Comments pages.

TROUBLE? If the links do not work, check the spelling of the filenames in the HREF property of the <A> tag. For some Web servers, the case (upper or lower) is also important, so you should make sure that the case matches as well.

Now you need to follow similar steps so that the Comments page links to the two other pages.

To add links in the Comments page to the Resume and References pages:

1. Return to your text editor, and then open the file **Comments.htm** from the Tutorial.02 folder on your Data Disk (you can close Refer.htm).

2. Locate the H4 heading at the top of the page.

3. Change the text "View My resume" to:

```
<A HREF="Resume.htm">View My Resume</A>
```

4. Change "References" on the same line to:

```
<A HREF="Refer.htm">References</A>
```

5. Save the changes to Comments.htm.

6. Open your Web browser, if it is not open already, and view Comments.htm. You should see the links shown in Figure 2-23.

| Figure 2-23 | LINKS ON THE COMMENTS PAGE |

new links

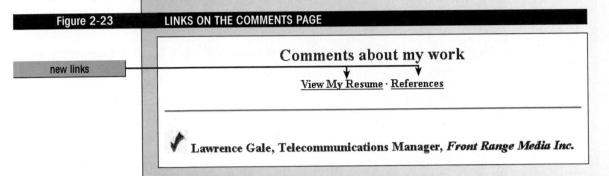

7. Click the two links to verify that you jump to the Resume and References pages.

Now that all the links among the three pages are set up, you can easily move among the three documents.

Linking to a Section of a Document

You might have noticed in testing your links that you always jump to the top of the destination page. What if you'd like to jump to a specific location elsewhere in a document, rather than the beginning? To do this, you can set anchors as you did in Session 2.1 and link to an anchor you create within the document. For example, to create a link to a section in the file Home.htm marked with an anchor name of "Interests," you would create an anchor in the Home.htm file at the section on Interest, and then you would enter this HTML code in your current document:

```
<A HREF="Home.htm#Interests">View my interests</A>
```

In this example, the entire text, "View my interests," is linked to the Interests section in the Home.htm file. Note that the pound (#)symbol in this tag distinguishes the filename from the anchor name (that is why you included the # symbol earlier when linking to anchors within the same document).

Mary wants to link the positions listed in the Employment section of her resume to specific comments from employers on the Comments page. The Comments.htm file already has these anchors in place:

- **GALE**, for comments made by Lawrence Gale, Mary's telecommunications manager
- **CARLSON**, for comments made by Karen Carlson, manager of Mountain View Bank
- **WU**, for comments made by Trent Wu of Computer Visions

Now you need to link the names listed in the Resume file to these three anchors in the Comments page.

To add links to the Resume page that jump to anchors on the Comments page:

1. With your text editor, reopen the **Resume.htm** file (you can close the Comments file).

2. Locate the Employment section in the middle of the Resume file. You need to bracket each job title with link tags that point to the appropriate comment in the Comments page. Leave in place any tags that format the text, such as the <P>, <I>, and <B> tags.

3. Move to the first job description and replace the title "Satellite Technician" with:

   `<A HREF="Comments.htm#GALE">Satellite Technician</A>`

4. Move to the next job description and replace the title "Technical Assistant" with:

   `<A HREF="Comments.htm#CARLSON">Technical Assistant </A>`

5. Move to the final job description, and replace the title "Salesperson" with:

   `<A HREF="Comments.htm#WU">Salesperson</A>`

6. Save the changes to the Resume file.

7. Open your Web browser and open **Resume.htm**. The job titles in the Employment section should appear as text links, as shown in Figure 2-24.

Figure 2-24	LINKS TO SPECIFIC LOCATIONS WITHIN THE COMMENTS PAGE

links in the resume that point to specific locations within the Comments page

Employment

Satellite Technician (Front Range Media Inc. 1998-1999): Monitored satellite uplink/downlink procedures to assure quality video transmissions. Aided technicians in the diagnoses and repair of transmission errors. Assisted in the assembly and maintenance of uplink facility.

Technical Assistant (Mountain View Bank 1996-1998): Managed data processing system. Trained users on data entry and report generation. Managed delivery service.

Salesperson (Computer Visions 1995): Sales and customer support in computers and electronics. Managed commercial accounts in Lake View and Crabtree locations.

Other Information

- References
- Comments on my work
- Go to Colorado State

8. Click the three links to verify that you jump to the appropriate places in the Comments page.

   TROUBLE? If you have a problem with your links, remember that anchors are case sensitive. Make sure you typed GALE, CARLSON, and WU in all uppercase letters.

9. If you are continuing to Session 2.3, you can leave your browser and text editor open. Otherwise, close them.

With these last hypertext links in place, you have given readers of Mary's online resume access to additional information. In the next session, you will learn how to point your hypertext links to documents and resources on the Internet.

Session 2.2 **QUICK** | **CHECK**

1. What is storyboarding? Why is it important in creating a Web page system?

2. What is a linear structure?

3. What is a hierarchical structure?

4. You are trying to create a system of Web pages for the play *Hamlet* in which each scene has a Web page. On each page you want to include links to the previous and next scenes of the play, as well as to the first scene of the play and the first scene of the current act. Draw a diagram of this multipage document. (Just draw enough acts and scenes to make the structure clear.)

5. What code would you enter to link the text "Sports info" to the HTML file Sports.htm?

6. What code would you enter to link the text "Basketball news" to the HTML file Sports.htm at a place in the file with the anchor name BBALL?

SESSION 2.3

In Session 2.2 you created links to other documents within the same folder as the Resume.htm file. In this session you will learn to create hypertext links to documents located in other folders and in other computers on the Internet.

Mary wants to add a link to her Resume page that points to the Colorado State University home page. The link gives potential employers an opportunity to learn more about the school she attended and the courses it offers. Before creating this link for Mary, you need to review the way HTML references files in different folders and computers.

Linking to Documents in Other Folders

Until now you've worked with documents that were all in the same folder. When you created links to other files in that folder, you specified the filename in the link tag, but not its location. Browsers assume that if no folder information is given, the file is in the same folder as the current document. In some situations you might want to place different files in different folders, particularly when working with large multidocument systems that span several topics, each topic with its own folder.

When referencing files in different folders in the link tag, you must include each file's location, called its **path**. HTML supports two kinds of paths: absolute paths and relative paths.

Absolute Pathnames

The **absolute path** shows exactly where the file is on the computer. In HTML you start every absolute pathname with a slash (/). Then you type the folder names on the computer, starting with the topmost folder in the folder hierarchy and progressing through the different levels of subfolders. You separate each folder name from the next with a slash. The pathname, from left to right, leads down through the folder hierarchy to the folder that contains the file. After you type the name of the folder that contains the file, you type a final slash and then the filename.

For example, consider the folder structure shown in Figure 2-25.

Figure 2-25   FOLDER TREE

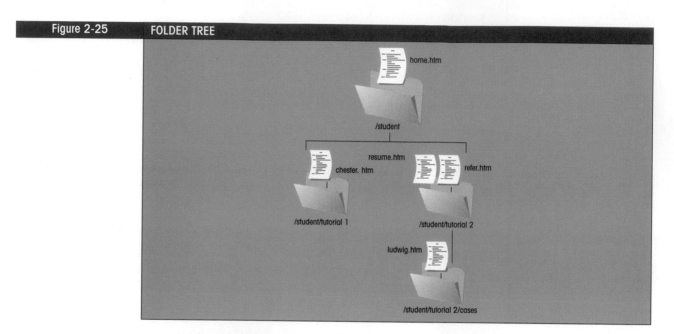

Figure 2-25 shows five HTML files contained in four different folders. The topmost folder is the student folder. Within the student folder are the tutorial1 and tutorial2 folders, and within the tutorial2 folder is the cases folder. Figure 2-26 shows absolute pathnames for the five files.

Figure 2-26   ABSOLUTE PATHNAMES

ABSOLUTE PATHNAME	INTERPRETATION
/student/home.htm	The home .htm file in the student folder
/student/tutorial1/chester.htm	The chester.htm file in the tutorial1 folder, a subfolder of the student folder
/student/tutorial2/resume.htm	The resume.htm file in the tutorial2 folder, another subfolder of the student folder
/student/tutorial2/refer.htm	The refer.htm file in the same folder as the resume.htm folder
/student/tutorial2/cases/ludwig.htm	The ludwig.htm file in the cases folder, a subfolder of the /student/tutorial2 folder

Even the absolute pathnames of files located on different hard disks begin with a slash. To differentiate these files, HTML requires you to include the drive letter followed by a vertical bar (|). For example, a file named "resume.htm" in the student folder on drive A of your computer has the absolute pathname "/A | /student/resume.htm".

Relative Pathnames

If a computer has many folders and subfolders, absolute pathnames can be long, cumbersome, and confusing. For that reason, most Web authors use relative pathnames in their hypertext links. A **relative path** gives a file's location in relation to the current Web document. As with absolute pathnames, folder names are separated by slashes. Unlike absolute pathnames, a relative pathname does not begin with a slash. To reference a file in a folder above the current folder in the folder hierarchy, relative pathnames use two periods (..).

For example, if the current file is resume.htm, located in the /student/tutorial2 folder shown in Figure 2-25, the relative pathnames and their interpretations for the other four files in the folder tree appear as in Figure 2-27.

Figure 2-27	RELATIVE PATHNAMES

RELATIVE PATHNAME	INTERPRETATION
../home.htm	The home.htm file in the folder one level up in the folder tree from the current file
../tutorial1/chester.htm	The chester.htm file in the tutorial1 subfolder of the folder one level up from the current file
refer.htm	The refer.htm file in the same folder as the current file
cases/ludwig.htm	The ludwig.htm file in the cases subfolder, one level down from the current folder

A second reason to use relative pathnames is that they make your hypertext links portable. If you have to move your files to a different computer or server, you can move the entire folder structure and still use the relative pathnames in the hypertext links. If you use absolute pathnames, you need to painstakingly revise each and every link.

Linking to Documents on the Internet

Now you can turn your attention to creating a link on Mary's resume to Colorado State University. To create a hypertext link to a document on the Internet, you need to know its URL. A **URL**, or **Uniform Resource Locator**, gives a file's location on the Web. The URL for Colorado State University, for example, is *http://www.colostate.edu/*. You can find the URL of a Web page in the Location or Address box of your browser's document window.

After you know a document's URL, you are ready to add the code that creates the link—again, the <A> code with the HREF property that creates links to documents on your computer. For example, to create a link to a document on the Internet with the URL *http://www.mwu.edu/course/info.html*, you use this HTML code:

```
<A HREF="http://www.mwu.edu/course/info.html"> Course
Information</A>
```

This example links the text "Course Information" to the Internet document located at *http://www.mwu.edu/course/info.html*. As long as your computer is connected to the Internet, clicking the text within the tag should make your browser jump to that document.

Linking to a Document on the Internet
- Locate the text or graphic you want to designate as the link.
- Before the text or graphic, place the tag <A HREF="*URL*"> where *URL* is the URL of the Web page you want to link to.
- After the text or graphic, insert the </A> closing tag.

In the Other Information section of Mary's resume, she wants to link the text "Go to Colorado State" to the CSU home page. You're ready to add that link.

To add a link to the Colorado State University page from Mary's Resume page:

1. If necessary, open your text editor, and then open the **Resume.htm** file that you worked on in Session 2.2 of this tutorial.

2. Locate the Other Information section near the bottom of the page.

3. Change the line "<LI>Go to Colorado State" to:

   ```
   <LI><A HREF="http://www.colostate.edu/"> Go to Colorado
   State</A>
   ```

4. Save the changes to the Resume file.

5. If necessary, open your Web browser and connect to the Internet.

6. Open the file **Resume.htm**. The Go to Colorado State entry should look like the text link shown in Figure 2-28.

| Figure 2-28 | LINK TO ANOTHER PAGE ON THE WEB |

Other Information

- References
- Comments on my work
- Go to Colorado State

link to Colorado State home page

Interested?

Contact Mary Taylor at mtaylor@tt.gr.csu.edu

7. Click the **Go to Colorado State** link. The Colorado State University home page shown in Figure 2-29 appears.

   TROUBLE? If the CSU home page doesn't appear right away, it might just be loading slowly on your system because it contains a large graphic. If the CSU home page still doesn't appear, verify that your computer is connected to the Internet.

| Figure 2-29 | COLORADO STATE UNIVERSITY HOME PAGE |

8. Click the **Back** button in your browser to return to Mary's resume.

Linking to Other Internet Objects

Occasionally you see a URL for an Internet object other than a Web page. Recall that one reason for the World Wide Web's success is that it lets users access several types of Internet resources using the same program. The method you used to create a link to the Colorado State University home page is the same method you use to set up links to other Internet resources, such as FTP servers to Usenet newsgroups (you'll learn what these are below). Only the proper URL for each object is required.

Each URL follows the same basic format. The first part identifies the **communication protocol**, the set of rules governing how information is exchanged. Web pages use the communication protocol **HTTP**, short for **Hypertext Transfer Protocol**. All Web page URLs begin with the letters "http". Other Internet resources use different communication protocols. After the communication protocol there is usually a separator, like a colon followed by a slash or two (://). The exact separator depends on the Internet resource. The rest of the URL identifies the location of the document or resource on the Internet. Figure 2-30 interprets a Web page with the URL:

```
http://www.mwu.edu/course/info.html#majors
```

Figure 2-30   INTERPRETING PARTS OF A URL

PART OF URL	INTERPRETATION
http://	The communication protocol
www.mwu.edu	The Internet host name for the computer storing the document
/course/info.html	The pathname and filename of the document on the computer
#majors	An anchor in the document

Notice that the URL for the Colorado State home page doesn't seem to have any path or file information. By convention, if the path and filename are left off the URL, the browser searches for a file named "index.html" or "index.htm" in the root folder of the Web server. Note that the path can be expressed in relative or absolute terms. This is the file displayed in Figure 2-29.

Before you walk Mary through the task of creating her final link, you take a quick detour to show her how to create links to other Internet resources, if needed. You might not be familiar with all the Internet resources discussed in these next sections. This tutorial doesn't try to teach you about these resources in detail; it just shows you how to reference them in your HTML files.

Linking to FTP Servers

FTP servers store files that Internet users can download, or transfer, to their computers. **FTP**, short for **File Transfer Protocol**, is the communications protocol these file servers use to transfer information. URLs for FTP servers follow the same format as those for Web pages, except that they use the FTP protocol rather than the HTTP protocol: ftp://*FTP_Hostname*. For example, to create a link to the FTP server located at ftp.microsoft.com, you could use this HTML code:

```
<A HREF="ftp://ftp.microsoft.com">Microsoft FTP server</A>
```

In this example, clicking the text "Microsoft FTP server" jumps the user to the Microsoft FTP server page shown in Figure 2-31. Note that different browsers will show the contents of the FTP site in different ways. Figure 2-31 shows what it might look like with Internet Explorer.

Figure 2-31	FTP SERVER AT FTP.MICROSOFT.COM

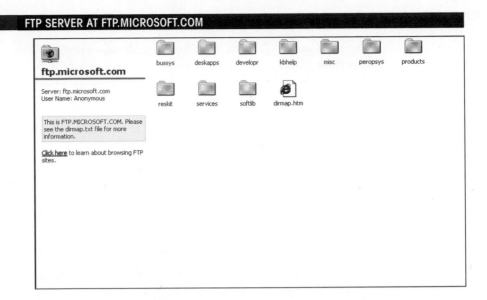

Linking to Usenet News

Usenet is a collection of discussion forums, called **newsgroups**, that lets users send and retrieve messages on a wide variety of topics. The URL for a newsgroup is news:*newsgroup*. To access the surfing newsgroup, alt.surfing, you place this line in your HTML file:

```
<A HREF="news:alt.surfing">Go to the surfing newsgroup</A>
```

When you click a link to a newsgroup, your computer starts your newsgroup software and accesses the newsgroup. For example, if you have the Outlook Newsreader program installed, clicking the above link will open the window shown in Figure 2-32.

Figure 2-32	ACCESSING THE ALT.SURFING NEWSGROUP

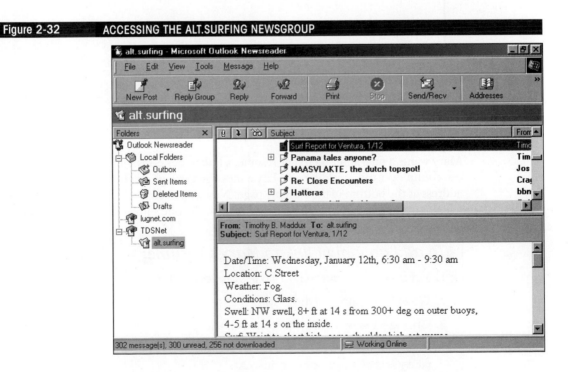

Linking to E-mail

Many Web authors include their e-mail addresses on their Web pages so that users who access these pages can easily send feedback. You can set up these e-mail addresses to act as hypertext links. When a user clicks the e-mail address, the browser starts a mail program and automatically inserts the author's e-mail address into the outgoing message. The user then types the body of the message and mails it. The URL for an e-mail address is mailto:*e-mail_address*. To create a link to the e-mail address davis@mwu.edu, for example, you enter the following into your Web document:

```
<A HREF="mailto:davis@mwu.edu">davis@mwu.edu</A>
```

If you click the text davis@mwu.edu and you have Microsoft Outlook installed as your default e-mail program, the window shown in Figure 2-33 appears.

Figure 2-33   SENDING MAIL TO DAVIS@MWU.EDU

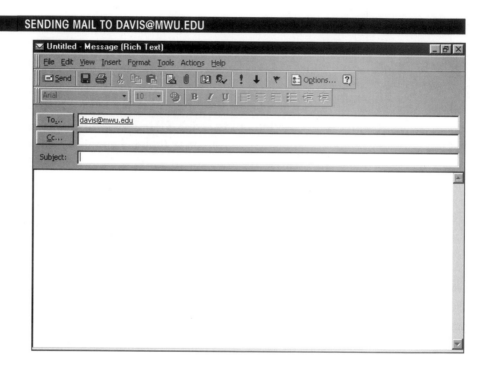

Adding an E-mail Link to Mary's Resume

Mary wants a final addition to her resume: a link to her e-mail address. With this link, an interested employer can quickly send Mary a message through the Internet. Mary placed her e-mail address at the bottom of the Resume page. Now you need to designate that text as a link so that when an employer clicks it, a window similar to the one shown in Figure 2-33 will open.

To add an e-mail link to Mary's resume:

1. Return to the Resume.htm file in your text editor.

2. Go to the bottom of the page.

3. Change the text "mtaylor@tt.gr.csu.edu" to

```
<A HREF="mailto:mtaylor@tt.gr.csu.edu">
mtaylor@tt.gr.csu.edu</A>
```

4. Save the changes to the Resume file.

5. Return to your Web browser and reload Resume.htm.

6. Move to the bottom of the page. Mary's e-mail address should look like the hypertext link shown in Figure 2-34.

   TROUBLE? Some browsers do not support the mailto URL. If you use a browser other than Netscape Navigator or Internet Explorer, check to see if it supports this feature.

| Figure 2-34 | MARY TAYLOR'S E-MAIL ADDRESS AS A HYPERLINK |

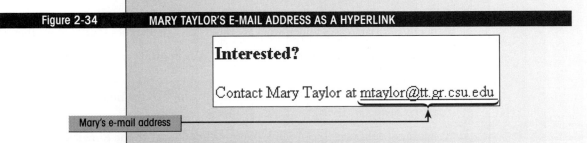

Mary's e-mail address

7. Click the hypertext link to Mary's e-mail address. See Figure 2-35.

| Figure 2-35 | MAIL MESSAGE WITH MARY TAYLOR'S E-MAIL ADDRESS AUTOMATICALLY INSERTED |

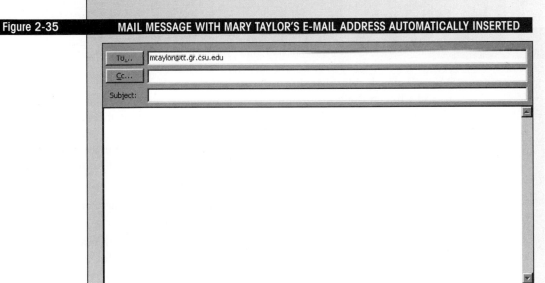

   TROUBLE? Your e-mail window might look different, depending on the mail program installed on your computer.

8. Cancel the mail message by clicking the Close button in the upper-right corner of the window. Mary's e-mail address is fictional, so you can't send her mail anyway.

9. Close your Web browser and text editor.

You show Mary the final form of her online resume. She's really thrilled with the result. You tell her the next thing she needs to do is contact an Internet service provider and transfer the files to an account on their machine. When that's done, Mary's resume becomes available online to countless employers across the Internet.

Session 2.3 QUICK CHECK

1. What's the difference between an absolute path and a relative path?

2. Refer to the diagram in Figure 2-25: If the current file is ludwig.htm in the /student/tutorial2/cases folder, what are the relative pathnames for the four other files?

3. What tag would you enter to link the text "Washington" to the FTP server at *ftp.uwash.edu*?

4. What tag would you enter to link the text "Boxing" to the newsgroup *rec.sports.boxing.pro*?

5. What tag would you enter to link the text "President" to the e-mail address *president@whitehouse.gov*?

REVIEW ASSIGNMENTS

Mary Taylor decides that she wants you to add a few more items to her resume. She wants to add a link at the bottom of her resume page that returns readers to the top. Also, in the Employment section, she wants to add the information that she worked as a tutor for Professor Ramirez at Colorado State University and link that job title to comments Professor Ramirez made about her in the Comments page. Finally, she wants to add a link to Colorado State's Department of Electrical and Computer Engineering, where she did a lot of her graduate work.

1. Open the **Resume.htm** file located in the Tutorial.02 folder on your Data Disk. You worked with this file over the course of this tutorial.

2. Save the file on your Data Disk in the Review folder with the same name, Resume.htm. This will leave intact the version that is in the Tutorial.02 folder.

3. Add an anchor tag around the H1 header at top of the page (Mary's name). Give the anchor the name TOP.

4. After the HTML line at the bottom of the page containing Mary's e-mail address, and before the </BODY> tag, enter a new paragraph with the line "Go to the top of the page." Change this text to a hyperlink, pointing to the TOP anchor you created in Step 3.

5. Move to the Employment section. After the paragraph describing Mary's experience as a salesperson, insert this paragraph: "Tutor (Colorado State): Tutored students in electrical engineering and mathematics." Format this paragraph using the same <P>, <B>, and <I> tags you used for the other job descriptions in the resume.

6. Change the text "Tutor" to a hyperlink pointing to the RAMIREZ anchor in the Comments page (this anchor already exists).

7. Move to the Other Information section, and add a new list item to the unsorted list: "Go to Colorado State Department of Electrical and Computer Engineering."

8. Change the new list item to a hyperlink pointing to the URL: *http://www.lance.colostate.edu/depts/ee/*.

9. Save the Resume.htm file and print it.

10. View the Resume.htm file with your Web browser. Make sure you open Resume.htm in the Review folder of the Tutorial.02 folder. Verify that all of the new links work correctly.

11. Print a copy of the Resume page as displayed by the browser.

CASE PROBLEMS

Case 1. *Creating Links to Federal Departments* As a librarian at the city library, you are creating a Web page to help people access the home pages for several federal government departments. Figure 2-36 lists each department's URL.

Figure 2-36

DEPARTMENT	URL
Department of Agriculture	http://www.usda.gov/
Department of Commerce	http://www.doc.gov/
Department of Defense	http://www.defenselink.mil/
Department of Education	http://www.ed.gov/
Department of Energy	http://www.doe.gov/
Department of Health and Human Services	http://www.dhhs.gov/
Department of Housing and Urban Development	http://www.hud.gov/
Department of Interior	http://www.doi.gov/
Department of Justice	http://www.usdoj.gov/
Department of Labor	http://www.dol.gov/
Department of State	http://www.state.gov/
Department of Transportation	http://www.dot.gov/
Department of Treasury	http://www.ustreas.gov/
Department of Veteran Affairs	http://www.va.gov/

You'll create an unsorted list containing department names, and then make each name a text link to the department's home page.

1. Start the text editor on your computer and open a new document.

2. Enter the <HTML>, <HEAD>, and <BODY> tags to identify different sections of the page.

3. Within the HEAD section, insert a <TITLE> tag with the text "Federal Government Departments".

4. Within the BODY section, create a centered H1 header with the text "A list of federal departments".

5. Create an unordered list of the department names shown in the first column of Figure 2-36. You can save yourself a lot of typing by using the Copy and Paste commands in your text editor (so that you don't have to type "Department of " each time).

6. Link each department name with its URL (shown in the second column of Figure 2-36).

7. Save the file as Depart.htm in the Cases subfolder of the Tutorial.02 folder on your Data Disk, print the file, and then close your text editor.

8. View the file with your Web browser, create a printout, and then close your browser.

Case 2. Using Graphics as Hypertext Links   You are an assistant to a professor in the Music Department who is trying to create Web pages for topics in classical music. Previously you created a Web page for her that showed the different sections of the fourth movement of Beethoven's Ninth symphony. Now that you've learned to link multiple HTML files together, you have created pages for all four movements.

Explore

The four pages are in the Cases folder of the Tutorial.02 folder on your Data Disk. Their names are: Move1A.htm, Move2A.htm, Move3A.htm, and Move4A.htm. You'll rename them Move1.htm, Move2.htm, Move3.htm, and Move4.htm so that you'll have the originals if you want to work on them later. Figure 2-37 shows the page for the third movement.

Figure 2-37

Beethoven's Ninth Symphony

✆ The Third Movement ☞

Sectional Form

1. A-Section
2. B-Section
3. A-Section varied
4. B-Section
5. Interlude
6. A-Section varied
7. Coda

View the Classical Net Home page.

You now need to link the pages. You've already placed graphic elements—the hands pointing to the previous or next movement of the symphony—in each file. You decide to mark each graphic image as a hypertext link that jumps the user to the previous or next movement.

1. Start your text editor and then open the **Move1A.htm — Move4A.htm** files in the Tutorial.02/Cases folder on your Data Disk, and save them as Move1.htm — Move4.htm in the Cases folder.

2. Within each of the HTML files you created in Step 1, edit the inline images, Right.jpg and Left.jpg, so that the Right.jpg inline image is a hyperlink pointing to the next movement in the symphony, and Left.jpg points to the previous movement in the symphony.

3. Within each of the four HTML files, change the text "View the Classical Net Home page." to a hyperlink pointing to the URL *http://www.classical.net/*. Save and print all four HTML files and then close your text editor.

4. Open the pages in your Web browser and verify that all of the links work correctly.

5. Print each page in the Web browser, and then close your browser.

Case 3. *Creating a Product Report Web Site*   You work for Jackson Electronics, an electronics firm in Seattle, Washington. You've been asked to create a Web site describing the company's premier flatbed scanner, the ScanMaster. There are three Web pages in the site: a product report, a fact sheet, and a sheet of frequently asked questions (FAQs). Your job is to add the links connecting the pages.

1. Start your text editor and then open the files **SMtxt.htm**, **Factstxt.htm**, and **FAQtxt.htm** in the Tutorial.02/Cases folder of your Data Disk and save the files as: Scanner.htm, Facts.htm and FAQ.htm, in the Cases folder.

2. Open the **Scanner.htm** file in your text editor, and add anchor names to the five H1 headers after the table of contents. Use the following anchor names: PR, SALES, STANDARD, PLAN, and LINKS.

3. Link the entries in the table of contents to the anchors that you created in Step 2.

4. Change the text "e-mail" in the second paragraph of the "Products Report Go Online" section to a hyperlink pointing to the e-mail address "jbrooks@Jckson_Electronics.com".

5. Go to the Links section of the document, and link the text "View the ScanMaster fact sheet" to the Facts.htm file. Link the text "View the Product Summary" to an anchor named SUMMARY in the Facts.htm file. Link "View the Features List" to the FEATURES anchor in Facts.htm. Link "View Ordering Information" to the INFO anchor in Facts.htm. Finally, link the text "View the FAQ sheet" to the FAQ.htm file. Save your changes to Scanner.htm file. Print the Scanner.htm file from your text editor.

6. Open the Facts.htm file in your text editor. Create anchors for each of the H2 headers with the names SUMMARY, FEATURES, and INFO.

7. Change the text "Return to the product report." at the bottom of the page to a hyperlink pointing to the Scanner.htm file. Save your changes. Print the Facts.htm file from your text editor.

8. Open the FAQ.htm file in your text editor. Change the last line to a hyperlink pointing to the Scanner.htm file. Print the FAQ.htm file from your text editor.

9. Open the Scanner.htm file in your Web browser and verify that all of your links work correctly.

10. Print each of the three resulting Web pages from your browser.

Case 4. *Create Your Own Home Page*   Now that you've completed this tutorial, you are ready to create your own home page. The page should include information about you and your interests. If you like, you can create a separate page devoted entirely to one of your favorite hobbies. Include the following elements:

- section headers
- bold and/or italic fonts
- paragraphs
- an ordered, unordered, or definition list

Explore ▶

- an inline graphic image that is either a link or the destination of a link
- links to some of your favorite Internet pages
- a hypertext link that moves the user from one section of your page to another

1. Create a file called Myhome.htm in the Cases folder of the Tutorial.02 folder on your Data Disk, and enter the appropriate HTML code.

2. Add any other tags you think will improve your document's appearance.

3. Insert any graphic elements you think will enhance your document.

Explore 4. Use at least one graphic element as either a link or the destination of a link.

5. Use your Web browser to explore other Web pages. Record the URLs of pages that you like, and list them in your document. Then create links to those URLs.

6. Test your code as you develop your home page by viewing Myhome.htm in your browser.

7. When you finish entering your code, save and print the Myhome.htm file, and then close your text editor.

9. View the final version in your browser, print the Web page, and then close your browser.

QUICK | CHECK ANSWERS

Session 2.1

1. <A NAME="CSU">Colorado State University</A>
2. <A HREF="#CSU">Universities</A>
3. Anchor tags should be placed within style tags such as the <H3> header tag.
4. <A NAME="PHOTO"> <IMG SRC="Photo.jpg"> </A>
5. <A HREF="#LINKS"> <IMG SRC="Button.jpg"> </A>
6. False. Anchor names are case-sensitive.

Session 2.2

1. Storyboarding is diagramming a series of related Web pages, taking care to identify all hypertext links between the various pages. Storyboarding is an important tool in creating Web sites that are easy to navigate and understand.
2. A linear structure is one in which Web pages are linked from one to another in a direct chain. Users can go to the previous page or next page in the chain, but not to a page in a different section of the chain.
3. A hierarchical structure is one in which Web pages are linked from general to specific topics. Users can move up and down the hierarchy tree.
4. A company might use such a structure to describe the management organization.
5. <A HREF="Sports.htm">Sports info</A>
6. <A HREF="Sports.htm#BBALL">Basketball news</A>

Session 2.3

1. An absolute path gives the location of a file on the computer's hard disk. A relative path gives the location of a file relative to the active Web page.
2. ../../home.htm

   ../../tutorial1/chester.htm

   ../resume.htm

   ../refer.htm
3. <A HREF="ftp://ftp.uwash.edu">Washington</A>
4. <A HREF=news:rec.sports.boxing.pro>Boxing</A>
5. <A HREF=mailto:president@whitehouse.gov>President</A>

HTML Extended Color Names

The following is a list of extended color names and their corresponding hexadecimal triplets supported by most Web browsers. To view these colors, you must have a video card and monitor capable of displaying up to 256 colors. As with other aspects of Web page design, you should test these color names on a variety of browsers before committing to their use. Different browsers may render these colors differently, or not at all.

Extended Color Names

COLOR NAME	HEXADECIMAL VALUE	PREVIEW	COLOR NAME	HEXADECIMAL VALUE	PREVIEW
ALICEBLUE	#F0F8FE		DARKPURPLE	#871F78	
ANTIQUEWHITE	#FAEBD7		DARKSALMON	#E9967A	
AQUA	#00FFFF		DARKSLATEBLUE	#6B238E	
AQUAMARINE	#70DB93		DARKSLATEGRAY	#2F4F4F	
AZURE	#F0FFFF		DARKTAN	#97694F	
BEIGE	#F5F5DC		DARKTURQUOISE	#7093DB	
BLACK	#000000		DARKVIOLET	#9400D3	
BLUE	#0000FF		DARKWOOD	#855E42	
BLUEVIOLET	#9F5F9F		DIMGRAY	#545454	
BRASS	#B5A642		DUSTYROSE	#856363	
BRIGHTCOLD	#D9D919		FELDSPAR	#D19275	
BRONZE	#8C7853		FIREBRICK	#8E2323	
BROWN	#A52A2A		FORESTGREEN	#238E23	
CADETBLUE	#5F9F9F		GOLD	#CD7F32	
CHOCOLATE	#D2691E		GOLDENROD	#DBDB70	
COOLCOPPER	#D98719		GRAY	#C0C0C0	
COPPER	#B87333		GREEN	#00FF00	
CORAL	#FF7F50		GREENCOPPER	#527F76	
CRIMSON	#DC143C		GREENYELLOW	#93DB70	
CYAN	#00FFFF		HOTPINK	#FF69B4	
DARKBLUE	#00008B		HUNTERGREEN	#215E21	
DARKBROWN	#5C4033		INDIANRED	#4E2F2F	
DARKCYAN	#008B8B		INDIGO	#4B0082	
DARKGOLDENROD	#B8860B		IVORY	#FFFFF0	
DARKGRAY	#A9A9A9		KHAKI	#9F9F5F	
DARKGREEN	#006400		LAVENDER	#E6E6FA	
DARKKHAKI	#BDB76B		LIGHTBLUE	#C0D9D9	
DARKMAGENTA	#8B008B		LIGHTCORAL	#F08080	
DARKOLIVEGREEN	#4F4F2F		LIGHTCYAN	#E0FFFF	
DARKORANGE	#FF8C00		LIGHTGRAY	#A8A8A8	
DARKORCHID	#9932CD		LIGHTGREEN	#90EE90	

COLOR NAME	HEXADECIMAL VALUE	PREVIEW
LIGHTPINK	#FFB6C1	
LIGHTSTEELBLUE	#8F8FBD	
LIGHTWOOD	#E9C2A6	
LIME	#00FF00	
LIMEGREEN	#32CD32	
MAGENTA	#FF00FF	
MANDARINORANGE	#E47833	
MAROON	#8E236B	
MEDIUMAQUAMARINE	#32CD99	
MEDIUMBLUE	#3232CD	
MEDIUMFORESTGREEN	#6B8E23	
MEDIUMGOLDENROD	#EAEAAE	
MEDIUMORCHID	#9370DB	
MEDIUMSEAGREEN	#426F42	
MEDIUMSLATEBLUE	#7F00FF	
MEDIUMSPRINGGREEN	#7FFF00	
MEDIUMTURQUOISE	#70DBDB	
MEDIUMVIOLETRED	#DB7093	
MEDIUMWOOD	#A68064	
MIDNIGHTBLUE	#2F2F4F	
MINTCREAM	#F5FFFA	
MISTYROSE	#FFE4E1	
NAVYBLUE	#23238E	
NEONBLUE	#4D4DFF	
NEONPINK	#FF6EC7	
NEWMIDNIGHTBLUE	#00009C	
NEWTAN	#EBC79E	
OLDGOLD	#CFB53B	
OLIVE	#808000	
ORANGE	#FF7F00	
ORANGERED	#FF2400	
ORCHID	#DB70DB	
PALEGOLDENROD	#EEE8AA	
PALEGREEN	#8FBC8F	
PALETURQUOISE	#AFEEEE	

COLOR NAME	HEXADECIMAL VALUE	PREVIEW
PINK	#BC8F8F	
PLUM	#EAADEA	
POWDERBLUE	#B0E0E6	
PURPLE	#800080	
QUARTZ	#D9D9F3	
RED	#FF0000	
RICHBLUE	#5959AB	
ROYALBLUE	#4169E1	
SADDLEBROWN	#8B4513	
SALMON	#6F4242	
SANDYBROWN	#F4A460	
SCARLET	#8C1717	
SEAGREEN	#238E68	
SIENNA	#8E6B23	
SILVER	#E6E8FA	
SKYBLUE	#3299CC	
SLATEBLUE	#007FFF	
SNOW	#FFFAFA	
SPICYPINK	#FF1CAE	
SPRINGGREEN	#00FF7F	
STEELBLUE	#236B8E	
SUMMERSKY	#38B0DE	
TAN	#DB9370	
TEAL	#008080	
THISTLE	#D8BFD8	
TOMATO	#FF6347	
TURQUOISE	#ADEAEA	
VERYDARKBROWN	#5C4033	
VERYDARKGRAY	#CDCDCD	
VIOLET	#4F2F4F	
VIOLETRED	#CC3299	
WHEAT	#D8D8BF	
WHITE	#FFFFFF	
YELLOW	#FFFF00	
YELLOWGREEN	#99CC32	

HTML Special Characters

The following table lists the extended character set for HTML, also known as the ISO Latin-1 Character set. Characters in this table can be entered either by code number or code name. For example, to insert the registered trademark symbol, ®, you would use either &reg or &#174.

Not all code names are recognized by all browsers. Some older browsers that support only the HTML 2.0 standard will not recognize the code name &times, for instance. Code names that may not be recognized by older browsers are marked with an asterisk. If you are planning to use these symbols in your document, you may want to use the code number instead of the code name.

CHARACTER	CODE	CODE NAME	DESCRIPTION
	&#00 - &#08		Unused
	&#09		Tab
	&#10		Line feed
	&#11 - &#31		Unused
	&#32		Space
!	&#33		Exclamation mark
"	&#34	&quot	Double quotation mark
#	&#35		Pound sign
$	&#36		Dollar sign
%	&#37		Percent sign
&	&#38	&amp	Ampersand
'	&#39		Apostrophe
(	&#40		Left parenthesis
)	&#41		Right parenthesis
*	&#42		Asterisk
+	&#43		Plus sign
,	&#44		Comma
-	&#45		Hyphen
.	&#46		Period
/	&#47		Forward slash
0 - 9	&#48 - &#57		Numbers 0 - 9
:	&#58		Colon
;	&#59		Semicolon
<	&#60	&lt	Less than sign
=	&#61		Equals sign
>	&#62	&gt	Greater than sign
?	&#63		Question mark
@	&#64		Commercial at
A - Z	&#65 - &#90		Letters A - Z
[	&#91		Left square bracket

CHARACTER	CODE	CODE NAME	DESCRIPTION
\	&#92		Back slash
]	&#93		Right square bracket
^	&#94		Caret
_	&#95		Horizontal bar
`	&#96		Grave accent
a - z	&#97 - &#122		Letters a - z
{	&#123		Left curly brace
|	&#124		Vertical bar
}	&#125		Right curly brace
~	&#126		Tilde
	&#127 - &#129		Unused
‚	&#130		Low single comma quotation mark
ƒ	&#131		Function sign
„	&#132		Low double comma quotation mark
…	&#133		Ellipses
†	&#134		Dagger
‡	&#135		Double dagger
ˆ	&#136		Caret
‰	&#137		Per mile sign
Š	&#138		Capital S with hacek
<	&#139		Less than sign
Œ	&#140		Capital OE ligature
	&#141 - &#144		Unused
'	&#145		Single beginning quotation mark
'	&#146		Single ending quotation mark
"	&#147		Double beginning quotation mark
"	&#148		Double ending quotation mark
•	&#149		Middle dot
–	&#150		En dash
—	&#151		Em dash
~	&#152		Tilde
™	&#153	&trade*	Trademark symbol
š	&#154		Small s with hacek
›	&#155		Greater than sign
œ	&#156		Small oe ligature
	&#157 - &#158		Unused
Ÿ	&#159		Capital Y with umlaut

CHARACTER	CODE	CODE NAME	DESCRIPTION
		*	Non-breaking space
¡	&#161	&iexcl*	Inverted exclamation point
¢	&#162	&cent*	Cent symbol
£	&#163	&pound*	Pound sterling
¤	&#164	&curren*	General currency symbol
¥	&#165	&yen*	Yen sign
¦	&#166	&brvbar*	Broken vertical bar
§	&#167	&sect*	Section sign
¨	&#168	&uml*	Umlaut
©	&#169	&copy*	Copyright symbol
ª	&#170	&ordf*	Feminine ordinal
«	&#171	&laquo*	Left angle quotation mark
¬	&#172	&not*	Not sign
–	&#173	&shy*	Soft hyphen
®	&#174	&reg*	Registered trademark
¯	&#175	&macr*	Macron
°	&#176	&deg*	Degree sign
±	&#177	&plusmn*	Plus/minus symbol
²	&#178	&sup2*	Superscript 2
³	&#179	&sup3*	Superscript 3
´	&#180	&acute*	Acute accent
µ	&#181	&micro*	Micro symbol
¶	&#182	&para*	Paragraph sign
·	&#183	&middot*	Middle dot
ç	&#184	&cedil*	Cedilla
¹	&#185	&sup1*	Superscript 1
º	&#186	&ordm*	Masculine ordinal
»	&#187	&raquo*	Right angle quotation mark
¼	&#188	&frac14*	Fraction one-quarter
½	&#189	&frac12*	Fraction one-half
¾	&#190	&frac34*	Fraction three-quarters
¿	&#191	&iquest*	Inverted question mark
À	&#192	&Agrave	Capital A, grave accent
Á	&#193	&Aacute	Capital A, acute accent
Â	&#194	&Acirc	Capital A, circumflex accent
Ã	&#195	&Atilde	Capital A, tilde
Ä	&#196	&Auml	Capital A, umlaut

CHARACTER	CODE	CODE NAME	DESCRIPTION
Å	&#197	&Aring	Capital A, ring
Æ	&#198	&Aelig	Capital AE ligature
Ç	&#199	&Ccedil	Capital C, cedilla
È	&#200	&Egrave	Capital E, grave accent
É	&#201	&Eacute	Capital E, acute accent
Ê	&#202	&Ecirc	Capital E, circumflex accent
Ë	&#203	&Euml	Capital E, umlaut
Ì	&#204	&Igrave	Capital I, grave accent
Í	&#205	&Iacute	Capital I, acute accent
Î	&#206	&Icirc	Capital I, circumflex accent
Ï	&#207	&Iuml	Capital I, umlaut
Ð	&#208	&ETH*	Capital ETH, Icelandic
Ñ	&#209	&Ntilde	Capital N, tilde
Ò	&#210	&Ograve	Capital O, grave accent
Ó	&#211	&Oacute	Capital O, acute accent
Ô	&#212	&Ocirc	Capital O, circumflex accent
Õ	&#213	&Otilde	Capital O, tilde
Ö	&#214	&Ouml	Capital O, umlaut
×	&#215	&times*	Multiplication sign
Ø	&#216	&Oslash	Capital O slash
Ù	&#217	&Ugrave	Capital U, grave accent
Ú	&#218	&Uacute	Capital U, acute accent
Û	&#219	&Ucirc	Capital U, circumflex accent
Ü	&#220	&Uuml	Capital U, umlaut
Ý	&#221	&Yacute	Capital Y, acute accent
þ	&#222	&THORN	Capital THORN, Icelandic
ß	&#223	&szlig	Small sz ligature
à	&#224	&agrave	Small a, grave accent
á	&#225	&aacute	Small a, acute accent
â	&#226	&acirc	Small a, circumflex accent
ã	&#227	&atilde	Small a, tilde
ä	&#228	&auml	Small a, umlaut
å	&#229	&aring	Small a, ring
œ	&#230	&aelig	Small AE ligature
ç	&#231	&ccedil	Small C, cedilla
è	&#232	&egrave	Small e, grave accent
é	&#233	&eacute	Small e, acute accent

CHARACTER	CODE	CODE NAME	DESCRIPTION
ê	&#234	&ecirc	Small e, circumflex accent
ë	&#235	&euml	Small e, umlaut
ì	&#236	&igrave	Small i, grave accent
í	&#237	&iacute	Small i, acute accent
î	&#238	&icirc	Small i, circumflex accent
ï	&#239	&iuml	Small i, umlaut
ð	&#240	&eth	Small ETH, Icelandic
ñ	&#241	&ntilde	Small N, tilde
ò	&#242	&ograve	Small o, grave accent
ó	&#243	&oacute	Small o, acute accent
ô	&#244	&ocirc	Small o, circumflex accent
õ	&#245	&otilde	Small o, tilde
ö	&#246	&ouml	Small o, umlaut
÷	&#247	&divide*	Division sign
ø	&#248	&oslash	Small o slash
ù	&#249	&ugrave	Small u, grave accent
ú	&#250	&uacute	Small u, acute accent
û	&#251	&ucirc	Small u, circumflex accent
ü	&#252	&uuml	Small u, umlaut
ý	&#253	&yacute	Small y, acute accent
þ	&#254	&thorn	Small thorn, Icelandic
ÿ	&#255	&yuml	Small y, umlaut

Putting a Document on the World Wide Web

Once you've completed your work on your HTML file, you're probably ready to place it on the World Wide Web for others to see. To make a file available to the World Wide Web, you have to transfer it to a computer connected to the Web called a **Web server**.

Your **Internet Service Provider (ISP)**—the company or institution through which you have Internet access—usually has a Web server available for your use. Because each Internet Service Provider has a different procedure for storing Web pages, you should contact your ISP to learn its policies and procedures. Generally you should be prepared to do the following:

- Extensively test your files under a variety of browsers and under different display conditions. Weed out any errors and design problems before you place the page on the Web.

- If your HTML documents have a three-letter "HTM" extension, rename those files with the four-letter extension "HTML." Some Web servers will require the four-letter extension for all Web pages.

- Check the hyperlinks and inline objects in each of your documents to verify that they point to the correct filenames. Verify the filenames with respect to upper and lower cases. Some Web servers will distinguish between a file named "Image.gif" and one named "image.gif." To be safe, match the uppercase and lowercase letters.

- If your hyperlinks use absolute pathnames, change them to relative pathnames.

- Find out from your ISP the name of the folder into which you'll be placing your HTML documents. You may also need a special user name and password to access this folder.

- Use **FTP**, a program used on the Internet that transfers files, or e-mail to place your pages in the appropriate folder on your Internet Service Provider's Web server. Some Web browsers, like Internet Explorer and Netscape Navigator, have this capability built in, allowing you to transfer your files with a click of a toolbar button.

- Decide on a name for your site on the World Wide Web (such as "http://www.jackson_electronics.com"). Choose a name that will be easy for customers and interested parties to remember and return to.

- If you select a special name for your Web site, you may have to register it. Registration information can be found at http://www.internic.net. This is a service your ISP may also provide for a fee. Registration is necessary to ensure that any name you give to your site is unique and not already in use by another party. Usually you will have to pay a yearly fee to keep control of a special name for your Web site.

- Add your site to the indexes of search pages on the World Wide Web. This is not required, but it will make it easier for people to find your site. Each search facility has different policies regarding adding information about Web sites to its index. Be aware that some will charge a fee to include your Web site in their list.

Once you've completed these steps, your work will be available on the World Wide Web in a form that is easy for users to find and access.

HTML Tags and Properties

The following is a list of the major HTML tags and properties. The three columns at the right indicate the earliest versions of HTML, Netscape, and Internet Explorer that support these tags. For example, a version number of 3.0 for Internet Explorer indicates that versions of Internet Explorer 3.0 *and above* support the tag or attribute. Both opening and closing tags are given where they are required (for example, <TABLE> … </TABLE>). A single tag means that no closing tag is needed.

You can view more detailed information about the latest HTML specifications at *http://www.w3.org*. Additional information about browser support for different HTML tags is available at *http://www.htmlcompendium.org/*.

Because the World Wide Web changes constantly, you should check this information against the current browser versions.

Properties are of the following types:

- *Character*   A single text character
- *Color*   A recognized color name or color value
- *CGI Script*   The name of a CGI script on the Web server
- *Document*   The file name or URL of a file
- *List*   List of items separated by commas, usually enclosed in double quotation marks
- *Mime-Type*   A MIME data type, such as "text/css", "audio/wav", or "video/x-msvideo"
- *Options*   Limited to a specific set of values (values are shown below the property)
- *Text*   Any text string
- *URL*   The URL for a Web page or file
- *Value*   A number, usually an integer

HTML supports six properties that are common to nearly all HTML tags.

COMMON PROPERTIES	DESCRIPTION	HTML	IE	NETSCAPE
CLASS=*Text*	The CLASS property is used to indicate the class or group to which a particular tag belongs.	4.0	3.0	4.0
DIR=*Option* (LTR | RTL)	The DIR property indicates the text direction as related to the LANG property. The LTR property value displays text from left to right, the RTL displays text from right to left.	4.0		
ID=*Text*	The ID property specifies a unique identifier to be associated with each tag. Unlike the CLASS property, an ID value can be associated with only a single tag.	4.0	3.0	4.0
LANG=*Text*	The LANG property identifies the language being used for the page content.	4.0	4.0	
STYLE="*Style declarations*"	The STYLE property is used to define an inline style for the tag.	4.0	3.0	4.0
TITLE=*Text*	The TITLE property is used to provide information about the tag and to identify the tag for scripts.	2.0	4.0	

TAGS AND PROPERTIES	DESCRIPTION	HTML	IE	NETSCAPE
Document-level Tags	Document-level tags are tags that specify the structure of the HTML file or control its operations and interactions with the Web server.			
<!>	The <!> tag is used for comments to document the features of your HTML file.	1.0	1.0	1.0

TAGS AND PROPERTIES	DESCRIPTION	HTML	IE	NETSCAPE
<BASE>	The <BASE> tag allows you to specify the URL for the HTML document. It is used by some browsers to interpret relative hyperlinks.	1.0	2.0	1.0
HREF=*URL*	Specifies the URL from which all relative hyperlinks should be based	1.0	2.0	4.0
TARGET=*Text*	Specifies the default target window or frame for every hyperlink in the document	4.0	3.0	2.0
<BASEFONT>	The <BASEFONT> tag specifies the default appearance of text in the document.	3.2	2.0	1.0
COLOR=*Color*	The color name or value of the text	4.0	1.0	
FACE=*List*	The font face of the text. Multiple font faces can be specified, separated by commas. The browser will try to render the text in the order specified by the list.	4.0	1.0	3.0
SIZE=*Value*	The size, in points, of the text font	3.2	2.0	1.1
<BODY> ... </BODY>	The <BODY> tag encloses all text, images and other elements on the Web page that will be visible to the user.	1.0	1.0	1.0
ALINK=*Color*	Color of activated hypertext links, links the user has pressed with the mouse button, but has not yet released	1.0	2.0	1.1
BACKGROUND=*Document*	The graphic image file used for the Web page background	1.0	2.0	1.1
BGCOLOR=*Color*	The color of the Web page background	3.2	2.0	1.1
BGPROPERTIES=FIXED	Keeps the background image fixed so that it does not scroll with the Web page		2.0	
BOTTOMMARGIN=*Value*	Specifies the size of the bottom margin, in pixels		4.0	
LEFTMARGIN=*Value*	Specifies the size of the left margin, in pixels		4.0	
LINK=*Color*	Color of all unvisited links	1.0	2.0	1.1
RIGHTMARGIN=*Value*	Specifies the size of the right margin, in pixels		4.0	
SCROLL=*Option* ("NO" | "YES")	Turns the scroll bars on and off (the default value is "YES")		4.0	
TEXT=*Color*	Color of all text in the document	1.0	2.0	1.1
TOPMARGIN=*Value*	Specifies the size of the top margin, in pixels		4.0	
VLINK=*Color*	Color of previously visited links	1.0	2.0	1.1
<HEAD> ... </HEAD>	The <HEAD> tag encloses code that provides information about the document.	1.0	1.0	1.0
<HTML> ... </HTML>	The <HTML> tag indicates the beginning and end of the HTML document.	1.0	1.0	1.0
<ISINDEX>	The <ISINDEX> tag identifies the file as a searchable document.	1.0	2.0	1.0
ACTION=*CGI Script*	Sends the submitted text to the program identified by *CGI Script*		2.0	2.0
PROMPT=*Text*	The text that should be placed before the index's text-input field	3.0	2.0	1.1

TAGS AND PROPERTIES	DESCRIPTION	HTML	IE	NETSCAPE
<LINK>	The <LINK> tag specifies the relationship between the document and other objects.	1.0	2.0	3.0
DISABLED	Disables the link relationship		4.0	
HREF=*URL*	The URL of the LINK tag, moves the user to the specified document	1.0	2.0	4.0
MEDIA=*Option* (ALL | AURAL | BRAILLE | PRINT | PROJECTION | SCREEN)	Specifies the destination medium for any linked information	4.0	4.0	
REL=*Option* (ALTERNATE | BOOKMARK | CHAPTER | CONTENTS | COPYRIGHT | GLOSSARY | HELP | INDEX | NEXT | PREV | SECTION | START | STYLESHEET | SUBSECTION)	Indicates the relationship type between the linked document and the current document	2.0	3.0	4.0
REV=*Option* (ALTERNATE | BOOKMARK | CHAPTER | CONTENTS | COPYRIGHT | GLOSSARY | HELP | INDEX | NEXT |PREV | SECTION | START | STYLESHEET | SUBSECTION)	Indicates the relationship type between the current document and the document specified by the HREF property	2.0	4.0	
TYPE=*Mime-Type*	The data type of the linked document (use "text/css" for linked style sheets)	1.0	2.0	4.0
<META>	The <META> tag is used to insert information about the document not defined by other HTML tags and properties. It can include special instructions for the Web server to perform.	1.0	1.0	1.0
CONTENT=*Text*	Contains information associated with the NAME or HTTP-EQUIV properties	1.0	2.0	1.1
HTTP-EQUIV=*Text*	Directs the browser to request the server to perform different HTTP operations	2.0	2.0	1.1
NAME=*Text*	The type of information specified in the CONTENT property	2.0	2.0	1.1
<STYLE> ... </STYLE>	The <STYLE> tag is used to enclose style declarations for the document.	4.0	3.0	4.0
DISABLED	Disables the style declarations		4.0	
MEDIA=*Option* (ALL | AURAL | BRAILLE | PRINT | PROJECTION | SCREEN)	Specifies the destination medium for the style information	4.0	4.0	
<TITLE> ... </TITLE>	The <TITLE> tag is used to specify the text that appears in the Web browser's title bar.	2.0	2.0	1.1
Block-level Tags	Block-level tags are used to format the appearance of large blocks of text.			
<ADDRESS> ... </ADDRESS>	The <ADDRESS> tag is used for information such as addresses and authorship. The text is usually italicized, and in some browsers it is indented.	2.0	2.0	1.0

TAGS AND PROPERTIES	DESCRIPTION	HTML	IE	NETSCAPE
<BDO> ... </BDO>	The <BDO> tag overrides the current direction of text.	4.0	5.0	
DIR=*Option* (LTR | RTL)	Specifies the text direction, LTR (left to right), or RTL (right to left)	4.0	5.0	
<BLOCKQUOTE> ... </BLOCKQUOTE>	The <BLOCKQUOTE> tag is used to set off long quotes or citations, usually by indenting the enclosed text on both sides. Some browsers italicize the text as well.	2.0	2.0	1.0
 	The tag forces a line break in the text.	2.0	2.0	1.0
CLEAR=*Option* (LEFT | RIGHT | ALL | NONE)	Causes the next line to start at the spot in which the specified margin is clear	3.0	2.0	1.0
<CENTER> ... </CENTER>	The <CENTER> tag centers the enclosed text or image horizontally.	3.2	2.0	1.1
<DFN> ... </DFN>	The <DFN> tag is used for the defining instance of a term,that is, the first time the term is used. The enclosed text is usually italicized.	2.0		2.0
<DIV> ... </DIV>	The <DIV> tag indicates a block of document content.	3.0	2.0	3.0
ALIGN=*Option* (LEFT | CENTER | JUSTIFY | RIGHT)	Horizontal alignment of the text within the <DIV> tag	3.0	3.0	3.0
<HR>	The <HR> tag creates a horizontal line.	1.0	2.0	1.0
ALIGN=*Option* (LEFT | CENTER | RIGHT)	Alignment of the horizontal line (the default is CENTER)	3.2	2.0	1.1
COLOR=*Color*	Specifies a color for the line		3.0	
NOSHADE	Removes 3D shading from the line	3.0	3.0	1.1
SIZE=*Value*	The size (height) of the line, in pixels	3.2	2.0	1.1
WIDTH=*Value*	The width (length) of the line, either in pixels or as a percentage of the display area	3.2	2.0	1.1
<H1> ... </H1> <H2> ... </H2> <H3> ... </H3> <H4> ... </H4> <H5> ... </H5> <H6> ... </H6>	The <H1> – <H6> tags are used to display the six levels of text headings, ranging from the largest (<H1>), to the smallest (<H6>). Text headings appear in a boldface font.	1.0	1.0	1.0
ALIGN=*Option* (LEFT | RIGHT | CENTER)	The alignment of the heading	3.0	2.0	4.0
<LISTING> ... </LISTING>	The <LISTING> tag displays text in a fixed width font resembling a typewriter or computer printout. This tag has been rendered obsolete by some newer tags.	2.0	3.0	1.0
<NOBR> ... </NOBR>	The <NOBR> tag prevents line breaks for the enclosed text. This tag is not often used.		2.0	1.1
<P> ... </P>	The <P> tag defines the beginning and end of a paragraph of text.	2.0	2.0	1.0
ALIGN=*Option* (LEFT | CENTER | RIGHT)	The alignment of the text in the paragraph	2.0	3.0	1.1

TAGS AND PROPERTIES	DESCRIPTION	HTML	IE	NETSCAPE
`<PLAINTEXT> ... </PLAINTEXT>`	The `<PLAINTEXT>` tag displays text in a fixed width font. It is supported by some earlier versions of Netscape, but in an erratic way, so authors should avoid using it.	2.0	2.0	1.0
`<PRE> ... </PRE>`	The `<PRE>` tag retains the preformatted appearance of the text in the HTML file, including any line breaks or spaces. Text usually appears in a fixed width font.	2.0	2.0	1.0
`<WBR> ... </WBR>`	The `<WBR>` tag, used in conjunction with the `<NOBR>` tag, overrides other tags that may preclude the creation of line breaks and directs the browser to insert a line break if necessary. This tag is not often used.		2.0	1.1
`<XMP> ... </XMP>`	The `<XMP>` tag displays blocks of text in a fixed width font. This tag is obsolete and should not be used.	2.0	2.0	1.0
In-line Tags	Inline tags modify the appearance of individual characters, words, or sentences from that of the surrounding text. Inline tags usually appear nested within block-level tags.			
`<A> ... </A>`	The `<A>` tag marks the beginning and end of a hypertext link.	1.0	1.0	1.0
ACCESSKEY=*Character*	Specifies an accelerator key for the element, which can be accessed by pressing the *Character* key along with the Alt key	4.0	4.0	
COORDS=*Value 1, value 2...*	The coordinates of the hotspot when the `<A>` tag is applied to an inline image; the coordinates depend on the shape of the hotspot	4.0		
Rectangle: COORDS=*x_left, y_upper, x_right, y_lower*				
Circle: COORDS= *x_center, y_center, radius*				
Polygon: COORDS= $x_1, y_1, x_2, y_2, x_3, y_3, ...$				
HREF=*URL*	Indicates the target, filename, or URL, to which the hypertext points	1.0	1.0	1.0
NAME=*Text*	Specifies a name for the enclosed text, allowing it to be a target of a hyperlink	1.0	2.0	1.0
REL=*Text*	Specifies the relationship between the current page and the link specified by the HREF property	1.0	2.0	
REV=*Text*	Specifies a reverse relationship between the current page and the link specified by the HREF property	1.0	2.0	
SHAPE=*Option* (RECT | CIRCLE | POLY)	The shape of the hotspot when the `<A>` tag is applied to an inline image	4.0		
TABINDEX=*Value*	Specifies the tab order in the form	4.0	4.0	
TARGET=*Text*	Specifies the default target window or frame for the hyperlink	4.0	3.0	1.0

TAGS AND PROPERTIES	DESCRIPTION	HTML	IE	NETSCAPE
TITLE=*Text*	Provides a title for the document whose address is given by the HREF property	1.0	2.0	
TYPE=*Mime-Type*	The data type of the linked document	4.0		
<ABBR> ... </ABBR>	The <ABBR> tag indicates text in an abbreviated form (for example, WWW, HTTP, URL).	4.0		
<ACRONYM> ... </ACRONYM>	The <ACRONYM> tag indicates a text acronym (for example, WAC, radar).	4.0	4.0	
<B> ... </B>	The <B> tag displays the enclosed text in bold type.	2.0	2.0	1.0
<BIG> ... </BIG>	The <BIG> tag increases the size of the enclosed text. The exact appearance of the text depends on the browser and the default font size.	3.2	2.0	2.0
<BLINK> ... </BLINK>	The <BLINK> tag causes the enclosed text to blink on and off.			1.0
<CITE> ... </CITE>	The <CITE> tag is used for citations. The text usually appears in italics.	1.0	2.0	1.0
<CODE> ... </CODE>	The <CODE> tag is used for text taken from the code for a computer program. The text usually appears in a fixed width font.	1.0	1.0	1.0
<DEL> ... </DEL>	The <DEL> tag is used to indicate that the text has been deleted from the document. Deleted text usually appears as strikethrough text.	4.0	4.0	
CITE=*URL*	Specifies the URL for a document that has additional information about the deleted text	4.0	4.0	
DATETIME=*Date*	Specifies the date and time of the deletion	4.0	4.0	
<EM> ... </EM>	The <EM> tag is used to emphasize text. The enclosed text usually appears in italics.	1.0	2.0	1.0
<FONT> ... </FONT>	The <FONT> tag is used to control the appearance of the text it encloses.	3.0	2.0	1.1
COLOR=*Color*	The color of the enclosed text	3.0	2.0	2.0
FACE=*List*	The font face of the text. Multiple font faces can be specified, separated by commas. The browser will try to render the text in the order specified by the list.	3.0	2.0	3.0
POINT-SIZE=*Value*	Point size of the text (used with downloadable fonts)			4.0
SIZE=*Value*	Size of the font in points, it can be absolute or relative. Specifying SIZE=5 sets the font size to 5 points. Specifying SIZE=+5 sets the font size 5 points larger than the size specified in the <BASEFONT> tag.	3.0	2.0	4.0
WEIGHT=*Value*	The weight of the font, ranging from 100 (the lightest) to 900 (the heaviest)			4.0
<I> ... </I>	The <I> tag italicizes the enclosed text.	1.0	1.0	1.0
<INS> ... </INS>	The <INS> tag is used to indicate that the text has been inserted into the document.	4.0	4.0	
CITE=*URL*	Specifies the URL for a document that has additional information about the inserted text	4.0	4.0	
DATETIME=*Date*	Specifies the date and time of the insertion	4.0	4.0	

TAGS AND PROPERTIES	DESCRIPTION	HTML	IE	NETSCAPE
<KBD> ... </KBD>	The <KBD> tag is used for text that appears as if it came from a typewriter or keyboard. Text is shown in a fixed width font.	1.0	2.0	1.0
<Q> ... </Q>	The <Q> tag indicates the enclosed text is a short quotation.	4.0	4.0	
CITE=URL	Specifies the URL for a document that has additional information about the quoted text	4.0	4.0	
<S> ... </S>	The <S> tag displays the enclosed text with a horizontal line striking through it.	4.0	2.0	3.0
<SAMP> ... </SAMP>	The <SAMP> tag displays text in a fixed width font.	1.0	2.0	1.0
<SMALL> ... </SMALL>	The <SMALL> tag decreases the size of the enclosed text. The exact appearance of the text depends on the browser and the default font size.	3.0	3.0	2.0
<SPAN> ... </SPAN>	The <SPAN> tag acts as a container for inline content.	4.0	3.0	4.0
DATAFLD=Text	Specifies the column of a data source that supplies bound data for use with the spanned text		4.0	
DATAFORMATAS=Option (TEXT | HTML)	Specifies whether the data in the data source column is formatted as plain text or as HTML code		4.0	
DATASRC=Text	Specifies the ID of the data source that is to be used with the spanned text		4.0	
<STRIKE> ... </STRIKE>	The <STRIKE> tag displays the enclosed text with a horizontal line striking through it. The <STRIKE> tag is being phased out in favor of the more-concise <S> tag.	3.2	2.0	3.0
<STRONG> ... </STRONG>	The <STRONG> tag is used to strongly emphasize the enclosed text, usually in a bold font.	1.0	1.0	1.0
_{...}	The <SUB> tag displays the enclosed text as a subscript.	1.0	3.0	2.0
^{...}	The <SUP> tag displays the enclosed text as a superscript.	1.0	3.0	2.0
<TT> ... </TT>	The <TT> tag displays text in a fixed width, teletype-style font.	1.0	1.0	1.0
<U> ... </U>	The <U> tag underlines the enclosed text. The <U> tag should be avoided because it can be confused with hypertext, which is typically underlined.	1.0	2.0	3.0
<VAR> ... </VAR>	The <VAR> tag is used for text that represents a variable. The text usually appears in italics.	1.0	1.0	1.1
In-line Object Tags	Inline object tags are used for inline objects such as graphics, multimedia files, and applets.			
<APPLET> ... </APPLET>	The <APPLET> tag, supported by all Java-enabled browsers, allows Web authors to embed a Java applet in an HTML document. It has been deprecated in favor of the <OBJECT> tag in HTML 4.0.	3.2	3.0	2.0

TAGS AND PROPERTIES	DESCRIPTION	HTML	IE	NETSCAPE
ALIGN=*Option* (ABSMIDDLE | ABSBOTTOM | ABSMIDDLE | BASELINE | BOTTOM | CENTER | LEFT | MIDDLE | RIGHT | TEXTTOP | TOP)	Specifies the alignment of the applet with the surrounding text	3.2	3.0	2.0
ALT=*Text*	Specifies alternate text to be shown in place of the Java applet	3.2	3.0	3.0
ARCHIVE=*URL*	Specifies the URL of an archive containing classes and other resources that will be preloaded for use with the Java applet	4.0		3.0
CODEBASE=*URL*	Specifies the base URL for the applet. If not specified, the browser assumes the same location as the current document.	3.2	3.0	2.0
CODE=*Text*	Specifies the name of the CLASS file that contains the Java applet	3.2	3.0	2.0
DATAFLD=*Text*	Specifies the column from a data source that supplies bound data for use with the applet		4.0	
DATASRC=*Text*	Specifies the ID of the data source that is to be used with the applet		4.0	
HEIGHT=*Value*	Specifies the height of the applet, in pixels	3.2	3.0	2.0
HSPACE=*Value*	Specifies the horizontal space around the applet, in pixels	3.2	3.0	2.0
MAYSCRIPT	Allows access to an applet by programs embedded in the document			4.0
NAME=*Text*	The name assigned to the Java applet	3.2	3.0	2.0
OBJECT=*Text*	Specifies a resource containing a serialized representation of an applet's state. It is interpreted relative to the applet's code base. The serialized data contains the applet's class name, but not the implementation. The class name is used to retrieve the implementation from a class file or archive.	4.0		
VSPACE=*Value*	Specifies the vertical space around the applet, in pixels	3.2	3.0	2.0
WIDTH=*Value*	The width of the applet, in pixels	3.2	3.0	2.0
\<AREA\>	The \<AREA\> tag defines the type and coordinates of a hotspot within an image map.	3.2	2.0	1.0
COORDS=*Value 1, Value 2…* Rectangle: COORDS=*x_left, y_upper, x_right, y_lower* Circle: COORDS= *x_center, y_center, radius* Polygon: COORDS= $x_1, y_1, x_2, y_2, x_3, y_3, …$	The hotspot coordinates, which depend on the shape of the hotspot.	3.2	2.0	1.0
HREF=*URL*	Indicates the target, filename or URL to which the hotspot points	3.2	2.0	1.0

TAGS AND PROPERTIES	DESCRIPTION	HTML	IE	NETSCAPE
SHAPE=*Option* (RECT | CIRCLE | POLY)	The shape of the hotspot	3.2	2.0	1.0
TARGET=*Text*	Specifies the default target window or frame for the hotspot	4.0	3.0	2.0
<BGSOUND>	The <BGSOUND> tag is used to play a background sound clip when the page is first opened.		2.0	
BALANCE=*Value*	Defines how the volume will be divided between two speakers, where *Value* is an integer between -10,000 and 10,000		4.0	
LOOP=*Value*	Specifies the number of times the sound clip should be played. LOOP can either be a digit or INFINITE.		3.0	
SRC=*Document*	The sound file used for the sound clip		2.0	
VOLUME=*Value*	Defines the volume of the background sound, where *Value* is an integer between -10,000 and 0		4.0	
<EMBED> ... </EMBED>	The <EMBED> tag is used to specify an object to be embedded in the document.		3.0	1.0
AUTOSTART=*Option* (TRUE | FALSE)	Specifies whether the embedded object should be started automatically when the page is loaded		3.0	1.0
ALIGN=*Option* (BOTTOM | LEFT | RIGHT | TOP)	Specifies the alignment of the embedded object with the surrounding text		3.0	1.0
ALT=*Text*	Text to display if the browser cannot display the embedded object		3.0	1.0
BORDER=*Value*	The size of the border around the embedded object, in pixels		3.0	1.0
HEIGHT=*Value*	The height of the embedded object, in pixels		3.0	1.0
HIDDEN=*Option* (TRUE | FALSE)	Specifies whether the embedded object is hidden or not			4.0
HSPACE=*Value*	The amount of space to the left and right of the image, in pixels		4.0	
TYPE=*Mime-Type*	Specifies the data type of the embedded object			4.0
UNITS=*Option* (EN | PIXELS)	Specifies the unit of measurement to be used with the embedded object			4.0
VSPACE=*Value*	The amount of space above and below the embedded object, in pixels		4.0	
WIDTH=*Value*	The width of the embedded object, in pixels		3.0	1.0
<IMG>	The <IMG> tag is used to insert an inline image into the document.	1.0	2.0	1.0
ALIGN=*Option* (LEFT | RIGHT | TOP | TEXTTOP | MIDDLE | ABSMIDDLE | BASELINE | BOTTOM | ABSBOTTOM)	Specifies the alignment of the image. Specifying an alignment of LEFT or RIGHT aligns the image with the left or right page margin. The other alignment options align the image with surrounding text.	1.0	2.0	1.1
ALT=*Text*	Text to display if the browser cannot display the image	2.0	2.0	1.1
BORDER=*Value*	The size of the border around the image, in pixels	3.2	2.0	1.1
CONTROLS	Displays VCR-like controls under moving images (used in conjunction with the DYNSRC property)		2.0	

TAGS AND PROPERTIES	DESCRIPTION	HTML	IE	NETSCAPE
DYNSRC=*Document*	Specifies the file of a video, AVI clip, or VRML worlds shown inside the page		2.0	
HEIGHT=*Value*	The height of the image, in pixels	3.0	2.0	1.1
HSPACE=*Value*	The amount of space to the left and right of the image, in pixels	3.0	2.0	1.1
ISMAP	Identifies the graphic as an image map (for use with server-side image maps)	3.0	2.0	2.0
LONGDESC=*URL*	The URL of a document that contains a long description of the image (used in conjunction with the ALT property)	4.0		
LOOP=*Value*	Specifies the number of times a moving image should be played (the value must be either a digit or INFINITE)		2.0	
LOWSRC=*Document*	A low-resolution version of the graphic that the browser should initially display before loading the high-resolution version		4.0	1.0
SRC=*Document*	The source file of the inline image	1.0	2.0	1.0
START=*Item* (FILEOPEN | MOUSEOVER)	Tells the browser when to start displaying a moving image file. FILEOPEN directs the browser to start when the file is open. MOUSEOVER directs the browser to start when the mouse pointer moves over the image.		2.0	
SUPPRESS=*Option* (TRUE | FALSE)	Suppresses the placeholder icon and any ALT text until the image is located (if SUPPRESS=TRUE)			4.0
USEMAP=*#Map_Namet*	Identifies the graphic as an image map and specifies the name of image map definition to use with the graphic (for use with client-side image maps)	3.2	2.0	2.0
VSPACE=*Value*	The amount of space above and below the image, in pixels	3.2	2.0	1.1
WIDTH=*Value*	The width of the image, in pixels	3.0	2.0	1.1
<MAP> ... </MAP>	The <MAP> tag specifies information about a client-side image map (note that it must enclose <AREA> tags).	3.2	2.0	1.0
NAME=*Text*	The name of the image map	3.2	2.0	2.0
<MARQUEE> ... </MARQUEE>	The <MARQUEE> tag is used to create an area containing scrolling text.		2.0	
ALIGN=*Option* (TOP | MIDDLE | BOTTOM)	The alignment of the scrolling text within the marquee		2.0	
BEHAVIOR=*Option* (SCROLL | SLIDE | ALTERNATE)	Controls the behavior of the text in the marquee. SCROLL causes the text to repeatedly scroll across the page. SLIDE causes the text to slide onto the page and stop at the margin. ALTERNATE causes the text to bounce from margin to margin.		2.0	
BGCOLOR=*Color*	The background color of the marquee		2.0	
DATFLD=*Text*	The column name in the data source that is bound to the marquee		4.0	
DATAFORMATAS=*Option* (TEXT | HTML)	Indicates the format of the bound data		4.0	

TAGS AND PROPERTIES	DESCRIPTION	HTML	IE	NETSCAPE
DIRECTION=*Option* (LEFT | RIGHT)	The direction that the text scrolls on the page		2.0	
HEIGHT=*Value*	The height of the marquee, either in pixels or as a percentage of the display area		2.0	
HSPACE=*Value*	The amount of space to the left and right of the marquee, in pixels		2.0	
LOOP=*Value*	The number of times the marquee will be scrolled (the value must be either a digit or INFINITE)		2.0	
SCROLLAMOUNT=*Value*	The amount of space between successive draws of the text in the marquee		2.0	
SCROLLDELAY=*Value*	The amount of time between scrolling actions, in milliseconds		2.0	
TRUESPEED	Indicates that the SCROLLDELAY property value should be honored for its exact value, otherwise any value less than 60 milliseconds is rounded up		4.0	
VSPACE=*Value*	The amount of space above and below the marquee, in pixels		2.0	
WIDTH=*Value*	The width of the marquee, in either pixels or as a percentage of the display area		2.0	
<NOEMBED> ... </NOEMBED>	The <NOEMBED> tag is used to display alternate content for older browsers that do not support the <EMBED> tag.		3.0	1.0
<OBJECT> ... </OBJECT>	The <OBJECT> tag allows authors to control whether data should be rendered externally or by a program, specified by the author, that renders the data within the user agent. (Most user browsers have built-in mechanisms for rendering common data types such as text, GIF images, colors, fonts, and a handful of graphic elements. To render data types not supported natively, user agents generally run external applications.)	2.0	1.0	1.1
ACCESSKEY=*Character*	Specifies an accelerator key for the object, which can be accessed by pressing the *Character* key along with the Alt key		4.0	
ARCHIVE=*URL*	Specifies the URL of an archive containing classes and other resources that will be preloaded for use with the object	4.0		
ALIGN=*Option* (TOP | BOTTOM | MIDDLE | LEFT | RIGHT)	Specifies the alignment of the embedded object, relative to the surrounding text	4.0	3.0	2.0
BORDER=*Value*	Specifies the width of the embedded object's border, in pixels	4.0	3.0	
CLASSID=*URL*	Specifies the URL of the embedded object	4.0	3.0	4.0
CODEBASE=*URL*	Specifies the base path used to resolve relative references within the embedded object	4.0	3.0	2.0
CODETYPE=*Text*	Specifies the type of data object	4.0	3.0	

TAGS AND PROPERTIES	DESCRIPTION	HTML	IE	NETSCAPE
DATA=*URL*	Specifies the location of data for the embedded object	4.0	3.0	2.0
DATAFLD=*Text*	Specifies the column from a data source that supplies bound data for use with the object		4.0	
DATASRC=*Text*	Specifies the ID of the data source that is to be used with the object		4.0	
DECLARE	Declares the object without installing it in the page	4.0		
HEIGHT=*Value*	Specifies the height of the embedded object, in pixels	4.0	3.0	2.0
HSPACE=*Value*	Specifies the horizontal space around the embedded object, in pixels	4.0	3.0	2.0
NAME=*Text*	Specifies the name of the embedded object	4.0	3.0	
STANDBY=*Text*	Specifies a message the browser should display while rendering the embedded object	4.0	3.0	
TABINDEX=*Value*	Specifies the tab order of the object when it is placed within a form	4.0	4.0	
TYPE=*Mime-Type*	Specifies the data type of the object	4.0	3.0	4.0
USEMAP=*URL*	The URL of the image map to be used with the object	4.0		
VSPACE=*Value*	Specifies the vertical space around the embedded object, in pixels	4.0	3.0	2.0
WIDTH=*Value*	Specifies the width of the embedded object, in pixels	4.0	3.0	2.0
<PARAM> ... </PARAM>	<PARAM> tags specify a set of values that might be required by an object at run-time. Any number of PARAM elements may appear in the content of an <OBJECT> or <APPLET> tag, in any order, but they must be placed at the start of the content of the enclosing <OBJECT> or <APPLET> tag.	3.2	3.0	1.0
DATAFLD=*Text*	Specifies the column name in the data source that is bound to the parameter's value		4.0	
DATAFORMATAS=*Option* (TEXT | HTML)	Specifies whether the data in the data source column is formatted as plain text or as HTML code		4.0	
DATASRC=*URL*	Specifies the URL of the data source from which to draw the data		4.0	
NAME=*Text*	Specifies the name of the parameter	3.2	3.0	2.0
VALUE=*Text*	Specifies the value of the parameter	3.2	3.0	2.0
VALUETYPE=*Option* (DATA | REF | OBJECT)	Specifies the type of the value attribute	4.0	3.0	
Form Tags	Form tags are used to create user entry forms.			
<BUTTON> ... </BUTTON>	Buttons created with the <BUTTON> tag function just like buttons created with the <INPUT> tag, but they offer richer rendering possibilities. For example, the BUTTON element may have content.	4.0	4.0	4.0
ACCESSKEY=*Character*	Specifies an accelerator key for the element, which can be accessed by pressing the *Character* key along with the Alt key	4.0	4.0	
DISABLED	Disables the button	4.0	4.0	

TAGS AND PROPERTIES	DESCRIPTION	HTML	IE	NETSCAPE
NAME=*Text*	Specifies the button name	4.0	5.0	
VALUE=*Text*	Specifies the initial value of the button	4.0	5.0	
TABINDEX=*Value*	Specifies the tab order in the form	4.0	5.0	
TYPE=*Option* (SUBMIT | RESET | BUTTON)	Specifies the type of button. Setting the type to BUTTON creates a pushbutton for use with client-side scripts.	4.0	4.0	
<FIELDSET> ... </FIELDSET>	<The FIELDSET> tag allows authors to group form controls and labels. Grouping controls makes it easier for users to understand the control's purpose, and simultaneously facilitates moving between fields.	4.0	4.0	
ALIGN=*Option* (TOP | BOTTOM | MIDDLE | LEFT | RIGHT)	Specifies the alignment of the legend with respect to the field set (see the <LEGEND> tag for more information)	4.0	4.0	
<FORM> ... </FORM>	The <FORM> tag marks the beginning and end of a Web page form.	1.0	1.0	1.0
ACTION=*URL*	Specifies the URL to which the contents of the form are to be sent	1.0	2.0	2.0
ENCTYPE=*Text*	Specifies the encoding type used to submit the data to the server	2.0	2.0	2.0
METHOD–*Option* (POST | GET)	Specifies the method of accessing the URL indicated in the ACTION property	2.0	2.0	2.0
TARGET=*Text*	The frame or window that displays the form's results	4.0	3.0	2.0
<INPUT> ... </INPUT>	The <INPUT> tag creates an input object for use in a Web page form.	1.0	2.0	1.0
ACCESSKEY=*Character*	Specifies an accelerator key for the element, which can be accessed by pressing the *Character* key along with the Alt key	4.0	4.0	
ALIGN=*Option* (LEFT | RIGHT | TOP | TEXTTOP | MIDDLE | ABSMIDDLE | BASELINE | BOTTOM | ABSBOTTOM)	Specifies the alignment of an input image (similar to the ALIGN option with the <IMG> tag)	1.0	2.0	1.1
ALT=*Text*	Alternate text description of image buttons for browsers that do not support inline images	4.0	4.0	
CHECKED	Specifies that an input check box or input radio button is selected	1.0	2.0	2.0
DISABLED	Disables the control	4.0	4.0	
MAXLENGTH=*Value*	Specifies the maximum number of characters that can be inserted into an input text box	1.0	2.0	2.0
NAME=*Text*	The label given to the input object	1.0	2.0	2.0
READONLY	Prevents the control's value from being modified	4.0	4.0	
SIZE=*Value*	The visible size, in characters, of an input text box	1.0	2.0	2.0
SRC=*Document*	The source file of the graphic used for an input image object	1.0	2.0	2.0
TABINDEX=*Value*	Specifies the tab order in the form	4.0	4.0	

TAGS AND PROPERTIES	DESCRIPTION	HTML	IE	NETSCAPE
TYPE=*Option* (CHECKBOX | HIDDEN | IMAGE | PASSWORD | RADIO | RESET | SUBMIT | TEXT | TEXTAREA)	Specifies the type of input object. CHECKBOX creates a check box. HIDDEN creates a hidden object. IMAGE creates an image object. PASSWORD creates a text box that hides the text as the user enters it. RADIO creates a radio button. RESET creates a button that resets the form's fields when pressed. SUBMIT creates a button that submits the form when pressed. TEXT creates a text box. TEXTAREA creates a text box with multiple line entry fields.	1.0	2.0	2.0
USEMAP=*#Map_Name*	Identifies the input image as an image map (similar to the USEMAP property used with the <IMG> tag)	1.0	2.0	2.0
VALUE=*Value*	Specifies the information that initially appears in the input object	2.0	2.0	2.0
WIDTH=*Value*	The width of the input image, in pixels	1.0	2.0	2.0
<LABEL> ... </LABEL>	The <LABEL> tag is used to create labels for form controls.	4.0	4.0	
ACCESSKEY=*Character*	Specifies an accelerator key for the element, which can be accessed by pressing the *Character* key along with the Alt key	4.0	4.0	
DATAFLD=*Text*	Specifies the column from a data source that supplies bound data for use with the label		4.0	
DATAFORMATAS=*Option* (TEXT | HTML)	Specifies whether the data in the data source column is formatted as plain text or as HTML code		4.0	
DATASRC=*Text*	Specifies the ID of the data source that is to be used with the label		4.0	
FOR=*Text*	Indicates the name or ID of the element to which the label is applied	4.0	4.0	
<LEGEND> ... </LEGEND>	The <LEGEND> tag allows authors to assign a caption to a FIELDSET (see the <FIELDSET> tag above).	4.0	4.0	
ACCESSKEY=*Character*	Specifies an accelerator key for the element, which can be accessed by pressing the *Character* key along with the Alt key	4.0	4.0	
ALIGN=*Option* (TOP | BOTTOM | LEFT | RIGHT)	Specifies the position of the legend with respect to the field set	4.0	4.0	
<OPTGROUP> ... </OPTGROUP>	The <OPTGROUP> tag is used to create a grouping of items in a selection list, as defined by the <OPTION> tag.	4.0		
DISABLED	Disables the group of option items	4.0		
LABEL=*Text*	Specifies a label for the option group	4.0		
<OPTION> ... </OPTION>	The <OPTION> tag is used for each item in a selection list. This tag must be placed within <SELECT> tags.	1.0	1.0	1.0
DISABLED	Disables the option item	4.0	4.0	
SELECTED	The default or selected option in the selection list	1.0	2.0	2.0
VALUE=*Value*	The value returned to the server when the user selects this option	2.0	2.0	2.0

TAGS AND PROPERTIES	DESCRIPTION	HTML	IE	NETSCAPE
<SELECT> ... </SELECT>	The <SELECT> tag encloses a set of <OPTION> tags for use in creating selection lists.	1.0	2.0	2.0
ACCESSKEY=*Character*	Specifies an accelerator key for the element, which can be accessed by pressing the *Character* key along with the Alt key	4.0	4.0	
ALIGN=*Option* (LEFT | RIGHT | TOP | TEXTTOP | MIDDLE | ABSMIDDLE | BASELINE | BOTTOM | ABSBOTTOM)	Specifies the alignment of an input image (similar to the ALIGN option with the <IMG> tag)	1.0	2.0	1.1
DISABLED	Disables the selection list	4.0	4.0	
MULTIPLE	Allows the user to select multiple options from the selection list	2.0	2.0	2.0
NAME=*Text*	The name assigned to the selection list	1.0	2.0	2.0
SIZE=*Value*	The number of visible items in the selection list	2.0	2.0	2.0
TABINDEX=*Value*	Specifies the tab order in the form	4.0	4.0	
<TEXTAREA> ... </TEXTAREA>	The <TEXTAREA> tag creates a text box.	1.0	2.0	1.0
ACCESSKEY=*Character*	Specifies an accelerator key for the element, which can be accessed by pressing the *Character* key along with the Alt key	4.0	4.0	
ALIGN=*Option* (LEFT | RIGHT | TOP | TEXTTOP | MIDDLE | ABSMIDDLE | BASELINE | BOTTOM | ABSBOTTOM)	Specifies the alignment of an input image (similar to the ALIGN option with the <IMG> tag)	1.0	2.0	1.1
COLS=*Value*	Specifies the height of the text box, in characters	1.0	2.0	2.0
DISABLED	Disables the text area	4.0	4.0	
NAME=*Text*	Specifies the name assigned to the text box	1.0	2.0	1.0
READONLY	Prevents the text area's value from being modified	4.0	4.0	
ROWS=*Value*	Specifies the width of the text box, in characters	1.0	2.0	2.0
TABINDEX=*Value*	Specifies the tab order in the form	4.0	4.0	
WRAP=*Option* (OFF | VIRTUAL | PHYSICAL)	Specifies how text should be wrapped within the text box. OFF turns off text wrapping. VIRTUAL wraps the text, but sends the text to the server as a single line. PHYSICAL wraps the text and sends the text to the server as it appears in the text box.		2.0	2.0
Frame Tags	Frame tags are used for creating and formatting frames.			
<FRAME>	The <FRAME> tag defines a single frame within a set of frames.	4.0	3.0	2.0
BORDERCOLOR=*Color*	Specifies the color of the frame border		4.0	3.0
FRAMEBORDER=*Option* (YES | NO)	Specifies whether the frame border is visible	4.0	3.0	3.0
FRAMESPACING=*Value*	Specifies the amount of space between frames, in pixels		3.0	
LONGDESC=*URL*	Specifies the URL of a document that contains a long description of the frame's content (used in conjunction with the TITLE property)	4.0		

TAGS AND PROPERTIES	DESCRIPTION	HTML	IE	NETSCAPE
MARGINHEIGHT=*Value*	Specifies the amount of space above and below the frame object and the frame borders	4.0	3.0	2.0
MARGINWIDTH=*Value*	Specifies the amount of space to the left and right of the frame object, in pixels	4.0	3.0	2.0
NAME=*Text*	Label assigned to the frame	4.0	3.0	2.0
NORESIZE	Prevents users from resizing the frame	4.0	3.0	2.0
SCROLLING=*Option* (YES | NO | AUTO)	Specifies whether scroll bars are visible (AUTO, the default, displays scroll bars only as needed)	4.0	3.0	2.0
SRC=*Document*	Specifies the document or URL of the object to be displayed in the frame	4.0	3.0	2.0
<FRAMESET> ... </FRAMESET>	The <FRAMESET> tag marks the beginning and the end of a set of frames.	4.0	3.0	2.0
BORDER=*Value*	The size of the frame's borders, in pixels		3.0	3.0
BORDERCOLOR=*Color*	The color of the frame borders		3.0	3.0
COLS=*List*	The size of each column in a set of frames. Columns can be specified either in pixels, as a percentage of the display area, or with an asterisk (*) indicating that any remaining space be allotted to that column (for example, COLS="40,25%,*").	4.0	3.0	2.0
FRAMEBORDER=*Option* (YES | NO)	Specifies whether the frame borders are visible		3.0	3.0
FRAMESPACING=*Value*	Specifies the amount of space between frames, in pixels		3.0	
ROWS=*List*	The size of each row in a set of frames. Rows can be specified either in pixels, as a percentage of the display area, or with an asterisk (*) indicating that any remaining space be allotted to that column (for example, ROWS="40,25%,*").	4.0	3.0	2.0
<IFRAME> ... </IFRAME>	The <IFRAME> tag allows authors to insert a frame within a block of text. Inserting an inline frame within a section of text allows you to insert one HTML document in the middle of another; both can be aligned with surrounding text.	4.0	3.0	
ALIGN=*Option* (ABSBOTTOM | ABSMIDDLE | BASELINE JUSTIFY | LEFT | MIDDLE | RIGHT | TEXTTOP)	Specifies the alignment of the floating frame	4.0	3.0	
FRAMEBORDER=*Option* (YES | NO)	Specifies whether the frame borders are visible	4.0	3.0	
HEIGHT=*Value*	Specifies the height of the floating frame, in pixels	4.0	3.0	
HSPACE=*Value*	Specifies the horizontal space around the inline frame, in pixels		3.0	
MARGINHEIGHT=*Value*	Specifies the amount of space above and below the frame object and the frame borders	4.0	3.0	
MARGINWIDTH=*Value*	Specifies the amount of space to the left and right of the frame object, in pixels	4.0	3.0	
NAME=*Text*	Label assigned to the frame	4.0	3.0	

TAGS AND PROPERTIES	DESCRIPTION	HTML	IE	NETSCAPE
NORESIZE	Prevents users from resizing the frame		3.0	
SCROLLING=*Option* (YES | NO | AUTO)	Specifies whether scroll bars are visible (AUTO, the default, displays scroll bars only as needed)	4.0	3.0	
SRC=*Document*	Specifies the document or URL of the object to be displayed in the frame	4.0	3.0	
VSPACE=*Value*	Specifies the vertical space around the inline frame, in pixels		3.0	
WIDTH=*Value*	Specifies the width of the floating frame, in pixels	4.0	3.0	
<NOFRAMES> … </NOFRAMES>	The <NOFRAMES> tag enables browsers that do not support frames to display a page that uses frames (the tag encloses the <BODY> tag).	4.0	3.0	2.0
Layer Tags	Layer tags are used to create overlapping content layers.			
<ILAYER> … </ILAYER>	The <ILAYER> tag is used to create an inflow layer with a relative position and which appears where it naturally would in the document.			4.0
ABOVE=*Text*	Specifies the name of the layer to be displayed above the current layer			4.0
BACKGROUND=*URL*	Specifies the URL of the layer's background image			4.0
BELOW=*Text*	Specifies the name of the layer to be displayed below the current layer			4.0
BGCOLOR=*Color*	Specifies the background color of the layer			4.0
CLIP=*top_x, left_y, bottom_x, right_y*	Specifies the coordinates of the viewable region of the layer			4.0
HEIGHT=*Value*	The height of the layer in pixels			4.0
LEFT=*Value*	Specifies the horizontal offset of the layer, in pixels			4.0
PAGEX=*Value*	Specifies the horizontal position of the layer			4.0
PAGEY=*Value*	Specifies the vertical position of the layer			4.0
SRC=*URL*	Specifies the URL of the document displayed in the layer			4.0
TOP=*Value*	Specifies the vertical offset of the layer, in pixels			4.0
VISIBILITY=*Option* (HIDE | INHERIT | SHOW)	Specifies whether the layer is hidden, shown, or inherits its visibility from the layer that contains it			4.0
WIDTH=*Value*	The width of the layer, in pixels			4.0
Z-INDEX=*Value*	Specifies the stacking order of the layer, relative to the other layers			4.0
<LAYER> … </LAYER>	The <LAYER> tag is used to create an inflow layer with an absolutely defined position in the document.			4.0
ABOVE=*Text*	Specifies the name of the layer to be displayed above the current layer			4.0
BACKGROUND=*URL*	Specifies the URL of the layer's background image			4.0
BELOW=*Text*	Specifies the name of the layer to be displayed below the current layer			4.0
BGCOLOR=*Color*	Specifies the background color of the layer			4.0

TAGS AND PROPERTIES	DESCRIPTION	HTML	IE	NETSCAPE
CLIP=*top_x, left_y, bottom_x, right_y*	Specifies the coordinates of the viewable region of the layer			4.0
HEIGHT=*Value*	The height of the layer, in pixels			4.0
LEFT=*Value*	Specifies the horizontal offset of the layer, In pixels			4.0
PAGEX=*Value*	Specifies the horizontal position of the layer			4.0
PAGEY=*Value*	Specifies the vertical position of the layer			4.0
SRC=*URL*	Specifies the URL of the document displayed in the layer			4.0
TOP=*Value*	Specifies the vertical offset of the layer, in pixels			4.0
VISIBILITY=*Option* (HIDE | INHERIT | SHOW)	Specifies whether the layer is hidden, shown, or inherits its visibility from the layer that contains it			4.0
WIDTH=*Value*	The width of the layer, in pixels			4.0
Z-INDEX=*Value*	Specifies the stacking order of the layer, relative to the other layers			4.0
List Tags	List tags are used to create a variety of different kinds of lists.			
<DD>	The <DD> tag formats text to be used as relative definitions in a <DL> list.	1.0	2.0	1.0
<DIR> ... </DIR>	The <DIR> tag encloses an unordered list of <LI> items formatted in narrow columns.	1.0	2.0	1.0
COMPACT	Reduces the whitespace between list items	2.0		
TYPE=*Option* (CIRCLE | DISC | SQUARE)	Specifies the type of bullet used for displaying each <LI> item in the <DIR> list			2.0
<DL> ... </DL>	The <DL> tag encloses a definition list in which the <DD> definition term is left-aligned, and the <DT> relative definition is indented.	1.0	2.0	1.0
COMPACT	Reduces the whitespace between list items	2.0	4.0	1.0
<DT>	The <DT> tag is used to format the definition term in a <DL> list.	1.0	2.0	1.0
<LI>	The <LI> tag identifies list items in a <DIR>, <MENU>, <OL>, or <UL> list.	1.0	2.0	1.0
TYPE=*Option* (A | a | I | i | 1)	Specifies how the list item is to be marked. A = uppercase letters, a = lowercase letters, I = uppercase Roman numerals, i = lowercase Roman numerals, and 1 = digits. The default is 1.	3.0	1.0	1.0
<MENU> ... </MENU>	The <MENU> tag encloses an unordered list of items, similar to a <UL> or <DIR> list.	1.0	2.0	1.0
COMPACT	Reduces the whitespace between menu items	2.0		
<OL> ... </OL>	The <OL> tag encloses an ordered list of <LI> items. Typically, ordered lists are rendered as numbered lists.	1.0	1.0	1.0
COMPACT	Reduces the whitespace between ordered list items	2.0		
START=*Value*	The value of the starting number in the ordered list	3.2	2.0	2.0

TAGS AND PROPERTIES	DESCRIPTION	HTML	IE	NETSCAPE
TYPE=*Option* (A | a | I | i | 1)	Specifies how ordered items are to be marked. A = uppercase letters, a = lowercase letters, I = uppercase Roman numerals, i = lowercase Roman numerals, and 1 = digits. The default is 1.	3.2	2.0	2.0
<UL> ... </UL>	The <UL> tag encloses an unordered list of <LI> items. Typically, unordered lists are rendered as bulleted lists.	1.0	1.0	1.0
COMPACT	Reduces the whitespace between unordered list items	2.0		
Type=*Option* (CIRCLE | DISK | SQUARE)	Specifies the type of bullet used for displaying each <LI> item in the <UL> list	3.2		2.0
Script Tags	Script tags are used for client-side scripts, including JavaScript and VBScript.			
<NOSCRIPT> ... </NOSCRIPT>	The <NOSCRIPT> tag is used to enclose HTML tags for browsers that do not support client-side scripts.	4.0	3.0	3.0
<SCRIPT> ... </SCRIPT>	The <SCRIPT> tag places a client-side script within a document. This element may appear any number of times in the HEAD or BODY of an HTML document.	3.2	3.0	3.0
DEFER	Specifies that the browser should defer executing the script	4.0		
EVENT=*Text*	Specifies an event that the script should be run in reaction to (this property must be used in conjunction with the FOR property)	4.0	4.0	
FOR=*Text*	Indicates the name or ID of the element to which an event, defined by the EVENT property, is applied	4.0	4.0	
LANGUAGE=*Text*	Specifies the language of the client-side script (see JavaScript for JavaScript commands)	4.0	3.0	3.0
SRC=*URL*	Specifies the source of the external script file	4.0	3.0	3.0
TYPE=*Mime-Type*	Specifies the data type of the scripting language (use text/javascript for JavaScript commands)	4.0	4.0	
Table Tags	Table tags are used to define the structure and appearance of graphical tables.			
<CAPTION> ... </CAPTION>	The <CAPTION> tag encloses the table caption.	3.0	2.0	1.1
ALIGN=*Option* (LEFT | RIGHT | CENTER | TOP | BOTTOM)	Specifies the alignment of the caption with respect to the table (the LEFT, RIGHT and CENTER options are supported only by Internet Explorer 3.0)	3.0	2.0	2.0
VALIGN=*Option* (TOP | BOTTOM)	Specifies the vertical alignment of the caption with respect to the table		2.0	
<COL> ... </COL>	The <COL> tag specifies the default settings for a column or group of columns.	4.0	3.0	
ALIGN=*Option* (CHAR | CENTER | JUSTIFY | LEFT | RIGHT)	Specifies the horizontal alignment of text within a column	4.0	4.0	
SPAN=*Value*	Specifies the columns modified by the <COL> tag	4.0	3.0	

TAGS AND PROPERTIES	DESCRIPTION	HTML	IE	NETSCAPE
VALIGN=*Option* (TOP | MIDDLE | BOTTOM)	Specifies the vertical alignment of text within a column	4.0	4.0	
WIDTH= *Value*	Specifies the width for each column or column group	4.0	3.0	
<COLGROUP> ... <COLGROUP>	The <COLGROUP> tag encloses a group of <COL> tags, and groups columns together to set their alignment properties.	3.0	4.0	
ALIGN=*Option* (CHAR | CENTER | JUSTIFY | LEFT | RIGHT)	Specifies the horizontal alignment of text within a column group	4.0	4.0	
CHAR=*Character*	Specifies a character with which to align the values in the column (a period usually is used to align monetary values)	4.0		
CHAROFF=*Value*	Specifies the number of characters to offset the column data from the alignment character specified in the CHAR property	4.0		
SPAN=*Value*	Specifies the columns within the column group	4.0	4.0	
VALIGN=*Option* (TOP | MIDDLE | BOTTOM)	Specifies the vertical alignment of text within a column group	4.0	4.0	
WIDTH= *Value*	Specifies the width of each column for the column group	4.0	3.0	
<TABLE> ... </TABLE>	The <TABLE> tag is used to specify the beginning and end of a table.	1.0	1.0	1.1
ALIGN=*Option* (CHAR | LEFT | CENTER | RIGHT)	Specifies the horizontal alignment of the table on the page (only LEFT and RIGHT are supported by Netscape 3.0 and Internet Explorer 3.0)	3.0	3.0	2.0
BACKGROUND=*Document*	Specifies a background image for the table		3.0	4.0
BGCOLOR=*Color*	Specifies a background color for the table	4.0	2.0	3.0
BORDER=*Value*	Specifies the width of the table border, in pixels	3.0	2.0	2.0
BORDERCOLOR=*Color*	Specifies the color of the table border		2.0	4.0
BORDERCOLORDARK=*Color*	Specifies the color of the shaded edge of the table border		2.0	
BORDERCOLORLIGHT=*Color*	Specifies the color of the unshaded edge of the table border		2.0	
CELLPADDING=*Value*	Specifies the space between table cells, in pixels	3.2	2.0	2.0
CELLSPACING=*Value*	Specifies the space between cell text and the cell border, in pixels	3.2	2.0	2.0
COLS=*Value*	Specifies the number of columns in the table, used for quickly calculating the size of the table		3.0	4.0
DATAPAGESIZE=*Value*	Specifies the number of rows that can be displayed in the table when data binding is used	4.0	4.0	
DATASRC=*URL*	Specifies the URL of the table's data source		4.0	

TAGS AND PROPERTIES	DESCRIPTION	HTML	IE	NETSCAPE
FRAME=*Option* (ABOVE | BELOW | BOX | HSIDES | LHS | RHS | VOID | VSIDES)	Specifies the display of table borders. ABOVE = top border only. BELOW = bottom border only. BOX = borders on all four sides. HSIDES = top and bottom borders. LHS = left side border. RHS = right side border. VOID = no borders. VSIDES = left and right side borders.	3.0	3.0	
HEIGHT=*Value*	The height of the table, in pixels or as a percentage of the display area		4.0	4.0
HSPACE=*Value*	Specifies the horizontal space, in pixels, between the table and the surrounding text			4.0
RULES=*Option* (ALL | COLS | NONE | ROWS)	Specifies the display of internal table borders. ALL = borders between every row and column. COLS = borders between every column. NONE = no internal table borders. ROWS = borders between every row.	4.0	3.0	
VSPACE=*Value*	Specifies the vertical space, in pixels, between the table and the surrounding text			4.0
WIDTH=*Value*	The width of the table, in pixels or as a percentage of the display area	3.0	2.0	2.0
<TBODY> ... </TBODY>	The <TBODY> tag identifies text that appears in the table body, as opposed to text in the table header (<THEAD> tag) or in the table footer (<TBODY> tag).	4.0	4.0	
ALIGN=*Option* (CHAR | LEFT | CENTER |RIGHT)	The horizontal alignment of text in the cells of the table body	4.0	4.0	
BGCOLOR=*Color*	Specifies a background color of the table body		4.0	
CHAR=*Character*	Specifies a character with which to align the values in the column (a period usually is used to align monetary values)	4.0		
CHAROFF=*Value*	Specifies the number of characters to offset the column data from the alignment character specified in the CHAR property	4.0		
VALIGN=*Option* (TOP | MIDDLE | BOTTOM)	The vertical alignment of text in the cells in the table body	4.0	4.0	
<TD> ... </TD>	The <TD> tag encloses the text that will appear in an individual table cell.	1.0	2.0	1.1
ABBR=*Text*	Specifies an abbreviated name for the header cell, used when displaying large tables on small screens	4.0		
ALIGN=*Option* (LEFT | CENTER | RIGHT)	Specifies the horizontal alignment of cell text	1.0	2.0	2.0
AXIS=*Text*	Specifies a name for a group of related table headers	4.0		
BACKGROUND=*Document*	Specifies a background image for the cell		4.0	4.0
BGCOLOR=*Color*	Specifies a background color for the cell	4.0	2.0	3.0
BORDERCOLOR=*Color*	Specifies the color of the cell border		2.0	
BORDERCOLORDARK=*Color*	Specifies the color of the shaded edge of the cell border		2.0	

TAGS AND PROPERTIES	DESCRIPTION	HTML	IE	NETSCAPE
BORDERCOLORLIGHT=*Color*	Specifies the color of the unshaded edge of the cell border		2.0	
COLSPAN=*Value*	Specifies the number of columns the cell should span	3.2	2.0	2.0
HEIGHT=*Value*	The height of the cell, in pixels or as a percentage of the display area	3.2	2.0	2.0
NOWRAP	Prohibits the browser from wrapping text in the cell	3.0	2.0	2.0
ROWSPAN=*Value*	Specifies the number of rows the cell should span	3.2	2.0	2.0
SCOPE=*Option* (COL | COLGROUP | ROW | ROWGROUP)	Specifies the table cells for which the current cell provides header information. A SCOPE value of COL indicates that the cell is a header for the rest of the column, a value of COLGROUP indicates that the cell is a header for the current column group, a value of ROW indicates that the cell is a header for the current row, and a value of ROWGROUP indicates that the cell is a header for the current row group.	4.0		
VALIGN=*Option* (TOP | MIDDLE | BOTTOM)	Specifies the vertical alignment of cell text	3.0	2.0	2.0
WIDTH= *Value*	The width of the cell, in pixels or as a percentage of the width of the table	3.2	2.0	2.0
<TFOOT> ... </TFOOT>	The <TFOOT> tag encloses footer information that will be displayed in the table footer when the table is printed on multiple pages.	4.0	4.0	
ALIGN=*Option* (CHAR | CENTER | LEFT | RIGHT)	The horizontal alignment of the table footer	4.0	4.0	
BGCOLOR=*Color*	Specifies a background color for the table footer		4.0	
CHAR=*Character*	Specifies a character with which to align the values in the column (a period is usually used to align monetary values)	4.0		
CHAROFF=*Value*	Specifies the number of characters to offset the column data from the alignment character specified in the CHAR property	4.0		
VALIGN=*Option* (TOP | MIDDLE | BOTTOM)	The vertical alignment of the table footer	4.0	4.0	
<TH> ... </TH>	The <TH> tag encloses the text that will appear in an individual table header cell.	1.0	2.0	1.1
ABBR=*Text*	Specifies an abbreviated name for the header cell, and used when displaying large tables on small screens	4.0		
ALIGN=*Option* (CENTER | CHAR | LEFT | RIGHT)	Specifies the horizontal alignment of header cell text	1.0	2.0	2.0
BACKGROUND=*Document*	Specifies a background image for the header cell		4.0	4.0
BGCOLOR=*Color*	Specifies a background color for the header cell	4.0	2.0	3.0
BORDERCOLOR=*Color*	Specifies the color of the header cell border		2.0	
BORDERCOLORDARK=*Color*	Specifies the color of the shaded edge of the header cell border		3.0	
BORDERCOLORLIGHT=*Color*	Specifies the color of the unshaded edge of the header cell border		3.0	

TAGS AND PROPERTIES	DESCRIPTION	HTML	IE	NETSCAPE
CHAR=*Character*	Specifies a character with which to align the values in the column (a period is usually used to align monetary values)	4.0		
CHAROFF=*Value*	Specifies the number of characters to offset the column data from the alignment character specified in the CHAR property	4.0		
COLSPAN=*Value*	Specifies the number of columns the header cell should span	1.0	2.0	2.0
HEADERS=*List*	Specifies of list of ID values that correspond to the header cells related to this cell	4.0		
HEIGHT=*Value*	The height of the header cell, in pixels or as a percentage of the display area	3.2	2.0	2.0
NOWRAP	Prohibits the browser from wrapping text in the header cell	3.0	2.0	2.0
ROWSPAN=*Value*	Specifies the number of rows the header cell should span	3.0	2.0	2.0
SCOPE=*Option* (COL | COLGROUP | ROW | ROWGROUP)	Specifies the table cells for which the current cell provides header information. A SCOPE value of COL indicates that the cell is a header for the rest of the column, a value of COLGROUP indicates that the cell is a header for the current column group, a value of ROW indicates that the cell is a header for the current row, and a value of ROWGROUP indicates that the cell is a header for the current row group.	4.0		
VALIGN=*Option* (TOP | MIDDLE | BOTTOM)	Specifies the vertical alignment of header cell text	3.0	2.0	2.0
WIDTH= *Value*	The width of the header cell in pixels or as a percentage of the width of the table	3.2	2.0	2.0
<THEAD> ... </THEAD>	The <THEAD> tag encloses header information that will be displayed in the table header when the table is printed on multiple pages.	3.0	3.0	
ALIGN=*Option* (LEFT | CENTER | RIGHT)	The horizontal alignment of the table header	3.0	3.0	
BGCOLOR=*Color*	Specifies a background color for the table cells within the <THEAD> tags		4.0	
CHAR=*Character*	Specifies a character with which to align the values in the table header columns (a period is usually used to align monetary values)	4.0		
CHAROFF=*Value*	Specifies the number of characters to offset the column data from the alignment character specified in the CHAR property	4.0		
VALIGN=*Option* (TOP | MIDDLE | BOTTOM)	The vertical alignment of the table header	3.0	3.0	

TAGS AND PROPERTIES	DESCRIPTION	HTML	IE	NETSCAPE
<TR> ... </TR>	The <TR> tag encloses table cells within a single row.	3.0	2.0	1.1
ALIGN=*Option* (LEFT | CENTER | RIGHT)	Specifies the horizontal alignment of text in the row	3.0	2.0	2.0
BGCOLOR=*Color*	Specifies a background color for the header cell	4.0	2.0	3.0
BORDERCOLOR=*Color*	Specifies the color of the header cell border		2.0	
BORDERCOLORDARK=*Color*	Specifies the color of the shaded edge of the header cell border		2.0	
BORDERCOLORLIGHT=*Color*	Specifies the color of the unshaded edge of the header cell border		2.0	
CHAR=*Character*	Specifies a character with which to align the values in the table row (a period is usually used to align monetary values)	4.0		
CHAROFF=*Value*	Specifies the number of characters to offset the column data from the alignment character specified in the CHAR property	4.0		
VALIGN=*Option* (TOP | MIDDLE | BOTTOM)	The vertical alignment of the text in the table row	3.0	2.0	2.0

EUDORA

Using the Eudora E-Mail Program

Eudora is an e-mail program that runs on your computer and communicates with an Internet mail server. You can use Eudora only if you are connected directly to the Internet on a university network (usually in a lab) or have a PPP or SLIP connection through an Internet service provider (ISP).

You can download and install a free version of Eudora from its publisher, Qualcomm, or from an Internet Web site such as DOWNLOAD.COM. You can install Eudora in one of three modes: Sponsored, Paid, and Light. In Sponsored mode, you will be able to use a fully functional copy of Eudora for free, but you will see advertisements in the program and in its messages, which subsidizes your free use of the program. In Paid mode, you pay a fee and get the fully functional software but do not see any advertisements. The Light mode of Eudora is free and provides users with basic program features but does not display any ads.

You can use any of the three Eudora versions to complete the steps in this appendix, which were written using the Light version of Eudora 5.1. A link to the Qualcomm home page appears in the Student Online Companion Web page for Appendix E. You can set the program mode for Eudora after installing it by clicking Help on the menu bar, clicking Payment & Registration, and then clicking the button for the mode that you want to use.

Note: The steps in this appendix assume that you have read and understand Session 3.1 in Tutorial 3, which covers basic e-mail concepts, and that you have installed Eudora on your computer.

To start and initialize Eudora for use on a public computer:

1. Click the **Start** button on the taskbar, point to **Programs**, point to **Eudora**, and then click **Eudora**. The Eudora program window opens.

   TROUBLE? If you do not see Eudora on your Programs menu, then Eudora is not installed on your computer, or it is installed in a different location. Ask your instructor or technical support person for help.

   TROUBLE? If a Note dialog box opens and asks if you want to change Eudora to your default mail program, click the No button.

   TROUBLE? If the New Account Wizard dialog box opens, click the Cancel button to close it.

   TROUBLE? If the Tip of the Day dialog box opens, click the Close button to close it.

2. If necessary, maximize the Eudora program window.

3. Click **Tools** on the menu bar, and then click **Options** to open the Options dialog box. If necessary, click the **Getting Started** button in the Category list box to display the start-up options.

4. Click in the **Real name** text box, and then type your first and last name, separated by a space.

   TROUBLE? If your account information already appears in the Options dialog box, skip to Step 9.

5. Press the **Tab** key to move to the Return address text box, and then type your full e-mail address (such as sharonkikukawa@yahoo.com).

6. Press the **Tab** key to move to the Mail Server (Incoming) text box, and then type the address of your incoming mail server. Usually, the mail server address is the word *mail* or *pop*, followed by a period, and then the remainder of your domain address (such as pop.yahoo.com). Ask your instructor or technical support person for the correct incoming mail server name to use.

7. Press the **Tab** key to move to the Login Name text box, and then type your login name, which is the same as your user name or user ID. Type only your login name (such as sharonkikukawa), and not the domain name.

8. Press the **Tab** key to move to the SMTP Server (Outgoing) text box, and then type the address of your outgoing mail server. Usually, the mail server address is the word *mail* or *smtp* followed by a period, and then the remainder of your domain address (such as mail.yahoo.com). Ask your instructor or technical support person for the correct outgoing mail server name to use. Figure E-1 shows the completed Getting Started information for a user named Sharon Kikukawa.

| Figure E-1 | ACCOUNT INFORMATION FOR SHARON KIKUKAWA |

9. Click the **Checking Mail** button in the Category list box.

10. If necessary, click the **Save password** check box to clear it. Clearing the Save password check box prevents Eudora from remembering your password so other users on your computer cannot access your account information after you exit the program.

11. Click the **Incoming Mail** button in the Category list box.

12. Make sure that the **Leave mail on server** check box does not contain a check mark, so your downloaded messages are deleted from the server when you request them on your computer. When this option is selected, any mail you download and read also stays on the mail server so you can access the mail from any computer.

13. Click the **OK** button to save the new settings and close the Options dialog box.

Now that you have created your user account, you can use Eudora to send a message.

Creating a Message

You use the **Composition window** to send a message. The title bar first displays the text "No Recipient, No Subject" until you enter information into the message header. The title bar then displays the recipient's e-mail address and the subject of the message. The Composition window toolbar includes buttons that allow quick access to many message features, such as the priority (importance) of your message, text styles, and a Send button.

The message header in the Composition window contains the To, From, Subject, Cc, Bcc, and Attached fields. The message body appears below the message header and contains your message.

Note: In this tutorial, you will send messages to a real mailbox with the address sharonkikukawa@yahoo.com. Follow the instructions carefully and use the correct address. Messages sent to this mailbox are deleted without being opened or read.

To send a message using Eudora:

1. Click the **New Message** button on the toolbar. Eudora opens the Composition window. The insertion point is positioned in the To field of the message header for you.

2. In the To field, type **sharonkikukawa@yahoo.com**, which is the recipient's full e-mail address consisting of a user name and domain name separated by the @ sign. Notice that the From field already contains your full e-mail address.

3. Press the **Tab** key to move to the Subject field, and then type **Eudora Test**.

4. Press the **Tab** key to move to the Cc field, and then type your full e-mail address so you will receive a copy of the message that you send.

TROUBLE? If you make a typing mistake, use the arrow keys to move the insertion point to a previous line, or within a line, and then correct the mistake. If the arrow keys do not move the insertion point up or down in the message header, press Shift + Tab or the Tab key to move the insertion point up or down, respectively.

5. Press the **Tab** key twice to move the insertion point to the message body, and then type **Please let me know when you receive this message. I'm testing Eudora and want to make sure that it is working properly.**

6. Press the **Enter** key twice to insert a blank line, and then type your first and last names to sign the message. See Figure E-2.

| Figure E-2 | SENDING A MESSAGE |

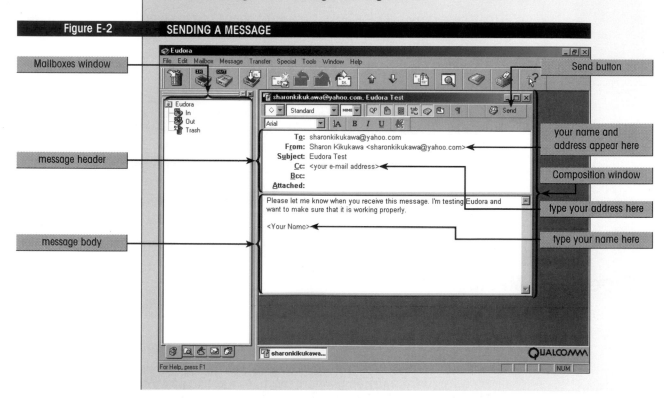

Before sending the message, you will verify that the Eudora options for sending a message are set correctly. Before sending any message, make sure that you verify the message body, the recipient's address, and the Cc address to ensure they are correct.

To check your mail send options and send your message:

1. Click **Tools** on the menu bar, click **Options**, and then click the **Sending Mail** button in the Category list to display the options shown in Figure E-3.

Figure E-3	CHECKING MAIL OPTIONS

Options

Category:

- Getting Started
- Checking Mail
- Incoming Mail
- **Sending Mail**
- Composing Mail

Return address:
`sharonkikukawa@yahoo.com`

Domain to add to unqualified addresses:

SMTP server:
`mail.yahoo.com`

☑ Allow authentication
☑ Immediate send
☑ Send on check

Secure Sockets when Sending
If Available, STARTTLS   Last SSL Info

OK   Cancel

your address and server information appear here

select this option to send messages immediately

Your message might not be sent to the mail server immediately, depending on how Eudora is configured. Eudora might queue the message and send it later at your command, or it might send the message when you exit the program. If you clear the Immediate send check box, Eudora will send your mail when you check for new messages. You will configure your program to send mail immediately after clicking the Send button.

2. If necessary, click the **Immediate send** check box to select it, and then click the **OK** button to close the Options dialog box.

3. Click the **Send** button on the Composition window toolbar to send the message.

TROUBLE? If the Enter Password dialog box opens, type the password for your mail account in the Password text box, and then click the OK button.

Now that you've sent a message, you can check for new mail.

Receiving Mail

Eudora can save delivered mail in any of several standard or custom mailboxes on your PC. Depending on your configuration, Eudora periodically communicates with the mail server to see if you have new mail. When you start Eudora, you enter a password so that Eudora can check to see if you have any new mail messages. Asterisks appear as you type each character to hide your password. After clicking the OK button, Eudora requests that the mail server deliver your new mail to your PC. Within a few seconds, any new messages appear in the In mailbox.

To check for new mail messages:

1. Click the **Check Mail** button on the toolbar to retrieve your new mail messages. (Refer to Figure E-4 for the location of this button.) After a few moments, any new mail messages are transferred to your PC and appear in your In mailbox.

TROUBLE? If the Enter Password dialog box opens, type the password for your mail account in the Password text box, and then click the OK button.

TROUBLE? If a New Mail! dialog box opens, click the OK button.

TROUBLE? If you do not receive any messages, then you either did not receive any new mail or you might be looking in the wrong mailbox. If necessary, double-click the In mailbox in the Mailboxes window. If you still don't have any mail messages, wait a few moments, and then repeat Step 1 until you receive a message.

TROUBLE? If you do not see the Mailboxes window on the left side of the Eudora window, click Tools on the menu bar, and then click Mailboxes.

2. Click the **Maximize** button on the In mailbox window to maximize it. Figure E-4 shows that you received a new message.

Figure E-4	RECEIVING A NEW MESSAGE

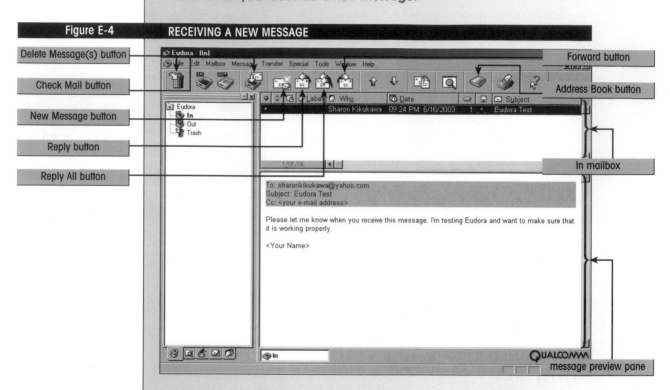

message preview pane

In the In mailbox and in other mailboxes, unread messages contain a dot in the first column. On the left side of the window is a list of available mailboxes, including the In, Out, and Trash mailboxes. You can create, delete, or rename mailboxes. Mailboxes let you organize your mail by type; you might create different mailboxes to store messages from different individuals or to group messages by project.

3. Double-click the **Eudora Test** message summary in the In mailbox to open the message.

4. Read the message, and then click the **Close** button on the menu bar to return to the In mailbox.

You can save new messages in different mailboxes by right-clicking the message summary in the list of messages, pointing to Transfer on the shortcut menu, and then clicking the mailbox to which to transfer the message. For now, you will leave the new message in your In mailbox.

Printing a Message

To print an e-mail message, select the message in the list of messages that you want to print, click the Print button on the toolbar, and then use the Print dialog box to select the desired print options.

> ### To print an e-mail message:
>
> 1. If necessary, click the **Eudora Test** message summary in the list of messages to select it.
>
> 2. Click the **Print** button on the toolbar. The Print dialog box opens. You can use this dialog box to change the default printer, the number of copies to print, or the pages to print, if necessary.
>
> 3. If necessary, select your printer, and then click the **Print** button (or the **OK** button) to print the message.

Your message is printed. Next, you'll transfer the message to a new mailbox.

Filing a Message

Eudora mailboxes provide a convenient way to file your e-mail messages by category. You'll create a new mailbox named Sharon Kikukawa in which to store the message you sent to Sharon. You can move mail from the In mailbox to any other mailbox to file it.

> ### To create a new mailbox and transfer a message to it:
>
> 1. Click **Mailbox** on the menu bar, and then click **New**. The New Mailbox dialog box opens.
>
> 2. In the Name the new mailbox text box, type **Sharon Kikukawa**, and then click the **OK** button. The Sharon Kikukawa mailbox is added to the Mailboxes window. When you create a new mailbox, its name is also added to the Transfer menu so you can transfer messages to it.
>
> 3. Click **Transfer** on the menu bar. The Transfer menu contains a list of your Eudora mailboxes.
>
> 4. Click →**Sharon Kikukawa** on the Transfer menu. The Eudora Test message is transferred from the In mailbox to the Sharon Kikukawa mailbox.

You also can create a new mailbox and transfer mail to it in one step by selecting the message to transfer, clicking Transfer on the menu bar, clicking New, typing a new name in the Name the new mailbox text box, and then clicking the OK button. Eudora will create the folder and transfer the new message to it at the same time.

Forwarding a Message

You can forward any message that you receive to one or more recipients. To forward a mail message to another user, open the mailbox containing the message, select the message, and then click the Forward button on the toolbar. Your e-mail address and name appear in the

From field of the message header, and the Subject field includes the word "Fwd" to indicate a forwarded message. Type the recipient's e-mail address in the To field and then click the Send button in the Composition window to send the message.

Replying to a Message

When you reply to a message, Eudora automatically creates a new message addressed to the sender, adds the word "Re" to the Subject field, and inserts the text of the sender's original message. To reply to a message, select the message to which you are replying, and then click the Reply button on the toolbar. To reply to the sender's message and to all addresses listed in that original message, click the Reply All button on the toolbar.

Deleting a Message

To prevent you from inadvertently deleting important messages, Eudora requires you to complete two steps to delete a message from your PC. First, you temporarily delete a message by placing it in the Trash mailbox. Then you permanently delete the message by emptying the trash.

To delete the message and mailbox, and then empty the trash:

1. Double-click the **Sharon Kikukawa** mailbox to open it, and then click the **Eudora Test** message, if necessary. You can select more than one message by holding down the Ctrl key and then clicking each message.

2. Click the **Delete Message(s)** button on the toolbar. You also can press the Delete key to delete selected message(s). The deleted message is sent to the Trash mailbox.

   TROUBLE? If you accidentally send a message to the Trash mailbox, double-click the Trash mailbox to open it, select the message that you need to restore, click Transfer on the menu bar, and then click the mailbox where you want to store the message.

3. Right-click the **Sharon Kikukawa** mailbox, and then click **Delete** on the shortcut menu to delete the mailbox that you created.

   To delete the message and mailbox permanently, you need to empty the trash.

4. Click **Special** on the menu bar, and then click **Empty Trash**. A warning dialog box opens to confirm your deletion.

   TROUBLE? If the warning dialog box does not open, this feature has been disabled on your system. Skip the next step.

5. Click the **Yes** button to empty the trash. After you empty the trash, you cannot recover the deleted items.

Even after you delete a message, the deleted message still occupies space. Normally, Eudora recovers this space as you send and receive messages. However, you can recover this space at once by clicking the Compact Mailboxes command on the Special menu.

You can set Eudora to warn you when you are about to transfer unread or unsent messages to the Trash mailbox. If you hear a warning sound or see a warning message box when you attempt to empty the Trash mailbox, check to make sure you have read all the messages before permanently deleting them. When Eudora finds unread mail in the Trash mailbox, the mailbox name appears in bold type. If this occurs, open the Trash mailbox and read any bolded messages.

Maintaining **an Address Book**

You can use an address book to create individual and group addresses. A group address is a single nickname that represents more than one individual e-mail address. When you want to send a message to someone listed in your address book, whether an individual or a group, you can type that person's nickname or full name, and Eudora will address the message automatically.

To create an address book entry:

1. Click the **Address Book** button on the toolbar to open the Address Book window.

2. Click the **New** button in the left side of the Address Book window. A new entry named "Untitled" is added to the Address Book and the fields for inserting a new address appear on the right side of the window.

3. In the Nickname text box, type **Sharon**, and then press the **Tab** key to move the insertion point to the Full Name text box.

4. Type **Sharon Kikukawa** in the Full Name text box, press the **Tab** key to move to the First Name text box and type **Sharon**, press the **Tab** key twice and then type **Kikukawa** in the Last Name text box.

5. Press the **Tab** key, and then type **sharonkikukawa@yahoo.com**. The completed entry for Sharon appears in Figure E-5.

| Figure E-5 | NEW ENTRY ADDED TO THE ADDRESS BOOK |

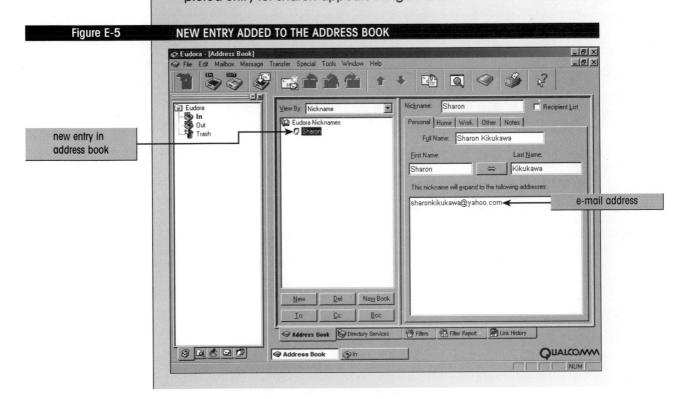

new entry in address book

e-mail address

> The entry is complete, so you can close the Address Book window and save your changes.
>
> **6.** Click the **Close** button on the menu bar to close the Address Book window, and then click the **Yes** button to save your changes. You return to the In mailbox.

You create a group address in a similar way—you open the Address Book, click the New button on the left side of the window, type the group's nickname in the Nickname text box, type the group's full name in the Full Name text box, and then type the e-mail address for each person in the group, separated by commas. Make sure that you save the group by closing the Address Book window and saving changes, or by clicking File on the menu bar, and then clicking Save.

Exiting Eudora

If you are using Eudora on a public computer, you should delete your user information from the program before exiting it and logging off your Internet connection, so other users won't see your stored user name and mail server information.

> ### To delete your mail account and exit Eudora:
>
> **1.** Click **Tools** on the menu bar, and then click **Options**. The Options dialog box opens.
>
> **2.** Click the **Getting Started** button in the Category list box, select your name in the Real name text box, and then press the **Delete** key.
>
> **3.** Repeat Step 2 to delete your Return address, Mail Server (Incoming) Login Name, and SMTP Server (Outgoing) names.
>
> **4.** Click the **OK** button to save your changes and close the Options dialog box.
>
> After deleting your personal information, you can exit Eudora.
>
> **5.** Click **File** on the menu bar, and then click **Exit**. Eudora closes.
>
> **6.** If necessary, log off your Internet connection.

BROWSER BASICS

With Netscape Navigator Version 4.7

Version 4.7 of the Netscape Navigator browser is still being used by many people and it is still being supported by the Netscape division of AOL. The current version of the browser at the time of publication is version 4.79. In this appendix, the figures reflect Netscape version 4.79, although the steps should work with any version 4.7 Netscape browser. You can use this appendix after completing Session 2.1; the case used in Tutorial 2, Browser Basics, continues in this appendix. You will learn how to configure the Netscape Navigator version 4.7 Web browser and use it to display Web pages and follow hyperlinks to other Web pages. You will learn how to copy text and images from Web pages and how to mark pages so you can return to them easily.

Starting **Netscape Navigator**

To be effective in searching the Web for the Sunset Wind Quintet, Maggie is sure that you will want to become familiar with Netscape Navigator, which is part of a suite of programs called Netscape Communicator. The other programs in the Communicator suite provide e-mail, discussion groups, real-time collaboration, and Web page creation tools. This overview assumes that you have Navigator installed on your computer. You should have your computer turned on so you can see the Windows desktop.

To start Navigator:

1. Click the **Start** button on the taskbar, point to **Programs**, point to **Netscape Communicator**, and then click **Netscape Navigator**. After a moment, Navigator opens.

   TROUBLE? If you cannot find Netscape Communicator on the Programs menu, check to see if a Netscape Navigator shortcut icon appears on the desktop, and then double-click it. If you do not see the shortcut icon, ask your instructor or technical support person for help. The program might be installed in a different folder on the computer you are using.

2. If the program does not fill the screen entirely, click the **Maximize** button on the Navigator program's title bar. Your screen should look like Figure F-1.

Figure F-1 NETSCAPE NETCENTER HOME PAGE

TROUBLE? Figure F-1 shows the Netscape Netcenter home page, which is the page that Netscape Navigator opens the first time it starts. Your computer might be configured to open to a different Web page or no page at all.

TROUBLE? If necessary, click View on the menu bar, point to Show, and if Personal Toolbar has a check next to it, click Personal Toolbar to deselect the check mark so your screen looks like Figure F-1.

TROUBLE? If a floating component bar, like the one shown in Figure F-2, appears anywhere in your window, click its Close button to anchor it to the right edge of the status bar.

Figure F-2 NETSCAPE COMMUNICATOR FLOATING COMPONENT BAR

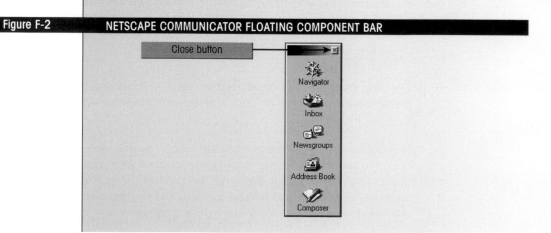

Now that you understand how to start Navigator, you tell Maggie that you are ready to start using it to find information on the Internet. To find information, you need to know how the Navigator toolbars and menu commands work.

Using the Navigation Toolbar and Menu Commands

The Navigation toolbar includes 11 buttons that execute frequently used commands for browsing the Web. Figure F-3 shows the Navigation toolbar buttons and describes their functions. (Depending on which version of Navigator you are using, you might see different toolbar buttons. Use online Help to get more information about buttons not pictured in Figure F-3.)

Figure F-3	NAVIGATION TOOLBAR BUTTONS	
BUTTON	**BUTTON NAME**	**DESCRIPTION**
Back	Back	Moves to the last previously visited Web page
Forward	Forward	Moves to the next previously visited Web page
Reload	Reload	Reloads the current page
Home	Home	Loads the program's defined start page
Search	Search	Opens a Web page that has hyperlinks to Web search engines and directories
Netscape	My Netscape	Opens a version of the Netscape's Netcenter page that you can customize
Print	Print	Prints the current Web page
Security	Security	Shows security information about the Web page that is currently displayed
Shop	Shop	Opens the Netscape Shopping directory page
Stop	Stop	Stops the transfer of a new Web page
N	Netscape Home Page (Netcenter)	Opens the Netscape Netcenter page

In addition to the toolbar buttons, the Navigation toolbar contains a toolbar tab that you can click to hide the toolbar so the window has more room to display a Web page in the Web page area. You can hide both the Navigation and Location toolbars so that the toolbar tabs fold up and remain visible, or you can hide the toolbars completely by using the options on the View menu, as you will see next.

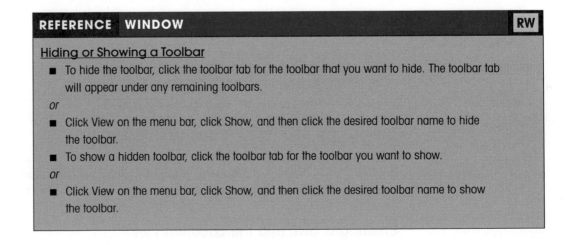

REFERENCE WINDOW   **RW**

Hiding or Showing a Toolbar
- To hide the toolbar, click the toolbar tab for the toolbar that you want to hide. The toolbar tab will appear under any remaining toolbars.

or

- Click View on the menu bar, click Show, and then click the desired toolbar name to hide the toolbar.
- To show a hidden toolbar, click the toolbar tab for the toolbar you want to show.

or

- Click View on the menu bar, click Show, and then click the desired toolbar name to show the toolbar.

> ### *To hide the Navigation toolbar and then show it again:*
>
> **1.** Click the **Navigation toolbar** tab, which appears on the left edge of the Navigation toolbar. The toolbar disappears and its toolbar tab appears under the Location toolbar.
>
> **2.** Move the pointer to the Navigation toolbar tab below the Location toolbar and notice that the message indicates that you are pointing to the Navigation toolbar.
>
> **3.** Click the **Navigation toolbar** tab. The Navigation toolbar appears above the Location toolbar.

You can use the toolbar tabs to hide or show the toolbars quickly. However, if you want to hide the toolbars and their tabs, you must use the View menu. The View menu commands are toggles. A **toggle** is like a push button switch on a television set; you press the button once to turn on the television and press it a second time to turn it off.

> ### *To hide the Navigation toolbar using the View menu:*
>
> **1.** Click **View** on the menu bar.
>
> **2.** Point to **Show** and then click **Navigation Toolbar** to hide the Navigation toolbar and its toolbar tab. To see the Navigation toolbar again, you repeat the same steps.
>
> TROUBLE? If the Navigation Toolbar does not have a check mark next to it, then the Navigation toolbar already is hidden. Go to Step 3.
>
> **3.** Click **View** on the menu bar, point to **Show**, and then click **Navigation Toolbar** to show the toolbar again.

Now you are ready to use the Navigation toolbar buttons and the menu commands to browse the Web.

Using **the Location Toolbar Elements**

Maggie explains that the Location toolbar contains five elements: the **Location toolbar** tab, the **Location** field, the **Page proxy** icon, the **Bookmarks** button, and the **What's Related** button. Figure F-4 shows these five elements.

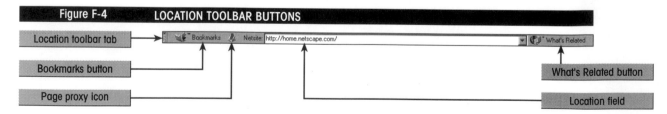

Figure F-4   LOCATION TOOLBAR BUTTONS

Hiding and Showing the Location Toolbar

You can click the Location toolbar tab or use the View menu commands to hide and show the Location toolbar, just as when you used the Navigation toolbar tab and the View menu commands to hide and show the Navigation toolbar. Clicking the Location toolbar tab hides the toolbar but keeps the tab visible so it folds up under any visible toolbars.

Entering a URL into the Location Field

Maggie tells you to use the Location field to enter URLs directly into Netscape Navigator. Marianna gave you the URL for the Miami Wind Quintet, so you can see its Web page.

REFERENCE WINDOW   **RW**

<u>Entering a URL in the Location Field</u>
- Click at the end of the current text in the Location field, and then backspace over the text that you want to delete.
- Type the URL to which you want to go.
- Press the Enter key to load the URL's Web page in the browser window.

To load the Miami Wind Quintet's Web page:

1. Click in the Location field; if it already contains text, click at the end of the text, and then press the **Backspace** key to delete it.

   TROUBLE? Make sure that you delete all of the text in the Location field so the text you type in Step 2 will be correct.

2. Type **www.course.com/newperspectives/internet3/** in the Location field to go to the Student Online Companion page on the Course Technology Web site.

3. Press the **Enter** key. The Location field's label changes from "Location" to "Go to" and the Student Online Companion Web page loads, as shown in Figure F-5. When the entire page has loaded, the Location field's label will change back to "Location."

| Figure F-5 | STUDENT ONLINE COMPANION WEB PAGE |

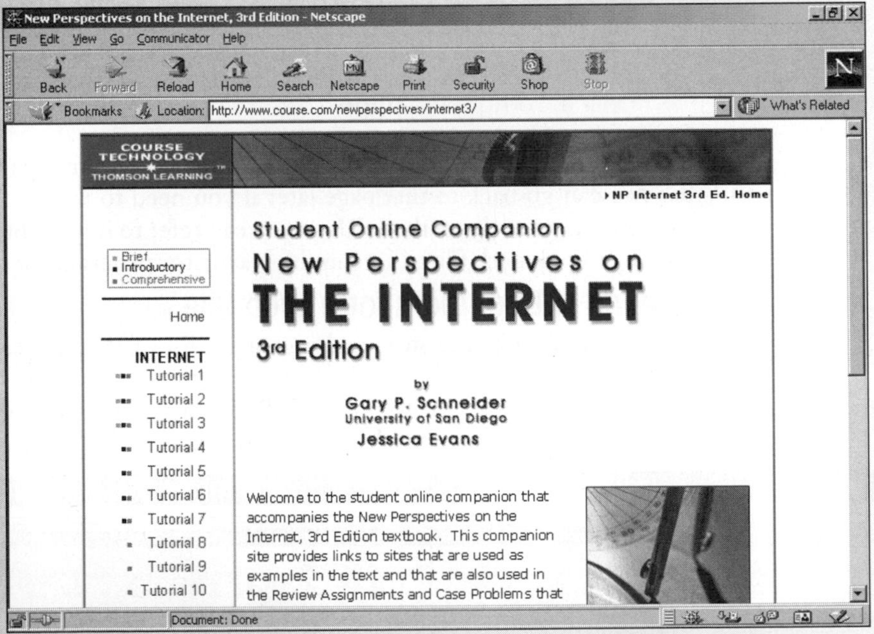

TROUBLE? If a Dial-Up Networking dialog box opens after you press the Enter key, click the Connect button. You must have an Internet connection to complete the steps in this appendix.

4. Click the link for the book you are using to open the main page, click the **Appendix F** link to open the page that contains the links for this appendix.

5. Click the **Miami Wind Quintet** link. The Web page opens, as shown in Figure F-6.

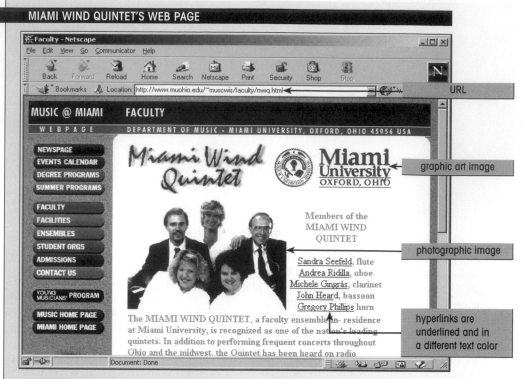

Figure F-6   MIAMI WIND QUINTET'S WEB PAGE

TROUBLE? The Miami Wind Quintet might change its Web page, so your Web page might look different from the one shown in Figure F-6. If this Web page is deleted from the server, you might see an entirely different Web page. However, the steps should work the same.

6. Read the Web page, and then click the **Back** button to return to the Student Online Companion page.

You like the format of the Miami Wind Quintet's home page, so you want to make sure that you can go back to that page later if you need to review its contents. Maggie explains that you can write down the URL so you can refer to it later, but an easier way is to store the URL in a bookmark file to save in the Navigator program for future use.

Creating a Bookmark for a Web Site

You use a **bookmark** to store and organize a list of Web pages that you have visited so you can return to them easily. You use the **Bookmarks** button to add new bookmarks, to open the Bookmarks menu, or to open the Bookmarks window. Figure F-7 shows a Bookmarks menu that contains bookmarks that are sorted into categories according to the user's needs.

Figure F-7   USING THE BOOKMARKS BUTTON TO OPEN THE BOOKMARKS MENU

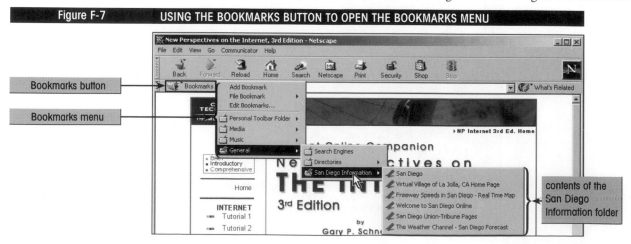

The hierarchical structure of the bookmark file is easy to see in Figure F-7. The six Web pages shown in the San Diego Information folder provide information about San Diego.

A **Bookmarks window** provides the same information as the cascading Bookmarks menus, but it also includes tools for editing and rearranging the bookmarks. For example, you can use the Bookmarks window menu commands to create new folders, or you can use the drag and drop method to move Web pages to another folder or to move folders to new locations. Figure F-8 shows the same set of bookmarks in the Bookmarks window, where you can see more details about the user's bookmarks and their organization.

Figure F-8	EXAMINING BOOKMARKS IN THE BOOKMARKS WINDOW

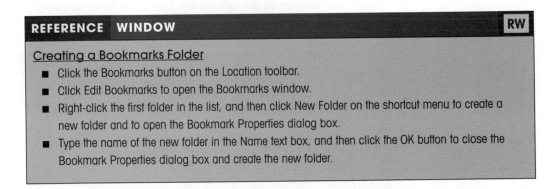

You decide to create a bookmark for the Miami Wind Quintet Web page. First, you will create a folder to store your bookmarks, and then you will save your bookmark in that folder. You might not work on the same computer again, so you will save a copy of the bookmark file to your Data Disk for future use.

REFERENCE WINDOW   RW

Creating a Bookmarks Folder
- Click the Bookmarks button on the Location toolbar.
- Click Edit Bookmarks to open the Bookmarks window.
- Right-click the first folder in the list, and then click New Folder on the shortcut menu to create a new folder and to open the Bookmark Properties dialog box.
- Type the name of the new folder in the Name text box, and then click the OK button to close the Bookmark Properties dialog box and create the new folder.

To create a new Bookmarks folder:

1. Click the **Bookmarks** button on the Location toolbar to open the Bookmarks menu, and then click **Edit Bookmarks** to open the Bookmarks window.

2. Right-click the first item in the Bookmarks window; usually, this item is "Main Bookmarks" or "Bookmarks for <name>," but it might have another title on your computer. After you right-click the first item, a shortcut menu opens.

3. Click **New Folder** on the shortcut menu to open the Bookmark Properties dialog box. The text "New Folder" appears selected in the Name text box. To change the new folder's name, you type the new name.

4. Type **Wind Quintet Information** in the Name text box, and then click the **OK** button to close the Bookmark Properties dialog box and create the new Wind Quintet Information folder in the bookmark file. The new folder should appear under the first item in the Bookmarks window, as shown in Figure F-9.

| Figure F-9 | CREATING A BOOKMARK FOLDER |

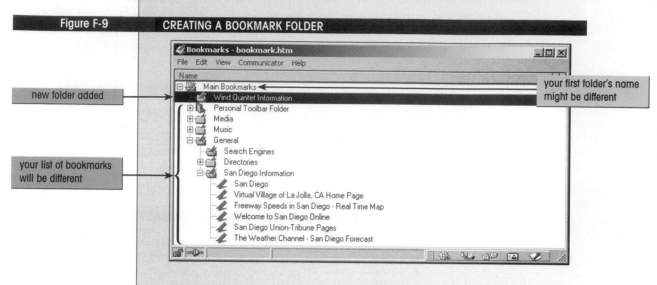

TROUBLE? It doesn't matter if your Wind Quintet Information folder appears in a different location—just make sure that the folder appears in the Bookmarks window.

5. Click the **Close** button on the Bookmarks window title bar to close the Bookmarks window.

Now that you have created a folder, you can save your bookmark for the Miami Wind Quintet's Web page in the new folder. However, first you must return to the Web page that you want to bookmark.

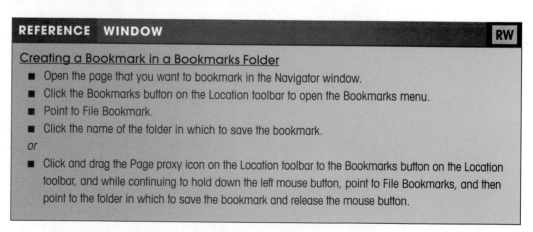

REFERENCE WINDOW   **RW**

Creating a Bookmark in a Bookmarks Folder
- Open the page that you want to bookmark in the Navigator window.
- Click the Bookmarks button on the Location toolbar to open the Bookmarks menu.
- Point to File Bookmark.
- Click the name of the folder in which to save the bookmark.

or

- Click and drag the Page proxy icon on the Location toolbar to the Bookmarks button on the Location toolbar, and while continuing to hold down the left mouse button, point to File Bookmarks, and then point to the folder in which to save the bookmark and release the mouse button.

To save a bookmark for a Web page in a folder:

1. Click the **Forward** button on the Navigation toolbar to return to the Miami Wind Quintet Web page.

2. Click the **Bookmarks** button on the Location toolbar to open the Bookmarks menu.

3. Point to **File Bookmark**, and then click the **Wind Quintet Information** folder. Now the bookmark is saved in the correct folder. You can test your bookmark by using the bookmark to visit the site.

4. Click the **Back** button on the Navigation toolbar to go to the previous Web page.

5. Click the Bookmarks button on the Location toolbar, point to Wind Quintet Information, and then click **Faculty**. The Miami Wind Quintet page opens in the browser, which means that you created the bookmark successfully.

   TROUBLE? If the Miami Wind Quintet page does not open, click Edit Bookmarks on the Bookmarks menu, make sure that you have the correct URL for the page, and then repeat the steps. If you still have trouble, ask your instructor or technical support person for help.

Because you might need to visit the Miami Wind Quintet page from another client computer, you can save your bookmark file on your Data Disk.

REFERENCE   WINDOW   **RW**

Saving a Bookmark to a Floppy Disk

- Click the Bookmarks button on the Location toolbar, and then click Edit Bookmarks to open the Bookmarks window.
- Click File on the menu bar, and then click Save As to open the Save bookmarks file dialog box.
- Click the Save in list arrow, and then change to the drive that contains your disk.
- Click the Save button to save the bookmark file and close the dialog box.

To store the revised bookmark file to your floppy disk:

1. Click the **Bookmarks** button on the Location toolbar, and then click **Edit Bookmarks** to open the Bookmarks window. When you save your bookmarks, you save all of the bookmarks, not just the one that you need: Netscape Navigator stores all of your bookmarks in a single file.

2. Click **File** on the menu bar of the Bookmarks window, and then click **Save As** to open the Save bookmarks file dialog box.

3. Click the **Save in** list arrow, change to the drive that contains your Data Disk (usually, this is 3½ **Floppy (A:)**), and then double-click the **Appendix.F** folder.

4. Make sure that **bookmark** appears in the File name text box, and then click the **Save** button.

   TROUBLE? Your computer might be configured to display file extensions, so you might see bookmark.htm in the File name text box, which is also correct.

   TROUBLE? If bookmark or bookmark.htm does not appear in the File name text box, click in the File name text box, type bookmark.htm, and then click the Save button.

5. Close the Bookmarks window.

When you use another computer, you can open the bookmark file from your Data Disk by starting Navigator, clicking the Bookmarks button on the Location toolbar, clicking Edit Bookmarks, clicking File on the menu bar, and then clicking Open Bookmarks File. Change to the drive that contains your Data Disk, and then open the bookmark.htm file from the disk. Your bookmark file will open in the Bookmarks window, and then you can use it as you practiced.

Hyperlink Navigation with the Mouse

Now you know how to use Navigator to find information that will help you with the Sunset Wind Quintet. Maggie tells you that the easiest way to move from one Web page to another is to use the mouse to click hyperlinks that the authors of Web pages embed in their HTML documents. You can also right-click the mouse on the background of a Web page to open a shortcut menu that includes navigation options.

To follow a hyperlink to a Web page and return using the mouse:

1. Click the **Back** button on the Navigation toolbar to go back to the Student Online Companion page, click the **Lewis Music** link to open that page, and then point to the **Instrument Accessories** hyperlink shown in Figure F-10 so your pointer changes to a pointing finger icon.

Figure F-10

LEWIS MUSIC HOME PAGE

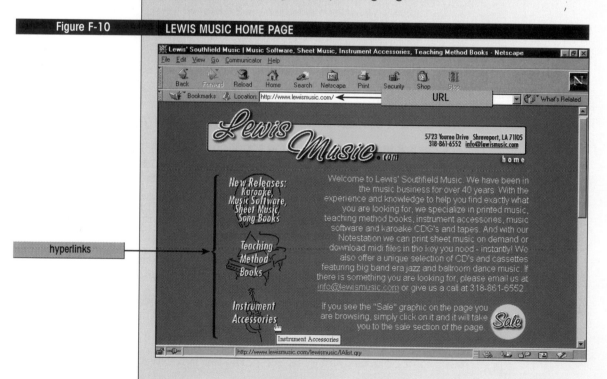

hyperlinks

2. Click the **Instrument Accessories** hyperlink to load the page. Watch the second panel in the status bar. When the shadow disappears, you know that Navigator has loaded the full page.

3. Right-click anywhere in the Web page area to open the shortcut menu, and then point to **Back**, as shown in Figure F-11.

Figure F-11   **USING THE SHORTCUT MENU TO GO BACK TO THE PREVIOUS PAGE**

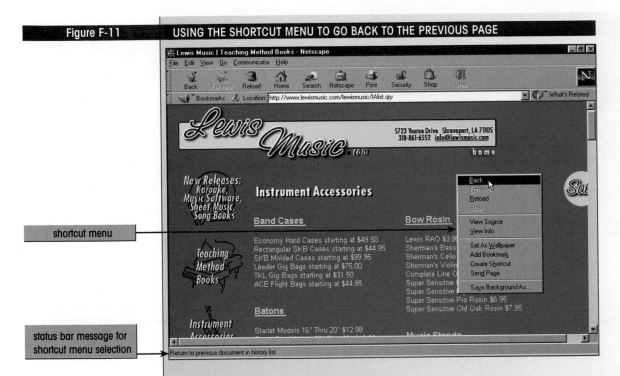

shortcut menu

status bar message for shortcut menu selection

TROUBLE? If you right-click a hyperlink, your shortcut menu will display a longer list than the one shown in Figure F-11, and the Back item will be third in the list instead of first. If you don't see the shortcut menu shown in Figure F-11, click anywhere outside of the shortcut menu to close it, and then repeat Step 3.

TROUBLE? Web pages change frequently, so the Instrument Accessories page you see might look different from the one shown in Figure F-11, but right-clicking anywhere in the Web page area will still work.

4. Click **Back** on the shortcut menu to go back to the Lewis Music home page.

5. Repeat Step 4 to return to the Student Online Companion page.

You are beginning to get a good sense of how to move from one Web page to another and back again, but Maggie tells you that you have mastered only one technique of many. She explains that the Navigation toolbar and the menu bar offer many tools for accessing and using Web sites.

Using the History List

In Session 2.1 of Tutorial 2 you learned that the Back and Forward buttons let you move to and from previously visited pages. These buttons duplicate the functions of the menu bar's Go command. Clicking Go opens a menu that lets you move back and forward through a portion of the history list and allows you to choose a specific Web page from that list. You also can open a full copy of the history list.

To view the history list for this session:

1. Click **Communicator** on the menu bar, point to **Tools**, and then click **History** to open the History window, as shown in Figure F-12.

Figure F-12	VIEWING THE HISTORY LIST

entries in your history
list will be different

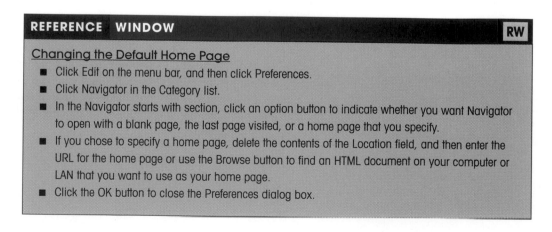

TROUBLE? The History window that appears on your computer might be a different size and contain different entries from the one that appears in Figure F-12. You can resize the window by clicking and dragging its edges. You can resize the columns in the window by clicking and dragging the edges of the column headers.

To return to a page, double-click the page in the list. You can change the way that pages are listed by using the commands on the View menu; for example, you can list the pages by title or in the order in which you visited them.

2. Click the **Close** button on the History window title bar to close it.

Reloading a Web Page

You learned in Session 2.1 of Tutorial 2 that clicking the **Reload** button on the Navigator toolbar loads again the Web page that currently appears in the browser window. You can force Navigator to get the page from the Web server by pressing the Shift key when you click the Reload button.

Going Home

The **Home** button displays the home (or start) page for your copy of Navigator. You can go to the Netscape Netcenter page, which is the software's default home page, by clicking the **Netscape Home Page** button on the Navigator toolbar. You cannot change the page that loads by clicking the Navigator Home Page button, but you can change the default URL that opens when you click the Home button by using the Preferences dialog box.

REFERENCE WINDOW   **RW**

Changing the Default Home Page
- Click Edit on the menu bar, and then click Preferences.
- Click Navigator in the Category list.
- In the Navigator starts with section, click an option button to indicate whether you want Navigator to open with a blank page, the last page visited, or a home page that you specify.
- If you chose to specify a home page, delete the contents of the Location field, and then enter the URL for the home page or use the Browse button to find an HTML document on your computer or LAN that you want to use as your home page.
- Click the OK button to close the Preferences dialog box.

To modify the Home navigation button settings:

1. Click **Edit** on the menu bar, and then click **Preferences** to open that dialog box.

2. Click **Navigator** in the Category list. See Figure F-13.

Figure F-13   CHANGING THE HOME PAGE

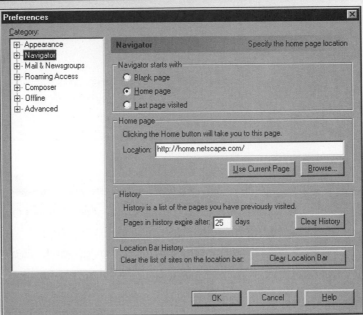

3. To have Navigator open with a **Blank page**, the **Home page** you specify, or the **Last page visited**, click the corresponding option button in the Navigator starts with section of the Preferences dialog box.

TROUBLE? You might not be able to change these and the following settings if you are using a computer in your school lab or at your office. Some organizations set the home page defaults on all of their computers and lock those settings.

To specify a home page, select the text in the Location field in the Home page section of the Preferences dialog box shown in Figure F-13 and enter the URL of the Web page you would like to use. If you loaded the Web page that you would like to be your new home page into Navigator before beginning these steps, you can click the Use Current Page button to place its URL into the Location field. You also can specify an HTML document on your computer or LAN by clicking the Browse button and selecting the disk drive and folder location of that HTML document.

4. Click the **Cancel** button to close the dialog box without making any changes.

Printing a Web Page

The **Print** button on the Navigation toolbar lets you print the current Web frame or page. You can use this button to make a printed copy of most Web pages. (Some Web pages disable the Print command.)

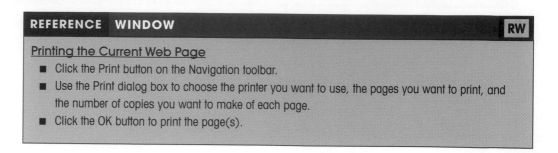

REFERENCE WINDOW   **RW**

<u>Printing the Current Web Page</u>
- Click the Print button on the Navigation toolbar.
- Use the Print dialog box to choose the printer you want to use, the pages you want to print, and the number of copies you want to make of each page.
- Click the OK button to print the page(s).

To print a Web page:

1. Click in the main (right) frame of the Student Online Companion page to select it.

2. Click the **Print** button on the Navigation toolbar to open the Print dialog box shown in Figure F-14.

Figure F-14   PRINT DIALOG BOX

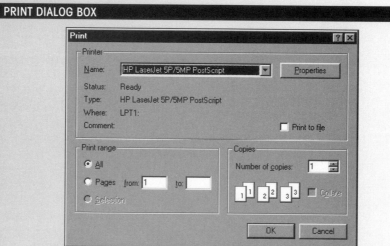

3. Make sure that the printer in the Name text box shows the printer you want to use; if necessary, click the Name list arrow to change the selection.

4. Click the Pages option button in the Print range section of the Print dialog box, type 1 in the from text box, press the **Tab** key, and then type 1 in the to text box to specify that you want to print only the first page.

5. Make sure that the Number of copies text box shows that you want to print one copy.

6. Click the **OK** button to print the Web page and close the Print dialog box.

Changing the Settings for Printing a Web Page

You already have seen how to print Web pages using the basic options available in the Print dialog box. You also learned how to store a bookmark so you can return to a Web page later. Usually, the default settings in the Print dialog box are fine for printing a Web page, but you can use the Page Setup dialog box to change the way a Web page prints. Figure F-15 shows the Page Setup dialog box, and Figure F-16 describes its settings.

Figure F-15	PAGE SETUP OPTIONS FOR PRINTING WEB PAGES

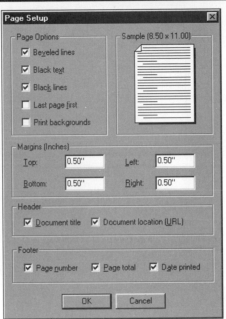

Figure F-16	PAGE SETUP DIALOG BOX OPTIONS

OPTION	DESCRIPTION	USE
Black text	Prints all of the text on a Web page as black	Use when the Web page contains text set in light colors, so it will be legible when printed.
Black lines	Prints all of the lines on a Web page as black	Use when the Web page contains light-colored lines, so they will be legible when printed.
Last page first	Reverses the normal order in which pages are printed	Some printers eject pages face up. Using this setting will correctly collate the Web page printout.
Print backgrounds	Prints a Web page background, if there is one on the page	You should leave this option off unless you are using a color printer. Backgrounds can render text and images illegible, and dark colors can waste your printer's toner or ink.
Margins	Use to change the margins of the printed page	Normally, you should leave the default settings, but you can change the right, left, top, or bottom margins as needed.
Header	Prints the Web page's document title and/or document location (URL)	Selecting these options lets you print the name and location of the page for later reference.
Footer	Prints the Web page's page number, the total number of pages, or the date that the page is printed	Selecting these options provides a record of the page number, total number of pages, and the date that you printed the page.

When printing long Web pages, another print option that is extremely useful for saving paper is to reduce the font size of the Web pages before you print them. To do this, click Edit on the menu bar, click Preferences, click the Appearance category, click the Fonts category, and then use the Size list arrow to decrease the size of the font used in the Web page. See Figure F-17.

| Figure F-17 | USING THE PREFERENCES DIALOG BOX TO CHANGE THE WEB PAGE FONT SIZE |

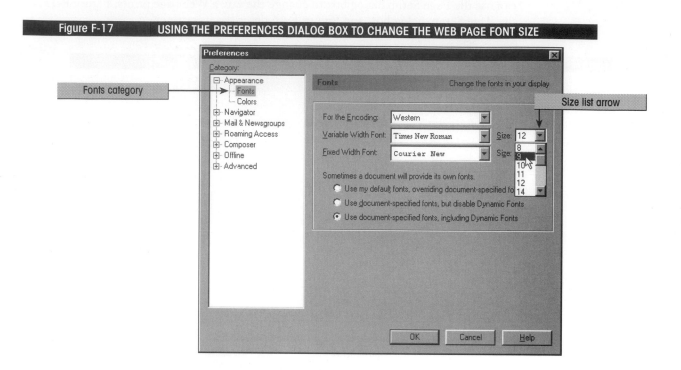

Checking Web Page Security Features

The **Security** button on the Navigation toolbar lets you check some of the security elements of a Web page. This button displays either an open padlock icon or a closed padlock icon. The icon on the Security button corresponds to the icon displayed in the left section of the status bar to indicate whether the Web page was encrypted during transmission from the Web server. **Encryption** is a way of scrambling and encoding data transmissions that reduces the risk that a person intercepting the Web page as it travels across the Internet can decode and read the page's contents. Web sites use encrypted transmission to send and receive information, such as credit card numbers, to ensure privacy. You can obtain more information about the details of the encryption used on a Web page by examining the Security Info window that opens when you click the Security button on the Navigation toolbar. Figure F-18 shows the Security Info window for an encrypted Web page after the user clicked the Security button on the Navigation toolbar.

Figure F-18	SECURITY INFO WINDOW FOR AN ENCRYPTED WEB PAGE

Netscape

Security Info

- **Security Info**
- **Passwords**
- **Navigator**
- **Messenger**
- **Java/JavaScript**
- **Certificates**
  - Yours
  - People
  - Web Sites
  - Signers
- **Cryptographic Modules**

Encryption

This page **was encrypted**. This means it was difficult for other people to view this page when it was loaded.

You can examine your copy of the certificate for this page and check the identity of the web site. To see the certificate for this web site, click **View Certificate**. For complete details on all the files on this page and their certificates, click **Open Page Info**.

View Certificate	Open Page Info

Verification

- Take a look at the page's Certificate.
- Make sure that this is the site you think it is. This page comes from

[OK] [Cancel] [Help]

Getting **Help in Netscape Navigator**

The Netscape Communicator suite includes a comprehensive online Help facility for all of the programs in the suite, including Navigator. You open the Help Contents window to use Help.

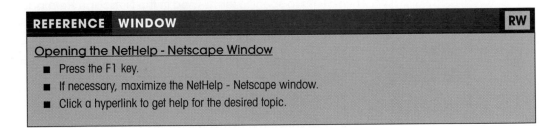

REFERENCE WINDOW   **RW**

Opening the NetHelp - Netscape Window
- Press the F1 key.
- If necessary, maximize the NetHelp - Netscape window.
- Click a hyperlink to get help for the desired topic.

To open the Navigator help window:

1. Press the **F1** key, and then click the **Maximize** button on the NetHelp - Netscape window, which provides help for all the programs in the Netscape Communicator Suite.

2. Click the **Browsing the Web** hyperlink to get help for the Navigator program. Examine the page shown in Figure F-19, and use the scroll box or scroll down button to move down the page.

Figure F-19 OPENING THE NETHELP - NETSCAPE WINDOW

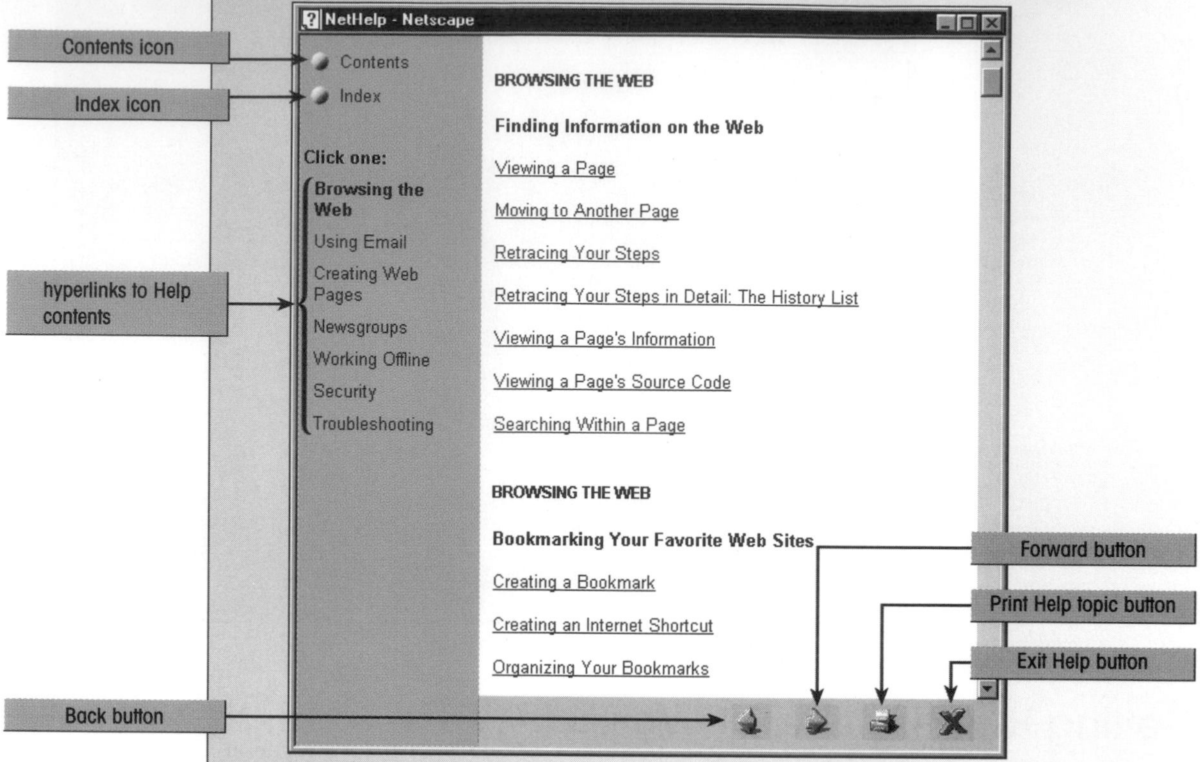

You can click any of the Contents hyperlinks to obtain help on the topics listed. You can also click the Index icon to obtain an alphabetized, searchable list of hyperlinks to specific terms used in the Netscape Help pages, or you can click the Find icon, which opens the standard Windows Find dialog box, and then enter search terms.

3. Click the **Close** button to close the NetHelp – Netscape window and return to Navigator.

You are now convinced that you have all of the tools you need to successfully find information on the Web. Marianna probably will be interested in seeing the Miami Wind Quintet Web page, but you are not sure if she will have Internet access while she's touring. Maggie says that you can save the Web page on disk, so Marianna can open the page locally in her Web browser using the files you saved on that disk.

Using **Navigator** to Save a Web Page

You have learned how to use most of the Navigator tools for loading Web pages and saving bookmarks. Now Maggie wants you to learn how to save a Web page. Sometimes, you will want to store entire Web pages on disk; at other times, you will only want to store selected portions of Web page text or particular graphics from a Web page.

Saving a Web Page

You like the Miami Wind Quintet's Web site and want to save the page on disk so you can send it to Marianna. That way, she can review it without having an Internet connection. To save a Web page, you must have the page open in Navigator.

REFERENCE WINDOW   **RW**

Saving a Web Page to a Floppy Disk
- Open the Web page in Navigator.
- Click File on the menu bar, and then click Save As to open the Save As dialog box.
- Click the Save in list arrow, and change to the drive on which to save the Web page.
- Accept the default filename, or change the filename, if you want; however, retain the file extension .htm or .html.
- Click the Save button to save the Web page to the floppy disk.

To save the Web page on your Data Disk:

1. Use your bookmark to return to the Miami Wind Quintet page.

2. Click **File** on the menu bar, and then click **Save As** to open the Save As dialog box.

3. Click the **Save in** list arrow, click the drive that contains your Data Disk (usually, this is **3½ Floppy (A:)**), and then double-click the **Appendix.F** folder. You will accept the default filename of mwq.html.

4. Click the **Save** button. Now the HTML document for the Miami Wind Quintet's home page is saved on your Data Disk. When you send it to Marianna, she can open her Web browser and then use the Open command on the File menu to open the Web page.

If the Web page contains graphics, such as photos, drawings, or icons, you should note that these items will not be saved with the HTML document. To save the graphics, right-click one in the browser window, click Save Image As, and then save the graphic to the same location as the HTML document. The graphics file is specified to appear in the HTML document as a hyperlink, so you might have to change the HTML code in the Web page to identify its location. Copying the graphics files to the same disk as the HTML document will *usually* work.

Saving Web Page Text to a File

Maggie suggests that you might want to know how to save portions of Web page text to a file so that you can save only the text from the Web page and use it in other programs. You will use WordPad to receive the text you will copy from a Web page, but any word processor or text editor will work.

Marianna just called to let you know that the quintet will play a concert in Grand Rapids on a Friday night, and she asks you to identify other opportunities for scheduling local concerts during the following weekend. Often, museums are willing to book small ensembles for weekend afternoon programs, and Marianna has given you the URL for the Grand Rapids Art Museum. You will visit the site and then get the museum's address and telephone number so you can contact it about scheduling a concert.

Copying Text from a Web Page to a WordPad Document

- Open the Web page in Navigator.
- Use the mouse pointer to select the text you want to copy.
- Click Edit on the menu bar, and then click Copy.
- Start WordPad or another word processor.
- Click Edit on the menu bar, and then click Paste.
- Click the Save button on the WordPad toolbar, and then save the file to the correct folder and drive using a filename that you specify.
- Click the Save button.

To copy text from a Web page and save it to a file:

1. Use the **Back** button to return to the Student Online Companion page, and then click the **Grand Rapids Art Museum** link to open that Web page in the browser window.

2. Click the **Information & Calendar** hyperlink to open the museum information page, and then click the **Map** hyperlink.

3. Scroll down to view the text below the map image. Click and drag the mouse pointer over the address and telephone number to select it, as shown in Figure F-20. The text changes color from black to blue as you click and drag the mouse pointer across it.

Figure F-20	SELECTING TEXT ON A WEB PAGE

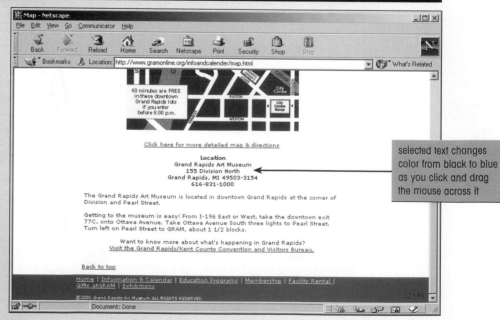

selected text changes color from black to blue as you click and drag the mouse across it

4. Click **Edit** on the menu bar, and then click **Copy** to copy the selected text to the Windows Clipboard.

Next, you can start WordPad and paste the copied text into a new document.

To start and copy the text into WordPad:

1. Click the **Start** button on the taskbar, point to **Programs**, point to **Accessories**, and then click **WordPad** to start the program and open a new document.

2. Click the **Paste** button on the WordPad toolbar to paste the text into the WordPad document, as shown in Figure F-21.

Figure F-21 **PASTING TEXT FROM A WEB PAGE INTO A WORDPAD DOCUMENT**

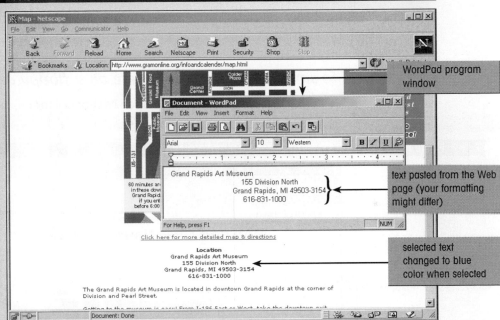

TROUBLE? If the WordPad toolbar does not appear, click View on the menu bar, click Toolbar to turn it on, and then repeat Step 2. Your WordPad program window might be a different size from the one shown in Figure F-21, which does not affect the steps.

3. Click the **Save** button on the WordPad toolbar to open the Save As dialog box.

4. Click the **Save in** list arrow, change to the drive that contains your Data Disk, and then double-click the **Appendix.F** folder.

5. Select the text in the File name text box, if any, type **GRAM-Address.txt**, and then click the **Save** button to save the file. Now the address and phone number of the museum are saved in a file on your Data Disk for future reference.

6. Click the **Close** button on the WordPad title bar to close it.

Later, you will contact the museum. As you examine the Web page, you decide that Marianna might like to have a copy of the street map of the area surrounding the museum that is included on the page.

Saving a Web Page Graphic to Disk

You decide that the Web page with directions and transportation information might be helpful to Marianna, so you decide to save the map graphic on your disk. You can then send the file to Marianna so she has a resource for getting to the museum.

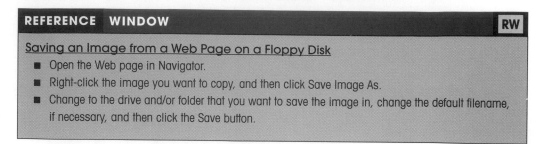

REFERENCE   WINDOW   RW

__Saving an Image from a Web Page on a Floppy Disk__
- Open the Web page in Navigator.
- Right-click the image you want to copy, and then click Save Image As.
- Change to the drive and/or folder that you want to save the image in, change the default filename, if necessary, and then click the Save button.

To save the street map image on a floppy disk:

1. Right-click the map image to open its shortcut menu, and then point to **Save Image As**, as shown in Figure F-22.

Figure F-22	SAVING THE MAP IMAGE TO DISK

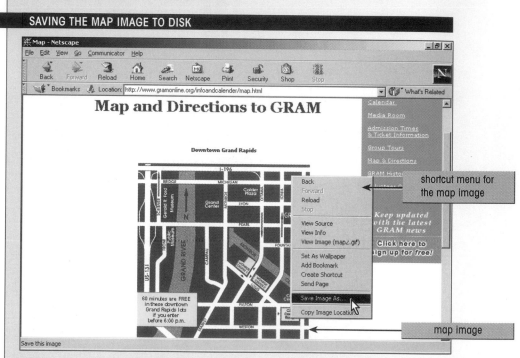

2. Click **Save Image As** on the shortcut menu to open the Save As dialog box.

3. Click the **Save in** list arrow, change to the drive that contains your Data Disk, and then double-click the **Appendix.F** folder, if necessary. You will accept the default filename, map2, so click the **Save** button. Now the image is saved on your Data Disk, and you can send the file to Marianna. Marianna can use her Web browser to open the image file and print it.

4. Close your Web browser and your dial-up connection, if necessary.

Now you can send a disk to Marianna so she has the Miami Wind Quintet Web page and a map that shows her how to get to the museum. Marianna is pleased to hear of your progress in using the Web to find information for the quintet.

TASK	PAGE #	RECOMMENDED METHOD	WHERE USED
HOTMAIL TASKS			
Address book, save to	WEB 3.67	See Reference Window: Adding a Contact to the Hotmail Address Book	Hotmail
Attached file, save	WEB 3.61	See Reference Window: Viewing and Saving an Attached File in Hotmail	Hotmail
Attached file, view	WEB 3.61	See Reference Window: Viewing and Saving an Attached File in Hotmail	Hotmail
Contact, add to address book	WEB 3.67	See Reference Window: Adding a Contact to the Hotmail Address Book	Hotmail
File, attach	WEB 3.59	Click the Add/Edit Attachments button, locate the file, click Attach	Hotmail
Group of contacts, add to address book	WEB 3.69	See Reference Window: Adding a Group to the Hotmail Address Book	Hotmail
Hotmail, start	WEB 3.53	Go to the MSN.com home page, click the Hotmail link, log into your account	
Hotmail account, set up	WEB 3.52	Start your browser, connect to the Internet, go to the MSN.com home page, click the Hotmail link, click the Sign Up link	Hotmail
Mail, compose	WEB 3.58	Open the Hotmail Home page, log into your account, click the Compose tab	Hotmail
Mail, delete	WEB 3.66	See Reference Window: Deleting an E-Mail Message Using Hotmail	Hotmail
Mail, delete permanently	WEB 3.66	Open the Trash Can folder, click the Empty Folder button, click OK	Hotmail
Mail, forward	WEB 3.64	See Reference Window: Forwarding an E-Mail Message Using Hotmail	Hotmail
Mail, print	WEB 3.65	Select the message, click the Printer Friendly Version link, click the Print button	Hotmail
Mail, read	WEB 3.60	Log into your Hotmail account, click the Inbox tab	Hotmail
Mail, receive	WEB 3.60	See Reference Window: Using Hotmail to Receive Messages	Hotmail
Mail, reply to all recipients	WEB 3.63	See Reference Window: Replying to a Message Using Hotmail	Hotmail
Mail, reply to sender	WEB 3.63	See Reference Window: Replying to a Message Using Hotmail	Hotmail
Mail, send	WEB 3.58	See Reference Window: Sending a Message Using Hotmail	Hotmail

TASK	PAGE #	RECOMMENDED METHOD	WHERE USED
Mail, spell check	WEB 3.59	Click the Tools list arrow, click Spell Check	Hotmail
Mail folder, create	WEB 3.64	Click the Home tab, click the View All Folders link in the Message Summary pane, click the Create New button, type the name of the folder, click OK	Hotmail
Mail folder, delete	WEB 3.67	See Reference Window: Deleting a Hotmail Folder	Hotmail

MICROSOFT INTERNET EXPLORER TASKS

TASK	PAGE #	RECOMMENDED METHOD	WHERE USED
Address book, open	WEB 3.30	Click the Addresses button	Outlook Express
Attached file, save	WEB 3.22	See Reference Window: Viewing and Saving an Attached File in Outlook Express	Outlook Express
Attached file, view	WEB 3.22	See Reference Window: Viewing and Saving an Attached File in Outlook Express	Outlook Express
Auto-Hide, turn on	WEB 2.19	Right-click the toolbar, click Auto-Hide	Internet Explorer
Contact, add to address book	WEB 3.30	See Reference Window: Adding a Contact to the Outlook Express Address Book	Outlook Express
Group of contacts, add to address book	WEB 3.32	See Reference Window: Adding a Group of Contacts to the Address Book	Outlook Express
Favorite, move to a new folder	WEB 2.24	See Reference Window: Moving an Existing Favorite into a New Folder	Internet Explorer
Favorites bar, open	WEB 2.21	Click the Favorites button	Internet Explorer
Favorites folder, create	WEB 2.22	See Reference Window: Creating a New Favorites Folder	Internet Explorer
File, attach in New Message window	WEB 3.18	Click the Attach button, locate the file, click Attach	Outlook Express
Full Screen, change to	WEB 2.19	Click View, click Full Screen	Internet Explorer
Help, get	WEB 2.32	See Reference Window: Opening Internet Explorer Help	Internet Explorer
History list, open	WEB 2.28	Click the History button	Internet Explorer
Home page, change default	WEB 2.28	See Reference Window: Changing the Default Home Page in Internet Explorer	Internet Explorer
Home page, return to	WEB 2.11	Click the Home button	Internet Explorer
Internet Explorer, close	WEB 2.10	Click the Close button	Internet Explorer, Outlook Express
Internet Explorer, start	WEB 2.16	Click the Start button, point to Programs, point to Internet Explorer, click Internet Explorer	
Internet Explorer window, maximize	WEB 2.10	Click the Maximize button	Internet Explorer, Outlook Express

TASK	PAGE #	RECOMMENDED METHOD	WHERE USED
Internet Explorer window, minimize	WEB 2.06	Click the Minimize button	Internet Explorer, Outlook Express
Internet Explorer window, restore maximized	WEB 2.10	Click the Restore button	Internet Explorer, Outlook Express
Lycos Chat, enter	WEB 8.11	See Reference Window: Entering a Lycos Chat	Internet Explorer
Mail, compose	WEB 3.18	Click the Create Mail button	Outlook Express
Mail, delete	WEB 3.29	See Reference Window: Deleting an E-Mail Message or a Folder in Outlook Express	Outlook Express
Mail, delete permanently	WEB 3.29	Open Deleted Items folder, click the message summary of the message to delete, click the Delete button, click the Yes button	Outlook Express
Mail, forward	WEB 3.26	See Reference Window: Forwarding an E-Mail Message Using Outlook Express	Outlook Express
Mail, move to another folder	WEB 3.27	Drag the message from the message list to a folder in the Folders pane	Outlook Express
Mail, print	WEB 3.28	Click the message summary, click the Print button, click the Print button again	Outlook Express
Mail, read	WEB 3.21	Click the message summary	Outlook Express
Mail, receive	WEB 3.21	Click the Send/Recv button	Outlook Express
Mail, reply to	WEB 3.25	See Reference Window: Replying to a Message Using Outlook Express	Outlook Express
Mail, send	WEB 3.18	See Reference Window: Sending a Message Using Outlook Express	Outlook Express
Mail, send and receive	WEB 3.20	Click the Send/Recv button	Outlook Express
Mail, spell check in New Message window	WEB 3.20	Click the Spelling button	Outlook Express
Mail account, set up	WEB 3.16	Click Tools, click Accounts, click the Mail tab, click the Add button, click Mail, follow steps in the Internet Connection Wizard	Outlook Express
Mail folder, create	WEB 3.27	Right-click the Inbox folder, click New Folder, type the name of the folder, click OK	Outlook Express
Mail folder, delete	WEB 3.29	See Reference Window: Deleting an E-Mail Message or a Folder in Outlook Express	Outlook Express
Mailing list, conceal your information in	WEB 7.15	See Reference Window: Concealing Your Information in a Mailing List	Outlook Express
Mailing list, identify list's members	WEB 7.14	See Reference Window: Retrieving Member Information from a Mailing List	Outlook Express

TASK	PAGE #	RECOMMENDED METHOD	WHERE USED
Mailing list, leave	WEB 7.16	See Reference Window: Leaving a Mailing List	Outlook Express
Mailing list, post a message to	WEB 7.10	See Reference Window: Posting a Message to a Mailing List	Outlook Express
Mailing list, retrieve archive filename list from	WEB 7.11	See Reference Window: Retrieving an Archive Filename List	Outlook Express
Mailing list, subscribe to	WEB 7.07	See Reference Window: Subscribing to a Mailing List	Outlook Express
News articles, read and send	WEB 8.32	See Reference Window: Reading and Sending Articles Using Outlook Newsreader	Outlook Newsreader
Newsgroups, search for using Google Groups	WEB 8.28	See Reference Window: Searching the Google Groups Directory	Internet Explorer
Newsgroups, search for using Tile.net	WEB 8.26	See Reference Window: Searching the Tile.net Directory	Internet Explorer
Outlook Express, start	WEB 3.16	Click the Start button, point to Programs, click Outlook Express	
Outlook Newsreader, start	WEB 8.31	See Reference Window: Starting Outlook Newsreader	Internet Explorer
Security, strengthen in Internet Explorer	WEB 9.39	Click Tools, click Internet Options, click the Security tab, adjust security settings, click OK	Internet Explorer
Start page, return to	WEB 2.28	Click the Home button	Internet Explorer
Toolbar, hide or show	WEB 2.19	See Reference Window: Hiding and Restoring the Toolbars in Internet Explorer	Internet Explorer
URL, enter and go to	WEB 2.20	See Reference Window: Entering a URL in the Address Bar	Internet Explorer
Web page, change print settings	WEB 2.30	Click File, click Page Setup	Internet Explorer
Web page, move forward to previous in history list	WEB 2.13	Click the Forward button	Internet Explorer
Web page, print	WEB 2.30	See Reference Window: Printing the Current Web Page	Internet Explorer
Web page, refresh	WEB 2.13	Click the Refresh button	Internet Explorer
Web page, return to previous in history list	WEB 2.13	Click the Back button	Internet Explorer
Web page, save to disk	WEB 2.34	See Reference Window: Saving a Web Page to a Disk	Internet Explorer
Web page, stop loading	WEB 2.13	Click the Stop button	Internet Explorer

TASK	PAGE #	RECOMMENDED METHOD	WHERE USED
Web page graphic, save	WEB 2.38	See Reference Window: Saving an Image from a Web Page to a Disk	Internet Explorer
Web page text, save	WEB 2.35	See Reference Window: Copying Text from a Web Page to a WordPad Document	Internet Explorer
Web pages, move between using hyperlinks and the mouse	WEB 2.25	See Reference Window: Navigating Between Web Pages Using Hyperlinks and the Mouse	Internet Explorer

NETSCAPE NAVIGATOR TASKS

TASK	PAGE #	RECOMMENDED METHOD	WHERE USED
Attached file, save	WEB 3.41	See Reference Window: Viewing and Saving an Attached File Using Mail	Mail
Attached file, view	WEB 3.41	See Reference Window: Viewing and Saving an Attached File Using Mail	Mail
Bookmark, create	WEB 2.46	Click Bookmarks, click File Bookmark, type a name for the bookmark, click OK	Navigator
Bookmark, create in a bookmarks folder	WEB F.08	See Reference Window: Creating a Bookmark in a Bookmarks Folder	Navigator
Bookmark, save in a folder	WEB 2.46	See Reference Window, Saving a Bookmark in a Bookmarks Folder	Navigator
Bookmark, save to disk	WEB F.09	See Reference Window: Saving a Bookmark to a Floppy Disk	Navigator
Bookmark file, save to a disk	WEB 2.47	See Reference Window: Saving a Bookmark to a Disk	Navigator
Bookmark folder, create	WEB 2.45	See Reference Window: Creating a Bookmarks Folder	Navigator
Bookmarks folder, create	WEB F.07	See Reference Window: Creating a Bookmarks Folder	Navigator
Bookmarks window, open	WEB 2.46	Click the Bookmarks button, click Manage Bookmarks	Navigator
Cookies, manage	WEB 2.55	See Reference Window: Managing Cookies with the Navigator Cookie Manager	Navigator
File, attach to message	WEB 3.38	Click the Attach button, click File, locate the file, click Open	Mail
Graphic, save from Web page	WEB F.22	See Reference Window: Saving an Image from a Web Page on a Floppy Disk	Navigator
Help, access	WEB F.17	See Reference Window: Opening the NetHelp - Netscape Window	Navigator
Help, get	WEB 2.57	See Reference Window: Opening Navigator Help	Navigator

TASK	PAGE #	RECOMMENDED METHOD	WHERE USED
History list, open	WEB 2.51	Click Tasks, click Tools, click History	Navigator
Home page, change default	WEB 2.52	See Reference Window: Changing the Default Home Page in Netscape	Navigator
Home page, change default	WEB F.12	See Reference Window: Changing the Default Home Page	Navigator
Home page, return to	WEB 2.11	Click the Home button	Navigator
Lycos Chat, enter	WEB 8.11	See Reference Window: Entering a Lycos Chat	Navigator
Mail, compose	WEB 3.38	Click the New Msg button	Mail
Mail, delete	WEB 3.47	See Reference Window: Deleting an E-Mail Message or a Folder Using Mail	Mail
Mail, delete permanently	WEB 3.47	Right-click the Trash folder in the Mail Folders pane, click Empty Trash Can	Mail
Mail, forward	WEB 3.45	See Reference Window: Forwarding an E-Mail Message Using Mail	Mail
Mail, print	WEB 3.46	Select the message, click the Print button, click OK	Mail
Mail, read	WEB 3.40	Click the Inbox folder, click the message in the message list	Mail
Mail, receive messages	WEB 3.40	See Reference Window: Using Mail to Receive Messages	Mail
Mail, reply to all recipients	WEB 3.44	See Reference Window: Replying to a Message Using Mail	Mail
Mail, reply to sender	WEB 3.44	See Reference Window: Replying to a Message Using Mail	Mail
Mail, send	WEB 3.38	See Reference Window: Sending a Message Using Mail	Mail
Mail, spell check	WEB 3.39	Click the Spell button	Mail
Mail, start	WEB 3.36	Click the Start button, point to Programs, point to Netscape 6, click Mail	
Mail, start	WEB 8.34	See Reference Window: Starting Netscape Mail	Navigator
Mail account, change settings	WEB 3.36	Click Edit, click Mail & Newsgroups Account Settings	Mail
Mail account, set up	WEB 3.36	Click Edit, click Mail & Newsgroups Account Settings, click Local Folders, click the New Account button, complete Account Wizard	Mail
Mail Address Book, add a card	WEB 3.48	See Reference Window: Adding a Card to the Mail Address Book	Mail

TASK REFERENCE

TASK	PAGE #	RECOMMENDED METHOD	WHERE USED
Mail folder, create	WEB 3.45	Right-click Inbox in the Mail Folders pane, click New Folder, type the name of the folder, click OK	Mail
Mail folder, delete	WEB 3.47	See Reference Window: Deleting an E-Mail Message or a Folder Using Mail	Mail
Mailing list, conceal your information in	WEB 7.15	See Reference Window: Concealing Your Information in a Mailing List	Mail
Mailing list, create	WEB 3.50	See Reference Window: Creating a Mailing List In Netscape Mail	Mail
Mailing list, identify list's members	WEB 7.14	See Reference Window: Retrieving Member Information from a Mailing List	Mail
Mailing list, leave	WEB 7.16	See Reference Window: Leaving a Mailing List	Mail
Mailing list, post a message to	WEB 7.10	See Reference Window: Posting a Message to a Mailing List	Mail
Mailing list, retrieve archive filename list from	WEB 7.11	See Reference Window: Retrieving an Archive Filename List	Mail
Mailing list, subscribe to	WEB 7.07	See Reference Window: Subscribing to a Mailing List	Mail
Navigator, close	WEB 2.10	Click the Close button	Navigator
Navigator, start	WEB 2.39	Click the Start button, point to Programs, point to Netscape Navigator (or Netscape), click Netscape 6	
Navigator window, maximize	WEB 2.10	Click the Maximize button	Navigator
Navigator window, minimize	WEB 2.10	Click the Minimize button	Navigator
Navigator window, restore maximized	WEB 2.10	Click the Restore button	Navigator
Netscape Netcenter, open	WEB 2.44	Click the My Netscape button on the Personal toolbar	Navigator
News articles, read and send	WEB 8.36	See Reference Window: Reading and Sending Articles Using Mail	Mail
Newsgroups, search for using Google Groups	WEB 8.28	See Reference Window: Searching the Google Groups Directory	Navigator
Newsgroups, search for using Tile.net	WEB 8.26	See Reference Window: Searching the Tile.net Directory	Navigator
Security, strengthen in Navigator	WEB 9.40	Click Edit, click Preferences, click Advanced, adjust security settings, click OK	Navigator
Start page, return to	WEB 2.11	Click the Home button	Navigator

TASK	PAGE #	RECOMMENDED METHOD	WHERE USED
Toolbar, hide	WEB 2.41	See Reference Window: Hiding or Showing a Toolbar in Navigator	Navigator
Toolbar, hide or show	WEB F.03	See Reference Window: Hiding or Showing a Toolbar	Navigator
Toolbar, show	WEB 2.41	See Reference Window: Hiding or Showing a Toolbar in Navigator	Navigator
URL, enter	WEB F.05	See Reference Window: Entering a URL in the Location Field	Navigator
URL, enter and go to	WEB 2.42	See Reference Window: Entering a URL in the Location Bar	Navigator
Web page, move forward to previous in history list	WEB 2.13	Click the Forward button	Navigator
Web page, print	WEB 2.53	See Reference Window: Printing the Current Web Page	Navigator
Web page, print	WEB F.14	See Reference Window: Printing the Current Web Page	Navigator
Web page, reload	WEB 2.13	Click the Reload button	Navigator
Web page, return to previous in history list	WEB 2.59	Click the Back button	Navigator
Web page, save	WEB F.19	See Reference Window: Saving a Web Page to a Floppy Disk	Navigator
Web page, save to disk	WEB 2.35	See Reference Window: Saving a Web Page to a Disk	Navigator
Web page, stop loading	WEB 2.13	Click the Stop button	Navigator
Web page graphic, save	WEB 2.62	See Reference Window: Saving an Image from a Web Page to a Disk	Navigator
Web pages, move between using hyperlinks and the mouse	WEB 2.48	See Reference Window: Navigating Between Web Pages Using Hyperlinks and the Mouse	Navigator
Web page text, save	WEB 2.60	See Reference Window: Copying Text from a Web Page to a WordPad Document	Navigator

FTP AND WINDOWS TASKS

Anonymous login using command-line FTP	WEB 6.04	Type anonymous, press Enter	FTP
Download file using command-line FTP	WEB 6.06	See Reference Window: Downloading a File Using Command-Line FTP	FTP

TASK	PAGE #	RECOMMENDED METHOD	WHERE USED
Downloading a file	WEB 6.10	See Reference Window: Downloading a File Using an FTP Client Program	FTP
End session using command-line FTP	WEB 6.06	Type quit, press Enter	FTP
Internet route, trace	WEB 6.36	Click the Start button, click Run, type command, click OK, type the URL to trace	Windows
Linked message, send	WEB 6.51	See Reference Window: Sending an E-mail Message Linked to a File in Briefcase	Yahoo!
List files and folders using command-line FTP	WEB 6.06	Type ls or type dir, press Enter	FTP
Open a connection using command-line FTP	WEB 6.06	Type open followed by connection URL, press Enter	FTP
Uploading a file	WEB 6.14	See Reference Window: Uploading a File Using FTP	FTP
Yahoo! Briefcase, delete file from	WEB 6.54	See Reference Window: Deleting a File from Briefcase	Yahoo!
Yahoo! Briefcase, upload a file to	WEB 6.47	See Reference Window: Uploading a File to Yahoo! Briefcase	Yahoo!

EUDORA TASKS

TASK	PAGE #	RECOMMENDED METHOD	WHERE USED
Entry, create in address book	WEB E.09	Click the Address Book button, click the New button, type the addressee's nickname, name, and e-mail address, click the Close button, click Yes	Eudora
Eudora, exit	WEB E.10	Click File, click Exit	Eudora
Eudora, start	WEB E.02	Click the Start button, point to Programs, point to Eudora, click Eudora	Eudora
Mailbox, create	WEB E.07	Click Mailbox, click New, type the new mailbox name, click OK	Eudora
Message, create	WEB E.04	Click the New Message button	Eudora
Message, delete	WEB E.08	Select the message, click the Delete Message(s) button	Eudora
Message, file	WEB E.07	Select the message, click Transfer on the menu bar, click the target mailbox	Eudora
Message, forward	WEB E.08	Select the message, click the Forward button	Eudora
Message, print	WEB E.07	Select the message, click the Print button	Eudora
Message, reply to	WEB E.08	Select the message, click the Reply button	Eudora
Message, send	WEB E.05	Click the Send button	Eudora
Messages, retrieve and read	WEB E.06	Click the Check Mail button, enter password, double-click the message	Eudora

The Internet Level I File Finder

Tutorial	Location in Tutorial	Name and Location of Data File	Files the Student Creates from Scratch
Tutorial 1		*There are no Data Files for Tutorial 1.*	
Tutorial 2			
	Session 2.1		
	Session 2.2		Wind Quintet Information\MiamiWind Quintet.htm Tutorial.02\WindQuintetBookmarks.html Tutorial.02\GRAM-Address.txt Tutorial.02\GRAM-Map.jpg
	Session 2.3		Wind Quintet Information\MiamiWind Quintet.htm Tutorial.02\MiamiWindQuintet.htm Tutorial.02\GRAM-Address.txt Tutorial.02\GRAM-Map.jpg
	Review Assignments		
	Case Problem 1		
	Case Problem 2		
	Case Problem 3		
	Case Problem 4		
	Case Problem 5		
Tutorial 3			
	Session 3.1		
	Session 3.2	Tutorial.03\Physicals.wri	
	Session 3.3	Tutorial.03\Physicals.wri	
	Session 3.4	Tutorial.03\Physicals.wri	
	Review Assignments	Tutorial.03\KAir.gif	
	Case Problem 1		Tutorial.03\signature.txt (if using Netscape Mail)
	Case Problem 2		Tutorial.03\Testing new BECO e-mail system.html (if using Outlook Express or Netscape Mail)
	Case Problem 3	Tutorial.03\Recycle.wri	Tutorial.03\signature.txt (if using Netscape Mail)
	Case Problem 4		
	Case Problem 5		Tutorial.03\Survey.* Tutorial.03\Completed Survey.*

*The file extension will reflect the default file extension of the word processor used.

The Internet Level II File Finder

Tutorial	Location in Tutorial	Name and Location of Data File	Files the Student Creates from Scratch
Tutorial 4		*There are no Data Files for Tutorial 4.*	
Tutorial 5		*There are no Data Files for Tutorial 5.*	
Tutorial 6			
	Session 6.1		
	Session 6.2		Tutorial.06\ws_ftple.exe *ar500enu.exe *winzip80.exe

Note: Due to large file sizes, students must download files marked with an asterisk to a hard drive, Zip disk, or network drive. Downloaded file sizes and filenames are subject to change.

... ernet ... DUE

Tutorial	Location in Tutorial	Name and Location of Data File	Files the Student Creates from Scratch
	Session 6.3	Tutorial.06\Memorandum.doc	Tutorial.06\Memorandum1.doc
	Review Assignments		Tutorial.06\eul3manl.pdf
	Case Problem 1		*Students will download a ping program of their choice to the Tutorial.06 folder or hard drive (depending on file size) if they have permission to do so.
	Case Problem 2		*Students will download a bookmark converter program of their choice to the Tutorial.06 folder or hard drive (depending on file size) if they have permission to do so.
	Case Problem 3		Tutorial.06\lusetup.txt
	Case Problem 4		Tutorial.06\f940.pdf Tutorial.06\f940ez.pdf Tutorial.06\f940pr.pdf
	Case Problem 5		

Note: Due to large file sizes, students must download files marked with an asterisk to a hard drive, Zip disk, or network drive. Downloaded file sizes and filenames are subject to change.

The Internet Level III File Finder

Tutorial	Location in Tutorial	Name and Location of Data File	Files the Student Creates from Scratch
Tutorial 7		There are no Data Files for Tutorial 7.	
Tutorial 8		There are no Data Files for Tutorial 8.	
Tutorial 9			
	Session 9.1		Tutorial.09/shockwaveinstaller.exe
	Session 9.2		
	Review Assignments		
	Case Problem 1		
	Case Problem 2		
	Case Problem 3		
	Case Problem 4		
	Case Problem 5		
Tutorial 10		There are no Data Files for Tutorial 10.	
Appendix E		There are no Data Files for Appendix E.	
Appendix F		There are no Data Files for Appendix F.	